A BROKE

Rule of Law, Human Rights and Democracy

Justice Surendra Kumar Sinha
Former Chief Justice of Bangladesh

Dedicated
to my beloved father
Late Lalitmohan Sinha

Table of Contents

INTRODUCTION

Of the organs of State, the judiciary is an essential and integral part and its independence is a prerequisite of a liberal democratic state. Bangladesh, which emerged through a war of independence against Pakistani occupation army in 1971, included democracy as one of the basic State principles in the constitution of 1972, and the constitution ensured the separation of judiciary from the executive, and the independence of judiciary. Part V1 of the constitution deals with the judiciary, which insists on independence of judiciary from executive interference. However, bureaucratic procedures and absence of political will of the succeeding governments have made the independence elusive. Besides, succeeding governments, both military dictators and civilian governments, have been averse to the idea of judicial independence and engaged in the process of subverting any efforts to curtail the executive's undue influence. Equally important is the significant changes judiciary in Bangladesh have undergone in the past four decades, through inclusion of highly skilled professionals, the introduction of technology, commitment to equal treatment of citizens, challenging the culture of impunity by trying the killers of the father of the nation and war criminals, and acting vigorously as a protector of civil liberties, to name but a few.

I had the opportunity and honor to observe this transformation and the hindrances as a participant of our judiciary since 1974 - rising from a practitioner at a lower level of the judiciary in the north-eastern district of Sylhet to the highest judicial position of the country, the Chief Justice of Bangladesh. But in 2017, after delivering the historic verdict upholding the independence of judiciary, I was forced to leave the country and resign, and exiled by the present government. It was unprecedented in the history of the judiciary. The unanimous verdict delivered by the highest court

1

of the country, with observations about the state of governance and tendencies of political leadership, was applauded by the citizens, lawyers, members of the civil society and drew significant attention of domestic and international media. However, it irked the power that be.

The series of unfortunate and unprecedented events, which led to the tension between the executive and the judiciary and subsequent improper and unethical action against a sitting Chief Justice began on September 17, 2014 when the Parliament amended the constitution to provide power of impeaching the judges of the higher judiciary to the members of the parliament. The Sixteenth Amendment of the constitution deleted the provision of removing the Judges from office through a highly powerful committee of peers called the Supreme Judicial Council (SJC). The SJC, as stipulated in the constitution, also allowed the offending judges to have defend themselves. Most importantly, the process was meant to protect the judiciary from being subjected to political vagaries and put an end to the pattern of serving political leaders rather than the citizens. On May 5, 2016, a special Bench of the High Court Division, by majority, declared the amendment unconstitutional. Soon after the verdict the MPs blasted the judges for nullifying the amendment and began displaying sheer disrespect to the judiciary. However, the State opted for an appeal which was heard by a seven-member Bench. It was incumbent on me to preside the Bench. On July 3, 2017, the Bench unanimously dismissed the appeal upholding the High Court Division's verdict. The complete text of the unanimous verdict with observations was made public on August 1, 2017.

Following the decision on September 13, the Parliament passed a resolution calling for legal steps to nullify the verdict. The Prime Minister and other members of her party and ministers blasted me for going against the wishes of the Parliament. Cabinet members including the Prime Minister begun smearing me, alleging misconduct and corruption. I was confined to my official residence, and lawyers, and judges were prevented to visit me, and the media was told that I am unwell and have sought medical leave. Several ministers announced I will travel abroad on medical leave. On October 14, as I was compelled to leave the country, I tried to clear the air in a public statement that I am neither unwell nor am I leaving the country for good. I was hoping that my physical absence combined with court's regular vacation will allow the situation to calm down and good sense will prevail, the government will understand that the essence of the verdict - upholding the independence of judiciary - is beneficial to the nation and the state. Finally, in the face of intimidation and threats to my family by the country's military intelligence agency called the Directorate General of Forces Intelligence, I submitted my resignation from abroad.

This book highlights my early struggle for survival and judicial life, experiences, challenges before the judiciary in Bangladesh, its struggle for independence; erosion of values in judicial service and of politicians: political interference and the state of nascent democracy; reflection of judicial mind on different issues; censuring public prosecutors' conduct in prosecuting cases; police excesses; impact of Emergency and the role of DGFI in extorting money from businessmen, and interference in the administration of justice. Also, the role of the Bar Council which has failed to stand with the court in defending its independence, due to partisan divisions.

This book provides intimate accounts of the developments which led to a tension between judiciary and executive in Bangladesh and my forced resignation. However, they are told as my life-long journey in quest of justice instead of trying to provide an assessment of the state of governance or the future pathway of the nation. Those are to be decided by the people of the country, who have never shied away from sacrifices for liberty, justice and equality. This autobiography is about how I became the first minority, both in terms of ethnicity and religion, Chief Justice in a Muslim majority country. This is also an account of the adverse situations I have endured to ensure the judiciary's independence. My journey through the tempest is also the journey of the nation through the whirlwind. As such, the book is relevant to those who try to understand contemporary Bangladesh, its trials and tribulations. Anyone interested in the relationship between the executive and the judiciary in developing countries, challenges of judiciary in fledgling democracies will find the book relevant.

This book will have more than served its purpose if it inspires the reader -- whether he or she is a lawyer or a politician; a teacher of Law College or a university; a layman, with belief that the vocation of a lawyer is an honorable vocation requiring the highest standards of rectitude, integrity and uprightness, or a judge. The book is yet incomplete since there are some errors and omissions in the citations and these are due to lack of access to books and various other relevant sources which I had in my collection but couldn't bring them when I left the country under duress. For some references I had to rely solely on my memory. Despite these hurdles, this book would not have been possible if not for the support of my well-wishers, most of whom were Bangladeshis living abroad. Under ideal conditions, I would have given them their due acknowledgement but fear of repercussions against them and their families, from the authorities who are hell bent on suppressing the truth, keeps me from mentioning their names. There are a few other errors in the book that could not be corrected due to the time constraint. I hope to correct them in the next revised and extended edition of the book. I hope this book will be a step forward in upholding democracy, rule of law and freedom of thought and expression of the people of Bangladesh.

Chapter 1
Early Life

I was born in Tilakpur, a village in Moulvibazar district, in present northeast Bangladesh. It is indeed a beautiful village on the bank of the Dhalai River which originates in India as a rivulet being only one foot deep in the summer. But in the rainy season it devastates village after village leaving innumerable people homeless. There my father late Lalit Mohan Sinha had his education in Normal High School and College in Shilchar, Cachar district, India, and attained his degree in Bengali literature which is equivalent to Bachelor of Arts. He started his profession as a school teacher at Batuli Ragana High School in Barlekha, Moulvibazar. My mother late Dhanabati Sinha was then studying in Karimganj of Cachar district staying in her elder sister's house.

My aunt (mashi) late Kokila Sinha was staying with her husband, who was a sub-registrar. As my aunt was very young, she felt very lonely, and to give company to her elder sister, my grandparents sent my mother to stay with her. The two sisters were born consecutively and therefore were very close. When my father was teaching in Raghana High School, he married my mother, who was very young then. On my father's side, he had one younger brother, late Bhubaneswar Sinha, who was more than six feet tall and had a healthy and slender body physique. He was not attentive to his education and wasted time playing with his friends, taking the advantage of my grandfather late Dhansaw Sinha, who studied in 'Tole' (Sanskrit school) and became a Pandit with a vast knowledge on recitation of Upanishads, Vedas and wrote scriptures on religious philosophy. My father preserved and recited them. Naturally, my grandfather had no interest in worldly affairs. Towards the south-western corner of our house we had a big mango tree and under the tree he set up a Mandir, calling it Brindaban, the Hindus' holiest place in Uttar Pradesh, India. In his Ashram, he taught 'Rakhal Dancing' (boys' dance) and performed Rakhal Nrittya every month with the villagers. Besides, he taught religious ceremonies, the Sree Geeta and Mahabharat every day to the villagers and entertained them with 'prasada' – fruits dedicated to the Deity.

Consequently, my uncle, taking advantage of my father's absence and my grandfather's lack of interest in worldly affairs, was not guided properly toward education. He remained busy with football and hockey. It was after my father's return in late 1947 that my mother taught my uncle at home and then got him admitted in the high school and, ultimately, he became a primary school teacher. My father had acquired a reputation as a teacher in Bengali literature, mathematics and he was particularly efficient in arithmetic (Patiganit).

We had farm land and cultivated various crops with permanent workers. We had two buffalos for ploughing besides innumerable cows for milk. My mother used to cook for the large joint family. It was a practice in the family that before going to school the men took care of the cows. My father joined Kaliprasad High School, Munshibazar, which is located about seven kilometers north from our house. The road was so muddy throughout the rainy season that it was not possible to attend school every day although he had a bicycle. So, he rented a house and stayed there with my elder brother who had been admitted to high school. Ultimately, my father joined Kamalganj High School at the thana headquarter in which I studied. My father inherited his father's behavior and was a cool-minded religious person. My mother, on the other hand, was a bit harsh toward all her children and she used to control the day to day affairs of her children. My parents had five sons and one daughter. One died from cholera while he was studying in Class V1.

I am the second of the four surviving brothers. My elder brother got a degree as an engineer and then he took up higher studies in Marine Engineering in London and served in the Mercantile Marine Department, Chittagong. My third brother is a banker, and my fourth brother is a dentist and currently a US citizen. My only sister Satyabhama studied in Women's College, Sylhet. All of us were given a proper education as my parents considered it important and made it a priority. My father's days used to begin

6

much earlier at dawn when he used to give tuition to some students at home. His capacity to feed his students' intellectual hunger by sheer brilliance and untiring zeal was praiseworthy.

My mother would share the bulk of household work along with raising her five children, and later on, after my uncle married for the second time, his wife, Maney my 'kakima', also helped my mother in doing the household chores. My mother was renowned for being a tough lady and I believe it was her instinct and hard work that made sure that all her children received a proper education and upbringing. I was kind of very unyielding in my childhood. I used to play in the afternoon and return home in the evening and developed a habit of eating a lot. I had another interest which I could not restrain and that was swimming in our small village river with my friends when flood inundated the area. I always had friends who were senior to me.

When I was old enough, along with my elder brother Narendra Kumar Sinha, I began to help the workers in the family farm while I was studying to lessen the burden on our parents. Aside from using the buffalos for ploughing we also utilized them for crushing sugarcane in the autumn, which we cultivated on the bank of the river. A huge chunk of land of about 25 bighas was used for cultivation of sugarcane which was diluviated by the Dhalai River.

I took my graduation in commerce from the Madan Mohan College in 1970 and was admitted to Chittagong University in the economics department. Since I had good grades in economics from college my professor advised me to take admission in economics at the university. The political atmosphere at the time was very volatile. My father was not inclined to let me study in Chittagong due to political disquiet and wanted me to join as a teacher in his school as a commerce teacher. As my father was reluctant to continue paying my educational cost at Chittagong due to security concerns I was confused whether to continue my education in Chittagong or leave. After three months I returned to Sylhet and got admitted to Sylhet Law College without my father's consent.

When my father came to know that I had been admitted to the law collage, he got furious and instructed me to return home. In fact, he had arranged an appointment for me at his school. In his view lawyers were liars and they earn money by lying. He could not imagine that an ideal teacher's son could be a lawyer and earn his livelihood by lying. Consequently, relations between my father and me got strained In clear language I had to tell him that I could not end my life as a school teacher and informed him that even without his financial support I would continue to study law. From then on, I met my expenses in Sylhet by tutoring students.

Meanwhile my uncle Bhubaneswar Sinha had been suffering from kidney disease from a young age. In the 1960s he had surgical operative treatment of his kidney disease and had his kidney stones removed at Kumudini Hospital, Tangail, a famous hospital during that time established by philanthropist Ranada Prasad Saha. Again, in the latter part of 1970 he had obstructions in discharging urine. Therefore, I brought him to Sylhet and had him admitted to Sylhet Medical College Hospital in the second week of March 1971. He would not eat the hospital food and I had to carry his food from Mashimpur where I was staying. Prof. Shamsuddin Ahmed, a renowned teacher in the surgery department removed his kidney stones about five or six days before March 25, 1971. As usual I brought him his food on March 25 at dusk on a bicycle. I noticed that his body temperature was very high and decided to stay the night with him despite his objections claiming the situation in the country was not normal.

There was tension in the city and it also reflected in the hospital. At dawn we heard sounds of processions toward Ambarkhana area chanting "Joy Bangla, Joy Bangla." Almost all the patients and others came out of the hospital compound saying that the country had been liberated. Within half- an- hour we heard sounds of indiscriminate firing. All the patients and everyone else returned inside the hospital and after about one hour the bullet injured persons were brought in one after another in rickshaws and vans. Within one hour about 70/80 injured were brought to the hospital and the emergency department was drenched in blood.

The hospital authority sent an ambulance for bringing Prof. Shamsuddin for the sake of the patients. As the situation was worsening my uncle told me to go back saying that my aunt might be very worried about me because I did not tell her that I would be staying the night and because I had come without my dinner.

So, with some hesitation I approached Mashimpur through Dariapara. But before I entered the main road toward Zindabazar I saw a large group of people were standing on the edge of the by lane and observing the situation. Some of them prevented me from going to the main road, because there was curfew; some others said there was no curfew. When we were talking we saw that a police jeep with a speaker was coming from Lamabazar toward Zindabazar announcing that curfew had been declared and hence no one should go out. Moments later an army jeep came toward us firing a machine gun indiscriminately. I jumped on my cycle and raced back to the hospital. I noticed that some of the people who were standing with me earlier had sustained bullet wounds.

Returning to the hospital I rushed into my uncle's cabin and fell on the floor. He had a temperature and his surgical stiches had not been removed. Even then he got down from his bed and asked whether I was also injured because there were blood stains on my clothes. He gave me a glass of water. Within a few minutes I came to full consciousness and narrated the harrowing incident to him. I told him other people beside me were hit by bullets and I had managed to survive with the help of my bike.

Thereafter I noticed that Prof. Shamsuddin Ahmed operated on the injured the whole day long without taking any rest. We did not have enough money and the food supply in the hospital fell short, so we did not have any food to eat. Hence, I went to meet the hospital super to ask for some bread and any other food. He replied that there was no supply of ration and even the regular patients could not be served breakfast, lunch or dinner. The hospital therefore authority decided that until conditions improved patients would be supplied with 'khichuri' (cooked mix of rice and lentil).

9

We had little money with us and I told my uncle that I would go and bring bread from a street vendor who was selling tea and bread near the south-western side of the hospital near Dariapara. The old Sylhet Medical College was in the west and the hospital in the east bifurcated by a road which passes through Dariapara and connects to the main road which goes from Lamabazar to Zindabazar. I found only a half-pound bread and brought it. We were put in an uncertain position: for two persons we had only half pound bread. We did not have any drinking water and started taking water from the bathroom tap. We lived on that one piece of bread for two days! While my uncle was pressing me to eat the bread and I was requesting him to have the bread as he was unwell. In truth we were eating only bits of the bread and taking them with a lot of water. When the curfew was lifted after 48 hours, to our awe, we noticed that half of the bread was still there. I told my uncle that the situation is completely uncertain, and I should somehow go home to bring some food and money.

After two days, the hospital returned to its hectic state and all the doctors and nurses got busy treating the patients with bullet wounds. I met Prof. Shamsuddin to see the condition of my uncle so that we could return home because of the uncertainty. He gave us some medications to heal the surgical wound, removed the bandage and advised me to take my uncle home and said that if the situation in the country became normal he would check on my uncle again after fifteen days. So, I brought him to Mashimpur on a rickshaw after eight days. Perhaps because of the mental pressure and the agony I suffered during those few days I developed a temperature that turned out to be typhoid.

There were rumors that all routes out of Sylhet were going to be closed. Therefore, either we should leave the city as soon as possible or it would be difficult for us to leave. Towards the last week of May my temperature was falling slightly and we along with four other families including my present wife's family started for our village in the morning. Arjun Babu, my wife's grandfather, was a very popular man who was the accountant general of Sylhet Zila Parishad. He had close relationships with the contractors of the Zila Parishad. One of the contractors arranged a truck for us which was on the opposite bank of the Surma River. We came out of the city and managed to cross the Surma by boat. I had to walk with the help of two people because till then I had not taken any food by mouth. We reached Tajpur Daakbanglow at dusk. We were received by local people and they supplied us with rice and lentil for cooking 'khichuri'. After two weeks I swallowed a bowl of khichuri and felt better.

On the following morning we started walking and sometimes took help of rickshaw vans, when available, to take the children and sick people till we reached Sherpur ferryghat. After crossing the Sherpur River we got a truck. The driver agreed to take us up to Srimangal. We reached Srimangal at around 3:00 PM and from there we started walking through the Srimangal-Bhanugah forest, more than 12 kilometers. It was an unimaginably arduous journey. There is a road between Srimangal and Bhanugach, but it was completely muddy. We did not feel any hunger or sickness; the only thing clawing in our mind was how to reach our destination without being confronted by the Pakistani Army. We traveled in a zigzag fashion and after crossing the Padmachera Tea Estate, we reached our maternal uncle's (Sonai Mama) house at the western-most portion of Madhabpur village Chingong. Sonai Mama loved me very much and seeing my health condition he persuaded us to stay the night. We took some puffed rice (muri) and water and started toward our village, which was about three kilometers away towards the northeastern corner intervened by the Dhalai River. We were determined to reach our home the same day because we thought that if we pass the night at my uncle's place it might so happen that we would not be able to walk if our physical distress worsened. Ultimately, we reached our home at around 9:00 PM.

After seven days at home I fully recovered. The road in front of our house passes from Moulvibazar town to Kumrarchara Tea Estate, the last point at the border with Tripura, India. The distance of this road is about 35 kilometers. The road was in a miserable state. Somewhere the depth of the wet mud was more than one foot and in spots it was dry. In the meantime, the Pakistani Army set up their camp at Shamsher Nagar Airport and took control of the Thana administration by forming a Peace Committee and started

11

recruiting razakars through their Peace Committee. The Army directed the villagers to make the road motor able with the help of the Peace Committee. Some radicals from Impala of Manipur, India came to support the Pakistan Army headed by one Sudhir of Meitai Manipuri and took refuge in Homerjan village. He started recruiting razakars from the Meitai of Manipuris. There was constant pressure on the villagers to repair the road, but there was no dry soil to fill up the potholes in the road because it was the rainy season.

I heard from one of my friends, Anil, that the army was looking for some young persons in the locality to give them the responsibility of the construction work instead of compelling them to join the razakar force. Whenever we heard that the army came to our locality, we used to take shelter in the paddy fields toward west where a vast area up to the Dhalai River had no habitation. Sometimes it continued from morning till dusk and in the process, leeches sucked our blood, but we could not move. It was an atrocious situation.

Finally, the Army managed to build the road by laying tree branches and filling earth over the branches. When the road was motorable the movement of the army was regular. Because the border toward the south is about 20 km away from my house. Possibly the Army thought of using the road as the defence against the infiltration of freedom fighters as the alternative road from Bhanugach to Patrokhola Tea Estate, which was a motorable road. At this time, I along with Gour Mohan decided to join the Mukti Bahini in India and took shelter in the Madhabpur village for crossing the border. We stayed there for three nights, but could not cross the border because the Army, in the meantime, had formed peace committees and Razakar groups up to the remote areas and the border was totally sealed. All along the border areas most of the population is from the Meitai sect of Hindus and Muslim Meitai sects. Their language is more common than that of the Bishnupriya sect of Manipuri to which I belong. These Meitai Hindus and Muslims are supporters of Pakistan. Consequently, it was difficult for us to cross the border. Some informers told us that the borders were completely closed as a precaution against infiltration of freedom fighters from India. So, after three days, I returned home, but Gour Mohan stayed in his sister's home at Madhabpur. Later on, I came to know that he managed to cross the border after fifteen days.

I used to pass almost all my days in the western paddy field and return home after dusk. Around September we were contacted by the freedom fighters who crossed the border through deep forest in the east to gather information about the army camp and their movements. We started giving them information, food, and when required shelter. In the last week of November, the first batch of Muktibahini entered our locality and we provided them shelter. I along with Anil collected rice, lentils, potato and cooked khichuri for them on the southern bank of Rajbari pond. On the second such event we were told by the Muktibahini to cook food for 20 people. It was around 2:30–3:00 PM. Abdul Mannan, a clerk of CO (Dev) office, who was a member of Meitai sect of Muslim and possibly the only SSC passed member of their community brought the Pakistan military from the western side by crossing the Dholai river and the Army, after crossing the river, opened brush firing with machine guns and attacked our village. We all fled towards the eastern side.

Some of us took shelter in Mangalpur and I took shelter at Chitlia, three kilometers to the east, in the house of Falguni Sinha, who was around my age, of the Meitai sect. Even though she was a Meitai, she had been my father's student and hence gave me shelter for two days. Since I had no winter clothes with me he gave me a Manipuri wrapper. I returned home after two days. My parents were worried that I had been killed by the military as I was missing for two days and scolded me. I told them that as I had links with the Muktibahini and worked for them as an informer, I took shelter at Chitlia. I feared that the military might target me at night and therefore as a precaution I did not return.

In the first week of December, the Muktibahini captured our village and the surrounding villages, then they captured the entire Thana. By December 12 our entire locality was under the control of the Muktibahini. After Gour Mohan and Mujibbahini forces came to our village, we went to kill Abdul Mannan. On suspecting our move, Abdul Mannan took shelter in a Muslim Meitai village in Tetaigaon. Then we learnt that one of my friends, who was a leader of the Muktibahini--I do not want to mention his name to avoid embarrassing him--gave Abdul Mannan shelter at his home. I asked him the reason for his behaviour and he told me that as he is a clerk of CO (Dev) office and he used to take lot of help from him. He had also attended Abdul Mannan's wedding reception. At that point, I developed a dislike for some of the freedom fighters. Jalalabadi, a college friend of mine, who was a leader of the Muktibahini took control of the Thana headquarter. After the liberation of the country all my friends took certificates of being freedom fighters. But I did not even make any attempt to collect one because of that reason.

Chapter 2

Struggle for Survival

Immediately after the war of liberation, I passed LL.B. in the second class securing the highest mark. My father completely disowned me and said that I should not give my identity as his son if I entered the law profession. After passing law, I had been facing with a lot of difficulties. Firstly, I had no accommodation in Sylhet; secondly, the economic condition of the country was very precarious; thirdly, it was not possible to carry on practicing law without the support of the family; and finally, joining with a good lawyer's chamber for training is a pre-condition to become a good lawyer. All this required support, and I had none. All my friends after passing law joined the local bar for survival. But I opted to stay in Sylhet because to become a good lawyer I had to practice in the district court, which was a challenging matter. I was not closely acquainted with any good lawyer in Sylhet. I only had formal relationships as student with senior advocates. At that time, most lawyers maintained their chambers till midnight, and unless a law graduate continuously worked as an article at a very reputed lawyer's chamber, he could not be a good lawyer.

In view of that fact I decided to join a good lawyer's chamber with the aim to prove that lawyers are not liars and that they are very respectable persons in society, if they become good lawyers. After discussing with my friends, I decided to join the chamber of Soleman Raja Chowdhury, a reputed criminal lawyer and a dignified person. He was also my teacher at Sylhet Law College. With a lot of hope and collecting enough courage one evening I went to the chamber of Chowdhury. I found there some clients and his junior Muniruddin Ahmed. On my arrival Chowdhury asked me the purpose of my visit and very politely I expressed my desire to him. I told him without hesitation that I belonged to a community which is known as Bishnupriya Monipuri, who are very simpleminded and most of them earned their livelihood by being teachers or cultivators.

Essentially this community lives a very simple life and is poor in comparison to other communities. i.e. Muslims, Hindus, Buddhists and Christians in the country. Even indigenous people in the hill districts hold higher posts in military, police and other civil posts because of quota facilities, and in Parliament they have representation, and a member of their community even gets ministerial position. On the contrary, there is no representation from the Bishnupriya Monipuri in the Parliament not to speak of any ministerial position, and no officer in the armed forces, high ranking police or administrative post and they are normally taken as people of inferior quality compared to the Muslims and Hindus, because of their financial and social status. So, advocate Chowdhury on the spur of the moment told me that he could not retain me as his junior and I should see other seniors. I was tremendously disheartened but preserved my positive mental attitude and bowed my head without replying anything and kept sitting there till he continued his work. I was adamant to work as his junior despite his unwillingness and promised to swallow any humility in the process of attending his chamber. I noticed that after some time his servant came and indicated to Chowdhury to come to the drawing room. Soon thereafter, Chowdhury with his junior Moniruddin went to the drawing room which is toward the northern side with a room in between. I realized that they took their tea, but did not offer me any, even though I was once his student. I felt insulted but did not express it.

On the following day I started attending the chamber regularly. Chowdhury did not look at me and his junior was not talking to me. I took a chair beside Muniruddin. Sometimes it so happened that a good number of clients crowded the chamber and Chowdhury required consultation with them. At such times he told me to sit on the back bench which was marked for his clients. Despite all this I continued attending his chamber for months together. I was convinced that if I would get a chance to take a dictation, Chowdhury would feel compelled to take me as his junior. From the handwriting and manner of dictation Moniruddin took, I was sure that I was much better than Moniruddin and Chowdhury would give preference to me as his junior. Soleman Chowdhury could not write with his right hand, after he had an

16

accident, so he signed with his left hand. It was always like a routine that Chowdhury took his tea without asking me, but I did not allow myself to feel humiliated with his behavior, because my only dream was to become his junior. Before long, my persistence and perseverance paid off and one stormy evening, I got my long-awaited opportunity. Coming through the storm and rain I got completely drenched. Despite that I waited in the verandah. At that time the door and windows were closed. I pressed the button for the doorbell and the door was opened by the boy. I entered the room and tried to dry my shirt with the help of the fan. After some time, some clients arrived but that evening Moniruddin did not come. I told the boy to inform Chowdhury about the arrival of the clients. It was the second occasion Chowdhury spoke to me. He looked at me and saw that my clothes were totally wet and simply expressed surprise that in this bad weather I had come without an umbrella. Maybe he was touched by my devotion and instructed the boy to bring a towel and told me that since I had come, he had some urgent drafting and asked me whether I could take dictation.

As soon as responded positively he started giving dictation. He found that I was much better and swift in taking dictation and my handwriting was also very good. After he finished the dictation he praised me for my English, noted that my handwriting was better and asked why I had not told him this. That evening he invited me to the drawing room and offered some light refreshment. I was so overwhelmed that somehow, I controlled my emotions and prayed to the Almighty for giving me this opportunity. On the following day both Moniruddin and I came to work. When the time for dictation came, Moniruddin was preparing to take dictation but Chowdhury prevented him saying, "You are senior, he (Suren) should be given some opportunity." I realized that Soleman Raja Chowdhury was satisfied with my performance. From that moment every day when dictation was necessary Moniruddin was sidelined and I was given the opportunity.

Another thing which worked in my favor was that every day I appeared at the chamber just after dusk, which Moniruddin never did because he had some clients in the magistrate's court. Naturally I was liked by Chowdhury. But I faced another problem.

17

Chowdhury was very miserly in matters of making payments. He used to give me Tk. 100 maximum twice a month or sometimes once. I was leading a very humble life, but it was still difficult to meet all the expenses. Eventually, a date for appearing before the Bar Council was fixed but I had no money at all to attend the examination at Dhaka. I requested Chowdhury to give me Tk. 500 for the exam and he instantly gave it. I had no coat, no shoes. So, I bought a coat from the second-hand market, got it altered and colored it black. When I appeared before the Bar Council, the viva-voce exam was taken by B.N Chowdhury, a reputed civil lawyer. He asked me from which bar I was attending. I told him from Sylhet. He said, "Oh, from Sylhet. A rich bar and the students are also well dressed." He asked me only one question relating to the difference between robbery, dacoity and theft. I replied correctly, and he was satisfied with my answer.

After the exam I enrolled as an advocate, but my luck did not favor me. I was facing acute financial crisis. I did not have my father's financial support and my senior was not giving me adequate money. My colleagues were attending the sub-divisional criminal courts and earning good money. They were earning money by signing bail bonds only but my senior in the chamber suggested that I not become a bail bond lawyer as it is not a dignified job. Hence as I did not sign bail bonds my income was low, and I could not bear my expenses. I had to realize that my survival was my priority and becoming a lawyer came after that. If I could not survive I could not be a lawyer. I also realized that unless I joined the Sub Divisional bar, I could not meet my expenses. I noticed that all my friends were economically solvent but I, on the other hand, could not earn my bread.

So, one fine day, rustling up some courage I told my senior that I had decided to join the Moulvibazar bar if he permitted me. My senior told me, certainly you join the Moulvibazar bar, because you are a lawyer of the district bar and you are mature enough to decide your future. He added, since I had already decided to join the local bar, he had no business to obstruct my decision. The following day, I came to Moulvibazar and went to the court. I was well received by senior reputed lawyers Abdul Muhit Chowdhury and Syed Abdul Matin, both were close relatives of my senior Soleman Chowdhury. They were known to me from before because of my attachment with Chowdhury.

Muhit Chowdhury was an eminent civil lawyer and he was appearing in Sylhet court for Tea Estate cases. I took a seat beside Muhit Chowdhury to watch the dealings of lawyers in a mufassil court. I noticed that whenever a brief was accepted, the lawyers had put up a long list of expenses, such as cost of paper, clerks, summons, notices, and peons' fees taka 60 to 65 to file a suit, Tk.50 to 60 as lawyer's fee, etc. I was so surprised with this process that I could not control the temptation and asked Muhit Chowdhury why he had to write a long list for filing a suit and did not ask for Tk. 200 or 250 at a time. He replied that if he asked for that amount of money, the client would leave at once. So, they were compelled to give a break up. But the full amount of money was retained for himself. The manner of practice in district and sub-divisional courts is far different. I could not indulge in this kind of procedure and was totally disheartened. Being frustrated I left for home in the evening and slept for seven days in a row without speaking to anybody.

After one week, I came to Moulvibazar and received a letter from my friend Akhter. He wrote that I left Sylhet without informing them and he heard from Soleman Raja Chowdhury that he was stunned by the manner I told him of my decision. Chowdhury also told Akhter that he saw in me the potential of becoming a good lawyer in future. He also admitted that I was facing financial difficulties which he realized but, according to him, it was only for a short time during my probationary period. Since now I had the license to practice as an advocate, it was the time to begin earning. Moreover, since I had the potential to become a good lawyer it was better for me to stay in Sylhet. The moment I read the letter, I rushed to Sylhet again and in the evening, I met my senior Chowdhury and informed him of my return. His happiness was beyond what I can describe. He told me that if someone wants to be a good lawyer he had to pass the ordeals of economic, physical and mental hardships. I started my second life there, but I continued to bedevil by lack of enough income to meet my expenses. As I could not attend the lower courts in bail matters, which were the main source of income for a junior advocate, I had no local client.

I was really struggling to survive and at that juncture Golam Kibria Chowdhury, a prominent civil lawyer and a close relation of Soleman Chowdhury, approached me to join his chamber. At that time, he had 12 juniors working with him, but even then, he could not manage because of the huge number of cases being filed every day. Golam Kibria Chowdhury was a very free, charming and generous type of lawyer. He earned a lot and spent money without reservation. He was also very liberal toward his juniors. I realized quickly that if I joined his chamber I could be financially solvent. But I could not avoid Soleman Raja Chowdhury, who was a dignified, honest and principled lawyer. He was very dependent on me mainly because, during trial of session's cases, one had to write down the statements of the witnesses promptly for cross examination, and I was satisfactorily doing that job. Accordingly, I told Golam Kibria Chowdhury that I could not leave the chamber of Soleman Raja Chowdhury since he is totally depending on me. It could be done only if he could get Soleman Chowdhury's consent. According to Golam Kibria Chowdhury, there was little scope of drafting in criminal matters but in the civil side a lot of drafting is necessary as my drafting was very good, he needed me in his chamber.

Ultimately, I could not avoid Soleman Chowdhury and decided that I would not leave his chamber. I proposed to work in the evening and in the morning from 6:00 to 10:00 at Golam Kibira's chamber. He agreed to my proposal. I started working in this manner and in the morning Golam Kibria Chowdhury used to give dictation, sometimes plaint and sometimes written statements. Every morning I used to complete two to three drafts and accompanied him to the court in his vehicle and every day he used to give me Tk. 20, which was substantial money at the time. Usually I used to go his chamber on an empty stomach and after getting the Tk. 20 I used to take my breakfast at the court canteen. This routine continued till 1977. Within this period, I had learnt a lot of civil and criminal matters, particularly the basics of civil and criminal law simultaneously. Toward the end of 1977, I realized, if I wanted to be a reputed lawyer I should shift to the Supreme Court of Bangladesh. My ambition to become a great lawyer would only then be fulfilled.

During this period, I had developed good relations with Sabita Ranjan Pal (S.R Pal), the best lawyer in Bangladesh at the time. As I used to come to Dhaka with briefs and engaged S.R Pal, this helped me greatly with my introduction with Pal. I was hesitant to switch over to the Supreme Court because in the Supreme Court prominent lawyers were practicing and without good financial support one could not survive as a lawyer there. During this period, I was spending much time in Dhaka causing inconvenience to the chambers of both Golam Kibria and Soleman Chowdhury. In fact, on one morning in January 1978, Soleman Raja Chowdhury rebuked me saying that a lawyer must be serious to his profession, but a lawyer who was indulging in "tout type of practice" sometimes in Sylhet and sometimes in Dhaka carrying briefs for the Supreme Court could not be a good law practitioner. He advised me either I should continue in Sylhet or leave Sylhet for Dhaka permanently. After four years of entering my profession, I had convinced my father that the profession of a lawyer is a dignified one. He acknowledged my argument and subsequently accepted my profession. It was primarily due to Soleman Chowdhury with whom he had a talk. My marriage ceremony was held under the arrangements of Soleman Raja Chowdhury and Suraiya Chowdhury, a venerable lady. The post wedding ceremony was also held at Soleman Chowdhury's residence. My father was convinced seeing the dignity of a lawyer like Suleman Raza Chowdhury and convinced that the lawyers are not liars. I realized the strong command of Suleman Raza Chowdhury and decided that I would finally move to Dhaka.

I finally moved to Dhaka in March 1978 with the ambition of developing a good relationship with S.R Pal. I had requested him to take me as his junior which he utterly refused. My high ambition to become a good lawyer by working with a very renowned lawyer was shattered. Whenever I told Pal that I had come to practice in the Supreme Court, he would say that it was a good decision but when I asked to join his chamber, he declined as if I was not known to him at all! Pal was an outspoken person and did not hesitate to express comments which he thought were proper.

I consulted about my predicament with late Advocate Abdul Hannan, who was close to me. He used to deal with revenue matters only. After hearing everything, he informed me that Sudhir Chandra Das (S.C. Das) had independent practice at that time and he was working with Pal. Hannan suggested that if I joined the chamber of S.C. Das, who was sharing the same chamber, I would have the opportunity to maintain contacts with Pal. I agreed to his suggestion and Abdul Hannan introduced me to S.C. Das. I started working with Das and when an opportunity came, I visited Pal. He was interested in gossiping with lawyers whenever he was free. I was confident that if I get a chance to work with Pal, I would be accepted by him. In this manner I continued for about six months keeping close ties with Pal in the chamber of S.C. Das and, in the evening, occasionally I used to visit Pal's chamber with Das. My relationship with S.R. Pal developed to some degree. S.R. Pal was dealing mostly with senior briefs and K.M. Saifuddin Ahmed was working with him. Saifuddin was a talkative person and not a serious lawyer. I realized that he had no depth of knowledge in law and his handwriting was also not good.

One afternoon, I was sitting in Das's chamber as S.R. Pal returned to the chamber from the court and finding me alone in the Das's chamber, wanted to know whether I had any business left at the court. Since I answered in the negative, he wished to know if I could accompany him to his residence for an urgent dictation of a writ petition. Since I was searching for such an opportunity, I readily accepted his offer. He took me to his home in his car and dictated the petition to me. Pal's drafting was very prompt, articulate, significant and concise. I took the dictation without any interruption because he was very prompt in dictating anything. Pal was so satisfied with my drafting he immediately gave me Tk. 500. He praised me and remarked that if I had joined his chamber, he could prepare cases without much difficulty. He offered me an opportunity to join his chamber, but at the same time remarked that

Sudhir would mind. He seemed to leave the matter to my discretion.

I told him frankly that initially I wanted to work with him (Pal) and with that expectation I had joined Das's chamber so that I would get an opportunity to remain in touch with his chamber. I was sanguine that if I got the opportunity, I would succeed in pleasing with my competency. From the following day, I started working with Pal and that was a most vital turning point in my life. Mainly because as Pal was a most prominent lawyer and his reputation was so high that almost all the judges would unhesitatingly take his opinion in case of any difficulty with points of law. Pal's conception was always very clear, and he could give opinions spontaneously without looking at the books. So usually all senior lawyers, sometimes judges, industrialists, businessmen and politicians used to come for consultations to his chamber.

I thus had the privilege of meeting those people even with my disadvantaged identity. Pal was not only a lawyer, but he was an institution by himself. His vast knowledge and command in law and language were acclaimed by people of various strata in the country. He seldom consulted any decision or any annotated book if any law point surfaced and when a question of law emerged, he consulted with the bare Acts. He advised me to know the law first and said if I did not understand on one reading, he advised me to read it twice, thrice and a hundred times and try to understand the meaning of the law. He added that once I understood the contents of the law to augment my understanding, I will have to consult the annotated books and decisions on the subject for more clarification.

Never did he attend the court with decisions other than the bare Acts and his arguments were precise on legal points. His legal and judicial integrity would be remembered from generation to generation. He was my mentor who shaped my life in understanding and grasping points of law on the facts of a given case. His extraordinary personality impressed and compelled me to be devoted in my profession. I learned from him the meaning of life and the meaning of the legal profession. He explained the law effortlessly giving only one or two grounds enough to grasp the point. The second benefit for me personally was that those clients who could not engage him were compelled to engage me in the expectation that I would be able to consult S.R. Pal. I started getting briefs from Chittagong and other parts of the country. Initially I was handling briefs chiefly from Sylhet but soon after I joined Pal's practice, I became a lawyer known in almost all the bars of the country. The third benefit which transformed me into a good lawyer was that whenever I accepted a brief I waited for the opportunity of consulting with my senior alone. And when I realized that he was in a good mood, I used to note down the grounds of my brief to be taken up in the matter. This helped me tremendously to argue the case on specific law points and to get a rule in any matter. In those days it was difficult even for senior advocates to get a matter admitted for hearing. Most of the lawyers of my standing did not dare to appear independently without a senior. Even lawyers with five to ten years' experience hesitated to move any motion without a senior. And yet I became an exception. This emboldened me, and I started arguments in the final hearing of matters against most senior Advocates like Syed Istaque Ahmed, Ashrarul Hossain, B.N. Chowdhury, Hamidul Hoque Choudhury, Abdul Malek, Zulmot Ali Khan, M.H. Khandaker, Khandaker Mahbubuddin Ahmed, T.H. Khan, and even S.R. Pal. The judges also started to treat me leniently because of my command of law and the superior drafting of my petitions.

I came in touch with eminent judges, lawyers and highly respected people through him. I think what I am today as well as my legal knowledge is largely due to what I learned from him. Before my elevation to the Bench, in fact, I had a roaring practice in the Supreme Court. For my sincerity, honesty, commitment as an advocate, and because of the support of my seniors from Sylhet and my long attachment with Pal, I remain a highly trusted member of the legal community. Additionally, my extraordinary devotion to law and jurisprudence, my forensic ability in analyzing and formulating legal arguments and a highly persuasive and distinctive way of placing them before the court, hugely helped me in developing a worthy personality in the legal profession.

Chapter 3

Elevation to the Bench

During that time, a lawyer over fifty years old used to be considered for elevation to the Bench though the Constitution provides for 10 years practice in the Supreme Court. When I was in my 40s, I was offered the office of judgeship. But on two successive occasions my name was dropped because of my age. ATM Afzal, the former Chief justice, on one occasion harmlessly remarked that my age was the barrier to my elevation although he was very eager to elevate me to the Bench. After the Awami League came to power in 1996, Abdul Matin Khasru, then minister in charge of the Ministry of Law offered me the office of the Deputy Attorney General. I declined the proposal and he was very much annoyed with me. There was a dearth of lawyers with experience in criminal law in the Attorney General's Office. I told him that I would accept any offer of becoming an Additional Attorney General, to which he said that Mahbubey Alam had been appointed to that position. I told him that during the previous government there were more than one Additional Attorneys General. He said that those appointments were in violation of the law. I told him that was not my problem, but I would not accept any offer less than an Additional Attorney General.

Though my name was in the list for appointment as a judge of the High Court Division from before, my name was dropped because of disagreement with Law Minister Abdul Matin Khasru in the first batch of elevation. In any case I was not much interested to become a judge because of my highly successful practice. My senior S.R. Pal also did not like the notion as it was not advisable to accept such an offer good by a good lawyer with a successful legal practice. At the time of recruitment of the second batch of judges Law Minister Khasru made three phone calls to my residence. My wife received the calls and he requested her to ask me to have a cup of tea with him. After the third call, my wife Shushma told me with some anger that since a minister was repeatedly calling me I should meet him adding that it is my duty to respond to his request. My wife advised me that if it was for elevation as a judge, I could decline his offer, but it was not fair to keep away without responding to him.

Ultimately, I went to meet the Law Minister in the late afternoon at the Pathokali Trust office located at the northern side of the then Sheraton Hotel, where he was doing his evening office. Sometimes thereafter, I noticed that Abdul Wahhab Miah arrived there with Advocate Syed Reza. I realized that Khasru was in the process of selecting some judges. As Md. Abdul Wahhab Miah came with Syed Reza, an Awami League leader from Comilla, I was confident that Syed Reza came for Abdul Wahhab Miah. After some discussions and tea, Syed Reza handed over the curriculum vitae (CV) of Wahhab Miah. Khasru also requested me to give him my CV and said that whatever misunderstanding we had previously should now be buried. He also told me that there was scarcity of judges with progressive thinking, so I should accept the offer. I told him that I would think over his offer and discuss with my wife. In course of our discussions, it was time for Maghrib prayers and we were about to leave. But Khasru requested me to wait for some time. After offering his prayers, he took me to another room and requested me by holding my hands that I should not refuse the offer. I then contacted my wife and intimated the desire of the minister. She told me that she would not express any opinion other than that it was indeed a respectable offer, but still I should think over the matter taking into consideration our financial condition.

At that time, I had a four-storey house in Madhubazar, West Dhanmondi, and Dhaka. After thinking about the financial condition, I decided to accept the offer and gave my CV to the law minister. He requested me to help in reorganizing the Attorney General's office and in selecting some judges. We discussed some time in choosing at least ten judges, but it was very difficult to select suitable persons. He told me that Syed Reza and some Awami League leaders were applying pressure to appoint Abdul Wahhab Miah. He said that two district judges would also be included and wanted to know about Mamtaz Uddin Ahmed. I suggested including Advocate Abdur Rashid. He was a progressive lawyer and a competent one. He accepted the proposal. Then I advised him to appoint at least two Deputy Attorneys General who could be selected for judgeship in due course. One was Syed Mahmud Hossain, the present Chief Justice, and another was Hasan Fayez Siddiqui. I told him that these two young lawyers are promising and would make good judges. Then he requested me to ask them to meet him.

The following morning, they met Law Minister Khasru and they were appointed Deputy Attorneys General. When my appointment was finalized, and the gazette notification was published, I called my junior, Mahbub Ali, now a Member of Parliament from the Awami League who was then working as Assistant Attorney General. I told him that he had worked with me for a considerable period and I wanted to hand over my 'sheresta' [briefs] to him. If he was ready to take the charge of my chamber, then I would take my oath of office. If he did not take the responsibility of the briefs within seven days, I would not take the oath. I had considered that I had about 4,000 plus briefs lying in my 'Sheresta' and unless I got a trusted lawyer, I would not accept the judgeship. Mahbub Ali responded by saying that he was supposed to visit China as a member of a government delegation and he needed one-months' time to take charge after his return from China. I advised him that if he could deal with briefs properly, he would be able to visit China every month with the income from the briefs. I told him clearly that he would have to give up his plan of visiting China and take charge of my briefs otherwise I would have to make a different decision. Advocate Mahbub Ali accepted my offer and on the following day he met Law Minister Matin Khasru and offered his resignation as Assistant Attorney General. Matin Khasru threw his letter of resignation and said there was a dearth of honest officers in the Attorney General's office, so he must withdraw the resignation. Mahbub Ali did not accept the direction of the Law Minister and came to me the following day and informed me about his resignation. Though a junior lawyer, Mahbub Ali is an honest lawyer and belongs to a very respectable family. He maintains honesty and dignity, but he did not have enough space in his house to keep four thousand briefs and requested me to allow him two months' time to keep the files in my residence. I told him that I could give him fifteen days' time and by then he must find a suitable place for storing the files. When he said that it was not possible to shift such a huge volume of briefs within fifteen days, I advised him to move them to my Supreme Court's chamber, which was shared with Advocate S.A Rahim, who rarely came to court. Mahbub Ali was sharing a chamber with Mahbubey Alam but the chamber was occupied with Alam's briefs. Mahbub Ali accordingly transferred the briefs as per my advice.

I took the oath on October 24, 1999 with seven other judges. Even after my elevation, I found no change in my mind, because I was attached to Pal, a reputed lawyer who commanded much more respect than an ordinary judge. Just fifteen days before our confirmation was due, the governing party changed and Bangladesh Nationalist Party (BNP) formed the government. I was sure that if I was not confirmed by the party in power, I would return to my practice. So, I was not too anxious. Mahmudul Amin Chowdhury was the Chief Justice at that time. Two days later, the Chief Justice wanted to know about my briefs and with whom they were lying. I told him that I had handed over the briefs to Mahbub Ali and disconnected the telephone. About four days thereafter, the Chief Justice called me and enquired about my briefs again. I was a bit annoyed about his questions and told him that I had already told him the briefs were with Mahbub Ali. I disconnected the line. Following this I was wondering why the Chief Justice (Mamun Bhai) had asked twice about my briefs, although he is known to me from the beginning of my profession at Sylhet. We sat in the same table of the Bar. There must be some reasons behind it, I thought. If I were not confirmed because of political reasons, I would have no objection. But if it was due to some other reasons, then I would have to think it over. I was certain of my integrity, capability and acceptability as a good judge by members of the Bar.

Sometimes thereafter I heard whispering that out of eight judges appointed along with me, three of them would not be confirmed, and I thought that among the three, one must be me. Nobody could say who were the other two, but my name was being told by almost everyone. Then I realized that there was a link between the Chief Justice's query and the ongoing rumor. Some lawyers including the vice-president of the Bar and judges were against my confirmation and they made representations to the Chief Justice which I heard later. Even then I kept silent and watched the progress. On the following morning, the personal assistant of the Chief Justice came to my chamber and told me, "Sir, I am happy to intimate that your name has been recommended for confirmation." I wanted to know the names of those along with me who else were recommended. He expressed his inability saying that he respects me like a father, so he gave the news about my confirmation. In the late afternoon, after court hours, I wanted to convey my congratulations to Abdul Wahhab Miah that he was going to be confirmed with a view to test his reaction. On the intercom I was surprised to overhear at that time that he was talking with Momtazuddin and I heard their discussions because of a cross connection. Justice Abdul Wahhab Miah was telling Justice Momtazuddin Ahmed in clear terms that Sinha would not be confirmed as he was a corrupt judge and that there were many allegations against him. On hearing the conversation, I became completely dumbfounded by the spread of the rumors against me and was bewildered that the person who took the leading part in this was none other than my close colleague.

After two days the gazette notification was published. I called the Chief Justice with a request to give me a short notice to meet him. He told me to visit him right away but, I said, I would want to meet him at his residence. He told me to come after Maghrib prayers. I reminded him that he knew me from my early days in the profession and about my connections with prominent lawyers. On the first occasion when he enquired about my briefs, I was not at all worried, but on the second occasion I became worried because even after knowing about my professional life he was asking about my briefs with a motive which I realized but as he was the only authority to recommend my confirmation, I thought that I should answer the correct reply and if I said more, it would tantamount to influence him, certainly it would be against the ethics. It was the Chief Justice who would recommend the judges who according to him were fit for confirmation. After the gazette notification, I came to clarify. Then I reiterated the story about the handing over the briefs to Mahbub Ali and told the Chief Justice that if he found anything misleading, I would not take oath despite the gazette notification. He can confirm this from Abdur Rahim. The Chief Justice was dissatisfied after hearing everything scolded me and told me I should have told him the story earlier. He said that a good number of lawyers and judges were against my confirmation and even the vice-president of the Supreme Court Bar Association (forgot his name, he hails from Barisal) made a representation to him. He took a lot of pressure for recommending my name. I told him that his recommendation must be independent and without influence. Though he had good relations with me from earlier days of our profession, I did not tell him because I was clear in my conscience that I did not commit anything unethical. He then told me that within six months of my elevation, the senior judges were determined to recommend me for confirmation on being satisfied with my judgments but because of the pressure he was confused.

Chapter 4

Emergency

After the Bangladesh Nationalist Party (BNP) formed the government in 2001, a good number of cases were filed against prominent leaders of the Awami League including leaders of Bangladesh Chhatra (Students') league. The president, vice-president and secretary of the student organization were put on detention. After their release, they were shown arrested in a dozen murder cases in different districts. I quashed all the cases in a habeas corpus petition in exercise of suo moto powers with guidelines to the police about showing arrest of an offender while in custody. I also released most of the Awami League leaders on bail. This enraged the government in power. Moudud Ahmed, then Law Minister openly criticized me on the floor of Parliament castigating me as a diehard Awami League supporting judge and for showing undue favor to Awami League leaders. I was extremely shocked by such criticism, which I saw as per advice of Abdur Rashid, a friend of mine with Channel-I, being broadcast directly from the Parliament.

This has become a convention being followed by both the biggest political parties: filing cases with a motive to take political vendetta whenever they come to power defeating the other party. Thereafter, the special intelligence department submitted reports against me with wild allegations of corruption which I came to know from late justice Sultan Hussain Khan, then Chairman of the Durnity Daman (Anti-Corruption) Commission. I asked him to get the matter investigated and said I was ready to face an inquiry. He said, it would create a very bad precedence and that the Constitution also does not permit such a procedure. I told him that this agency will not stop in their endeavors to vilify me. I also knew why this department was showing so much interest to castigate me as corrupt judge.

A deadlock ensued about the appointment of the Chief Advisor. The Awami League protested the appointment of K.M. Hasan, and ultimately Hasan himself declined to become the Chief Advisor. President Dr. Yajuddin Ahmed assumed the office of Chief Advisor by-passing the provisions of the Constitution. There was total lawlessness due to the movement by the Awami League. Ultimately the army intervened, and it was due to the pressure from international organizations that unless a credible election is presented by the government with the participation of all political parties, the Bangladesh members of the peace keeping force deployed by the United Nations would be sent back. This created some commotion in the armed forces rank and file. Yajuddin Ahmed was compelled to step down due to the pressure of the army, Emergency was declared in the country, and Dr. Fakruddin Ahmed was appointed as the Chief Advisor. While the Bangladesh Awami League was happy with the outcome, the other main political party was demoralized. During all this development Justice B.K. Das's wife suddenly died (in 2007) and hearing the news I rushed to his residence. A few minutes later Suranjit Sengupta, a senior prominent leader of the Awami League also arrived there. We were very close to each other. Suranjit could not control his happiness on the declaration of Emergency and gave credit to his party's achievement as if his party, the Awami League, had come to power. He said, it is a matter of time before the formation of the next government by his party. Seemingly he even forgot that we went there to express our grief to the bereaved family, particularly to B.K. Das.

Suranjit was about to leave saying that he had some engagements. I stopped him saying, "Hello leader, before you depart I have something to say, please sit down." I told him that leaders like him were the people dancing due to the declaration of Emergency without making a political evaluation of the situation. I told him that apparently, he had forgotten about the consequences of the imminent danger caused to the country. "You've foolishly welcomed the army without understanding the impact. Your party would be the first target and take it for granted, you are not getting any election in the near future." When I explained to him the reasons, it appeared to me that he was a bit confused but left saying, "Let us see." My apprehension proved true within a few days. The first target of the army was Sheikh Hasina, President of the Awami league. She was arrested in connection with some cases filed in the meantime for alleged corruption even though she was not the immediate past prime minister. Meanwhile, more political leaders were arrested after the consolidation of power by the army.

After about six months, I was informed by the Registrar that President Yajuddin Ahmed had invited me at Bangabhaban the following afternoon. When I went to meet him, I found that his Military Secretary Major General Mohammad Aminul Karim was with him with a file in his hands. Initially I did not harbor any doubt, rather I was thinking that I was called to be given a special assignment. However, my assumption proved false within a minute. The President told me that I had to resign. On query, he told me that there were serious allegations of corruption against me. I told him that this report was false and that he should think over the matter again. At that point the Military Secretary was trying to say something while looking at the file in his hand. I stopped him saying that he was not supposed to talk with me because I was invited by the President.

I told the President that I would not resign in this manner and reminded him that I would not even get my pension benefit if I resigned. Then he said to me that the government would give me double the amount if I agreed to his proposal. Even if I wanted to go to India, the government would afford me all facilities. I said sorry and told him to think over the matter again and I left even without taking the tea offered to me. Chief Justice Md. Ruhul Amin was away from the country and three days after his return I narrated the incident and sought his advice. He told me to perform my judicial work without succumbing to the pressure. By then Brigadier General Ameen, who was also known as Behari Ameen, had been posted to the DGFI. He started creating pressure on me to step down. One day the Military Secretary to the President wanted to talk with me through the Supreme Court telephone exchange. I refused to talk with him. Dr. Kamal Hossain was in the U.K. and on getting information, he sent his daughter Barrister Sara Hossain, an activist and social worker, to my Kakrail residence with the message that I should not do anything till his return. Then I received a letter from the President's Secretariat to intimate my opinion regarding the talk between myself and the President. Dr. Hossain in the meantime had returned from abroad and met me in my chamber and handed over a written reply. I showed him the one prepared by me. On reading my reply, he emotionally said that it was far better than his. I replied directly to the President that both of us had taken oath under the Constitution: that the Constitution has delineated both of our duties and responsibilities specifically and that he should refrain from doing anything which violates his oath under the Constitution. Thereafter the matter subsided.

Chapter 5

Ailment, Treatment, and Elevation to Appellate Division

In 2009 I became sick with Lower Gastrointestinal cancer. Unfortunately, almost six months elapsed before doctors confirmed the diagnosis. In adition to my extreame physical sufferings, emotional torment descended on me when I started to believe that my days were suddenly numbered. After extensive discussions the doctors decided to treat me with radiation and chemotherapy. Following the second dose of chemotherapy I felt so crippling sick that I prayed to Almghty to take my life instead of so much pain and distress.

At this point of time, I got a phone call from Law Minister Barrister Shafique Ahmed telling me that the government had decided to elevate me to the Appellate Division. I declined his offer explaining that my condition was perilous, and I did not even know the chances of my survival. Moreover, the doctors were unable to say anything about the impact of the treatment till six weeks had elapsed. He told me that everyone in Bangladesh and the government were hoping that I would recover soon, and that unless I was elevated to the Appellate Division, the hearing of the Bangabandhu Murder Case would not be possible. I told him that due to my health condition, it would not be possible on my part to take the responsibility. After six or seven days he called me again and wanted to know the condition of my health. By that time my chemotherapy was just over leaving only two or three radiotherapy sessions. I told him that the nauseas feeling was almost over, and I was able to take some fluid orally. He requested me to return to Bangladesh after the treatment was complete and added that if necessary special arrangement would be made for my transportation and the government would take care of that.

I thought that there was no use of staying further in Singapore wasting a huge amount of money and decided to return to

Bangladesh. Accordingly, in mid-June, I returned to Dhaka. On July 15, 2009 I took oath along with Md. Abdul Aziz, B.K. Das and A.B.M. Khairul Haque. I was the junior most judge. I superseded Sikder Mokbul Haque. I had no control over the supersession, but it was criticized by journalist Mizanur Rahman Khan of the daily Prothom Alo. Sikder Mokbul had six months more time and I could have been accommodated after six months. As a result, Justice Sikder Mokbul and his family were much angered by the supersession.

I came to know later that the Chief Justice had constituted a Bench with Tofazzal Islam, Md. Abdul Aziz, B.K. Das, Md. Mozammel Hossain and me for hearing the Bangabandhu murder appeal. Although there were about six more senior judges, all of them were not able to be in the Bench because some of them felt embarrassed and Fazlul Karim and A.B.M. Khairul Haque had heard the appeal in the High Court Division. The equation was clear as to why I superseded Sikder Mokbul Hossain. Though all the judges were senior and efficient, they had little conception in criminal law and except for me all other members of the Bench were comfortable in dealing with civil matters. After taking oath, I went to Singapore for a final check-up and the doctors believed the results of the treatment were positive and that there were only 10-15 percent chances of relapse. The day I heard the news, the first thing that came to my mind was that I would see my granddaughter who arrived on Earth in the meantime. One of my well-wishers in Singapore was Siddiqui, a resident there who helped me greatly throughout my treatment although I had no acquaintance with him previously. I requested him to help me purchase a gold chain for the new member of a younger generation... After disposal of the Bangabandhu Murder case, I went to U.S. for a second opinion. The doctors upon examination of my medical records and preforming blood tests advised me to scrap all the papers and not to consult any doctor other than Dr. Chong of Singapore, stating that he was one of the best oncologists in the world and had treated me properly. They added that if I had not consulted the proper doctor, my fate would have been different.

Chapter 6

Fazlul Karim's Appointment as Chief Justice

M.M. Ruhul Amin, the then Chief Justice, was due to retire on December 22, 2009. He had superseded Md Tofazaal Islam and Mohammad Fazlul Karim. Md Tofazaal Islam became the 17th Chief Justice and took oath on December 23, 2009 and retired on February 7, 2010. He was in office for less than two months. He was made Chief Justice because he presided over the Bench which heard the Bangabandhu Murder case. He also superseded Mohammad Fazlul Karim, who was bent upon becoming the next Chief Justice of Bangladesh. The only plus point in his favor was that he was the third judge in the High Court Division who had heard the Bangabandhu Murder appeal after the dissenting verdict delivered by Md. Ruhul Amin and Khairul Haque while hearing the main appeal in respect of maintaining the conviction of two or three accused. Md. Fazlul Karim was entrusted as third judge to hear the appeal who was against the line of political thinking of the Awami League. The office of Chief Justice was made political for a long time and it was beyond comprehension that anyone would become the Chief Justice outside the political line of thinking.

His name was also not considered during the caretaker government because he heard the appeal of the Bangabandhu murder case and MM Ruhul Amin, who was junior to him, was made the Chief Justice. Fazlul Karim had the tenacity and perseverance to continue in judicial works despite being superseded twice. His only aim and object were to become Chief Justice of Bangladesh because his father-in-law Justice Imam Uddin was also a Chief Justice. He was moving heaven and earth to become the 18th Chief Justice. On the other hand, A.B.M. Khairul Haque also wanted to become the Chief Justice after retirement of Justice Tofazzal Islam. He had worked only a few months in the Appellate Division because he was elevated with me in July 2009. The point in his favor was that he had delivered the verdict of the Fifth Amendment to the Constitution and Bangabandhu Murder appeal.

Mohammad Fazlul Karim was a Barrister and as was Law Minister Shafique Ahmed. They had a special connection, but Shafique Ahmed had little power in the selection process and the Prime Minister alone was the authority although the Constitution empowered the President of the country to appoint the Chief Justice. Even at some point, Mohammad Fazlul Karim came to my residence twice to seek my help for his selection. There was serious persuasion on behalf of Mohammad Fazlul Karim. Ultimately somehow, he convinced late Akhtaruzzaman Babu, who was a powerful MP from Chittagong. The Chittagonians had their soft corner for their friends irrespective of their political identity. Akhtaruzzaman was successful in convincing the Prime Minister in favor of Md. Fazlul Karim. The government was in a dilemma; on the one hand, A.B.M. Khairul Haque was a very junior judge in the Appellate Division and, on the other hand, Md. Fazlul Karim had managed to reach the Prime Minister through Akhtaruzzaman. Though there were two other judges who were senior to Khairul Haque they were out of consideration. At the eleventh hour, the Law Minister and I had a telephonic discussion. In the evening of the same day I told Fazlul Karim that night would be the crucial one as the decision on the next Chief Justice would be made. I told him I would let him know the final decision at night. Just immediately before making the decision, Shafique Ahmed rang me at around 11.00 PM to receive assurances from Mohammad Fazlul Karim that if he was chosen as the Chief Justice he would not embarrass the government. I rushed to Fazlul Karim's house at around 11.30 PM and found him sitting in the drawing room with his wife. He was of course very happy to know the positive outcome. I communicated the message of the Law Minister to Fazlul Karim. He was a physically challenged person but the moment I entered the room, he was so anxious that he stood up with the help of stick. I asked him not to stand up. He caught my right hand and told me, "I always looked at you like my younger brother. I will do whatever you want me to do." I was surprised by his words and expressed my anxiety that he should not belittle himself for an office he was going to hold which was an exalted one. Standing there I communicated the words used by Fazlul Karim to the Law Minister and gave the phone to Fazlul Karim to speak with the Law Minister.

Thus Justice Md. Fazlul Karim became the Chief Justice of Bangladesh. After he assumed the office, he recommended some advocates for elevation as additional judges including Md. Ruhul Quddus and Khasruzzaman. But immediately after publication of the names, there was a report in the newspapers that both Md. Ruhul Quddus and Khasruzzaman had criminal records while studying in the university. In fact, those were political cases. Nevertheless, the Chief Justice did not invite these judges for taking oath. It was an embarrassing situation for me, the Law Minister, the government and others, who had recommended him as the Chief Justice. The government was annoyed about this event. A few days later a group of judges which included me along with Chief Justice Karim visited South Korea for a program arranged by the Korea International Cooperation Agency. After the orientation program, I invited the Chief Justice to my room for a few minutes for an emergency discussion. I requested the Chief Justice to change his decision and save us from embarrassment by taking on those two judges. I reminded him the night when he gave me his words and more so because those two names were recommended by him. The Chief Justice stoutly denied deviating from his decision. Thereafter, his relationship with the government was not strained. He was in office for about seven months and twenty-one days. Those two judges took oath after A.B.M. Khairul Haque took office. He was appointed on November 30, 2010 superseding MA Matin and Shah Mominur Rahman. Both took long leave instead of resigning till Khairul Haque retired on May 17, 2011. Thereafter, Mohammad Mozammel Hossain was appointed as the Chief Justice on May 18, 2011, superseding Abu Nayem Mominur Rahman. Soon thereafter, the latter resigned.

When Khairul Haque was the Chief Justice the strength of the Appellate Division had reduced to three members only: besides the Chief Justice there were Mohammad Mozammel Hossain and me. The government was delaying filling the posts with a view to avoid Md. Abdul Wahhab Miah. There was enormous pressure on the court and the load of work could not be transacted with only three judges. During that time Abdul Wahhab Miah was the senior most judge of the High Court Division. While the government was reluctant to elevate him to the Appellate Division, it was also apprehended that if other junior judges were appointed there might be a commotion in the Supreme Court Bar because he was not aligned with the political ideology of the Awami League and he had close relations with lawyers of the opposition political party. He was involved in bar politics and the Supreme Court Bar was dominated by pro-BNP lawyers and Md. Abdul Wahhab Miah was popular to them. He had been secretary of the Bar Association twice. He was lobbying robustly for his elevation. At one point of time he even started behaving abnormally in open court and it was the talk of the day in the Bar Association and judges' quarter.

He was so ambitious that he wanted to occupy the office of the Chief Justice from the day he was elevated as additional judge and he expressed his intention on one occasion in my presence at the Bangladesh Bar Council. The Bangladesh Bar Council was conducting a training course for lawyers. Barrister Amirul Islam was the chairman of the program. Former and sitting judges and senior lawyers used to conduct the classes. One day retired Justice AM Sadeque, an amiable and well-behaved judge, was waiting in the room meant for the judges. At that time Sadeque enquired about judicial works from Abdul Wahab Miah and me and praised us saying that we had a bright future and would be able contribute much the judiciary. Abdul Wahhab Miah responded by stating, if God forbids, Justice Sinha would remain as Chief Justice for more than three years and he would be the Chief Justice for 11 months, although he was senior to me in terms of enrollment in the Supreme Court, but because of age seniority, Sinha was given seniority at the time of elevation. I knew Md. Abdul Wahhab Miah from before in which sense he was making the comment was clear to me and I avoided in making any comment.

Obaidul Hasan and M. Enayetur Rahim were junior to Abdul Wahhab Miah when they were practicing at the Bar. They along with Syed Rezaur Rahman were involved in the Jatiya Ainjibi Samity, a parallel lawyers' forum headed by Advocate Khandker

Mahbuddin Ahmed. The biggest such forum was Samannita Ainjibi Samity headed by Shamsul Hoque Chowdhury. Naturally Obaidul Hasan and Enayetur Rahim had a soft corner and close relations with Abdul Wahhab Miah. These two judges were going door to door for the elevation of their senior to the Appellate Division. They used to visit to my chamber almost once a week and after exchange of greetings, I used to ask them whether they had any business with me. I knew the purpose of their visit but pretended knowing nothing. They knew that I am man of very strict personality and did not dare raise the issue at any point. They are in the habit of saying; "Sir, we've come to convey Salams to you."

One weekend morning Mahbubey Alam came to my official residence at Kakrail for discussion on a private matter. We were then on very good terms because of our progressive thinking. He is a thoroughly progressive-minded gentleman and has a weakness in Rabin Dra Sangeeta and occasionally arranged Rabindra Sangeet programs at his residence sometimes inviting Indian singers for selected audiences. Abdul Wahhab Miah could not imagine that the Attorney General would be at my residence and I noticed a bit of embarrassment in him on seeing the Attorney General. Mahbubey Alam and Abdul Wahhab Miah were on good terms, but they kept a distance from one another due to their different political thinking, although when they met they behaved as if they were close friends. This kind of exchange of views appeared to me meekly and I used to enjoy the moment whenever they met each other. As observed above, Mahbubey Alam was a very progressive man, while although Abdul Wahhab Miah pretended to be progressive minded, his performance and conduct proved otherwise. Despite knowing everything about him, Obaidul Hasan and Enayetur Rahim kept their closeness with Abdul Wahhab Miah and they were very much interested in his elevation.

However, both Obaidul Hasan and Enayetur Rahim belonged to strong Awami League leaning families. Obaidul Hasan's younger brother Sajjad, an additional secretary, was working as private secretary to the Prime Minister and he is very close to the Prime Minister. Enayetur Rahim's younger brother is a whip of the

Parliament where the Awami League is in the majority. I realized the purpose of Abdul Wahhab Miah's to my residence and requested him to have a cup of tea with us. He was hesitating in the presence of Attorney General Mahbubey Alam saying that since we were discussing something confidential his presence would not be befitting. After taking tea, Wahhab Miah wanted to leave but I came out from my chamber requesting the Attorney General to wait for a while. Out on the verandah Abdul Wahhab Miah embraced me and said, "Friend, forgive me if I'd offended you. Please help me to be elevated to the higher bench."

It was the first time he expressed regrets and asked for my forgiveness. But I told him that still I treated him as my close friend and I would be happy if he was elevated to the Appellate Division and that I would not be standing in his way. It seemed to me he relaxed after this assurance. When I returned to the waiting Attorney General, Mahbubey Alam in his usual fashion laughingly asked me that certainly Abdul Wahhab Miah had come to lobby for his elevation. I smiled. Then Mahbubey Alam said, "This gentleman has polluted the High Court Division and committed blunders and if he was elevated, there would be serious complications in the administration of justice."

Ultimately however Abdul Wahhab Miah managed to get his name included along with those of Nazmun Ara Sultana, Syed Mahmud Hossain, Muhammad Iman Ali and Hasan Adbul Foez Siddique for the elevation. The last three judges were much junior to him. Later, I had an occasion to meet the Prime Minister and she asked about the judiciary and at one point she told me that she was compelled to appoint Md. Abdul Wahhab Miah because of Law Minister Anisul Haque. I came to know later that Wahhab Miah met the Law Minister and embraced him and somehow convinced him to pursue the matter of his elevation with the Prime Minister. Anisul Haque subsequently admitted to me that he had made an error and due to this he was facing a lot of criticism from the Prime Minister.

On many occasions I performed the office of Chief Justice as the Chief Justice was touring not only during holidays but also during court hours regularly. On one occasion, while I was in charge, I noticed a news item published in the daily Jugantar regarding corruption of one Faruk Ahmed. The report provided of case numbers. Faruk Ahmed had retired as Special Judge, Dhaka, a few days earlier. It had been alleged that he had indulged in serious corruption in the last six months before retirement. Soon after reading the news I went to inspect that court. I had inspected some of the cases mentioned in the report and noticed that the said officer delivered judgments on two or more cases in a day. He did not follow the procedure for attendance of witnesses and by examining one or two witnesses, without waiting for the arrival of other witnesses, closed the prosecution cases and delivered judgments acquitting the accused. I inspected only two months' judicial records and in two months he had disposed of about one hundred cases most of which were matters of gold smuggling or cases relating to smuggling of other valuable goods. I found collusion of the public prosecutors as it was revealed on inquiry of the Bench Assistants and lawyers. Moreover, without the help of the Public Prosecutors he could not deliver judgments in such a manner. I directed the Bench Assistants and other officials to bring a printer for printing the records of the cases so that I could submit a report on that day because on the following day the Chief Justice would resume his office.

I noticed that in cases which were not ready for hearing, he framed charge and fixed the following day for trial and after examining one witness, he closed the prosecution case and delivered his judgment. After bringing the record, I sat at the Judicial Service Commission at night and dictated the report. I finalized the report by 10:00 PM and directed the Registrar to keep open the office till I returned. Gigantic corruption and fraud were practiced by the officer in acquitting huge number of sensational smuggling and corruption cases. I submitted a detailed report pointing out that since the officer had retired, the Durnity Daman Commission (ACC) would take legal action against him and directed the Ministry not to give his pension benefits until the investigation was complete. I also pointed out that due to shortage of time, I could not inspect other cases and requested the Chief Justice to hold an inquiry with another judge of the High Court Division in respect of cases heard by Faruk Ahmed in the preceding two months. This

43

news was somehow leaked to the media and published the following day. The Chief Justice on coming to know asked me why I had submitted the report without waiting for his return and requested me to withdraw the report promptly. I told him that I had only pointed out whatever irregularities I found, and this type of officer cannot be exonerated. He, being the Chief Justice, could keep the report concealed without communicating to the Ministry and the ACC or in the alternative he could withdraw the report in exercise of his power. But I could not withdraw the report after submission.

This officer was known to be corrupt and his name was proposed by the Ministry on three occasions and the GA Committee, the highest body headed by the Chief Justice and three senior judges of the High Court Division to oversee the transfer and postings of judicial officers, refused the proposal even though the Chief Justice had pressured the members of the committee to approve the proposal due to the persistent demand from the Ministry. This officer hailed from Kishoreganj and the Chief Justice was also of the same locality. But the judges refused to approve the proposal. At one stage one judge threatened to resign from the Committee if the Chief Justice insisted on Faruk Ahmed'posting to Dhaka. The Chief Justice then reconstituted the GA Committee and approved the proposal. When the fact was brought to the attention of the Law Minister, he did not make any comment. In respect of another judicial officer on one occasion the Prime Minister asked me how a judicial officer can leave the country after passing judgment and how he could afford to stay abroad. I told her that it would be better to ask her Law Secretary because he was brought at the instance of the Ministry. There were innumerable incidents of this nature.

Normally I do not allow lawyers to make irrelevant submissions and cannot tolerate dawdling of lawyers at the hearing of any matter. I always preferred disposal of cases without wasting the court's time but some judges do not have any interest in clearing the docket; rather they are happy if lawyers can be made happy and allow irrelevant submissions. I had once noticed that a lawyer was making irrelevant submissions while I was presiding over a Bench and Md. Abdul Wahhab Miah was asking questions with a view to linger the submission of the lawyer.

Finding no alternative, I intervened and asked the lawyer to answer the question of law involved in the case. Suddenly Justice Abdul Wahhab Miah started shouting in open court and saying things like "I could not tolerate him and could not allow him to ask any question. I always suppressed him" and so on. By nature, Wahhab Miah's voice was very loud. When he was talking with any person supposedly normally someone would feel that he was squabbling. It is a court tradition that whenever the presiding judge intervened in a matter during a hearing, the puisne judges would cease talking. Thus, decorum was maintained. It is a tradition being practiced over centuries. Naturally, I felt embarrassed due to the misbehavior of Abdul Wahhab Miah in open court. I immediately came down from the court. So naturally all the judges followed me. After entering the chamber, I requested Abdul Wahhab Miah with folded hands in front of the other judges, "Don't create any scene like this in open court breaking all decorum." This would send the wrong message to the Bar and added, "I tender my unconditional apology if I've committed any mistake. Please come and sit in court to transact the business of the day." I calmed the situation for the time being in the interest of justice with a view to keeping harmony among the judges. I believe, even if there is a misunderstanding it should not affect our judicial work.

During that period, I was fortunate enough to have played a vital role in the administration of justice, commanded respect from all because of my swift grasp of points of law in most matters, and accordingly was able to play a pivotal role in the policy matters of the judiciary bypassing the Chief Justice.

Chapter 7

Judicial Service Commission

I was appointed the Chairman of the Judicial Service Commission although Md. Mozammel Hossain was senior to me. The Judicial Service Commission is housed in a few rooms of the Judicial Training Institute (JTI). There was acute space scarcity for officers and staff. So, without delay I initiated a development program for vertical extension of the JTI building by three floors for proper accommodation. I knew that the government machinery moves very slowly, but I had a very short period to complete this work otherwise the project would be frustrated. I had the advantage that then Finance Secretary Fazle Kabir, a sound and sober, intelligent gentleman, was a member of the Commission. On one occasion, he himself volunteered that he knew me for a long time and he was one of my admirers. I told him that unless he supports me it would be difficult to complete the development of the Commission. He extended his hands willingly and assured me that whenever any genuine development would be necessary, he would provide the fund.

I directed my Secretary Farid Ahmed Sibli, a brilliant senior officer, to expedite the preparation of drawing and other paper work for vertical extension of the building. He had very good links with the officers and within a very short time the paper work for the extension of the building was prepared. Then I approached the Finance Secretary for the necessary fund. Once we received the fund and finalized plan I deputed an officer to oversee the development work. Meanwhile some brilliant officers were recruited in the Commission by removing some existing ones. Besides officers, I used to convene meetings with the engineers entrusted with the work. At one stage, I noticed that the contractor could not complete the project and the remaining fund was returned to the government after the end of the financial year. This annoyed me hugely because bringing back the fund after returning it would take time. I directed the contractor to continue his work and assured him that I would take care of the finance. Due to my persistent pressure, I surmise, the contractor abandoned the work.

I directed the office to forfeit his security money and directed the office to appoint a new contractor without delay. A new contractor was appointed but there was delay in providing the fund chiefly because of the Law Ministry's tardiness in communicating with the Finance Ministry. I deputed an officer to liaise with the Finance Ministry and thus the project was completed within two years.

I had selected each item of the fittings of floors, toilets and purchasing the furniture. I arranged a conference room, two viva-voce examination rooms, a library, waiting room for the resource persons and another conference hall in the top floor. It was designed by me. Initially the hall was raised in the similar manner by putting grills and walls as are normally done. I told them that the hall should be installed with colored glasses without any wall in the manner the foreign countries made wall with glass. The contractor and engineer were confused with my advice. But I insisted on, to see the beautification of the Dhaka city from the hall and ultimately, I could prevail upon them. It is one of the most beautiful, well-built halls. Whenever foreign dignitaries visited the Commission they were entertained in that hall. They all praised seeing the architectural design and its interior design and beautification. Even the floors were so beautifully decorated that they commented that it is the best building they ever seen in Dhaka. I set up a new modern library with a huge collection of books and installed three computers in the middle of the room, with which other libraries in the world could be visited through digital means. I appointed a qualified librarian to look after the library.

The viva-voce exam rooms were in fact unused the whole year except for 10/15 days a year and sometimes even longer. I directed the office to convert the rooms in such a manner that they could be used as arbitration centers. The charge for each arbitration sitting was fixed at taka. 6,000. After the library and the arbitration center began operating, the retired judges who used to conduct arbitration proceedings were very happy and they used to recommend the venue at Judicial Service Commission. I kept the rent of the venue a bit lower than other private stakeholders arrange venue for arbitration. The arbitration proceedings are held in two shifts and the money is deposited in the government fund. In fact, the expense of the Commission can be borne out of the income through arbitration proceedings. I also set up an archive in the Commission, a gymnasium and a suite for accommodation of two guests keeping in mind that everywhere outside the country the judiciary maintains a guest house where visiting judges are provided. In all Indian States, there are separate guest houses for judges. So, whenever any judge intending to visit Bangladesh, the Chief Justice must face an awkward position. He must approach to the Law Minister, Attorney General or Foreign Minister to accommodate the guest at a 5-star hotel. After the suite was opened, judges from India and other countries are accommodated there. Because, the judges visiting our country contacted the Chief Justice for accommodation. The Chief Justice was put in an embarrassing position. Now the problem is solved. After I became the Chief Justice, I earmarked House No-1 of the Supreme Court judges' complex as the rest house after renovating it. The Supreme Court is now equipped with a world class guest house.

In course of time, when I noticed that all question papers of public exams for the judiciary were leaked I talked with my officers about finding a solution that would prevent these episodes. I have entrusted two officers with the task and I directed the Commission office to make provisions for online acceptance of applications from prospective candidates. Under the existing system whenever an examination is scheduled to be held, the candidate must collect the application form from certain branches of the Sonali Bank only. In that case the applicant from remote areas of the country and who are residing abroad had to travel long way to collect the form. For improvement of the Commission's exam process, I visited India, the UK, Scotland, Singapore and Indonesia and wanted to know their systems. I sought help from our Scotland counterparts to provide help in digitizing our system. They expressed their eagerness if any proposal was sent to them with our requirements. The examinations are held in three phases. The first examination was for screening out about sixty percent of candidates. Out of 5,000 to 8,000 candidates, selection is to be made only 100 or less. It was heavy task. There was provision for setting question by two examiners and then the questions were sent to a moderator for finalization. I decided that the procedure should be maintained but none of the questions prepared by examiners or moderators are finally kept in the examination. I used to sit with the Secretary for finalization of questions in such a twisted manner that it was difficult to imagine for the examiners how the questions were so changed. On one occasion the Public Service Commission also sought our help to improve their standard.

Our problem is that we were confined to certain laws beyond which we could not go. In the schedule of the Rules, the syllabus for the examination is restricted. Naturally, the question setters had to repeat many questions. In the Judicial Service Commission meetings, we adopted resolutions many times and requested the Law Secretary to amend the rules for setting questions according to the discretion of the Commission. In each meeting the Law Secretary assured us that he would do the needful, but we did not find any fruitful result. In the meetings the Janaproshason Secretary, the Finance Secretary, a professor of a public university attended, but no result ensued. On one occasion I asked the Law Secretary the reason for the delay. On hearing his reply, I was surprised. His reply was that if any Chairman aligned with the ideology of the BNP or Jamaat was appointed, he would set up questions in such a manner that they would ignore the history of our liberation war and progressive thinking. I told him that similar incident could happen at the PSC too. Moreover, if he could change the rules, what would stop the other political parties to alter the rules after coming to power?

The Law Secretary in fact made the Commission unworkable. I recollect an incident which was very pathetic. As per rule, within December 31, the Law Ministry was required to submit next year's requisition for selection of candidates. In the academic session, possibly of 2013, no requisition was sent despite repeated requests. Sometime in April, he sent a requisition for 24 candidates. According to our estimation more than one hundred candidates could be recruited. I sent an officer to show the Law Secretary about the prospective vacant posts, which were about 150. The reasoning and the argument of necessity fell on deaf ears. He did not issue any modified requisition. We thought since an examination process is huge, and it was not the worthy of our time and energy to initiate an exam process for only 24 candidates. We could not persuade the Law Secretary to change his mind. At one point, he said that if he modified the requisition he would be sent to jail. I showed him the chart of officers who were supposed to go on retirement and it would take only ten minutes to calculate. Ultimately, we were able to convince him to send requisition for 54 candidates, although there were 150 vacant posts.

The examination process was lengthy that it takes one and a half years to complete. The Ministry takes six months for gazette notification after police verification. We felt the adverse effect of this cumbersome process in 2015 and 2016. There was acute shortage of Assistant Judges. After appointment of an officer he cannot become a full-fledged judge in a couple of years. He requires training and he must undergo a departmental examination after two years of appointment. To turn out a mature judicial officer it takes six to seven years. Consequently, if the appointment process is delayed, the litigants suffer due to shortage of courts. In 2016, the Chairman had published notification for appointment of around 100 candidates, but he was compelled to publish results of 300 candidates. There is lot of difficulty in the recruitment of more than 100 candidates in a batch, because after their recruitment, some of the officers who were at the top in seniority would be promoted to the level of Additional District Judges but some of their batchmates would remain as Senior Assistant Judges, thus creating embarrassment for them.

I also introduced various modifications in the examination system. The first process is after submission of application, there was a system of decoding the applicants and the coding was made so secretly that only a member of the Commission who is trusted is given the task for decoding. Then the question papers were prepared in the similar way that followed in the preliminary. Three sets of questions were prepared through three examiners on a subject and sent to the moderators and the chairman finalized one set of question changing altogether in different manner those prepared by examiners and moderators to avoid the possibility of leakage and repetition. We discovered that most of the question papers were leaked from BG Press. Therefore, we decided that not only the question papers, but the answer scripts should also be prepared by the Commission despite its inadequate number of staffs. Nevertheless, we purchased three printing machines and thence onward we printed all the question papers and answer scripts and the Commission became self-sufficient. By the time I left the Commission, it had been transformed into a self-sufficient institution. The system became foolproof to the extent that even if the Chairman of the Commission wanted to make a candidate successful, he would not be able to do so. We had prepared a video cassette to display the transparency of our new system. After looking at the video, our New Delhi counterpart greatly appreciated our mode of exams and told us that he would introduce a similar system in the next exam in New Delhi.

As Chairman of the Commission, as I've recounted earlier, I visited many countries to acquaint myself with the various processes followed elsewhere. While in India I met the Chief Justice of India and other senior judges and held an official meeting in which the senior most judge and other high officials were present. Our High Commissioner was also present during the discussions. There I sought cooperation for the training of the judges of the Supreme Court in the National Judicial Training Institute, Bhopal. Chief Justice Altamas Kabir assured us of arranging the necessary training, adding that Pakistani, Sri Lankan, Nepalese and Bhutanese judges were availing the training opportunity there. During my tenure as Chief Justice the first batch of judges attended their training there.

In Indonesia, when I met the Chief Justice and the Chairman of the Judicial Appointment Commission I came to know that they select brilliant young law graduates from the universities for training as judges and for other positions. They called this "Green Harvesting". The same system is followed in Singapore and South Korea as well. The best students are selected as judicial officers and the second batch of good students are appointed as public prosecutors and the last batch can practice in the courts as lawyers. I also talked with the Attorney General whose rank is equivalent to a cabinet minister. I have been to the Judicial Training Institute in Indonesia and seen the trainers' training program. I had the privilege of speaking a few words in both the training programs at the request of my counterpart who was a woman in charge of the Commission. I apprised them of our strong judicial heritage and the functioning of the court system. In UK and Scotland, the appointment process is completely different from other countries. The Commissions are headed by laymen and other members are judges of the highest courts and members of different communities who have practical knowledge of socio-political affairs. Even judges of the highest court are selected based on applications filed by the candidates. In England, even a magistrate's minimum eligibility for appointment is Barrister with experience of not less than ten years.

Chapter 8
Charitable Work

After the disposal of the Bangabandhu murder appeal, I came to New York for my second checkup and confirmed that my treatment in Singapore was accurate and was advised again that I need not consult any oncologist other than the Singapore consultant. It was indeed a tremendous relief and the removal of agony from a life-threatening disease. I was boosted with new energy to give proper attention toward the administration of justice and determined that if I could overcome a life-threatening disease, I would try to make innovative change in the judiciary. From New York I went to Boston to meet my younger brother Dr. Ananta Kumar Sinha and visited Harvard University. I was also contemplating purchase of some books. My brother was happy to see me and gave me some money to repay the loan I had taken for my treatment. I asked them to send the money to my account maintained with Sonali Bank, Supreme Court branch.

I thought that since I had received a second shot at life I should utilize the money for charitable purposes and it would be most appropriate if the charity was dedicated to the memory of my parents. I registered "Lalit Mohan & Dhanabati Trust" and opened a fixed deposit account in the name of the charity and kept twenty-five lac taka in it with a view to meet the expenses from the interest, with the specific provision that in no case the fixed deposit money would be withdrawn. With the help of my brother-in-law Dr. Nanda Kishore Sinha and some villagers we had opened a library 'Lalit Mohan Gonogranthagar' (public library) in memory of my father. The trust assumed responsibility for the library aiming to modernize it and a permanent librarian was appointed. Over a period I purchased books worth about thirty lac takas for the library.

The library was started in a room of my outer house and in another room a computer training center with about fifteen computers was started with the object of training local boys and girls free of cost and to confer a computer diploma on passing. I appointed two permanent teachers for training and the center got registered with the Technical Education Board so that the students can officially utilize the certificate to be given after completion of training. The students are undergoing three and six months training courses there. About forty-five students are trained round the year. The number of books and manuals is increasing as also the number of students. Therefore, the training center cannot continue to be accommodated in the present location because two other outer rooms are occupied by my security detail. Hence, I arranged a piece of land of seven decimal for construction of a four storey building for extending the library and accommodating the students. A two-storied building has already been constructed and the library has been shifted to the first floor with the computer training center in two rooms of the ground floor. Other rooms are also used for the library. I have a personal library with a huge collection of books on law, philosophy, and autobiography of great personalities, history and literature valued above fifty lac takas. I have meanwhile donated my books to the charity.

Our area is mainly populated by our community's people and in my Thana about forty percent of the population is Hindu. Hindus are cremated on the banks of river and small water body. No permanent or modern cremation ground is available and dead bodies are cremated with wood. These cremation grounds are washed away during the rainy season by heavy rain and gushing flood waters. Since it is a rain-prone area, sometimes the rain continues for two days. In such conditions if one dies, the bereaved family must wait till the rain stops. Dry wood is also not available during the rains. The total cremation of a body requires a large quantity of wood and takes at least seven to eight hours to be completed. The use of wood and bamboos causes profound environmental depletion. To remove the difficulties, I procured about twenty-five decimals of land near the Dhalai River, raised a boundary wall for protection, installed a semi-deep tube well, planted trees around the land and started construction of a modern cremation ground. I have already spent about thirty lac taka and it will require a further amount of more than about fifty lac takas. I had hoped to complete the work from my pension benefits but the government for reasons not known to me has not given my pension funds although Justice Md. Abdul Wahhab Miah, who resigned after me got his benefits immediately after resignation. If the project is complete, all dead bodies of Moulvibazar districts can be cremated without cost in a short time. Our area is developed in communication and carrying of a dead body from the remotest area will hardly take thirty to forty minutes.

I also undertook a project for paying the education cost of some poor students from graduation to post graduation level and I had been providing for around thirty to thirty-four students Tk 2000 to 2500 every month for the last six to seven years regularly. But due to compelling circumstances beyond my control the project had to be stopped from October 2017. I feel for those poor students who cannot continue with their education. I am totally unable to help them at this moment although they are contacting my charity office regularly in the hope of getting help. I also try to help the needy families who cannot marry off their daughters or cannot perform Shradha ceremony on the death of near ones. To these people I give a lumpsum grant of Tk 15,000 to 20,000. I distribute clothes to Muslims twice a year and to the Hindus once during Durga Puja. Besides, my charity distributes blankets every year during winter.

All these charitable works are done in the name of my parents. I did not do anything in my name; but in the neighboring village Madhabpur the villagers started a school and college in my name and requested me to inaugurate it. I was very embarrassed that the institution was named after me. However, when an institution for education has been set up I felt compelled to contribute some ten-lac taka to the educational institution from my pocket. Madhabpur village is possibly the biggest one in our thana and most of the people of the village is illiterate. Finally, however the institution, "Justice Surendra Kumar Sinha School and College," was inaugurated by Education Minister Nurul Islam Nahid. I had wished to launch a sewing training program but could not implement it yet due to a shortage of space although I have collected some sewing machines. In this project five employees are already working and at present my elder brother is managing it in my absence, but I fear whether he will be able to properly undertake all work including pisciculture, which I have been developing in three ponds with a substantial investment.

Chapter 9

Role in the Formation of ICT

Among the agendas of the Bangladesh Awami League in the 2008 parliamentary elections was that if it came to power the government would bring the offenders of war crimes, crimes against humanity and genocide to justice. Ultimately, the Awami League managed to form the government and in the process of implementation of its agenda, it wanted to set up a tribunal in the old High Court building. Shafique Ahmed, Justice Abdur Rashid and I were working on the matter, because Shafique Ahmed wanted our help in the selection process of the prosecutors and judges. I suggested Rana Das Gupta, a prominent lawyer of Chittagong, to be included as a member of the tribunal. Mohammad Nizamul Haque was selected as Chairman of the tribunal as he was involved in the process of "Gonoadalat" (people's court) in a symbolic trial of perpetrators of war crimes.

After getting the green signal, I requested Rana Das Gupta to come to Dhaka as soon as possible. I took him to Abdur Rashid's residence and we had several discussions. Rana Das Gupta was reluctant to give up his lucrative practice he had developed in Chittagong. We convinced him to sacrifice his profession for the cause of the nation. Unwillingly he consented to our proposal. It was communicated to the Law Minister. Subsequently, for reasons not known to us we learnt that Rana Das Gupta was dropped from the list of possible members of the tribunal. Then we suggested his name as chief prosecutor. But Tipu Sultan was picked for the job because he had close relations with the Law Minister and other high ups, although he was already very senior in age. I subsequently noticed that even in the list of prosecutors Rana Das Gupta's name was not included.

It may be mentioned that I was requested to convince Rana Das Gupta and accordingly I requested him to come to Dhaka. Nizamul Haque along with two members ATM Fazle Kabir and AKM Zahir Ahmed, a retired District Judge, were chosen for the constitution of the tribunal. In place of Rana Das Gupta, Zahir Ahmed was selected. It was a bad selection which the government realized later. But in the meantime, a lot of misgivings were generated. The work of the tribunal was not progressing properly. Md Nizamul Haque was unnecessarily wasting time by writing lengthy orders-- even at the time of disposal of petty applications. Naturally, the accused would try to delay the trial of the cases. It is the task of the Chairman of the tribunal to ensure the administration of the tribunal and he must have appropriate knowledge on case management system.

Generally, it was expected that Nizamul Haque produce favorable results in the handling of the cases mainly because he had knowledge on criminal law as he had worked with late Aminul Haque for a considerable period. Everybody thought that he was a good choice. But instead the selection produced negative results. He could not conclude the trial even one case in a year. He was pursuing me, off and on, for his elevation to the Appellate Division and simultaneously he was lobbying for giving him a position like the Chief Justice, or at least close to that position.

Whenever he came to meet me I advised him to expedite the trial process and at least dispose of one or two cases. His name cannot be considered for elevation to the Appellate Division unless he disposes of at least one case. Ultimately, the Law Minister, Air Commodore (retired) AK Khandker, the Planning Minister and the Chairman of the Sector Commanders' Forum, also the Deputy Chief of the Liberation Forces, wanted to constitute another tribunal as the trial did not get momentum. Though the country was functioning under a parliamentary form of government, it was so only on paper. Even after the amendment to the Constitution in 1991 changing the form of government, the country was being run, in reality, as in a presidential form by setting up the Prime Minister's Secretariat and strengthening the Prime Minister's Office. All decisions were being made by the Prime Minister's Office irrespective of whether it was an Awami League or BNP government. The Law Minister therefore had little power to exercise discretion in any policy matter. Shafique Ahmed and AK Khandaker met the Prime Minister with a proposal to set up another tribunal. The Prime Minister outright rejected their proposal saying that the tribunal was constituted as a political decision with a view to fulfil the election pledge. But there was little scope of success and have any result in the process. Later, I came to know that the two senior ministers did not utter a single word when the Prime Minister refused their proposal and returned with broken hearts.

Shafique Ahmed then contacted me with a request to persuade the Prime Minister for setting up another tribunal. According to him, if I lobbied with the Prime Minister, I would be able to convince her. I was reluctant to interfere in the matter because I was thinking that as a sitting judge it was not fair for me to talk with the Prime Minister over an executive matter and I told the Law Minister that after two Senior Ministers' proposal had been turned down by the Prime Minister, I would not like to get involved in the matter again lest she refused again, which would put me in an awkward position. He repeated that it was his firm conviction that if I requested the Prime Minister, the idea could be implemented. Shafique Ahmed is a very sound, polite gentleman. We regard him as a gentleman par excellence. His firm belief left me in a dilemma. I told him that I would think over the matter again.

Then I decided that it was the demand of most people who knew that the people had suffered during the war of liberation. We sacrificed three million lives and more than 100,000 people had lost their limbs, some of them were maimed forever and 200,000 females had lost their chastity. As a citizen of this country, besides being a judge, I have an obligation to the nation. I also realized that if the country had not been liberated at the call of Bangagbandhu Sheikh Mujibur Rahman, I would have ended up as a teacher of a school or at best as a lawyer of the sub-divisional court. Independence not only gave a flag to the nation, it gave new life to the thinking of persons who had survived and could lead the country better than who had been ruling our country in the past. I became the judge of the highest court because of the country's independence and I could not deserve more power or prestige from the country other than by showing respect to the souls of the martyrs. If it is my belief, it was an obligation on my part to try to persuade the Prime Minister once again and if any favorable result could be achieved from my endeavor, it would be a great honor and respect for the sacrifice made by our courageous freedom loving people. So, I decided to approach the Prime Minister. Accordingly, I requested a meeting with the Prime Minister at a secret place. I got a favorable reply within few hours. This emboldened me in my belief that I would be able to convince the Prime Minister

When we met I told the Prime Minister the purpose of my meeting. The moment I raised the point, I felt she reacted sharply. Then she became emotional and explained to me the suffering she had undergone in getting justice for the trial of those who had murdered her parents and younger brothers. She told me how much money she spent for collecting and safeguarding witnesses and said the mental pressure she withstood was beyond comprehension. She was intensely interested in putting the offenders to justice, but she had to cross a lot of hurdles. Given that backdrop she straightaway rejected the proposal of the Ministers. She frankly conceded that corruption was rampant, and since the offenders were powerful persons having money and muscle, and they could influence any official or witness and this could not be tackled by the administration all the time. Moreover, forty years had elapsed in the meantime, and it was extremely difficult to collect witnesses as most of them are not alive now. She had set up the tribunal chiefly to meet her election pledge and there was nothing more than that she was prepared to do. She was still in a highly emotional state even after she had spoken for 15/20 minutes while I heard her without any interruption. I realized if I inserted any comment she would take exception. After she had completed expressing her opinion I noticed she relaxed a bit. I then started to submit my plea. I told her that I was a judge of her father's case and knew everything upon conclusion of the hearing of the case. I found many loopholes in the trial, but these were because of the lapse of time and changes in the political scenario in the country.

But the war crimes trial was completely different from her parents killing case, I explained. Bangababdhu's murder case was tried under the general law and it was an obsolete law for which she had to undergo a lot of troubles. But in respect of offences of crimes against humanity, the procedure is totally different. The prosecution or for that purpose the government need not take so much pain in collecting evidence to prove a charge in the manner she had collected evidence in her father's assassination trial. I further explained to her in brief the process of trial of the cases, mode of recording evidence and the admissibility of evidence which are totally distinct from the earlier trial. Under the new system, affidavit evidence is admissible, newspaper reports are available, video reports and photographs are also admissible, no matter from where it was collected. Most of the evidence can be collected from the national archives and some of them can be collected from freedom fighters' possession. The process can be expedited if the government provided enough money and right persons were selected for the purpose. I told her that the selection of the First tribunal was not proper and there were errors.

After hearing me out on the differences between trials under general and special laws, I noticed a change in the Prime Minister's demeanor. Then she took out her diary and wanted to know what the requirements were for setting up another tribunal and how the trial process could be expedited. I told her that the first thing was to give some resources like laptops to the investigation agency, prosecutors and judges. Then I talked about the selection of prosecutors. I told her that only four prosecutors would be required to be appointed. I added, if another tribunal was set up she would get results within six months. She assured me of that if the list of prosecutors was sent to her she would arrange for their appointment and take steps for setting up the second tribunal. Subsequently, within fifteen days the Prime Minister fulfilled her commitment.

I informed the Law Minister about the result of the talk. He was very happy and was keen to initiate the process. But he could not arrange for the lawyers I had suggested to him. In the meantime, the Skype controversy involving Nizamul Haque became public. In the conversation he had taken my name three to four times. On behalf of the offenders, recusal petition was filed against me when the appeals hearing began. I declared that I was not feeling embarrassed because I did not speak to Nizamul Haque regarding the trial of the cases or touched on the merit of the cases or even anything about trial process. Whenever he came to me for elevation to the higher bench, I told him that he had to conclude trial of at least one or two cases before his name could be considered for elevation.

On behalf of the convicted accused, it was pointed out that I had directed Nizamul Haque to hang one or two accused. Nizamul Haque had said, "I told Sinha Babu to take me in the Appellate Division, but he told me to dispose of one or two cases." The accused misinterpreted his version claiming that I had directed him to hand down capital punishment to one or two accused. Moreover, since he could not conclude any of the trials, the appeals were not on any verdict of Justice Nizamul Haque. There was thus no legal bar for me to sit in the Bench to hear the appeals. Nizamul Haque was compelled to resign after publication of the Skype conversation in the newspapers. Then the question arose about the selection of chairmen of the two tribunals. I talked with Obaidul Hasan and M Enayetur Rahim. Obaidul Hasan responded that if he was given any responsibility, he was ready to take charge. But Enayetur Rahim was reluctant claiming his father was an MP and his brother is also an MP. If he is appointed as the chairman of a tribunal, objections might arise. Ultimately Fazle Kabir was appointed Chairman of Tribunal-1 and Obaidul Hasan was made Chairman of Tribunal-2. After the retirement of Fazle Kabir, Enayetur Rahim became the Chairman of Tribuanl-1. The trial of the cases gained some momentum after the constitution of two tribunals. The first judgment was delivered in Abdul Quader Mollah's case.2

References:

1. The Constitution of Bangladesh (XXII) Amendment Act, 1991
2. Criminal Appeal Nos. 24 and 25 of 2013

Chapter 10
Appointment as Chief Justice of Bangladesh

About three months before the date of retirement of Justice Md. Mozammel Hossain, various stories were circulating regarding the appointment of the next Chief Justice. Shamsuddin Chowdhury was trying hard to become the next Chief Justice and the other speculation was that Nazmun Ara Sultana, having been the first lady Judge as Munsif, District Judge, Judge in the High Court and the Appellate Divisions, was a possible choice as the Chief Justice. Even i that came to pass, I would have a chance of becoming the Chief Justice after her retirement. Moreover, the Prime Minister and the Speaker being females, the Prime Minister could show to the world that three branches of the State are headed by females in Bangladesh. It would be a historical event as nowhere in the world there was such a coincidence. Shamsuddin Chowdhury was scampering from earth to heaven for his selection. Even that if that happened there was also a likelihood of my becoming the Chief Justice as he would retire before Nazmun Ara Sultana.

On the other hand, Md. Abdul Wahhab Miah was very anxious about such rumors. Although he knew that he would not be chosen for that office, his apprehension was that if those judges were appointed, they were junior to him, he would have no other alternative but to resign. But in case of my appointment, he would continue till my retirement on January 31, 2018. Accordingly, he was repeatedly requesting me to contact the Prime Minister and other policy makers so that I was not superseded. I told him that, I did not know whether I would be appointed to the office, but I am sure that Shamsuddin Chowdhury would not be taken into consideration for the office of the Chief Justice for he was not at all competent to occupy that office. Additionally, the Prime Minister was mature and competent enough to know right from wrong. She would not choose the junior most judge of the court as the chief justice. I also told him that I am the last person to approach on my behalf to occupy the exalted office.

It may be recalled, the conduct of Shamsuddin Chowdhury was beyond the control of the Chief Justice, when he was in the High Court Division. On different occasions, his Bench was changed and even then, he was passing orders recklessly against public servants and issued contempt rules without just cause and directed them to appear in person in court. He kept them standing throughout the court hours and then adjourned the matters. The government was also embarrassed by his conduct. While sitting in a writ Bench, he interfered with pure and simple criminal matters ignoring the grounds of the constitution of his Bench which was not authorized to adjudicate on those matters. On one occasion I persuaded the Chief Justice to change the constitution of the bench. Ultimately finding no other alternative, the government thought that he should be elevated to the Appellate Division so that he would not be able to pass such orders since he was the junior most judge and would have no such authority.

About his appointment, there was an interesting story. Though he had close friendship with Chief Justice Mohammad Mozammel Hossain, the latter did not recommend his name. As per provisions of the Constitution the President shall appoint the judges after consultation with the Chief Justice.2 the President appointed him without such consultation, when Shamsuddin Chowdhury was in London. The appointment was displayed in the TV scroll. On noticing the action of the government, the Chief Justice contacted the Law Minister saying that his name should be dropped. Shafique Ahmed, the Law Minister, wanted my advice in this regard. I told him not to worry about it, and instead to inform the Chief Justice that the government was thinking seriously about the amendment of Article 96 of the Constitution for removal of the judges of the Supreme Court by a resolution of supported by most two-third members of Parliament on the ground of proven misbehavior or incapacity. As a matter of fact, former Chief Justice Khairul Haque, Suranjit Sengupta MP and some other MPs were seriously pressing the Prime Minister to introduce such a provision by amending the Constitution. Murad Reza, the Additional

Attorney General, who oversaw the Attorney General's office as the Attorney General was out of the country, rushed to my official residence and intimated me that serious complications would arise if the Chief Justice was not eager to accept Justice Shamsuddin Chowdhury. I told him that I already had advised the Law Minister in this regard. Despite that I along with Murad Reza was trying to contact Justice Shamsuddin Choudhry in London to return immediately. After finally collecting the contact number from his wife we called him and advised him to return to Bangladesh on the next available flight. Murad Reza and I told him the reason and he assured us that he would try. But in the meantime, we got a message that the Chief Justice, frightened by the news of the possibility of a constitutional amendment after having been informed by the Law Minister, called the latter declaring that he had no objection to the appointment of Shamsuddin Chowdhury.

I was clear in my mind that anyone amongst Nazmun Ara Sultana or Syed Mahmud Hossain might be appointed Chief Justice if the Prime Minister did not feel comfortable to appoint a minority member of the community in a Muslim majority country. I had also definite information that the Prime Minister was willing to recommend my name but was seriously weighing the impact of the appointment of a member from a minority community as the Chief Justice of Bangladesh. I, however, felt that under the circumstances then prevailing in the country, there was no reason on her part not to appoint me as the Chief Justice. I had also decided that if I was not selected, I would step down immediately. But I did not disclose my feelings to anyone. Meanwhile though, Abdul Wahhab Miah was so anxious that he was pressurizing me every alternate day to maintain a liaison with the hierarchy so that my name was recommended. I told him in clear terms that I was the last person to request anybody in the selection of a candidate for the exalted office. But I assured him that in no case Shamsuddin Chowdhury would be appointed.

Ultimately about seven days prior to the date of retirement of Mohammad Mozammel Hossain, Law Minister Anisul Haque wanted to meet me at a secret location. I told him to come to the Judicial Service Conference Hall which was just the right place for such a meeting. Accordingly, in the late afternoon the Law Minister came and congratulated me on my selection as the next Chief Justice of Bangladesh, telling me that it was decided in a meeting in the Bangabhaban with the President, the Prime Minister and himself. I kept the matter concealed, but the following day there were strong rumors that Shamsuddin Chowdhury would be appointed as Chief Justice. On hearing the rumors, I was laughing to myself; but the more the rumors spread the more concerned Abdul Wahab Miah became. I noticed that he could not concentrate his mind in the administration of justice. One day I sternly urged him that he should give attention to his work and should not pay heed to rumors. If destiny favored me, I would be selected as the Chief Justice, but assured him that Shamsuddin Choudhury had no chance even for consideration as a prospective candidate. Under the constitutional mandate it is the President's power to select and appoint the Chief Justice. But in Bangladesh the President is holding no power at all. It was not only during that period but had been all along after the presidential system was abolished. Wahab Miah left my chamber with a broken heart. As always, a day or two before oath-taking was to take place, it was published in the media that I had been selected as the next Chief Justice of Bangladesh. Accordingly, I took oath of office on July 15, 2015. It was a historic moment because no member of any minority community had ever occupied such an exalted office in a Muslim-majority country in the world.

As a convention, on the day of taking the oath, a felicitation for the Chief Justice is held. I had fixed the time at 10:30 AM for the purpose. It was a memorable occasion. I also realized that irrespective of the political polarization, all lawyers would join in the felicitation, although on the last five or six occasions, only a fraction of lawyers of the ruling party attended the occasion. It was for the first time the lawyers of the AL, BNP, Jamaat and Ganotantrik Forum attended. Courtroom number one was packed and left with no space inside the room, many lawyers were standing on the western and southern verandahs of the building. Therefore, I directed to my Registry to arrange extra chairs outside the courtroom and speaker so the lawyers there could hear the proceedings.

In reply to the felicitations, I told the lawyers that my priority would be to reform the judiciary. Among first actions:

a) Judicial reforms;
b) Ensuring the utilization of courts allocated full time in judicial work, i.e. sitting in court and rising according the agreed time;
c) Digitization of the entire Judiciary;
d) Bringing discipline to the Judiciary;
e) Restoring public confidence in the judiciary;
f) Making the Judiciary function without interference from the Executive;
g) There would be no mentions in court and no fixation of any matter for early hearing while cases would automatically be listed in the daily Cause List on the basis of the order of the judge -in- chamber;
h) Curtailing holidays of the Supreme Court;
i) Signing judgments and orders expeditiously not later than six months from the date of delivery;
j) Increasing the court rooms and the number of judges.

It may be mentioned that during my predecessor's tenure the court wasted about one and half hours every day. That is, though the time for the sitting of the court is 9:00AM, the court usually sat at 9:30 to 9:45AM. And again, after a recess, the court was scheduled to sit at 11:00 AM but we usually sat between 11:30 and 11:45 AM and rose at 1:00 PM in place of 1:15 PM. I had performed the functions of the Chief Justice many times when Chief Justice Md. Mozammel Hossain was away from the country. But when I wanted to sit in court on time Justice Abdul Wahhab Miah prevented me, saying that when I would be the Chief Justice, I would fix the time table, but the old system would be followed till the retirement of Chief Justice Mozammel Hossain. Other judges remained silent, meaning they were supporting Abdul Wahhab Miah's view. So, I could not set a definite schedule. When I disclosed the details of the sitting of the court, judges were compelled to sit with me in time.

Another problem related to the wastage of time during mention of cases every Sunday. There used to be a long queue of lawyers every day. They mentioned that their cases were so urgent that they had fixed the matters with the chamber judge as per the direction of the Chief Justice, but the cases were not posted on the list. When I was sitting beside the Chief Justice I used to think of all the time wasted by him. But I was helpless. There were allegations of corruption regarding taking advantage by way of wealthy persons getting their cases listed in exchange of money. Sometimes lacs of taka were paid to some designated persons and it was an open secret.

There were also reasons for these. The former Chief Justice did not constitute a second Bench with senior most judges or the second senior most judge but sat with all the seven judges hearing miscellaneous petitions. It was such a laughable matter that senior lawyers were why we did not constitute a second Bench. I felt embarrassed and said that it was the prerogative of the Chief Justice. When the Chief Justice fixed two or three appeals of the convicted accused for crimes against humanity under the ICT Acts of 1973, he constituted a second Bench headed by Nazmun Ara Sultana. Never during his tenure of three years and eight months had the former Chief Justice ever given any independent Bench to me. I had the opportunity to preside the bench when he was abroad.

The Judiciary is of course a vital organ of the State. Normally whenever a new Prime Minister or President assumes office, s/he visits the National Mausoleum to pay respect to the martyrs by placing wreaths. Even foreign dignitaries including visiting presidents and prime ministers are taken there on the first day of their visit. But never had any Chief Justice visited the National Mausoleum to show respect to the martyrs. So, after the felicitation ceremony was over, I told all the judges that I would go to the mausoleum for laying wreaths to pay my respect to the martyrs. All of them expressed their willingness to accompany me. It was a memorable occasion. The GOC of the 9th Division and the local parliament member received the Chief Justice and the accompanying judges. Media people and people in general gathered there and I laid floral wreaths at the National Mausoleum officially and then wrote comments in the visitors' book. This event was also widely appreciated by media.

On the following day, I constituted two Benches, one was with me as the Chief Justice, and the other one presided over by Justice Abdul Wahhab Miah and both the courts started working simultaneously. I directed the office to enlist all the cases which were not posted in the daily Cause List and prevented the lawyers from mentioning cases in open courts and thus wasting time. Within six months of my assumption of office, there was a complete change in the atmosphere at the Supreme Court and at one point I found that I did not find enough lawyers after the recesses. I disposed of around one hundred to one hundred twenty cases on petition day and twelve to fifteen appeals on appeal day. About sixty to seventy percent petitions were disposed of in open court by dictation, a practice that was not prevalent previously in the Supreme Court. The orders and judgments were available within a week or two, sometimes in a day. So, the litigants were relieved of their long agony due to not getting orders from the court and the lawyers were also happy.

Another improvement I was able to make was to restrict dawdling of lawyers on any matter. Within a minute or two, I brought out the point. The lawyers were sometimes found unprepared to meet the queries. All complicated matters were disposed of within five to six minutes. In no case I allowed a petition to take up more than ten minutes. Previously this would be heard for hours together. The net result was that the disposal rate increased by more than sixty percent. It so happened that after one year, some lawyers were not even interested to dispose of their cases and sometimes they were uneasy when their cases were listed.

I had directed the office to enlist the cases year-wise and the cases were appearing in the daily Cause List serially without interference and without any illegal financial transaction. I found no appearance of lawyers in old cases. Sometimes, I granted Suo moto leave when I found law points asking someone advocates-on-record siting in the front desk. There was another precedent in the court that even after dismissal of a suit by three courts, at the time of dismissing of leave petition a lengthy judgment was delivered. I stopped this practice and disposed of those petitions in concise orders. A petition which has no merit at all does not require a lengthy judgment taking up unnecessary time of the court and thus the process also helped in disposing of cases expeditiously. The judges were also relieved of unnecessary pressure and work load. I encouraged my brother judges to write short orders and while granting leave we passed short leave granting orders that enabled the judges to sign the orders very quickly. Previously I found some leave granting orders were not signed in three years---a period during which the appeal could have been disposed of. There was a radical change in the system of work at which the litigants, the lawyers and the judges were all happy. But the bench readers had to take a lot of pressure because of the huge number of cases handled.

Tahmina Anam, a writer and anthropologist and author of 'A Golden Age', wrote an article in 'The International New York Times' of February 9, 2015, where while writing about 'oborodh' (obstruction) she said, "Clashes with police and random acts of violence occur on a daily basis, schools and factories are closed, businesses are failing, and in the capital the simple act of getting from one side of town to the other has become dangerous. Amid this grim news, there is a small glimmer of light: the appointment of Surendra Kumar Sinha, a Hindu and the first minority Chief Justice in this Muslim-majority country." She added, 'Justice Sinha has already indicated that he wishes to modernize the judiciary. On Jan.18, in his first public address since being sworn in, he proposed the reform of colonial-era laws and a sustained effort to improve the efficiency of the courts. He also urged the judiciary to take a close look at itself and work harder, with greater transparency and in more democratic ways. If only Justice Sinha had been around a dozen years ago, when the judicial system came crashing into my own household...Justice Sinha has proposed doubling the number of judges and has called for more automation of the courts' administrative functions. The law is not like antique to be taken down, admired and put back on the self' she said. He wants his courts to enjoy the 'full public confidence and credibility of all.' In the current political climate, it is difficult to find cause for celebration. Nor does it mean that Bangladesh's treatment of minorities has fundamentally changed. There is a culture of repression in the legal system, too, that is alarming. And the mandate for the head is not an easy one: to strengthen the integrity and political neutrality of our courts. Justice Sinha's appointment is no panacea. But if he stands by his opening remarks, Justice Sinha can be that leader."

Among other international print media praising my appointment were The Economic Times of India, General Knowledge of India, Eduncle; Pakistan Defence, Jagran Josh of India and The Guardian of Britain in which a detailed report progressing from the time of my appointment as Additional Judge, Appellate Division, performing functions as Chairman of the Judicial Service Commission, presentation of papers in different seminars abroad, etc. were highlighted. On social media platforms as well, there were more than 10,000 comments praising my appointment and hoping that there would be a revolutionary change in the judiciary during my tenure.

During the tenure of the former Chief Justice, there was serious squabbling between Abdul Wahhab Miah and AHM Shamsuddin Chowdhury that led to such an extreme situation that they did not speak to each other. Justice Abdul Wahhab Miah's view was that Shamsuddin Chowdhury does not show any respect to him and in course of his conversation Shamsuddin Chowdhury would intervene. He had no courtesy, manners and good behavior as a judge. Shamsuddin Chowdhury's version was totally otherwise. He used to demean Abdul Wahhab Miah. It was a convention being followed that whenever a judge of the higher court goes on retirement, a lunch is arranged by the other judges in honor of the retiring judge. Similarly, a farewell lunch was also arranged for Mozammel Hossain on his last working day. Mozammel Hossain and Shamsuddin Chowdhury were very close to each other being barristers. I requested the Chief Justice to resolve the dispute because I was apprehending that if such dispute persisted, it would be difficult to work in a harmonious atmosphere. The dispute was accordingly resolved.

One morning, Abdul Wahhab Miah came to meet me in a very foul mood and told me that I am being the guardian of the judiciary I must look after the prestige and dignity of the judges. I told him that as the Chief Justice, I would not hesitate to do anything to uphold the prestige of the judiciary and wanted to know what had happened to him. He brusquely told me that he had decided to issue contempt proceeding against the Law Minister the following day and came for my permission. I wanted to know from him what had happened and why he was so seriously agitated against the Law Minister. When I heard his reason of harboring anger toward the Law Minister, I was extremely embarrassed. It seemed that the Law Minister on the previous day commented at a forum that the judges were delaying the preparation and signing of judgements, and as a result, the litigants were suffering. Abdul Wahhab Miah took the statement of the Law Minister personally because he was always late in delivering judgments. I told him that since he was the senior most judge he should not do something like that. Because the Law Minister without mentioning the name of any judge had made a general statement which was correct. If he were to issue a contempt proceeding, it would prove that he was late in delivering judgments, which was true; and secondly, being the senior most judge, if he behaved in such a way, what the junior judges would learn from him, I enquired.

I said I was embarrassed by the conduct of the judges of the High Court Division in issuing contempt proceedings on flimsy grounds and cited the example of Sahmsuddin Chowdhury. Abdul Wahhab Miah realized my sentiment and left. It may be recalled, except for one or two, most of the judges were taking long time in writing judgments. It came to my notice that Abdul Wahhab Miah had three-year-old judgments in the High Court Division when he was elevated to the Appellate Division. Shamsuddin Chowdhury had also kept about 300 plus judgments when he was elevated to the Appellate Division. Some of the judges retired while they had judgments unsigned for two to three years prior to the date of their retirement.

Though Mohammad Mozammel Hossain also showed his eagerness to elevate Abdul Wahhab Miah to the Appellate

Division, he could not totally rely on him. I was convinced about his mindset over an incident. After assuming office, Mozammel Hossain began going on foreign trips. Whenever an invitation came, whether it was befitting for a Chief Justice to visit was not a concern to him. He went to the U.S. and Canada along with some other judges as head of the delegation to see case management and other related matters on a trip financed by the UNDP. During each vacation or long holiday, Mozammel Hossain used to be away on one or two foreign trips. On one occasion, before a court holiday, I arranged a tour program as the Chairman of the Judicial Service Commission. A few days before my journey, I wrote a letter to the Chief Justice seeking permission to leave the country. The Chief Justice told me that he was also planning to visit Singapore to attend a seminar and requested to delay my foreign trip till his return. I told him that my program was finalized about six months ago and I had already purchased my ticket and it was not possible to change my schedule. The Chief Justice was going out with the Registrar and some other judges. Later, I came to know that he changed the names of members of his entourage and included the name of Abdul Wahhab Miah. After their return, I wanted to know from Abdul Wahhab Miah whether he had delivered a paper at the seminar. He told me that just two days before the trip he was included in the delegation by the Chief Justice. He simply visited Singapore without participating in any discussion. Mozammel Hossain arranged his trips by giving charge to Nazmun Ara Sultana, because he did not feel secure to give charge to Abdul Wahhab Miah. If all the trips of Justice Mozammel Hossain are scrutinized, this will become clear. If we do not have respect and confidence over a brother judge, it is unhealthy for the judiciary, and I have seen some who play double roles by pretending to show cordiality externally only.

Reference:

1. *Article 95(1) of the Constitution.*

Chapter 11

Backlog of Cases

There is a huge backlog of cases both in the lower and higher judiciary. In the lower courts about three million cases are pending while in the High Court Division there are about three hundred thousand cases. In the Appellate Division, despite huge pressure, I did not allow the docket to rise. Still there are about 15,000 cases pending. I was concerned about the huge number of cases and I was convinced that the present obsolete laws will not meet the challenges of burgeoning dockets. I identified several reasons for the continued increase despite commendable rise in rate of disposal. It was necessary to initiate a few urgent and doable steps. I believed that the time had come to implement business management practices in judicial administration and replicate diverse winning strategies from various other disciplines to usher in reforms. All are agreed that the judiciary is a very vital pillar of democracy that a robust and quick justice delivery system is essential to invite foreign investment in this era of globalization, and among nations vying for international investment Bangladesh has a decisive edge because of its inexpensive manpower.

Unless the judiciary is improved, it will be difficult to attract international investments. It is an undeniable fact that our judiciary has an extremely poor infrastructure in comparison of neighboring countries. This needs to be upgraded urgently. The allocation of funds for the judiciary has been abysmally low. If this unjust situation remains unadressed, crimes will be perpetrated, and a sense of helplessness, dismay and disgust will set in the minds of the people against the Executive. Such despondency enables undesirable elements in society to move in and settle disputes with muscle and money. For a just order in society strengthening of the entire judicial framework is of paramount importance. Therefore, all the infrastructure needs related to the institutional development, such as, accommodation of judicial officers while performing judicial work, rich libraries, high-end IT infrastructure and functional conveniences for judges, lawyers, and litigants---all must be made available without delay. With that end in view, within a few months of my appointment I chalked out a plan and calculated the shortage of courtrooms which must be constructed on an emergency basis and the digitization of the system in phases. Consequently, I handed over a plan to the Prime Minister in the interest of the judiciary pointing out that those developments related to the overall development of the country. A few days thereafter I noticed in dismay that the Prime Minister sent those papers to the Law Ministry with a view to bury the project.

Clearance of backlog must have the highest priority and appropriate measures should be taken to address the appalling situation. The first step is to increase the number of courtrooms and the number of judges. Increasing their number is not an easy task because one cannot become a competent judge in two to three years. Experience and judicial training are indispensable in becoming a mature judge. Hence the initial step must be increasing the number of judges and to deal with the vacuum it is necessary to raise the retirement age of District Judges as a temporary solution. Recruitment of about five hundred judges and giving them training and performing judicial works. Experience is a precondition for a judge to maturate. There are various reasons for a lack of professionally competent judges. And the chief cause for this shortage is the number of cases among a large population. Bangladesh has possibly the lowest number of judges compared to other countries. Even we cannot compare favorably with Bhutan and Nepal, two small countries. The second reason is the obsolete laws prevailing in the country. The colonial rulers promulgated most of the laws keeping in mind the objective of effectively ruling the country and collect revenues. With that end in view, the parent laws, e.g. Code of Civil Procedure, Code of Criminal Procedure, the Penal Code, the Evidence Act, Transfer of Property Act, Limitation Act, and Easement Act were promulgated.

These laws are still in force even after the transformation into a totally sovereign country. Most of those laws are directly in conflict with the ethos, objects and spirit for which our freedom fighters sacrificed their lives and additionally do not reflect the core values of our Constitution. We cannot claim to have become independent in 1947 because we were under the hand of another set of rulers. In fact, till 1971 we did not get the taste of independence politically, socially, culturally, and economically, and we were deprived of freedom of thought, freedom of expression, freedom of employment and freedom of language. The pending cases cannot be heard and disposed of under the existing laws, with the present strength of manpower, infrastructure and facilities available. The colonial laws must be dismantled. Some of the provisions in the Penal Code were promulgated with the goal of controlling and penalizing the "rebellions".

These laws are in direct conflict with the fundamental rights enshrined in our Constitution. The Code of Criminal Procedure is totally obsolete and after the abolition of Chapters XVIII and XXI, it lost its efficacy. The amendments made in the Code directly conflict with other provisions. Under the present formulation of the Code an offender even if he commits a heinous crime like murder or rape followed by murder or dacoity with murder cannot be kept in judicial remand beyond fifteen days. I made observations in a case and cautioned the Attorney General and the Law Minister to make corresponding amendments to the law, but nothing has been done yet. The offender must be released on bail if no investigation is completed within this time. Section 344 of the Code does not cover the field because it was included to cover the field of Chapter XVIII. There are hotchpotch provisions prevailing in the in trial of complaint and police cases provided in Chapter XX of the Code. Similarly, Civil Procedure Code is also not workable after the amendments. There should be substantial changes in Order XXI of the Code.

Though India kept the Code of Civil Procedure 1908 it amended the Code in such a way that the provisions are not conflicting. We could not make corresponding amendments and the net result is the multiplication of proceedings. Some provisions of the Code are applicable in holding trial of recovery of outstanding loans by the Loan Recovery Act, but there are a lot of inconsistencies. I wanted to harmonize the provisions by pronouncement of a judgment with a view to protect of right of property of innocent persons whose property has been mortgaged with the banks by taking loans by deceitful means, but I could not harmonize the inconsistencies even in my decision. There are a lot of inconsistencies in every legislation which deserve to be scrapped totally and substituted with new laws to be recommended by a strong Law Commission with experts from lawyers, professors, laymen and judges, and basic laws must be promulgated in consonance with the spirit of our liberation struggle and the Constitution by slashing out the colonial mindset. The infrastructure available now is not at all suitable to take the load of the cases being filed, the manpower strength must be increased three-fold. There must be enough judicial training institutes in every district and a central judicial academy should be established in Dhaka for training of judges of all segments. They should be provided with adequate training on case management and court management.

There should be a law compelling the litigants to resolve their disputes by arbitration compulsorily and if a litigant disowns the arbitration award and institutes litigation and lost should be burdened with the costs covering the entire expenditure of the litigation the court's time, the opponent's harassment and lawyer's fees. In respect of criminal law also, except felonies, pre-bargaining procedure should be introduced in the administration of criminal justice. It is basically a pre-trial negotiation before the prosecution and the accused in which the accused agrees to plead guilty to a charge in return of some concession from the prosecution. There are three types of plea bargaining: in charge bargaining the accused pleads guilty to reduced charges; in sentence bargaining the accused pleads guilty to a reduced the sentence; in fact, bargaining negotiation involves an admission to certain facts in return for an agreement not to introduce certain facts into evidence. This system is one of the alternatives to deal with large sections of criminal cases.68

Chapter 12

Judicial Reforms

In our country, one of the very first priorities should be enhancing the quality of justice that is at the core of human existence and welfare of society. In fact, it is the fundamental goal of all societies in the world. We, as a nation, were deprived of justice from our colonial rulers since even after Partition we were ruled for about 24 years by Pakistan. We were deprived of human rights, human values, rule of law, and right to public service, right to trade and business, and most certainly democracy---all of which are the foundation of a civilized society. We were deprived of our proper share of revenue for the development of our roads, schools and colleges, and setting up industries even though a major portion of the entire country's revenue was earned by our province. We were treated as a colony by a minority.

But immediately after independence, the judiciary was neglected by all the successive governments in power although the judiciary played a vital role in maintaining rule of law within its limited powers and resources. If we compare with other Organs of State, the ratio of funds provided by the governments to the judiciary used to fall to the bottom of the list. The judiciary contributed remarkable results to the state and its citizenry and was the only institution in which people had trust. Access to fair, inexpensive, speedy and substantive justice is a basic universal human right. To ensure compliance of this basic human right, judicial reforms in various countries have been made in the last few decades. But Bangladesh remained an exception. Universally it is accepted and acknowledged that for proper functioning of democracy and rule of law it is imperative to carry out judicial reforms from time to time.

Even a developed country like the United Kingdom made several changes in its judiciary. After the passing of the Constitutional Reforms Act 2005, the latest major changes have been described as the most significant since the Magna Carta of 1215. This Act establishes the Lord Chief Justice as President of the courts of

England and Wales and Head of the Judiciary. The House of Lords was substituted by Supreme Court resulting in complete independence of the judiciary. In its 1000 years of judicial history, the judiciary for the first time was officially recognized as a fully independent organ of the state having its own independent system, staffs, budget and building.

Similarly, reforms were made in China, Brazil and some Latin American countries while the first two countries named also maintained a tremendous pace of economic development. In China the State Council of the People's Republic released a White Paper on October 9, 2012 on "Judicial Reform in China." This paper highlighted the changes undertaken over the last decade and referred to the main objectives of such reforms aiming to safeguard justice and focusing on optimizing the allocation of judicial functions and power, enhancing protection of human rights and judicial capacity, practicing the principle of "judicature for the people" and finally digitization of the judiciary.

Brazil is a fast-developing economy with a legal system in the civil law tradition. It did not follow the doctrine of stare decisis. But after an amendment to the Constitution in 2004, the Supreme Court began to follow the tradition of stare decisis with a view to minimizing the docket size and to preserve the people's perception and respect toward the judiciary. A bill of law for the new Code of Civil Procedure has almost been finalized with the aim of minimizing the time for the final disposal of litigations. If it is implemented, it would usher in a revolutionary change in procedural law in Brazil. Similarly, Cambodia, Ecuador, Chile, Mexico, Peru, Guatemala and Panama have carried out significant judicial reforms.

Some Asian countries like India and Sri Lanka have already implemented the digitization process and their judiciary can now compete with developed countries like the UK, US, Canada and Australia. Despite the modernization of the judiciary long before the US, Australia, Canada and South Africa have carried out judicial reforms a decade ago. When I visited China and Russia, I could not believe my eyes when I saw the digitization process had reached the remotest corners of these two big countries. My Russian counterpart showed me by pushing a button the judicial work of a District Court in progress about 7,000 miles away in Siberia, talked with the president of the court and introduced me!

In the Supreme People's Court of the People's Republic of China, electronic monitors have been installed on the walls of a big room. On these monitors all judicial activities throughout the county are being seen. The entire process---from filing of a case up to the final stage---is completed under the digitization process. Witnesses are examined in video conferences in both China and Russia. I noticed an urgency in the mind of the judicial hierarchy and the Executive to modernize the judicial system. According to them, if the judicial process is not developed in comparison with the development of the country, the economic progress would be hampered. Because, according to them, foreign investors are always interested in their investments and the expeditious return on their investment if any litigation cropped up.

According to the Chinese authority, they were inviting chief justices of different nations of the world as well as other judges by arranging seminars for their understanding of advances made in other counties. I was invited twice as Chief Justice of Bangladesh and the invitation was made by the highest authority of China. I attended one seminar and I was given the opportunity of giving the opening and valedictory speeches despite the presence of other chief justices. In the next seminar, I sent Foez Siddiqui as the representative of the Chief Justice of Bangladesh. After the seminar Foez Siddqui told me that a big electronic portrait of mine was displayed at the venue on the assumption that I would attend the seminar.

In Bangladesh a huge number of cases are pending in the lower courts and in the Supreme Court. The litigants are deprived of justice due to lengthy procedure. It is due to many reasons:

   i.   obsolete laws,
   ii.   shortage of judges,
  iii.   shortage of courtrooms,

iv.   no checks and balances in monitoring the judges' performance,

v.   repeatedly seeking additional time by the lawyers while the courts are liberal in granting them time, and

vi.   long holidays enjoyed by the judges of the Supreme Court. If we want to reduce the docket in the High Court Division, there is no alternative other than reducing the number of holidays drastically.

It was not that after becoming Chief Justice I wanted to reduce holidays for showing "revolutionary" change. When I was in the High Court Division, Syed Mudassir Hossain was the Chief Justice, and I wrote a letter to all the judges for consideration in a Full Court meeting for reducing holidays on the ground that a large number of cases were pending and we could not deal with them; that the litigants were being deprived of the fruits of their litigation during their lifetime and that we were having long holidays which made our work to suffer. Except Syed Mahmud Hossain, none supported me. The issue was dropped without discussion

The system of long holidays was introduced by the British judges in the early 19th century when the communication between India and England was by sea from Bombay. It took 21 days to travel by sea and, therefore, during the autumn they took long holidays to visit their relatives. The number of cases in those days in the superior court was low and, therefore, there was no backlog of cases. Now we have millions of cases. We are afforded with maximum facilities including emoluments in comparison with other public servants at the cost of the tax payers. It is against our conscience to enjoy holidays of about six months a year. In South Korea, the judges of the Supreme Court enjoy only 21 days a year. Other Commonwealth countries drastically reduced their holidays. Our very mode of calculation of holidays is faulty. For instance, if we enjoy 15 days holiday in a month, we exclude weekly holidays; if we take vacation for the entire month of June, we calculate it as 22 days by excluding weekly holidays. This calculation is not right. The weekly holidays should not be excluded in calculating days off. But in case of taking leave, weekly holidays are included.

Another interesting thing is, we exclude government holidays if we count holidays during festivities. Yet another error is that senior judges start calculating holidays from the month of November for the next year keeping their judgments pending for months and even sometimes years together. In their computation they decide for how many days they would enjoy vacation the next year. This is totally unheard of in any country. The normal procedure is to decide how many days judges would work in a year. It is a prevailing system in the US, UK, India and other countries. We are obviously an exception. Therefore, in the Full Court meeting in 2015, I placed a list of 201 working days for 2016.

All the senior judges headed by Md. Abdul Wahhab Miah charged me and wanted to know why I had fixed the holidays without discussing with them. I told them, it is the practice prevailing everywhere. I even entreated them to reduce at least 10 days from the holidays. Abdul Wahhab Miah, Nazmun Ara Sultana, Muhammad Iman Ali and some other senior judges of the High Court Division in a concerted manner insulted me explicitly. My officers were shocked and commented the judges were not even courteous while discussing with the Chief Justice. I told them that I was not hurt with their behavior because I wanted to reduce vacation time not for my personal gain but for the benefit of the judiciary. Hence, I did not mind at all, but rather I felt pity for them. They acted against their conscience ignoring their past. They forgot that they became judges and after confirmation they forgot the purpose for which they were appointed.

I noticed that some judges of the High Court Division did not sit in court at the proper time and some of the judges even did not sit in the afternoon session after recess. I told them to sit and rise from the court by adhering to the schedule because if they do not maintain the court's time, how could we compel the judges of the lower judiciary to maintain court timings. The litigants' perception of judges would suffer. They did not respond to my request. In a Full Court meeting, I again raised the issue and requested them to maintain the court's time. I made surprise visits at 2:30 PM and found that most of the judges did not sit in court. I noticed that some of the judges came to court after 11:00 AM although court hour starts at 10:30 AM.

Finding no other alternative, I directed the Registrar General to close the Supreme Court's main gates at 10:30 AM. Some judges took exception to my new step, but I did not listen to their objection. Lawyers also informed me that due to closure of the main gate they were facing difficulties in coming in. I told them that I took the action for a limited period for compelling the judges to come in time and that they have two other alternative access roads. It can be perceived that global issues are becoming increasingly prominent because of globalization and liberalism. In the world of business and investment pressure on the governments to reform comes from both local and foreign interests. Therefore, it is time to make urgent judicial and legal reforms in our country not only to clear the backlog of cases but also to ensure that all cases are decided promptly.

The main causes for delay in disposing of cases besides the above are:

a) inadequate infrastructure in the subordinate courts;
b) inadequate supporting staff;
c) non-availability of modern technology, such as computer and digitization; (d) inadequate use of technology for classification of cases;
d) inadequate use of modern technology in identifying the infrastructure or dead cases;
e) unavailability of video recording and video conferencing facilities;
f) inadequate use of case management system;
g) delay in filling up existing vacancies;
h) frequent adjournment of cases
i) inadequacy of training of the judges.

Besides, it is not possible with the existing manpower to dispose of the pending cases even in 50 years from now even if no new case is added. So, it is high time to employ time tested alternative methods of dispute resolution, such as, arbitration, conciliation and mediation with vigor by amending the laws. Government is the biggest litigant in Bangladesh. It must ensure that litigation may be initiated, or appeals may be filed only in genuine and bonefide cases. Nowadays a practice has developed that in government, semi-government and autonomous bodies' cases, even after losing in the apex court, review petitions are filed after a long delay. I confronted the lawyers on these issues, like, review petitions being filed after losing the case and belatedly. Their answer was simple: The authorities wanted a review for their own defense in case they are charged for not filing review petitions. The departmental heads and executives must appreciate the fact that they have been given those positions with responsibilities. They were not chosen for the job to cause unnecessary costs to the government and adding to the burden of the courts.

Our vision should be a modern judiciary aligned with the standard in the neighboring countries. An efficient legal and judicial system delivers quick and quality justice that reinforces the confidence of people in the rule of law. It facilitates investment and production of wealth, enables better distribution of justice, promotes basic human rights and enhances accountability and democratic government. However, at the same time the Executive should look toward better training of the judges of the higher judiciary. At present the higher judiciary does not possess any judicial academy for training of judges. As Chief Justice, I wrote a letter to the Prime Minister for allocation of land suitable for the establishment of a judicial academy for the training purposes of members of the higher judiciary. As I did not get any response, I personally requested the Prime Minister to allot a piece of land measuring not less than 25 acres. The Prime Minister was surprised on hearing the size of the land asked for. I told her that Nepal, a mountainous state, and Jammu and Kashmir, another hilly provincial state of India, own judicial academies on over 40 acres of land. I requested her to allot such an area outside Dhaka City, perhaps in Keraniganj, Savar or Gazipur.

For a long time, it was held that there was no need for special education or training for members of the judiciary. Initially it was believed since they had already studied law in different universities and had subsequently carried on with their legal practice it was more than enough for them to the judges. This previous trend has changed remarkably. In the last half century, the earlier belief changed with the French establishing one of the earliest judicial academies. The United States of America followed them. Now almost all countries of the world, including India, have underscored the importance of creating training and development programs for the judiciary. If we seriously need to look at judicial reforms, we need to look at the context of knowledge creation within the judiciary; its importance to understand the changing dimensions of law and justice; and to empower the judges to be able to engage with contemporary issues relating to law and justice. The University College in London has established UCL Judicial Institute, a research center that brings to the forefront the importance of research and capacity building for the judicial process. This is inextricably connected to training and development that are needed for the members of the judiciary. The United States in collaboration with Duke University Law School established an Institute of Judicial Studies. Law is a dynamic discipline and if this dynamism of the law has to be brought into the judicial system it is essential that judicial education is imparted by establishing judicial academies.

The continuing education plan for Ontario Court Judges, the National Judicial Institute and Judicial Education Program is to expand the range of professional opportunities available for new and experienced judges. These education plans are based on the three objectives of maintaining and developing professional competence, maintaining and developing social awareness, and encouraging personal growth. Collectively, the development of this structured judicial education programs helped1 promote enhanced judicial decision making and provided greater consistency in continuing the education, increased resources, provided support and training opportunities for judges from all backgrounds.

When I was practicing in the district court, I noticed that District and Sessions Judges were taking up miscellaneous petitions, that is, bail petitions, criminal and civil motions in the morning session and after the recess they regularly sat in court and held trials of complicated session's cases and heard appeals. For the last ten to twelve years, the District and Sessions Judges seldom rise after recesses, which I noticed in course of my inspections in different district courts. I advised them to keep enough cases for covering the entire day transacting judicial business. My advice bore no result, because whatever report I submitted were not addressed by the Chief Justices and the Ministry of Law. So, after tackling the pressure of lawyers to dispose of urgent matters pending for a long time, I decided to visit the district courts randomly.

This was for two reasons:

1. After the separation of the Magistracy in 2007, the construction of Magistracy buildings was very slow and in some districts site selection was not finalized. The court buildings which were undertaken for construction were delayed for years together. This was also due to lack of monitoring by the Ministry of Law and the corruption of the contractors in collusion with the engineers. As a result, the judicial officers were sharing courts and chambers, sometimes three judicial officers shared one court. It was very dismal to observe that a female judicial officer had to share a chamber with a male judicial officer in some stations, and

2. Compelling the judicial officers to utilize the time allocated for judicial works and also to give priority to the old cases.

I requested the District Magistrates to provide two or three rooms from their offices, which were earlier used as criminal courts by the Executive Magistrates. Some District Magistrates honored my request, some of them expressed their inability by enumerating excuses. I held judicial conferences and, in such conferences, Public Prosecutors, Government Pleaders, Presidents and Secretaries of the Bar, Executive Engineers, Civil Surgeons, Superintendents of Police, sometimes, BGB Sector Commanders, RAB Commanders, District Magistrates, Additional Districts Magistrates, all judges and judicial magistrates attended. I heard the problems being faced by the judiciary and advised them by providing guidelines. Sometimes the police, the district magistrates and others wanted to know of the solutions to their problems and whenever possible I solved them on the spot. Judicial officers were confused about inconsistency in judgments. I explained to them the correct legal positions.

Moreover, there were many defects in medical evidence being filed in criminal cases. I directed the Civil Surgeons to advise the doctors who issue autopsy reports and medical certificates promptly pointing out the defects which in most cases related to elopement of young girls. The doctors were not issuing proper medical reports of age since they did not follow the minimum procedure while ascertaining the age by ossification tests. While issuing medical certificates of grievous injuries, they submitted reports on guesswork on superficial examination of wounds without ascertaining the injury by X-ray. Sometimes they even submitted faulty reports as regard cause of injury by sharp pointed or blunt weapons.

The BGB while patrolling border and remote areas often seized smuggled goods, but they do not follow the procedures provided in Sections 100-103 of the Code of Criminal Procedure. I explained the defects and told them that due to their lack of proper preparation of seizure lists, the smugglers were getting the benefit of doubt. The police officers lack knowledge in Evidence Act and all the time we found faulty investigation reports in sensational cases. I noticed in several cases that though the accused were convicted by the trial court and affirmed by the High Court Division, I was compelled to acquit the convict due to defect in collection of legal evidence to connect the accused to the case and because of delayed examination of witnesses by the investigation officers. I pointed out these defects to the police officers and advised them to direct the investigation officers to rectify those defects. Additional District Magistrates are empowered to deal with proceedings under sections 107, 133, 144, 145 of the Code of Criminal Procedure and mobile courts. Most of the proceedings were found defective. I made the Executive Magistrates conscious of the defects and asked them to rectify those. I explained the position in law. This is the reason the judicial conferences used to take three to four hours. I enjoyed those conferences because in those conferences I gathered practical knowledge of the field officers who frequently face problems and I clarified their defects. After the conferences the officers often expressed their satisfaction and said that they benefitted very much from the explanations and guidance given to them which they had never experienced previously.

In the meetings, I directed the District Magistrates and Executive Engineers to expedite the construction and selection of the sites of the court buildings. This resulted in momentum gained in the progress of construction work. In some districts, there was unusual delay in fixing the date for inaugurating the buildings, such as, in Chittagong, Moulvibazar, Habiganj and some other districts. As I declared the opening of the court buildings, the authority had to complete the works by compulsion.

On one occasion, I attended a conference in Moulvibazar district and when I was returning at 1:00 AM, I noticed that the workers were working at that time also. I was very shocked and admonished the Chief Judicial Magistrate and the Executive Engineer for exerting such pressure on the workers. They frankly replied that as I had fixed the date for opening the complex, they had no alternative but to complete the work quickly. In one district, possibly Jessore, the work was closed for about two years. On inquiry I came to know that the contractor had left the work on the plea of his inability to complete the work at the rate quoted by him because in the meantime the price of construction materials had gone up. I told the local authority to forfeit his security money and take legal action against him. Later I came to know that due to my threats the work was completed within six months.

In Moulvibazar the project was approved in the first phase, but due to delay in the site selection work on the site could not be started. District Magistrate Mukhlesur Rahman informed me that unless I intervened the work would not be started even within a decade. He came to meet me in my village home at about 11:00 PM. Normally I did not use the Circuit House whenever I had any program either official or unofficial in Moulvibazar, despite scarcity of space at my home. As I remember, I passed one or two nights---due to the fact that the programs continued till midnight---in the Circuit House during my 18 years in the highest court. When the District Magistrate came to see me, I was performing the functions of the Chief Justice. I told the District Magistrate that on the following day at 10:00 AM I would lay the foundation of the building, if the political parties supported me. The District Magistrate took ten minutes time and spoke with the leaders of the political parties and the mayor of the City Corporation. The District Magistrate subsequently reported that none of the leaders would oppose whatever decision I made.

Accordingly, I advised him to arrange a meeting at the Circuit House at 9:00 AM and fixed the time for laying the foundation at 10:00 AM. I also advised him to convey the message to the Executive Engineer for arranging necessary materials. It may be recalled that the present magistracy building is owned by the court, but the space was not enough. There was a khas land toward the northern side of the existing building but due to political pressure that khas land was allotted in favor of an organization of the government and the selection of the site of the magistracy building was selected about three kilometers away from the present building, over which three suits were filed, and injunctions were issued. The lawyers were not agreeable to construct the magistracy building at a distant place. In the meeting I sought opinion from leaders of all political parties and lawyers. They gave me full authority to decide and promised that my decisions would be accepted by them.

So, I told them I would lay the foundation of the magistracy building at the present site and make arrangements to hand over the adjacent land by cancelling the earlier allotment in favor of the Shishu Academy. I also advised the District Magistrate to take immediate measures in this regard. The District Magistrate told the meeting he would allot the land in favor of the magistracy building within next seven days. I expressed my desire to lay the foundation at that time. At this time some of them told me about the injunction about which I knew already. They were eager to withdraw the suits. Within 45 minutes, we concluded the meeting and marched toward the site on foot and laid the foundation stone. Thereafter, I came to know that the District Magistrate had allotted more land for the magistracy building than the lawyers had demand. Now one of the best judicial buildings has been established at that site.

One of the problems I noticed regarding delay in construction was lack of monitoring by the Ministry of Law, noncooperation of some of the District Magistrates in selecting the site, and corruption in the construction work. Normally a work order is given to a politician in power, who has no work experience. As soon as he gets the work order, he would engage a sub-contractor retaining a margin of fifteen to twenty percent. The sub-contractor also had to pay to different agencies their unwritten shares. As a result, he would find his own margin of profit dwindling if he completed the construction. Consequently, he would adopt other devices, like persuasion, lobbying, etc. to increase the cost of the project on the plea that prices of construction materials had gone up. In most cases, the sub-contractors managed the increase the expenditure in connivance with the local hierarchy after taking two or three "running" bills, utilizing the money on other projects and thus delaying construction. A post of director was created in the Ministry of Law to oversee the execution of the construction plans. Normally a senior level officer in the rank of District Judge was appointed. When I became the Chief Justice, the director had retired from his service and no new director was appointed despite demands from the Supreme Court. In the Ministry of Law, there was a scarcity of senior officers and the department was run by some junior officers. The senior most officer, who was even senior to the Secretary-in-Charge, was made Registrar of the Supreme Court. The next senior officer was the Secretary of the Ministry of Law, Abu Saleh Sheikh Mohammad Johirul Haque. He was appointed the Deputy Secretary in the law ministry. Within a few days he was promoted to the position of District and Sessions Judge. After the secretary was elevated to the Bench, no senior officer was appointed in his place. Abu Saleh Sheikh Mohammad Johirul Haque managed to assume the office of Secretary-in-Charge and his junior officers were serially given the charge of the next higher posts to transact their business. As a result, I found a shambolic condition in the Ministry.

As per precedent, the Ministry used to make proposals for postings and promotions in different courts in the country. Sometimes, I noticed, in busy courts like in Chittagong, two Joint District Judges are working in place of five or six officers and in a district like Lakhsmipur, three or more Joint District Judges were working. I noticed that 6/7 Judicial Magistrates and 17 MLSS (lower-level staff) were posted in Khagrachhari. But, one or two magistrates would be sufficient to deal with the cases there, whereas those officers could have been accommodated in Chittagong where four or five more Judicial Magistrates are required. This way the officers were posted without any thorough field assessment and there was no competent officer in the Ministry to make recommendations after overall evaluation of the position in the field. The Ministry also failed to send replacement of an officer when a proposal for transfer of an officer was made. If the proposals were made simultaneously two officers could join the vacant posts, but if an officer is withdrawn from a station the court remains vacant for an indefinite period. It was pointed out to the Ministry that the proposals suffered delays of three to four months and thus caused backlog of cases. Moreover, the number of cases fixed for hearing faced a deadlock because the other judicial officer who would be in charge of the court would hear only urgent petitions without taking up regular matters, mainly because he too was overworked and could not hold trials of other courts' matters.

Following this method, we would never solve the problem particularly because the recommendations were normally made on a random basis. The officers who were working in so-called good stations, such as Dhaka, Chittagong, Khulna and Sylhet were retaining the same stations repeatedly. While the officers who were working in remote stations and choukis were not getting any chance to serve in Dhaka, Chittagong, Khulna and Sylhet. Normally if an officer worked in a station for three years, he could be posted in the same station again but in another capacity. There should be rotation of officers on a regular basis and all officers should be treated equally. I found the same set of officers was recommended for posting in Dhaka. I opposed such recommendations and told the Ministry that the officers who worked in Dhaka should not be allowed to work there again.

Whenever I changed the recommended postings, the Ministry would not issue the Government Order (GO) and the court had to remain vacant for months together. Thus, the posting of Chief Metropolitan Magistrate, Dhaka, was delayed for about six months. The Ministry recommended an officer who did not have a good reputation. I opposed the proposal and directed my Registry to write to the Ministry that henceforth the Supreme Court would not approve any proposal for the posts of District and Sessions Judge, Metropolitan Sessions Judge, Chief Metropolitan Magistrate and Chief Judicial Magistrate from among officers who did not possess reputation and that only honest and efficient officers would be appointed to those posts.

In Dhaka, I recommended an officer as Chief Metropolitan Magistrate who was working as an Additional District and Sessions Judge, at the instance of the Ministry but the Ministry did not issue the GO and held it up for six months but ultimately it was compelled to issue the GO. Similar incident happened in the case of the Chief Judicial Magistrate, Dhaka. Whenever I brought this matter to the Law Minister, he told me that the government is in favor of posting officers who adhered to their line of thinking. I told the Minister that I am the last person to appoint any officer who has an unacceptable record as judicial officer. As regards to the proposal I had made, according to him, he was not belonging to the government's line of thinking. I countered by saying, if he was brought to Dhaka at the instance of the Ministry and worked honestly, why he could not be appointed as the Chief Metropolitan Magistrate, Dhaka. He did not have response. He said that officers who were not following the government's line of thinking--- even if honest---could not be posted because in certain cases they could inflict damage on the government.

I made it clear to the Minister that the Judges were not engaged in politics and whatever political affiliation they might have had in their student life, they had given up long ago. And after working ten to fifteen years in judicial service, they cannot be stigmatized as pro-opposition political party supporters. Secondly, I advised him that a pool of officers should be selected in the manner the government selected Deputy Commissioners (DCs) and

Superintendents of Police (SPs) in the districts. In respect of postings of DCs, most honest and efficient officers are selected from amongst the serving officers and no disputed officer having a blemished reputation was posted as DC.I told him that if the DCs are appointed why could we not appoint the best officers in judicial posts. He did not agree to my proposal, but I did point out to him that most of the time the ministry concerned recommended disputed officers for Dhaka and Chittagong.

Even when the deadlock in the judicial service was not resolved after bringing it to the knowledge of the Minister, I directed my office to write to the Law Secretary asking him to meet me on a day. Despite the receipt of the letter, the Secretary left for Rajshahi without intimating the Supreme Court Registry. I took the matter seriously and brought it to the attention of some cabinet ministers. The ministers on hearing the issue expressed their bewilderment and said they found it incredible that the Law Secretary, known as an amiable officer, would show such disrespect to the Chief Justice. I discussed the matter with the senior judges and when the matter was disclosed publicly, the Law Secretary came to meet me one evening. I told him that his discourteous conduct was unpardonable. I reminded him that I had taken the matter very seriously. He then seemed to realize the gravity of the situation and sought unconditional apology. I told him that since the Law Secretary---who is none other than a judicial officer---had displayed disobedience to the Chief Justice I had to direct him to provide an explanation in writing. Subsequently all the officers posted in the Ministry came with written replies seeking unconditional apology and the matter was finally resolved.

Later the Law Secretary came and informed me that in the cabinet meeting he was not allowed to sit in the designated chairs meant for the Secretaries; rather the Secretaries were treating him like a Deputy Secretary. He therefore requested me to recommend his name as Secretary. Since I was always fighting for the dignity, prestige and status of all judicial officers, especially because the judicial officers were being neglected by the Secretaries and whenever any proposal for upgradation of their status was made there was opposition from the Secretaries, I did not have to think much and recommended his name to get the rank and status of Secretary. Accordingly, he was made the Secretary in the Law Ministry.

I also found that there was no gradation list of the judicial officers. In the absence of such a roster, I had faced many problems when appointing an inquiry officer against any officer for corruption charges, because a junior officer cannot investigate charges against a senior office. I wrote to the Ministry of Law to prepare the gradation list, but they could not do so. In every department of the government as well as in the sector corporations, gradation lists had been prepared and existed. Accordingly, I directed the Registry to prepare a gradation list. The Registry issued a notice to all judicial officers to intimate their position and, after a thorough examination, the gradation list was published at the annual judicial conference. The judicial officers were naturally extremely pleased to finally receive the gradation list. The Ministry is now following this list. I also issued numerous circulars to the courts providing with guidelines and one of the guidelines was the District and Sessions Judges must hold trial of cases and hear of appeals in the morning session, and criminal, civil motions and bail matters in the afternoon session. I passed this order when I realized that the District Judges were explaining to me that in the afternoon, after recess, lawyers were not available and therefore they were not sitting in the afternoon. I personally checked some District Judges' courts at 2.30 PM or 3.00 PM, but nobody answered the calls. The peons sometimes received the calls and said that the Judge had left the court. When I issued the circular, some senior lawyers were annoyed because the lawyers were interested in the hearing of bail petitions and injunction matters in the morning. They are not interested to appear in trial of suits, session's cases and appeals.

On one occasion, I visited Narsingdi and all the senior lawyers came to me and requested that I withdraw the Circular. Their version was that they being senior lawyers wanted to work in the morning session and at lunch time they returned home and took rest. I told the lawyers that doctors were advising that senior persons should take little food and continue working to avoid heart ailments. I told them that I had issued the Circular in the interest of the senior lawyers who normally would return home and eat a heavy lunch that would cause heart diseases. Secondly, if they attended trials of cases, the junior lawyers would learn from them the art of cross examination of witnesses. This was a practice which I myself had learned from my senior in the district court. The lawyers got the message and did not proceed further on this matter.

In addition, I issued other circulars on many topics ranging from directing the judges to issue certified copies to the parties without delay; to inspect sections on regular basis; to hold judicial conference every month and so on. These circulars and guidelines infused momentum into the administration of justice in the lower courts. It was also reported by the District Judges in course of my inspection that they have been facing with acute shortage of employees and they could not proceed with the appointment process without the prior permission of the Ministry. I was also told that the third and fourth-class employees were appointed from other districts and usually they left their stations on Thursday afternoon and sometimes did not return to work on Sunday or Monday on various pretexts. I noticed too that 17 low-level employees who had been posted to Khagrachhari district court were all from Rangpur and Rajshahi areas. The District Judge told me that they remained absent for 15 or 16 days a month and, he said, since they were from other districts it was not possible to issue summons to them in remote areas.

Hence, I issued another circular directing the District and Sessions Judges, Metropolitan Session Judges, Nari-O-Shishu Nirajaton Daman Tribunals and Chief Judicial Magistrates to appoint 3rd and 4th class employees from the local districts and they should start the process without seeking any permission from the Ministry of Law. It was pointed out to me that the Ministry of Law had issued a circular to the courts directing them that there should not be any appointment to vacant posts without prior permission of the Ministry. This had created a deadlock in all districts. The Judges could not transact business smoothly for shortage of supporting staff. The circular was issued by the Ministry of Establishment now Janaproshason. It was for the government departments and sector corporations to the effect that no appointment could be made without the approval of the concerned ministry. This Circular was not applicable to the District Courts because the District Courts are under the Supreme Court.9 Neither the government nor the Ministry of Law can control or have supervision authority over it. There were complaints from the local Bars that outsiders were being appointed in different sections and they were not regularly available and, as a result, the litigants were facing serious problems in taking copies and do other related work.

On one occasion, I got a case of a similar nature, in which some employees were working for five years in Tangail. They were transferred from one station to other. Their salaries were stopped claiming they were appointed in the revenue set up beyond the time schedule fixed by the Ministry. The selection process was delayed by seven days only. When the matter came up for hearing, on behalf of the State the Additional Attorney General produced the Circular of the Ministry of Janaproshason (Establishment). On inquiry whether this circular was applicable for recruitment in the lower judiciary, he could not give any proper reply. On the strength of the circular, the Law Minister used to send an officer from the ministry with a list whenever the process of appointment was started, and a process of exam and recruitment was conducted, and the District Judges were compelled to make appointments as per the ministry's list. It was also reported by the lawyers that in each appointment, the officer concerned used to take five to six lakh taka and the outsiders were normally selected. I declared the circular void and directed the District Judges to continue the recruitment process without any approval from the ministry, so far as the vacant posts were concerned. From thence, recruitments are being made independently and the local people are getting priority and only in technical posts, if local appropriate people are not available, candidates from neighboring districts are appointed. After the verdict and after the appointment process was regularized, it was reported that the Secretary of the Ministry of Law threatened the judicial officers that they would have to face unpleasant consequences after my retirement. The Law Minister was so annoyed that one day he came to my office and told me that he could appoint 2/3 political supporters, but due to the judgment, he was facing many inconveniences. I told him that the appointment process had become so corrupted by a section of officers, the administration of justice was hampered, and the Chief Justice felt compelled to take actions for the interest of dispensing justice and eliminate corruption in the appointment process.

The entire budget for the lower judiciary was given to the Ministry of Law. But the Chief Justice noticed that the judges were recording evidence manually and the copying section was issuing handwritten certified copies because of shortage of typewriters. Lately supply of typewriters had been stopped and even though computers were supplied down to the Union Parishad level none was supplied by the ministry to the District Courts. Accordingly, the Chief Justice called a meeting with the Secretaries concerned to simplify the work order and harmonize it. The Cabinet Secretary Mohammad Shafiul Alam, who was the Secretary of the Ministry of Land, including some other Secretaries and the Law Minister were present. In the day-long program different issues were discussed. All of them praised the initiatives and expressed their willingness to improve the spheres which needed to be improved in the lower judiciary. I pointed out, at one juncture that due to shortage in supply of computers judicial work was greatly hampered and requested the Law Secretary to provide 700 computers while the rest of the computers would be provided by the Chief Justice. The Law Secretary assured supply of the computers, but not a single computer was supplied. Whenever I visited district courts, I used to carry five to six computers with me. In this way, phase by phase, I had supplied computers from the Supreme Court budget.

All government offices were taken under the digitization program, but the judiciary was left out of consideration. I took the issue to the Law Minister, the Finance Minister and the Prime Minister. But none paid any heed to my request. Thereafter I took up the digitization program on my own with the help of the UNDP and, as a test case, I started the program with the Magistracy of Sylhet. Shortly after digitization we noticed that the disposal of cases in that Magistracy was four times higher than in other courts. On being encouraged by the pace of work I decided to initiate digitization in all courts. Initially it was decided to start the process in Dhaka, Chittagong, Rajshahi and other large courts. I contacted the Minister for State in charge of the Ministry of Information and Communication Technology Junaid Ahmed Palak. He appeared to me to be a very energetic, spirited young politician.

As soon as I brought up the issue he gladly accepted my proposal and he displayed great interest in the digitization process. He sent some of his experts for exchanging views in this regard and after assessing the requirements intimated my office that about Tk 400 crore would be needed for digitizing the judiciary. I invited Junaid Ahmed Palak and when he came to my office, he learnt about the amount of money required for the project. After consultation with him, I invited Planning Minister AHM Mostafa Kamal for a cup of tea and when he was in my office I requested him to grant the necessary Tk 400 crore for the project from the development budget. He agreed and included it in the pre-ECNEC meeting and asked the Supreme Court Registry to send an officer to that meeting.

This was for the first time an officer of the Supreme Court attended a pre-ECNEC meeting. The officer noticed that six officers from the Ministry of Law opposed the project at the meeting. Their main objection was that the Ministry itself would manage, control and oversee the entire digitization program. The worst ministry in the government is the Ministry of Law. It had even failed to construct the magistracy buildings in nine years

And I had to personally involve myself in the site selection process in some districts. As for the digitization program, the IT Ministry had already undertaken the scheme in other sectors and it had the needed experts, while the Ministry of Law did not have any expert. With the intervention of the Secretary of the Planning Commission---who commented that the Chief Justice was very active and energetic in the development of the judiciary and did a lot for it---the project was approved in the pre-ECNEC meeting, but it could not pass through the ECNEC because of the objection from the Ministry of Law. When I came to know about this I was very shocked that the Ministry of Law was working against the interest of administration of justice instead of the development of the judiciary.

Amongst the urgent development work undertaken in the Supreme Court one was the improvement of the Registry. When I assumed the office of Chief Justice Kuddus Zaman was the Registrar and the Supreme Court was run by one Registrar, two Additional Registrars, and some other officers in the junior level. Zaman was an efficient and honest officer. But he lacked judicial experience. I told him that I would send him to a district of his choice as District and Sessions Judge, but I could not keep him as Registrar. Though initially he appeared shocked but a moment later he smiled and said that whatever order I would give he would obey. The objective was that unless the Registry was improved with the infusion of efficient officers, the Chief Justice would not be able to perform his duties effectively. Moreover, with few exceptions, Chief Justices usually had little previous experience in administrative matters. Therefore, among the first things I kept in mind was that there had to be improvement of the Registry office by bringing in efficient officers.

I proposed the name of Farid Ahmed Shibli, who was then a Senior District Judge and Secretary of the Judicial Service Commission. He was an efficient dignified man of principle. He had good command of the English language and had also obtained higher training in Canada. But my proposal was met with objection from the Ministry of Law claiming he did not belong to their political ideology. I told the Minister that if Shibli could be the Secretary of the Judicial Service Commission under MM Ruhul Amin, Tozammel Hossain, ABM Khairul Haque and me for about six-seven years and had performed his work efficiently, why he could not be appointed Registrar. Earlier, he had worked as Additional Registrar of the Supreme Court as well. I had thought that since he had served as Additional Registrar, he could be the best Registrar. I informed the Minister that it is my priority to bring in officers of my choice in the Registry and the government had nothing to do with this matter. The Law Minister ultimately approved the proposal and sent Kuddus Zaman as District and Sessions Judge of Dhaka.

The first thing I advised the new Registrar to do was to reshuffle the Registry by bringing efficient officers from the field irrespective of their race, color and belief. I believed that the Chief Justice would remain busy with heaps of work since he must administer justice and look after the administration of the Supreme Court and lower judiciary. So competent and efficient officers would infuse momentum in the work of the office of the Chief Justice. As per his advice, the officers were selected, among them, Anisur Rahman as Secretary to the Chief Justice, Farzana Yasmin as Deputy Registrar and another female officer as Assistant Registrar. Of note here is that Farzana Yasmin was the first female Deputy Registrar.

The Chief Justice maintains two secretaries, one for the Appellate Division and the other for the High Court Division. The secretaries used to be posted by promotion from the position of Bench Officers and Bench Readers, which are essentially clerical jobs. I found strange that a Secretary to the Chief Justice was appointed from a clerical post. I therefore appointed an Additional District Judge Anisur Rahman as Secretary to the Chief Justice in the Appellate Division. Since many dignitaries, judges, ministers, chiefs of foreign aid agencies and ambassadors, among others, used to come to meet the Chief Justice and he must remain busy with many kinds of responsibilities, I believed if a competent officer was posted as the Chief Justice's secretary he could receive the guests properly and converse with them before the Chief Justice was available.

I told the Law Minister that if the Speaker and Ministers could have Private Secretaries in the rank of Deputy Secretary and Joint Secretary, why the Chief Justice could not maintain a Secretary in the rank of an Additional District Judge. The Law Minister could not counter my plea plausibly and moved the file and ultimately it was approved. So, for the first time a higher judicial officer was appointed as Secretary to the Chief Justice. This helped me a lot particularly since the former Chief Justices used to come to the Supreme Court for drawing their pension and other benefits and they could not be received properly by the officers. After this change all the former Chief Justices and other retired judges praised me for appointing a judicial officer as the CJ's Secretary. Secondly, I had noticed that the retired judges, former Chief Justices, ambassadors, social workers, donor agency heads used to come to meet with the Chief Justice but there was no proper arrangement for them to sit. The judges, including myself, were therefore compelled to stand at the front door of the Chief Justice's chamber for interviews. The High Court Division judges have only 45 minutes of recess and in that time, they had to eat lunch, pray, and meet the Chief Justice. They could not be met at a time, because some had personal issues to talk with the Chief Justice. Apart from that the President and Secretary of the Bar, senior lawyers, the Attorney General also used to come to meet with the Chief Justice. Accordingly, I arranged one room for the Judges and foreign dignitaries with all amenities and for the lawyers another room. After this arrangement, all the judges were very pleased, and they used to recount their past ordeals when meeting the Chief Justice. I told them that there is hardly any difference between a Chief Justice and the other judges; they are all brothers. The difference is that the CJ was given some extra work for the smooth administration of justice. He is being the guardian of the Constitution should also look after the difficulties being faced by the judges. Previously the situation was so dire that there was not even a toilet for the use of a visiting dignitary.

Another problem which used to bother me hugely was the delay in writing judgments by the judges. Sometimes they took 3/4 years. This was done mostly by AKM Khairul Haque, Md. Mozammel Hossain, AHM Shamsuddin Chowdhury, Md. Abdul Wahhab Miah and a few others. When Md. Mozammel Hossain was the Chief Justice the lawyers complained in court that they did not get the judgments even after three years. A most embarrassing instance occurred when all seven judges were constituting the Bench and a lawyer mentioned a matter, possibly relating to Gulshan Club, which was disposed of about three years back, but the judge did not deliver the judgment. When the Chief Justice asked about the judgement, the lawyer produced a slip mentioning the name of AHM Shamsuddin Chowdhury. Despite the Chief Justice's direction, the judge took six months to finalize the judgment.

Previously we delivered judgment in the High Court Division in open court but subsequently the judges adopted a policy of not dictating the judgment in open court but instead declared the verdict absolute or discharged or dismissed or allowed. Lawyers were complaining that as the judgments are Witten after long delays, almost in all cases, the judges did not discuss the points argued by them and, as a result, when the matters were heard, I pointed out points that had not been raised in the High Court Division. The lawyers' answer was that they argued for a long time and showed grounds taken in the High Court Division. This was totally unethical. So, I directed the judges to dictate their judgments in open court, but it yielded little result.

Another bad precedent that had developed was keeping the judgment without expressing opinion and the judges used to write the judgments after retirement. Md. Mozammel Hoque kept about 70-80 judgments and AHM Shamsuddin Chowdhury retained more than 300 judgments. He even kept some judgments of the High Court Division. I issued a circular prohibiting judges from writing judgments after retirement. The judiciary acts as a natural umpire which keeps checks on the exercise of power by other organs of the State to ensure that the rights of citizens are not trampled on contrary to the law. When the judiciary enjoys such a special position in the functioning of the State it is also saddled with the onerous duty of discharging its functions efficiently and without delay. It is universally known that a judge finally speaks through his judgment. The Pakistan Supreme Court observed that the cases where judgments were withheld by courts for a considerable period are frowned upon and disapproved.

In another case, the same Supreme Court, in the case of a judgment passed after one year and three months, set it aside on the reasoning that it was against natural justice and it fundamentally did not satisfy the concept of proper judicial dispension. It was of the view that there is rule of violation of a judicial decision. The Constitution provided that a judge shall hold office until he attained the age of sixty-seven years. He subscribes to an oath under Article 148 so long he would hold such office to faithfully discharge the duties and protecting, preserving and defending the

Constitution. But after the retirement he did not remain a judge and any judgment delivered by him is void because he had become functus officio. He cannot hold the office of a judge of the Supreme Court because his oath covers only the period of office.

After I had issued the Circular there was serious tension among the members of the Cabinet including the Prime Minister? Their apprehension was that the Constitution's Thirteenth Amendment would become void because ABM Khairul Haque delivered his opinion long after his retirement. Some ministers met me and even castigated me as one to cause damage to the government. On one occasion the Prime Minister brought up the issue with me and asked why I was issuing controversial orders. She told me that ABM Khairul Haque wanted to make a hold a press conference, but she had prevented him. She added that since the practice was already being followed why I had raised the point. On hearing her I laughed and told her, yes ABM Khairul Haque wrote the judgment after retirement but what about my judgment. All the judges signed the short order while all of them were in office and I wrote a separate judgment. I told her she would not allow any minister or secretary to sign an official file after retirement even if they inadvertently they kept a matter pending. The Prime Minister after getting the explanation remained silent. As per my direction all judgments of Md. Mozammel Hossain and Shamsuddin Chowdhury were rewritten by sitting judges. I did not allow any judge who had retired from the High Court Division to sign judgments. The bad precedents have been eliminated and now all judges are mindful to complete their judgments before retirement.

After having successfully implemented these improvements, I realized that the beautification of the Supreme Court should be undertaken so that people who came to the court would feel that they have entered the temple of justice. If the atmosphere was appropriate they would develop a sense of getting justice here. So, I decided to extend the size of the Registry. Previously there was a demand for the establishment of a Supreme Court Secretariat. The government did not pay any heed to it. I realized that if I raised this point it would not be implemented during my tenure. Hence, I proposed the upgradation of the position of the Registrar to

Registrar General and under him there would be two Registrars, one for the High Court Division and another for the Appellate Division, and under them Deputy Registrars and Assistant Registrars would be appointed.

Simultaneously I presented a program for setting up a section under the name 'Research Wing'. After much tussle and back and forth of communication, I managed to get approval for the expansion of the Registry office. Then I appointed Syed Aminul Haque as the first Registrar General. He was in the Ministry as a Joint Secretary. After the elevation of Farid Ahmed Shibli to the Bench as Additional Judge of the High Court Division, I succeeded in appointing Syed Aminul Haque. This provided momentum in the work of the Registry. I also set up the IT department with required experts to digitize the Supreme Court completely. As part of the beautification process, I took up the inner garden had flower bushes planted and the entire court compound was cleaned up including the extended the Supreme Court building toward the north and deputed the Special Officer to look after the beautification project.

I noticed that the Supreme Court Bar car park was very small, and cars were being parked all around the court premises. Half of the car park was covered with bushes and garbage. I directed the Registry to clean up the place and directed the Ministry concerned for carpeting the area for additional parking space. Thus, while the lawyers got double the space than previously, vehicles of litigants were prevented from parking within the court premises. There was a road in the western side of the Supreme Court which passed between Suhrawardy Uddyan and the three national leaders' mausoleum. The road was unusable because a big portion of the road in the middle at the entrance of the Uddyan was taken over by slum dwellers. I evicted the encroachers with the help of police and directed the Works Department to build a spacious road. Ultimately the road was opened, and it was named Nyan Sarani (Justice Road).

I noticed that the judges had their hair cut either at the New Market or the officers club or some other private places. Sometimes they had to wait for a long time to get their turn. It was not pleasing to see judges have hair trimmed at public places. The Chief Justice and other judges are not safe when using such public places. The army, police and administrative officers have their own barber shops, but the Supreme Court had no such facility. Though the former Chief Justice had opened a Judges' Corner in the extended court building, due to shortage of fund he could not arrange any recreational facilities. In the process of improving the Judges' Corner I had arranged to set up two modern barber shops for male and female judges including their spouses. I constituted a committee to manage the Judges' Corner and advised them to expand the facilities for the judges. The Judges' Corner had a badminton court, but it could not be used in the rainy season. They wanted me to build an indoor sports complex with modern facilities. I arranged funds for it with the help of the Ministry of Sports and constructed a modern standard complex in the north of the extended building which can also be used as a conference hall. The committee also approached me for funds for starting a bakery and canteen for the judges. I arranged the needed funds and a modern bakery, and a canteen were established. Since the Judges' Corner became self-sufficient the management committee arranged 'Boisakhi Mela' on Pohela Boishakh and observed all national festivities while organizing blood donation programs every year on the 15th of August.

During Ramadan, hosting iftar parties by various departments including the President and the Prime Minister has become a part of our culture. The Army, Police and other departments also arrange grand iftar parties. The Chief Justice is invited to all such occasions. But the Supreme Court could not host any iftar which, I felt, was damaging to the reputation of the court. I asked the Registry to arrange an iftar party in the very first year of assumption of my office inviting the President, the Prime Minister and some Ministers, Secretaries who relate to the judiciary, senior lawyers and officers of the office of the Attorney General. Though there was heavy rain, that party was arranged in an open space of the extended building. The officers arranged the waterproof canopy in such a manner that the rain did not create any hindrance. The performance of the first Iftar party in such inclement wealth, the items served in the Iftar to the guests were so delicious that they praised. The President, Prime Minister, Speaker, three service chiefs were present. The second year the iftar was arranged in the indoor sports complex. The President was very pleased with the arrangement and advised us to continue with the program every year.

There was no space for a daycare center for the children of the employees of the Supreme Court. I saw that the female workers were facing many problems while attending office keeping their new born babies at home. So, I decided to open a daycare center. Female employees were appointed to look after the babies. Food and milk were also arranged. But I could not arrange a daycare center like the one Bangladesh Secretariat has due to shortage of space. However, since the process had been started, I hoped it would be improved in the future and could be shifted to a suitable location. Keeping this thing in mind, I asked the government to shift the International Crimes Tribunal (ICT) from the Old High Court building to another place so that the museum, the daycare center, the bank and post office could be accommodated there.

I raised the problems with the Prime Minister specifically because it had been falsely reported to the Prime Minister that there was enough vacant space in the extended building, which was occupied by the Roads and Highways Department. I told the Prime Minister that not an inch of land was lying vacant and that she had been misinformed by interested quarters who do not want the appropriate institutionalization of the Supreme Court. I came to know later that the Prime Minister got a report from an intelligence agency suppressing the facts. On one occasion when the Law Minister came to the Supreme Court, before we started our discussions, I requested him to look in the extended building so that all misunderstandings could be erased. I took him to the different sections of the building and showed him how the employees were working in a noxious environment without proper air and light. I showed him where the employees were sitting with piles of files around them which might fall on them. I also showed him the condition of the Record Room where there was not even an inch vacant space and every day thousands of files were added to the Record Room. The Supreme Court being a Court of Record2 all files are required to be preserved. In more developed countries, including India, the records are kept in digitized form.

The Minister was convinced, and I initiated a program to digitize the records. Therefore, I invited State Minister for IT Junaid Ahmed Palak. He visited our Record Room and was convinced that the records should be kept in digitized form. But his wishes could not be implemented till higher authorities approved the project. I pointed out to the relevant Ministers that, if God forbid, any fire occurred in the Supreme Court particularly in the Record Rooms, there would be a colossal damage to the nation which could not be assessed in terms of money. Accordingly, I submitted a project profile for the construction of a building towards the middle section of the Supreme Court and extended the building providing provisions for underground floors for keeping records where fire could not cause any damage to them. A police sub-station would be set up for the security of the records of the Supreme Court as well as accommodation for a clinic for the officers of the Supreme Court. The project was finally sent to the cold storage for reasons not known to the Chief Justice although the Law Minster was in favor of the project.

In Commonwealth countries particularly where the Westminster type of governments are working, it was a convention that a national judicial conference is held which is attended by the Chief Executive of the government, Finance, Law and Home Ministers and their Secretaries and all the judges. A meaningful and workable judiciary is necessary to build the country as a State for the welfare of the people and unless the Executive branch extended its hands, rule of law cannot be established. At the conference field level officers would point out the difficulties they were facing in the administration of justice while the Chief Justice in his speech highlighted his programs to be implemented, so that the Chief Executive of the government could realize and direct the ministries concerned to take appropriate measures by providing funds and security.

This convention is not followed in Bangladesh. It is because though we inherited the British legacy of the administration of justice, after the Partition, Pakistan was ruled by the military for a long period of time. There was no rule of law in the true sense in Pakistan and the judiciary was neglected and the Chief Justices did not follow traditions. After the independence, there was scope for the Chief Justices of Bangladesh to arrange such programs, but they did not do so. As a result, the convention was given a pass. I realized that unless these things were brought to the notice of the Executive, there could not be any positive change in the judiciary. On the other hand, the Ministry that was supposed to initiate the development programs was instead hindering the programs.

Accordingly, I arranged a National Judicial Conference in December 2015, when the civil court was on vacation. The Prime Minister and other related Ministers and Secretaries were invited. The intimation was sent to the Prime Minister's office two months prior to the event. The Bangabandhu International Conference Center was also booked for the program to accommodate about 1600 judges. There was no response from the Prime Minister's office despite repeated reminders from the Registry office. I came to know from some source that the Prime Minister was persuaded to avoid the conference. I was naturally extremely shocked particularly because the Prime Minister was always attending conferences some of which were not even suitable for the Chief Executive. She was attending all functions and seminars of the bureaucrats, police, military and other organizations. She used to attend functions like inaugurating a building but avoided the most vital gathering. So, without waiting for any reply, I rushed to the Bangabhaban to meet the President. President Abdul Hamid gladly accepted the invitation and said that in such an august gathering, he should have been invited earlier. The President had a program in Sylhet on that day. He directed the organizers to delay the program by an hour so that he could attend our program. On seeing the packed auditorium with judges and, equally significantly, with 40 percent audience being women, he was enormously delighted and told me that if he had no program in Sylhet he would have spent the whole day with the judges and would have taken his lunch with them.

Judicial officers from every corner of the country attended the occasion and it was an innovation for them which they had never experienced. I ate lunch at a table where the junior Assistant Judges were taking lunch, although arrangements for the Chief Justice and other judges were made separately. But the result was that the junior officers were immensely happy getting me with them. The next judicial conference was also fixed for December 2, 2016. Before sending any invitation to the Prime Minister, the Principal Secretary to the Prime Minister came to meet with me for some special purpose. I informed him that despite my invitation to the Prime Minister during the last judicial conference her absence had created a bad precedent. I also said that I would not invite her to attend the next conference if she did not wish to attend. He then wanted to know whether any "unusual demand" would be made to the Prime Minister. I told the Principal Secretary that it was beyond belief the Prime Minister's office had imagined that the Prime Minister would be invited to a judicial conference to embarrass her, particularly when the Chief Justice, Ministers and other judges would be present. I explained to him the purpose and necessity of holding such conferences and cited examples from other countries. The Principal Secretary was convinced, and a signal was received to invite her. The Supreme Court officially invited her and there was confirmation from the Prime Minister's office that she would attend the program.

As mentioned earlier, there is always a tug of war between the Ministry and the Supreme Court over postings and transfers of the judicial officers and promulgation of Disciplinary Rules for the judicial officials. On the question of Disciplinary Rules, the matter was ultimately brought to the attention of the Prime Minister. On one occasion I met her and said that if an officer of her department flatly declined her direction, what would be the working condition of the Prime Minister's office and what would be her reaction if she found that despite such insubordination, she had no power to dismiss him. It would not have been practical on her part to transact business with such errant officers. This was what was happening in the judiciary. There was practically duel administration in the lower judiciary because of conflicting provisions in the Constitution.3

Only seven days before the conference it was unofficially reported that the Prime Minister would not be attending the conference, but there was no intimation. The Registry could not reach the Prime Minister's Office and one or two days before the conference, it was said that the Prime Minister would remain busy with other work, so she could not attend. At this stage, there was a possibility of inviting the President. It was also reported from the Prime Minister's Office that since the President was attending the conference, the Prime Minister declined to attend. But as a matter of fact, the President was not even invited. Nevertheless, the conference was held in a congenial atmosphere, but the Law Minister and the Law Secretary were also conspicuously absent. For the Law Secretary it was reported that he had gone to Chennai for his wife's treatment and the Law Minister was admitted to hospital for a hernia operation.

The date of the conference had been fixed six or seven months ago, and they were properly invited and agreed to attend the conference. But it became very clear that the Executive in a planned manner avoided the conference. After the conference, I decided to organize the next conference in 2017 with a different format. I would invite the Chief Justice of India from whom the judges would be able to learn about the improvement that he had done in the judiciary. I also directed the Registry to distribute one laptop to each of the judicial officers and arrange funds accordingly. The process of purchasing of laptops was also initiated. But my destiny did not allow me to remain present in Bangladesh as the Chief Justice. Therefore, as reported, the conference was held in a very perfunctory environment, and after the lunch almost all judicial officers left the venue. The laptops were, not distributed among the officers even though I had arranged for the purchase of the laptops. It was due to lack of efficient officer in the Registry.

The Supreme Court's condition was so precarious at the time I assumed office, it even could not print a diary for the judges, Bench Officers and Personal Officers of the judges, although all departments of the government used to publish diaries and supplied them to us. In the judiciary, particularly for the Bench Officers and Personal Assistants, a diary is indispensable. The

Personal Officers are required to maintain the judges' daily schedule of work and to enable them to remind the judges about their programs. The judges had to wait for the arrival of calendars and diaries from other government departments and business houses. I directed the Registrar General to print diaries every year in December and distribute those among the judges, Bench Officers, Assistant Bench Officers and other officers of the Supreme Court. This practice was begun in 2015.

I had undertaken and implemented many development programs and activities.

a) New link road between the Supreme Court and the Bangla Academy;
b) Beautification of the Supreme Court, 5-km road, garden lighting, fountain, landscape, carparking area of the Supreme Court;
c) New administration building under process;
d) Annexed-2 building under process; (e) Procurement of security materials, bag scanner, archway etc.
e) New chambers for judges and other dignitaries, new court no-10,
f) Renovation of all judge's chambers;
g) Renovation of administrative sections,
h) New waiting room for the guests of the Chief Justice;
i) Indoor sports complex;
j) Day care center;
k) Renovation of judge's lounge,
l) Renovation and beautification of corridor of main building, installation of legal aid office;
m) Providing support to judge's corner by furniture, equipment, monthly cash contribution, canteen and bakery;
n) Arranged training for all judges in India;
o) Holding national judicial conference for judges;
p) Development of 5-year strategic plan for Supreme Court;
q) Developed new performance and evaluation system and software for judges of the subordinate courts;
r) Publication of first judicial policy for the subordinate judiciary;

s) Amendment of Criminal Rules and Orders;
t) steps to amend of recruitment Rules and Disciplinary Rules of both the Divisions;
u) Installation of CCTV camera covering the entire area of Supreme Court;
v) Iftar Programs;
w) New gradation list for judges of subordinate courts;
x) Developed E-filing for Supreme Court;
y) developed software for jail appeal cases;

z1) Research Unit;

z2) Prepare new delegation of power policy;

z3) Administration and financial arrangement for smooth running of the administration of the Supreme Court;

z4) New entitlement guideline for medical treatment abroad;

z5) Complaint box in front of the Registrar General's office;

z6) Renovation of medical center;

z7) Renovated the Chief Justice's official residence replacing the old gates and naming the house as 'Nyan Bhabhan', beautification of the garden by installing two fountains;

z8) Judge's Rest House.

I also improved the libraries of the Supreme Court. There are two libraries, one for the Appellate Division and the other for the High Court Division. The Appellate Division's library was arranged just towards the southern corner room contiguously next to the Chief Justice's court room and the High Court Division library was in the old court building. The former Chief Justices did not give much attention to the modernization and relocation of the libraries. After the annex court building started functioning, most of the High Court judges started sitting in courts in the annex building. It was difficult for only three or four staff to function well in the libraries. There was no qualified librarian in the library of the High Court

Division. I had to appoint a qualified librarian and two qualified assistant librarians for each of the libraries. I sent the Appellate Division librarian along with another for training to the Indian Supreme Court library. When I had visited the Indian Supreme Court library, I had noticed that the library was very well organized. The librarian had a PhD degree in library science. The librarians also used to help the judges in preparing speeches for various functions. The library is possibly the biggest court library in Asia is being managed so scientifically that within minutes they could collect the books requisitioned by the judges from different benches. I wanted to know from the librarian about his experience. He was highly impressed by the very developed system in the Indian library. I told him that now he should utilize that experience in modernizing our libraries. His first duty was to shift both the libraries from their present locations. I directed the Registry to arrange suitable places in the annex building for the High Court Division's library so that it could be easier for judges to get the necessary books. I also directed him to depute an officer for shifting and improvement of the library. The Appellate Division library is shifted to the former place of the High Court Division library. After the shifting of the library, the room is converted to a court room which was previously used as court and now it can be used as court no-3 for the Appellate Division.

Besides I introduced e-library in the Supreme Court which was the digital format library. A software, KOHA, was developed for both the libraries. With KOHA more than 80,900 books were enlisted. The essential feature of a book, i.e. total number of pages, writer's name, bibliography, abstract, name of the book, etc. are described in the software. The system is very user friendly and also made it easier for the librarians in the management of the books. The users of library, especially the judges of the Supreme Court, can access the entire library online and see the necessary books. Previously the Supreme Court librarian's status was of a third-class employee which I upgraded to an officer, and the High Court librarian's position was also in the process of final approval when I left the court, because all librarians now have master's degree in library science.

Despite non-cooperation from the government with budgets, I undertook the digitization process in the Supreme Court. The first program I took up was the publication of the daily cause lists online in November 2015. Under this system, cause lists of both the Divisions of the Supreme Court are published online. To make the system sustainable and "Operational manual" has been drafted by the Research Unit of the Supreme Court. The Bench officers, staff of the Bench Section and IT Department give impute of cases to make online cause list more user friendly. IT Department converted into PDF format and upload in the website. There are two mobile apps available in the Supreme Court using which the following information can be accessed:

i. the litigants can be informed about the result of the case even at a remote place;

ii. they are usable on a simple smart phone;

iii. the lawyers and litigants can get the upcoming cause lists 12 hours ahead of the hearing;

iv. results can be found immediately after orders and judgments are passed;

v. corruption among the Bench Officers and court staff in listing, upgrading, downgrading cases from the daily cause lists has been totally abolished;

vi. through using such options lawyers and litigants can easily access their cases;

vii. lawyers and litigants can get information about the item which has been taken up for hearing at any time;

viii. there is opportunity to get both printed hard copy and soft copy of the cause lists. However, I failed to persuade the lawyers to stop printing the daily cause list from the BG Press, although I proposed to them that I would arrange monitors in the Bar library to follow the progress of the cases being heard by the Benches and the daily cause lists would be regularly uploaded to save public money. With the saved money, more development programs could be undertaken. Even new apps have been added to check the number of pending cases of any particular lawyer. We also introduced a system so that lists can be uploaded by the lawyers and their clerks and introduced a database using which litigants can monitor the status of their cases.

Every year we must pay BG Press twenty crore taka for printing the daily cause lists. For printing the cause list, the Supreme Court now requires only one hundred taka, but the lawyers contribute Tk. 500 per month. So, a huge amount of money was wasted for printing the daily cause list. Accordingly, I called upon the Supreme Court Bar to download the cause list and print those instead of obtaining printed copies. But the lawyers were bent on printing the cause list. I even told them that, if needed, I would arrange training for downloading the daily cause list and put up monitors in the Supreme Court Bar for monitoring the cases being heard by different Benches. I also prepared a program by application of which each of the lawyers could find out the serial numbers of cases pending in different courts. The lawyers prevented me from stopping the printing of the list. I told them that the Patna High Court stopped printing of cause lists in 1978 and around 2000 all courts in India stopped printing daily cause list. Due to objections raised by the lawyers the digitization process for cause list could not be implemented yet.

Another fact that disturbed me much was coming to know that hardened criminals could manage to get released from jail by forging the signatures of the judges in collusion with some corrupt officials of the court. So, I directed the Registrar General to issue notice upon all Bench Officers and all Presiding Judges holding criminal jurisdictions to inform the office the names and case numbers of the accused in favor of whom bail had been granted. Simultaneously, I directed the Registrar General to intimate the concerned courts about granting of bails by the High Court in respect of the accused person and mention the list. I also directed him to communicate to all jailors that no accused should be released from custody without verification from the Supreme Court. After introduction of this system, though there was check in forgery, some judges, Bench Officers and the lawyers were not happy. For the judges the procedure put extra pressures on Bench Officers while the lawyers told me that this process created delay in releasing the accused. I did not listen to their objections and continued the process and directed the office to create another wing under the name 'Research Center' and proposed to the government the sanction of some judicial officers with supporting staff pointing out specifically that this would bring advantage to the government. Often corrupt litigants, after taking lease of a fishery or quarry or a ferry ghat or property, obtained stay order from the High Court Division for a temporary period but continued to enjoy the property for indefinite periods. And as mentioned earlier, hard-edged criminals also managed to be released from jails by forging signatures. All these corrupt practices would be rectified if a Research Wing could be established.

When I used to visit the district courts, the Deputy Commissioners would complain to me that they could not get up-to-date orders of different cases and, as a result, even after the expiration of the lease period, the lessees profited from government property for indefinite periods and thus affected revenue collection. I spoke to the Law Minister explaining the situation and requested him to expedite the matter. The Law Minister supported my proposal and assured me of cooperating in this regard. I also requested the Janaproshashon (Establishment) and the Finance Secretaries to co-operate in the improvement of the Registry of the Supreme Court in the interest of the government. I monitored the progress of the issue by deputing an officer to keep tabs on the file. But ultimately—and sadly--our officers could not trace where the relevant file was concealed. Even after waiting for one year when we had no result I got an opportunity to meet the Prime Minister at a State function. I explained to her how the project for improvement of the Supreme Court would serve the interest of the country. In reply the Prime Minister told me that this would require many officers and involvement of substantial money. I responded by telling her that no new officers would be required to be hired, only 5 to 6 judicial officers from the field could be deputed in implementing the project. Her reply was that, even if those officers were deputed, they would require support staff involving huge monetary expenses. I got her reply and did not say anything more to her. She gets whatever she desires from the judiciary, continues in power without holding national elections properly in by presenting inaccurate interpretation of our judgment in the

Thirteenth Amendment case, but continues to be hostile toward the improvement of the Judicial Branch.

In the meantime, I directed the Registry to find out a new software that would expedite the communication of bail granting orders on the same day without waiting to obtain a copy from the court. This would obviously reduce corruption and expedite the process. I had collected some brilliant judicial officers in my Registry who had vast knowledge on IT. With their assistance the IT Department worked out a method in which the entire process of communication was digitized. After a bail order was signed by a judge, the signed copy is sent to the criminal miscellaneous section where it is noted in the file and signed by an Assistant Registrar deputed for the purpose. Thereafter the order is sent to the IT Section which then scans it and gives it a web reference number and finally posts it on the Supreme Court website. The district courts can verify it online to ascertain the authenticity of the bail order quickly and decide for releasing the prisoner.

I can honestly claim that no Chief Justice other than Mahmudul Amin Choudhury ever tried to reduce court holidays. There was no endeavor to modernize the judiciary, not to speak of digitizing it. No attempt was made by anyone to enhance the strength of the Registry for transacting court business except claiming to set up a secretariat which would be a futile attempt because they had not read the mindset of the Executive. All the time we accepted the government's dominance over us and it reached such a position that the Executive wanted to treat us as a department of the Executive. For the first time I asserted the Supreme Court's role as guardian of the Constitution. It is an Organ of the State, not an organ of the government. This raised eyebrows among some and started a conspiracy to somehow humiliate and undermine me.

I did not want the unlawful acts conducted by the Executive Magistrates in the name of mobile court exercising judicial powers to arrest, taking an offender in custody and awarding sentence. In the schedule of the Mobile Court Act, 2009 new laws were included. Some provisions of the Penal Code, Madak Drabya Niyantran Ain (Narcotics Control Act), and some other offenses in the schedule, are not only unconstitutional but also contrary to the Code of Criminal Procedure and Masder Hossain judgment. These offenses are exclusively triable by tribunals and courts created by the Code of Criminal Procedure and special laws. For some offenses the penalty is death sentence, but the Executive Magistrates are trying them and were awarding two to three months' sentence. I showed the Law Minister the illegal provisions included, and he was convinced but then he said that he had kept a file on his table for a quite long time despite pressure from the Executive to extend the powers of the so-called mobile courts.

The Principal Secretary and Janaprashasan Secretary met me for resolving the issue. I told them that the law was faulty, and it should be re-enacted by repealing the existing one. The Prime Minister, who has little elementary knowledge of law, wanted to know from me whether I wanted the judges to administer judicial works on the roads and added that some countries had expressed satisfaction with the outcome of this law. My only regret in my judicial career is that I could not get time to settle issues relating to this law after hearing the appeal although I had granted leave to examine this law. It is an affront to the judiciary and violative to the fundamental laws in its application. Consequently, the top-level officers who were transacting business of the government keeping close touch with the Prime Minister were unhappy with me. This obstructed me from concluding judicial reform work.

Reference:

1. *Civil Petition No. 2532 of 2014, Bangladesh v. Md. Abul Kalam Azad*
2. *Article 109 of the Constitution.*
3. *Article 108 the Constitution.*
4. *Articles 109 and 116 of the Constitution.*

Chapter 13

Responsibilities of Chief Justice

Besides essential judicial work the toughest job for a Chief Justice is the constitution of different Benches of the High Court Division. It is an extremely difficult chore. In India, I came to know in course of discussions with Altamas Kabir and TS Thakur, former Chief Justices, that they did not have a choice in the allocation of cases to different Benches. They use a computer program for the allocation of cases and thus the judges have no choice. But our case is completely different because our appointment procedure is totally political ignoring the constitutional mandate. The Executive is not concerned with quality and, therefore, the Chief Justice must consider many things, among them the most important is eligibility of the presiding judge to resolve the subject properly. ATM Afzal, former chief justice, told me on one occasion that the constitution of Benches and allocation of cases are the most challenging tasks. After assuming office, I realized that it was indeed a tough job. You must keep in mind the number of cases of different nature pending in court. All judges are dependable on all subjects. They have shortcomings on different laws, but the Chief Justice must get the necessary work done by them. Most of the judges are interested to preside over a Division Bench and wanted motion powers in criminal matters and their second choice was writ motion powers.

After writ matters were fragmented into different groups, they lost their importance. I did it intentionally. Some judges were in the habit of issuing rule and stay orders without caring about the merit of the petition and its consequence. Opinions of different Benches vary; one Bench might take cognizance of a matter, but another could decline to do so on the same issue. Some judges took cognizance of matters which were already settled by the apex court. Criminal matters are also fragmented in different groups but even then, power of motions on bail matters was given top priority. Some of the judges are very qualified and knowledgeable but as they had not practiced in civil and criminal matters they did not have good grasp of those laws. There were myriad similar factors

119

to take into consideration when allocating cases and constituting benches. Worst of all was that some of them had reservations about sitting with judges and sometimes they even squabbled in open court.

Secondly, I also had to keep in mind the capacity of the judges in having a proper understanding of a subject so that we could the best decisions. In some instances, lawyers are not keen to appear before a judge for hearing. Some judges taking advantage of that opportunity would rise from the court although there was still more than one hour left. Some judges were not interested in a subject of law allocated to him and so he would perform his responsibility in a perfunctory manner. Some judges even complained to me that they were not given important jurisdictions without realizing whether he would be able to deal with the matter. Additionally, they would point out that a judge junior to him was given Division Bench power.

Some judges are reluctant to dispose of first appeals which involve power that is very important because right to property is involved in those appeals and lot of critical facts and law points are required to be assessed. I was left with very limited option to allocate business of this power since to hear these matters one must have a good grip on evaluation of evidence and law. Nowadays, there is a dearth of civil lawyers and judges. Earlier most prominent lawyers used to appear in those matters and every lawyer would not show an impudence to appear in those matters. So, I constituted Benches according to my estimation of judges who were suitable to deal with such matters without worrying about whether anyone took exception or not. I did not even consider the issue of seniority in taking these decisions.

Jail appeals are always neglected because poor litigants were not able to engage lawyers and judges do not like to dispose of a matter in the absence of lawyers. So, I gave priority to these appeals and gave the responsibility to almost all criminal Benches to hear them every Thursday. I also constituted benches consisting of additional judges with senior judges to dispose of jail appeals on weekends at home. One judge is physically challenged, and he could not sit on the court. I gave him the constitution of jail appeals with a senior, who would discuss with the senior in his chamber in case of necessity. These steps helped much in the disposal of undefended appeals. My second priority was to monitor the sections for which I allocated some officers to inspect the different sections regularly. I noticed that huge number of criminal miscellaneous cases and writ matters which infrastructures are pending in the section. I instructed an officer to direct section to supply list of those cases and then directed different Benches to dispose of them for reducing the docket. I also made surprise visits to the sections. This helped me in keeping the employees at their desks till the office hour ended. Thirdly, my attention was also focused on the process of promotions of employees and constituted a committee to recommend for promotions of senior employees if s/he had the requisite qualification.

Even though it may not be relevant at this point, but I must describe an incident which I had experienced. As per the Constitution and the practice being followed, the Chairman and the Members of the Public Service Commission (PSC), the Comptroller and Auditor General are required to take oath before the Chief Justice in the Supreme Court Judges' lounge. On one occasion, Dr. Mohammad Siddique, the PSC Chairman, after taking oath of some members of the Commission conceded that after I had assumed the office of the Chief Justice the oath taking ceremony had become very elegant. Previously the Chief Justice alone administered the oath without participation of the other judges and they used to carry snacks for light refreshment. I instead directed that whenever any such program is arranged, it should be scheduled after 2:00 PM so that the other judges of the Appellate Division could attend. Since these were in effect state functions on the Supreme Court premises they were our guests and so they should be cordially received and entertained as honorable guests. I therefore ensured the presence of the all the judges of the Appellate Division and arranged refreshments for all the guests. After the formal function a very cordial interaction used to follow among the judges of the Apex Court and members and officers of the PSC.

Another crucial task of the Chief Justice is to oversee the administration of justice in the district courts. It is common practice prevailing now that some lawyers boycott judges on very nominal issues. If any officer was strict in granting bail, they would boycott that officer to press for his withdrawal. I was very firm in this regard and told the lawyers that if they took the law into their own hands I would not withdraw that officer. If they had any problem they must inform the Chief Justice and then I would consider their grievance. I did not succumb to their pressure and told them that they would face inconvenience unless they attended the court because I would not withdraw a judge with a cloud over him from a station. If such an officer were sent to another district, the lawyers there would also adopt the same posture. Normally in such circumstances I used to entrust one judge of the High Court Division who belonged to that district to amicably settle the dispute, and this process was very helpful.

Chapter 14

Participation in Seminars and Conferences

As Chief Justice I attended a seminar arranged by the 'International Conference of Jurists' held in Mumbai, India from March 27 to March 29, 2015. There I was awarded with the prestigious 'International Jurist Award' for my extraordinary contribution in the field of 'Administration of Justice'. I participated 'Regional Consultative Meeting on Judicial Service Commission Model Law' in Kualalumpur, Malaysia from June 9 to June 11, 2015. I delivered a lecture on 'Contribution of the Judiciary of Bangladesh in Strengthening Rule of Law and Democracy 'on October 5, 2015 at the Gujrat National Law University, Gujrat, India. In this seminar The Governor and the Chief Minister graced the occasion. Then I opened the new modern Auditorium. During a visit to India organized at the behest of the dynamic Indian Prime Minister Narendra Modi, I met President Pranab Mukherjee at the Rashtrapati Bhaban and the Prime Minister Narendra Modi at his official residence. On my first interaction Pranab Mukherjee completely charmed me. His simplicity, intelligent remarks, steady but forceful low voice, the topics he discussed convinced me that he is a well-read intellectual and possesses a commanding personality. He was truly appropriate for the high office of the President of India. One can easily pass an entire day listening to him. He has a sublime soul, is a versatile jurist, and a graceful example of dignity and refinement. He started with the Constitution of India and I noticed the vast knowledge of constitutional law he possess---it was as if he was teaching constitutional law to me, while in his presence I felt like a novice in constitutional law. He critiqued the judgments of the Supreme Court regarding the appointment of judges through a collegium system saying that the judges drafted the Constitution and treated it as if they were lawmakers. They had usurped the power of Parliament. He pointed out two judgments of the Supreme Court.1 According to the President, the Supreme Court seized power to appoint judges through a collegium without any warrant in the Constitution in defiance of Ambedkar's views. At the end he gifted me some books written by him.

From the Rashtrapati Bhaban, I was directly taken to the Prime Minister's official residence. There was only a woman interpreter with us. The Prime Minister spoke in Hindi, although he is fluent in English, which I knew from two previous occasions. In the beginning the Indian Prime Minister asked about my Gujrat visit and the areas I had visited. It was a very organized tour and I was treated as a state guest. On the first day of my visit, the Governor arranged a grand dinner in my honor in which all judges of the high court, cabinet ministers and high-level government officials attended. I congratulated Narendra Modi for arranging such a tour and thanked him the honor given to me. I also congratulated him for establishing the first university of Forensic Science and Technology, a unique institution in the world, and the Gandhi museum, a very modern museum with two big auditoriums, the construction of which was completed in six months when he was the Chief Minister of Gujrat.

Narendra Modi is an institution by himself. He is a self-made personality, politician and an unquestioned nationalist. His eyes and expression led me to believe that after Nehru, this was the dynamic leader for India who was born for take the country to a height which would dominate the world one day. We had very cordial discussions for over one and half hours on various issues. The Prime Minister assured me of giving all cooperation and help in the administration of justice in Bangladesh including training facilities of judges in the Forensic University in Gujrat and the National Judicial Academy in Bhopal. After my arrival from India, I heard whispering in the government and particularly in a powerful elite intelligence agency that I did not accompany our High Commissioner in New Delhi intentionally as I had secret discussions with the Indian Prime Minister. As a matter of fact, I had no idea whether the High Commissioner, who was with me at the Rashtrapati Bhaban, would be allowed to accompany me or not. He did not tell me anything though he knew my schedule.

Later I also attended the 16th Conference of Chief Justices of Asia and the Pacific region held in Sydney, Australia, from November 6 to November 9, 2015. In 2016 I attended the '10th Chief Justices 13th SAARCLAW' from March 04 to March 07, 2016 in Nepal. Later I attended the conference on Effective Adjudication of Terrorism Cases held at the United Nations Security Council, New York, USA. I stayed in the Millennium Hotel just opposite to the UN headquarter. Prior to the conference we were taken to General Assembly conference hall, the Security Council room and other important halls where different conferences are held throughout the year. When we were taken for the lunch to the main cafeteria I found two Bangladeshi workers who had been there for a long time. On seeing me they came forward and introduced themselves. They served me special salads and desserts besides the usual menu. They were very happy to meet me and wanted to take photographs with me. They told me that had met politicians, diplomats, ministers and people from other segments of society but, they felt, my visit was special as no Chief Justice from our country had ever attended any meeting there. They added, my presence there was extra-special to them particularly because, according to them, I had made revolutionary changes in the judiciary which they came to know from their relatives and the media.

I also came to know from them and other diplomats that only six seats are reserved for Bangladesh and no other person can enter the General Assembly Hall when the assembly is in session, although we learn from the media that every year more than hundred delegates come from Bangladesh to attend the General Assembly session at the cost of the public exchequer. In 2009 a total of 227 Bangladeshi delegates came to attend UN General Assembly Session with the Prime Minister, while in 2013 the number was 134, and in 2014 the number of delegates from Bangladesh to the UN General Assembly Session was 178.1(a) I learnt that huge amounts of foreign currency are spent every year unnecessarily. If there is no need for additional personnel, why should the state bear their expenses? No one is above the law; not even the Chief Executive of the country. Hence, she cannot spend superfluous foreign currency to cover expenses for employees or officers who have no role in the programs.

125

I placed a remarkable contribution in the discussion concerning counter-terrorism. I also attended the '19th Annual International Judicial Conference' from May 18 to May 16, 2016 in USA. It is an honor to have the privilege to participate the Committee established pursuant to UN Resolution No 1373(2001). In that conference I took part in a panel discussion on the 'Regional Effort to Support the Judiciaries of South Asia in the Effective Adjudication of Terrorism Cases' in ECOSOC Chamber in the UN Headquarter, New York from 3:00 PM to 6:00 PM on March 9, 2016. I also participated in an event of exchange of views from Supreme Court of South Asia on Adjudicating Terrorism Trials from 9:00 AM to 12:30 PM in the Lipton D'agostino Hall, New York University School of Law. I played a very effective and vibrant role in all the sessions.

In the briefing at the UN terrorism conference I stated that terrorism, in any form, has been one of the constant concerns affecting every country in the 21st century. In many countries of the world it has been one of the most pronounced threats to peace, security and stability. The international community's understanding of the term 'terrorism' has undergone transformations over time. Sami Zeidan, a Lebanese diplomat and scholar, had observed: "There is no consensus on the definition of terrorism. The difficulty of defining terrorism lies in the risk it entails in taking positions. The repercussion of the current preponderance of the political over the legal value of terrorism is costly, leaving the war against terrorism selective, incomplete and ineffective."2 I mentioned that while condemnation of terrorist activities by the international community has been unanimous and unequivocal, the efforts so far taken to combat this phenomenon have been occasionally marred by differences of approach.

Regarding our government's approach, I pointed out that Bangladesh has demonstrated a firm commitment to combating domestic and transnational terrorist groups and the government's zero tolerance approach had made it harder for transnational terrorist groups to operate in or establish safe havens in our country. Even then, risks and vulnerabilities posed by certain fringe terrorist elements remain a threat to our national security. In one sensational case, I said, in 2006, the masterminds behind the banned terrorist outfit 'Jama`atul Mujahideen Bangladesh' (JMB) were found guilty and sentenced accordingly on charge of murdering two young judges in a remote south-western district of the country.

I also quoted3 what the apex court had observed: "Islam is a religion of peace. It is derived from the word 'Salam' meaning peace. Using the holy name of Islam, the perpetrators have engaged in a wild, mad struggle jeopardizing the law and order of the country resulting in killing of innocent people as has been done in the present case of killing two judges. Islam does not encourage use of force in the matter of religion." I also underscored the enactment of the Anti-terrorism Act, 2009 with provisions to deter certain terrorist activities and bring to justice the perpetrators, abettors and other accomplices including those who provide funding. In 2013, I informed the conclave, the law was further amended wherein a list of International Conventions, Instruments and Protocols had been incorporated, and violation of any provision of those instruments had been made punishable. One of the notable provisions of the Act is its extraterritorial application.

It provides: 4 "If any person commits an offence in any foreign country and then takes shelter in Bangladesh which, if committed in Bangladesh, would be punishable under this Act, the said offence shall be deemed to have been committed in Bangladesh and the provisions of this Act shall apply to the said person if he cannot be extradited to a foreign State having jurisdiction over the said offence." I made observations saying that it is well acknowledged that without effective regional and international cooperation it would not be possible to combat and defeat terrorism and financing terrorism. The South Asian Association for Regional Cooperation (SAARC) had been sensitive to the challenges posed by terrorism since the outset and adopted the SAARC Convention on Suppression of Terrorism at its 3rd Summit held on November 1, 1987. The convention stipulated that it was "required that each state should refrain from organizing, instigating, assisting or participating in the acts of civil strife or terrorist acts in another state or acquiescing in organized activities within its territory directed towards the commission of such acts."

South Asian Judiciaries, I said, may share their experiences with each other in respect of disposal of cases relating to terrorism. The South Asian countries may actively consider setting up a Judicial Research Academy where joint research studies could be conducted about the various dimensions of counter-terrorism legislations and adjudication of terrorism related cases. The Regional Toolkit being developed by Counter-Terrorism Executive Directorate also looks like a sound initiative. Although I am personally not yet quite familiar with the Toolkit, from what I have gathered, it could be a useful exercise to implement and validate the Toolkit in the national level in our region, particularly through our respective Judicial Training Institutes. The higher judiciary in the region should also be involved in discussions concerning breaking the nexus between terrorism and violent extremism, on one hand, and transnational organized crimes, illicit financial flows, and external financing, on the other hand.

The judiciary may also help propagate the messages of a culture of peace, non-violence and tolerance through its verdicts and pronouncements. And finally, I summed up saying that terrorism has no country and it is a threat to the entire human race and humanity. As a peace-loving country, Bangladesh is fully committed and ready to fight against terrorism and support all meaningful steps taken by the international community to combat the menace and I am sure that our intentions and endeavors will take us to the desired goal through our concerted efforts to a better future, which is not only the demand for the present, but also the next generation.

In New York University School Law in reply to a question regarding what the biggest challenges judges are facing in terrorism cases, I said the biggest challenges emanate from weak investigation reports and prosecution in relation to counter-terrorism cases. Despite the stringent counter-terrorism legislations in place, there still are different levels of understanding about their application among the law enforcement and investigation agencies, which often results in relatively weaker submission of charge sheets and resulting charges.

All our neighboring countries have National Judicial Academies to serve the training and research needs of the judges, government attorneys, government legal officers, judicial officers, private practitioners and others who are directly involved in the administration of justice. But it is very disappointing that we do not have that type of academy. These academies are the crying need for effective adjudication of terrorism cases. These academies should help establish a modern and independent judiciary offering contemporary training facilities and opportunities for exchange views on challenges and best practices relating to the application of existing norms and standards in relation to adjudicating cases including counter-terrorism cases.

As a practice being followed by me for long, whenever I visit a country I purchase some books—kind of a second priority. I expressed my desire to our ambassador at the Permanent Mission Masud bin Momen, a career diplomat, low speaker and a perfect gentleman. His wife is a well-educated lady with a personality to go with it. Her quality as a good cook may be compared with a qualified trained chef of Bangladeshi dishes. Momen took me to the Strand Book Store at 828 Broadway on 12th Street, Manhattan. It is possibly one of the biggest libraries in the world. One may pass the entire day visiting the library. With such a huge amount of choice I felt indecisive about which books to select because each and every book seemed like my favorite. I purchased nine books hoping that on my next visit I would purchase more. This bookstore also sells second hand books in excellent condition. When leaving I ran into an employee of Bangladeshi origin working there for more than twenty years. He got extremely emotional on seeing me and wanted to entertain me. However, I managed leave by letting him take a photograph with me.

I also attended '29th LAWASIA Conference and Golden Jubilee Celebration' in Sri Lanka and presented a significant speech. I also attended the '3rd Asian Judges Symposium on Environment from September 16 to September 18, 2016 in Philippines. I joined

'Bangladesh Law Society' in New York, USA. I also attended seminars on 'National Initiative towards Strengthening Arbitration from October 14 to October 25, 2016, held in USA and India respectively. In Indian seminar the President opening speech seminar and the Prime Minister delivered the valedictory speech. I also attended the conference on 'The 2nd China South Asia legal Forum' arranged by China Law Society from October 14 to October 17, 2016. In the conference I was honored to give the opening and valedictory speeches. In this seminar the senior most Police Bureau member graced the occasion.

Over time I attended and participated in many law conferences. The last was the Asia Pacific Chief Justices conference in Japan. It was one of the biggest conferences and more than 35 Chief Justices and other 15 judges of the apex courts from different countries attended. There were five sessions and only ten Chief Justices including myself were key speakers. My topic was 'Role of Courts Regarding Family Issues and Protecting Violence against Women in Bangladesh'. It was a challenging issue around the globe but more so in the 3rd world countries. It varies in nature and extent in different countries depending on the financial conditions, rule of law, democracy and literacy of women. Bangladesh being a Muslim majority country, I realized, most of the countries wanted to hear me expound on the subject, especially on custody of minor children of broken families, marriage, dowry, violence against women, etc.

Initially I thought the other Chief Justices and social activists weren't sure what to expect from me because Bangladesh is a poor Muslim majority country. But in fact, it is different from other Muslim countries of the world. I told them we have one of the best constitutions in the world. Rule of Law, protection of life and property and democracy are enshrined in it. The government is changed according to democratic processes. The Prime Minister, Speaker, the leader of the opposition and another large political party's chairperson are women. Six women judges were working in the High Court Division and in the lower judiciary 35 percent of judges are women—a figure far above many developed countries like US, UK and even India.

I added for the protection of women and children we have a good number of laws. I mentioned those laws and said that we had established Family Courts in every district court. We even diluted religious sanctions in cases relating to custody of minors because we give top priority to the welfare of the minor while deciding custody issues. If the court finds that the welfare of the minor would not be protected, s/he would not be given custody in accordance with personal law. Courts do not hesitate to give custody of a male or female child beyond the prescribed age limit. In matters of maintenance and dower the courts lean toward the women. I also explained the philosophy of marriage, which I have discussed in another chapter.

After my speech, almost all judges expressed their satisfaction that Bangladesh judiciary had attained tremendous height which can be compared with any other country. They told me after my speech that initially they had a poor opinion about the Bangladesh judiciary but after my deliberations they adopted a much better estimation of our judiciary. The Chief Justice of China wanted to know whether there was any Shariah court in our country. I told him that under a modern Constitution there was no place for Shariah court. I explained to him the tenets and functioning of our Constitution and said that the rule of law was being maintained. Following the discussion, he requested me to give five or six constitutional judgments including the then recent Constitution 16th amendment judgment, a topic that was much discussed among them.

According to him, Chinese economic development was progressing rapidly, and they were looking forward to developing human rights in their country. His final statement was totally unexpected. He said, he wanted to keep my judgments in the museum of the highest court and wanted my signatures on the first page. The Chief Justices of Malaysia and Pakistan disclosed that as shariah courts are functioning as per their constitutions they worked within limitations. It is my pride to mention here that whenever I attended a seminar everywhere my counterparts were telling by themselves that I am a Hindu by faith though listening their conservativeness I felt so proud. But possibly I was expecting

131

something more forgetting that though we achieved independence sacrificing three million martyrs, our leaders forget them of their thirst for power.

When I was in The Hague I visited the International Criminal Court and the International Court of Justice and had detailed discussions with my counterparts. At International Criminal Court they wanted to know about the trials for crimes against humanity. I appraised them of the successful completion of trials of about 20 cases without outside help and assured them that the trials were being held impartially by affording all facilities to the defense. We have provisions of review against any order under our law though we do not follow the customary international law because in the presence of domestic law covering the field, international law could not prevail. We had already settled this point before the International War Crimes Tribunals were created.5 I mentioned that we respect international laws but if those laws or provisions had not been incorporated into our domestic law, they are they are not enforceable in national courts.

While visiting Russia I executed an MOU with Russia and as part of cooperation. The Chief Justice of Russia visited our country on my invitation in October 2017. He is the only Chief Justice of a superpower ever to have visited Bangladesh. Though I was in Dhaka and still the Chief Justice, I could not meet him as I was under house confinement. It is shocking for me and disgraceful for the country that I was not allowed to talk with him. This incident surely undermined our government's position because only a few days earlier we had met in Tokyo at the Asia Pacific Region's Chief Justices Conference and had talked about his forthcoming tour of Bangladesh. We had exchanged gifts and he knew that I was still the Chief Justice and that I was not sick. As happens most often we gave precedence to narrow interests than to the national interest. The government did not know what talks and cooperation in the judiciary to be made between us. Those points were not addressed, and we are deprived of many things for the judiciary due to my absence.

References:

1. *(1993) 4 SCC 441 and (1998) 7 SCC 739*

1(a). Daily Manavjamin, May 17, 2018

2. *Sami Zeidin, Spoke on Terrorism, 36 Cornell International Law Journal (2004) page: 491-492*
3. *Sheikh Abdur Rahman v. State, 15 BLT (AD) 326*
4. *Section 5 of the Act, 2013*
5. *Hossain Mohammad Ershad v. Bangladesh, 21 BLO(AD) 69; Bangladesh v. Sheikh Hasina, 60 DLR(AD) 90; and Criminal Appeals Nos. 24-25 of 2013; Abdul Quader Mollah v. Government*

Chapter 15

Reflection of Judicial Mind on Different Issues

Crimes against Humanity (A)

Crimes against humanity are certain acts that are deliberately committed as part of a widespread systematic attack or individual attack directed against civilians or an identifiable part of the civilian population. The first prosecutions for crimes against humanity had taken place at the Nuremberg Trials. These crimes have since been prosecuted by other international courts. Unlike war crimes, crimes against humanity can be committed during both peace and war. They are not isolated or sporadic events but are part either of a governmental policy or a wide practice of atrocities tolerated or condoned by a government or de facto authority. Murder, massacre, extermination, dehumanization, genocide, ethnic cleansing, deportation, unethical human extermination, extrajudicial punishment including summary execution, state terrorism or state sponsored terrorism, death squad, kidnapping and forced disappearance, unjust imprisonment, enslavement, torture, rape, political repression, racial discrimination, religious persecution, and other human rights abuses may reach the threshold of crimes against humanity if they are part of a widespread or systematic practice.1A

In 1993 the UN Security Council established the International Criminal Tribunal for the former Yugoslavia (ICTY) and expanded the list of criminal acts used in Nuremberg to include imprisonment, torture and rape. Subsequently in 1994 the Security Council established the International Criminal Tribunal for Rwanda (ICTR), pursuant to the genocide that had taken place from April to July 1994. In this Charter, the requirement was added that the inhuman acts must be part of a systematic or widespread attack against any civilian population on national, political, racial or religious grounds. The Permanent International

Criminal Court came into force in 2002 and in its founding treaty, the Rome Statute, expanded the horizon of offences. The offences include1B (a) murder; (b) extermination; (c) enslavement; (d) deportation or forcible transfer of population; (e) imprisonment or other severe deprivation of physical liberty in violation of fundamental rules of international law; (f) torture; (g) rape, sexual slavery, enforced prostitution, forced pregnancy, enforced sterilization, or any other form of sexual violence of comparable gravity; (h) persecution against any identifiable group or collectively on the grounds of political, racial, national, ethnic, cultural, religious, gender as defined in paragraph 3, or other grounds that are universally recognized as impermissible under international law, in connection with any act referred to in this paragraph or any crime within the jurisdiction of the Court; (i) enforced disappearance of persons; (j) the crime of apartheid; (k) other inhumane acts of a similar character intentionally causing great suffering, or serious injury to body or to mental or physical health.

Naturally, the first appeal of Abdul Quader Mollah was heard because it was the first case tried by the Tribunal. I am the author of the judgment in presence of the Chief Justice because he endorsed me to express the opinion of the court. In course of hearing of the appeal, a crucial point on question of law was raised on behalf of the convict that the tribunal erred in law in convicting Quader Mollah without following Customary International Law (CIL) which is applicable in the case, inasmuch as, an offence of crime against humanity attracts CIL on two broad reasons, (1) article 47(3) of the Constitution expressly recognizes that genocides, crimes against humanity and war crimes fall under international law; (2) the short title, the long title and the Act1 expressly provides the detention, prosecution and punishment under international law. I disposed of the point holding that though the tribunal has invested with the power to try any person for violation of "any other crime under international law" this does not mean that the tribunal is bound to follow CIL. It is not correct to infer the constituent elements of crimes against humanity as recognized under the international law must be present for convicting a person. When a person irrespective of nationality will

135

be charged with "any other crime under international law," he may claim his right to follow CIL, though the Act is based on the foundation of International Legal Instruments or in the alternative, the Act was structured in conformity with international standards, in consultation with international experts and the legislature has excluded those offences to be followed under International Law.

The offenders of former Yugoslavia and Cambodia were tried under International Law in accordance with the Rome Statute with the help of international experts. But we have our own statute and we have inherited a legacy of administration of justice for more than three hundred years. There was a provision that any State party which has not accepted the amendment to the Rome Statue, can withdraw from this Statue with immediate effect.2 Further a look into the provisions of our Act will reveal that it is a domestic law. The offences mentioned in the Rome Statue and those mentioned in our Act are distinct. The offences mentioned in section 3 of our Act were not in existence when the Rome Statute was corrected on November 10, 1998, January 12, 2001 and January 16, 2002; these came into force on July 01, 2002. These are quite distinct offenses and these offences will not be applicable to all domestic tribunals as would be evident from the preamble "emphasizing that international criminal court established under this Statute that shall be complementary to national criminal jurisdiction."

Since the tribunal was constituted under the Act of 1973, it has no jurisdiction over a national, ethnic or religious group or any civilian population or persons other than any individual or group of individuals or organizations or any member of any armed, defense or auxiliary forces unless he commits crimes mentioned in section 3(2) in the territory of Bangladesh. More so, under the Rome Statue the accused has a right to challenge the jurisdiction of the court.3 and while applying the law, the court shall consider the State, the elements of crimes and its rules of procedure and evidence. The national laws of States which are not inconsistent with the Rome Statue shall be applicable to the ICT. Therefore, the Rome Statue has no primacy over the national law. Our apex court held4 that local laws both constitutional and statutory are not always in consonance with norms contained in international human rights instruments. If domestic laws are not clear enough or there is nothing therein, the national courts should draw upon the principles incorporated in the international instruments. But in cases where the domestic laws are clear and inconsistent with the international obligation, the national courts will be obliged to respect national laws. In another case5 our apex court had held that our courts will not enforce the covenants and conventions even if ratified by the State unless these are incorporated in municipal laws. International conventions could be recognized upon ratifications but could be applied only when its provisions are incorporated in our municipal laws and thus for enforcing any international covenants under any convention to which our country is a signatory. The provisions of the convention must be incorporated in our domestic law.6

English and Indian superior courts also took similar views.7 It is a trite to observe that there is no such thing as a standard of international law extraneous to a domestic law of a kingdom to which appeal may be made.8 Though international convention could be recognized upon ratification, it could be applied in our country when its provisions are incorporating our municipal laws and thus for enforcing any international covenants under any convention to which our country is a signatory, the provisions of the convention have to be incorporated in our domestic law. The US Supreme Court also observed9 that law is a universal obligation and no statue of one or two nations can create obligations for the world. Like all the laws of nature it rests upon the common consent of civilized communities. It is in force, not because it was prescribed by any superior power but because it is accepted as a rule of conduct. Every nation must be the final judge for itself, not only of the nature and extend of the duty but of the occasions on which its exercise may be justly demanded.10 It was also observed that international organizations are established by States through international agreements and their powers are limited to those conferred on them in their constituent document. The Security Council has the authority to make decisions that are binding on all member States when it is performing its primary responsibility of maintaining international peace and security.

Individuals are generally not regarded as legal persons under international law. Their link to the State is through the concept of nationality which may or may not require citizenship. Though some international practices and obligations are treated as peremptory norms (Jus Cogens), a breach of such peremptory norms does not entail any penal sanction upon the State. I concluded my opinion, besides observing other points, that the CIL developing international crimes does not impose penal sanction upon an individual unless the domestic law assimilates the said concepts of international crimes into the body of domestic law.

After disposal of the appeal on merit two review petitions were filed by convict Abdul Quader Mollah.11 On behalf of the State a preliminary objection was raised about the maintainability of the review petitions claiming in view of Article 47A (2)12 review petitions are not maintainable from the judgment of the appeal in the absence of any provision for review in the Act. I held that the provisions in the Constitution are a non-obstante clause. But a combined reading of the provisions of the Act suggests the intention of the legislature that the trial of offences specified in the Act should be concluded expeditiously. However, an appeal is essentially the continuation of the original proceedings. When a right of appeal is conferred by a statue, it becomes a vested right and, therefore, where the right of appeal exists it is a matter of substance, not of procedure and, therefore, it cannot be said that the appellate court cannot invoke its inherent power, if it finds it necessary to meet the ends of justice or to prevent the abuse of the process of the court.

There is an inherent right to a litigant to a judicial proceeding and it requires no authority of law to see the correctness of the judgments. An appeal being the continuation of the proceeding, in effect, the entire proceedings are open before the appellate authority and it has the power to review the evidence subject to statutory limitations prescribed. A right of appeal carries with it a right of rehearing in some way. The primary functions of the court are to do justice in respect to causes brought before it, then on principle it is difficult to accede to the proposition that in the absence of specific provision the court will shut its eyes if a wrong or an error is detected in its judgment. Courts are meant to do justice and must deem to possess as a necessary corollary inherent in their constitution all the powers to achieve the end and undo the wrong. It does not confer any additional jurisdiction on the court; it only recognizes the powers which it already possessed.

If the law contains no specific provisions to meet the necessity of the case, the inherent power of a court merely saves by expressly preserving the court which is both a court of equity and law, to act according to justice, equity and good conscience and make such order as may be necessary for ends of justice or to prevent the abuse of the process of the court. It is an enabling provision by which an inherent power is vested in a court so that it does not find itself helpless in administering justice. The court can use its inherent powers to fill up the lacuna left by the legislature while enacting law or where the legislature is unable to foresee any circumstance which may arise in a case. There is a power to make such order as may be necessary for the ends of justice and prevent the abuse of the process of the court. The inherent powers of the court are in addition to and complementary to the powers expressly conferred upon it by other provisions of the law. They are not intended to enable the court to create rights for the parties, but they are meant to enable the court to pass such orders for ends of justice as may be necessary.

The court is conscious that it cannot rewrite, recast or reframe the legislation for the very sound reason that it has no power to legislate. It cannot add words to a statue or read words into it which are not there. A court shall decide what the law is and what it should be. A court of course adopts a construction which will carry out the presumed intention of the legislature but cannot legislate itself. The court should not give beneficial construction where by giving such construction it would virtually legislate a position either by addition, alteration or substitution of words where the words used in a statue are capable of only one meaning from which the court may not depart; and when the provision is unambiguous and does not give rise to any doubt as to its meaning. Where two alternative constructions are possible, the court must choose the one which would be in accord with other parts of the

139

statute and ensure smooth, harmonious working and eschew the other which leads to absurdity, confusion or fiction, contradiction and conflicts between its various provisions, or undermines or tends to defeat or destroy the basic scheme and purpose of the enactment.13

There is a presumption that the authors of a statute intend results that are both rationale and coherent and that human behavior is guided by reasons and purpose and is seldom bizarre. It is, therefore, necessary to apply the principle of logic, both deductive and inductive, particularly in excluding from consideration facts and circumstances which are not relevant for determination of issues raised14 where, by use of clear and unequivocal language, capable of only one meaning, anything enacted by the legislature may be enforced however harsh or absurd or contrary to common sense the result may be. However, the literal construction would defeat the obvious intention of the legislature and would produce a wholly unreasonable result, the court must do violence to the words to achieve that obvious intention and produce a rational result.15 it is because, it may be presumed that the legislature does not intend to produce any absurd result. If two interpretations of a provision are possible the court will lean in favor of that construction which avoids absurdity and ensures smooth working of the system, which the statues seek to regulate.

If the court is vested with full power for seeking complete justice, there is no reason why the exercise of that power would not be applicable in respect of a matter coming up before it in the form of a decision by a lower tribunal. There is no reason why that power in its full scope should not also be applicable for reviewing a judgment delivered by the highest court of the country if there is necessity within the meaning of the expression "complete justice" in exercise of that power. Accordingly, I held that the court has ample power to give such directions as are necessary for the ends of justice. This power has been recognized and exercised by issuing necessary directions to fill in the vacuum till such time the legislature steps in to cover the gap. This power is not restricted by statutory enactments, but it should be used sparingly. Accordingly, I held that the review petition was maintainable.

Killing of Natun Chandra Singha (A-1)

Salauddin Qader Chowdhury had faced trial before the tribunal on 18 counts of serious offences, like killing, abduction, torture, compelling Hindus to leave the country, concealment of dead bodies, etc. Evidence disclosed that he was directly involved in those crimes and he had set up a torture center at his house. The tribunal found him guilty of charges 2, 3, 4, 5, 6, 7, 8, 17 and 18 and sentenced him 20 years on two counts, death on three counts, and 5 years on two counts. He filed an appeal in the highest court and the court after hearing the appeal 16 by judgment dated July 29, 2015 allowed the appeal in part acquitting him in respect of count number 7 and maintained the conviction and sentence in respect of charge nos. 2, 3, 5, 6, 8, 17 and 18. He was sentenced to death in respect of count numbers 3, 5, 6 and 8. Of the said charges charge number 3 is a very sensitive one. I will discuss this charge only.

The incident took place on April 13, 1971 at around 9:30 to 10:00 AM. Natun Chandra Singha, the founder of Kundeshwari Owshadhaloy, was brutally killed. In support of the charge the prosecution examined two eye witnesses, Gouranga Singha and Gopal Chandra Das. Gouranga stated that he along with Gopal Chandra was on the first floor of Natun Chandra Singha's Kundeshwari Owsadhalay and saw from there that Salahduddin Quader Chowdhury with some Bengali and military personnel came to the spot. They pulled Natun Chandra Singha out of the Mandir (temple). The military personnel and Salahuddin Quader Chowdhury shot at him. A case was lodged with the Rauzan Police Station by Satya Ranjan in 1972. Profulla Chandra, another witness corroborated witness Gouranga Singha. Gopal Chandra stated that he was the principal of Kundeswari Women's College and at the time of occurrence, he was on the first floor of the Kundeshwari complex. He said that he and Brazahari saw the incident from the window. Salahuddin Quader Chowdhury and the army personnel talked for a bit with Natun Babu and then left.

Sometimes thereafter, they came back. They saw the Pakiastani force and Salahuddin Quader Chowdhury enter the temple, drag out Natun Chandara from the temple and brought him out onto the

141

courtyard fired at him indiscriminately and then they left. In support of the charges the prosecution had examined forty-one witnesses and provided a series of documentary evidence showing the participation of the offender. The defense took a plea of alibi and examined some witnesses. Its main case was that Salahuddin Quader Chowdhury was not present in Chittagong, he was initially in Karachi, then moved to Punjab for studying at Punjab University and in the later part of September he left for the UK for higher studies. In support of his plea, it examined some witnesses and some documents. However, it failed to produce reliable documents in support of his study in Punjab or in London. The tribunal and the apex court did not find his plea credible and held that the accused had utterly failed to prove that he had left for then West Pakistan in March 1971. The court also disbelieved the documentary evidence filed in support of the alibi plea and held that the oral and documentary evidence produced by the prosecution was reliable. The apex court maintained his conviction in respect of eight counts including the brutal killing of Natun Chandra Singha.

Against the said judgment Salahuddin Quader Chowdhury filed a review petition.17 in the review petition the defense had produced a duplicate certificate dated May 22, 2012 issued by the University of Punjab certifying that Salahuddin Quader Chowdhury obtained Bachelor of Arts degree from the department of political science in the examination held in August 1971. Another duplicate certificate attested by the Vice Chancellor and Registrar of Punjab University and authenticated by an officer of the Foreign Ministry of Pakistan and some other letters and documents were also filed. Initially he filed a testimonial issued by a professor of the department of Political Science, University of Punjab, issued on January 24, 2013. The Court believed that the testimonial was a forged one. In the review matter he produced a duplicate certificate of the university. In support of the alibi plea it was submitted in circumambulation that this duplicate certificate proved that Salahuddin Chowdhury was in Pakistan in September 1971.

I discarded the plea observing why he could not produce the certificate before the tribunal or at the appellate stage, although he had procured many affidavits and other papers in 2013 from Pakistan. Even then it was submitted again and again on the question. A duplicate certificate was apparently a forged paper which was detected on my first glance. But I did not make any query and kept silent with a view to affording the lawyer an opportunity to improve it if possible. Other members of the Bench, Nazmun Ara Sultana and Hasan Foez Siddique were making one or two queries of the counsel while Syed Mahmud Hossain kept silent. I was of the view that if I could draw the attention to the forgery, the counsel would be put in an embarrassing position at the very initial stage. Since a death sentence had been passed, the council should be afforded time.

The council did not go into the merit of the matter, and there was little scope to make submission on facts in review matters. I realized that the counsel would be tired at one point of time and when he would finish leaving no other point I would point out the forgery. After arguing about one and half hours, I noticed that the counsel was making only one submission, that Salahuddin Quader Chowdhury's absence from the scene of occurrence is proved from the duplicate certificate. On his behalf no other submission was made. I made it clear to the counsel that if he could satisfy me about Salahuddin Quader Chowdhury's claim of studying at Punjab University in 1971 I would be in favor of allowing a review of the matter and persuade my other colleagues to follow me. The counsel felt satisfied that the Chief Justice was confining the hearing only on one point and hence it would be very easy for him convince the court.

I asked him to place the duplicate certificate again and queried whether, on the face of it, he could detect any forgery in procuring it. The counsel seemed confused on point that I was doubting the genuineness of the duplicate certificate. When he failed to follow my query, I pointed out that this certificate was issued in 2012 and the defense did not produce it in the tribunal even though it was in his possession. The counsel then replied that an application for the copy was filed earlier, but he received it in November 2015.If it was issued on May 22, 2012, there was no reason not to produce it in the tribunal; but he could not meet the point. The second point I asked him related to which academic session was the accused admitted in Punjab University and obtained degree in 1971. In the certificate, his academic session was shown as 1971. I pointed out that there was no scope for receiving a Bachelor of Honors degree in one year. When he noticed the defect, the counsel replied that the accused studied in Dhaka University and then he transferred his credit to Punjab University in 1971. It is not at all the defense plea that the accused was initially admitted to Dhaka University and then completed his degree in Punjab University.

During the Pakistan period honors degree course was of three years course and recently it had been turned into a four-year course. I asked the counsel whether he could produce any scrap of paper that the accused had studied in honors course in 1969 or 1970 in Dhaka University. I also wanted to know whether there was any provision for transferring credits from one university to another university in 1971. The counsel felt embarrassed to reply to my query. When I pointed out that the certificate was a spurious document, the counsel seemed very shaky. Then I drew his attention to whether he had any other point to argue on merit. He frankly conceded that he had no case on merit save and accept the plea of alibi. Then I repeated that the duplicate certificate was a forged one and given that fact should the court take judicial notice of it. The counsel realized the sentiment of the court as to on which point we were underlining and he sat down without saying anything.

References:

1A. Margaret M. DeGuzman, "Crimes Against Humanity" RESEARCH HANDBOOK ON INTERNATIONAL CRIMINAL LAW, Bartram S. Brown, ed., Edgar Elgar Publishing, 2011

1B. Rome Statute of International Criminal Court, Article

1. International Tribunal Act, 1973
2. Article 124 XI of the Rome Statue
3. Article 19 of the Rome Statue
4. Hussein Muhammad Ershad v. Bangladesh, 21 BLD (AD) 69
5. Bangladesh v. Sheikh Hasina, 60 DLR (AD) 90
6. Ms. Supermax International v. Samah Rajor Blade Industries, 2ADC 593
7. J.H Rayner Ltd. V. Department of trade and Industry, (1990) 2 AC 418; Apparel Export Promotion Council v. V.A.K Chopra, AIR 1999 SC 625
8. Mortensen v. Peters (1906) 8F (J) 93
9. The Scotia, 81 US (14WAII) 170 (1872)
10. Joseph Story, Commentaries on the Conflict of Laws, p 24-38
11. Criminal Review Petition Nos. 17-18 of 2013
12. Article 47A (2) of the constitution
13. Andhra Pradesh v. LVA Dikshitlu, AIR 1979 SC 193
14. 'The Role of Logic' in Reed Dickenson's "The Interpretation and Application of Statues."
15. CIT v. National Jaj Traders, AIR 1980 SC 485
16. Salahuddin Quader Chowdhury v. Chief Prosecutor, Criminal Review Appeal No. 122 of 2013
17. Criminal Review Petition 63 of 2015

Constitutional Convention (B)

While in the High Court Division I have pronounced some momentous judgements, among those one is the "Ten Judges" case on constitutional convention, and two other cases are criminal matters. I have also given decisions on a few other significant cases, but I am unable to discuss them here in the absence of references. The two cases mentioned above are on the interpretation of Section 167 of the Code of Criminal Procedure relating to remanding an offender and showing him arrested while in custody in connection with another case, and procedure of trial and the applicability of law governing the field in the absence of specific provision in the law.1 In ten judges case2 Twelve Additional Judges were appointed during the period of a government formed by the Bangladesh Awami League. After the BNP formed the government in 2001, those judges were not confirmed after completion two years, despite recommendation made by the Chief Justice. A writ petition was filed by ten of them in the High Court Division. A Special Bench was constituted by the Chief Justice for hearing the matter. I was a member of the

Bench. Though there was no provision for consultation with the Chief Justice by the President in appointing the Judges a constitutional convention was in practice that the President appointed the judges prior to consultation with the Chief Justice.

While expounding on the constitutional convention, I held that constitutional conventions are rules of political practice which are regarded as binding by those to whom they apply. But they are not laws and are not promulgated by Parliament. Many conventions had developed in the US relating to the election of the President, the formation, selection and functioning of the President's cabinet, senatorial approval of certain political appointments and other matters. In this connection Sir Ivor Jennings observed that "a single precedent with a good reason may be enough to establish a rule." According to K.C Wheare, "Convention can become law also by judicial recognition. Once it is established to the satisfaction of the court that a convention exists, and it is operating then the convention becomes a part of the constitutional law of the land," and can be enforced in like manner. We accordingly directed the non-confirmation of 10 judges was a violation of the Constitution and therefore illegal. Accordingly, we made the rule absolute and directed the government to issue gazette notification for confirming and reinstating them. The Judges were appointed by the President.

In the Saifuzzaman Case, Liaqat Sikder and Mohammad Rafiqul Islam, the President and Vice-President were arrested on January 25 under section 54 of the Criminal Procedure Code, when they were coming out of 'Sudha Sadan', the residence of Sheikh Hasina, the Chairperson of the Presidium of the Awami League, and were put under detention. A habeas corpus petition was filed on their behalf. The High Court Division declared the order of detention without any lawful authority and directed to release them forthwith. When they were about to be released from the jail, they were shown arrested in a murder case at the jail gate. They obtained bail in that case and now of their release from custody, they were again shown arrested in another case. In this manner they were shown arrested in 12 different cases from different parts of the country ranging from Rajshahi to Chittagong. Finding no other alternative, they moved another habeas corpus petition. I noticed that the orders showing those detainees arrested were in contravention of Section 167 of the Code of Criminal Procedure and accordingly made the rule absolute with the direction to the police to follow guidelines. (Appendix) 2(a)

The third case relates to an offence punishable under the provisions of the Payment of Wages Act, 1936A. Under the said Act a worker may file a complaint against his employer if the employer did not make payment of the worker's wages after employing him. The offence is punishable under the Act, but the law is totally silent regarding procedure of trial and the applicability of law in such a trial. There are conflicting decisions of the High Court Division regarding the maintainability of complaint in the absence of law and procedure of trial of cases relating to such offences. The trial of such offences was stopped for two years in the Labor Court, which entertained the complaints but did not proceed with the trial due to conflicting decisions. Shah Abu Nayeem Mominur Rahman and Md. Ayes Uddin constituting the Division Bench referred the matter to the Chief Justice for constituting a Full Bench for settling the law points.

I was included in the Bench and resolved the law point in a few minutes and expressed the opinion of the Full Bench.3 I held that in the absence of procedure in the law, the provisions of Code of Criminal Procedure will be applicable in view of section 5(2) of the Code. Section 5 of the Code provides for the trial of offences under the Penal Code and the trial of offences under other laws. Sub-section (2) of Section 5 states that all offences under special or local laws shall be tried in accordance with the provisions of the Code of Criminal Procedure if the provisions of special or local laws are not inconsistent with the Code or are silent regarding the procedure. It was a major judgment early in my life as a judge. But I am unable to quote the observations, findings and citations in the absence of any reference or judgment with me.

References:
1. *10 Judges Case*
2. *Saifuzzaman Md. V. State, 56 DLR 324*
2(a) Ibid, 2(b) Ibid
3. *Code of Conduct (Appendix)*

Bangabandhu Murder Case (C)

One of the darkest chapters in our country's history is the killing of our Father of the Nation, Bangabandhu Sheikh Mujibur Rahman and other members of his family who were in the house including a child of barely four years leaving alive only his two daughters who were abroad. The murders were brutal, cruel, motived and intentional. They killed the youngest son Russel ignoring his entreaties. The killers are comparable with wild animals, otherwise there was no excuse for killing the women who were all innocent. Besides Bangabandhu's wife, two newly married wives of his sons were also brutally killed. Mahatma Gandhi, the father of the nation of India, was killed by a fundamentalist but ours was totally inhuman and cruel. After the killing spree the authority in power wanted to obviate the process of putting the killers to justice by promulgating a black law under the name Indemnity Ordinance. There lies a big difference between India and Bangladesh. If the rule of law is recognized as by the nations of the world, even rulers tremble because of the rule of law. If we cannot come out from the archaic line of thinking, such killings are likely to continue. We cannot claim to be a civilized nation even if we develop our economic condition. There are many rich countries in the world, compared with per capita income, but they do not maintain internationally recognized rule of law and democracy. They do not command respect in the world. But much poorer countries which possess about a quarter amount of per capita income are commanding respect.

We can, however, respect our judiciary which we inherited from the British rule. The Britons developed a strong judiciary with a view to preserving law and order for their own interest and introduced common law systems. There was aberration in the Pakistan judiciary and this trend was reintroduced in Bangladesh by the post-1975 regimes. But the judiciary rose to the occasion whenever it got a congenial atmosphere. It declared the black law had no force of law particularly as no authority can prevent the offenders being brought to justice; the law shall its take its own course; and the killers cannot escape a trial after committing such heinous crimes. The then authority committed a further wrong by "rewarding" the killers. So, the court held the trial and sentenced the perpetrators to death. In the appellate forum there was a split verdict in respect of some offenders. This was rectified by the highest court which settled the law points.

During the hearing of the Bangabandhu Murder Case I was totally disappointed. Veteran lawyers like the late lamented Sirajul Haque along with some senior lawyers appeared on behalf of the prosecution. But it was so badly prosecuted that it was beyond belief. But the defense also made similar mistakes in pointing out the major mistakes on behalf of the prosecution even though veteran lawyers Abdur Razzak Khan and Khan Saifur Rahman appeared along with other lawyers. The point related to criminal conspiracy. On the question of criminal conspiracy, the prosecution relied on oral evidence: the confessions of Lt. Colonel Faruk Ahmed, Lt. Col (artillery) Mohiuddin Ahmed and Lt. Colonel Sultan Shahriar Rashid Khan. The High Court Division as well as the trial court considered the confessional statements of these three accused while finding the accused guilty of the charge of criminal conspiracy.

To prove a case on charge of criminal conspiracy, the court is required to consider the Section 10 of the Evidence Act. A statement made after a conspiracy has been terminated on achieving its objects could not be used as substantive evidence or as corroborative evidence. Anything said, done or written by any one of such persons in reference to their common intention, after the time when such intention was first entertained by any one of them used in Section 10 of the Evidence Act are not capable of being widely construed, so as to include a statement made by one conspirator in the absence of the other with reference to past acts done in the actual course of carrying out the conspiracy, after it has been completed. The common intention signifies a common intention existing at the time when the thing was said, done or written by one of them. But it would be a different matter to hold that any narrative or statement to a third party after the common intention or conspiracy no longer operating and ceased to exist is admissible against other party. There is then no common intention of the conspirator, to which the statement can have reference.1 I persuaded the presiding judge to accept my view. He was initially hesitant but when I explained to him the object and the meaning of section 10 of the Evidence Act and the views taken by the Judicial Committee of the Privy Council, he agreed with me. We ignored the confessions of Faruk Rahman, Sultan Shahriar Rashid and Mohiuddin Ahmed and disposed of the appeal based on ocular and circumstantial evidence.

After conclusion of hearing all the judges unanimously decided that the opinion should be expressed by the Presiding Judge of the Bench. I felt that it was the best and a most propitious part of my career that as a member of the Bench which heard the Bangabandhu Sheikh Mujib Killing Case finally I could add something substantive which would assist in keeping my name in the history books. On coming to know about my addition to the verdict, other judges also started adding their opinions separately. In preparing the judgment, Mohammad Tofazzal Islam was a tad confused on the question of criminal conspiracy and use of evidence on such charges. When I brought to his notice the opinions of the Privy Council and Supreme Courts of India and Pakistan, he was convinced and prepared his opinion in consultation with me. Other members also endorsed it and wrote their opinions on other points avoiding this crucial element.

I have exhaustively explained the non-admissibility of confession in a charge of criminal conspiracy, and the procedure in admitting digital evidence. Abruptly the whereabouts of Justice Mohammad Mozammel Hossain could not be known after the delivery of the judgment orally in open court. No contact could be made with him and no favorable reply was given about him from his residence. It was stated from his house that he was sick. It took more than three weeks' time after the preparation of the final judgment by Mohammad Tofazzal Hossain and other judges that it was detected that Mohammad Mozammel Hossain was secretly writing his own opinion that delayed the process of signing the judgment.

Article 49 of the Constitution provides that the President shall have power to grant pardon, reprieves and respites and to remit, suspend or commute any sentence passed by any court, tribunal or other authority.13 This power is independent of the power given by sections 401, 402 and 402A of the Code of Criminal Procedure in respect of suspension and remission of sentence and commutation of punishment.14 Where the law prescribes a minimum sentence the court cannot reduce it but the President can do so under Article 49 since the power comes from the Constitution. It cannot be modified, abridged or diminished by Parliament. Therefore, the President can grant clemency to a prisoner even after confirmation of death sentence by the court. The power of pardon also includes the power of granting general amnesty.15

Lord Macaulay, in the introduction to the Penal Code, pointed out that a sentence of transportation is one "likely to be regarded with particular terror by Hindoos (Hindus), largely because of their dread of crossing 'the black water', the loss of caste which a journey overseas entails and of the uncertainty whether they will ever see their homes again." The object and purpose have been clearly explained by the Chairman of the Law Commission while recommending the report of the Commission. Therefore, there is no doubt that the sentence has been preserved for its deterrent effect and because in certain cases it may be both useful and desirable to send convicts to isolated islands. After the partition a convict is sent to penal servitude to serve his sentence in local prison.

Therefore, under no stretch of the imagination it can be said that life imprisonment means thirty years in total in prison to be served by a prisoner. It means a sentence of imprisonment for the whole of the remaining period of the convicted person's natural life. Section 57 of the Penal Code is only for calculating fractions of terms of punishment and provides that imprisonment for life shall be reckoned as equivalent to imprisonment for thirty years for the specific purpose mentioned therein.16 A sentence for life would ensure till the lifetime of the accused as it is not possible to fix a particular period of the prisoner's death and remissions given under the rules could not be regarded as a substitute for a sentence of transportation for life. Though under the relevant rules a sentence for imprisonment for life is equated with the definite period of twenty years, there is no indefeasible right of such a prisoner to be unconditionally released on the expiry of such particular term, including remissions, and that is only for the purpose of working out the remissions that the said sentence.

References:

1. *Section 57 of the Penal Code*
2. *Criminal Appeal Nos. 15-16 of 2010, Ataur Mridha alias Ataur v. State*
3. *Rokeya Begum v. State 4 CLR (AD) 147*
4. *Ordinance No. XL1 of 1985*
5. *Section 45 of the Penal Code*
6. *Sections 84 of the Penal Code and 401 of the Code of Criminal Procedure*
7. *Ibid*
8. *Gopal Binayek Godsey v. State, AIR 1961 SC 600*
9. *Code Bangladesh*
10. *Section 41 of the Code of Criminal Procedure*
11. *K. M Nanavati v. State of Maharastra, AIR 1961 SC 112*
12. *Ramdeo Chowhan v. State of Assam, AIR 2001 SC 2231*
13. *Article 49 of the Constitution*
14. *State v. Eliadah MaCord, (1927) 2 BLC (AD) 1*
15. *Punjab v. Jogindarsingh, AIR 1990 SC 1396*
16. *Bangladesh v. Kazi Shaziruddin (2007) 15 BLT (AD) 95*

Conduct of Public Prosecutor (D)

At this moment I can recollect a case in a Dhaka Court. The present Food Minister Advocate Quamrul Islam was the Public Prosecutor of Dhaka during 1999-2001. The dead body of one Jalal, an informer of DB police, was recovered from the rooftop water tank of the DB office building sometime in 2000. After investigation it was revealed that Jalal was killed by the DB officials who dumped the body in the rooftop water tank. The case was ultimately sent for trial before the Sessions Judge, Dhaka. One morning I read a news item in the Daily Star that the victim's wife was claiming that she was going to court on every given date, but the public prosecutor took adjournment of the case on the plea that no witness had turned up and told her to go back and come to court the next month for hearing. She was the informant and prime witness for the prosecution. On reading the news, I felt extremely dismayed. I was then an additional judge and sitting with Ali Asgar Khan having jurisdiction of criminal Bench with motions. I showed the report and requested the senior judge to do justice for this illiterate woman. Ali Asgar Khan agreed to my proposal and asked for my opinion. I told him that unless we took cognizance of the reporting Suo moto, the victim's wife would not get justice in the hand of the Public Prosecutor, who is known to have corrupt predilections. Accordingly, we issued a Suo moto rule upon the State to explain why the Public Prosecutor in charge of the case should not be withdrawn from the case and that another neutral Public Prosecutor should not be appointed at the cost of the State. After the issuance of the Suo moto rule, the matter was reported on the front pages of different newspapers. Some Ministers of the cabinet contacted me to drop the matter for the prestige of the Public Prosecutor and assuring that he would conduct the case properly. I told them that the matter had received so much publicity nothing could possibly done, and, in any case, I had nothing much to do since a presiding judge was involved in the matter. The matter was accordingly posted in the list for hearing. Veteran lawyers appeared at the hearing and wanted discharge of the rule for maintaining the prestige of the Public Prosecutor. On perusal of the record we noticed that after framing of charges two years had elapsed and, on each occasion, the Public Prosecutor had taken adjournments on the plea that witnesses had not turned up. We were stunned at the conduct of the Public Prosecutor and we were satisfied that the Public Prosecutor was influenced by the accused who were very influential persons and the PP did not perform his responsibility fairly. Accordingly, we made the rule absolute, relieved the Public Prosecutor from conducting the case and directed the Home Ministry to appoint an independent veteran lawyer from the Bar as per choice of the victim's wife at the cost of the State. We also held that the victim's wife and witnesses should be given police protection till the conclusion of the trial. Within six months from that direction, the trial was concluded with the conviction of the accused.1 It may be noted that from before that time there was deterioration in the process of appointment of Public Prosecutors, Government Pleaders and other law officers in the Attorney General's office.

Reference:

1. *Daily Star v. State, 53 DLR 155*

Doctrine of Judicial Review (E)

This doctrine was unknown in judicial history till 1803. It is a doctrine propounded by a great American judge John Marshall, the then Chief Justice. In the American Constitution there is no provision like our Article 7 of the Constitution prescribing that "if any other law is inconsistent with this Constitution that other law shall, to the extent of the inconsistency, be void." Or a provision like Article 26 which stated, "The State shall not make any law inconsistent with any provisions of this part, and any law so made shall, to the extent of such consistency, be void." It was a most remarkable case which changed the concept of governmental power in a State and the checks and balances of a government in the functioning of the administration. While deciding the case the antecedents in American colonial experience, and its taproots in the declarations of fundamental rights of Englishmen back to Magna Carta. Marshall kept in mind that early in American history the colonial experience of living under a parliamentary system with no check on the Legislative or Executive branch, except that of popular will in a limited way, led America's Founding Fathers to feel strongly the need for limitations on all branches of government. Montesquieu greatly influenced the notion of separation of powers within the government itself in order that each branch might act as a sort of brake upon the others.

As the system worked in those days, one of the checks exercised by the Supreme Court involved measuring Executive or Legislative actions against the Constitution whenever a challenge to such actions was first brought within the framework of a case or controversy and then brought within the "appellate jurisdiction" of the court. Marshall kept in mind that in the Constitutional Convention of 1887 the "propertied classes" regarded a Supreme Court and an independent Federal Judiciary as a source of protection against the egalitarian popular government advocated by Jefferson. They could not fail to be aware that the exercise of such powers by the judiciary must in some way involve limitations on legislative and executive actions.1

It is true that the American constitution makes no reference to the theory in defining judicial power, but Chief Justice Marshall viewed that constitutional adjudication was inherent in the very nature of a written constitution and he enunciated the doctrine as part of federal jurisprudence and seized the opportunity to assert the power of the court to measure an act of Congress by the yardstick of the Constitution. Ours is totally different and our Constitution has clearly given the judiciary the power of scrutinizing the legality or authority of the Parliament to enact any law contrary to the Constitution. Consequently, our Supreme Court is armed with such powers which our Founding Fathers realized at the time of drafting the Constitution that such powers should be preserved because of the antecedents of colonial experience. It would not be an exaggeration to argue that whatever might be the reason for John Marshall to exercise such power, it was the usurpation of judicial power because it was not basic power. The American people accepted the doctrine and therefore, although Jefferson termed it usurpation of power, the Executive bowed to the wishes of the people and it remains part of the American system. Our Executive whittled down the power given by the Constitution and did not give weight to the people's feelings and wishes, and thus whittled down their rights.

I noticed some inconsistent judgements of our highest court on the question of exercise of such power in a given case and without looking at the dictum on the given facts, those decisions were given, and taking advantage of the inconsistency, some lawyers rampantly file writ petitions for judicial review in respect of promotion, transfer, suspension and dismissal of public servants, although Administrative Tribunals had been set up by the government for covering that field. The net result was the piling up of cases over those matters and the government could not transfer a public servant as a punitive measure and, accordingly, I decided to finally resolve the issue. The apex courts of different countries settled law points and the US Supreme Court is a pioneer in this regard, though it has overruled some of its previous decisions.

Article 111 of the Constitution empowers our apex court to declare any law to be binding and Article 112 says that all authorities, Executive and Judicial, in the Republic shall act in aid of the Supreme Court. The expression "law" used in Article 111 includes the decisions on any point of law by the apex court of the country. Common law has traditionally adhered to the precedents of earlier cases as a source of law. This principle, known as stare decisis, distinguishes the common law from the civil law system which gives great weight to codes of laws and the opinions of scholars explaining them. Under stare decisis, once the court has answered a question the same question in other cases must elicit the same response from the same court in that jurisdiction. The principle of stare decisis not always applied with uniform strictness. Stare decisis to be effective if its jurisdiction of one highest court what the law is in a precedent case. The US Supreme Court served as a body of precedents resolving conflicting interpretations of law and dealing with issues of first impression. Whenever this court decided an issue it became a judicial precedent. The US Supreme Court rarely overturns one of its own precedents, but when it does, the ruling usually signifies a new way of looking at an important legal issue. As for example, in a landmark case2 the court ignored stare decisis renouncing a legal precedent that had legitimized racial segregation for almost 60 years.

The power of judicial review was given to the High Court Division under Article 102 of the Constitution. The power can be exercised by the High Court Division under clause (1) for the enforcement of any of the fundamental rights conferred by Part III of the Constitution; and clause (2) empowers the High Court Division to exercise judicial power if no other equally efficacious remedy is provided by law. Article 117 of the Constitution is a non-obstante provision, by which provisions are made to establish one or more Administrative Tribunals to exercise jurisdiction in respect of matters relating to the terms and conditions in the service of the Republic and award penalties and punishment. Clause (5) of Article 102 clearly excludes the other courts from entertaining proceedings or making any order in respect of any matter falling within the jurisdiction of the Administrative Tribunal. This led to filing of various writ petitions by different public servants. The High Court Division traveled to the extent that it even interfered with the order of transfer of a public servant from one station to another. Ultimately, I constituted the Full Bench and resolved the point. In course of arguments, it was pointed out that no equally efficacious remedies are available in the Administrative Tribunal and, therefore, the aggrieved public servants are compelled to seek remedy in the High Court Division for the enforcement of fundamental rights.

While deciding the case we considered the cases of Masder Hossain, 3 Mujibur Rahman, 4 Anwar Hossain Chowdhury, 5 Khandaker Delwar Hosain, 6 Ehteshamuddin, 7 Ismail Haque, 8 Mushtaque Ahmed, 9 Helaluddin Ahmed, 10 and Shaheda Khatun, 11 and overruled the dictum in cases relating to Shaheda Khatun, Ehteshamuddain, Ismail Haque, Mushtaque Ahmed and Helaluddin Ahmed. We decided the matters on different premises and contexts. We distinguished the cases and took the view that except on limited scope challenging the vires of the law or if there is violation of fundamental rights, the power of the High Court Division is totally ousted under clause (5) of Article 102 read with Article 117 (2). If a public servant or an employee of a statutory corporation wants to invoke his fundamental rights in connection with the terms and conditions of service, he must lay the foundation in the petition about the violation of fundamental rights

157

by sufficient pleadings. A malaise action or collusion or arbitrary order or a disputed question of fact and law is within the jurisdiction of the tribunal and the tribunal is competent to decide the question of malafide or collusion or arbitrariness in taking the decisions. On the question of jurisdiction, the tribunal also has the power to decide the said point. I distinguished the dictum in Shaheda Khatun holding that the action complained of is found to be coram non-judis, without jurisdiction or malafide as found in the case was based on decisions on different premises and the said views cannot be applicable in-service matters.

I also considered the cases of Junnur Rahman BSRS,12 Delwar Hossain Miah,13 Mohammad Abdul Halim Miah,14 Shafiuddin Ahmed,15 Shamsunnahar,16 Mahbubuddin Ahmed,17 Member Administrative Tribunal,18 Enayetullah,19 Mohammad Salahuddin Talukder,20 Delwar Hossain Mollah,21 Md. Shamsul Islam Khan,22 Abdul Halim,23 Ruhul Amin,24 and held that though the Act did not authorize the tribunal to pass any interim order, it can use its inherent powers to fill up the lacuna left by the legislature while enacting law or where the legislature is unable to foresee any circumstance which may arise in any particular case, inasmuch as the tribunal has all trappings of a civil court and it is not a persona designata and, therefore, it can issue interim orders in appropriate cases.25

We fixed some civil appeals along with civil petitions analogously for hearing.26 Santosh Kumar Saha was a judicial officer. The authority drew up a departmental proceeding on allegation of corruption. He was put on suspension. The inquiry report was misplaced in the Ministry of Law. Ultimately the Ministry of Law recommended for exonerating him from the charges to the Supreme Court and to withdraw his suspension order on January 17, 2002. The Supreme Court did not approve the proposal. Again, the Ministry sent another letter to drop the proceedings against him. The Supreme Court rejected the proposal and directed the Ministry to issue a second show-cause notice. He then sought judicial review of the said order, but the Supreme Court rejected the petition. Subsequently it was detected that the suspension order was not placed before the General Administration Committee and therefore the suspension order was illegal. His prayer was also rejected. He again moved the High Court challenging the suspension order and disciplinary proceedings. This time the High Court Division made the rule absolute.

When the matter was heard, I had considered all previous decisions of judicial review.27 I formulated seven points, among those, the crucial issues were: (i) whether a disciplinary action taken against an officer of the Judicial Service of the Republic can seek judicial review against such action; (ii) whether the General Administration Committee (GA Committee) can ignore a recommendation of the Executive to exonerate an officer of the lower judiciary and direct the concerned Ministry to take penal action; (iii) whether judicial review in the High Court Division is available in respect of the terms and conditions of service of an employee in the service of the Republic; (iv) whether the Administrative Tribunal is competent to examine the constitutional validity of a statutory provision; and (v) whether the administrative tribunal can pass interim orders so as not to frustrate the proceedings pending before it.

The tribunal was constituted as a forum substitute, alternate or co-equal to the High Court Division. The judicial review by the High Court Division in respect of the terms and conditions of service of the Republic has been deliberately excluded by clause (2) of Article 117. The tribunals are not meant to be like the High Court Division or the subordinate court over which the High Court Division can exercise both judicial review and superintendence. The tribunals are not in addition to the courts described in Chapters I and III.

Clause (2) of Article 44 provides that Parliament may empower any other court to exercise "all or any of those powers,' that is, for enforcement of the rights conferred by Part III, but this power cannot be so conferred affecting the powers of the High Court Division. The power of judicial review given to the High Court Division is a constitutional power, which can be exercised by it based on an application moved by a citizen and this power has been specifically preserved for a citizen to invoke such right/privilege in the High Court Division under Article 102(1). Judicial review vested in the High Court Division under Article 102(1) is one of the basic structures of the Constitution and it cannot be taken away by Parliament. Parliament in exercise of its legislative power cannot curtail the constitutional jurisdiction conferred on the High Court Division. Parliament can confer upon the administrative tribunal in exercise of its legislative power the power of judicial review of administrative actions and nothing more. In Mujibur Rahman, the apex court noticed Article 44(1), but it has totally ignored the tenor of Article 44(1). By creation of tribunals Parliament cannot curtail the powers of the High Court Division given under Article 102(1) to issue writs, directions and orders.

The High Court Division's power is extensive. It is a court of record and it has the power of contempt. It has control and superintendence over the courts and tribunals subordinate to it. The High Court Division's power is constitutional while the power of the tribunal is legislative, and the tribunal has been created by a subordinate legislation. The Constitution guaranteed the High Court Division not to become a mere appendage to the administration. The basic human freedoms, including freedom of religion and the rights of all minorities – religious, cultural, linguistic--will not cease to exist because these are guaranteed rights and will be enforceable on the application of a citizen in the High Court Division. These powers cannot be exercised by a tribunal created under Article 117(2). After the creation of administrative tribunals, the jurisdiction of the High Court Division in service matters and its propriety which it had exercised must be exercised by the tribunal established under Article 117(2). If this provision is taken into consideration with Article 44(2), there will be no confusion in concluding that an effective alternative institutional mechanism for judicial review in respect of service matters has been created by Parliament.

Under our constitutional dispensation particularly, Articles 44(2) and 117(2), it is possible to set up an alternative mechanism in place of the High Court Division for providing judicial review in respect of the terms and conditions of service to the Republic and other public organizations. Over a span of time after the creation of administrative tribunal, there is no doubt that a service jurisprudence has been developed in the country to the satisfaction of the litigants. Initially there was confusion in the minds of some as to whether the tribunal will be able to address and adjudicate upon the problems properly since the tribunal is manned by a District Judge who has no expertise in these fields. I find no serious infirmity on the question of judicial review of administrative actions by the tribunal. The public servants and other litigants have accepted the system.

Thus, it is possible to set up an alternative institution in place of the High Court Division for providing judicial review. The debates and deliberations spread over almost two decades for exploring ways and means for relieving the High Court of the load of backlog of cases and for assuring quick settlement of service disputes in the interest of the public servants as also the country cannot be lost sight of while considering this aspect. The tribunal under the scheme of the Act would take over a part of the existing backlog and a share of the normal load of the High Court Division. The tribunal has been contemplated as a substitute and not as supplemental to the High Court Division in the scheme of administration of justice. To provide the tribunal as an additional forum from where parties could go to the High Court would certainly have been a retrograde step considering the situation and circumstances to meet which the innovation had been brought about. Thus, barring of the jurisdiction of the High Court Division can indeed not be a valid ground of attack. (S.P Sampath Kumar)

There is no command or any necessary intention in the Constitution that the tribunal or the appellate tribunal is to be construed as a forum substitute, alternate or co-equal to the High Court Division. There cannot be any doubt in holding the view that the jurisdiction and powers conferred upon an administrative tribunal is an alternative forum with the object to relieve the High Court Division from the huge backlog and Parliament has been given the power to establish such a tribunal subject to certain limitations without affecting the fundamental rights of a citizen. All the fundamental rights enshrined in Part III are not inalienable;

some of them are conditional. This clause (2) of Section 117 contains in Part VI. It is a forum created by Parliament providing for judicial review with an object to relieve the High Court Division of the burden of huge backlog of cases and ensuring quick disposal of service related matters in an alternative dispute resolution mechanism. The Constitution has empowered Parliament to give such power of judicial review to a tribunal.

The bar of jurisdiction to entertain a writ petition on any of the above matters is a measure for effective, expeditious and satisfactory disposal relating to service disputes of public servants and the power of judicial review in respect of those matters by the High Court Division has been debarred by clause (5) of Article 102 read with clause (2) of Article 117. There is thus a forum where matters of importance and grave injustice over service matters can be brought for determination. One may pose a question as to what nature of jurisdiction a tribunal is barring the judicial review of the High Court Division. This tribunal has all the powers and jurisdiction relating to the terms and conditions of persons in the service of the Republic that were being exercised by the High Court Division. This is a new alternative dispute resolution mechanism. There are courts under the prevailing laws in the country by which both the High Court Division and the District Courts exercise such powers.

Parliament in exercise of its legislative power has also given concurrent jurisdictions to the High Court Division and the Sessions Judges under section 498 of the Code of Criminal Procedure. This power has been given to a court subordinate to the High Court Division with a view to enabling the litigants to avail of prompt and less expensive criminal justice from the lower tier of the judiciary. The difference between these two enactments is that under the Code of Criminal Procedure the power of judicial review has been given to the High Court Division from the judgment of the Sessions Judges, but in respect of service matters, the appellate power of judicial review has been given to the administrative appellate tribunal and then to the apex court. The object is to afford the service holders the avenue to get prompt and less expensive relief in a lower tier of the judiciary. And the final power of judicial review has been given to the highest court on limited matters only on the question of law.

Under the Indian provision of laws, though there is an enabling provision in clause (3) of Article 32 of the Constitution empowering Parliament provide to any other court the power to exercise all or any of the powers exercisable by the Supreme Court, no such legislation was made in India till 1985, when Part XIV containing Articles 323A and 323B were inserted. This Article 323A is almost in pari materia to Article 117(1) of our Constitution. By Article 323A Parliament has given power to constitute a Central Administrative Tribunal and by Article 323B the State Legislature has been given the power to constitute Administrate Tribunals at the State level.

In India there was no separate provision like Articles 44 and 101 of our Constitution; but similar provisions have been incorporated in clauses (1) and (3) of Article 32, but no such provision is included in Article 226 with the result that in case of violation of fundamental rights, its citizens can move the Supreme Court only under Article 32. Whatever other remedy may be open to a person aggrieved, he has no right to complain under Article 32 if there is no infringement of fundamental rights. Article 32 is included in Part III in the Chapter on fundamental rights, but Article 102 of our Constitution is included in Part VI under the heading 'The Judiciary'.

As regards Acts passed by the legislature, judicial legislation enabled modification and reinforcement principally in four ways: (1) by applying to them the rules of statutory construction; much law is created in this way; (2) or the judiciary may decide that a certain statute is unconstitutional or is not unconstitutional as the case may be, and thus, either destroy it altogether, or in order to save it, may greatly modify its effect and in a large measure thwart the interest of the legislature; (3) or in construing any statute, the judges may impute a narrow meaning to certain words used or a liberal meaning, as the case may be, and thus modify and mold the law to their own notions of justice and the public good; (4) or a statute may be ignored altogether in some important particulars and a new law created by the judiciary.

There are three organs of the State, of them, the Judiciary is of course one, but if the higher judiciary is equated with the lower judiciary, there will be chaos and confusion. In the early 1980s Canada experienced a fundamental change in its political and legal structures. The new Constitution28 came into effect declaring itself to be "the Supreme law of Canada." The new Constitution further decreed that "any law that is inconsistent with (its) provisions is, to the extent of the inconsistency, of no force or effect."29 Judicial review under the Canadian system "refers to any form of judicial assessment of legal validity of government action (typically legislation) under a constitutional Charter of Bill of Rights." It has been observed by W.J. Waluchow30 that judicial assessment is such as one finds in Canada and the United States, or under sections of a nation's constitution that outline basic civil rights, like equality and freedom of association.

All judicial reviews - all manner of adjudication by courts – are itself an exercise of judicial accountability – accountability to the people who are affected by a judicial pronouncement. In the United States, the Attorney General's Department exercises some of the functions of a Ministry of Justice, together with numerous congressional committees and ad-hoc commissions. Each of these national institutions has certain merits and deficiencies. There is no doubt that the Constitution is the supreme law of the country and, therefore, any court or tribunal can exercise any of the provisions of the Constitution, but about judicial review in respect of legislative actions, this power has been restricted to the High Court Division in our Constitution. When the constitution itself has preserved the right of a citizen to move the High Court Division for infringement of fundamental rights against any administrative action, such power cannot be exercised by any tribunal other than the one established by the Constitution. This power has been assigned to the High Court Division as will be evident from Articles 7(2) 26(2), 44(1), 101 and 102(1).

Article 101 provides that the High Court Division shall have such original, appellate and other jurisdictions and powers that are conferred on it by the Constitution or any other law. To invoke the fundamental rights conferred by Part III of the Constitution, any person aggrieved by the order, action or direction of any person performing the functions in connection with the affairs of the Republic, the forum is preserved for the High Court Division. The conferment of this power cannot be curtailed by any subordinate legislation -- it being the inalienable right of a citizen. This power cannot be conferred upon any tribunal by Parliament in exercise of legislative power or by the High Court Division or the Appellate Division in exercise of its power of judicial review.

The apex court itself noticed in Mujibur Rahman that "The Tribunals are not meant to be like the High Court Division or subordinate court over which the High Court Division of the Supreme Court exercises both judicial review and superintendence. The tribunals are not in addition to the court described in Chapters I and III of Part VI. There is no command nor any necessary intendment in the Constitution that the tribunal or appellate tribunal is to be construed as a forum substitute, alternate or co-equal to the High Court Division." Here possibly the court has overlooked Article 44(2) of the Constitution. The Constitution has conferred legislative power to promulgate law empowering a court to exercise all or any of the powers of fundamental rights. Though Parliament has such power, this clause is to be read not in isolation. Parliament's power is limited to the extent of giving powers of judicial review of administrative actions only and not more than that. There is no dispute that there is provision in the Constitution in Article 117(2) conferring upon Parliament the power to establish administrative tribunals to exercise judicial functions relating to the terms and conditions in the service of the Republic, "including the matters provided in Part IX."

The government has established the tribunals with effect from June 5, 1981, both for exercising the original and appellate jurisdictions, and another forum for judicial review of the judgment of the administrative appellate tribunal.31 The appellate tribunal has been created with three members, the chairman shall be a person

165

who is or has been or is qualified to be a judge of the Supreme Court, and two other members of whom one shall be a person who is or has been an officer in the rank of Joint Secretary and the other person who is or has been a District Judge. So, practically the power of a Division Bench of the High Court Division has been given to the administrative appellate tribunal. The composition of the appellate authority by including a high-level administrative officer with specialized knowledge will be better equipped than the judicial officers to dispense with prompt justice. On the contrary, there is no provision for appeal under the Indian Act of 1985 and the High Court's power of judicial review was ousted except the Supreme Court's power under Article 136. So, our provision is more comprehensive to some extent so far as it relates to the creation of an appellate forum than that of India except the power for issuing interim order by our tribunal.

Under our constitutional scheme, there is no doubt that the power of judicial review in respect of legislative action has not been conferred upon the tribunal by subordinate legislation. If the right to move the High Court Division is guaranteed and this power having been conferred on the High Court Division by the Constitution, it cannot be said that for enforcement of that right and the right to judicial review under Article 102(1) is guaranteed if a citizen's fundamental rights are infringed. The remedy for enforcement of that right is conferred by the Constitution under Article 102(1). Therefore, the exercise of this power by the High Court Division cannot be curtailed or taken away by Parliament. Only the Supreme Court, the creation of the Constitution itself, can exercise that power. If the entire scheme of the Constitution is looked at, it will appear that of the three organs of the State created by the Constitution the judiciary is headed by the Supreme Court, and the other two organs are the Legislature and the Executive. These three organs are independent and not dependent one on the other organs but in a unitary form of government these three organs must work harmoniously with a view to avoiding any conflict in the administration of justice. Each organ is, therefore, supplementary to the other. The framers of our Constitution were conscious about the independence of the judiciary and to protect it from any future encroachment they gave full independence to the Supreme Court in the administration of justice.

Therefore, it is the Supreme Court alone which is empowered to examine whether any law is inconsistent with the Constitution. Parliament has been given legislative powers under Article 65 to promulgate laws, but this power is circumscribed by limitations and if it exercises any power which is inconsistent with the Constitution, it is the Supreme Court which being the custodian of the Constitution and manned by judges who are oath-bound to protect the law and to examine it in this regard. The Supreme Court is the only organ of the State to see that all laws are in consonance with the Constitution. Hence where the Constitution confers the power upon the Supreme Court to strike down laws, if found inconsistent, such power cannot be delegated to a tribunal created under subordinate legislation. In the alternative, the Supreme Court cannot delegate its power of judicial review of legislative action to a tribunal, on the principle that the don of a limited power cannot, by the exercise of that very power, convert the limited power into an unlimited one or a delegate cannot exercise the same or more power than the delegator.

So, apart from the Constitution, Parliament can confer any other power upon the High Court Division by subordinate legislation. Similarly, as to the powers of the Appellate Division, sub-Clause (c) of clause (2) of Article 103 provides that if the High Court Division "has imposed punishment of a person for contempt of that Division; and in such other cases as may be provided by Act of Parliament" an appeal shall lie as of right. I am of the view that the Framers ought to have included the latter part of sub-clause (c), such as, "and in such other cases as may be provided for by Act of Parliament" by a separate sub-clause because the empowerment of these two powers conflict with each other.

If we compare the constitutional provisions between ours and the Indian, the Indian Constitution is more comprehensive than ours so far as it relates to making of interim orders in urgent cases with a view to preserving the subject matter of the litigation in status-quo for the time being. Such an order is necessary for equitable considerations and it is an extraordinary relief, which is normally granted in accordance with reasons and sound judicial principles. It is not a grace or on default of any person. It is passed in the interest of justice and it is necessary in order to prevent the abuse of the process of law, or to prevent wastage or to maintain the situation as on date or from recurrence of certain incident which was existing as on the date presenting such application.

If the original constitution empowers Parliament to give power to a court or a tribunal all or any of the powers of the High Court Division, why can it not empower "alternative powers" to the tribunal as opposed to "substitutional" as observed by the Supreme Court of India. But in no case it can be treated as co-equal to the High Court Division to deal with all matters in respect of the terms and conditions of persons in the service of the Republic, including matters provided in Part IX the services of Bangladesh. However, I am unable to endorse the views taken by the Supreme Court of India in Chandra Kumar (Supra) that "The Tribunals are competent to hear matters where vires of statutory provisions is questioned."

Under our Administrative Tribunals Act, the powers have been given to the administrative tribunal under section 4 to hear and determine applications made by any person in the service of the Republic or of any statutory public authority in respect of the terms and conditions of his service including the person's rights or in respect of any action taken in relation to him as a person in the service of the Republic or of any public authority. So, the tribunal can adjudicate in relation to only the terms and conditions of service of any public servant or of any statutory public authority. Though an exclusive jurisdiction has been invested upon the tribunal, it has no power to nullify any law, rules or regulations. The tribunal has been given limited power in relation to those mentioned in Sub-Section (1) of section 4.

Article 102(1) has not been retained in the fundamental rights chapter as has been done in India, but in view of Article 44(1) it is akin to fundamental rights. Similarly, the observation that the enforcement of fundamental rights is available only when "no other equally efficacious remedy is provided by law" is also not a correct view, since, whenever there is infringement of fundamental rights, any person can move the High Court Division for judicial review of the administrative action under Article 102(1). The question of equally efficacious remedy arises only when it will exercise power under Article 102(2) i.e. writ of certiorari and other writs mentioned in sub-clauses (a) and (b) of clause (2). If there is an alternative remedy, the High Court Division's power is debarred. It is only in exceptional cases that it can exercise this power. Under clause (2) of Article 102 a citizen cannot invoke judicial review of legislative action. Judicial review under this clause is not available if there is "any other equally efficacious remedy" as provided by law. Justice Mostafa Kamal rightly observed that this power of judicial review of legislative action is exclusively preserved to the High Court Division under Article 102(1).

There is thus no gainsaying that if the vires of any law is challenged notwithstanding ouster of the jurisdiction of the High Court Division by an Act of Parliament, the High Court Division has power of judicial review to examine the constitutionality of the law. Our apex court ignoring the ouster of the jurisdiction of the High Court Division by a legislative provision observed the High Court Division is yet entitled to exercise its power of judicial review under Article 102 if the action complained of before the High Court Division is found to be Coram non judice, without jurisdiction or taken malafide.

Except on the limited scope challenging the vires of the law or if there is violation of fundamental rights, the power of the High Court Division is totally ousted under clause (5) of Article 102 read with Article 117(2). If a public servant or an employee of a statutory corporation wants to invoke his fundamental rights in connection with his terms and conditions of service, he must lay the foundation in the petition of the violation of the fundamental rights by enough pleadings in support of the claim. It will not suffice if he makes evasive statements of violation of his fundamental rights or by making stray statements that the order is discriminatory or malafide. A malafide action is a disputed question of fact and law, and the tribunal is, therefore, competent

169

enough to decide the question of malafide or collusion or arbitrariness in taking the decision. The expression "malafide" has a definite significance in legal phraseology and the same cannot emanate out of fanciful imagination or even apprehensions but there must be existence definite evidence of bias and actions which cannot be attributed to be otherwise bonafide. By themselves these would not amount to be malafide unless the same is accompanied with some other facts which would depict a bad motive or intent on the part of the authority and the same cannot be decided in summary proceedings in writ jurisdiction.

Similarly, if an order is said to be without jurisdiction or is contrary to law, the appropriate course open to the applicant is to plead to the tribunal and ask for vacating the order or action. It is altogether within the tenor of the tribunal. "Coram non judice" is a Latin phrase which means "not in the presence of a judge". It is a legal term typically used to indicate a legal proceeding held without a judge, in an improper venue such as before a court which lacks the authority to hear and decide a case in question or without proper jurisdiction. I find no cogent ground why the tribunal cannot deal with these issues. The observations made in Shaheda Khatun that if the action complained as is found to be coram non judice, without jurisdiction or malafide, judicial review is available based on the decisions on different premises and the said views cannot be applicable in-service matters in presence of an alternative forum, and this forum is created as per provisions of the Constitution. It is to be borne in mind that no case can be an authority on facts. The tribunal is created as an alternative forum of the High Court Division in respect of specific purposes. If any administrative action is found without jurisdiction or coram non judice or malafide, the tribunal is competent to deal with the same and adjudicate these issues satisfactorily. These issues are within the constituents of the administrative tribunal. If the order complained of was passed by an officer who is not competent, the order would be without jurisdiction. If the rules provide for the constitution of a domestic tribunal with designated persons but the tribunal was constituted by persons not authorized by the rules, the action would be coram non judice. If the decision is taken malafide out of vengeance or with motive to take revenge, in all those cases the tribunal can strike down the action taken against the applicant.

There is no reason to restrict the powers of the tribunal by judicial pronouncement. These matters are within the powers of the tribunal and, therefore, if a public servant wants to challenge the actions under Article 102(1), it will be barred under clause (2) of Article 117. In sub-section (3) it is provided that the member of the tribunal is among persons who are or have been District Judges. The expression "District Judge" has been described in the Civil Courts Act, 1887 as a senior most judicial officer of Civil Courts. In the classification of "Courts" under the Civil Courts Act, Clause (a) provides, 'the Court of District Judge'. Section 18 provides the ordinary jurisdiction of the District Judge which says: save as otherwise provided by an enactment for the time being in force, the jurisdiction of the District Judge.

So, according to Civil Courts Act, the office of the District Judge is a Civil Court and not a persona designata. Therefore, for all practical purposes the tribunal or the appellate tribunal is exercising powers of a civil court and disposing of civil disputes determining the terms and conditions of service. The rights to his office, privileges, promotion, and pension rights are included within such jurisdiction. The tribunal has power to substitute the heirs in case of death of the applicant. The tribunal has been given the power under section 7B to amend the pleadings. In section 8(2), it is provided that the decision of the administrative tribunal be binding upon the parties, that is, the government. Again, in section 10A, it is provided that the administrative appellate tribunal has the power to punish for contempt of its authority or that of the administrative tribunal, as if it were the High Court Division of the Supreme Court. The language used in section 10A is self-explanatory that the tribunal has been created as an "alternative" forum of the High Court Division in respect of matters mentioned above. It can also initiate execution proceeding for enforcement of the judgment. Therefore, the tribunal or the appellate tribunal has all the trappings of a civil court.

The tribunal is not powerless since it has all the trappings of a civil court and, in proper cases, it may invoke its inherent power and pass interim orders with a view to preventing abuse of the process of the court or the mischief being caused to the applicant affecting his right to promotion or other benefits. But the tribunal shall not pass any such interim order without affording the opposite party affected by the order an opportunity to being heard. However, in cases of emergency, which requires an interim order in order to prevent the abuse of the process and in the event of not passing such order preventing such loss, which cannot be compensated by money, the tribunal can pass an interim order as an exceptional measure for a limited period not exceeding fifteen days from the date of the order unless the said requirements have been complied with before the expiry of the period, and the tribunal shall pass any further order upon hearing the parties. While prescribing the powers of the tribunal, it is specifically provided that "a Tribunal shall have all the powers of civil court." Monetary compensation cannot be measured while considering the status of an officer. An officer's dignity, status, privilege, position in office, etc. cannot be measured in terms of money

The inherent powers of a tribunal remind the judges of what they ought to know already, namely, that if the ordinary rules of procedure result in injustice in any case and there is no other remedy, it can be broken for the ends of justice. This power furnishes the legislative recognition of the age-old and well-established principle that every tribunal has inherent power to act ex debito justitiae, i.e. to do that real and substantial justice and the administration of which alone it exists to prevent abuse of the process of the court. This power can be exercised when no other power is available under the procedural law. Nothing can limit or affect the inherent power of a tribunal to meet the ends of justice since it is not possible to foresee all possible circumstances that may arise to provide appropriate procedures to meet all those situations. All tribunals, whether civil or criminal, possess this power in the absence of any provision, as inherent in their constitution, all such powers as are necessary to do the right and to undo a wrong in the course of administration of justice on the principle "quando lex aliquid alique, concedit, conceditor, it sine quo res ipsa eshe non potest" i.e. when the law gives a person anything it gives him that also without which the thing itself cannot exist.

Therefore, while exercising this power the tribunal is to consider whether the exercise of such power is expressly prohibited by any other provision and if there is no such prohibition then the tribunal will consider whether such power should be exercised or not on the facts of a given case. We cannot overlook the fact that the primary function of the judiciary is to do justice between the parties who bring their causes before it. If the primary function of the court is to do justice in respect of causes brought before it then on principle it is difficult to accede to the proposition that in the absence of specific provision the court will shut its eyes even if a wrong or an error is detected in its judgment. To state it otherwise, courts are meant for doing justice and must be deemed to possess as a necessary corollary as inherent in their constitution all the powers to achieve the end and undo the wrong. It does not confer any additional jurisdiction on the court; it only recognizes the inherent powers which it already possesses.

If the law contains no specific provisions to meet the necessity of the case the inherent power of a court merely saves by expressly preserving to the court which is both a court of equity and law, to act according to justice, equity and good conscience and make such orders as may be necessary for the ends of justice or to prevent the abuse of the process of the court. It is an enabling provision by which inherent powers have been vested in a court so that it does not find itself helpless for administering justice. The tribunal can use its inherent powers to fill up the lacuna left by the legislature while enacting a law or where the legislature is unable to foresee any circumstance which may arise in a case. There is a power to make such order as may be necessary for the ends of justice and to prevent the abuse of the process of the tribunal. The inherent powers of a tribunal are in addition to and complementary to the powers expressly conferred upon it by other provisions of the Act of 1973. They are not intended to enable the tribunal to create rights for the parties, but they are meant to enable the tribunal to pass such orders for the ends of justice as may be

173

necessary. Considering the rights which are conferred upon the parties by substantive law to prevent abuse of the process of law, it is the duty of all tribunals to correct the decisions which run counter to the law.

References:

1. *The Constitution and Chief Justice, Marshall, p-384*
2. *(Brown v Board of Education, 347 US 483, 74S. CT. 686, 98 L.ED. 873 (1954)), the Supreme Court repudiated the separate but equal doctrine it endorsed in Plassy v. Ferguson, 163 US 537,16S.CT.1138, 41L, Ed. 256 (1896)).*
3. *Masder Hossain, 52 DLR (AD) 82*
4. *Mujibur Rahman v. Bangladesh 44 DLR (AD) 111*
5. *Anwar Hossain Chowdhury v. Bangladesh 41 DLR (AD) 165*
6. *Khandker Delwar Hossain v. Bangladesh (Italian Marble Works 62 DLR (AD) 298*
7. *Ehtesham Uddin v. Bangladesh 33 DLR (AD) 154*
8. *Ismail Haque v. Bangladesh 34 DLR (AD) 125*
9. *Mustaque Ahmed v. 34 DLR (AD) 222*
10. *Helaluddin Ahmed v. 45 DLR (AD) 81]*
11. *Shaheda Khatun v. Administrative Appellate Tribunal, 3 BLC (AD) 155*
12. *Junnur Rahman v. BSRS 51 DLR (AD) 166*
13. *Delwar Hossain Miah v. Bangladesh 52 DLR (AD) 120*
14. *Government v. Mohammad Abdul Halim Miah, 9 MLL (AD) 105*
15. *Secretary v. Shafiuddin Ahmed 2 MLR (AD) 257*
16. *Shamsunnahar v. Secretary 3 MLR (AD) 68*
17. *Bangladesh v. Mahbubuddin Ahmed 3 MLR (AD) 121*
18. *Bangladesh v. Member, Administrative Tribunal 6 MLR (AD) 181*
19. *Bangladesh v. AKM Enayetullah 11 BLC (AD) 2001*
20. *Bangladesh v. Salahuddin Talukder 15 BLT (AD) 60*
21. *Delwar Hossain Mollah v. Bangladesh 15 BLT (AD) 124*
22. *Md. Shamsul Islam Khan v. Secretary 8 BLT (AD) 64*

23. *Bangladesh v. Abdul Halim 13 BLT (AD) 120*
24. *Ruhul Amin v. District Judge 38 DLR (AD) 172*
25. *Bangladesh v. Santosh Kumar, Civil Appeal No. 159 of 2010*
26. *Ibid*
27. *Mujibur Rahman v. Bangladesh 44 DLR (AD) 111; SP Sampad Kumar v. Union of India AIR 1987 SC 386; Minarva Mills AIR 1980 SC 1789; RK Jain v. Union of India 1993 SC 1769; Anwar Hossain Chowdhury v Bangladesh 41 DLR (AD) 165; Khandker Delwar Hossain v. Bangladesh (Italian Marble Works) 62 DLR (AD) 298; Ehteshamuddin v. Bangladesh 33 DLR (AD) 154; Ismail Haque v. Bangladesh 34 DLR (AD) 125; Mustaque Ahmed v Bangladesh 34 DLR (AD) 222; Helauddin v. Bangladesh 45 DLR (AD) 1; Siddique Ahmed v. Bangladesh 65 DLR (AD) 8; Khalilur Rahman v. Md. Kamrul Ahsan 11 MLR (AD) 5; Bangladesh v. Md. Abdul Halim 9 MLR (AD) 166; Delwar Hossain Miah v. Bangladesh 52 DLR (AD) 120; Secretary v. Shafiuddin Ahmed 2 MLR (AD) 257; Shamsunnahar Begum v. Secretary 3 MLR (AD) 68; Bangladesh v. Mesbahuddin Ahmed 3 MLR (AD) 121; Bangladesh v. Administrative Tribunal 6 MLR (AD) 181; Bangladesh v. AKM Enayetullah 11 BLC (AD) 201; Bangladesh v. Salahuddin Talukder 15 BLT (AD) 60; Md. Shamsul Islam Khan v. Secretary 8 BLT (AD) 64; Delwar Hossain Mollah v. Bangladesh 15 BLT (AD) 124; T & T Board v. Md. Shafiul Alam 8 BLT (AD) 225; Bangladesh v. Abdul Halim 13 BLT (AD) 120; Ruhul Amin v. District Judge 38 DLR (AD) 172*
28. *The Constitution Act, 1983*
29. *Schedule V, Part-1, of the Constitution Act, 1982*
30. *W. J Waluchow, a Common Law Theory of Judicial Review*
31. *Act VII of 1981 and Act XXIII of 1991*

Legitimate Expectation (F)

The "doctrine of legitimate expectation" has been defined as a promise made in the shape of a statement of policy or a procedure adopted by the administrative authority, which may give rise to a legitimate expectation and it has been established as a corollary to the principle of "promissory estoppel." It "arises when there is a promise which the promiser should reasonably expect to induce action or forbearance of a definite and substantial character on part of promise and which does induce such action or forbearance and such promise in binding if injustice can be avoided only by enforcement of promise."1 This doctrine is an equitable doctrine. A representation made by one party for influencing the conduct of another party and to be acted upon him will in general be enough to entitle him to assistance of the court of equity for the purpose of such representation. If there is no such representation or an agreement to issue license or registration, the claimant cannot plead for issuance of license under the principle of promissory estoppel. Before a person claims entitlement of a license on the doctrine, it must be proved (a) there was a representation of promise in regard to something to be done in future; (b) the representation or promise was intended to affect the legal relations of the parties and intended to act accordingly; and (c) it is one which the other side has acted to his prejudice.

Legitimate expectation is a doctrine which is akin to that of promissory estoppel. The concept of legitimate expectation can be traced back to European Community Law. According to the doctrine, where a person is the victim of an unfavorable decision taken by a public authority, this may amount to an infringement of that person's legitimate expectation, where, for example, the decision contradicts an earlier promise or course of conduct on the part of the public authority. A person may have a legitimate expectation of being treated in a certain way by an administrative authority even though he has no legal right in private law to receive such treatment. The expectation may arise from a representation or promise made by the authority, including an implied representation, or from consistent past practice.2

An aggrieved person is entitled to invoke judicial review if he can show that a decision of a public authority affected him by depriving him of some benefit or advantage which in the past he had been permitted to enjoy and which he could legitimately expect to be permitted. To continue to enjoy either until he was given reasons for its withdrawal and the authority to comment on those reasons or because he has received an assurance that it would not be withdrawn before he had been given the opportunity of making representation against the withdrawal. The claimant's legitimate expectation arising from the regular practice or consultation which he could reasonably expect to continue gave rise to an implied limitation on the authority's exercise of the power.3

Thus for a legitimate expectation to arise the decision of the administrative authority must effect such person either (a) altering the rights or obligations of that person which are enforceable by or against him by private law, or (b) depriving him of some benefit or advantage which (i) he has in the past been permitted by the decision maker to enjoy and which he can legitimately expect to be permitted to continue to do until some rational ground for withdrawing it has been communicated to him and he has been given an opportunity to comment thereon, or (ii) he has received assurance from the decision maker that they will not withdraw without first giving him an opportunity or advancing reasons for contending that they should not be withdrawn. When a public authority has permitted to follow a certain procedure, it is in the interest of good administration that it should act fairly and should implement its promise so long an implementation does not fulfil.4 Ibid

The doctrine imposes a duty to act fairly. Of course, such promise or undertaking must not conflict with his statutory duty, or his duty, in exercise of a prerogative power. By declaring a policy, he does not preclude any possible need to change it, but then if the practice has been to publish the current policy, it would be incumbent on him in dealing fairly to publish from the new policy, unless again that would conflict with his duties. Had the criteria here needed changing for national security reasons no doubt the executive could have changed them. Had those reasons prevented him also from publishing the new criteria, no doubt he could have refrained from doing so. Had he even decided to keep the criteria but depart from them in a single case for national security reasons, no doubt those reasons would have afforded him a defense to judicial review.5

A mere reasonable or legitimate expectation of a citizen, in such a situation, may not by itself be a distinct enforceable right. But failure to consider and give weight to it may render the decision arbitrary, and this is how the requirement of due consideration of a legitimate expectation forms part of the principle of non-arbitrariness, a necessary concomitant to the rule of law. Every legitimate expectation is a relevant factor requiring due consideration in a fair decision-making process. Whether the expectation of the claimant is reasonable or legitimate in the context is a question of fact in each case. Whenever the question arises, it is to be determined not according to the claimant's perception but in the larger public interest wherein other more important considerations may outweigh what other method would have been the legitimate expectation of the claimant. A bonafide decision of the public authority reached in this manner would satisfy the requirement of non-arbitrariness and withstand judicial scrutiny. The doctrine gets assimilated in the rule of law and operates in the legal system in this manner and to this extent.6

For legal purposes, an expectation cannot be the same as anticipation. It is different from a wish, a desire or a hope nor can it amount to a claim or demand on the ground of a right. However earnest and sincere a wish, a desire or hope may be and however confidently one may look to them to be fulfilled, they by themselves cannot amount to an enforceable and a mere disappointment does not attract legal consequences. A pious hope even leading to a moral obligation cannot amount to a legitimate expectation. The legitimacy of an expectation can be inferred if it is founded on the sanction of a law or custom or an established procedure followed in regular and natural sequence. Again, it is distinguishable from a genuine expectation. Such an expectation should be justifiable, legitimate and protectable. Every such legitimate expectation does not by itself fructify into a right and therefore it does not amount to a right in the conventional sense.7

A change in policy can defeat a substantive legitimate expectation if it can be justified on Wednesbury reasonableness. The choice of the policy is for the decision maker and not for the court. The legitimate substantive expectation merely permits the court to find out if the change in the policy which is the cause for defecting the legitimate expectation is irrational or perverse or one which no reasonable person could make.8 In an English case it was held that a board's duty to act fairly was no more than a duty to decide the application honestly without bias or caprice. They were not under a duty to give their reason for refusing.9

There are different types of legitimate expectations: (a) the doctrine of legitimate expectation has no substantive effect; it merely gives protection against procedural unfairness; (b) the concept is used to refer to the claimant's interest in some ultimate benefit which he hopes to retain. It is the interest itself rather than the benefit that is the substance of the expectation. It existed only in public law by way of judicial review, but the claimant must apply for judicial review in time. If there is a requirement of procedural fairness it is superfluous to say that procedural fairness is a legitimate expectation. (Ibid) A procedure not otherwise required by law in the protection of an interest must be followed consequent upon some promise of practice.10

The elements of estoppel are generally claimed where there is a representation in any form, a declaration, act or omission, the representation must have been the existence of a fact, the representation must have been made under circumstances which amounted to an intentional causing or permitting belief in another, that is to say, the person must have believed the representation to be true and that person must have acted on the belief so induced and thus to change his former position to his prejudice. Lord Denning argued "the crown cannot escape by saying that estoppels do not bind the crown for that doctrine has long been exploded. Nor can the Crown escape by praying in aid the doctrine of executive necessity, that is, the doctrine that the Crown cannot bind itself to fetter its future executive action."11 This view was expressed following two earlier views.12 the above view was overruled in Howell v. Fallmouth Boat Construction Company13 case. It was observed, "When the Crown or any other person, is entrusted, whether by virtue of the prerogative or by Statute, with discretionary powers to be exercised for the public good, it does not when making a private contract in general terms, undertake and it may be that it would not even with the use of those powers, and in the exercise of the discretion."

Generally, a State is not subject to an estoppel to the same extent as an individual or private corporation. Otherwise, it might be rendered helpless to assert its power in government. Therefore, as a rule the doctrine of estoppel will not be applied against the State in its governmental, public or sovereign capacity. An exception however arises in the application of estoppel to the State where it is necessary to prevent fraud and manifest injustice.14

The government cannot divest itself the rights incidental to its office by conduct which in the case of a private person would amount to estoppel and in characterizing the demand of tax. The doctrine of estoppel cannot be allowed to impede the proper exercise of public of statutory functions by State or public authorities.15 in public law the most obvious limitation on the doctrine of estoppel is that it cannot be invoked to give an authority or powers which it does not in law possess. Estoppel within the meaning of the Evidence Act means (i) there must be a representation by a person or by his authorized agent to another in any form or declaration, act or omission; (ii) the representation must have been of the existence of a fact and not of promises de future or intention which might or might not be enforceable in contract; (iii) the representation must have been meant to be relied upon; (iv) there must have been belief on the part of the other party and in its truth; (v) there must have been action on the fate of that declaration, act or omission, that is to say, the declaration, act or omission must have actually caused another to act on the faith of it, and to alter his former position to his prejudice or detriment; (vi) the misrepresentation or conduct or omission must have been the proximate cause of leading the other party to act to his prejudice;

(vii) the person claiming the benefit of estoppel must show that he was not aware of the true state of things; if he was aware of the real state of affairs or had means of knowledge, there can be no estoppel; and (viii) only the person for whom the representation was made or for whom it was designed can avail himself of it. A person is entitled to plead estoppel in his own individual character and not as a representative of his assignee.15

This doctrine will apply in all civilized countries, that if a man, either by words or by conduct has intimated that he consents to an act which has been done, and that he will offer no opposition on it although it could not have been lawfully done without his consent, and he thereby induces others to do that from which they otherwise might have abstained, be cannot question the legality of the act he had so sanctioned, to the prejudice of those who have so given faith to his words or to the fair inference to be drawn from his conduct: generally speaking, if a party having an interest to prevent an act been done has full notice of its having been done, and acquiesces in it, so as to induce a reasonable belief that one consents to it, and the position of others is altered by their given credit to his sincerity he has no more right to challenge the act to their prejudice than he would have had it been done by his previous license. The above view expressed by the Judicial Committee of the Privy Council has been approved by our court.16

The Supreme Court of India later on after evaluation of all decisions from home and abroad summed up the doctrine as: (i) The key of promissory estoppel is not available against the exercise of the legislative functions of the State; (ii) the doctrine cannot be invoked for preventing the government from discharging its functions under the law; (iii) when the officer of the government acts outside the scope of his authority, the plea of promissory estoppel is not available. The doctrine ultra-vires will come into operation and the government cannot be held bound by the unauthorized acts of its officers; (iv) when the officer acts within the scope of his authority under a scheme and enters to an agreement and makes a representation and a person acting on that representation puts himself in a disadvantageous position the court is entitled to require the officer to act according to the scheme and the agreement or representation. The officer cannot arbitrarily act on his mere whim and ignore his promise on some undefined and undisclosed grounds of necessity or change the conditions to the prejudice of the persons who had acted upon such representation and put himself in a disadvantageous position; (v) the officer would be justified in changing the terms of the agreement to the prejudice of other party on special considerations such as difficult foreign exchange position or other matters which have a bearing on the general interest of the State.17

These are the established norms and doctrines on which a claimant can seek judicial review if his claim is refused by the authority in power. In Bangladesh it generally happens every year that during the rainy season the poor fishermen used to go to the deep sea for catching fish with trawlers and drowned due to cyclones and tides in the mighty Bay of Bengal. Innumerable fishermen lost their lives. Accordingly, the government stopped issuing of license for fishing in deep water with trawlers unless the trawlers are built with steal body based on an expert report submitted on May 20, 1997.

There was illegal catching of fish in the deep sea by Thai fishermen. The government seized many trawlers with wooden body used by the encroachers and ultimately published tenders for selling those trawlers in auction with the clear condition that no purchaser could claim any license for catching fish in deep sea water with those trawlers. The purchasers participated in the bids by filing affidavit that they would not claim license for fishing the in deep sea of the Bay of Bengal. Based on their undertaking, the authority sold the trawlers to them. Some of the purchasers sold the trawlers to third parties, some of them took loans from different commercial banks and renovated the trawlers at huge expenses and then they claimed license to the Mercantile Marine Department for catching fish in the deep water of the Bay.

Since the government had taken a policy of not allowing any wooden body trawler to exploit fish in the deep sea and in view of the undertakings given by them, the authority refused their claims in due course that led to filing of different writ petitions by the owners of those trawlers in the High Court Division. Some of them obtained interim orders from the High Court Division and managed temporary licenses for fishing in the deep sea. The government moved the apex Court against those orders. A seven-member Bench heard the matters18 and the court with Justice Mohammad Mozammel Hossain, the Chief Justice, Md. Abdul Wahhab Miah, Nazmun Ara Sultana, Syed Mahmud Hossain, Muhammad Iman Ali, Mohammad Shamsul Huda and I dismissed the appeals by a majority.

The majority opinion was written by Md. Abdul Wahhab Miah, who observed that it is not the government's case that "the fishing trawlers sold in the auction for any other purpose and definitely the writ petitioners did not purchase those for using them as firewood or as scrap. It is the writ petitioners' case that they have been repeatedly asking the writ respondents to give registrations and licenses to go for deep sea fishing and in support of their said case they had annexed their applications to the writ petitions. More so, when the writ petitioners specifically asserted in the writ petition that they had been engaged in deep sea fishing, and purchased the respective trawlers", they did so in violation of their undertakings and therefore, they were not entitled to any equitable relief in a court of law.

Is it enough to give relief on the doctrine of legitimate expectation? There is nothing in the pleadings in the writ petitions that the Mercantile Marine Department assured them of issuing licenses for fishing in the deep waters if they purchased the trawlers from the government in auction and renovated them. Save and except a mere statement that the claimants had acquired the right of legitimate expectation by purchasing the trawlers in auction, there is no other statement whatsoever in their respective writ petitions. It may be said that it is the mere perception that they would get license or had a wish or desire or a hope of getting a license. The majority opinion failed to note that it is a policy decision of the government that a wooden body trawler would not be allowed to catch fish in the deep sea. Moreover, in the tender document it was clearly spelt out that the trawlers to be sold could not be used in deep sea fishing. The purchasers also gave undertakings by affidavits that they would not claim any license for catching fish in the deep sea. These undertakings shielded them from claiming licenses for catching fish in the deep sea under the doctrine of estoppel. Further, the conditions attached to the tender documents that the purchasers could not claim any license for fishing in the deep waters which debarred them the right of legitimate expectation of getting a license for that purpose. They were not debarred to catch fish locally. This is the simple answer to the opinion expressed by the majority.

A person seeking judicial review must show that the decision of the authority deprived him of some benefit or advantage which in the past he had been permitted to enjoy and which he could legitimately expect to be permitted to continue to enjoy either until he was given reasons for its withdrawal or from the existence of a particular practice which he could reasonably expect to continue gave rise to an implied limitation on the authority's exercise of power. A mere representation will not generate an enforceable legitimate expectation. If there is a change in policy or position in the public interest by a rule or by legislation a question of legitimate expectation would not arise. A bonafide decision of the public authority would not satisfy the requirement of arbitrariness and withstand judicial scrutiny. Where the public authority represents that it will not act in a way unless the authority realizes from its representation it cannot give rise to a legitimate expectation because a legitimate expectation cannot be the same as anticipation.

The modern trend points to a judicial restraint in the administrative action. The court must guard against encroaching beyond its proper bounds, and more so since the only restraint upon it is self-restraint.19 It is not the function of a judge to act as a super board or with the zeal of pedantic schoolmaster substituting its judgment for that of the administrator.20 Therefore, there is no gainsaying that the majority opinion is based on numerical numbers other than the established norms and/or on the philosophy of law. These cases lead to the conclusion of pointing fingers at the lawyers that the standard of drafting of pleadings had deteriorated, and the judges administer justice at their whim.

References:

1. *J. Black's Law Dictionary*
2. *Sarad Chander Dey v. Gopal Chandra laha 19 IA 203; Bangladesh Parjatan Corporation v. Mofizur Rahman 46 DLR (AD) 44; Civil Service Union v. Minister for Civil Service (1984) 3 A11 ER 935; and Halsbury's laws of England, 4th Edition.*
3. *Attorney General of Hong Kong v. NG Yuen Shill, (1883) 346 (PC)*
4. *Ibid*
5. *R v. Secretary of State (1987) A11 ER 518*
6. *Food Corporation of India v. Kamdhenu Cattle Feed Industries Ltd. (1993) 1 SCC 71*
7. *Union of India v. Hindustan Development Corporation, AIR 1994 SC 988; Bangladesh Textiles v. Nasir Ahmed Chowdhury 7 MLR (AD) 265*
8. *Punjab Communications Ltd. v. Union of India, AIR 1999 SC 1801*
1. *Mclnnes v. Onslaw Fain (1978) 3 A11 ER 211*
2. *R v. Devon County Council, 1995 1 A11 ER 73*
3. *Robertson v. Minister of Pensions (1949) 1 KB*
4. *Rederiaktiebloget Amphitrite v. The King (1921) 3 KB 500 and Reilly v. The King (1934) AC 176 (179)*
5. *Howell v. Falmouth Boat Construction Co. 1951 AC 837*
6. *American Jurisprudence, second edition, para 123, page 783*
7. *Excise Commission v. Ramkumar, AIR 1976 SC 2237 and Wad, Adminstrative Law, 4th Edition*
8. *Jitram Shibkumar v. State of Haryana AIR 1980 SC 1285*
9. *Section 115 of Evidence Act and Chhaganlal v. Narayan Das, AIR 1982 SC 121*
10. *Government of Bangladesh v. Satellite Fisheries Ltd. Civil Appeal Nos. 127-138 of 2005*
11. *Trop v. Dulles, 2L Ed 630 356 US (1957) and Tata Cellular v. Union of India AIR 1996 SC 11*
12. *The Administrative Law by Bernard Schwartz, page-584*

Common Intention, Common Object, Culpable Homicide and Dying Declaration (G)

Common intention under section 34 of the Penal Code means, if two or more persons intentionally do an act jointly, it is just the same as if each of them has done it individually. Common intention requires a prior consent or pre-planning. It is the intention in the commission of the crime and the offender can be convicted if such an intention has been shared by all the accused. Such a common intention should be anterior in point of time of the commission of the crime but may also develop at the spot when such crime is committed. The constructive liability under this section would arise if (a) there is a common intention to commit a criminal act, and (b) there is participation of all the persons in committing such an act in furtherance of that intention. The expression "common intention" mentioned in section 34 of the Penal Code does not create a substantive offence while the expression "common object" prescribed in section 149 though creates a substantive offence, but law does not prescribe any separate sentence. Almost in all cases we commit mistakes in their application in a given case. To understand the application of section 34, we usually ignore sections 35, 37, 39 of the Penal Code. Common intention requires a prior consent or planning of doing an act jointly by two or more persons. It is very difficult to procure direct evidence of such intention and it must be inferred in most of the cases from the acts or conduct of the accused and such other relevant circumstances. Mere accompanying a person with an offender cannot infer common intention. Common intention is attracted only if an accused shared a common intention and not where they shared only similar intentions. It is only those who had participated in the crime that would be held responsible for its commission.

To attract the culpability under section 149 it must be borne in mind that this provision does not create a new offence but deals with vicarious liability of the members of the unlawful assembly for the acts done in prosecution of common object and for such offence as its members knew to be likely to be committed in the prosecution of that common object. This provision requires primarily that a person should be a member of an unlawful assembly, that in the prosecution of the common object of that assembly an offence should be committed by a member of that assembly, and that the offence should be of such a nature that members of the assembly knew the offence likely to be committed in prosecution of their common object. The first essential element of common object is the commission of an offence by any member of an unlawful assembly; the second essential part is that the offence must be committed in prosecution of the common object of the unlawful assembly or must be such as the members of that assembly knew to be likely to be committed in prosecution of the common object.1

Common object contains two parts. The first part of the section means that the offence to be committed in the prosecution of the common object must be one which is committed with a view to accomplishing the common object. In order that the offence may fall within the first part of the offence it must be of which the accused were members. Even if the offence committed is not direct prosecution of common object of assembly it may fall under section 149 if it can be held that the offence was such as the members knew was likely to be committed.2 Under this section, a person who is a member of an unlawful assembly is made guilty of the offence committed by another member of the same assembly, in the circumstances mentioned in the section, although he had no intention to commit that offence and had done no overt act except being present in the assembly and sharing the common object of that assembly.

Both sections 34 and 149 deal with constructive criminality. Section 149 besides containing a declaratory provision creates, unlike section 34, a distinct offence also. It is because the substantive offence under section 141 of the Penal Code of unlawful assembly is also involved in section 149. So, where specific charge is necessary to bringing an offender under section 149 that is not necessary in section 34. In respect of common object, a prior meeting of minds is not necessary, which is necessary in common intention that presupposes prior concert. Sometimes, common intention and common object overlap. In such cases as common intention is involved in common object, if there is charge under section 149, the omission of section 34 would not in any way prejudice the accused and so would not matter.

On the other hand, if they do not overlap conviction under section 34 without notice to the accused of constructive criminality would certainly be wrong if it would cause prejudice to the accused. Common intention presupposes prior consent and it requires a pre-arranged plan. There must have been a prior meeting of minds. Common intention differs from common object in that the latter does not require prior concert and a prior meeting of minds before the commission of the offence and can develop an unlawful object after the people get there. To convict persons vicariously under section 34 or section 149, it is not necessary to prove that every one of them had indulged in overt acts. But there must be material to show that the overt act or acts of one or more of the accused was or were done in furtherance of the common intention of all the accused or in prosecution of the common object of the members of the unlawful assembly. In case, such evidence is lacking the accused cannot be held liable for the individual act of anyone of them.3

Common intention is anterior in time to the commission of the crime. But common object speaks of an offence committed by any member of an unlawful assembly in prosecution of the common object of that assembly. The distinction is of vital importance. The aspects of the accused persons likely to cause that would be relevant under section 149 and not under section 34 for the obvious reason that under section 34 it has to be established that there was common intention before participation by the accused.4 These two sections have a some resemblance, but it cannot be said that both have the same meaning.5 In a charge under section 34 there is active participation in the commission of the act; under section 149 liability arises by reason of the membership of the assembly with a common object, and there may be no active participation at all in the perpetration or commission of the crime. Section 34 merely lays down a rule of law while section 149 creates a definite head of criminality. Common intention is the decisive test under section 34 but the common object of the members of the unlawful assembly is the basis of section 149. Participation in the criminal act is the gist of the offence under section 34 while membership of the unlawful assembly is the foundation of liability under section 149.

Section 35 does not create any substantive offence at all and no charge is required to be framed under this section. This section should be read with section 34, which also does not create any specific offence, but lays down the principle of constructive liability. Section 34 requires that there must be a general intention shared by all the persons concerned in the offence when several persons unite with a common purpose to do any criminal offence, all of those who assist in the accomplishment of the object would be equally guilty. Therefore, the provisions of Sections 34 and 35 are complementary, since, the principle embodied in section 35 supplements the principle embodied in section 34.

Section 34 deals with an act following a common intention while section 35 deals with an act following not joint but a like intention. It is limited to offences which are independent of intentional knowledge, that is, those cases which cannot be presumed but must be expressly proved. The accused has nothing to rebut until the prosecution has established criminal intention or knowledge on the part of each of the accused. Say for example, A and B beat C, because of which C dies. If it is proved that A and B had the common intention of killing C, they would both be liable for murder. However, if it is found that A had intended to kill C while B had intended to merely cause hurt, then A will be liable for murder and B will be liable for the injury caused by him according to the nature of the injury. So naturally their sentences will be different.

Sections 34 and 35 create responsibility for the total result of the acts by which the victim sustained grievous hurt or succumbed to injury. However, section 35 requires the existence of "knowledge or intent" on the part of each of the accused before he can be held liable provided that the knowledge or intention is necessary to execute the act criminal. If the criminal act is the result of a common intention, then every person who did the criminal act with the common intention would be responsible for the total offence irrespective of the share which each of them had in its perpetration. If section 35 is applied, then even if all the accused persons participated in the killing, they cannot be sentenced for the similar period. If the offender who participated in the killing did not have any intention to kill the victim, his sentence would be either under section 304 Part I or II or under sections 326 or 325 or 324 of the Penal Code, but if the person had the requisite intention to cause death, then his offence would attract section 302 of the Penal Code.6 Ibid

Sometimes courts distinguish between criminal knowledge and criminal intention done by several persons who join in the acts with such intention or knowledge. The responsibility is shared by each offender individually if the act which is criminal only by reason of certain criminal knowledge or intention is done by each person sharing that knowledge or intention.7 But irrespective of whether the acts done by the accused are similar or diverse, if they are not done in furtherance of common intentions, say, if one intends to cause death and the other intends to cause grievous injury, then there is no common intention of both the accused. Therefore, their offence and criminal liability will be different.

Homicide was in the earliest times regarded by common laws as an act so serious as to admit of no excuse and there were very few exceptions and no gradations of liability in the ancient doctrines under which a man was held strictly accountable for any death which could be traced to his active conduct. But over time and by a process not only have grounds of excuse been extended but various degrees of liability have been established in those cases where the killing of a man cannot wholly be excused. The result is that homicides now be distinguished as

a) Justifiable;
b) Excusable;
c) Murder;
d) Suicide;
e) Manslaughter;
f) Infanticide;
g) Child destruction.

The old maxim of homicide is "actus non facit reum nisi mens sit rea"8 has been most frequently cited as the fundamental requirement of criminal liability. Therefore, every case of homicide in common law must be examined to ascertain if each essential ingredient is present.

When this is done it will be found that much of the obscurity and confusion in which law of this matter is involved can be dissipated.9 Culpable homicide within the meaning of section 299 of the Penal Code contains three ingredients of causing death of a person, namely (a) with the intention of causing death; (b) with the intention of causing such bodily injury as is likely to cause death; and (c) with the knowledge that the offence is likely by such act to cause death. If any of the clauses attracts section 300, then it is culpable homicide amounting to murder. But if the answer is in the negative, the offence would be culpable homicide not amounting to murder punishable under the first or the second part of section 304 depending respectively on whether the second or third clause of section 299 is applicable. If the answer is found in the positive but the case comes within any of the exceptions enumerated in Section 300, the offence would still be a culpable homicide not amounting to murder.10

The Legislature has accepted the recommendation of Lord Macaulay and two other reports of Law Commission for addition of "Explanation 2" as justified adding "the meaning of the Commissioners we conceived to be is that, whereas in countries in which medical treatment is common, it is difficult to suppose that a person inflicting a slight wound on another could contemplate his death as a probable result, such a result may be supposed to enter into his contemplation in a country where bad medical treatment is far more common than good, and therefore, the definition of homicide ought not to exclude death resulting from a slight wound as the primary or original cause."11

In this connection I reproduced 'Explanation 2' for clarification. This explanation lays down that no man can be heard to say that he did not cause that death because it might have been prevented by resorting to proper remedies and skillful treatment. It is difficult to suppose that a person who has inflicted a slight wound on another could contemplate of death as a probable result, such a result may be supposed to enter his contemplation in a country where bad medical treatment is far more common than good, and, therefore, the definition of homicide ought not to exclude death from a slight wound as the primary or original cause. If the injury was so severe that, in the ordinary course, it was enough to cause death it is homicide. But if the injury was not mortal and death was due to other supervening causes, such as, gangrene or fever, brought by bad treatment, then the course would be justified in holding that the death was not due to the injury as its causa causans.12Without intervention of charge any circumstance where death is caused by bodily injury, the person who causes such bodily injury shall be deemed to have caused the death, although by resorting to proper remedies and skillful treatment the death might have been prevented.13***

Now taking the above principles in mind I will discuss a case14 Ibid in which some accused including accused Mamun assassinated Abul Kalam Peada at around 8:00 PM on August 23, 1999 at a tea stall while he was returning home from work. The trial court sentenced all the accused except one to death under sections 302/34 of the Penal Code. The High Court Division, however, commuted the sentence of Mamun, but maintained the sentence of life imprisonment of another accused, Khalil, who is also an appellant in the case under Sections 302/35 and 148 of the Penal Code. The High Court Division is of the view that the bodily injury inflicted by Mamun was not enough in the ordinary course of nature to cause death and all the accused cannot be grouped in one category as having intended the same result. However, the blow by Khalil on the chest of the victim attracts 'Thirdly' of section 300 of the Penal Code that is to say, the injuries were sufficient in the ordinary course of nature to cause death. The victim died in the hospital after eight days and the medical evidence showed that the victim sustained five injuries and the opinion was that the victim developed "gas gangrene" which caused the death.

According to medical jurisprudence14, "the remote causes of death operating secondarily from the injury amongst other are septic infection of wound causing septicemia or gangrene etc." The author observed that under the law in England remote causes of death due to injury are responsible, if they occur within a year and a day after the infection of the injury. If a secondary factor supervened the cause of death, then 'Explanation 2' of section 299 is attracted in the case. Therefore, it is not necessary to investigate whether clause 'Thirdly' of section 300 is attracted to the case. Or in the alternative, it is not necessary that there should be an appreciable passage of time between the formation of intent and the act of common intention taking place as it may be formed in the spur of the moment. The facts proved by the prosecution beyond doubt that the accused caused the injuries with an intention of causing grievous injuries which were likely to cause death. Therefore, the accused committed an offence punishable under Part-1 of section 304 of the Penal Code which provides that the act by which the death is caused is done with intention of causing death or such bodily injury as is likely to cause death. The High Court Division was wrong in altering the conviction of the accused under Sections 302/35 of the Penal Code.

In another case, 15 Mustafizur Rahman was done to death at 2:30 PM on May 7, 1996. Besides five eye witnesses, the victim himself made a dying declaration implicating six persons including five to seven unknown persons. The tribunal awarded death sentence to accused Tofael Ahmed alias Joseph and Kabil Sarker to life imprisonment. The High Court Division maintained the conviction and sentence relying upon the dying declaration and the ocular evidence. In course of hearing the counsel of the accused did not press an appeal on behalf of Kabil Sarker but pressed for commutation sentence of Tofael Ahmed Joseph claiming from the facts established by the prosecution, it is not a case for awarding death sentence to Joseph.

Sometimes lawyers appear in court upon superficial consideration of the materials or, though had considered the case minutely, could not find the point of law involved in the case. This leads the court to give proper attention while disposing of an appeal in which cessation of life or imprisonment for life is involved. It is the trend of the Bar, which has developed in around ten to twelve years, that they left the matter to the discretion of the court without taking pains of analyzing the evidence on record and the laws applicable in each case. So, the court gives proper attention in disposing of such cases taking in view that the apex court, being the final court, will settle the law points finally, and if it delivers a judgment based on the submission of the lawyer without looking at the law points involved in the matter, the courts subordinate to it including the High Court Division might be confused if the decision is not proper.

I noticed that the dying declaration of the victim Mustafizur Rahman was so clearly worded, structured and the way the declarant made the disclosure of the accused persons with such precision that it created a doubt as to whether the declaration was true and voluntary, or it was tutored one. The dying declaration appeared to me as one made by a normal person who had suffered no injury not to speak of being at a stage about to die. He stated that Masum shot at his leg with a .05 pistol. There was no inconsistency in the statement or dropping a word or two or the possibility of making moaning of utterances. If someone makes a dying declaration after sustaining an injury the tone should be half-articulate, babbling, broken or half-broken or repeated breaking or split. It is a condition precedent that the person or officer who records the statement must record all utterances of the declarant at the time of recording the statement. He should not record it in his own version or modify the version of the declarant for getting the correct meaning. The exact version of the maker should be left for the consideration of the court and it will decide on a bare reading of that statement along with other evidence on record as to whether it was the true version of the person. If the language of the recording officer is found in a clear narrative version, then the court may raise suspicions about the entire statement.

It is now settled that if the court believes the declaration is true, voluntary and free from being tutored, the court can base its conviction relying on it. In the case in hand, the evidence revealed that the parties were at loggerheads. If the declaration does not stand a normal test, it is far worse than an ordinary statement because the maker is not subjected to cross examination by the accused. Therefore, the court takes utmost care to rely upon such statement considering the facts and circumstances of a given case.

194

It is our common experience that people have a tendency of telling a lie and sometimes the victims make exaggerated statements implicating innocent persons with guilty one(s) to satisfy their sense of revenge. As the maker does not appear in the trial court, it is difficult for the court to infer whether the maker made the statement with the aid of someone else and it is also not clear the manner in which the maker receives a question and replies to it. The court, however, can assess the manner and demeanor of a witness who is cross examined in its presence and then after scrutiny believe the witness or discard the evidence of the witness. Only after the most scrutiny is applied to all physical circumstances as they appear from the evidence, is it possible to decide whether it can be said, with a degree of certainty which is made obligatory for reaching a conclusion of guilt, that account given by the maker of the way he met his death is worthy of belief. 16

In the matter of administration of criminal justice, taking in view the present state of our society, the assessment of evidence, whether the statement of a witness or a person who is dead, is essentially an exercise of human judgment to evaluate to find out what is true and what is false. Generally, in our country the habit, unfortunately now judicially recognized, that people do add innocent persons along with the guilty to satisfy their sense of revenge and to put the other side to the utmost grief. It is difficult to lay down a rigid rule that a person who is injured and is under an apprehension that meeting his death would suddenly be gifted, as if by a magic transformation, with a clean conscience and purity of mind to shed all age-old habits and deep-rooted rancor and enmities. Even assuming that the pangs of conscience are there at the time of making a false charge, the question arises whether this pangs are strong enough to fortify him to resist the promptings and persuasions of his relations and others who may be surrounding him at the time and incite him to support the pattern of the charge which they have chosen to make against the accused, whether innocent or guilty. It is for this reason, a scrutiny of dying declarations like the statements of interested witnesses become necessary. The maxim "falsus in uno falsus in omnibus" has all along been discarded by the court.17

I acquitted Kabil Sarker giving him the benefit of doubt, since, besides the dying declaration there were insufficient reliable evidence. However, I found accused Masum who is an FIR (First Information Report) named accused and the other witnesses also proved his involvement, but the High Court Division gave him benefit of the doubt and commuted Joseph's sentence on the reasoning that the victim died after 13 days of the occurrence and the medical evidence proved that the death was due to septicemia shock resulting from the bullet injuries. So, there is no doubt that a secondary cause intervened in the cause of death which developed after the operative treatment of the victim. Because septic shock is derivative from the noun septicemia, which means blood poisoning, especially caused by bacteria or their toxins. I could not but arrive at the conclusion that the injuries inflicted on him was not enough in the ordinary course of nature to cause the death in order to attract the clause "Thirdly" of section 300 of the Penal Code. Therefore, clause (b) to section 299 of the Penal Code is attracted in the case, that is to say, the injuries caused by Joseph be such that the deceased might die as a result of such injuries or the deceased might have survived if no secondary cause intervened. These two eventualities were probable. The word "likely" used in section 300 in the sense of more likelihood cannot be inferred from the facts proved. The use of the word likely may denote a lower degree of likelihood of death. It is in that sense the word likely is used to distinguish between the offence falling under section 302 and falling under section 304 of the Penal Code. There is higher degree of likelihood to cause the death because of the injuries caused by accused Joseph and thereby his act attracts Part 1 of section 304 of the Penal Code.

References:

1. Chikkarange Gowda v. State of Mysore, AIR 1956 SC 731
2. Devilal v. State of Rajsthan AIR 1971 SC 1444
3. Rambilash Singh v. State of Bihar AIR 1981 SC 193
4. William Slaney v. State of Maddhya Pradesh AIR 1956 SC 116; and Baredra Kumar Ghosh v. King Emperor AIR 1925 PC 1
5. Khalil Peada v. the State, Criminal Appeal Nos. 05-06 of 2010
6. Ibid
7. Ibid & Anda v. State of Rajsthan AIR 1964 SC 148

8. *A. Rallonale, Law of Homicide (1937) 37 Law Review 701 and 1261*
9. *Russell on Crime, 11th Edition, p 451*
10. *State of Andhra Pradesh v. VR Punnayya AIR 1977 SC 45*
11. *Penal Law of India, Dr Sir Hari Singh Gour, 11th Edition*
12. *Lord Hale, p 482*
13. *Ibid*
14. *Modi's Medical Jurisprudence*
15. *Criminal Appeal No. 51 of 2009 and 4 of 2010; Tofael Ahmed Joseph v. State*
16. *Abdur Razzak v. State 17 DLR (SC) 1*
17. *Tawab Khan v. State 22 DLR (AD) 130; and Nurjahan Begum v. State, 42 DLR 130*

Bar Council (H)

Must be kept pure and clean. It must be kept unpolluted. Administration of justice is not I came across a case1, the point in question in appeal was whether a judicial officer after holding a judicial office for a period of about ten years in subordinate courts can be permitted to practice in the district courts. A District and Sessions Judge is the highest office in the lower judiciary and on attaining the age of superannuation, he retires, but he is entitled to practice if he obtains a certificate from the Bangladesh Bar Council. Rule 65A (II) of the Bangladesh Legal Practitioners2 Code provides that a retired judicial officer is debarred from practicing before any subordinate court. But he can practice in the High Court Division. Annually about hundred judicial officers retire and enroll as advocates. Most of them live in their own district headquarters and they are practicing in the district courts, but because of the above Rules, they cannot practice. The said rule has been challenged by a former judicial officer. The High Court Division was of the view that this restriction is violation of Articles 31 and 40 of the Constitution.

The Bar Council is empowered to relax the rules for a lawyer to practice in the High Court Division for a period of two years if the applicant is called to the Bar in the UK or has obtained higher

197

second class in LL.M. or the applicant, holding a law degree, has held a judicial office for a total period of at least ten years. There is precondition that a lawyer is generally enrolled in the Bangladesh Bar Council to practice in the district court after obtaining a law degree certificate from a recognized law college or university. An arbitrary action can be proved by any person raising a plea and it can be done by showing that the action is uninformed by reason, in that there is no discernible principle on which it is based, or it is contrary to the prescribed mode of exercise of power. No doubt arbitrary power ordinarily violates equality; but it is simply not true that whatever violates equality must be arbitrary. The large number of decided cases, before and after Rayapppa, makes it obvious that many laws and executive actions have been struck down as violating quality without them being arbitrary.3

The question of arbitrariness in restricting former judicial officers to practice in the district courts does not arise. Rather by imposing such restrictions the Bar Council has performed the responsibility reposed in it with a view to maintaining the canons of ethics befitting an honorable profession. Article 31 guarantees the protection of law that no action detrimental to life, liberty, body or reputation or property shall be taken against any citizen except in accordance with law. The concept is akin to the due process clause contained in the Fifth and Fourteenth Amendment of the American Constitution. From the substantive point of view, a law is violative of Article 31 if it is demonstrably being unreasonable or arbitrary. It may be stated in another way: that a rule creating serious hardship shall be declared void on the ground of lacking unreasonableness. More clearly, a law shall pass the test of Article 31 if there is a rational relationship between the provision of the law and the legitimate governmental objective sought to be achieved.

The primary duty cast upon the court is to see the existing economic condition and the current values of society with reference to which reasonableness and fairness of law and procedure will have to be judged. The principle of equality does not mean that every law must have universal application to all persons who are not by nature, attainment or circumstance in the same position. There are varying needs of classes of persons often requiring separate treatment. Therefore, it cannot be said that all laws have not be made uniformly applicable to all people. Equality does not mean that the legislature is not competent to exercise its discretion or make classifications. This principle does not take away State power of classifying persons for legitimate purposes. A classification to be valid must rationally further the purpose for which the law is enacted4 to pass the test of constitutionality, the classification made in the legislation must satisfy that the classification is logically correct, that it must be founded upon some intelligible differentia which distinguish the persons or things grouped together from others left out of the group, and the differentia must have a rationale relation or nexus to the object sought to be achieved by the statute in question.5

The Bar Council has differentiated a person who held a judicial office for a period of ten years to be eligible for enrollment as an advocate in the High Court Division. The relaxation of conditions makes him a different class and after his enrollment he cannot be equated with another class of advocates who have not held a judicial office. A classification may be made on different bases according to objects, occupation or the like. A classification may be justified if it is not palpably arbitrary – it is real and substantial. If there is reasonable classification that may be treated as a class by itself.6

The case was challenged for violation of Article 40 of the Constitution, which guarantees freedom of occupation or trade or business, subject to any restriction by law. There is no doubt that every citizen is entitled to take any occupation or profession if he is qualified for the job. But it is circumscribed by restrictions. To claim a right under the rule the claimant must show, for instance, that rule 65A (II) violates his rights to practice his profession in the district court. A person can complain of a violation of fundamental rights if he can establish that the right claimed is a legal right, and it is a fundamental right. The Bar Council allowed them to practice in the High Court Division directly, a right which is denied to the other categories of advocates. It has not curtailed the rights of the applicants. They have not acquired any privilege or right to practice in the subordinate courts after retirement from service. The Bar Council restricts them on the assumption that in the subordinate courts their direct junior colleagues are administering justice and if they can practice in any subordinate court that would be unethical, undignified and prestigious. The officer who had worked with them is put in an embarrassing position when they would appear before him in a court. Among the main tasks of lawyers are not only professional but also public utility service. To manage the lawyers' ethical side and good conduct the Bar Council promulgated the Conduct Rules.7

The lawyers are a class in the society and trusted with the task of protecting the rights of the citizens and it can be achieved only if they respect the models of integrity, imbued with the spirit of public service and render their honorable responsibility in upholding the rule of law while maintaining dignity. Thereby the rights of the citizens will be secured. They are expected to contribute sufficiently toward the maintenance of rule of law and, therefore, they must maintain norms of correct conduct. An independent judiciary is the key to upholding the rule of law in a society. That independence may take a variety of forms across different jurisdictions and systems of law. Once citizens lose confidence in the fairness of the legal system, they may turn to other means to assert their basic rights and this inevitably results in violence and loss of human life.

Y.K Sabhawal, the former Chief Justice of India, in an article7 stated, "Cases of breach of professional conduct by the lawyers cannot be brushed aside as stray cases of aberration. Cumulatively, they have the effect of undermining the legal profession and eroding confidence of the public at large in the judicial administration and, therefore, a phenomenon that cannot be brooked. If allowed to snowball, misconduct by the legal community can lead us to anarchy that could threaten the continuity of rule of law. In the large interest of the doctrine of justice because of which, and for which, we exist." Lawyers, hence, must bear in mind that they are not mere legal craftsmen functioning to represent their clients, but their responsibility is also toward the larger economic development of society where the people's interest comes ahead of private interest.

Sabhawal again stated in another article, "The noble profession of law is founded on great traditions. It is not a business. It is a part of a scheme of a welfare State where the larger public good takes precedence over all narrow personal interests. Members of the legal profession are answerable to the social conscience of the society and have moral and social obligation towards that section of the society which is unable to protect its lawful interests. The Code of Conduct developed by the Bar Council reminds each member of the legal profession of his social responsibilities. Lawyers are duty-bound to contribute in a large measure in building a classless egalitarian social order so that the fruits of the goal of socio-economic justice reach the poorest of the poor and in this direction, they are expected to be driven by compassion and humanitarian approach so that they can collaborate with the State policy."

A lawyer owes a duty to be fair not only to his client, but also to the court as well as to the opposite party in the conduct of the case. Administration of justice is a stream which something which concerns the Bench only. It concerns the Bar as well. The Bar is the principal ground for recruiting judges. Nobody should be able to raise a finger about the conduct of a lawyer. Judges and lawyers are complementary to each other. The primary duty of the lawyer is to inform the court as to the law and facts of the case and to aid the court to do justice by arriving at the correct conclusions. Good and strong advocacy by the council is necessary for the good administration of justice. Consequently, the council must have freedom to present his case fully and properly and should not be interrupted by the judges unless the interruption is necessary.8

The Bar Council acts as the protector of the purity and dignity of the profession. The function of the Bar Council in entertaining a complaint against advocates is needed when the Bar Council has reasonable belief that there is a prima facie case of misconduct and a disciplinary committee is entrusted with the enquiry.9 "A glance at the Functions of the Bar Council, and it will be apparent that a rainbow of public utility duties, including legal aid to the poor, is cast on these bodies in the national hope that the members of this monopoly will serve society and keep to canons of ethics befitting an honorable order. If pathological cases of member misbehavior occur, the reputation and credibility of the Bar suffer mayhem and who, but the Bar Council is more concerned with and sensitive to this potential disrepute the few black sheep bring about? The official heads of the Bar i.e. the Attorney General and the Advocates General too are distressed if a lawyer 'stoops to conquer' by resort to soliciting, touting and other corrupt practices."10

The professional ethics and conduct of an advocate cannot adhere to a stroke or be maintained by a former judicial officer after being enrolled as an advocate if he can appear before a subordinate officer who had worked under him. If he appears before a subordinate officer the public perception toward him would erode, and if such an advocate attempts to gain any special consideration, the judge would hesitate to review matters. That is why the judges of the High Court Division have been restricted to practice in the High Court Division. The question is if a judge of the High Court Division after retirement appears before a judge who worked in the same Bench under him, people's perception toward him might not be respectful, even if he makes any order in favor of such a lawyer in accordance with the law.

Some interesting cases presented themselves to me11 which were heard analogously along with the above matter. Professor Munirul Haque claimed to be the Vice-Chancellor of Darul Ihsan University while Professor Akbaruddin Ahmed claimed for a direction upon the government to appoint him as the Vice-Chancellor of the said university. Professor Dr Rahmat-E-Khuda was appointed the Vice-Chancellor of the said university and his appointment was challenged by another group. Dr. Saifullah Islam claiming to be the Vice-Chancellor also sought a direction to appoint him the Vice-Chancellor of the said university. The university was opened on various campuses in Dhaka City, Savar and Uttara Residential Model Town. It was rumored that the university was not adhering to the education programs in accordance with the guidelines given by the University Grants Commission and opened different outer campuses and was indulging in selling bachelor's and master's certificates in different subjects. The Bangladesh Bar Council did not recognize the graduation certificates in law for the enrollment of some students in the preliminary test examination, and that led to the filing of another writ petition seeking direction upon the Bangladesh Bar Council to allow them to sit the exam.

The petitions were filed on behalf of Savar group, Dhanmondi group, Ashulia group and Uttara group, that is to say, different persons opened universities in different locations of the country in the same name and issued certificates in law in exchange of money. The old law12 was repealed and replaced by a new law13. Under the new law, a private university is required to obtain temporary license for the operation of an educational curriculum and such a license cannot be extended beyond seven years with precondition that if any university is established in Dhaka and Chittagong it must own at least one acre of land and outside the city the university must own two acres of land. Darul Ihasan was initially a trust in Dhanmondi and operated at the Dhanmondi campus.

A great academic jurist14 had wanted to set up the legitimacy of judicial governance. According to him, present day judges who may have had nothing to do with written a constitution when it was framed but by reason of their position as judges should become and must act like partners of the framers of the constitution- because a constitution is an ongoing project and will always be an ongoing project-to interpret a historical document in the best possible light. He invoked the idea of constitutional convention of democracy wherein judicial review occasioned by a charter of rights ensures the democratic pedigree of legislation by benchmarking the values found in the content of law, rather than in the process of law making. 'Judicial activism' and 'judicial review' remarked, 'All judicial review – all manner of adjudication by courts – is itself an exercise in judicial accountability – accountability to the people who are affected by the judge's rulings (if punitive contempt power is kept in check). That accountability is evidenced in critical comments on judicial decisions when judges behave as they should (as moral custodians of the Constitution); the function they perform enhances the spirit of constitutionalism.' Some of our modern-day judges – whether in India or elsewhere – do not always realize the solemnity and importance of the functions they are expected to perform. The ideal judge of today, if he is to be a constitutional mentor, must move around, in and outside the court, with the Constitution in his pocket, like the priest who is never without the Bible (or the Bhagavad Gita). Because, the more you read the provisions of our Constitution, the more you get to know how to apply its provisions to present-day problems.15 "That sometimes some men and women who sit on the Bench are not conscious of the extent (or limits) of such power, or do not have the sensivity to exercise judicial restraint when warranted, only means that those few men and women are just not equal to the supremely difficult task of judging entrusted to them under the Constitution. It only indicates that perhaps it is time we adopted a better method of selection of judges for our higher judiciary.16]

While exercising power of judicial review it is to be borne in mind that the test of reasonableness, whenever prescribed, should be applied in each individual Statute impugned and no extra standard or general pattern of reasonableness can be pattered in reasonableness can be laid down by the court. The nature of right alleged to have been infringed – the purpose of restriction imposed, the extent an urgency of evil sought to be remedied thereby, this proportion of the imposition – the prevailing condition at the time should all enter the judicial mind. In evaluating circumstances of the given case, it is inevitable to see that the social philosophy and scale of values of the judge's participation in the decision should play an important part and the limit of their interference with legislative judgment in such cases only be directed by their sense of responsibility and self-restraint. To judge the quality of reasonableness no abstract or a fixed principle can be laid down for universal application. This will vary from case to case. In delivering a judicial verdict, the court is required to observe the changing conditions, the value of human life, social philosophy of the Constitution and prevailing conditions. The court should not take a rigid or dogmatic but an elastic and pragmatic approach to the facts of the case and the issues in the situation.17

A vital philosophical point surfaced when matters relating to Darul Ihsan University were heard. There was total restriction on various students in appearing in the Bar Council examinations. If leave is granted the disposal of the appeal would take years and it would hamper the career of a huge number of students. Since all the parties were present, I opted to hear the matters summarily. It was also submitted at the Bar that admission of students in LL.B. honors course in some universities was withheld. The syllabus and number of students admitted in a private university and the enrollment process of advocates in the Bar Council remained stagnant. Under the circumstances the lawyers who appeared on behalf of the other universities including the Attorney General wanted the matters to be disposed of summarily.

There was a demand from a section of lawyers that the court should stick to the age limit of the applicants to become advocates. This submission was made taking into consideration that if a person after being removed from service on moral turpitude is entitled to enroll as advocates under the existing law, he will undermine the noble profession, and this will erode the confidence of the people in judicial administration. The question was whether a court can debar a person who having obtained an LL.B. degree left the country and failed to face the Bar Council. Is it desirable for the court to debar him from facing the Bar Council in the absence of any law after staying abroad for 30 years? In this connection the lawyers argued that in India the State Bar Councils prescribed the age limit of 45 years for enrollment in the Bar. The Supreme Court quashed the said age limit on the reasoning that this cannot be done because many people enrolled as lawyers after retirement.

There have been paradigm shifts over the last two and half decades in the socio-economic condition of the country. This has also contributed to new challenges for the judges and lawyers. However, considering the mammoth changes that have taken place, hardly any change has been injected in the body of the legal profession and legal education in Bangladesh to cope up with the new challenges in legal practice. Historically, and at least up to the time of market liberalization in Bangladesh, the legal profession was largely based on typical civil disputes (almost all relating to land litigation) and criminal disputes (almost all relating to classic offences as covered by penal statutes), but now the horizon of legal practice had flourished into new dimensions where the old-fashioned attitude in resolving modern legal dispute is measurably inadequate and outdated.

The concept of citizens' rights has entered a new era; the courts are coming up with creative interpretations of constitutional rights; young, talented and highly educated judges are offering new notions of rights and remedies; corporate lawyering and corporate legal responsibility (including intellectual properties) is completely a new field of practice. And of course, this digital age has posed to us entirely a new phenomenon of legal challenges including forensic evidence which has already revolutionized law and legal practices. All these new challenges are already surrounding our society and we urgently need several brilliant lawyers and judges who can face these new challenges and ensure a stable society. To comprehend all these new symptoms of legal development and to ensure a judiciary which understands the sensitivity of the people and the demands of the modern age we need lawyers and judges who possess an inexhaustible spirit of fighting evil with an indestructible commitment to the establishment of rule of law in society.

Toward the late 1960s and 1970s, there had been a vibrant and healthy nexus between lawyers and the legal education institutions. But these days much is lacking in this regard. Many highly reputed lawyers used to regularly teach in universities and law colleges. This connection is now almost non-existent unfortunately. A good practice has died, but it should not preclude us from attempting to create new practices. Legal academia and legal profession must have a very close tie; it is the demand of the time because the legal profession in Bangladesh is now at a crossroads. The veteran lawyers and judges are retiring or are absent from the courts due to old age. But the indications from emerging lawyers who are supposed to replace them are not always greatly promising. A crisis in legal genus is looming near the horizon of our country

Already there is much depletion in the standard of lawyers practicing all over the country. Due to socio-economic changes, except a few, lawyers are now more money-driven rather than knowledge-driven. In many cases we find severe dearth of evidence in pleadings related to the points at issue. Many have been seen conducting cases with deplorable levels of superficial knowledge about facts and applicable laws relating to the case. The result is disastrous; final verdict goes against the party having three previous judgments in his favor due to sheer incompetency of his counsel. Similarly, in criminal matters prosecutors conducting he prosecution cannot even lead relevant evidence to prove the charge and sometimes it so happens that the counsel appearing for the defense rectifies the defects of the prosecution by cross examination or offering suggestions to the witness! If university teachers can practice in the court the Bar will be enriched because they not only teach law but also do research in that field. Legal academia and legal practitioners together will have to contribute in reshaping our collective conscience of jurisprudence capable of catering to the new legal challenges surfacing due to rapid changes in local and global economy and cutting-edge technology.

These have more to do with decent society than the rule of law. For instance, judicial enforcement of rights by courts does not necessarily guarantee public understanding and support for those rights; such understanding and/or awareness needs to be inculcated and can only be achieved through education. And if lawyers are to be educators, they must be trendsetters inspiring public confidence.18 "But the (Englishman) will now say lawyers are idiots. He may say they are too expensive. He may say they are too wealthy. But he will, and does, respect them. The law may fall into disrepute, but lawyers do not, unless they themselves create the circumstances in which they can become disreputable."19 He expressed his anxiety about the profession of law in developed countries and said, "Their position is servants of society." Those days are gone and if we do not rethink over the matter and look at our predecessors in the profession, about their etiquette and behavior, I believe we will face disastrous consequences since everywhere politicians are out to grab power leaving aside principles, political science, humanity and good governance. It is only the lawyers who can be saviors in this milieu. There is therefore an urgent need to rediscover and reaffirm the profession's moral foundation that will help refurbish its image. These are issues which should be investigated by the elected bodies of Bar Councils and it is not an issue for the court to decide; it may only express an opinion in this regard.

The Bar Council has a significant role to oversee the standard of law education in public and private universities as well as in law colleges so that law degrees are conferred properly. It must also see as to whether the universities and colleges are teaching law students suitably and whether they have qualified teachers for undertaking such education because ultimately these law graduates will become judges and lawyers. We have been noticing for a considerable period that the new entrants in the profession from the universities and law colleges, with some exceptions of course, are performing at a very poor standard. This is due to lack of proper education and training. We hope that the Bar Council shall prescribe/give guidelines to all the universities and colleges teaching law subjects and conferring law degrees on students. It should compel them to follow the syllabus on subjects to be taught, which should be uniform, and in case of violation, it would not recognize the law degree of such an institute. If it cannot restrict the recognition of those students who have obtained law degree from universities and colleges which do not teach basic law subjects and have no permanent qualified teachers on all subjects of law, the standard of law graduates will continue to decline.

There are allegations that Darul Ihsan University and some other private universities have set up campuses in remote areas and they are involved in selling law graduation certificates in exchange of money. This type of allegation should be taken up most seriously and violators should be brought to justice. It is the high time for the Bangladesh Bar Council to frame rules in accordance with Article 40(2) (t) with prior approval of the government to oversee the standard of legal education being given by the universities and colleges. In the absence of appropriate Rules, it is not desirable to interfere in the internal management of the universities and colleges. Such conditions may be attached in accordance with Article 27(1) (D) of P.O.46 of 1972. I have also given some guidelines to be followed by the Bar Council and the universities.21

References:

1. *Civil Appeal No. 235 of 2014 with Civil Petition Nos. 276-2764, 2777-2779, 2498-2880, 3016-3570, 3577 and 2873 of 2016, Bangladesh Bar Council v. AKM Fazlul Karim*
2. *The Bangladesh Legal Practitioners and Bar Council Rules, 1972*
3. *HM Seervai, Constitutional law of India, page-437*
4. *Massachussetes Boar of Retirement of North Georgia, (1976) 427 US 307*
5. *SA Sabur v. Returning Officer, 41 DLR (AD) 30; Ramkrishna Dalmia v. Justice Tendulkar, AIR 1958 SC 538*
6. *Maneka Gandhi v. India AIR 1978 SC 597; Romana Shetty v. International Airport Authority AIR 1979 SC 1628; Ajoy Hashia v. Khalid Mujib AIR 1981 SC 487; DS Nakara v. India AIR 1983 SC 130; AL Kalra v. P & E Corporation of India AIR 1984 SC 1361*
7. *Bar Council Canons of Professional Conduct and Etiquette*
8. *Role of Bar in a Democracy*
9. *P.D Gupta v. Ram Murti, AIR 1998 SC 283*
10. *Bar Council v. Debholkar, AIR 1975 SC 2092*
11. *Justice Krishna Iyer*
12. *IBIB Writ Petition (CP Nos. 276-2764 of 2016)*
13. *The Private University Ain of 1992*
14. *The Private University Ain of 2010*
15. *Roland Dowkin, Law's Empire 1986*
16. *Before Memory Fades, Fali S. Nariman*

17. *Chief Justice Sir Edward Coke, Remade regarding the powers of the court to correct errors and misdemeanors and also all manner of misgovernment.*
18. *Pathumma v. Kerala, (1978) 2 SCR 537*
19. *Predman, Law of Justice (1999), Sweet and Maxwell*
20. *Before Memory Fades, Lord Leslie Scarman, NZ*
21. *Guidelines**

Impact of Commercialization (I)

My long association with the legal fraternity, both as lawyer and judge, has led me to believe that about 60 percent of the litigants lose their case due to improper conduct, lack of knowledge or negligence or corruption of the lawyers of the parties. Law is a subject which must be perceived in clear conception. Law is the enterprise of subjecting human conduct to governance by rules. Unlike most modern theories of law, this view treats law as an activity and regards a legal system as the product of a sustained purposive effort, 1 We must understand that many of its characteristic problems are moral in nature. We need to put ourselves in the place of the judge faced with a statue extremely vague in its operative terms yet disclosing enough in its preamble and objective the judge considers plainly unwise. If we attempt to offer a neutral concept of law, we find that "rule of law" simply means "existence of public order". It means organized governments, operating through various instruments and channels of legal command. In this sense, all modern societies live under the rule of law---fascists as well as socialist and liberal states.2 It is perfectly obvious that a system of legal rules may lose its efficacy if it permits itself to be challenged by lawless violence. Sometimes violence can only be restrained by violence. Hence it is quite predictable that there must normally be in society some mechanism ready to apply force in support of the law in case it is needed. But this no sense justifies treating the use or potential use of force as the identifying character of law. Modern science depends heavily upon the use of measuring testing apparatus; without such apparatus it could not have achieved what it has. But no one would conclude on this account that science should be defined as the use of apparatus for measuring and testing. So, it is with law. It is precisely when the legal system itself takes up weapons of violence that we impose on it the most stringent requirement of due process. This body of law is administered with integrity and in case of disputes, is interpreted and applied by the courts. If an infraction is established the State, pursuant to court order, levies a fine in the form of a deduction from the traders as deposit.3

If we look at the motives of litigation or what motivates litigation and delays, the larger goal being justice delivery, an analysis of the problem will reveal that as a primary area by reason of a shortcoming in our legal education system, enough attention is not paid to the distinction between fact, law, and application of law. The term "fact" has a variety of meanings.4 It may signify a state of things, i.e. an existence or a motion; an event or incident or occurrence; and act, action or deed; a thing done; an effect produced or achieved; a reality as distinguished from supposition or opinion; a truth as distinguished from fiction. Facts can be both physical and psychological. All rights and liabilities depend on and arise out of facts.

The idea of law to Kant's practical reason is the realm of purposes realized by volition. Stammer concludes his opinion.5 (a)] Just law is the highest universal point in every study of the social life of men; (b) it is the only thing that makes it possible to conceive, by means of an absolutely valid method, of social existence as a unitary whole; (c) it shows the way to a union with all other endeavors of a fundamental character which aim likewise at right consciousness; the concept of law gives the formal and universal elements of law. The idea of law directs all possible means and purposes towards one aim, i.e. to say; (i) The community of purposes; (ii) The fact that man, as a reasonable being is an end in himself.

Law can be classified into two parts, i.e. substantive and procedural. In the broad sense, substantive law may be defined as those rules and standards of general application by which the State regulates human affairs; i.e. defines the rights and duties of

211

citizens. The part which deals with procedures for enforcing those rights and duties and is designed to manage ongoing litigation is called procedural law. Briefly, law means the one which is laid down by legislature as Statute or by the course of time as common law or any custom or usage, having the force of law.6 There is an interlink between (a) questions of fact; (b) questions of law, (c) mixed questions of facts and law. We study law, get a degree, follow it up with enrollment and enter the legal profession. To earn money within the four corners of ethics is a career goal. For a long time, the judiciary very strongly believed that there is need for any education. The idea of judicial education around the world anthemic to the role of a judge itself. What they had already studied in law colleges and universities and then moved on to carry it into legal practice was more than sufficient for them to be judges. Then, following the efforts of the United States and other parts of the world, the situation underscored the importance of creating and developing programs for the judiciary. If you look at the University College in London, they have established what is known as a UCL judicially institute and an important research center, which brings to the forefront be importance of research and capacity building for the judicial process. This is inextricably connected to training and development that is needed for members of the judiciary. We know that law is a dynamic discipline and not constant; and if this dynamism of law must be brought within the judicial system, it is necessary that judicial education needs to move beyond the judicial academies and should go into law schools. In fact, there are now very innovative programs that are being implemented around the world.

A plot of land with a building located at Gulshan, a very posh area of capital Dhaka City, was taken on lease from RAJUK by Inge Flatz, an Austrian citizen married to a Pakistani. The house was leased to Barrister Moudud Ahmed in 1981. She also executed a power of attorney to look after the property. The property was declared abandoned in 1972 and the Austrian government wanted to get the property released without success. In June 1984, Inge Flatz executed a power of attorney in favor one Mohsin Darbar empowering her with all powers of sale etc. The said attorney executed an agreement for sale of the property with Manzur

Ahmed, elder brother of Barrister Moudud Ahmed. Manzur Ahmed filed a suit for specific performance of the contract, 7 and the suit was ultimately dismissed. On appeal in the High Court Division, the appellate court decreed the suit and directed the government to execute and register the sale deed.

When the matter came up before the apex court, 8 various complicated questions arose. On behalf of the government some documents were filed showing that Ms. Flatz died on March 30, 1985 before the institution of the suit. It was claimed by the government that Mohsin Darbar, Inge Flatz's attorney, a fake person and the agreement for sale and the power of attorney were also forged. No consideration was paid to Inge Flatz and, therefore, the suit and the decree were nullity. Manzur Ahmed claimed that the documents produced at the late stage of the proceeding were not admissible in evidence and the court should not take cognizance of them, even if it is found that Inge Flatz had died. It was further claimed that Manzur Ahmed should be given an opportunity to take legal steps for substitution and the case should be remanded to the trial court. Various other complicated questions of law were also raised about the abandoned character of the property and some other related points.

On perusal of record I noticed that no service of summons of the suit was served upon Ms. Flatz at any point of time. A summon was sent through the Bangladesh embassy to Austria and it was reported that Inge Flatz had died long ago. On behalf of Manzur Ahmed an application for substitution of the heirs of Ms. Flatz was filed on September 25, 1994. So Manjur Ahmed acknowledged the death of Ms. Flatz. But instead of taking proper steps, proceeded with the suit and ultimately based on an application made for the substituted service of summons, the court allowed the prayer on September 28, 2009. Even after the dismissal of the suit, Manzur Ahmed filed an appeal against Inge Flatz, a dead person in the High Court Division. Inge Flatz had died leaving her husband Ehsan and a son, but subsequently she divorced her husband.

Documents in support of the death were: a) an inheritance declaration filed in the district court in Brengenz dated April 01,

1985 by her son Karim Franz Solaiman and the court accepted the prayer; b) the minutes of the treaties dated September 26, 1985 which were permitted by the court; c) renouncement of the inheritance of the widower Mohammad Ehsan stating that he had no claim over the property of Inge Flatz on April 01, 1985. These were documents relating to the final decision in the hereditary proceedings. Besides those papers, some other documents were produced, such as: a letter written by judge of the district court Bregenz dated September 05, 2012 intimating the Attorney General that Inge Flatz died on March 30, 1985 with other of her date of birth, her marital status, her residence and the property at Gulshan. These were certified copies of the court supplied by the judge along with a death certificate, which were duly notarized by the Notary Public authenticated by the Bangladesh Embassy in Bonn, Germany. These papers clearly showed that Ms. Flatz died on March 30, 1985. But the suit was instituted on January 23, 1993. The death of Inge Flatz was also admitted by Manzur Ahmed and he filed an application on December 30, 2005 in the High Court Division for amendment of the plaint making the government the principal defendant in the suit so that the principal defendant, i.e. the government may be directed to execute a sale deed in his favor in the absence of Inge Flatz.

Under the Evidence Act, 10 there is provision prescribing the mode of proving the contents of various official documents, public acts, proceedings of legislature, etc. Clause (6) of Section 78 relates to the proof of any other documents of any other class in a foreign country "by original", or by a copy certified by the legal keeper thereof, with a certificate under the seal of a Notary Public, or of a Bangladesh Consul or diplomatic agent, certified by the officer having the legal custody of the original, and upon proof other character of the document according to the law of the foreign country. A public document in a foreign country should be certified by the legal keeper of the original documents, or of a Consul General and there shall be proof of the character of the document according to the law of the foreign country. These copies were duly certified by the keeper of the documents with certificates under the seal of a Notary Public. This clause lays down three conditions for admitting public documents of this nature, but the admission of judicial record is not a condition precedent for drawing the requisite presumption under Section 86 of the Evidence Act. Except the birth and death certificates, other documents are from the judicial record. In the hereditary proceedings, the date of death of Inge Flatz had been mentioned as "30.03.1985" and this date corroborates the date mentioned in the death certificate, which is also a public document. Therefore, conditions laid down in Clause (6) of Section 78 have been fulfilled and there is no legal bar to admit them in evidence.

When a document, whether private or public, has been filed for admittance in evidence, the court may draw an inference for certain facts in supersession of any other mode of proof.11 That inference will remain as proved until contrary is proved by the opponent. A copy of the judgment certified by the legal keeper of the original within the meaning is that under section 78(6) of the Evidence Act, three conditions must be complied with before a document can be admitted in evidence. A foreign document may be proved by the original or a certified copy to be certified by the legal keeper with a certificate by a Notary Public or of a diplomatic office of Bangladesh to the effect that the copy is certified by the legal keeper of the original, upon proof of the character of the document. If these conditions are fulfilled, the document may be presumed to be genuine and accurate. A perusal of section 78(6) of the Evidence Act makes it clear that apart from the two certificates – one from the legal keeper of the original documents and the other from the Consul General – there shall also be proof of the character of the document according to the law of the foreign country before the document is admitted. It is a condition precedent.

Proof can also be given by placing before the court facts giving rise to presumptions, rebuttable or irrefutable. Section 86 of the Evidence Act lays down that a court may presume the genuineness and accuracy of any document purporting to be a certified copy of any judicial record of any foreign country if such a copy is duly certified in the manner and according to the rules in use in the country for certification of copies of judicial records. To give rise to this presumption, it is not necessary that the judgment of the foreign country should have already been admitted in evidence.

While section 78(6) of the Evidence Act lays down three conditions for admitting the judgment in evidence, the admission of the judicial record is not a condition precedent for drawing the requisite presumption under Section 86 of the Evidence Act. The presumption may be drawn before the said record is admitted.

To ascertain whether there is the requisite certificate, viz., a certificate issued by any representative of the Central Government in the country concerned to the effect that the said document was certified in the manner commonly in use in that country for the certification of copies of judicial records. The requisite certificate makes the document admissible and not vice versa. If it is presumed to be genuine and accurate, it shows its character, viz., it is a genuine judgment made by the court. If the three conditions laid down in section 78(6) of the Evidence Act are fulfilled, the document can legitimately be admitted in evidence, and if it is admitted, the document by its own force establishes that the aforesaid three conditions for the enforceability of the awards have been fulfilled.12

The mode of proof of public documents mentioned in section 78 is permissive and, therefore, the court is not precluded from having other modes of proof. A public document may be proved by production of the original or by a certified copy under section 77 or in the manner prescribed in section 78. A foreign judicial record is a public document and may be proved by a copy certified in the manner prescribed by sections 78(6) and 86 of the Evidence Act.13 Documents regarding the death of Inge Flatz are relating to the judicial proceedings, except the birth and death certificates, but all those documents have been issued by the keeper thereof duly authenticated by the Notary Public and attested by the Embassy of Bangladesh. As regards the birth and death certificates, these are clearly written in English and public documents. The date of death of Inge Flatz has also been mentioned in the hereditary proceedings. Besides, the letter issued by the District Court of Bregenz was also in English. The Judge of the District Court of Bregenz clearly mentioned that Inge Flatz died on March 30, 1985 leaving a son and husband. This English-language letter was also duly countersigned by the president of the court and also attested by the embassy. This date tallies with the date mentioned in the death certificate which is also in English and in the original death certificate it was also written in different languages including English.

In a suit for specific performance, which is also based on contract in view of section 23 of the Specific Relief Act, which provides that the specific performance of a contract may be obtained by "the representative in interest for the principal..." Representative in interest includes alien, transferee or legal representatives after death. Each of them may sue or may be sued for specific performance of the contract provided that the contract is not dependent on the learning, skill, solvency or any personal quality of such contracting party, or there are no terms in the contract that his interest shall not be assigned. Under the above rule, a suit ordinarily abates only against the deceased defendant, unless there are circumstances which would cause an abatement as against one to operate as abatement against all.

Order 22, Rule 4(3) of the Code of Civil Procedure lays down in express terms that if no application is made, the suit would abate in so far as the interest of the deceased is concerned. If the court can deal with the matter in controversy so far as regards the right and interest of the plaintiff or the defendant, other than the deceased defendant, it shall proceed with the suit and decide it. The heirs of the deceased defendant, who are not party to the suit, will not be bound by the decree and, in that sense, the decree will not be effective against the heirs. If an effective decree can be passed against the other defendants, the whole suit cannot abate. The question of abatement of the whole suit depends on whether the defendant was such a necessary party that his absence would result in the dismissal of the whole suit. However, if the deceased was a proper party the suit would not abate as a whole. It depends upon the facts of each case.14

The suit being specific performance is nullity in the eyes of the law since Inge Flatz died before the institution of the suit. Even if the suit is remanded no fruitful purpose would be served, because the main defendant died before the filing of the suit with knowledge to

Manzur Ahmed. Suit not abated but itself is a nullity. I was stunned on noticing how a lawyer like Barrister Moudud Ahmed with hordes of veteran lawyers conducted the suit from the beginning had failed to rectify the defects in the trial court. He lost the property, a very valuable one for badly conducting the matter and misconception of law. However, as noticed, the way Barrister Moudud Ahmed was evicted from the house was inhuman and against all canons of law. He was not even afforded an opportunity to remove his valuable articles. He has been residing in the house for a long time. It seemed that though the judgment of the apex court was not a politically motivated one, the conduct of the government proved that it was politically motivated. A more deplorable part of the government's action was that just within seven days of the eviction, the land was handed over to the police department for residential purposes, although the police department had been given more than 100 acres of land at Purbachal contiguous to Bashundhara and Jamuna Future Park. There are other agencies which have no accommodation at all. The higher judiciary has no training academy which a demand of the day is. But the government preferred the police's accommodation was more preferential than a National Judicial Training Academy.

References:

1. *Morality of Law, Lon L. Fuller, page 106*
2. *Law and Social Change (1951), Professor Friedman, page 281*
3. *The Morality of law*
4. *Section 3 of the Evidence Act, 1872*
5. *Article 152 of the constitution*
6. *Theory of Justice by Stammler*
7. *The suit number: 179 of 1999*
8. *Civil Appeal No. 81 of 2004, Chairman RAJUK v. Manzur Ahmed*
9. *Order 5, Rule 20 of the Code of Civil Procedure*
10. *Section 78 of the Evidence Act*
11. *Sections 79-90 of the Evidence Act*
12. *Badat & C v. East India Trading Company AIR 1964 SC 538*
13. *Haranund Chetlangia v. Ramgopal Chettangia*

Tenancy Law (J)

Tenancy laws were promulgated by the British Parliament for securing its interest in the colonies and to realize rent from the citizens in possession. Different tenancy laws were applicable in our country. The most well-known law was the Bengal Tenancy Act, 1885 which was applicable to entire Bengal except Sylhet, where the Sylhet Tenancy Act was applicable. After the partition two laws in succession were promulgated by the government with the help of British drafters; one was The Non-Agriculture Tenancy Act, 1949 applicable to municipal areas and The State Acquisition and Tenancy Act, 1950 which is applicable to cultivable lands. By these statues, the Zamindari and Talukdari systems prevailing in the country were abolished on payment of compensation and annuities to the owners. The status of the "raiyots" was upgraded to "maliks" (owners). The peasants from the rural areas flocked to the cities mainly to cosmopolitan cities because they could not get proper price of their produce. Instead they preferred the work of pulling rickshaws, opened shops as street vendors and in this way the cities were crowded with huge numbers of people.

As a result, the suburbs were included in the city areas and various supermarkets were built without proper planning and, as a result, most of the City Corporations are suffering from acute traffic problems. Though the acquisition of land receiving interest was taken away by the government long ago, a new class of landlords has cropped up in city areas and, taking advantage of faulty laws, this group acquired most of the lands in city areas and remained owners despite receiving large amounts of money from the tenants like the market price from the supermarkets. The net result was that the land owners developed their lands by constructing multistoried buildings and let out the spaces to shop owners and businessmen for office space by taking huge amount as "salami" from them. The tenants remained tenants forever despite payment of massive amounts money and continued to pay monthly rent generation after generation and thereby a section of land owners comprehensively defied the purpose for which the new tenancy laws were promulgated.

I came across one case1 in which a supermarket was constructed in a stylish area, namely Gulshan Market No-1. The owners took lease of the land from RAJUK (Rajdhani Unnayon Kartripakkha), constructed a multistoried building and leased out space to 725 lessees as shops. The shop owners formed a cooperative society for their internal management and were carrying out business since 1977. The owners started various devices to somehow evict them for constructing a new multistoried building after demolition of the old one. Since the price of space for a shop in that area had gone up by more than hundred times, an officer of RAJUK made a surprise visit with an Executive Magistrate and found unauthorized constructions. The magistrate disconnected the electricity line and fined the owners. The tenants made entreaties to reconnect electricity, but they received no fruitful results. Suddenly a fire broke out in a portion of the building in 2003 and the building became unfit for occupation by the business owners. The owners of the building thereupon served notices on the shop owners to vacate for demolition of the building. Various litigations cropped up over the matter and it reached up to the highest court.

Ultimately against some interim orders, the matter came before us. One petition was filed by the business owners and another was filed by the building owners. The documents executed between the landlords and tenants revealed that the tenants have the right to transfer possessions of shop space with prior written consent of the landlords on payment of certain amounts. There is another stipulation that even if the landlords transfer the property, the tenancy shall continue, and the new purchaser would attorney the tenants. An arbitration clause was also incorporated for resolving disputes amicably. The landlords received vast sums of money at the time of execution of deeds as consideration of "sale of possession" of shops. Some of tenants paid about Tk 2.14 lakh for a space of 250 sq. Ft. and some of the tenants paid Tk 6.50 lakh for similar space. The price was almost like the value of the space, but the landlords did not execute proper sale deeds in favor of the tenants the possession along with proportionate space of land was not transferred by executing legal instruments.

Lease2 of immovable property is a "transfer of a right to enjoy such property, made for certain time, express or implied, or in perpetuity, in consideration of a price paid or promised, or of money, a share of crops, service or any other thing of value, to be rendered periodically or on specified occasions to be transferred by the transferee, who accepts the transfer on such terms." Such a contract vests in the lessee a right of possession for a certain time, it operates as a conveyance or transfer, and is a lease. It may be said otherwise that it is a transfer of a right of enjoyment of immovable property for a certain period. The price mentioned in Section 105 according to the Transfer of Property Act is taken as "premium."

If a payment is a consideration being made for possession such as "salami," it is a premium within the meaning of the law. This premium cannot be taken as advance of rent, advance of right. "Salami" is a payment by the tenant as a present or as price for parting by the landlord with his rights under the lease of a holding. It is a lump sum payment as consideration for what the landlord transfers to the tenant. Salami is not rent. The point at issue in that case was whether salami falls within the meaning of "agricultural income" for assessment of tax.3

Section 105, therefore, brings out the distinction between a price paid for a transfer of a right to enjoy the property and the rent to be paid periodically to the lessor. When the interest of the lessor is parted with for a price, the price paid is a premium or salami. But the periodical payments made for the continuous enjoyment of the benefits under the lease are rent. The former is a capital income and the latter a revenue receipt. There may be circumstances where the parties may camouflage the real nature of the transaction by using clever phraseology. In some cases, the so-called premium is in fact advance rent and in others rent is deferred price. It is not the form but the substance of the transaction that matters. The nomenclature used may not be decisive or conclusive, but it helps the court, having regard to the other circumstances, to ascertain the intention of the parties.4

When the interest of the lessor is parted with for a price, it is a price paid as "premium" and it cannot be taken as advance toward the payment of rent. The monthly payments are made for the continuous enjoyment of the benefits under the lease and this payment is called rent. In case of payment of "premium" it is a consideration paid by the tenant for being let into possession for creating a lease. If the landlord parted with an interest for a price the tenant's status is upgraded. Rent is a periodical payment. It is usually reserved for yearly, monthly or quarterly payment and it becomes due at the end of each such period. The Transfer of Property Act does not define an agreement to lease, but Section 2(7) of the Registration Act, 1908 defines "lease" as including "a counterpart, kabuliyat and an undertaking to cultivate or occupy." It is an inclusive definition and used in generic term having many species in it. The legislature deliberately gives an inclusive definition. A lease of immovable property is a transfer of right to enjoy such property made in the manner specified in Section 105. Section 17 of the Registration Act prescribes a deed which is required to be registered compulsorily including those mentioned in Clause (d) such as, "leases of immovable property from year to year, or for a term exceeding one year, or reserving a yearly rent." So, deeds mentioned in Clause (d) of Section 17 would cover the cases of documents which do not involve a present or immediate transfer of the lessee's right.

A lease is a contract outlining the terms under which one party agrees to rent property owned by another party. It guarantees the lessee, the tenant, and the use of an asset and guarantees the lessor, the property owner or landlord, regular payments from the lessee for a specified number of months or years. Both the lessee and the lessor face consequences if they fail to uphold the terms of the contract.5 An agreement between the two parties which entitles one of them merely to claim the execution of a lease from the other without creating a present or immediate demise in his favor is not an agreement to lease within the meaning of section 2(7).

In construing the documents, it is necessary to remember that they have been executed by laymen without legal assistance, and so it must be liberally construed without recourse to technical considerations. The heading of the documents, though relevant, would not determine their character. It is true that an agreement would operate as a present demise although its terms may commence at a future date. Similarly, it may amount to a present demise even though parties may contemplate to execute a more formal document in future. In considering the effect of a document we must enquire whether it contains unqualified and unconditional words of present demise and includes the essential terms of a lease. Generally, if rent is made payable under an agreement from the date of its execution or other specified date, it may be said to create a present demise. Another relevant test is the intention to deliver possession. If possession is given under an agreement and other terms of tenancy have been set out, then the agreement can be taken to be an agreement to lease. As in the construction of an agreement to lease, regard must be had to all the relevant and material terms; and an attempt must be made to reconcile the relevant terms if possible and not to treat many of them as idle surplus age.6

The Registration Act requires the transfer of possessory right to be registered. The landlords had acknowledged the receipt of money against the sale price of possession, but the deeds were not registered. Section 53A of the Transfer of Property Act gives statutory recognition of the doctrine of part performance. To obviate the eventuality that a parole agreement relating to land has partly been performed by one party and yet by reason of some technical defect, as want of the necessary registered document, such party cannot compel the other to perform his part of the contract. Where one party has performed his part of the agreement in the confidence that the other party would do the same, it would be a fraud upon the former to suffer the latter's refusal to work to his prejudice. Section 53A of the Transfer or Property Act protects the interest of the transferee in possession which is used as a shield against the transferor/owner. Even if a person purchases the property from the real owner, the purchaser would disentitle the person, in possession based on unregistered deed, from disturbing his possession of which he is in possession pursuant to an agreement. Since there has been acceptance of salami toward sale of possession, Section 53A7 will be used as a shield against the owners to oust the tenants. In cases of lease, the legislature has recognized that the equity of part performance is an active equity as in English law and is enough to support an independent action by the tenants.8

The Registration Act 9 protects the rights of the person in possession pursuant to an agreement. A document which is required to be registered10 can either create a right in immovable property or be received as evidence of such right. The documents of lease can be used for collateral purposes of possession to prove the agreement for sale of the property. There can be one mode of transfer of immovable property (a) by registered instrument, and (b) by delivery of possession, and a sale cannot be affected in any other way. The ownership of the property does not pass until registration is affected. Though there is strict restriction to claim any premium, salami or rent more than one month in advance, 11 the landlords are always taking advance of more than one month from the tenants and the tenants are handicapped in the hands of mighty landlords. The law12 enjoins the tenants to have electricity connection without the permission of the landlords. The tenants have apparent rights to continue as tenants even though no registered instruments were executed in their favor. But they have acquired interest in the premises by reason of payment of money toward sale of possession and their interest is protected under Section 53A.

References:

1. *Civil Petition No. 2209 of 2016 and 1059 of 2016, Banichitra Protishthan Ltd v. Bilkis Begum*
2. *Section 105 of Transfer of Property Act, 1882*
3. *Board of Agricultural Income Tax v. Sindhu Rani AIR 1957 SC 729*

4. *Commission of IT v. Panbari Tea Company, AIR 1965 SC 1871*
5. *Investopedia*
6. *Trivenibai v. Lilabai, AIR 1959 SC 620*
7. *Transfer of Property Act*
8. *Manik Lal Mensuekhbhai v. Hormusji Jamshedji, (1950) SCR 75*
9. *Section 49 of the Registration Act, 1908*
10. *Ibid Section 17*
11. *Section 10 of the Premises Rent Control Act, 1991*
12. *Ibid Section 33*

Medical Education (K)

Medical education is, obviously, related to the practice of being a medical practitioner, and includes the initial training to become a physician or additional training thereafter for fellowship. Entry level medical education programs are tertiary-level courses undertaken at a medical school or college. In general, the initial education is given at a medical school or college. Traditionally initial medical education is divided between practical and clinical studies. The former consists the basic sciences, such as anatomy, physiology, biochemistry, pharmacology and pathology. The latter consists of teaching in the various areas of clinical medicine such as internal medicine, pediatrics, obstetrics and gynecology, psychiatry, general practice and surgery. Medical programs are using system-based curricula in which learning is integrated and several institutions are doing this. The practice of medicine, i.e. diagnosing, treating and monitoring disease is directly affected by the ongoing changes in both national and local health policy and economics.[1] There is a growing call for health professional training programs to not only adopt more rigorous health policy education under leadership training,[2] but to apply a broader sense to the concept of teaching and implementing health policy through health equity and social disparities that largely affect health and patient outcomes.[3]

In Bangladesh the private medical and dental colleges have been admitting a huge number of students without following the guidelines and circulars on taking large amounts of money from the students.4 The 2011 guidelines provide that a student would be eligible to get admission if s/he scored highest mark out of 200, 100 marks to be calculated on the basis of GPA score in the Secondary School Certificate and Higher Secondary School Certificate examinations, and 100 marks in written test. It was also provided that a student scoring 120 marks in the merit list would be eligible for admission. Challenging the decision, Bangladesh Private Medical College Association (BPMCA) filed a writ petition. A Bench of the High Court Division made the rule absolute and made direction accordingly. Another group of students of 10 private medical colleges filed another writ petition and the students got a favorable order. Pursuant to the latter judgment, the students were admitted to the medical colleges. An appeal against the said judgment5 had been filed in the apex court. Two other writ petitions were filed, but the appeal and the petitions were dismissed.

Subsequently the principals of private medical colleges made applications for registration of the names of the students to Dhaka University, which refused to register the names. In the meantime, the students' first year professional MBBS examination became due. Accordingly, on the application of another petition, the High Court Division directed the university authority to issue registration cards to the students. Against such a direction the university obtained a stay order from the apex court. The private medical colleges were admitting students for the academic sessions 2013-14 and 2014-15 by securing judgment from High Court Division. Ultimately, it so happened that the private medical colleges started flouting the circulars of the government and universities and admitted students without checking the results of the students purely based on money taken from them. They utilized the sentiments of the students and secured orders from High Court Division for their admission.

Under such circumstances, the apex court realized that the private medical colleges played a trick to utilize the sentiment of the students and obtained interim orders from the High Court Division. The court issued Suo moto notice upon the chairmen and principals

226

of the private medical colleges to explain why they should not be proceeded against by imposing penalty for violation of the decisions of the government and the university for admission of 153 students in their colleges. Showing cause they stated that they admitted the students in pursuance of the orders of the High Court Division, that the university is corum-non-judice in introducing the cut-off mark; "that the colleges did not give admission to any student who did not secure 40 marks in the written exams, and that it was only after the judgment of the High Court Division they admitted the students". It is to be noted that the university authority issued a circular prescribing the criteria for admission of students in medical and dental colleges directing that the students must secure 40 marks out of 100 in the written exam.

In course of the hearing I noticed that the private medical colleges had admitted the students without caring about the decisions and circulars of the government and the university. This could not be countenanced particularly in respect of medical education for the students would be the future life saviors of the next generation. Their only plea was that they got the students admitted in pursuance of the orders of the High Court Division. We noticed that in one judgment that the High Court Division itself noticed that the ministry concerned, and the university were acting on their whim without bothering to adhere to their guidelines. I further noticed that the judgment referred to by the private medical colleges was on a different issue and those judgments are not applicable in respect of medical colleges in view of the amendment to the circular and decisions of the university.

Accordingly, I held that the Academic Council of Dhaka University is responsible for the maintenance of the standard of education and examination within the university's jurisdiction and shall exercise such powers which are imposed by its statute. Medical and Dental Council Ain (Act) empowers the Bangladesh Medical and Dental Council to recognize the appropriate and competent education to be given by the colleges; to recognize the students obtaining degrees from other colleges outside Bangladesh; and to settle the admission of degree and post degree courses. No rules, no guidelines or regulation for admission of students had been formulated by it. The object of promulgation of the Act was to monitor the standard of medical education and to recognize the medical and dental graduates and post- graduates both from home and abroad, but it retains no power to confer degrees on students. Though there is a provision to register the students of recognized institutions, the colleges sought registration of the students with Dhaka University from which it may be inferred that the law had not been implemented in full swing. If the Council has the power to regulate the standard of education given by the medical and dental colleges, it can't compel the university to relax the criteria for admission of students. So, the law has no force in law and the admission criteria and other related matters for maintaining the standard of education of medical students were to be regulated by the university and that was why they needed registration with Dhaka University.

The medical and dental council law will not prevail over the university Statue since the medical and dental students are obtaining degrees from the university. The university Statutes have the force of law and the university regulates the criteria for admission of medical students' syllabus. The Medical and Dental Council law was promulgated to regulate medical education and it has the power not to recognize a degree certificate issued by any public university in or outside Bangladesh. It can also suggest the universities to incorporate any subject or course for education. If the universities do not follow its advice, it may withhold recognition of students obtaining certificates from the said university, yet it cannot compel the universities to relax the guidelines for admission since the university is the sole authority to issue medical graduate certificates within its jurisdiction.

In view of the above, the students legally cannot get a direction from the universities to get their admission registered unless they satisfy the criteria and guidelines given by the university, because it issues the graduation certificates. The power to coordinate the standard of education lies with Parliament. It has the power to prevent disparity in the standard of education by different universities by promulgating laws. But this does not mean that Parliament can interfere with the internal administration of the university. A decision is flawed if it is illegal and if the authority contravenes or exceeds the terms of the power which authorizes the making of that decision, but judicial review is available against such decisions. The task for a court of law in assessing whether a decision is illegal is essentially one of construing the content and scope of the instrument conferring the duty or power upon the decision maker. The court is to determine whether an authority has made an error in law in making the decision. There are several issues that arise in public law that makes the court's task more complex. This task is made easier where the purpose is clearly defined or where the considerations which the body must consider in arriving at its decision are clearly spelled out. In such cases the court requires the decision-maker to consider the specified considerations and ignore the irrelevant. The students were admitted by the colleges concerned in pursuance of the judgment passed on a writ petition. Though the High Court Division discussed the minutes of the resolution of the Ministry of Health and Family Welfare, the issue of scoring 40 in written exam was not an issue in the writ petition. The High Court Division declared that "the admission procedure for MBBS/BDS courses for all Medical Colleges, Government or Private, be done by the Bangladesh Medical and Dental Council in accordance with the Bangladesh Medical and Dental Council Act and for the ensuing year, i.e. 2014-2015 admission of MBBS/BDS students be done "by ignoring the threshold cutoff marks."

The students were admitted by different colleges on a misinterpretation of a judgment of the High Court Division. The High Court Division directed the admission procedure to be made in accordance with the Bangladesh Medical and Dental Council Act ignoring the threshold cutoff marks. The colleges also admitted students by securing the judgment from the High Court Division and in the next session as well they admitted students in violation of the decisions of the government and universities by using the sentiments of the students. There are some issues which are unsuited for judicial administration while there are a good number of reasons why the court may exercise its discretion.

The decision involving a policy, utilitarian calculation of public good, about the level of taxation and public expenditure are constitutionally in the realm of public legislature and not judicially reviewable. The court will not interfere with a policy decision merely because it feels that another policy decision is fairer or wiser or more scientific of more logical.6 the same principle is applicable in the case of admission of students, because, it is the policy decision of the universities to get the students admitted after fulfilment of certain criteria. The authority which is authorized by law to deal with a subject should be allowed to perform its duty and responsibility in accordance with laws that govern the subject. The High Court Division usurped the power not sanctioned by law. Every organ of the State should be allowed to perform its responsibility in accordance with their respective laws. If the court interferes with their internal administration and the eligibility of admission of students in any university, this will tantamount to exercise of power not vested in law. The court should refrain from interfering with the internal administration of an authority if such authority does not contravene the law. It can intervene only in those cases where there is infraction of law in taking decisions affecting the right of a citizen. The court shall always keep in mind while exercising its power of judicial review that it has not transgressed the jurisdiction of any authority transacting its business.

The private medical and dental colleges utterly violated the Statutes of Dhaka University and admitted the students and thereby they have gambled with the students for their personal gains. Their conduct is deprecated, and they are to be dealt with severely. Accordingly, I directed a contribution of one crore taka each by the private medical colleges as penalty to be paid to certain charitable organizations, failing which, they would be debarred from getting students admitted in the next academic year. The students could have their registration subject to the above condition.

References:

1. *Steinberg, Michael, Introduction: Health Policy and Health Care Economics*

2. Schwartz, R.W: Pogge, C. "Physician Leadership: Essential Skills in a Changing Environment." American Journal of Surgery; Bee, Rebekah E, Lockwood, Charles J, "Medical Education and Health Policy."
3. Heiman, Harry: Smith, L Lerrisa; Mekool, Marissa; Mitchell, Denise N; Roth Bayer, Carey "Health Policy Training: A Review of the Literature
4. Civil Petition No. 2274 of 2016
5. Civil Appeal No. 147 of 2015
6. Belco Employees Union v. India (2002) (2) SCC 3330

Enemy Property (L)

The Defense of Pakistan Rules was promulgated on September 6, 1965 and a majority portion of the properties of Hindus were declared Enemy Property. The object of promulgation of the law was the protection of the properties of the minorities so that no local person misappropriates the property and, secondly, so that the owners cannot take money after selling the properties to the enemy country, i.e. India. Though there was cessation of war within 17 days between India and Pakistan after the Tashkent Pact between General Ayub Khan, President of Pakistan and Lal Bahadur Shastri, Prime Minister of India, under the mediation of Prime Minister Kosygin of the Soviet Union, the emergency declared by President Ayub Khan was not withdrawn till February 16, 1969. It happened due to the oversight or inefficiency of the authority entrusted with the responsibility. Practically there was cessation of war on paper, it continued for three years. This was the mode of government being run by the Pakistani regime. On the following day, February 17, 1969, General Ayub Khan promulgated Ordinance 01 of 1969, the Laws Continuance Order. After the bloody holocaust, majority were Hindus, they dreamt of living peacefully in their ancestral land. Bangabandhu Sheikh Mujibur Rahman, after return from incarceration, declared that one of the cornerstones of the new country would be religious tolerance, and the State would be secular. The Hindus thought that their past sufferings were over, and they would be treated as equals in the eye of law.

Within a few years their hopes were proved to be myths. The laws which were promulgated during the illegal period and were sought to be justified by the Ordinance 01 of 1969 were kept in force by the subsequent government treating the Hindu properties as "enemy properties." Even after the independence and the execution of the Friendship Treaty1 on March 19, 1972 for 25 years executed between India and Bangladesh, India remained an "enemy alien country" and the property of the Hindus who had left the country continued as enemy property under the new name of the Vested and Non-Resident Property.2 In the definition clause, "Non-resident" means one who is not, or has ceased to be, a permanent resident of the territory now comprising Bangladesh or who has acquired a foreign nationality but does not include a person who is an evacuee as defined in Article 2(c) of the Bangladesh (Regulation of Evacuee Property) Order, 1972. "Non-resident Property" means any property owned by a non-resident but does not include any property which (i) is owned by any person who is a citizen of the State which, at any time after March 25, 1971, was at war with, or engaged in military operation, against the Republic of Bangladesh (ii)(iii)(iv)(v). Hence this definition excludes any property owned by any person who is a citizen of a State which was not at war in 1971 with Bangladesh even if such a person had taken citizenship of India after 1965.

Even the law was renamed, it still retained the fundamental ability to deprive a Bangladeshi citizen of his property simply by definition of that person as an enemy of the State, leaving the country through abandonment of property is cited is the most common reason for this, and it is frequently the case that Hindu families who have one or several members leaving the country due to religious atrocities as well as political reasons have their property confiscated due to labeling as enemy. This would be evident if we see the decrease in population. In 1961 the figure of Hindu citizens in the East Pakistan stood at 18.5 percent. After liberation the reduction in the population had come down to pre-partition level. Hindus continue fleeing from the country in smaller numbers, but the percentage is not negligible. In 1974 the percentage was 13.5 and in1981, 12.1. After declaration of Islam as the State religion in 1989, in 1991 the percentage of Hindus came down to 10.5% of the population.3

An estimated 29,900 Hindus from five districts have sought refuge in India. Substantial numbers fled from Comilla --10,000, Natore -- 12,000, Chittagong -- 5,000, Jhenidah -- 500, and Pabna -- 600. Thirty-three temples in nine districts have been damaged, among them, Khulna 4, Pabna 3, Jamalpur 3, Chittagong 2, Bogra 2, Comilla 3 and Barisal 4.4

Much of the property of murdered Hindu politician Dhirendra Nath Dutta was confiscated by the Bangladesh government after independence in 1972 because Dutta's body was never found after he was arrested by the Pakistani Army during the Bangladesh Liberation War. An affidavit was brought forward that it could not be concluded that Dutta had not voluntarily left the country. The family property of Nobel Prize-winner Amartya Sen had been confiscated by the Pakistan government. In 1999, the Bangladesh government announced that it was investigating opportunities to return the property to Sen's family.5 the daily Sangbad reported on March 27, 1977 that at that point of time, according to the government's own figures, 702,335 acres, 2882 sq. km of cultivable land, and 22,835 homes were listed as enemy property (ibid). Professor Abul Barakat6 in his report demonstrated that 925,050 Hindu households (40% of Hindu families in Bangladesh) had been affected by the Enemy Property law, including 748,850 families dispossessed of agricultural land. The total amount of land lost by Hindu households because of this discriminatory act was estimated at 1.4 million acres (6,640 sq.km), which is equivalent to 53 percent of the total land owned by the Hindu community and 5.3 percent of the total area of Bangladesh. The survey also showed the beneficiaries of the land grab and such acts cut across all party lines. The political affiliations of the beneficiaries of appropriated property were:

- Bangladesh Awami League 44.2%
- Bangladesh Nationalist Party 31.7%

- Jatiya Party 5.8%
- Jamaat-i-Islami 4.8%
- Others 13.5%

There is no logic behind continuing with the provision of retaining the properties of Hindus as enemy properties within the meaning of the Defense of Pakistan Rules, 1965. There were agitations for repealing the law, but the government did not pay any heed to it. Even the "Debuttor (religious property dedicated to the name of God) properties were treated as enemy property. A deity is a supernatural being considered divine or sacred. The Oxford dictionary defines "deity" as a "God" or "Goddess" of a polytheistic religion; or anything revered as divine. Other notable characteristics include a belief in the existence of "aatman" (soul), and reincarnation of one's "aatman". Still many Debuttor properties are enlisted as enemy property and the local administration did not mutate the record of rights in the name of the deity. A deity is generally taken as a spiritual symbol by its believers. In legal terms, the property is treated as God's property. A deity cannot travel or take shelter in an enemy country like India and, therefore, the question of treating the deity's property as that of an enemy does not arise at all. It is beyond any norm or ethics. The property does not belong to any individual. The property of the deity is being managed by "Shebait" or "pujari" or by a management committee. Such persons are not the owners of the deity's property; they are merely caretakers of the property and are looking after the interest of the deity. So, if a "Shebait" or any member of the managing committee leaves this country or takes shelter in an "enemy country" like India, the deity's property cannot be treated as enemy property. The property remains in the country. Therefore, by no stretch of the imagination the status of the property ever changes.

Tarapur Tea Estate, located in the heart of Sylhet town, and naturally it was considered valuable property. One Baikuntha Chandra Gupta purchased the garden on June 10, 1882 in favor of deity Sree Radha Krishna Jiew and dedicated the tea estate in the name of the deity on July 2, 1892 for the maintenance of the deity and charitable purposes. Though the property was managed by the

"Shebait", it was declared enemy property in 1968. The "Shebait" and other family members were brutally killed by the Pakistani Army leaving minor boy Pankaj Kumar Gupta.

There were various litigations over the declaration of the tea estate as enemy property. This tea estate was ultimately declared as property of the deity. Pankaj Kumar Gupta after attaining majority managed the property as a "Shebait" of the deity. On September 16, 1968, as alleged by one Abdul Hye and his father Ragib Ali, Pankaj Kumar applied to the government for permission to transfer the tea estate in their favor. The government accorded permission and pursuant thereto the "Shebait" executed a 99-year lease of the tea estate in favor of Abdul Hye on February 12, 1990 and appointed him as "Shebait" of the deity. Some interested persons got a memo issued from the government questioning the takeover of the tea estate which led to the filing of a writ petition in the High Court Division challenging the government action.

A criminal case was also filed against Abdul Hye and his father Ragib Ali. The High Court Division declared the government memo without lawful authority.7 Ragib Ali set up a medical college with a hospital, a housing estate and a supermarket by removing tea plantations. I held that a religious trust was created and if the property is dedicated to the deity for the worship or service of the idol, it cannot be alienated by anyone. A religious trust by way of Debuttar can come into existence only when a property is dedicated for worship or service of an idol. When there is an endowment in favor of an established idol, no trust in the legal sense of the term can possibly come into being -- it is only the moral duty of the person who installed the deity or his heirs to carry on the worship in such a way as they think proper in accordance with the deed of endowment. A property can be given to an idol either at the time when it is consecrated or at any subsequent period.   Therefore, a question arises about the dedication of the property. When a property is given absolutely by a pious Hindu for worship of an idol the property vests in the idol itself as a juristic person. This is quite in accordance with Hindu philosophy and has been uniformly accepted in a long series of decisions by different courts.8

The properties of the law vest in the trustee whereas in case of an idol or Sansthan they do not vest in the manager or Shebait. Under Hindu law no mode or form of creating a dedication is prescribed. If such dedication is not evidenced by a document, it can be established by consent and satisfactory evidence of conduct of the parties and user of the property which shows the extinction of the private secular character of the property and its complete dedication to charity. What is necessary to be established is that not only there is a clear and unequivocal intention to dedicate but also that such intention was in fact carried into effect.9 a trust would be denominated a religious or charitable trust if it is created for the purposes of religion or charity. Two things, therefore, require to be considered in this connection: (a) what are religious and charitable purposes? (b) What is a trust? Religion is absolutely a matter of faith with individuals or communities, and it is not necessarily theistic, i.e. Buddhism. The expression "religious purpose" is understood where the purpose or object is to secure the spiritual well-being of a person or persons according to the tenets of the religion which they believe in.10

Lewin in his well-known treatise on the "Law of Trusts" defines "Trust" to be a "confidence reposed in some other, not issuing out of the land, but as a thing collateral, annexed in privacy to the estate of the land, for which cestui que trust has no remedy but by Subpoena in the Chancery."

Hindu concepts of religious and charitable gifts have been operative under two heads: "Istha" and "Purtta". The compound word Istha-Purtta has been retained in the writings of all Brahminical sages and commentators down to modern days. By Istha is meant Vedic sacrifices, and rites and gifts in connection with the same. Purtta, on the other hand, means other pious and charitable acts which are unconnected with any one or Vedic sacrifice. The meaning of the two expressions has been discussed elaborately by Pandit Pran Nath Saraswati in his "Tagore Law Lectures" on the Hindu Law of Endowments. In the Hindu Law system, there is no line of demarcation between religion and charity. The Hindu religion recognizes the existence of a life after death, and it believes in the law of "karma" according to which the good or bad deeds of a man produce corresponding results in the life to come. If we look into the essentials of dedication for religious and charitable purposes, we will find that there are various works of this kind where the subject of gift or dedication has been elaborately discussed, among others, of Danakhanda by Hemadri, namely Purta Kamalakar and Dana Kamalakar by Kamalakar Bhatta; Pratistha Mayukha of Nikantha and Pratistha Tattwa of Raghunandan (B.K. Mukherjea, ibid).

In every act of dedication, there are two essential parts, one of which is called "Sankalpa" or the formula of resolve, and the other "Utsarga" or renunciation. The ceremony, as Mandalik points out, always begins with a Sankalpa, which after reciting at the time of gift with reference to age, year, season, month, etc. states the object for which the founder is making the gift. Utsarga, on the other hand, completes a gift by renouncing the ownership of the founder in the thing given. If we examine the details on how Debutter is managed and administered, there is no doubt that it is in an ideal sense that the dedicated property vests in an idol. The person so entrusted must, of necessity, be empowered to do whatever may be required for the service of the idol and for the benefit and preservation of its property, at least to as great an extent as the manager of an infant heir. If this were not so, the estate of the idol might be destroyed or wasted, and its worship discontinued for want of necessary funds to preserve and maintain it.11

This human ministrant of the deity, who is its manager and legal representative, is known by the name of Shebait in Bengal and Northern India. He is the person entitled to speak on behalf of the deity on earth and is endowed with the authority to deal with all its temporal affairs. As regards the temple property, the manager is in the position of a trustee, but as regards the service of the temple and the duties that appertain to it he is rather in the position of the holder of an office of dignity. The exact position of a Shebait or manager cannot be said to be altogether beyond the range of controversy, though much of the earlier theories has now been discarded. The relation of a Shebait to the Debutter property is not that of a trustee to trust property under English law. It is held that the "endowments of a Hindu Math are not 'conveyed in trust', nor is the head of the math a 'trustee' to regard to them, save as to specific property proved to have been vested in him for a specific object."

In English law the legal estate in the trust property vests in the trustee who holds it for the benefit of the cestui que trust. In a Hindu religious endowment, the entire ownership of the dedicated property is transferred to the deity or the institution itself as a juristic person, and the Shebait is mere a manager. The Judicial Committee of the Privy Council held that a trust in the sense in which the expression is used in English law is unknown in the Hindu system, pure and simple. Hindu piety found expression in gifts to idols and images consecrated and installed in temples, to religious institutions of every kind, and for all purposes considered meritorious in the Hindu social and religious system. Under the Hindu law the image of a deity of the Hindu pantheon is a juristic entity, vested with the capacity of receiving gift and holding property.12

Under Hindu law apostasy was certainly a disqualification in the heir and excluded him from inheritance. This was removed by the Cast Disabilities Removal Act, 1850 (Act XXI of 1850), about ordinary property; the fact that a Hindu has become a convert to some other religion does not entail forfeiture of his heritable rights. This Act XXI of 1850 has been repealed by Section 2 of Act VIII of 1973. By this Act, namely the Bangladesh Laws (Revision and Declaration) Act, 1973, some laws promulgated in British India have been repealed including Act XXI of 1850. So, the consequence of such repeal is that a convert from Hinduism could inherit the property of Hindu Law by Act XXI of 1850, but after the repeal by Act VIII of 1973 he disinherits it. The position as it stands now is that a Hindu apostate is disqualified from being the heir and in the succession of his paternal property. If that being so, a non-Hindu cannot become a Shebait or pujari of the deity. He cannot carry on the worship or the management of the property of the deity.

An idol is a juristic person in whom the title of the property vests. The personality of the idol might, therefore, in one sense, be said to be merged in that of the Shebait. A Shebait, like a trustee in English Law, cannot delegate his duty to another, no matter whether such other is a stranger or co-trustee. The rule is founded on the maxim "delegatus non potest delegary."13 So by no stretch of the imagination the Shebait can transfer the entire Debutter property even with the permission of the government. I summed up my opinion by formulating some guidelines.14

References:

1. *Treaty of Peace and Friendship between the Government of India and the Government of the People's Republic of Bangladesh dated March 19, 1972*
1. *Vested and Non-Resident Property (Administration) Act, 1974.*
2. *Bangladesh Bureau of Statistics (data, www.bangla.net/nbd/ana_voll?religion.htm)*
3. *A white paper on the 1500 days of Persecution of Minorities in Bangladesh by Shariyar Kabir, Ekattor Ghatak Dalal Nirmul Committee, Dhaka, 2005, Vol.1*
4. *Vested Property Act (Bangladesh), Wikipedia.*
5. *Professor Abul Barakat of Dhaka University, Inquiry into Causes and Consequences of Deprivation of Hindu Minorities in Bangladesh through the Vested Property Act, (Published in 2000)*
6. *Civil Appeal No. 163 of 2009, Bangladesh v. Abdul Hye*
7. *Kalanka Devi Sansthan v. MRT Nagpur, AIR 1970 SC 439*
8. *East Pakistan v. Kshitidhar, 16 DLR (SC) 457 and Manakono Das Matharami Reddy v. Durddukasi Shubha Rao AIR 1957 SC 797*
9. *The Hindu Law of Religious and Charitable Trusts, B.K Mukherjee*
10. *Proshonna Kumari Debya v. Golab Chan Baboo (1875) LR 21A 145*
11. *Vidya Bharathi Thirtha v. Bulusamu Iyer, LR 48 IA 302*
12. *Speight v. Gaunt, 22 Ch, D 727*
13. *Guidelines; page 42-47 (a-q)*

Alluvion and Diluvion (M)

Bangladesh is a very small country with India surrounding it on three sides and the Bay of Bengal being in the south. The country is covered with many rivers mostly originating in India. So, in the dry season all the rivers dry up because India has obstructions on the water flow upstream for irrigation and hydro-electricity generation while during the rainy season all the water gates are opened resulting in larger flows of water inundating vast areas of the country. Toward the south tidal waves during cyclones also inundate houses, roads and crop fields. So essentially Bangladesh is regularly subject to alluvion and diluvion phenomena and hence it is a common feature of our country because of its geographical location. Sometimes the abundance of river flows from the Himalayas wash away village after village during the rainy season. There was no law for the protection of the lands which are washed away by the tides of the rivers and the sea. A land owner having a vast area of cultivable land becomes a homeless man in a day or two. Therefore, the question of ownership of the land accreted after a few years of diluvion often arises. A similar case appeared before us for decision.[1]

Kazem Uddin's ancestral land on the bank of Padma River diluviated in 1947 and then he shifted to Char Bhadrashon. From there he shifted to Jhaokanda in Dhaka District. He purchased some land which was also diluviated in 1991. He purchased some land in Dohar and that land was also diluviated in 1992. To resolve the issue the Ministry of Land issued a circular upon all Deputy Commissioners directing them to take steps which were diluviated in situ under the substituted provision of law[2] with prospective operation and that the new amended provision in 1994 would not be applicable in respect of those land which were diluviated and illuviated prior to July 13, 1994. The previous tenancy law[3] was amended in 1929 inserting a provision[4] providing that tenants' right in the diluviated land could be deemed to have been surrendered and extinguished if the tenant obtained any abatement of rent in respect of such diluvion. Such extinction of right would not affect the accrual of his right of accretion of the said land if it was available to him under any other law. This law was also changed in 1938. Then a new law5 came into operation with a drastic change in tenancy law which is termed as "confiscatory piece of law." But in the law section 86 was inserted which is similar to previous section 86A of Bengal Tenancy Act.

Part V of the Act contains section 86 which came into force in Dhaka on August 1, 1963 and Faridpur on August 5, 1963. Till such dates, in view of section 80 of the Act of 1950, the provisions of the Bengal Tenancy Act regulated the field of diluvion and alluvion of land in those districts. The deviation from the provisions of the Bengal Tenancy Act under the aforesaid provision is that there cannot be automatic abatement of rent in the case of loss of land by diluvion and there would be proportionate abatement of rent which might be considered by the Revenue Officer on the application of the tenant. The subsistence of right on the re-appeared land of the tenant of such diluviated land shall continue within twenty years of loss or has re-appeared for the period which was lost or for four years whichever is less subject to the condition regarding the total area of land that could be retained under sections 20 or 90 of the Act. If the total area of land in possession of the tenant exceeds the ceiling, his right of re-possession of the re-appeared land would be extinguished, and the said land shall vest in the government.

This provision was again amended.6 the new provision was also amended.7 Again it was amended in 1994.8 so this provision ensured the subsistence of the title to the land lost by diluvion on the re-appearance of the land within a period of thirty years notwithstanding the abatement of rent or tax. The other difference between these two provisions is that under the present provision the right of possession after re-appearance shall be exercised initially by the Collector who shall make a survey of the land so re-appeared and after completion of survey, he shall allot the land to the tenant whose land was lost provided that the quantity of land in his possession together with the land alluviated shall not exceed sixty standard bighas and the excess land shall vest in the government. Apparently, the right, title and interest of the tenant or his successor shall subsist in the land from the date of substitution of section 86 if the land diluviated re-appear within thirty years from that date. The legislature is totally silent about the operation of the substituted provision by Act XV of 1994, whether this provision shall have prospective or retrospective effect, but I find no ambiguity in the language used in it. It is said, "The right, title and interest of the original tenant or his successor-in-interest shall subsist....." The legislature has used the word "shall", that is, the right of the tenant shall subsist in respect of diluviated land if such land re-appears within thirty years of loss, that is, if the re-appearance of the diluviated land takes place in future. Under the previous provision limited retrospective operation was given to the loss of land by diluvion which took place before the commencement of the substituted provision, but under the present provision such language was deliberately omitted.

There were conflicting views on the issue.9 the new substituted Sub-section (2) of section 86 clearly says that the right, title and interest of the tenant shall subsist during the period of loss by diluvion and the tenant or his successor can claim right to the said land if it re-appears within a period of thirty years of loss. The meaning of this sub-section ensuring the right of the tenant or his successor is so clear that his right subsists if diluvion and alluvion take place after coming into force of Section 86 substituted by Act XV of 1994. There cannot be any explanation other than this. The Secretary of the government gave the explanation of this substituted provision that if the land is diluviated prior to July 13, 1994, the amended provision would not be applicable in respect of that land. It is significant to note that in the introductory clause the words "Notwithstanding anything contained in any other law for the time being in force" have been used instead of using the words "in the Act". There is no reference to the law contained in the Act of 1950. The intention of the legislature is thus clear to conclude that if the land diluviated before July 13, 1994, the tenant cannot claim right, title or interest of the alluviated land even if the land re-appears within thirty years from July 13, 1994. The tenant or his successor can claim title on the re-appeared land within thirty years of loss if the diluvion took place after July 13, 1994. I concluded my opinion by summing up guidelines to be followed by revenue officers.10

References:

1. *Civil Appeal No. 364 of 2002, Bangladesh v. Md. Kazem Uddin Miah*
2. *Section 86 of the State Acquisition and Tenancy Act*
3. *The Bengal Tenancy Act, 1885*
4. *Section 86A*
5. *Act of 1950*
6. *President's Order No. 135 of 1972, Effetive from 4th November 1972 substituting section 86*
7. *Ordinance No. LXI of 1975*
8. *Act XV of 1994*
9. *Syed Nizamuddin Mohsin v. Bangladesh 41 DLR (AD) 141 and Mannan v. Kulada Ranjan 31 DLR (AD) 1995*
10. *Guidelines; Para I - IX*

Environment, Ecology, and Conservation (N)

The combined influence of biotic and abiotic factors around an organism that interact and influence the life and behavior of it are caused due to environmental degradation. It has specific influence in the formation and functioning of life. The surrounding light, air, water and temperature have specific influences on plants, animals and microorganisms in nature. All of which interact with each other to form the environment. So, life and environment are inseparable from each other, as food and shelter are two important factors for survival. Ecology is a branch of biology that deals with the interaction of organisms with the environment and vice-versa. The total number of individuals of a given population is termed as the population size. The number of individuals of a population in a specified area is known as population density; it is the number of individuals per unit of a given population. The number of people per unit area, e.g. one sq. km. in Dhaka City; number of

243

earthworms in each area per acre of land; number of planktons found per liter of water in a pond are good examples. Bangladesh has been formed from the alluvial plains slanting from north to south, intercepted by the rivers Padma, Jamuna, Brahmaputra, Meghna and their tributaries. Though Bangladesh falls under the temperate zone, yet the influence monsoon air has a great impact on it.

The degradation of environment has direct impact on humans especially in populated areas. It may also affect vegetation, wildlife, soil, water, etc. Environmental degradation is the disintegration of art or deterioration of environment through consumption of asset, for example: air, water and soil; and the destruction of environment and eradication of wildlife. It is characterized as any change or aggravation to nature's turf seen to be pernicious or undesirable. Ecological effect of degradation is created by the consolidation often effectively substantiate and expanding human population and constantly expanding commercial developments. It occurs when natural resources are depleted, and the environment is compromised in the form of extinction of species, pollution of air, water and soil, and rapid growth in population. Environmental degradation is one of the greatest threats that are being looked at now in the world today. Environmental issues can be seen in long term ecological effects, some of which can demolish the whole environment.

Some environmental life species require substantial area to help provide food, living space and other different assets. These creatures are called area specific. A more basic cause of environmental degradation is land damage. Numerous weedy plant species, for example, garlic and mustard, are both foreign and obtrusive. A rupture in the environmental surrounding provides a chance for the growth and spread of pollution in whatever form, whether it is in the air, water, land or noise and they are harmful to the environment. Air pollution contaminates the air that we breathe and this causes health issues. Water pollution degrades the quality of water that we use for drinking purposes. Land pollution results in degradation of earth surface because of human activities. Noise pollution can cause irreparable damage to our ears when exposed to continuous loud sound.

Rapid population growth puts strains on some natural resources which result in degradation of our environment. More population means more demand for food, clothes and shelter. These also result in deforestation which is another factor of environmental degradation. Deforestation, i.e. the felling of trees may be to make way for more homes and industries. Rapid growth of population and urban sprawl are two of the major causes of deforestation. Use of forest land for agriculture, animal grazing, harvesting for fuel wood and logging are some of the other causes of deforestation. Deforestation contributes to global warming as decreased forest size generates greenhouse gases adversely affecting the environment. Landfills pollute the environment and destroy the beauty of the city. Landfills within the city are due the large amount of waste that gets generated by households, industries, factories and hospitals. Landfill poses a great risk to the health of the environment and the people who live there. Landfills produce foul smell when burnt and cause environmental degradation. Human health is at the receiving end because of the environmental degradation. Areas exposed to toxic air pollutants can cause respiratory problems, pneumonia and asthma. Ozone layer is responsible for protecting us from harmful ultra-violet rays. The presence of chlorofluorocarbons and hydro-chlorofluorocarbons in the atmosphere is causing the ozone layer to deplete. As it will deplete, it will permit harmful radiation back to earth.

I am now concerned about a case of landfills in the suburb of Dhaka City in the west. In 1997 RAJUK prepared a masterplan known as Dhaka Metropolitan Development Plan (DMDP) for Dhaka City and its surrounding areas identifying areas of floodplains, rivers, waterbodies, sub-flood flow zones (SFFZ) to protect the safety, health and welfare of the common people from negative environmental impacts and to protect and preserve the natural drainage system to ensure their continuing and proper functioning. The masterplan in clear terms earmarked prohibited residential, commercial and industrial development including raising the level of land through earth filling in flood flow/sub-

245

flood flow zones. It identified nineteen spatial planning zones (SPZ) out of which seventeen comprising the area between Savar and Dhansona in the west and present Dhaka established area in the east which is a low-lying area across the Turag River and its canals and is designated as an SFFZ area within which Aminbazar area in Savar has fallen as part of Sub-Flood Flow Zone. The DMDP has identified that there have been many private development schemes approved by RAJUK especially in Aminbazar area on the south on the Dhaka-Aricha road which will have considerable negative impact on the environment. The DMDP recommended that all such development permits should be withdrawn and that no new ones should be allowed.

Despite such prohibition, Metro Makers & Developers Ltd (MMDL) has undertaken a development project near Amin Bazar which is situated within the SPZ and earmarked as SFFZ and has started earth-filling work in the substantial part of the zone with an object to implement an unauthorized non-permitted satellite township under the name Modhumoti Model Town (MMT). RAJUK prohibited illegal earth filling, but MMDL did not pay any heed to it and that led to filing of a public interest litigation by the Bangladesh Environmental Lawyers Association (BELA).1 the object of promulgating Act of 1950 was mainly in liquidation of rent receiving interest of landlords. Under the said Act relaxation of holding ceiling of land is made in respect of large scale farming through use of machinery or for large scale dairy farming; land held for cultivation of tea, coffee or rubber; and land held for cultivation of sugarcane for manufacturing sugar. Another legislation2 restriction was imposed on retaining a total quantity of land by a family of more than 100 standard bighas and land more than that quantity shall be surrendered to the government.

There was also restriction for purchase or acquiring or by any other means and area of land beyond such limitations. There is another legislation3 by which the total quantity of agricultural land which may be held by a family has been reduced to 60 standard bighas. Yet another piece of legislation was promulgated by the government.4 the object of this law is to protect the environment, improve environmental standard and control and mitigate pollution of the environment, and violators thereof are liable to punishment. Still another legislation, 5 was enacted for preservation of waterbodies as per masterplan within the metropolitan areas restricting earth filling in river, canal and water reservoir and violators will be punishable under the Act.

MMDL undertook the project in Bilamalia and Baliarpur Mouzas under Savar Police Station which was already included in the DMDP and RAJUK has control over those areas. But MMDL did not get any permit from RAJUK. After coming into force of the laws mentioned above prior permission of the government is necessary for conversion of agricultural land of those two mouzas to housing projects. The Joladhar Ain [Waterbody Act] prohibits change of the existing nature of any land without prior permission. MMDL has been developing the area by filling earth to make it suitable for constructing buildings even though for such development work prior permission of the relevant authority is necessary.6 the new masterplan shows that development must be compatible with the existing rural nature, i.e. the development should be undertaken for housing projects without disturbing the natural flood flow. But if the development work by filling earth for a housing scheme is made this would disturb the flood flow.

The right to a healthy environment is now to be found in several regional human rights instruments, such as the Additional Protocol to the Inter-American Convention of Human Rights, popularly known as the San Salvador Protocol. In the Stockholm Declaration of 1972, it was declared that "man has the fundamental right to freedom, equality and adequate condition of life, in an environment of a quality that permits a life of dignity and wellbeing and he bears a solemn responsibility to protect and improve the environment for present and future generations." The UNGA Resolution No. 45/94 recalled the language of the Stockholm Declaration. All global and human rights bodies have accepted the link between environmental degradation and internationally guaranteed human rights.

The right to life has been used in a diversified manner---this includes the right to survive as a species, quality of life, the right to

247

live with dignity and the right to livelihood. Right to life includes the right of enjoyment of pollution free water and air for full enjoyment of life. The notion that the public has a right to expect certain lands and natural areas to retain their natural characteristics is finding its way into the law of the land. The need to protect the environment and ecology has been summed up by David B. Hunter, University of Michigan: 7

Another major ecological tenet is that the world is finite. The earth can support only so many people and only so much human activity before limits are reached. This lesson was driven home by the oil crisis of the 1970s as well as by the pesticide scare of the 1960s. The current deterioration of the ozone layer is another vivid example of the complex, unpredictable and potentially catastrophic effects posed by our disregard of the environmental limits to economic growth. The absolute finiteness of the environment leads to the unquestionable result that human activities will at some point be constrained. Human activity finds in the natural world its external limits. In short, the environment imposes constraints on our freedom; these constraints are not the product of value choices but of the scientific imperative of the environment's limitations. Reliance on improving technology can delay temporarily, but not forever, the inevitable constraints. There is a limit to the capacity of the environment to service ... growth, both in providing raw materials and in assimilating by-product wastes due to consumption. The largesse of technology can only postpone or disguise the inevitable.

Professor Barbara Ward echoed in similar language: "We can forget moral imperatives. But today the morals of respect and care and modesty come to us in a form we cannot evade. We cannot cheat on DNA. We cannot get around photosynthesis. We cannot say I am not going to give a damn about phytoplankton. All these tiny mechanisms provide the preconditions of our planetary life. To say we do not care is to say in the most literal sense that 'we choose death'."

MMDL has purchased 169.91 bighas of land and it also claimed that it had acquired 550 acres of land by different deeds for implementation of its project. The acquisition of such a huge chunk of land is affected by law.8 Rule of law requires that the authorities concerned are under obligation to see that no one violates the law in implementing any project in a restricted area. The Revenue Officer and the Chairman of RAJUK cannot, therefore, permit any person or company or firm to use any land without complying with the due requirements of laws. The public authorities should enforce the laws strictly so that pollution or other environmental harm should not cause injury to human beings. MMDL utterly violated the laws and has been implementing the housing project and therefore it is void. Protection of the environment is not only the duty of the citizen, but it is also the obligation of the State and its organs including the courts to check the violation of laws. Therefore, MMDL is under an obligation to pay damages for mitigating the hardship of the third-party purchasers if they do not want to take back their monies paid to them since they have illegally acquired, advertised and sold plots suppressing material facts from them violating the laws. I therefore gave guidelines and directions to be followed by the authority.9

References:

1. *Civil Appeal No. 253-256 of 2009*
2. *The Bangladesh Land Holding (Limitation Order 1972)*
3. *Land Reforms Ordinance 1984*
4. *Bangladesh Poribesh Sangrakkhon Ain, 1995 (Environment Protection Act)*
5. *The Jaladhar Sangakkhon Ain, 2000 (Preservation of Waterbodies Act)*
6. *The Building Construction Act, 1952*
7. *An Ecological Perspective on Property: A Call for Judicial Protection of the Public's Interest in Environmentally Critical Resouces, Published in Harvard Law Review, Vol, 12, 1988, page 331*
8. *Article 3 of PO 98 of 1972*

Legislative Incompetency (O)

In a democracy it is accepted that the public should have full access to the law-making process. It generally has gone unnoticed, however, that governmental bodies, which should remain open to the public for their deliberations, may nevertheless adopt laws with little or no publicity being given to those enactments. Under the ancient Anglo-American common-law doctrine, a law may take effect from the moment it is signed, or an administrative rule may penalize conduct immediately after it is voted on, with no obligation on the lawmakers to publicize or promulgate their enactments. Public policy dictates that there ought to be a more rigorous and imaginative approach to promulgation. Though the common law of England is the foundation of US law to the extent that it is not repugnant to domestic law, a small number of important British Statutes in effect at the time of the Revolution have been independently reenacted by US States. The US enacted all federal laws in conformity with the Constitution. Their national language is English, but they changed the spelling of different words, accents, ignored verb and still follow the old system of measurement.

Even after nearly half a century of independence, we have retained almost all parent laws enacted by the colonial powers. Some of the penal provisions of the Penal Code and some provisions of the Code of Criminal Procedure are inconsistent with the Constitution. Even then we have retained them after the Constitution came into force. We did not try to re-promulgate these two important Codes. We failed to improve both the parliamentary procedures and the drafting wing of the Ministry of Law. It is due to lack of institutionalization of both the branches. No government in power made any endeavor to institutionalize them. These two branches, in my estimation, should be kept out of politics and endeavors should be taken to improve them. A political party may form the government for a period and another political party may come to power. These political parties will try to implement their political ideology for the welfare of the people and the people will be the ultimate decision makers which will be reflected in the next election after evaluating the programs of the parties, even though the laws promulgated will remain in force during the tenure of different political parties. Those laws cannot be repealed in a day even if the other political party after coming to power feels that the laws prepared by the former political party in power were against their line of thinking and philosophy. For example, The Special Powers Act, 1974 was promulgated by Bangladesh Awami League. All opposition political parties termed it as a black law. But those political parties after coming to power used the said "black law" as an instrument to victimize and harass the workers and leaders of Awami League.

I can cite innumerable examples like the ones prevailing in our country. After a new law comes into force it creates rights and liabilities for the citizens. Therefore, if a political party that has newly come to power wants to repeal any law promulgated during the rule of the other political party, it has to consider the impact and consequences of repealing the law. Laws are promulgated mainly for the welfare of the people and proper administration of justice. Therefore, it is the bounden duty of the political parties in power to institutionalize the drafting wing of law and Parliament and to appoint qualified and competent persons for drafting laws. Since when a bill is placed in Parliament, it is sent for scrutiny to the concerned Standing Committee1 the members of the Standing Committee must have knowledge and expertise in law. It can be improved if competent persons specialized in law are nominated ignoring egotism and parochial mindset. After their recommendation it is again sent to Parliament for discussion. The parliamentarians thereupon examine the bill and recommendations and express their opinions. The procedure prevailing in Parliament is totally different. The members of Parliament do not perform their responsibilities reposed upon them. They treat the matter of legislation as routine work and approve the bills as laws. Even if a parliamentarian wants to amend a provision and he happens to be a member of the opposition political party, his suggestions are ignored or negated by the ruling party. The net result is that most laws remain faulty all the time.

It is found that just immediately after gazette notification and becoming an Act of Parliament or a law, the government comes with an amendment. These amendments are made so rapidly and secretly it is very difficult for the people, the lawyers and judges to know of these amendments. I had a bitter experience in this regard. I was presiding over a Bench in a civil matter regarding an amendment of pleadings. I pointed out to the counsel that the courts are always liberal in allowing amendments taking the view that litigation should be disposed of finally, and in case there are some defects in the pleadings, these would give rise to a multiplicity of proceedings. Therefore, with a view to stop further litigation over the same subject the court is always in favor of such amendments subject to some limitations.

The counsel appearing for the petitioner argued that the law has been amended in the meantime.2 I had no knowledge about the amendment, although the amendment was made one year back. On reading the amendment, I was astonished to find that the amendment was made ignoring all legal decisions right from the Privy Council and all through the highest courts of India, Pakistan and Bangladesh. There was so much ambiguity that nothing had been mentioned in the amended provision about the pending proceedings. About 1.5 million suits were pending and due to lack of knowledge of the lawyers, there are defects in almost all pleadings. The amendment of pleading continues up to the apex court.

The legislature should have clarified the effect of the amendment by providing a savings clause. Previously if an amendment was made about a provision or if any new legislation was enacted on the same subject matter, there used to be a savings clause prescribing the mode of applicability of the law in the pending proceedings. The legislature these days makes amendments to different laws without looking to the consequence as if it were performing routine work. There were three previous laws prior to the coming into force of the present Money Laundering (Protirodh) Ain, 2012. The first law on the subject was the Foreign Exchange Regulation Act, 1947. Keeping this alive, the Money Laundering Prevention Ordinance, 2008 was promulgated. Subsequently the

Ordinance was repealed by the Money Laundering Prevention Act, 2009. This law was also replaced by the Money Laundering Act, 2012.

The significant thing to be noted here is there remains confusion regarding its applicability. Suppose an incident took place in 2000 but the offence is detected in 2013. This caused an embarrassing position for us in deciding a case of a political leader. In more developed countries most of the parliamentarians have a background in law and they possess vast knowledge on law, even sometimes they possess more expertise in law than senior lawyers and judges. A politician, who holds a ministerial function in a particular ministry, may not be so qualified, but if the law is clear, specific, leaving no ambiguity, he will not do any wrong or even if he intends to do something contrary to the law, he will not be able to do so because officers with extensive knowledge would not allow him to do anything which is beyond the law.

I also find in politicians or policymakers or officers, who are involved in the process of making decisions in promulgating a new law, a lack of some sort of foresight in these matters. The net result is that laws are promulgated one after another on the same subject matter preserving the inconsistencies with each other. Sometimes they use the expression "notwithstanding anything containing in any other law" in such cases. When such an expression is used, the new law will prevail over the other law. It is the plain and simple meaning and the court treats it as such. But we find similar expressions are used in all amendments to new laws over the same subject matters and, under such circumstances, the court is put in a dilemma as to which provision should prevail. This is mainly due to lack of foresight or knowledge. Besides the Money Laundering Prevention Act, the present Artharin Ain (Finanacial Institutions Loan Recovery Act) is in force repealing two succeeding laws on the same subject. On the question of trial of offenders of crimes committed on women and children, the first law was "Cruelty to Women (Deterrent Punishment) Ordinance 1983. This legislation was followed by "Nari-O-Shishu Nirjaton (Bishesh Bidhan) Ain, 1995" and the present legislation on the same subject is "Nari-O-Shishu Nirajton Daman Ain, 2000". This law was also amended drastically in 2003. So, we find three successive legislations on same subject. If the first legislation was drafted properly, after taking suggestions from lawyers, NGOs working in the field and judges, there would have been no need for promulgating two subsequent laws. Even the legislature could have overcome the pains of legislating two successive laws if it had given thought over the first legislation and made corresponding amendments curing the defects with a savings clause.

Similarly, the "Durniti Daman Commission Ain" (Prevention of Corruption Act) was also promulgated in a similar fashion. It has so many defects that if it is followed in the strict sense, no offender can be brought to justice even within a period of ten to fifteen years, not to speak of apprehending an offender who has committed serious crimes under the said law. The present system is made workable only by way of giving guidelines by the apex court. Finding no other alternative, I directed the present chairman of the Anti-corruption Commission, Iqbal Mahmud, after handing over a judgment, to give guidelines to the officers concerned after a thorough reading of the judgment. Under the existing system, there was restriction of arresting an offender even if it was found by an officer of the Commission that an offender had committed an offence in his presence, because prior permission from the Commission was necessary to arrest the offender. I told him that if the offender flees with incriminating materials it would be difficult on the part of the Commission to collect evidence, since in the meantime the offender would destroy the incriminating materials.

In the United States, all the Senators are very knowledgeable in law which is evident from their performances. In the judicial arena of US, some expressions like "Super Precedence" or "Super Duper Precedence" or "Super-Stare Decisis" in constitutional law are used because of their repeated reaffirmation by the court.3 The term "Super Precedence" surfaced in the Roberts4 (present Chief Justice) confirmation hearings in 2005, when late Senator Arlen Specter of Pennsylvania, Chairman of the Judiciary Committee, asked Roberts whether he agreed that cases like Roe5 had become "Super Precedence" or "Super Duper Precedence"--- that is, they were so deeply embedded in the fabric of law they would be especially hard to overturn.6 In the hearing, Roberts never directly answered the question except to say that he agreed with the doctrine of Stare-Decisis. He has said that the Planned Parenthood v. Kasey7 decision reaffirming Roe is itself "a precedent on whether or not to revisit Roe v. Wade" (supra-precedent).

Chief Justice Roberts has said he does not want the court to be viewed as a forum where "partisan matters would be worked out." In the hearing Roberts implicitly, repudiated identity politics in decision making. He famously gave an interesting response to Senator Schumer's question as to "what kind of justice John Roberts would make". He said that he would be an objective "umpire" calling "balls and strikes" and not a pitcher or a batter. He said, "Judges and justices --- are like umpires. Umpires don't make the rules, they apply them. The role of an umpire and a judge is critical. They make sure everybody plays by the rules, but it is a limited role. Nobody ever went to a ball game to see the umpire."8

Analogies are always dangerous; yet one must love the comparison with baseball. In the Senate hearing he went on to testify that he had no agenda:

"Mr. Chairman, I came before the Committee with no agenda. I have no platform. Judges are not politicians who can promise to do certain things in exchange for votes. I have no agenda, but I do have a commitment. If I am confirmed, I will confront every case with an open mind. I will fully and fairly analyze the legal arguments that are presented. I will be open to the considered views of my colleagues on the bench, and will decide every case based on the record, according to the rule of law, without fear or favor, to the best of my ability, and I will remember that it's my job to call balls and strikes, and not to pitch or bat."9

Senator Grassley asked: Well, is there any room in constitutional interpretation for the judge's own values and beliefs?

Roberts: No, I don't think there is….. You don't look at your own values and beliefs. You look outside yourself to other sources. This is the basis for, you know, that judges wear black robes, because it does not matter who they are as individuals. That's not going to shape their decision. It's their understanding of law that will shape their decision.10 Ibid

Arlen Specter asked a question on whether his religion would cause a problem to him as a Supreme Court Justice in deciding whether to overrule certain highly charged cases like Roe v. Wade as reaffirmed in Casey.

Roberts answered: There had been a question raised about your personal views and let me digress from Roe for just a moment because I think this touches on an issue which ought to be settled. When you talk about your personal views, and as they may relate to your own fate, would you say that your views are the same as those expressed by John Kennedy when he was a candidate and he spoke to the Greater Houston Ministerial Association in September in 1960, "I do not speak for my charge on public matters, and the charge does not speak for me?"

Roberts: I agree with that, Senator, yes.

Chairman Specter: And did you have that in mind when you said, "there is nothing in my personal views that would prevent me from fully and fatefully applying the precedent as well as Casey?"

Roberts: Well, I think people's personal views on this issue varied from a number of sources, and there's nothing in my personal views based on fates or other sources that would prevent me from applying the precedents of the court under principle of Stare-decisis.11 Ibid

Why did I bring up the transcript of the US Senate Committee on Judiciary on the nomination of the Chief Justice of the highest court? It is to show how the system works with checks and balances. Secondly, it is said, the President of the US is the most powerful man on earth, but he cannot impose anything at will in State affairs unless and until the Senate approves it, particularly on the question of appointments to the constitutional posts or passing of a bill by the Senate. Even no President can pass any law or manage to pick up any individual of his choice to the constitutional posts without the approval of the Senate even if his party enjoys a majority in the Senate. Thirdly, the above questions and answers are displaying to us how intelligent and conversant in law are the Senators. They have a grasp of all important decisions of the US Supreme Court on any issue with precision. Can we claim our lawmakers have such depth of knowledge in law and the pronouncements of the highest court of the country? My respectful answer would be: No. Some of our parliamentarians have law backgrounds, some of them practice regularly in the Supreme Court, but I find that their knowledge in law is superficial. Whenever a question is put to them on any fact or law over a matter for which they appear, except for one or two, instead of giving an answer they smile looking toward the Bench. Their body language speaks and leads the court to believe that they are so busy with other political activities that they find little time to go through the facts and law meticulously when they appear in court.

One may pose a question whether our government could provide such facilities to a lawmaker in our country in the manner a Senator in the US is privileged to have. True, a nation like ours we cannot provide them with such facilities. Even then the question will arise whether we are as backward as what the US was in 1803. My answer is an emphatic "No". In 1803, if we look at history, Washington DC's roads were full of mud, almost one foot deep. The judges, the senators and representatives of the House used to sit in one building. There was no accommodation for them in Washington DC when the seat of the government was shifted from Pennsylvania to Washington DC. US Congressmen were more educated and learned than we had in 1960s, 1970s, 1980s, and 1999s, even today with exception of one or two. The simple reason for the fact that we still lag is that we did not try or believe in institutionalizing the departments and organs of the State. We believe and still believe in our own name, fame and power without caring about the nation.

I made those remarks and even travelled to the US to show the difference between our law-making system and the US law-making arrangement only because America was not of the same status in the early part of the Nineteenth Century. The founding fathers and subsequent politicians wanted to develop their country as a Class One nation and they ultimately succeeded. Even today we as a nation do not try to develop our country along the similar principles or ideology or mindset. Our country is sharply divided on the issue of the development of our nation. I believe that at least on one or two points the politicians should unite to build our nation together to transform us into a respectful country, and we can achieve this goal only when all the politicians join their hands ignoring their ego, feeling of superiority in thinking or learning. Secondly, we must have an intense sense of patriotism to build ourselves as a nation. We have seen from the media that even in India all leaders of political parties sit together to resolve problems when Parliament becomes unworkable on an issue. We have seen that all the parliamentarians voted to pass the GST Bill. We have also seen that all the parliamentarians voted in favor of a bill placed in the house for the appointment of judges of the higher judiciary and the Chief Justice.

But our experience shows that if a ruling political party placed a bill for the welfare of the people, the opposition members oppose it for the sake of opposing only. We have not seen for a long time the leaders of all political parties come together even for a cup of tea on any national occasion. We have seen that on the invitation of present Indian Prime Minister Narendra Modi, Sonia Gandhi attended a program and discussed the problems of the country. We may have political differences, but we must respect all members of Parliament irrespective of their political ideology because they were elected by their constituents who are people of their locality. Even if his party holds fewer numbers of seats in Parliament, he is being the representative of the people who are sovereign, it is their mandate that we should respect.

I have expounded all this to underline the issue of lack of qualified persons nominated and elected as representatives of the people and, as a result, our laws remain obsolete and defective. In this connection, I would like to cite one case.11 In this case the constitutionality of Section 6(2) of the Nari-O-Shishu Nirjaton (Bisesh Bidhan) Ain, 1995 and Section 34 of the Nari-O-Shishu

Nirjaton Daman Ain, 2000 were challenged. One Sukur Ali was sentenced to death under the Ain (Act) of 1995 for sexually assaulting to death of a minor girl Sonia Akhter, 7 years old. The trial court sentenced him to death, the High Court Division confirmed the sentence and the apex court also maintained the sentence. A review petition was also filed in the apex court and it was also rejected. Because as per law12 & 13 a mandatory sentence of death is provided for the offence. Thereafter, the convict along with another moved a writ in the High Court Division challenging the vires of the law. The High Court Division refrained from declaring the law unconstitutional observing that when the legislature prescribes any punishment as mandatory, the hands of the court become a simple rubber stamp. However, the High Court Division granted certificate14 formulating points that the constitutionality of the law should finally be settled by the apex court. Since "the punishment prescribed in section 6 (2) of the Ain is such that if the 'Bisesh Adalot' finds the accused guilty it can do no more than to impose the mandatory punishment of death."

We found defect in the certificate granted by the High Court Division in that if it grants a certificate, it ought to have formulated the point on which the certificate was granted containing, inter alia, that the case involves a question of law as to the interpretation to the Constitution or that the question is a substantial one.15 We noticed a pertinent question in the Acts of 1995 and 2000, which require to be addressed and accordingly we took up the point. We also noticed that some of the offences in the 1983 law are also included in the schedule of the Special Powers Act, 1974. This law was replaced, and the law of 1995 was passed and then this law was also replaced and the present law, the Nari-O-Shishu Nirjatan Ain, 2000 was promulgated. In the present law, the horizon of offences has been expanded and alternative sentences in respect of all offences except one has been provided. A savings clause was provided in it stating that the cases instituted or pending for trial under the repealed law including the appeals shall continue as if the Ain of 1995 has not been repealed.

It may be noted here that the European Community has abolished the death sentence. In America also, some States have abolished the death sentence. But we cannot abolish sentence of death because our social conditions and cultural values are completely different from those of the western countries. However, we have safeguards while awarding a death sentence. If an offender commits an offence which is punishable by death, he is provided with a defense counsel in the absence of his lawyer and will be provided with documents for the filing of an appeal if he is convicted by the trial court. Our Constitution guarantees equal protection of law: State cannot take any action against a citizen detrimental to his life otherwise than in accordance with law, and finally, no citizen shall be subjected to cruel or inhuman treatment.16

One of the important concepts of rule of law is legal certainty. The United States constitution declares that "No State shall deny to any person within its jurisdiction the equal protection of laws."17 This provision is equal to our provisions of the Constitution. The United States forbids "Class Legislation but does not forbid classification which rests upon reasonable grounds of distinction. It does not prohibit legislation, which is limited either in the objects to which it is directed to by the territory within which it is to operate." It only requires that all persons are subjected to such legislation shall be treated alike under like circumstances and conditions both in privileges conferred and, in the liabilities, imposed.18

On the question of equal protection of law, it was observed the court has frequently held that the legislative authority, acting within its proper field, is not bound to extend its regulation to all cases which it might possibly reach. The legislature "is free to recognize degree of harm and it may confine its restrictions to those classes of cases where the need is deemed to be clearest." If the law presumably hits the evil where it is most felt, it is not to be overthrown because there are other instances to which it might have been applied. There is no 'doctrinaire requirement' that the legislation should be couched in all embracing terms."19 On the question of classification of the legislature, it was observed in another case: "Classification must have relation to the purpose of the legislature. But logical appropriateness of the inclusion or exclusion of objects or persons is not required. A classification may not be merely arbitrary, but necessarily there must be great freedom of discretion, even though it results in ill advised, unequal, and oppressive legislation..... Exact wisdom and nice adaptation of remedies are not required by the 14th Amendment, nor the crudeness nor the policy nor even the injustice of state laws redressed by it."20

In our Penal Code some for offences the maximum sentence has been prescribed. But no minimum sentence has been prescribed and it is left with the discretion of the court. Even in a murder case, there is maximum sentence, but though a minimum sentence is provided, the court is left with the discretion to alter the conviction and award a lesser sentence. A wide discretion has been given to a court in awarding sentences in different provisions of the Penal Codes except in section 303. There is rational ground for making this provision, since, "whoever being under sentence of life commits murder shall be punished with death." In those days, when the Penal Code was enacted, jail officials were Englishmen and with a view to preventing assault by the indigenous people on white officers they had in their mind one kind of case. That is why it was observed that "the primary object of making the death sentence mandatory for an offence under this section seems to be to give protection to the prison staff."21 So the purpose of keeping such a provision was with a motive. Moreover, section 303 fastens the special requirement of murder with the definition of "culpable homicide". By and large, murders are committed by a person more on a variety of motives which operate on the mind of the offender, whether he is under a sentence of life imprisonment or not. Such motives are too numerous and varied too innumerable, but hate, lust, sex, jealousy, gain, revenge, weaknesses to which human flesh is subject are common for the generality of murders.

The authors of our Penal Code in many cases have not fixed a minimum as well as a maximum sentence for an offence. But in respect of some heinous offences: offences against the State, murder, attempt to commit murder and the like, they had thought it right to fix a minimum sentence.22 The authors had in mind that where there is a statutory maximum sentence, it should be reserved for the worst type of offence falling within the definition of offence. The Penal Code prescribes minimum sentence of seven years under sections 397 and 398, but for other offences there is no minimum.

Sentencing an offender is an important branch of the law. The International Union of Criminal Law of the French group in 1905 recommended that "there should be organized in the faculties of law. Special teaching theoretical and practical for the whole range of penal studies (and) the certificate in penal studies awarded should be taken into consideration for nomination to and advancement in the Magistracy.23 Subsequently the Ninth International Prison Congress in 1925 resolved at its London meeting that "judicial studies should be supplemented by criminological ones. The study of criminal psychology and penology should be obligatory for all who wish to judge in criminal cases. Such judges should have a full knowledge of prisons and similar institutions and should visit them frequently." But they are wanting in our country as in many other countries as well.

The main purpose of the sentence, broadly stated, is that the accused must realize that he has committed an act which is not only harmful to society of which he forms an integral part but is also harmful to his own future, both as an individual and as a member of the society. Punishment is designated to protect society by deterring potential offenders as also by preventing the guilty party from repeating the offence. It is also designed to reform the offender and reclaim him as a law-abiding citizen for the good of the society. Reformatory, deterrent and punitive aspects of punishment thus play their due roles in judicial thinking while determining the question of sentences. In modern civilized societies, however, the reformatory aspect is being given somewhat greater importance. Too lenient as well as too harsh sentences both lose their efficaciousness. One does not deter and the other may frustrate thereby making the offender a hardened criminal. The courts have always had in mind the need to protect society from persistent offenders but at the same time they are not oblivious to the system prevailing in the country for it has not gone for in cutting out the risk of conviction of innocent persons because of the peculiar character of the people and of the law-enforcing agencies.24

The Supreme Court of India has struck down section 303 of the Penal Code as violative of Articles 14 and 21 of the Indian Constitution on the philosophy that no person shall be deprived of life and personal liberty except in accordance with law.25 If the law has given to the judge a wide discretion in the matter of sentencing to be exercised by him after balancing all the aggravating and mitigating circumstances of the crime, it will be impossible to say that there would be at all any discrimination, since facts and circumstances of one case can hardly be the same as the facts and circumstances of another. .... The judicial decision must depend on the facts and circumstances of each case and what may superficially appear to be an unequal application of the law may not necessarily amount to a denial of equal protection unless there is shown to be present in it an element of intentional and purposeful discrimination .... Further, the discretion of judicial officers is not arbitrary, and the law provides for revision by superior courts of orders passed by the subordinate courts. In such circumstances, there is hardly any ground for apprehending any capricious discrimination by judicial tribunals. Crime as crime may appear to be superficially the same but the facts and circumstances of a crime may vary widely and since a decision of the court about punishment is dependent on a consideration of all the facts and circumstances, there is hardly any ground for challenge under Article 14.26

The preponderance of judicial opinion is that the structure of prevailing criminal law underlines the policy that when the legislature has defined an offence with enough clarity and prescribed the maximum punishment therefor, a wide discretion in the matter of fixing the degree of punishment should be allowed to the court. The policy of the law in giving a very wide discretion in the matter of punishment to the court has its origin in the impossibility of laying down standards. In Jagmohan Singh, an example was given in respect of an offence of criminal breach of trust punishable under section 409. The maximum sentence prescribed is imprisonment for life and the minimum could be as low as one day's imprisonment and fine. It was observed from the above that if any standard is to be laid down about several kinds of breaches of trust by persons referred to in that section, it would be an impossible task.

All that could be reasonably done by the legislature if they told the court that between the maximum and the minimum prescribed for an offence, it should, on balancing the aggravating and mitigating circumstances as disclosed in the case, judicially decide what would be the appropriate sentence. The judicial decision must depend on the facts and circumstances of each particular case and what may superficially appear to be an unequal application of the law may not necessarily amount to a denial of equal protection unless there is shown to be present in it an element of intentional and purposeful discrimination. The discretion reposed on a judicial officer is not arbitrary and the law provides for revision by superior courts. In such circumstances, there is hardly any ground for apprehending discrimination by a judicial tribunal. In Jagmohan, the Supreme Court declined to declare the death sentence unconstitutional on the reasonings that the court is primarily concerned with all the facts and circumstances in so far as they are relevant to the crime and how it was committed, and since at the end of the trial the offender was liable to be sentenced, all the facts and circumstances bearing upon the crime are legitimately brought to the notice of the court.

A very wide discretion in fixing the degree of punishment is allowed to the trial judge except for the offence of murder, for which the court must pass a sentence of imprisonment for life, and for a limited number of offences in respect of which the penalty is fixed by law including those offences for which the sentence of death must be pronounced. About most offences, the policy of the law is to fix a maximum penalty, which is intended only for the worst cases, and to leave to the discretion of the court the determination of the extent to which in a particular case the punishment awarded should approach to or recede from the maximum limit. The exercise of this discretion is a matter of prudence and not of law, but an appeal lies against any sentence not fixed by law, and, if leave is given, the sentence can be altered by the court. Minimum penalties have in some instances been prescribed by the enactment creating the offence.27

In awarding the maximum sentence in respect of an offence the position of law prevailing in our country is a bit different. It is provided in our Code of Criminal Procedure that if the prosecution wants to award the maximum/enhanced sentence for the offence charged against an offender, it shall be stated in the charge the fact of his previous conviction of any offence or the punishment of a different kind for a subsequent offence as well as the date and place of the previous conviction. However, a statement of previous conviction in the charge is not necessary where such conviction is to be taken into consideration, not for the purpose of awarding enhanced sentence under section 75 of the Penal Code but merely for the purpose of the punishment to be awarded within the maximum fixed for the offence charged. This however does not deter the court or tribunal from awarding the maximum sentence if the act of the offender is an intentional and brutal one. Whenever a criminal law provides for a mandatory sentence for an offence there is a possibility that there may be considerable variations in moral blameworthiness, despite the similarity in legal guilt of the offenders upon whom the same mandatory sentence must be passed. In the case of murder, a crime that is often committed in the heat of passion, the likelihood of this is very real; it is perhaps more theoretical than real in the case of large scale trafficking in drugs, a crime of which the motive is cold and calculated with equal punitive treatment for similar legal guilt.28

It follows that the decision as to the appropriate penalty to impose in the case of murder should be taken by the judge after hearing submissions and, where appropriate, evidence on the matter. In reaching and articulating such decisions, the judges will enunciate the relevant factors to be considered and the weight to be given to them, having regard to the situation in Saint Lucia. The burden thus laid on the shoulders of the judiciary is undoubtedly heavy, but it is one that has been carried by judges in other systems. The judges of Saint Lucia will discharge this new responsibility with all due care and skill.29 Ibid

In the Bahamas, two persons were convicted for murder and sentenced to death under Section 312 of its Penal Code. This provision was challenged to the extent that persons, other than pregnant women, charged with murder must be punished to death was unconstitutional. The Privy Council upon hearing the constitutional question formulated the principle for arbitrary sentence of death:

"(A) It is a fundamental principle of just sentencing that the punishment imposed on a convicted defendant should be proportionate to the gravity of the crime of which he has been convicted. (b) The criminal culpability of those convicted for murder varies very widely. (c) Not all those convicted of murder deserve to die. (d) Principles (a), (b) and (c) are recognized in the law or practice of all, or almost all states which impose the capital penalty for murder. (e) Under an entrenched and codified Constitution of the Westminster model, consistent with the rule of law, any discretionary judgment on the measure of punishment which a convicted defendant should suffer must be made by the judiciary and not by the executive." The conclusion of the Privy Council's opinion is that Section 312 should be construed as imposing a discretionary and not a mandatory sentence of death. So construed, it was continued under the 1973 Constitution of Bahama. The death sentences were quashed, and the cases remitted to the Supreme Court for consideration of appropriate sentences.30

In a Ugandan case the Supreme Court observed, the Constitution provides for the separation of powers between the Executive, the Legislature and the Judiciary. Any law passed by Parliament which has the effect of tying the hands of the judiciary in executing its function to administer justice is inconsistent with the Constitution. It also agreed with Professor Sempebwa, for the respondents, that the power given to the court under Article 22(1) does not stop at confirmation of conviction. The Court has the power to confirm both conviction and sentence. This implies a power not to confirm, implying that the court has been given discretion in the matter. Any law that fetters that discretion is inconsistent with this clear provision of the Constitution.31

The Kenyan Court of Appeal also expressed similar views, i.e. the imposition of the mandatory death penalty for offences is neither authorized nor prohibited in the Constitution. As the Constitution is silent, it is for the courts to give a valid constitutional interpretation on the mandatory nature of the sentence. Mandatory death sentence is antithetical to fundamental human rights and there is no constitutional justification for it. A convicted person ought to be given an opportunity to show why the death sentence should not be passed against him. The imposition of a mandatory death sentence is arbitrary because the offence of murder covers a broad spectrum. Making the sentence mandatory would therefore be an affront to the human rights of the accused. Section 204 of the Penal Code is unconstitutional and ought to be declared a nullity. Alternatively, the word "ought to be construed as "may".32

It is on record that within a space of 12 years, our legislature promulgated laws on the subject repeatedly prescribing a hard sentence leaving nothing for the courts to exercise its discretionary power on the question of awarding sentence. In the Ordinance of 1983 a similar nature of offence was prescribed in Section 7 providing alternatively for sentence of death or imprisonment for life. What prompted the legislature to make a U-turn in seizing the discretionary power of the tribunal in the matter of awarding the sentence is not clear. In the preamble nothing was mentioned to infer the intention of the legislature which prompted it to promulgate such a draconian law. It was simply stated that "It was desirable to promulgate law for committing serious offence towards women and children and a special law is required to be promulgated. The legislature abruptly took away the alternative sentence. Sub-section (2) of Section 6 provides, "If any person killed a woman or child by committing sex or after such commission of sex he would be sentenced to death." There are two parts in this sub-section: the first part carries the meaning that if someone causes the death of a child or woman in committing rape is discernable. The second part is that after the commission of rape, if the victim dies then also the offender will be sentenced to death.

The legislature is totally silent under which eventuality if the death is ensued, the offender will be sentenced for the offence. If secondary causes intervened in the death, the offender certainly cannot be held responsible for causing death by rape. There is a total lack of reasonableness in the provision that even if the offender is a minor or an old person the court is left with no discretionary power in the matter of awarding alternative sentence on extraneous consideration, which a core is sentencing principle, i.e. giving a sentence proportionate to the offender's culpability or gravity to the offence. Additionally, if the offender is a minor or an infirm person, the court is left with no discretion.

If a similar offence is committed under the Ain (Act) of 1995 by more than one person all of them will be sentenced to death. Suppose five persons are involved in the commission of the crime, of them two directly participated in the commission of rape and other three persons abetted the offence. If these three persons are sentenced to death with the other two, it will be contrary to norms and sentencing principles which are being followed for over a century. Sub-section (4) also provided that if more than one person sexually assaulted a woman or child causing death after such rape, they will also be sentenced to death. This provision is so vague and indefinite that the courts cannot have any discretionary power to exercise particularly in a case where there is no direct evidence for causing rape and the case rests upon circumstantial evidence. However, if the court finds that the circumstances are such that the offenders are responsible for causing the rape to the victim, it will be logical to award the death sentence to all in the absence to direct evidence.

In all cases while awarding a sentence of death, which is a forfeiture of the life of a person, the court always insists upon direct evidence. In the absence of direct evidence, it is very difficult to conclude that the accused had sufficient means in the act of rape. But since only one sentence is provided for the offence, the courts are left with no option other than to award the death sentence. This is totally inhumane and illogical. A law which is not consistent with notions of fairness and provides an irreversible penalty of death is repugnant to the concepts of human rights and values, and safety and security and the fundamental rights enshrined in the Constitution.

No law which provides for it without involvement of the judicial mind can be said to be constitutional, reasonable, fair and just. Such law must be stigmatized as arbitrary because such provision deprives the tribunal in the administration of justice independently without interference by the legislature. These provisions while purporting to impose mandatory death penalty seek to nullify those statutory structure under sub-sections (3) and (5) of Section 367 of the Code of Criminal Procedure, though these provisions are contained in general law, in the absence of prohibition, in view of section 5(2) of the Code of Criminal Procedure, they cover the field. A provision of law which deprives the court the use of its beneficent discretion in a matter of life and death, without regard to the circumstances in which the offence was committed and, therefore, without regard to the gravity of the offence cannot but be regarded as harsh, unfair and oppressive. The legislature cannot make relevant circumstances irrelevant, deprive the court of its legitimate jurisdiction to exercise its discretion not to impose death sentence in appropriate cases. Determination of appropriate measures of punishment is judicial and not an executive function. The court will enunciate the relevant facts to be considered and weight to be given to them having regard to the situation of the case.

Therefore, I have no hesitation in holding the view that these provisions are against the fundamental tenets of our Constitution that all citizens are entitled to equal "protection of law", that State shall not "discriminate against any citizen on grounds only of religion, race, cast, sex or place of birth and that to enjoy 'the protection of law,' and to be treated in accordance with law, and only in accordance with law, is the inalienable right of every citizen, wherever they may be, and of every other person for the time being in Bangladesh, and in particular no action detrimental to the life, liberty, body, reputation or property of any person shall be taken except in accordance with the law and that no person shall be subjected to torture or cruel, inhuman, or degrading punishment or treatment.33 Therefore, those provisions are ultra vires of the Constitution and, accordingly, they are declared void.

While legislating the Ain (Act) of 2000, similar provisions have been provided in sub-sections (2) and (3) of section 9 providing alternative sentence. This shift in the attitude of the legislature, on the question of sentence within a space of five years justifies the unreasonableness in the repealed law. However, in Section 11(Ka) of the Ain of 2000, it is provided that if death is caused by husband or husbands, parents, guardians, relations or other persons to a woman for dowry, only one sentence of death has been provided leaving no discretionary power for the tribunal to award a lesser sentence on extraneous considerations. This provision is to the same extent ultra vires of the Constitution, inasmuch as, there is vagueness and uncertainty in determining the appropriate measure of punishment. When it is said, "any person demands dowry on behalf of the husband." there is scope for victimizing any person by implicating in the offence and the tribunal will be left with no discretionary power to award an alternative sentence. Since I held that Sub-sections (2) and (4) of Section 6 of the Ain of 1995 and Sub-sections (2) and (3) of Section 34 of the Ain of 2000 are ultra vires the constitution, despite repeal of the Ain of 1995, all cases and appeals pending under the repealed Act shall be regulated under the said law, but on the question of imposing sentence, the sentences prescribed in respect of those offences shall hold the field until new legislation is promulgated. I held that there was total absence of proper application of the legislature's mind in promulgating those laws, which may be rectified by amendments.

In respect of section 303 of the Penal Code, the punishment shall be made in accordance with section 302 of the Penal Code. I declared that despite repeal of Nari-O-Shishu Nirjatan (Bishesh Bidhan) Ain, 1995, the pending cases including appeals may be held under the repealed Ain, while dealing with the question of sentence the alternative sentences provided in the corresponding offences prescribed in the Nari-O-Shishu Nirjatan Daman Ain, 2000 shall be followed. I concluded my opinion by giving guidelines: 33(i) (a) sub-sections (2) and (4) of Section 6 of the Nari-O-Shishu Nirjatan (Bishesh Bidhan) Ain, 1995, sub-sections (2) and (3) of Section 34 of the Nari-O-Shishu Nirjatan Daman Ain, 2000 and Section 303 are declared ultravires the Constitution. (b) Despite repeal of the Ain of 1995, the pending cases and pending appeals in respect of those offences shall be tried and heard in accordance with the provisions of the Ain of 1995, but the sentences prescribed in respect of similar nature of offences in the Ain of 2000 shall be applicable. (c) There shall be no mandatory sentence of death in respect of an offence of murder committed by an offender who is under a sentence of life imprisonment.

References:

1. *Article 76(2) (a) of the constitution*
2. *Order 6 Rule 17 of the Code of Civil Procedure*
3. *Richmond Medical Center for Women v. Gilmore, 219 F. 3d 376, 376-377 (4th Cir. 2000) Notwithstanding Senator Ted Cruz, who clerked for Luttig on the Fourth Circuit before he cleared for Chief Justice Rehnquist, praised Luttig in the Second Republican Presidential debate as a "Rock-Ribbed Conservative."*
4. *Present Chief Justice, Federal Supreme Court of the US*
5. *410 US 113 (1973)*
6. *By Jeffrey Rosen, "Do you believe in 'Super Precedence?'?" New York Times, October 30, 2005, Available at: http://www. Nytimes.com/2005/10/130/weekinreview/so-do-you-believe-in-superprecedent.html.*
7. *505 US 833 (1992)*
8. *Transcription of Hearings of the US Senate Committee on the Judiciary on nomination of John G Roberts, Jr to be Chief Justice of the United States, page 55*
9. *Ibid page 56*
10. *Ibid 178*
11. *Ibid page 146*
12. *Civil Appeal No. 116 Of 2010, Criminal Petition No. 374 of 2011, and Jail Petition Nos. 18 of 2008, 3 of 2009, 1 of 2010, 8 of 2010, 16 of 2010, 2-3 of 2011, 5, 7 & 8 of 2012, BLAST v. Bangladesh.*
13. *Section 6(2) of the Nari-o-Shishu Nirjatan (Bisesh Bidhan) Ain. 19995*
14. *Article 103(2) (a) of the Constitution*
15. *PATRICK Reyes v. The Queen, 1A 64 of 2001, Bachan Singh v. State of Punjab (19800 2 SCC 375 and Matadeen v. Pointu-Pointu (1991) 1AC 98.*
16. *Articles 27, 31, 32 & 35(5) of the Constitution*

17. *The Fourteenth Amendment of the US Constitution.*
18. *Professor Willes dealing with the Fourteenth Amendment*
19. *West Coast Hotel Co. v. Parrish (1936) 300 US 379*
20. *Heat & Milligan Mfg. Co. v. Worst (1907) 207 US 338*
21. *Indian 42nd Law Commission Report.*
22. *Proceedings of the Legislative Council of the Governor General of India, Ed 1856 page 718*
23. *Rdzionwiez L, In Search of Criminology, Ex 1961, page 70*
24. *B.G Goswami v. Delhi Administration (1974) 3 SCC 85*
25. *Mithu v. State of Punjab (1983) 2 SC 277*
26. *Jamohan Singh v. State of UP (1973) 1 SCC 20*
27. *Halsbury's Laws of England, 4th Edition, Vol II, page 487*
28. *Ong Ahachuan v. Public Prosecutor, (1981) AC 648*
29. *Ibid*
30. *Bowe v. The Queen, (2006) 1 WR 1623*
31. *Attorney General v. Susan Kigula, Constitutional Appeal No. 3/2006*
32. *Godfrey Ngotho Mutiso v. Republic, Civil Appeal No. 17/2008*
33. *Guidelines*

Revenue Matters (P)

Revenue is the backbone of a country. Taxation is the central part of modern public finance. The main objective of taxation is raising revenue. A high-level of taxation is necessary in a welfare state to fulfill its obligations. Taxation is used as an instrument of attaining certain social objectives, i.e. as a means of redistribution of wealth and thereby reducing inequalities. Taxation in a modern government is thus needed not merely to raise the revenue required to meet its ever-growing expenditure on administration and social services but also to reduce the inequalities of income and wealth. Taxation is also needed to draw away money that would otherwise go into consumption and cause inflation to rise.1 (a) one of the government's main object is to collect taxes and revenues. The process involves many actors including the revenue collection office, accounting office, tax payers, tax assessors, etc. The more modern technology is used the more revenue can be collected and the country's development work can be implemented. After assuming office, I gave much attention to revenue matters because revenue is the backbone of a country's development programs. The number of taxpayers in our country is very low in comparison to India, the UK and the US. About half the number of Income Tax References is pending in India compared to the number of taxpayers in our country, and India has about one-fourth the number of Tax References than the UK. (The comparison between India and the UK was given by Nani Palkiwala.)

Our laws are also obsolete and the rate of taxes, advance income tax, VAT, customs duty, etc. is not in conformity with the law. Besides, there is lack of proper implementation of taxes and duties. Taking advantage of faulty laws, some businessmen, business houses, entrepreneurs and individuals in collusion with corrupt officials evade payment of taxes and duties at the proper rates and instead pay at a rate two to three times lower. Over-invoicing and under-invoicing is another field to evading taxes and siphoning huge amounts of the difference to foreign countries. While I was in Toronto, Canada, some months back I was shown an area having very palatial houses and the locality was known to be the costliest township. It is called "Begum Para" (Madams' Neighborhood), where the wives and children of politicians, businessmen and high-ranking officials are residing.

In the US also almost all owners of big business houses, ministers, politicians and high-ranking officials own business enterprises and houses in posh areas. I met a businessman of Bangladeshi origin whom I had known from before. He told me that he was offered by a very high-level Bangladeshi official to keep some million dollars on his behalf at an exchange rate of ninety taka per dollar provided he agreed. They siphoned the "black money" through money dealers, particularly the differences in amounts of money by under- and over-invoicing while importing and exporting items.

I constituted six Benches for hearing revenue matters excluding the jurisdiction of other benches and chose the presiding judges in whom I had confidence. The system worked tremendously well. There was improvement in the collection of revenue of the government, even during the three months of abnormal condition

273

after this present government formed its cabinet as the country was totally at a standstill due to blockade of roads. Imports and exports collapsed almost totally, and the government was unable to cover up the deficiency by collecting revenue from the businesses and industries. After disposal of the cases by the courts the collection of revenue gained momentum. In this connection I remember a case in which almost all the members of a renowned business house and possibly the richest families of our county were involved in a criminal case over evasion of tax. In a financial year the business house procured a balance sheet from a chartered accountancy firm showing zero income for the purpose of taxation and by another balance sheet through another firm showed business of Tk.2500 crore and by producing this balance sheet it obtained loan over Tk.2500 crore from Sonali Bank. Naturally a criminal case was filed by the Anti-Corruption Commission against all the members of the family. They were tried in absentia and convicted by the Special Judge. They somehow managed a judgment in their favor from the High Court Division in writ jurisdiction although law provides for an appeal from the conviction. On appeal by the Revenue Department, a most prominent lawyer appeared on their behalf. He could not support the judgment because there is uncontroverted evidence. The writ petition itself is not maintainable. After hearing was over, I kept the matter for the following day for order. A high-ranking officer of an elite intelligence agency (DGFI) in the rank of a Colonel wanted my permission to meet me. He was a very tall figure and told me that the litigants were very close to them and that their agency was interested in the matter. Therefore, I should show leniency toward them. I kept looking at him and was thinking about the audacity of the officer. I told him that he should not come to the court premises in future. I called the law minister and handed over his identity card to him and narrated the incident to him. I told him that he should bring the matter to prime minister's knowledge since she was directly dealing with the department so that no officer of the department could dare to interfere in the administration of justice. Md. Nojibur Rahman, present Principal Secretary, who was the Chairman of the National Board of Revenue during the relevant time, expressed his gratitude to me for helping him in collecting revenue for the government.

I want to turn to an income tax matter in respect of one of the biggest charitable organizations in the country. It is not my object to demean the organization. I had very little knowledge of tax matters, therefore I wanted to learn by expressing opinion on the matter. The organization is known as Bangladesh Rural Advancement Committee (BRAC) whose tax assessment had been stalled from assessment year 1993-94. The point of law involved in the matter was whether donation of Tk. 677,520,000.00 received for charitable purposes was invested on other projects without intimation to the Deputy Commissioner of Taxes and the income derived therefrom was claiming exemption from payment of tax. The point has public importance because there is no decision on this issue in our jurisdiction and similar points may arise in future. The High Court Division answered the question in the negative without assigning any reason observing that another Bench disposed of the point holding that since the assesses had distributed the profits to the general members and spent the income for charitable purposes, the income is not liable to taxation.

The first condition of exemption is that the income derived from property held under trust must be wholly for religious and charitable purposes. The word "property" has not been defined in the Income Tax Ordinance, 1984. In the absence of a definition, we may take the literal meaning of the word "property". According to the Concise Oxford English Dictionary, Tenth Edition, "property" means "a thing or things belonging to someone; a building and land belonging to it; shares or investments in property; law ownership; a characteristic of something," etc.1

The meaning of the expression "property" has come for consideration in different jurisdictions and the expression "charitable purpose" though defined in the Ordinance, different courts have provided elaborate discussions on the issue as to whether the heirs may take the property as beneficiary subject to a charge in favor of a charity allowable limit, it is only the excess amount accumulated, and not the entire income of the trust, which becomes entitled to exemption. The accumulated income in respect of which the conditions of sub-para (2) of Para 1 of the Sixth Schedule are satisfied is entitled to exemption. If the assessee has complied with the above provisions, he is entitled to as of right the exemption under the Sixth Schedule, Part A. Subsequent non-application of the accumulated income to the right purposes and failure to continue the investment to deposit the accumulated income in the permissible limit are to be dealt with in accordance with the law and the assessee cannot take any exception in this regard.

Thus, to enjoy exemption to the full extent, the question is whether the total income or a portion of the income of the trust property has to be applied to the continuity in the assessment year for charitable purposes. On a plain reading of this provision there is no ambiguity that section 44 read with the Sixth Schedule, Part A, can have application unless the source of income is the same property and, further, the property is held under charitable trust or other legal obligation wholly or in part for a religious or charitable purpose.2

The assessee would get some exemption, since, it is a registered charitable and social welfare organization and it carries on its activities mainly on donations and income derived from business on accumulation of the donations without spending the total amount on charitable purposes under sections 44-47 of the Income Tax Ordinance. The question therefore arose whether the assessee received donation wholly for charitable purposes and in that case, this only will be exempt from payment of tax. However, in respect of some assessment years it was found that the source of income was from industrial concerns and profit earned by investing money in business organizations. Though it claimed that the money was used for charitable purposes, these incomes which it derived from business will not be exempted from payment of tax since it derived income from other sources. Even if it is assumed that it has received donations for charitable purposes, it did not use the entire amount for charitable purposes, rather it invested the money in other business establishments and earned income from those business establishments. Sub-paragraph (2) of Paragraph 1 provides that if any income is not applied or is not deemed to have been applied to charitable or religious purposes in Bangladesh during the income year but is accumulated, or finally set apart, for application to such purposes in Bangladesh, such income shall not be included in the total income of the income year of the assessee provided that the assessee fulfils the conditions. If the assessee does not spend the entire amount of donation on charitable purposes, it can invest the unutilized portion with prior permission of the Deputy Commissioner of Taxes. But it cannot accumulate or set apart the amount so received exceeding ten years. It is not that the assessee has invested the money received by way of donation for charitable purposes with prior permission of the Deputy Commissioner of Taxes. Therefore, the assessee will not be or is not entitled to get the exemption as claimed in view of Section 44(1) read with Part a of Sixth Schedule. The income can be said to be for charitable purposes if it is utilized for the said purposes without diverting that income to other fields after receiving the donation. This is what is disclosed on a plain reading of Paragraph 1, Part A, of the Sixth Schedule of the Ordinance.

Though in general, income from property held in trust wholly for religious or charitable purposes is exempt from income tax, when the said property is a "business" then two alternative conditions have been imposed for getting that exemption: one condition is that the business is for the trust, that is, a religious or charitable institution. A trust is discouraged from entering business with trust properties unless such business is directly related to the objectives of the trust. This restriction having been imposed by a conscious act on the part of Parliament it is not within the court's power to dilate the restriction by liberal interpretation ignoring the language of the statute. This court held that the trust will not be entitled to exemption of tax and maintained the tribunal's decision.3 there is an amendment in the law. In place of word "property" used in paragraph 1(1) of the Sixth Schedule, the words "house property" have been substituted by Finance Act, 2001 and after the word 'obligation' the words "or from operation of microcredit by such trust or obligation" have been substituted by the Finance Act, 2002. An explanation has also been added in sub-paragraph (1) by the Finance Act, 2001 providing that the provisions of this paragraph shall not apply in the case of non-governmental organizations registered with the NGO Bureau.

The return shows the source of income, besides grants received from donors, was from money invested in three commercial organizations: (a) Aarong (b) BRAC Printers (c) BRAC Dairy. It also earned income from house property and from other sources, not disclosed. Though it derived income by lending money for interest, it is non-taxable income in view of the amendment, but the other sources are totally commercial and in no way related to charitable purposes mentioned above. Exemptions are allowable in respect of income derived from the operation of microcredit business by an NGO registered with NGO Bureau and donations received for charitable purposes provided the entire amount of donation is utilized for the same purpose during the financial year only. Even though the trust's objects are charitable, the presence of ancillary or secondary object of non-charitable nature does not prevent taxation – if among several objects of trust, the trust carries on trade or business it can do so subject to the condition of relaxation with prior permission and not otherwise.

The essential conditions to create a charitable trust are: (a) a declaration which is binding on the settlor; (b) setting apart definite property and the settlor depriving himself of the award ship thereof; (c) statement of the objects for which the property is thereafter to be held i.e. beneficiaries. If a fund is collected for charitable purposes and a portion thereof is found to contain real elements of trust present therein as management, its nature and utilization of the said amount will be entirely taken within assesses volition and not be exempted from taxation. In the definition of the clause "charitable purpose" though the words "not involving the carrying on of any activity for profit" have not been used in the manner the Indian definition has been used, a plain reading of this definition vis-a-vis the amendment made to paragraph 1(1) of the Sixth Schedule, Part A, the intention of the legislature is clear that the trust may carry on activities for profit for a limited purpose, that is to say, any income derived from operations of microcredit by a trust which is registered with the NGO Bureau and that if any income is not applied to charitable purposes and is accumulated or set apart for a period not exceeding ten years, and to be invested with intimation to the Deputy Commissioner of Taxes mentioning the purpose of accumulation in government or other securities approved by the government or Post Office savings account.

In this paragraph the word "applied" in place of the word "spent" has been used. These two words "applied" and "spent" should not be equated. Actual payment of funds is irrelevant for the purposes of finding out whether there has been application of funds. There is nothing on record to infer the purpose for which the assessee BRAC was constituted, but if the object falls within the words "advancement of any object of general public utility" in section 2(15), all the incomes derived by the assessee would not be a charitable purpose within the meaning of the law as above. If there are several objects of a trust, some of which are charitable, and some are non-charitable and the trustee in its discretion applied the income or property or house property to other purposes, the income would not be regarded as charitable and no part of its income would be exempt from tax.

Where the main and primary object of a trust are distributive, each and every one of the objects must be charitable in order that the trust might be taken as a valid charity.4 But if the primary or dominant purpose of a trust is charitable, another object which by itself may not be charitable, which is merely ancillary or incidental to the primary or dominant purpose, it would not prevent the trust from being a valid charity.5

So, whether the object which is said to be non-charitable is the main or primary object which is charitable. In this connection the Supreme Court of India in Andhra Chamber of Commerce (Supra) held that if the primary purpose be advancement of objects of public utility, it would remain charitable even if an incidental entry into the political domain for achieving that purpose, the promotion of or opposition to legislation concerning that purpose was contemplated." It is the object of public utility which must not involve the carrying on of any activity for profit and not its advancement or attainment. What is inhibited by the last ten words is the linking of an activity for profit with the object of public utility and not it's linking with the accomplishment or carrying out of the object. It is not necessary that the accomplishment of the

279

object or the means to carry out the object should not have involved in an activity for profit. That is not the mandate of the newly added words. What these words require is that the object should not involve the carrying on of any activity for profit. The emphasis is on the object of public utility and not on its accomplishment or attainment. The true meaning of these last ten words is that when the purpose of a trust or institution is the advancement of an object of public utility, it is that object of public utility and not its accomplishment or carrying out which must not involve the carrying on of any activity for profit.6 Ibid Mere contribution to a fund would not entitle him to the exemption claimed.

Sub-paragraph (2) of the Sixth Schedule provides that if the income of the trust is not wholly used for charitable purposes during the income year or the unused amount is set apart for application to other purposes subject to the condition that the trust by notice in writing seeks permission of the Deputy Commissioner of Taxes. The purpose for which the income is being accumulated or set apart which shall not exceed ten years, or the said money is invested in any government security or any other security approved by the government and not otherwise. Admittedly, the assessee did not intimate the Deputy Commissioner of Taxes of accumulation of money for using the same for business purposes. He has not invested the accumulated income in accordance with law. Though the assessee has been doing business besides microcredit programs and other commercial business, and the income which has been shown is not derived wholly from house property held under trust, therefore, it will not get exemption. BRAC did not use the income totally for charitable purposes. After utilizing of a portion of the income for charitable purposes, it utilized a substantial portion in business and industrial purposes. It would get exemption if the income was derived from donations for charitable purposes, and the income was used solely for charitable purposes. It had not fulfilled these two conditions.

If a trust was created for charitable purposes and it entered business with trust property, such business is not directly related to the objective of the trust. The business is carried on meeting the expenses of the employees of the trust or for the livelihood of some other persons, but the proviso has restricted the scope and general exemption. Moreover, after the amendment of paragraph 1, the assessee cannot get the benefit of exemption, since, it failed to show that the income had been derived from the house property only. The explanation made it clear that sub-paragraph (1) shall not apply in the case of an NGO registered with the NGO Affairs Bureau. The trust has been registered under the Societies Registration Act and registered with the NGO Bureau, and therefore, it will not get the benefit of paragraph 1, Part I of the said schedule. The assessee transferred BRAC Printer's income from taxable account to non-taxable account; that the income from Aarong Craft Project was not correct and added the income under Section 33 of the Ordinance. We found no infirmity in the assessment.

References:

1.a Public Finance, Wikipedia

1. *Section 44(1) of the Income Tax Act, 1944*
2. *Guru Estate v. CIT, 48 ITR SC 53*
3. *36 DLR (AD) 166*
4. *Mohammad Ibrahim v. Commissioner of Income Tax*
5. *Commissioner of Income tax v. Andhra Chamber of Commerce (1955) 55 ITR 722 (SC)*
6. *Ibid*

Loan Recovery Legislation (Q)

In Bangladesh, the management of the financial sector is very weak due to various reasons. The laws are defective and there are no checks and balances in the administration mainly of the public banks. In public sector banks the political parties, after coming to power, appoint political persons at the helm of the banks. Governance failings and appointment of politically linked people

281

to the boards of public banks have been contributing to defaults on large loans, frequent scams and poor recovery of stolen money. These open the door for corruption, money laundering and financial crime risks, according to the Mutual Evaluation Report (MER) of the Asia/Pacific Group on Money Laundering (APG). In the report, the Australia-based inter-governmental body fighting money laundering, said better government steps were needed to freeze assets early on during investigation and to bring back the money that had been laundered. Default loans in Bangladesh stood at Tk 111,347 crore as of April 2016, said Finance Minister AMA Muhith in parliament on Monday. Just before the Awami League-led alliance assumed power in early 2009, the amount was Tk 35,000 crore. Since 2009, the government had appointed politically linked people to the boards of public banks, much to the dismay of the central bank. The recent APG report, prepared after its mission to Bangladesh late last year, referred to the $467 million loan scam of Sonali Bank (discovered in 2012); fraud involving $337 million of BASIC Bank between 2010 and 2012; and the embezzlement of $51 million from Janata Bank.

The report said, "Significant involvement of politically exposed persons in the board and management [of state banks] and failings of internal controls and governance were common factors ...." It added that politically exposed persons were present as beneficiary owners or directors/managers of banks, securities firms and other businesses. Abdul Hye Bachchu, the former BASIC Bank chairman, was blamed for damaging the bank through large-scale irregularities. Until 2009, BASIC was one of the best-run banks in the country. Despite Bangladesh Bank's reservations, the government had appointed Bachchu for a second-term. A year before the APG's mission to Bangladesh in 2016, the Anti-Corruption Commission had filed 56 cases in connection with the BASIC Bank scam but Bachchu was not accused in any of the cases. "To date, no assets have been attached or frozen. Despite the BFIU [Bangladesh Financial Intelligence Unit] efforts to investigate, no monies have yet been uncovered in bank accounts that were able to be frozen under the BFIU powers," said the APG. But in January this year Finance Minister AMA Muhith told The Daily Star, "I don't think that he [Bachchu] will escape the due process of law." Bachchu cannot go abroad without approval of the authorities, Muhith added.

In 2015, the finance minister also expressed frustration. "Despite my efforts, I could not take a particular culprit to jail as people like him enjoy support from our [party] men. And that is why, I am extremely disappointed," the daily Prothom Alo quoted him as saying on June 30, 2015. Speaking about a loan scandal in Rupali Bank in November 2014 last year, Muhith said there was a time when we used to place people on the board on political considerations. But this has stopped. "Not that we are always successful, as bad hats also make their way onto the boards," he added. About the BASIC Bank's case, the APG said it was evidence of the authorities' poor use of formal and informal channels when large amounts of proceeds of crime were being taken out of Bangladesh. "... The authorities were aware of a significant amount of monies being sent to Malaysia, but no formal requests for assistance had been made at the time." The money laundering risks did not appear to have been well assessed in the country's national and scrotal risk assessment exercises, the report noted.

The APG, however, appreciated that Bangladesh had made significant progress since its last evaluation in 2009, reflecting political commitment and leadership in anti-money laundering and countering terror financing. It said the inter-agency work to assess terror financing risks showed strength, but more work was needed to assess foreign terror finance threats. The APG praised the Bangladesh Financial Intelligence Unit (BFIU) of the central bank for seeking and receiving cooperation from its Malaysian counterparts regarding money flowing out of Bangladesh and sharing the results with the relevant law enforcement agencies.

The APG said Bangladesh should increase its use of mutual legal assistance (MLA) and extradition systems to make international requests for information and evidence. MLA is a method of cooperation between states for obtaining assistance in the investigation or prosecution of criminal offences. The report said Bangladesh Bank's supervision of a branch of Sonali Bank in 2012 identified evidence of corruption-related fraud by Sonali Bank's client, Hallmark Group, and its related fictitious companies. Supported by the BFIU, the ACC investigated actions of companies, including Hallmark Group, over the allegation of embezzlement of about $454 million. The APG, however, said the ACC did not pursue asset tracking and provisional measures during the enquiry. The BFIU did freeze 258 bank accounts, worth $4.2 million, whilst the ACC investigated. During the investigation stage, the High Court Division passed an order restricting the sale or transfer of all assets of the group.

The APG said the court order came in response to an application made by an interested advocate of the High Court Division, not the ACC. Bangladesh had four money laundering convictions and one acquittal until late 2016. Three of the four convictions were made in absentia, according to the APG. At least 214 more money laundering cases are under trial, it said. "Resource constraints and process challenges with the courts and trials lead to very lengthy legal processes and hinder effective money laundering investigations and prosecutions," observed the APG. Overall levels of confiscation were low, it said, adding that the law enforcement agencies generally did not effectively trace, restrain and manage proceeds of crime at an early stage in the investigations, which led to limited ability to recover the money.

Ibrahim Khaled, a former deputy governor of Bangladesh Bank, said loans given through corrupt practices could be laundered abroad but it was tough to trace the money as it is mostly laundered through illegal channels. He also touched upon the example of BASIC Bank, saying, "The money of BASIC Bank has been looted." Zaid Bakht, chairman of state-owned Agrani Bank, said there were incidents of loan money being taken out of the country. "This is mainly done through over-invoicing. In a case of over-invoicing, a borrower opens a letter of credit involving money that is much higher than the amount needed for the import." He said loans approved through corruption and bowing to political pressure were difficult to recover. In the current fiscal year 2017, the government has set aside Tk 2,000 crore to recapitalize the scam-hit state-owned banks. With this money, the total bailout amount is Tk 13,655 crore in the last eight years. Bangladesh is due to take over the APG co-chair role for 2018-2020 and will host an annual meeting during its two-year term.1

Chairman and directors of the banks and these political persons by using their political influence sanctioned huge amounts of loans to different persons of their line of thinking and corrupt businessmen in exchange of money. Not only that, activities of government supported labor leaders, interference of officials with political affiliations, inability to face political pressure, lack of competence in understanding land-related documents (as in most cases bank loans are approved by taking land as collateral). It is mostly due to legal advisors who are appointed on. There are allegations that in many cases directors are involved in looting public sector banks such as Sonali Bank, Janata Bank, Agrani Bank, Rupali Bank, Basic Bank, Krishi Bank etc. Many of them took big loans, sometimes using the names of their relatives and family members.

It has been seen since the independence of the country that even after passing almost half a century we continue to falter in our endeavors to build the nation. It is mainly, as I think, due to a lack of foresight among our politicians in power, corruption in the administration, apathy of the political leaders to develop institutions in the country while everyone is interested to consolidate power by using both money and muscle ignoring his capability and the interest of the country. Almost all people with any power in any sector are always driven by a need to make more money. It is even evident from the fact that just immediately after the liberation, when there was a shortage of food, clothing, medicines etc., and many people with the right connections rushed to take licenses for dealership of various commodities for making easy money. The manipulation of the stock market is another example of the urge to earn at a rapid pace. In this instance, companies which had not gone into production placed their shares in the Stock Exchanges and the value of those shares jumped hundred times higher than their face value. Naturally the result was the market collapsed and many innocent people who had invested their hard-earn funds or savings made with the expectation of purchasing a plot of land in Dhaka for their next generation became beggars within only a few days. Some of them committed suicide but the perpetrators remained beyond the reach of the law enforcement agencies. Yet another example is that a section of people jumped into the business of education by setting up private universities, medical and dental colleges, and often the certificates from these mushrooming institutions had extremely little, if any, value.

When someone started a business for profit, others jumped in such businesses without any knowledge of the subject. I have come across a massive number of cases in which the public banks could not realize money from the loan defaulters. The persons who took loans did not utilize the entire fund on the project; instead they sometimes transferred a great portion of the money abroad, sometimes they used the money to purchase properties and vehicles, sometimes they spent it on leading a lavish life at home and abroad, and ultimately could not pay the bank dues. When the bank took steps for realization of the loans it was detected that the documents of title mortgaged with the bank were forged or, if genuine, there was over-valuation of the property.

The banks could not take legal action against the officials responsible because by that time they were retired or gave up the job or left for elsewhere. The litigation dragged on for years together due to faulty laws. Even after getting a decree the banks could not realize the outstanding loans due to over-valuation of the properties. Banks had also advanced money purportedly for import of goods with fake documents when the importer did not import any goods. The best example in this connection is draining off the money equivalent to $344 million from the Sheraton Hotel branch of Sonali Bank by Tanvir Mahmud, Managing Director of the Hallmark Group, in connivance with bank officials. Sometimes people became what are known as briefcase industrialists/businessmen and obtained loans from banks showing papers only. The result, as expected is that all public banks are now on the verge of collapse.

As noted, the defects in law can be found in another example from the following case.1 (a) this case relates to only .03 acre of land decreed exparte.2 Lal Miah and his two brothers purchased 2.34 acres of land from different persons. Lal Miah died leaving two brothers and two sisters. One of the brothers sold .03 acre of land to one Habibur Rahman. He again sold a similar area of land to another person. Another brother Chan Miah also sold .03 acre of land to different persons. One of the purchasers again sold .05 acre of land to the plaintiffs by two different deeds. They obtained permission to construct a four storey building. Later, they came to know that the above decree was passed against them and accordingly filed suits for declaration of title in respect of .03 acre of land.

The trial court decreed the suit, but on appeal the High Court Division set aside the decree on the reasoning that the suit was not maintainable in the presence of alternative remedy of appeal under the Artha Rin Adalot Ain (Loan Recovery Court Act). Under the said law there is a provision for depositing in cash or security money of a certain percentage of the decretal amount within a statutory period as a pre-condition of filing appeal. A petition for setting aside exparte decree can be filed, but there is a condition of depositing money by security, but the difficulty is that they were not parties to the suit. The Artha Rin Adalot Ain is a special law. As per prevailing laws where there is remedy or any provision for recourse to law, the provisions of the law shall prevail over the general law. The suit was instituted in the ordinary civil court under the general law. Now the question was whether the civil case was maintainable in the presence of alternatives available under the special law. The High Court Division was in dilemma and granted a certificate for determination of the law by the apex court.

Section 9 of the Code of Civil Procedure confers the jurisdiction upon a civil court to adjudicate upon a right or obligation except to grant a substantive right or action which must be established by a statute or common law, that is to say, the right to recover damages under the law of tort. The jurisdiction of a civil court is all embracing except to the extent it is excluded by an express provision of law or by clear intendment arising from such a law. This is the purpose of section 9 of the Code of Civil Procedure.3 A suit in respect of property is suit of a civil nature.4 In every case where the dispute has the characteristic of affecting one's right then it is not only civil but is also of civil nature.5

Where the cognizance of a specified type of suit which is ousted either expressly or impliedly that the jurisdiction of the civil court would be ousted to entertain such a suit. The general principle is that a statute excluding the jurisdiction of a civil court should be construed strictly.6 A provision seeking to bar the jurisdiction of a civil court requires strict interpretation and the court will normally lean in favor of a construction upholding retention of jurisdiction.7 Normally all disputes between the parties of a civil nature would be adjudicated by a civil court. There is no absolute right in any one to demand that his dispute is to be adjudicated only by a civil court. Access to a civil court, which is an important vested right in every citizen of the country, implies the existence of the power of the court to render justice according to law. Where the Statute is silent and a judicial intervention is required, courts strive to redress grievances according to what is perceived to be principles of justice, equity and good conscience.8 Where the action challenged is without jurisdiction, civil court's jurisdiction is not ousted.9 An express bar is where a statute itself contains a provision that the jurisdiction of a civil court is barred, as in section 182 of the Income Tax Ordinance, 1984.

The jurisdiction of a civil court to entertain a suit, though of a civil nature, may be barred if it is so provided in a statute. There are, in fact, many statutes which have made provisions specifically ousting the jurisdiction of civil courts in specified matters. Section 26 of the Union Parishad Ordinance has put a clear bar to the determination of election dispute by any court except the Election Tribunal.10 Section 102 of the Waqf Ordinance debars a civil court to question the decision of the Waqf Administrator except as otherwise expressly provided in the Ordinance.11 An implied bar may arise when a suit provides special remedy to an aggrieved party, that is, a right of appeal contained in a statute.12 Where the legislature acts within its power, it is not open to the civil court to question the legality of an enactment.13

It is an ordinary principle of law that the court will not interfere with the management of a company acting within its power. If a court has no jurisdiction to try a suit, it goes to the very root of the matter and it is a case of inherent lack of jurisdiction. Preponderance principle is that the jurisdiction of a civil court to deal with civil causes can be excluded by a special law to deal with special subject matters. But the said law must expressly provide for such an exclusion. The presumption to be drawn must be in favor of the existence rather than exclusion of the jurisdiction. The questions for ascertaining such an issue are (a) whether the legislature's intent to exclude arises explicitly, and (b) whether the statute provides for adequate and satisfactory alternative remedy to a party aggrieved by an order made under it. Exclusion of jurisdiction of a civil court is not readily to be inferred unless law regarding exclusion of jurisdiction has been laid down.14 When a question as regards jurisdiction arises, the court has always the inherent jurisdiction to examine whether it has jurisdiction.15 Civil Courts have always the jurisdiction to determine whether a court of special jurisdiction is acting in accordance with the law or within the limits prescribed by law or in conformity with the fundamental principles of judicial procedure. As such determination in effect amounts to determining the extent to which the jurisdiction of civil court is ousted.16

The preamble of the Ain (Act) indicates the object of promulgating it. It is for realization of loan by financial institutions by amending the prevailing laws which the legislature felt was a necessity to integrate the law. The expression Financial Institute has been defined in section 2(Ka) and includes the Janata Bank. The word "loan" means advance, loan, overdraft, banking credit, discounting bills, guarantee, indemnity, letter of credit, etc. Section 3 says that the Ain shall prevail over any other law which is inconsistent with the Ain. Section 5 empowers the exclusive jurisdiction of the Artha Rin Adalat to adjudicate disputes relating to the realization of a loan by a financial institution. It is said, notwithstanding anything contained in any other law, subject to the provisions of sub-sections (5) and (6), all suits relating to realization of loans by a financial institution shall be instituted before the Artha Rin Adalat established under section 4 of the Ain and to be disposed of in the said Adalat (Court). This Adalat shall be constituted by a gazette notification and though it is a civil court within the meaning of Civil Courts Act, 1887, the officer of the Adalat cannot adjudicate any civil or criminal case other than a suit relating to a "loan".

A plain reading of these provisions clearly show that it is a special law and this law shall prevail over any other law and the object is the realization of loans by a financial institution; and the suit shall be filed and adjudicated by the Artha Rin Adalat constituted under the said Ain. These provisions do not prohibit specifically or impliedly a citizen from establishing his title in a civil court in respect of any property which has been mortgaged with a financial institution. The provisions of the Code of Civil Procedure will be applicable in filing and adjudicating a suit under the Artha Rin Adalat Ain, if those provisions are not inconsistent with the provisions of the Ain. In filing a suit against the principal debtor, the financial institution may implead the third-party mortgagor or the third-party guarantor, if he is involved in the loan. These are the three categories of persons against whom a suit of this nature can be filed seeking relief. There is no scope under the scheme of the Ain to implead in the category of defendants other than those mentioned above or any third party as defendant. The judgment, order or decree of the Artha Rin Adalat can be jointly and severally executable.

The execution proceeding shall be proceeded against all judgment debtors subject to the condition that the Adalat shall execute the decree against the principal debtor and subsequently against the third-party mortgagor or the third-party guarantor for the recovery of the loan. There is a second proviso providing that if the third-party mortgagor or third-party guarantor repays the total amount of the dues, the decree can be transferred in their favor and that they can also realize the total amount against the principal debtor. A third party is neither a necessary nor a proper party in a suit for realization of a loan against debtors. Therefore, neither section 19 nor section 41 has provided any provision to redress the grievances of a third party in respect of a mortgaged property. If someone takes loan from a bank by mortgaging another's property by deceitful means or by resorting to forgery or collusion or misrepresentation, the Adalat cannot adjudicate the issue. Sub-section (5) of section 6 has specifically provided the parties against whom a suit under the Ain can be filed. Other than those persons, there is no scope under the Ain to implead any person to add as a defendant in the suit.

It is only section 32 of the Ain which enables a third party to file objection against the decree in execution proceedings within a period of 30 days subject to payment of 10 percent of the decretal amount. This section is included in Chapter VI for execution of decree. If the scheme of the law does not authorize the Adalat to decide the title of a third party in respect of the mortgaged property, how then can it decide the right, title and interest of a third party in an execution proceeding is difficult to comprehend. The only right given to a third party is to file such objection in accordance with the Code of Civil Procedure. It is said that objection can be filed in accordance with the provisions of the Code of Civil Procedure. A third party who has right, title and interest in the decretal property has limited scope to file an objection against the attachment of the property in dispute or sale of the attached property in execution of a decree. He has also a right to file a suit under order 21, rule 103 and this provision can be applied even after exhausting remedies provided in rules 98, 99 and 101 of order 21 of the Code. A suit under rule 103 is a special remedy. The proviso to section 42 of the Specific Relief Act does not debar the suit if the plaintiff does not ask for recovery of possession or other consequential relief because he has been dispossessed by the process of the court over a property which he has right, title and interest.

Procedures prescribed by rules 97-102 are summary in nature and not intended for decision after hearing oral evidence and the conclusion is subject to the result of a suit under rule 103. Therefore, in view of sub-section (1) of section 32 of the Ain that while a third party can pray for setting aside the decree or order, the provisions of the Code of Civil procedure will be applicable, we find no cogent ground to prevent a third party from filing a suit to establish his title to in the property sold in execution of a decree in view of order 21 rule 103 since the said provision appears in order 21 under the heading Execution of Decree and Orders.

References:

1. *"Public Bank Scams: Problems left to persist", a report by Rejaul Karim Byron and Reaz Ahmed, published in The Daily Star, July 16, 2017*
2. *1(a). Civil Appeal Nos. 25 & 26 of 2013 and Criminal Petition Nos. 227 of 2012, 1587 of 2017, 1134 of 2015, Sikandar Ali v. Janata Bank Ltd.*
3. *Mortgage Suit No. 35 of 1995 (Narayanganj)*
4. *Union of India v. Sir Shadilal Sugar, AIR 1980 ALL 379 (FB) Dhulabhai v. S, AIR 1969 SC 78*
5. *Secretary of State v. Fahim Dannisa, ILR 13cal 95(PC) and Didar Ahmed Chowdhury v. Faruque Ahmed, 27 DLR (AD) 138*
6. *PMA Metropolitan v. Marthoma, AIR 1995 SC 2001*
7. *Dhruv Green Field Ltd v. Hukam Singh, (2002) 6 SCC 416; Secretary of State v. Mask, AI 1940 PC 105; Solaiman Bibi v. Administrator, 45 DLR 727; Md. Shahidullah v. Abdus Sobhan 1996 BLD 423*
8. *Dwarka Prasad v. Ramesh Chandra, AIR 2003 SC 2696*
9. *MV Elizabeth v. Harwan Investment, AIR 1993 SC 1014*
10. *Sardara Singh v. Sardara Singh (1900) 4SCC 90*
11. *Rafiqul Islam v. Mostafa Kamal, 42 DLR (AD) 137*
12. *Syed Masud Ali v. Asmatullah, 32 DLR (AD) 39; Director Housing and Settlement v. Howlader, 9BLC (AD) 51; Bangladesh v. Basharat Ullah, 42DLR (AD) 91 & Shahabuddin Chishti v. RAJUK 18 BLT (AD) 501*
13. *NDMC v. Satish Chan, AIR 2003 SC 3187*
14. *BWDB v. Syed Moazzem Hossain, 1BLC (AD) 13*
15. *State of Andhra Pradesh v. Manjeti Lakhsmi Kartharao, AIR 2000SC 2220; Secretary v. Mask AIR 40 PC 105; Church of North India v. Lavajibbai Ratanjbbai, AIR 2005 SC 2544*
16. *Nur Mohammad v. Mainuddin, 39 DLR (AD) 1; Rouf v. Hamid 17DLR (SC) 515*
17. *Amir Hasan v. Sheobakash 11 cal 6(PC)*

Presumption of Muslim Marriages (R)

I found an interesting case of claiming maintenance by Momtaz Begum1 against her husband. She claimed that though her marriage with Anwar Hossain was solemnized, according to Mohammedan law, but no "kabinnama" was registered. Thereafter they lived as husband and wife together for a considerable period of time---about 3 years---in a rented house. The marriage was duly consummated. With the passage of time, Anwar Hossain became greedier and started demanding dowry and, on her failure to pay dowry, she was driven out of the house. She instituted a suit for maintenance. The trial court decreed the suit and it was affirmed by the lower appellate court, but the High Court Division reversed the judgment. While hearing the appeal various questions were raised, such as whether non-registration of a marriage under Mohammedan Law made the marriage illegal or non-existent, (b) whether continuous cohabitation of three years as husband and wife coupled with their conduct infer a presumption as to a legal marriage.

I held that a marriage contracted without witnesses is irregular but not void. An irregular marriage is one which is not unlawful by itself but unlawful for something else, as where the prohibition is temporary or relative or when the irregularity it raises for an accidental circumstance such as absence of witnesses. Though among Sunnis the presence of witnesses is necessary to the validity of a marriage, their absence only renders it invalid, which is cured by consummation. A marriage may be proved directly if presumptively: by means of oral testimony of the witnesses present at the marriage or by documentary evidence in the shape of a deed of marriage; presumptively by a statement of the parties or by evidence of conduct and reputation. When court must form an opinion as to the relationship of one person to another, the opinion expressed by conduct as to the existence of such a relationship of any person, who is a member of a family or otherwise, has special means of knowledge on this subject is a relevant fact. Illustration :(a) section 50 asks the question is whether A and B were married.

The fact that they were usually received and treated as husband and wife is relevant.

So, when the question arises as to the presumption of marriage, the opinion expressed by conduct as to the existence of such a relationship and not merely as to that relationship. It is for the court to weigh such evidence and come to its own opinion as to the relationship in question. When the court has formed an opinion as to the relationship of one person to another, the opinion expressed by conduct, as to the existence of such relationship, of any person who as a member of the family or otherwise has special means of knowledge on this subject, is a relevant fact.

I summed up my opinion as under: (1) where it is proved that the parties cohabited continuously and for a long time as husband and wife and were treated as such by their relatives and friends. (2) Neither party has acknowledged that he or she was married to the other, and the other party has confirmed or acquiesced in the acknowledgement. After this pronouncement, a section of Muslim fanatic demonstrated with placards in front of Baitul Mokarram National Mosque for a review of the judgment. One day Justice Abdul Wahhab Miah criticized me saying, "Do you know what the repercussion among the Muslims was after the disputed verdict!" I told him I was not concerned with the reaction of my verdict, but I was concerned about the law and its impact on society. The days of keeping a concubine by a powerful moneyed person have been over for long. I understood the reasons behind his concern about the verdict because of his mindset.

Reference:

1. *Momtaz Begum v. Anwar Hossain, Civil Appeal No. 139 of 2003*

Customary Law (S)

Rangamati, Bandarban and Khagrachhari, these three districts constituted the Chittagong Hill Tracts. The government divided the region into three districts. From before the Regulation 19001 came into effect, the hill people were governed by their own customary laws. Normal laws applicable to the other regions of the country were not applicable there. The hill people were normally lived in or around Kaptai river valley mainly because the area was fertile. They used to produce one crop a year, which is commonly known as "Jhum Chash." During the 1960s, the Pakistan government constructed a dam on the Kaptai River for generation of hydroelectricity and as a result the entire fertile land, the houses of the tribal people including the house of the Chakma king all were inundated by water. The government did not make any alternative arrangement for the rehabilitation of the tribal people. Finding no other alternative, the tribal people scattered in deep hilly areas and had to live miserable life.

After the independence of the country, sometime from 1975 onwards, the government started relocating of people from the plains, a majority of whom were Muslims, in the area and the local administration allotted them "khas" (public) land. Among the rehabilitated people, some convicted persons who came with a view to avoid sentences taking advantage of the situation took shelter in the region. They were also allotted khas land. Some of the rehabilitated people, who were known criminals, committed rapes and abductions of local women. The hill people were not given allotment of any plain land. As a result, a section of tribe's people revolted, took shelter in Tripura, India, and formed an armed group under the name Shanti Bahini. There were a lot of causalities due to the armed conflict between the terrorists and the law enforcement agencies.

There was lawlessness in the region and it continued till 1997 when the Bangladesh government and leaders of the Shanti Bahini entered a treaty and pursued the armed cadre to lay down their arms. All refugees who took shelter in Tripura returned to Bangladesh. Thereafter, in pursuance of that pact the government promulgated Ain XII2 and some other laws.   There was a judgment in the High Court Division that Regulation 1900 was a dead law after the Pakistan Constitution 1962 came into force and, therefore, the tribal people will not get special status under Regulation 1900. While in the High Court I delivered a judgment that Regulation 1900 is applicable to the hill people.

A dispute arose as to whether the Land Appeal Board Ain4 has jurisdiction to hear a dispute arising out of a judgment passed by the Deputy Commissioner and Divisional Commissioner in civil suits in exercise of powers under Regulation 1900. I held that Regulation 1900 is a special law that applied to several parts of the former British Empire including Burma now Myanmar, where indigenous people inhabited. The piece of legislation was promulgated in accordance with the laws, customs and systems prevailing among the people of Chittagong Hill Tracts. It safeguards a wide body of laws of land, forest and other natural resources of the indigenous people in the hill districts. Under the law the Deputy Commissioner was given the jurisdiction in respect of civil, revenue and other related matters and the Divisional Commissioner was given power to hear criminal matters.

Customary laws comprise customs that are accepted as legal requirements or obligatory rules of conducts, practices and beliefs that are so vital and intrinsic a part of a social and economic system that they are taken as laws. The normative force of customary law may be felt within a community but may also create a legal and moral expectation that it will

Be recognized beyond the original community. The prevailing laws in the country are not applicable to the hill districts and only those provisions which are not inconsistent with the Regulation and Rules are applicable. Though our Constitution does not provide any special status for the indigenous people residing in Chittagong Hill Tracts, Clause (2) of Article 19 of the Constitution is noteworthy in that the state shall adopt measures to remove social and economic inequality between man and man and to ensure the equitable distribution of wealth among citizens, and of opportunities in order to attain a uniform level of economic development throughout the country.

Article 23 however, states that the state shall adopt measures to conserve the "cultural traditions and heritage of the people, and so to foster and improve the national language, literature and the arts that all sections of people are afforded the opportunity to contribute towards and to participate in the enrichment of national culture." Under this provision the culture, heritage and tradition of the indigenous people have been recognized. Article 42 states that "subject to any restrictions imposed by law, every citizen shall have the right to acquire, hold, transfer or otherwise dispose of property, and no property shall be compulsorily acquired, nationalized or requisitioned save by authority of law." Coupled with this provision, Clause (4) of Article 28 enjoins the State to make special provisions in favor of women and children or for the advancement of any backward section of citizens.

I concluded my opinion that under the scheme of our Constitution the composition of the local government has been provided in Chapter III which contains Articles 59 and 60 in every administrative unit of the government in accordance with law, but the laws promulgated for the three hill districts are completely different from the other districts. This distinction is significant and in the absence of any provision recognizing the special status of the hill districts, there is implied recognition of special status of the Chittagong Hill Districts. The Regional Parishad (Council) has been given legislative power as well in relation to the Chittagong Hill Tracts to advice and recommend to the government to remove inconsistencies between Regulation 1900 and the Hill District Parishad Ain, 1989.

Moreover, another law, The Parbatya Chattagram Bhumi Birodh Nispatti Commission, which existed on March 26, 1971, had been given force of law in whole or any part of the territories of Bangladesh. Thereafter the Bangladesh Laws (Revision and Declaration) Act, 1973 was promulgated for adapting, modifying, amending laws in force "in territories now in Bangladesh". This law empowered the Commission to dispose of land related dispute brought before the Commission in accordance with laws, customs and systems prevailing in the Chittagong Hill Tracts with power to declare land grants illegal and to restore possessions. Though civil and criminal courts are constituted for the administration of justice, the dispensation of justice in civil matters is to be decided in accordance with the existing laws, customs and usages of the district concerned except cases arising out of family laws and other customary laws of the tribes which shall be tried by the Mouza Headmen and Circle Chiefs. These laws have not impeded the indigenous peoples' traits, customs and traditions, rather they have been safeguarded.

Despite the introduction of courts, the respective system of administration of customary laws and other local laws and practices remain unaffected. Family Laws are excluded within the jurisdictions of the civil court. Where special provision is made in a special statute dealing with a special subject, the resort should be that law instead of a general provision which is exercisable, or which is available under extraordinary circumstances only. Since the Regulation has been promulgated with the object of giving special privilege to the indigenous people of the three hill districts to protect and safeguard their culture, traditional practices and customs, they should not fall prey to the tactics of unscrupulous people.

The idea of Customary Law concerns the laws, practices and customs of indigenous people and local communities. "Custom" is understood as a "rule of conduct, obligatory on those within its scope, established by long usages." Customary laws and protocols are central to the very identity of indigenous peoples. The normative force of customary law may be felt within a community but may also create a legal or moral expectation that it will be recognized beyond the original community. The full effect of customary law may only be understood with reference to the social and community context to understand why customary law rights, such as those in folklore, are binding, it is necessary to examine more closely the nature and significance of the social and political structure of tribal societies. (Kuruk P. African Customary Law and Protections of Folklore, Copyright Bulletin, xxxvi, No 2, 2002)

In another case which led to a question to decide whether the Chittagong Hill Tracts Regulation is dead law or is still in force in the hill districts. It relates to refund of Tk 1,77,296.26 paid as advance income tax and VAT for manufacturing canned jam, jelly and fruit juices. The High Court Division discharged the rule on the reasoning that the Regulation is a dead law relying upon Case 47 of the Supreme Court. It was urged that the expression "excluded area used in the Government of India Act 1935, was amended in the Constitution of 1962 for the expression "Tribal Area" on January 10, 1964.

I held that after the independence by the Bangladesh (Adaptation of Existing Laws) Order, 1972 the Regulation 1900 has not been deleted, meaning thereby the government recognized Regulation 1900 as a subsisting law. Besides, Article 149 of the Constitution saved Regulation 1900. In recognition of the Regulation the government appointed the Mong Chief following Rule 48 of the Rules and, therefore, it recognized the Rules framed in exercise of powers of Regulation 1900. The government also promulgated Chittagong Hill Tracts Forest Transit Route 1973; Bhumi Khatian Parbotta Chattagram Ancholik Parishad Ain, 1998; and in recognition of the Accord executed on December 2, 1997, the government constituted a Commission for resolving the disputes relating to land. Though civil and criminal courts were set up, the courts would be regulated by Regulation 1900 which is still in force and that by amendment of Section 7 of the Regulation, the three hill districts, i.e. Rangamati, Bandarban and Khagrachhari have been constituted. Additionally, by amendment of the Section 8 of the Regulation three separate sessions' divisions have been constituted to be headed by Sessions Judges in the respective session's division. The Sessions Judges have been given power of taking cognizance of any offence as a court of original jurisdiction. But under the Code of Criminal Procedure, the Sessions Judges cannot exercise power of taking cognizance of any offence as a court of original jurisdiction. Therefore, there is no doubt that the government still recognizes the customs and usages of the tribal people of the Hill districts.

References:

2. *Chittagong Hill Tracts Regulation 1900*
3. *Parbattya Chattagram Ancholik Parishad Ain, 1998 (CHT Local Parishad Ain, 1998.)*
4. *(A) Parbattya Zila Parishad Ain, 1989, (b) Khagrachari Zila Parishad Ain, 1989 and (c) Bandarban Zila Parishad Ain, 1989.*
5. *Land Appeal Board Ain, 1989*

Absorption of Employees in the Revenue Set up (T)

After the independence of the country, the economic condition was completely wrecked. There was no proper communication system within the country as almost all the bridges and culverts had been blown up. There was zero foreign reserve, there was little electricity, shortage of food, dearth of clothing. The general election was held within a very short period after the adoption of the Constitution on November 4, 1972 effective from December 16, 1972. The government took different development programs with aid given from the donors. These development projects continued for years together.

Vast numbers of employees were appointed in development projects mostly on political grounds without following the rules. Sometimes appointments were in such a way that a much higher number of employees were appointed than required for the project. Some departments and organizations recruited employees following the procedures required for appointments of employees in accordance with the procedures being followed by the Public Service Commission. Some projects were extended from time to time, and some projects were abolished. After a project was implemented, sometimes a new project was undertaken with fund procured from other donors and some organizations changed the nomenclature of the posts. The appointments were made purely on temporary basis with clear terms that on expiry of the projects the employees cannot claim any right to continue in service. Some of the employees were employed on daily basis, some of them on monthly basis and some of them on no-work-no-pay basis, and some of them were appointed on muster-roll basis.

There were no subsisting service rules for the appointment of those employees. Naturally the government did not regularize their services in the revenue budget. Ultimately due to the pressure of some employees, the government formulated a rule providing the criteria of regularizing in the revenue set up. Most of the employees filed different writ petitions in the High Court Division for absorption in the revenue budget. The High Court Division made all the rules absolute directing the government to absorb them in the revenue set up with a direction to pay arrear salaries and other benefits without noticing that most of the employees were appointed on contract basis for projects. Therefore, they could not claim to continue in the service on the doctrine of legitimate expectation. Most of the Benches of the High Court Division without going through the appointment letters, and without application of mind, and with no importance to the tenor and applicability or doctrine of legitimate expectation gave the direction. I noticed that if the High Court Division's judgments were maintained, the government would be overburdened with a huge number of employees with little or no real basis, a burden not appropriate for an economy like ours.

On the other hand, it is also true that some of the employees worked for about 20/25 years and after such a long service, if they were unemployed, they would face profound financial hardships because they would not get any government job due to age limitation. These realities exerted heavy pressure on me to decide the matter: one was the humanitarian aspect, and the other was the legal aspect. Ultimately, I concluded that if the humanitarian aspect was given precedent over the legal aspect, the ends of justice would be defeated. The court should not be swayed by emotions and extraneous considerations. Accordingly, we heard a bunch of cases together and persuaded the brother judges to approve my view and gave guidelines to be followed by the departments in absorbing the employees in the revenue budget.

The first conditions were that the employees should be absorbed in accordance with the Rules of 2005 and the employees must be the ones who had been employed in development projects defined in the rules, subject to having requisite qualifications for the said posts. The second consideration was that whenever a post was lying vacant in the revenue set up, the department should absorb him in accordance with the rules provided that such employee was appointed following procedures prescribed for appointment in public employment. Next, such an employee must have the requisite qualifications seeking absorption and he must have continuity in service in the project. The employee also must have satisfactory service record before his case was considered for regularization. If an employee's rank and status did not relate to the post advertised by the department, such employee would not be considered for employment. The employees who were appointed on monthly pay basis would only be eligible for consideration for absorption subject to the availability of posts. He cannot claim as of right absorption in the revenue budget. The appointing authority shall maintain strictly the prevailing quota system existing in public service. In respect of muster-roll basis employees, their cases should be considered sympathetically if they had the requisite qualifications subject to availability of vacancy.

Police Excesses (U)

Shamim Reza Rubel, a BBA student, died in police custody after being arrested under Section 54 of the Code of Criminal Procedure. A public outcry occurred with protests by members of the public, political parties, lawyers, teachers, students and human right activists. His father, a retired government official, demanded a judicial enquiry. Sheikh Hasina, the Prime Minister, and Begum Khaleda Zia, leader of the opposition, visited the bereaved family members. A one-person judicial probe committee was constituted with Justice Habibur Rahman Khan to inquire into the incident involving Shamim Reza Rubel, find out the perpetrators and make recommendation on how to prevent such incidents in future. The Commission made several recommendations. Ain O Shalish Kendra, one of the writ petitioners submitted a chart after a thorough survey throughout the country about custodial deaths and tortures in the hands of police. Several NGOs and personalities filed a writ petition seeking direction upon the police to refrain from exercise of unwarranted abusive power under sections 54 and 167 of the Code and to strictly exercise the power of arrest and remand within the limits established by law.

The High Court Division upon hearing the parties made the rule absolute and directed the government to make amendments to certain provisions of the Code of Criminal Procedure in the light of the recommendations made by the Commission. The matter ultimately came up to the apex court at the instance of the government. In disposing of the appeal, I considered the laws of different countries relating to arrest, detention and taking an offender to police remand, the standard norms to be practiced by the department, the international treaties and conventions, and made observations touching on the findings of the High Court Division's recommendations and my opinion.

There is no doubt that the present the Code of Criminal Procedure, promulgated about 118 years ago by an imperial government, was primarily for use in a colony as this subcontinent was then. If the scheme of the law is investigated there will be suspicions enough that the colonial power made this law with an object to suppress their subjects with a unified law so that different religious systems for administration of justice were brought under a unified system. This would be easier to them to rule the country more easily so that it could realize revenues from the subjects by means of oppressive measures. Therefore, the penal laws and procedural laws were promulgated against the rule of law and the administration of criminal justice. The Executives were given the power to administer justice at the Magistracy level and in the trial of sessions cases the Session Judges had no power to take cognizance of an offence triable by them unless and until the accused was committed by Executive Magistrates under Chapter XVIII of the Code. Even the evidence of a witness recorded in the presence of an accused person by a Magistrate in a session triable case can be used in the subsequent trial, i.e. such evidence is put in under Section 288 of the Code.

There were three Chapters XX, XXI and XXII under which different offences were triable by Executive Magistrates. Chapter XXI has been deleted, Chapter XX has been substantially amended, and Chapter XXII which empowered the High Courts and Sessions Courts to hold trials in certain matters has also been substantially amended recently. There are corresponding amendments in each chapter of the Code apart from deleting some chapters. There is no doubt that excessive powers had been given to the police officers and Executive Magistrates. Though the power of the Executive Magistrates has been taken away pursuant to the direction given by this court in Masdar Hossain, the powers of the police officers which are being exercised from the period of colonial rule have not been amended at all with the result that the police officers are using excessive abusive powers against the peace-loving people taking advantage of the language used in the Code. As a result, the rule of law which is the foundation of our Constitution, which we achieved with the sacrifice of three million martyrs and molestation of two hundred thousand women and girls, is being violated in every sphere of life.

The Universal Declaration of Human Rights was drafted by the Human Rights Commission after receiving a detailed report on the prosecution evidence at the Nuremberg trials. The killing of "useless eaters", the Einsatzgruppen orders to kill indiscriminately, the gas chambers, Mengele experiments, "night and fog" decrees and the extermination projects after Kristallnacht were at the forefront of their minds and provided the examples to which they addressed their drafts.1 Democracy cannot be isolated from the rule of law. It has a nexus with rule of law. Unless democracy is established in all fields of a country the rule of law cannot be established. The rule of law is the foundation of a democratic society. Judiciary is the guardian of the rule of law. If the judiciary is to perform its duties and functions effectively and remain true to the spirit with dignity and authority, the courts must be respected and protected at all costs.

Today, Dicey's theory of rule of law cannot be accepted in its totality. Rather Davis2 gives seven principal meanings of the term "rule of law":

a) law and order;
b) fixed rules;
c) elimination of discretion;
d) due process of law or fairness;
e) natural law or observance of the principles of natural justice;
f) preference for judges or ordinary courts of law to execute authorities and administrative tribunals;
g) judicial review of administrative actions.

It has been said that no contemporary analysis of rule of law can ignore the vast expansion of government functions which has occurred because of both the growing complexity of modern life, and of the minimum postulates of social justice, which are now part of the established public philosophy in all civilized countries. Over the recent years, recognition of the importance of the rule of law and the significance of the independence of the judiciary has increased remarkably. The prime responsibility of the judiciary is to uphold the rule of law and it is the rule of law which prevents the ruler from abusing his powers. Simultaneously, we should keep in mind that the judiciary alone does not possess a magic wand to establish rule of law in the country.

Rule of law means all organs of a State shall maintain the rule of law in all spheres of the Executive and administrative branches, the government, its officers including law enforcing agencies, as well as people's representatives must protect, preserve and maintain the rule of law. If there is aberration in one branch of the government, it will reflect in the judiciary as well. To discharge its onerous responsibility of protecting and enforcing the rights of the citizens of a country the judiciary has to be seen to be impartial and independent. Unless the public accepts that the judiciary is an independent entity, they would have no confidence even in an unerring decision taken by a court exercising its jurisdiction fairly. Unless the rule of law is established the citizens of a country will be deprived of the fruits of justice. The concept of the rule of law has different facets and has meant different things to different people at different times.

Professor Brian Tamanaha has described the rule of law as "an exceedingly elusive notion giving rise to a rampant divergence of understandings and analogous to the notion of the food in the sense that everyone is for it, but have contrasting convictions about what it is."3 It is an essential principle of the rule of law that "every executive action, if it is to operate to the prejudice of any person must have legislative authority to support it."4 Entick v. Carrington, Lord Atkin in Eshugbayi Eleko5 opined that "no member of the executive can interfere with the liberty or property of a British subject except on the condition that he can support the legality of his action before a Court of Justice." It has been stated by Soli J. Sorabjee in a lecture that it needs to be emphasized that there is nothing western or eastern or northern or southern about the underlying principle of the rule of law. It has a global reach and dimension. Rule of law symbolizes the quest of civilized democratic societies, be they eastern or western, to combine that degree or liberty without which law is tyranny with that degree of law without which liberty becomes license.

In the words of the great Justice Vivian Bose of the Indian Supreme Court, the rule of law "is the heritage of all mankind because its underlying rationale is belief in the human rights and human dignity of all individuals everywhere in the world." Rule of law provides a potent antidote to executive lawlessness. It is a salutary reminder that wherever law ends, tyranny begins. In the developed as well as developing countries due to the prevalence of the rule of law, no administrator or official can arrest or detain a person unless there is legislative authority for such action. In those countries a Police Commissioner or any other public functionary cannot ban a meeting or the staging of a play or the screening of a movie by passing a departmental order or circular which is not backed by law. The rule of law ensures certainty and predictability as opposed to whimsicality and arbitrariness so that people can regulate their behavior according to a published standard against which to measure and judge the legality of official actions. Experience testifies that absence of the rule of law leads to executive highhandedness and arbitrariness.

In the Constitution Eighth Amendment case, 7 and Kesavananda Bharati8, the apex courts of Bangladesh and India held that the rule of law is one of the basic features of the Constitution. In I.R. Coelho, 9 it is stated that the rule of law is regarded as part of the basic structure of the Constitution. Consequently, the rule of law cannot be abolished even by a constitutional amendment. This manifests the high status accorded to the rule of law in Indian constitutional jurisprudence. The apex courts of this subcontinent did not hesitate to make such orders or directions whenever necessary when it came to its notice that the rule of law was violated and vigorously enforced the rule of law in practice. Rule of law must not be confused with rule by law. Otherwise rule of law would become an instrument of oppression and give legitimacy to laws grossly in violation of basic human rights. There is a certain core component in respect of basic human rights of the people and for human dignity. Otherwise, commission of atrocities and gross violation of human rights could be justified by pointing to the mere existence of a law.'6 ibid

Andrew Le Sueur, Maurice Sunkin and Jo Murkens in Public Law, Text, Cases, and Materials10 have aptly summarized the main ideas associated with the rule of law as follows. Compliance with the law: "Like citizens, the Government and public bodies must act in accordance with the law and must have legal authority for actions which impinge on the rights of others. The requirement of rationality: The rule of law implies rule by reason rather than arbitrary power or whim. To comply with the rule of law, decisions must be properly and logically reasoned in accordance with sound argument. The rule of law and fundamental rights: The rule of law requires the protection of the fundamental rights of the citizens against the Government. If we summarize the above treatise on public law we find, whenever one speaks of law, it must satisfy at least the prerequisite that it guarantees basic human rights and human dignity and ensures their implementation by due process through an independent judiciary exercising power of judicial review. Absent of these requirements the rule of law would become a shallow slogan.

Lord Justice Stephen Sedley of the Court of Appeal in the UK observed: "The irreducible content of the rule of law is a safety net of human rights protected by an independent legal system. Custodial violence, including torture and death in the lock-ups, strikes a blow at the rule of law, which demands that the powers of the executive should not only be derived from law but also that the same should be limited by law. Custodial violence is a matter of concern. It is aggravated by the fact that it is committed by persons who are supposed to be protectors of the citizens. It is committed under the shield of uniform and authority within the four walls of a police station or lock-up, the victim being totally helpless...It cannot be said that a citizen 'sheds off' his fundamental right to life the moment a policeman arrests him. Nor can it be said that the right to life of a citizen can be put in 'abeyance' on his arrest. If the functionaries of the government become law breakers, it is bound to breed contempt for law and would encourage lawlessness and every man would have the tendency to become law unto himself thereby leading to anarchy. No civilized nation can permit that to happen. The Supreme Court as the custodian and protector of the fundamental and the basic human rights of the citizens cannot wish away the problem. State terrorism is no answer to combat terrorism. State terrorism would only provide legitimacy to terrorism. That would be bad for the State, the community and above all for the rule of law."11

The preamble to our Constitution declares "rule of law" as one of the objectives to be attained. The expression "rule of law" has various shades of meaning and of all constitutional concepts, the rule of law is the most subjective and value laden. The concept is intended to imply not only that the powers exercised by State functionaries must be based on authority conferred by law, but also that the law should conform to certain minimum standards of justice, both substantive and procedural. Rule of law is the subordination of all authorities, legislative, executive and others to certain principles which would generally be accepted as characteristic of law, such as the ideas of the fundamental principles of justice, moral principles, fairness and due process. It implies respect for the supreme value and dignity of the individual. The minimum content of the concept is that the law affecting individual liberty ought to be reasonably certain or predictable; where the law confers wide discretionary powers, there should be adequate safeguards against their abuse; and unfair discrimination must not be sanctioned by law. A person ought not to be deprived of his liberty, status or any other substantial interest unless he is given the opportunity of a fair hearing before an impartial tribunal; and so forth.

The rule of law demands that power is to be exercised in a manner which is just, fair and reasonable and not in an unreasonable, capricious or arbitrary manner leaving room for discrimination. Absence of arbitrary power is the first essential of the rule of law upon which our constitutional system is based. Discretion conferred on the Executive must be confined within the defined limits and decisions should be made by the application of known principles and rules and, in general, such decisions should be predictable and the citizen should know where he stands. A decision without any principle or rule is unpredictable and is the antithesis of a decision in accordance with the rule of law. Rule of law contemplated in the Constitution concerns the certainty and publicity of law and its uniform enforceability and has no reference to the quality of the law.

The framers of the Constitution, after mentioning "rule of law" in the Preamble, took care to mention the other concepts touching the qualitative aspects of law, thereby showing their adherence to the concept of rule of law. If the Preamble to the Constitution is read in its proper perspective, there remains no doubt that the framers of the Constitution intended to achieve "rule of law". To attain this fundamental aim of the State, the Constitution has made substantive provisions for the establishment of a polity where every functionary of the State must justify his action with reference to law. "Law" does not mean anything that Parliament may pass. Articles 27, 31 and 32 have taken care of the qualitative aspects of law. Article 27 forbids discrimination in law or in State actions, Articles 31 and 32 imported the concept of due process, both substantive and procedural, thus prohibiting arbitrary or unreasonable law or State action.

The Constitution further guarantees in Part III certain rights including freedom of thought, speech and expression to ensure respect for the supreme value of human dignity. Though the Constitution contains provisions to ensure rule of law, the actual governance has nullified rule of law in the country. No right can compare with the right to life without which all other rights are meaningless and rule of law can play its most significant role in this aspect. But the tolerant and rather approving attitude of successive governments in respect of extrajudicial killings by the law enforcing agency in the name of "cross fire" and "shoot out" and very lately "encounter" has seriously dented the operation of rule of law so much so that it will not be a misstatement to say that rule of law for the common men in the country exists only in the pages of the Constitution.12 It must be remembered that the rule of law is not a one-way traffic. It places restraints both on the government and individuals. If the underlying principles of the rule of law are to become a reality in governance as also in our lives, no doubt laws, are necessary, but they alone are not enough.

In addition, fostering of culture based on rule of law is imperative. The only true foundation on which the rule of law can rest is its willing acceptance by the people until it becomes part of their own way of life. Therefore, we should strive to instill a rule of law temperament, rule of law culture at home, in schools, colleges, public places, utility service locations, parks, even mosques, temples and other holy places. We must respect each other in our respective holy places. We should strive for the universalization of its basic principle. Our effort should constantly aim at the expansion of the rule of law to make it a dynamic concept which not merely places constraints on the exercise of official power but facilitates and empowers progressive measures in socio-economic rights of the people. That indeed is the moral imperative for the civilized world.

Justice Vivian Bose made a very remarkable observation by posing a question as to why it should be respected by all segments of citizenry: "Because we believe in human worth and dignity. Because, on analysis and reflection, it is the only sane way to live at peace and amity with our neighbors in this complex world.

Because it is the only sane way to live in an ordered society."13 We eagerly look forward to the day when the quintessential principles of the rule of law, namely, the protection and promotion of all human rights and the human dignity of all human beings is universally accepted. One hopes that in a world torn by violent sectarian and religious strife the rule of law with its capacious dynamic content becomes the secular religion of all nations based on tolerance and mutual respect. It should be borne in mind that progress is the realization of utopia.

We must earnestly strive to realize this utopia which is a moral imperative for the civilized world. Unjust laws have troubled lawyers, political scientists, judges, civil society and philosophers since they first reflected on the legal standards by which people govern themselves. Unjust laws raise difficult questions about our understanding of law, our aspirations for our laws, our obligations to one another, and our government's responsibilities to each of us. From Aristotle and Aquinas to Hart and Fuller, the debate about these questions has continued for millennia, and it will endure for as long as people need law to order their societies and to guide their lives. There are several ways that a law might be unjust. It might prohibit or curtail conduct that should be permitted. It might permit conduct that should be prohibited. It might apply or enforce unfairly and otherwise unobjectionable law. People can and will disagree about whether and in what way a law is unjust.

If a law is unjust then the question may arise by what legal basis, if any, a judge can resist and attempt to correct that injustice. It seemed that it might help clarify discussions to have a specific example of an unjust law in mind. An example of an unjust law is one that is permitting government-sanctioned racial discrimination or violation of human rights. If a defense is needed, that racially discriminatory laws are unjust. Of course, someone might imagine a polity in which racially discriminatory laws are not necessarily unjust. That racially discriminatory laws are paradigmatically unjust refers to the related experiences of common law nations regarding, for example, treatment of indigenous populations and the political and constitutional history of the United States with respect to slavery and legalized racial segregation and subjugation.14

Courts have a solemn obligation to test any law to see if the law is just and therefore capable of being called a law in the truest sense of the word; if not then there is no option left with a judge but to declare that law an unjust law. Because a judge is under no obligation to work as a mere instrument of implementing and explaining law like a machine, if he does so then this would be the highest form of injustice one can imagine in a democratic polity. And to understand this subtle level of injustice done by unjust law the judges must have the moral compass and sensitivity to recognize injustice and feel its sting; and they must have the strength of character and the will to act on their convictions, even when they must act alone. And as a final point, the role of judges in a situation when they are confronted with in a paradox in expounding a law: If people need laws to govern themselves and if these laws are made by people, some of these laws will be unjust. If the threat of unjust laws persists, people will and should consider how judges ought to best address that threat and its occasional actualization.

To this point, consideration of these problems has left judges with three possibilities. But mendacity, abnegation and acquiescence are not the only options. The common law tradition and legal principles permit and require more from judges. Judges must develop the law. That, too, is a fundamental aspect of their legal obligations. Sometimes, as in cases involving unjust laws, development demands that judge's subject government action to the rule of law. This should not elicit fear or frustration. The common law has always functioned this way, and common law judges have always, in one form or another, fulfilled this function. The common law tradition recognized long ago what we sometimes still lose sight of today: only when the waters are pure can we hope to see down to the riverbed. Ibid

This protection must be afforded not only when the Statute is wholly or partially silent as to the procedure to be adopted, but also when a procedure has been prescribed by Statute and the statutory authority has tried to carry out its functions according to such procedure, but in doing so has violated the principles of natural justice. The courts are jealous to ensure that when an authority trips into a pitfall the citizen does not suffer because of an arbitrary act of the authority. A police officer's power to arrest under section 54 is discretionary and, notwithstanding the existence of the conditions specified in the section, it may be desirable in the circumstances of a case to simply make a report to the Magistrate instead of arresting the suspected persons. A police officer can act under clause (1) of section 54 only when the offence for which a person is to be arrested is a cognizable offence.

Such person must, as a fact, have been concerned in such an offence or there must have been a reasonable complaint made or credible information received that he has been so concerned. If the person arrested is a child under nine years of age, who cannot under section 82 of the Penal Code commit an offence, the arrest is illegal. Where a complaint is made to a police officer of the commission of a cognizable offence but there are circumstances in the case which lead him to suspect the information, he should refrain from arresting persons of respectable positions and leave the complainant to go to Magistrate and convince him that the information justifies the serious step of the issue of warrants of arrest.

There was no provision in the Codes of 1861 and 1872 enabling an arrest without warrant on credible information as to the person to be arrested being concerned in a cognizable offence. Such a provision was introduced for the first time in the Code of 1882. The words "credible information" include any information which, in the judgment of the officer to whom it is given, appears entitled to credit in the instance. It need not be sworn information. The words "credible" and "reasonable" have reference to the mind of the person receiving the information. A bare assertion without anything more cannot form the material for the exercise of an independent judgment and will not therefore amount to "credible information". The grounds "reasonable suspicion" and "credible information" must relate to definite averments which must be considered by the police officer himself before he arrests a person under this section. A complaint of a cognizable offence recorded by a Magistrate and sent by him to the police for investigation and report is enough information justifying arrest under section 54 of the Code of Criminal Procedure, 1898.

Similarly, if information that a warrant of arrest has been issued against a person in respect of a cognizable offence, it may justify action being taken under the said section. Where from a report of a chowkidar that certain persons were dacoits the police officer called them to surrender, but the latter resisted and fired shots at the officer, the latter was justified in arresting those persons. Where a police officer suspecting that certain pieces of cloth which a man was carrying early in the morning, was stolen property, went to him and questioned him and having received unsatisfactory answers, arrested him, he was entitled to arrest him because reasonable suspicion exists of his being concerned of a cognizable offence. Where a person was found armed lurking at midnight in a village inhabited by persons well known to the police as professional dacoits, there was a reasonable suspicion against the person of being concerned in a cognizable offence.

But this does not mean that the powers of police are limited only by their own discretion as to what persons they may arrest without warrant. Their powers in this respect are strictly defined by the Code. To act under the first clause, there must be a reasonable complaint or reasonable suspicion of the person to be arrested having been concerned in a cognizable offence. What is a "reasonable" complaint or suspicion must depend upon the circumstances of each case; but it should be at least founded on some definite fact tending to throw suspicion on the person arrested, and not on a mere vague surmise.

Section 60 of the Code states that a police officer making an arrest without warrant shall, without unnecessary delay and subject to the provisions contained as to bail, take or send the person arrested before a Magistrate having jurisdiction in the case, or before the officer in charge of a police station. Section 61 of the Code states that no police officer shall detain in custody a person arrested without warrant for a longer period than under all the circumstances of the case is reasonable, and such period shall not, in the absence of a special order of a Magistrate under section 167, exceed twenty four hours exclusive of the time necessary for the journey from the place of arrest to the Magistrate's Court. The Magistrate exercising his jurisdiction under section 167 performs judicial functions and not executive power, and therefore, the Magistrate should not make any order on the asking of the police officer. The object of requiring an accused to be produced before a Magistrate is to enable him to see that a police remand or a judicial remand is necessary and to enable the accused to make a representation he may wish to make. Since a remand order is a judicial order, the Magistrate must exercise this power in accordance with the well-settled norms of making a judicial order. The norms are that he is to see whether there is a report of cognizable offence and whether there are allegations constituting the offence which is cognizable. Non-disclosure of the grounds of satisfaction by a police officer should not be accepted.

Whenever a person is arrested by a policeman during investigation he is required to ascertain his complicity in respect of a cognizable offence. The entries in the diary afford the Magistrate the information upon which he can decide whether or not he should authorize the detention of the accused in custody or upon which he can form an opinion as to whether or not further detention is necessary. The longest period for which an accused can be ordered to be detained in police custody by one or more such orders is only 15 days. Where even within the 15 days' time allowed under this section the investigation is not completed, the police may release the accused under section 169. Sub-section (3) of section 167 requires that when the Magistrate authorizes detention in police custody, he should record his reasons for so doing.

The object of this provision is to see that the Magistrate takes the trouble to study the police diaries and to ascertain the actual conditions under which such detention was asked for. The law is jealous of the liberty of the subject and does not allow detention unless there is a legal sanction for it. So, in every case where a detention in police custody is ordered, the Magistrate should state his reasons clearly. He should satisfy himself that (a) the

315

accusation is well-founded, and (b) the presence of the accused is necessary while the police investigation is being held. The mere fact that the police say that the presence of the accused was necessary to finish the investigation, will not be enough to order detention.

To order a detention of the accused to get from him a confessional statement or that he may be forced to give a clue to stolen property is not justified. Similarly, it is improper to order detention in police custody on a mere expectation that time will show his guilt or because the accused promised to tell the truth or for verifying a confession recorded under section 164 or because though repeatedly asked the accused will not give any clue to the property. Section 167 is supplementary to section 61 of the Code. These provisions have been provided with the object to see that the arrested person is brought before a Magistrate with the least possible delay to enable him to judge if such person must be kept further in police custody and also to enable such person to make representation in the matter. The section refers to the transmission of the case diary to the Magistrate along with the arrested person.

The object of the production of the arrested person with a copy of the diary before a Magistrate within 24 hours fixed by section 61 when investigation cannot be completed within such period that the Magistrate can take further course of action as contemplated under sub-section (2) of section 167. Secondly, the Magistrate is to see whether the arrest of the accused person has been made on the basis of a reasonable complaint or credible information or a reasonable suspicion exist of having been concerned in any cognizable offence. Therefore, while making an order under sub-section (2), the Magistrate must be satisfied with the requirements of sections 54 and 61, otherwise the Magistrate is not bound to forward the accused either in the judicial custody or in police custody. The "diary" referred to in sub-section (1) is a special diary referred to in section 172 of the Code read with Regulation 68 of Police Regulations, Bengal. The Code clearly provides that the police officer is bound to transmit to the nearest Magistrate a copy of the entries in the diary in relation to the case whenever any person is arrested and detained in custody and produced before a Magistrate within a period of 24 hours.

A perusal of regulation 68 makes it clear that the diary should contain full unabridged statement of persons examined by the police to give the Magistrate a satisfactory and complete source of information which would enable him to decide whether or not the accused person should be detained in custody. Section 167(1) requires that copies of entries of the diary should be sent to the Magistrate with the object to prevent any abuse of power by the police officer. The object of use of special diary under section 172 of the Code has been well explained by Edge, Chief Justice. The early stages of investigation which follows on the commission of a crime must necessarily, in the vast majority of cases, be left to the police and until the honesty, capacity, discretion and judgment of the police can be thoroughly trusted, it is necessary for the protection of the public against criminals for the vindication of the law and for the protection of those who are charged with having committed a criminal offence that the Magistrate or Judge before whom the case has been sent for investigation or for trial should have the means of ascertaining whether the information was true, false or misleading, which was obtained day to day by the police officer who was investigating the case and what were the lines of investigation upon which the police officer acted.15

Section 172 relates to the police diary made in respect of a case under inquiry or trial by the court which calls for it. It is incumbent upon a police officer who investigates the case under Chapter XIV to keep a diary as provided by section 172 and the omission to keep the diary deprives the court of the very valuable assistance which such a diary can give. The investigation officers do not have any discretion to take decision as to whether he will or will not record the events during investigation in the case diary. This is a compulsory statutory duty for every officer to record all the events in the case diary. This is the duty of the Officer-in-Charge to make sure that officers subordinate to him shall record necessary entries in the case diary properly.

A case diary is an indicator of how good and intelligent a police officer is. It is, however, to be noted that the case diary is a confidential document. So, it may not be claimed by the accused person at any time for assessing and scrutinizing its entries. A criminal court is free to ask for the case diary at any stage of the proceedings. But, the case diary cannot be used as evidence in the trial. A case diary is written as the investigation progresses. It is, therefore, obligatory to record the case diary every day when investigation is taking place. The writing of the case diary must not be held up at the end of the day. It is always wise to write the case diary in the place where investigation is conducted. The quick and immediate writing up of case diary helps recording every little detail of the investigation properly. This sort of case diary truly reflects the nitty-gritty of the police investigation. The case diary needs to be recorded as the case advances during the investigation. In most cases, the police officers have developed a bad habit of writing case diary long after conclusion of investigation or after a few days of the investigation. It is not at all a promising approach when the police officers follow such a procedure. This is a compulsory requirement for an investigation officer to record the case diary without any apparent failure.

The case diary must refer to the proceedings in the investigation of an alleged offence. It is a mandatory duty for such officer to record every day's progress of the investigation. The case diary must include entries of necessary information for each of the days when investigation is in progress. Sometimes the investigation officers neglect the examination of the witnesses on the first day of the visit of the place of occurrence and after consuming days together record the statements in a single day. This process is totally unauthorized. In every case the investigation officers must record the statements of the witnesses present expeditiously on the first day or the following day if the FIR discloses the names of the witnesses who are acquainted with the facts of the case. Section 157 of the Evidence Act in unambiguous language stated that the admissibility of a previous statement that should have been made before an authority legally competent to the fact "at or about the time", when the fact to which the statement relates took place.

The object of section 157 if the Evidence Act is to admit statements made at a time when the mind of the witness is still so connected with the events as to make it probable that his description of them is accurate. But if time for reflection passes between the event and the subsequent statement it not only can be of little value but may be dangerous and as such a statement can be easily brought into being. Every detail in connection with the investigation into the offence must clearly be recorded without fail. It is to be noted that in section 172(1) of the Code the word "Shall" has been used which definitely indicates "mandatory". So, a case diary must be recorded, and all the details as mentioned in the section 172(1) of the Code must be recorded without any failure by the police officer in charge of investigation of an offence

The entries of the case diary may not be referred to the court at the instance of the accused person. The accused in such a case can seek permission to use the case diary to show contradictions in the prosecution case. The police officer, therefore, has scope to see the case diary during his examination-in-chief for the purpose of refreshing memory. If the police officer thinks that his case diary can be helpful in giving appropriate testimony, he may request the court to permit him to use the case diary for refreshing his memory while giving evidence. Keeping the case diary under safe custody is an important task. The case diary is the picture of the entire result of the investigation and other regarding the topography of the place of occurrence, the probability of approach of the offender to the scene, the direction of retreating and the location of the probable witnesses, etc. The activities of the police investigation officer can very well be looked after by the senior police officers going through the records of the case diary.

When any person dies while in the custody of the police, the nearest Magistrate empowered to hold inquests shall, and, in any other case mentioned in section 174, clauses (a), (b) and (c) of sub-section (1) any Magistrate so empowered, may hold an inquiry into the cause of death either instead of, or in addition to, the investigation held by the police officer, and if he does so, he shall have all the powers in conducting it which he would have in holding an inquiry into an offence. The Magistrate holding such an inquiry shall record the evidence taken by him in connection therewith in any of the manners. Section 176 of the Code enables a Magistrate to hold inquiry into a suspicious death. The language used in this section does not depend merely upon the opinion of the police officer but that there should be a further check by a Magistrate to hold an independent inquiry. The object of holding the inquiry is to elucidate the facts of unnatural death before there is any reasonable suspicion of the commission of any offence and when such grounds exist, the inquiry comes under the Ain (Act) of 2013.16

Wide powers have been given to a police officer to arrest a person on suspicion. A police officer should not exercise his power of arrest on his whims and caprice merely saying that he has received information of a person being involved in a cognizable offence. He is required to exercise his power depending upon the nature of the information, seriousness of the offence and the circumstances unfurled not only in the complaint but also after investigation based on information or complaint. To make the point clearer, the police officer shall not exercise the power arbitrarily violating the dignity, honor, liberty and fundamental rights of a citizen. These rights are inherent and inalienable, and enshrined in Articles 32 and 33 of the Constitution so that no one can curtail the same. These rights are required to be scrupulously protected and safeguarded because the effective enforcement of fundamental rights will prevail over subordinate laws. In clause "Firstly" of section 54, the words "credible information" and "reasonable suspicion" have been used relying upon which an arrest can be made by a police officer. These two expressions are so vague that there is chance for misuse of the power by a police officer, and accordingly, I hold the view that a police officer while exercising such power, his satisfaction must be based upon definite facts and materials placed before him and basing upon which the officer must consider for himself before he takes any action. It will not be enough for him to arrest a person under this clause that there is likelihood of cognizable offence being committed.

Before arresting a person on suspicion, the police officer must carry out investigation based on the facts and materials placed before him without unnecessary delay. If any police officer produces any suspected person in the exercise of the powers conferred by this clause, the Magistrate is required to be watchful that the police officer has arrested the person following the directions given by the court and if the Magistrate finds that the police officer has abused his power, he shall at once release the accused person on bail. In case of arresting of a female person in exercise of this power, the police officer shall make all efforts to keep a lady constable present. If it is not possible by securing the presence of a lady constable which might impede the course of arrest or investigation, the police officer must record the reasons either before arrest or immediately after the arrest by assigning lawful reasons.

Under the present scheme of our Code, a Magistrate has no power to detain such an offender beyond fifteen days. Under the proviso to sub-section (1) of section 344 of the Code the court has power to remand from time to time but such remand shall not be for a period exceeding fifteen days at a time. This section empowered the court to pass such order when Chapter XVIII of the Code was in existence but after the deletion of this Chapter, the Magistrate cannot pass such an order. Because the language used in this sub-section (i) is such that the court if it thinks it fit it may postpone/adjourn "any inquiry or trial." The power of inquiry under Chapter XVIII by a Magistrate in respect of an offence exclusively triable by a Court of Sessions has been deleted. If the trial of an offence commences in the court of sessions, the Magistrate does not possess any power to remand an accused person. It is the trial court which will pass necessary orders if it thinks fit. But before the trial commences and after expiry of fifteen days' time provided in sub-section (2) of section 167, the law does not permit the Magistrate to direct a suspected accused person to be detained in judicial custody. Under the scheme of the Code as it stands now, a Magistrate/Judge having power to take cognizance of an offence has no power to direct the detention of an accused person in judicial custody, if he thinks fit, beyond a period of fifteen days from the date of production in court after arrest by a police officer in respect of a cognizable offence.

The Code is totally silent to deal with an accused person who is allegedly involved in a cognizable offence if the police officer fails to conclude the investigation of the case within this period. If the Magistrate has no power to direct such accused person to be detained in judicial custody, he will be left with no option other than to release him on bail till the date of submission of the police report. Normally in most cases the police officers cannot complete the investigation within the stipulated period sanctioned by law and they usually take years together. The detention/remand of an accused person beyond fifteen days by order of the Magistrate is not only an exercise of power not sanctioned by law but also violative of Article 32 of the Constitution.

It is, therefore, necessary to take legislative measures authorizing the judicial magistrate to direct such offenders in judicial custody if the investigation cannot be concluded within the stipulated time. If no legislative measure is taken, the State cannot take any exception if the Magistrates/Courts direct the release such accused persons irrespective of the nature of their complicity in the incidents under investigation. I allowed three months moratorium period for the interest of justice and to maintain the law and order in the country, but in presence of specific constitutional provisions protecting rights of a citizen the court cannot remain a silent spectator for an indefinite period. Till today the government has not amended the law.

After driving out two colonial powers, one of course mostly through negotiations and the other by sacrificing three million martyrs, we cannot detain and prosecute an offender with a draconian law. Firstly, the object of the Code for which it was implemented on this soil does not exist now. The present procedures for holding trials by the Magistrates and courts of session are inadequate and conflicting. Secondly, some of the provisions, particularly, sections 54, 167, Chapters VII, XX, XXII, and some provisions in Chapters XV, XVI and XXXII are inconsistent with the Constitution and the judgment in the Masder Hossain case. In fact, the present Code is not at all suitable for the administration of criminal justice after so many changes that had been made in the meantime and it is high time to promulgate a new Code.

Our Constitution was enacted under the dynamic leadership of the Founding Fathers of the Nation clearly depicted the importance of rule of law and independence of judiciary. Therefore, we all must strive to implement the dream of the Father of the Nation. Otherwise, the independence which we have achieved sacrificing so many lives will be meaningless and the struggle against the British colonial occupation for about 200 years and the 24-year long struggle against the Pakistani autocratic rulers and our nine months sanguinary fight against the occupation army will render all ineffective and useless. The guidelines embodied in the historical speech of March 7, 1971 delivered by Bangabandhu Sheikh Mujibur Rahman, will also be diminished in its spirit. The long-cherished independence achieved after huge sacrifices should not be frustrated only for a few members of law enforcing agencies. If we do so it will be preposterous for us to continue as an independent sovereign State in the world with dignity and self-respect. The image of a State is dependent upon the way its judiciary administers justice for the common people. It should be kept in mind that the very nature of the job of law enforcing agencies is to respect the law even when their lives are at stake. Crime control remains an important function to them. They entered the job knowing the responsibilities reposed on them. It is known to them what the objects and purposes are of raising a police force or an equivalent force in a country.

In our country we find no concern of the police administration about the abusive powers being exercised by its officers and personnel. This department has failed to maintain the required standard of integrity and professionalism. There is aberration in other departments as well, but these departments should not be compared with law enforcing agencies because of the philosophy based upon which responsibilities have been reposed on them. Their duties and actions are always dependent on public approval, particularly during periods of crises. They must secure and maintain public respect, and this will decrease crimes in the country. Looking at the law and order situation, I have reasons to believe that it has forgotten its core value that it is accountable to the community it serves and, that at the same time, prevention of crimes is its prime operational priority. Conversely it is seen that the rate of crime is on the rise. It is not known whether the department has adopted any policy to develop a set of values so that the people have faith and confidence in it. Most of the time it is noticed that the force is following the old principles and policies that were followed during the colonial period. Their behavioral attitude must be developed in conformity with the present values and rights.

Even after the Constitution is in operation, its attitude toward the citizenry has not changed. The police administration, particularly its chief, must oversee training of recruits to reduce the use of coercive force. He should strive to rebuild mutual trust and respect between its force and the citizenry especially in communities that have been subjected to heavy stop-and-frisk techniques. The department's head must keep in mind the remark of its precursor Robert Peel who founded first police force in 1829: "Police should maintain a relationship with the public that gives reality to the historic tradition that the police are the public and the public are the police." If he forgets this prime philosophy and leaves behind a demoralized force, it will be much harder for his successor to combat crimes and uphold human values.

After delivery of the judgment17, there were repercussions within the law enforcement agencies, particularly the police department and Rapid Action Battalion (RAB). The departments' heads met me saying that they came to call on me for a courtesy visit and for my blessings and guidance. After discussing one or two points, suddenly they raised points about the judgment regarding the direction given upon the Judicial Magistrates for taking cognizance of offence against the police officials who took an offender on remand but could not produce him due to death in "crossfire" or "encounter" for detection of crimes. According to them, the offenders are so trained and stubborn that normally they did not disclose their involvement in the crime; that terrorism is on the rise and has increased tremendously; that the offenders manage to collect different sophisticated devices and techniques and it would be difficult on the part of the law enforcers to cope with them and that the offenders collect sophisticated arms through syndicates but the government could not provide these to match those. As a result, they must resort to the changed interrogation techniques and in course of such interrogation, some officers might apply excessive pressure causing death to the offenders. Another version offered by them was that the law enforcement agencies are public servants and taking the offenders on remand is a part of public duty with a view to unearthing the criminals and recover the arms; but if they are subjected to criminal prosecution their moral strength to detect crimes would diminish and, as a result, the law and order situation might deteriorate. From a reliable source I came to know that the officers even met the Prime Minister with a demand for repealing Act of 2013. I told the officers that if the terrorists resorted to modern tactics in committing terrorism, the law enforcers should also be trained in similarly so that they can take up the challenge.

These types of acts of terrorism are not committed in Bangladesh alone. It is a global menace. They must collect techniques from developed countries too. Before the delivery of the judgment, it was a common practice that an offender used to be taken on police remand and he could not be produced in the court on the plea that in course of interrogation the offender disclosed the location where he had concealed the weapons and accordingly they would go to the area with the offender at dead of night. On getting the scent of the presence of the police, the terrorists attacked the police and in course of the cross firing, the offender tried to escape and was killed in the crossfire. Two crucial points surfaced from their explanation. Firstly, if the offender discloses the location where he had concealed the arms, the arms could have been recovered during the day. There was no reason on the part of the police to take the offender to an isolated place at dead of night for any purpose. If the offender admits that he has kept concealed arms at a place, what could be the reason for the police to go for the recovery at such unusual hours?

The law provides that after recovery of arms, a proper seizure list is to be prepared under sections 100/103 of the Code of Criminal

Procedure. If the procedure is not followed, the recovery would be doubtful, and the accused will get the benefit of doubt. It is not practicable on the part of the police officers to collect seizure list witnesses at that time. Secondly, how was the offender able to escape in course of the cross firing because he had been taken in a handcuffed condition and he would not be let free when the miscreants attacked them. There must be one police personnel to guard him. Not only that, he is normally affixed to a bar in the police vehicle or remained in a hand cuffed condition. If the offender discloses the location of a house where his cohorts with arms are kept hiding, it is their duty to cordon the house the whole night and start operation during the day. This would reduce risks to the lives of the police personnel or casualty of any innocent person staying in the neighborhood.

So, the explanation provided by the law enforcement agencies is self-contradictory and not acceptable. They seem to have gotten into the habit of introducing concocted stories after killing the offender. These are in fact sort of cold-blooded killings, which may be termed as lynching and they are a serious type of offence. Police officers cannot take the law in their own hands and kill any person even if he is a hardcore terrorist without the process of law. Their primary responsibility is to maintain law and order in their locality; to detect crimes; apprehend the offenders and make proper investigation about the involvement of the offender in the crime; and bring him to court for trial. In the judgment I have pinpointed the responsibility of s police officer, 18 formulated guidelines to be followed by the Magistrates, 19 Judges and Tribunals.20 After the judgment, there is remarkable change in the killing of offenders while in police custody. But it was for a limited period. Now that they reintroduced their old habit of lynching innocent persons on the plea of nabbing drug paddlers. The prime minister, home minister and some so called columnists and intellectuals have supported their actions. It is none of the business of the law enforcing agencies to have a final say as to one is a drug paddler.

References:

1. *Entic v. Carrington, 1765 EWHC KB J98, 95 ER 1807*
2. *Eshugbayi Eleco v. Officer Administering the Government of Nigeria, 1913 Appeal No, 43 of 1930*
3. *D.K Basu v. State of West Bengal (1997) 1 SCC 416*
4. *Responsibilities and Guidelines**
5. *Guidelines to Magistrates and Courts*

Responsibilities of Law Enforcing Agencies:

I.   Law enforcement agencies shall at all times fulfill the duty imposed upon them by law, by serving the community and by protecting all persons against illegal acts, consistent with the high degree of responsibility required by their profession.

II.   In the performance of their duty, law enforcement agencies shall respect and protect human dignity and maintain and uphold the human rights of all persons.

III. Law enforcement agencies may use force only when strictly necessary and to the extent required for the performance of their duty.

IV.   No law enforcement agencies shall inflict, instigate or tolerate any act of torture or other 388 cruel, inhuman or degrading treatment or punishment, nor shall any law enforcement agencies invoke superior orders or exceptional circumstances such as a state of war or a threat of war, a threat to national security, internal political instability or any other public emergency as a justification of torture or other cruel, inhuman or degrading treatment or punishment.

V.   The law enforcing agencies must not only respect but also protect the rights guaranteed to each citizen by the Constitution.

VI.   Human life being the most precious resource, the law enforcing agencies will place their highest priority on the protection of human life and dignity.

VII. The primary mission of the law enforcing agencies being the prevention of crime, it is better to prevent a crime than to put the resources into motion after a crime has been committed.

Police Guidelines:

I.   The police officer making the arrest of any person shall prepare a memorandum of arrest immediately after the arrest and such officer shall obtain the signature of the arrestee with the date and time of arrest in the said memorandum.

II.   The police officer who arrested the person must intimate to a nearest relative of the arrestee and in the absence of the relative, to a friend to be suggested by the arrestee, as soon as practicable but not later than 6(six) hours of such arrest notifying the time and place of arrest and the place of custody.

III.   An entry must be made in the diary as to the ground of arrest and name of the person who informed the police to arrest the person or made the complaint along with his address and shall also disclose the names and particulars of the relative or the friend, as the case may be, to whom information is given about the arrest and the particulars of the police officer in whose custody the arrestee is staying.

IV.   Copies of all the documents including the memorandum of arrest, a copy of the information or complaint relating to the commission of cognizable offence and a copy of the entries in the diary should be sent to the magistrate at the time of production of the arrestee for making the order of the magistrate under Section 167 of the Code.

V.   If the arrested person is taken on police remand, he must be produced before the Magistrate after the expiry of the period of such remand and in no case he shall be sent to the judicial custody after the period of such remand without producing him before the Magistrate.

VI.	(vi) Registration of a case against the arrested person is sine-qua-non for seeking the detention of the arrestee either in police custody or in the judicial custody under Section 167(2) of the Code.
VII.	If a person is produced before a magistrate with a prayer for his detention in any custody, without producing a copy of the entries in the diary as per item No.(iv) above, the Magistrate shall release him in accordance with Section 169 of the Code on taking a bond from him.
VIII.	If a police officer seeks an arrested person to be shown arrested in a case who is already in custody, the Magistrate shall not allow such prayer unless the accused/arrestee is produced before him with a copy of the entries in the diary relating to such case.
IX.	On the fulfillments of the above conditions, if the investigation of the case cannot be concluded within 15 days of the detention of the accused under Section 167(2), the Magistrate having jurisdiction to take cognizance of the case or with the prior permission of the Judge or Tribunal having such power can send such accused person on remand under Section 344 of the Code for a term not exceeding 15 days at a time.
X.	The Magistrate shall not make an order of detention of a person in judicial custody if the police forwarding the report disclose that the arrest had been made for the purpose of putting the arrestee in preventive detention.
XI.	It shall be the duty of the Magistrate, before whom the accused person is produced, to satisfy that these requirements have been complied with before making any order relating to such accused under Section 167 of the Code.

Impact of Emergency (V)

During the period of emergency declared on January 11, 2007, the joint forces led by army officers arrested most of the politicians, businessmen and owners of big business houses of Bangladesh without showing any cause. Some of them were subjected to inhuman torture, some of them were compelled to attend their interrogation cell in the morning and compelled them to wait till dusk without affording minimum facilities and released them with a direction to come back the following day. This process continued from days to months. Aside from some of them being tortured, some were incarcerated, some were put under detention, and some of them who could arrest left the country. The country was submerged in anarchy with the result that business houses were bound to close their businesses; millions of people became jobless; the economy was collapsing. There was shortage of food grains too.

With a view to meet emergency monetary difficulties, the joint forces compelled many businessmen to pay money by checks, drafts or in other forms in the name of advance income tax and VAT. The businessmen had no fund to meet the demand, but under compulsion they arranged funds by borrowing from commercial banks or their near ones. In this manner they collected about Tk 1200 crores and deposited the money with the Bangladesh Bank. Bangladesh Bank opened a suspense account No. 0900-for the government and kept the money in the said account. After the withdrawal of emergency and following elections some businessmen demanded the money back from the Bangladesh Bank without any result. The government though realized the money could not be utilized because the money was not legally realized; rather it was extorted and then deposited in a suspense account.

The businessmen finding no other alternative sought judicial review in the High Court Division by filing different writ petitions for refund of the money. The High Court Division made the rules absolute and directed the Bangladesh Bank to refund the money. Bangladesh Bank preferred appeals to the apex court.1 though the litigants claimed the money upon the government, the latter did not contest the cases. Only Bangladesh Bank contested the matters claiming that the account was maintained by the government and Bangladesh Bank had received the money on behalf of the government. It was further claimed that Directorate General of Forces Intelligence (DGFI) deposited the said pay orders for onward collection from banks.

Bangladesh Bank claimed to have merely acted on behalf of the government. The vital point involved in these issues were that though the money was collected against alleged evasion or non-payment of taxes and duties by different business houses as revenue for the government, in the absence of filing any affidavit by the government, the money extorted by an intelligence department taking the abnormal situation of the country into consideration can be retained by the Bangladesh Bank. The petition for judicial review is decided by affidavit evidence and if an allegation is made against the person holding the office of the Republic and if he does not deny the statements of facts made by the applicant, the court shall presume that the statement is true.2

The Bangladesh Bank was founded with the object to the managing monetary and credit systems of Bangladesh and stabilizing the domestic monetary value and maintaining a competitive "External par value of Bangladesh Taka" toward fostering growth and development of country's productive resources in the best national interest. The functions of the Banks were

a) to formulate and implement monetary policy;
b) to formulate and implement intervention policies in foreign market;
c) to give advice to the government on the interaction of the monetary with fiscal and exchange rate policy, on the impact of various policy measures on the economy and to propose legislative measures it considers necessary or appropriate to attain its objectives and perform its functions;
d) to hold and manage official foreign reserve of Bangladesh;

e) to promote, regulate and ensure a secure and efficient payment system including the issue of bank notes; and

f) to regulate and supervise banking companies and financial institutions. None of these objects cover the retention of the money of individuals in a suspense account collected by an intelligence agency.

Documents including circulars filed by Bangladesh Bank revealed that Account Nos. 0100 to 0200 relate to the National Parliament; 0300 relates to the Prime Minister's Office; 0400 to the Cabinet Division; 0600 the Election Commission; 0700 to Public Administration; 0800 to the PSC; 0900 Finance Division;0901 Internal Loan Interest; 0903 Treasury Bill; 0904 to Means and Ingredients; 1000 to the Comptroller General;1100 Internal Resources Division;1101 to VAT;1102 Income Tax;1103 Customs Duty;1104 to Supplementary Duties;1105 others and NBR;1106 to the National Savings Project, principal amount;1107 National Savings Project Interest. So obviously in no case either Account No. 900 or 0900 relates to collection of revenue for the government.

As regards the columns of relevant forms for collecting of income tax it was recited that "It must be deposited by challans irrespective of anything said in levels 2 & 3 if there is mentioning code from 01 to 0111, DGFI in their affidavit admitted that it collected the money as revenue of the government by force, but according to it, the officer who collected the money was responsible for the same. Lt. Colonel Saiful Islam Hawladar posted in DGFI office and he collected the checks and drafts and acknowledged in receipts in the DGFI official form stating that he "received the said pay order." Mohammad Moazzem Hossain, Lt Colonel for Director General, received Tk. 60 crore only in favor of Bangladesh as rant of out of court settlement." In another letter of the Bangladesh Bank, in the prefix, it was mentioned, "Sena Sadar Puraton Officers Mess, Dhaka Senanibash, taka 60 Crores." The Governor of Bangladesh Bank endorsed in the said letter that he had received the money from the military and directed the office to intimate the fact to the Finance Ministry.

Therefore, there is no doubt that DGFI officials collected the money with force as advance income tax during the abnormal situation in the country. A question was raised by the Bangladesh Bank that the money was deposited in the Consolidated Fund of the government and hence the same cannot be refunded without an Act of Parliament. The procedure for dealing with Money Bill is contained in Article 81. It says that any imposition, regulation, alteration, remission, repeal of any tax, the borrowing of money, or the giving any guarantee by the government or amendment of any law relating to financial obligations of the government, the custody of Consolidated Fund, the payment of money into, or issue or appropriation of moneys from that fund and the imposition of charge upon the Consolidated Fund or the alteration or addition of any such charge are included, and the imposition of a charge upon the Consolidated Fund has to be made by a Bill.

However, any imposition or alteration of fine or other pecuniary penalty or levy or payment of license fee or a fee or charge for any service rendered cannot be included in a Money Bill. Government can collect any tax under the Act of Parliament, but any fine or imposition of any penalty or levy any license or charge cannot be included in the Money Bill and, therefore, they may be taken outside the ambit of the Consolidated Fund. Revenue receipts by the government or loans raised by the government and all moneys received by it in repayment of loan formed part of the Consolidated Fund. But moneys collected and deposited with the Bangladesh Bank directly are not revenues of the government since those moneys have not been kept in government account numbers 1101, 1102, 1103, 1104 and 1105.

Tax revenue is paid in order of standing charges especially interest payments on the national debts from the Consolidated Fund. The constitutional provision says that no money can be withdrawn from the Consolidated Fund without an Appropriation Act passed by Parliament. The disputed money had been kept in Account No. 0900 and it was an ascertained amount and there was no legal bar in refunding the money at the direction of the court. The control of public finance is an important function of Parliament, but it can neither levy tax nor spend money for itself without an authorization. Article 83 gave protection against arbitrary or illegal extraction which can be enforced through court proceedings. A taxpayer is made to pay tax, but he can also recover the money if the tax is sought to be levied without following the monetary provisions. Where there is an expressed prohibition of imposing and realizing tax, the action of the government or its officials or any official or any office instrumentalities in transgressing that prohibition must be regarded as an exercise of power without jurisdiction. Tax is levied by local authorities or revenue department under statutory powers. A tax cannot be levied or collected merely by an Executive fiat or action without there being a law to support the same. Therefore, no tax can be levied or realized by the government or its officials without any sanction of law. The DGFI illegally raised the money and therefore the Bangladesh Bank cannot retain the money.

After the above findings and conclusions, I made some remakes about the DFI (Defense Forces Intelligence) which was later renamed DGFI on August 24, 1976. Before that the organization worked under the name NSI (National Security Intelligence) as the sole intelligence agency in Bangladesh. However, from external threat of foreign military, the force was reorganized. The role of DFI was only limited to sharing intelligence with the armed forces. After renaming it DGFI, the government made a massive modification in the organizational structure of the agency and it was transformed from defensive to an offensive intelligence unit. Its primary role is to specialize in the collection, analysis and assessment of military intelligence. Its purpose is to collect, collate and evaluate and disseminate all services strategy and topographical intelligence about the law and order situation, armed forces and to ensure counter intelligence and security measures for the Bangladesh armed forces.

So evidently this force cannot usurp the powers of the revenue department. A defense force is an asset of the country. The primary responsibility of raising a defense force in a country is for ensuring national security including securing its borders and approaches; to defend the country's sovereignty; to contribute to and if necessary lead peace and security operations; to protect the country's wider interest by contributing to international peace and security and international rule of law; to contribute to whole-of-government efforts at home and abroad in resource protection, disaster relief, and humanitarian assistance; peace-keeping, crisis management and humanitarian relief operations; protection of internal security; defend scientific research and development; defense procurement and purchases etc. In short the obligation of the military went beyond their primary purpose of battling the external enemy as there is a perceptible shift toward internal security involving deactivating terrorists, winning the hearts and minds of aggrieved people of the country, riot control, saving lives during natural disasters, and military diplomacy.

References:

1. *Civil Appeal Nos. 340-342 and 332-339 of 2015*
2. *R.P Kapur v. Sarder Pratap Singh, AIR 1961 SC 1117; Maddhya Pradesh Indutries Ltd. v. Income Tax Officers, AIR 1970 SC 1011; and Jagdish Prasad v. State of Bihar, AIR 1974 SC 911*
3. *Article 90(3) of the Constitution*

Role of Defence Forces (W)

During the independence of Bangladesh, the armed forces played a pivotal role in the liberation of the country and it has been fully a structured organization officially as the Bangladesh Armed Forces with the Bangladesh Army, Bangladesh Navy and Bangladesh Air Force. The Bangladesh Coast Guard under the Home Ministry plays a stronger role in anti-smuggling, anti-piracy and protection of off-shore resources. Sometimes it provides support to the civil authority on disaster relief and internal security. The Army fought tribal insurgents in the Chittagong Hill Tracts (CHT). Bangladesh Navy effectively sees off economic aggression of Myanmar in the seas of Bangladesh. Since the late 1980s, the Armed Forces have earned international reputation by working as part of the UN Peacekeeping Mission in different countries of the world. They have been recognized as a disciplined and well-trained national institution that can tackle critical national phases.

There is also a dark side to these forces. Some aberrated officers and soldiers participated in the killing of the Father of the Nation Bangabandhu Sheikh Mujibur Rahman and other members of his family and his kith and kins. Some of them committed heinous crimes like the killing of four national leaders in Dhaka Central Jail. Some of them brutally killed President Ziaur Rahman. A section of military officials declared martial laws in 1975 and 1982. Its intelligence force DGFI could not detect the mutiny in the then BDR headquarter now Border Guard Bangladesh (BGB), although most of the officers were from the Army. These national forces cannot avoid the responsibility of these dark chapters of our nation. It is hoped that these forces will take the pride of glory by overcoming the incidents mentioned above and command respect from the hearts and minds of the citizenry.

The incident of what has been popularly dubbed as "seven-murder" case in Narayanganj in April 2014 was so brutal and horrific that it shocked the conscience of the nation. Some army personnel deputed to the Rapid Action Battalion (RAB) were directly involved in the killing. The investigating agency could not dare to apprehend them despite confirmation that they were the killers. The Supreme Court rose to the occasion and directed that whoever was involved in the incident should be severely dealt with and directed the investigation agency to proceed with the investigation of the case independently. Thereafter the investigation agency apprehended the army officers and the whole gamut of murder was revealed to the nation. This helped the government to take credit in not interfering with the administration of justice. But if the Supreme Court did not intervene in the matter, public sentiment might have gone to such an extent that it would have been very difficult for them to continue in power for long.

I had the occasion to discuss with a high-ranking officer in the Army of the rank of a Major General who was posted in a very responsible position. In course of discussions I noticed that the officer was brilliant, nationalist, professional and wanted to uphold the Army's glory, dignity and respect. While we were eating breakfast, I expressed my opinion regarding the army without any hesitation, i.e. the defense forces were unconsciously heading toward criticism from a section of the people. I told him that our defense forces are assets of the country. But because of the aberration and ambition of some past and present officers, the image which they deserve was decaying day-by-day. I also told him that it was a suicidal decision to depute defense forces personnel in RAB and Coast Guard along with other officers of police, Ansar and BGB. The Army, Navy and Air Force officers should be kept away from such duties and thus should not be allowed to work in civil administration, because whenever a disciplined force can mix with civilians and get involved in daily law and order situations, the possibilities of distortions in their mindset and mottos are larger.

The officer took the point very seriously and agreed with my opinion that the hierarchy of the Army was seriously thinking not to bring back those officers to the defense forces for maintaining its image. I thanked and felicitated him and advised him that if the Army could overcome the problem, its glory would revive in the manner of many members of the American Defense Forces who are regarded as the more acceptable and popular than some politicians, social workers or professionals from other spheres.

I had also the advantage of exchanging views with some senior Armed Forces officers in the rank of Brigadier Generals and Major Generals. The former Generals were acquainted with me at the ROAWA Club, when I was a lawyer. I had close links with some high-ranking officers and after becoming the Chief Justice in some social gathering I had the opportunity of exchanging views with some Generals. I was very delighted in meeting with them. They knew me well and wanted to talk with me on different issues particularly the judiciary. They appreciated my endeavors in improving the judiciary. I was so impressed on coming to know their views, viz. their apprehension about the degradation of the values of a section of officers and politicians, and about polluted politics in the country. They wanted to improve the present judicial system and encouraged me to take leadership in improving law and order and the administration of justice. I told them that without cooperation from different segments of people it would be difficult for me to bring about dramatic changes in the judiciary alone since it is one of the most neglected branches of the State. I pointed out the amount of money allocated to the judiciary. They could not imagine how the judiciary can run with such nominal amount of fund.

I met some other senior Army, Navy and Air Force officers at the time of their visits to the Supreme Court with the National Defense College members. Every year high ranking officers, even officers from other countries who were attending the National Defense College courses visit the Supreme Court. After arrival the NDC members are given a reception by the officers of the Supreme Court. They can sit in different courts to see the proceedings and some departments and thereafter they meet the Chief Justice in the judges' conference room. The Registrar General delivers the welcome speech followed by a presentation and interactive session, question and answer session, address by the Chief Justice, exchange of crests and gifts, vote of thanks, group photo session, light refreshment and departure. Photos are available in photo gallery of the Supreme Court website.

In the first such meeting after I became the Chief Justice I felt embarrassed that the military officers gifted a token to the Chief Justice, but I could not offer any gifts to them. When I asked the Registrar General to give them some gifts, he informed me that the Supreme Court does not have any such convention to present anything to outsiders and foreign dignitaries. After the program, I directed the Registrar General to arrange some gift items inscribed with the symbol of the Supreme Court for the visiting dignitaries. Thereafter on each occasion we could give gifts and improved the quality of light refreshment, because when such meetings are finished it is about lunch time. At the time of refreshment most of the visitors wanted to take photographs with me. They appeared to me so intelligent and dignified, they deserved adoration from any respectable person. They frankly admitted that I did a lot of improvement in the judiciary which they could understand from their relatives and media reports. They praised my efforts to improve the country's judiciary and conceded that one day they would become civilians after retirement and, therefore, the judiciary being the backbone of the country, its improvement should have been initiated long ago. Anyway, they hoped that if this process continues the Bangladesh judiciary would set an example in the international arena. They also wanted to bring the Army officers' right under the jurisdiction of the Supreme Court when their rights are infringed as is possible in India. I told them that would be very difficult in Bangladesh because we have achieved our independence in 1971, but the Army, Navy and Air Force are being regulated by laws promulgated by Pakistan. The Army Act was promulgated in 1952, the Navy Ordinance in 1961 and the Air Force Act in 1953. These laws were not amended as yet and were promulgated to suit the purposes of some Generals. I told them that there are a lot of loopholes in the laws which I came to know after a thorough reading of matters relating to the Armed Forces when some criminal matters relating to their involvement in ordinary criminal courts were heard. Also, in course of the hearing of the Presidential reference after the BDR mutiny, I had the occasion to read those laws. Due to such conversations I had a very good opinion of most of the officers that they have vast knowledge in international affairs and socio-economic and political issues of the country, and some of them have good knowledge in philosophy and political science and they want the welfare of the country. But they felt handicapped in the hands of some hierarchy who, taking advantage of their power and position, wanted to dominate them improperly.

I came to know from a close look at our forces that we could not totally shed the thinking, ideology, professional attitude and behavioral approach from the Pakistani forces' line of thinking. The forces of the US have totally changed their line of thinking, training, organizational set up and professionalism and made them different from British defense forces. Today the United States' military is America's most trusted institution. And the most honored figures in modern American life at the start of the 21st Century are the soldiers, marines, airmen, and sailors. Who built this dominant high-tech military machine? It was not the Founding Fathers. The leading architect of this historic project is General William Westmoreland, the man who commanded the military forces during the Vietnam War. Today an otherwise politically polarized public finds common identity in its uniformed service members. And Since the 1970s, the number of Americans expressing trust in the military has increased to an astounding 76 percent. The poll shows, the military is increasingly respected. They are more respected than politicians, Congressmen, social workers etc. It is only Westmoreland switched to all-volunteer-army on getting good students without criminal records as cadets and recruits and treating them as military professionals.

Following Westmoreland's lead, Abrams, DePui and Weynd gave new shape to the armed forces with ground breaking strategies for managing and training the new soldiers. They created performance standards to measure their training and skill. Together they literally rewrote the basic manual on strategies for fighting wars.1 India has also changed its forces' line of thinking, training pattern, organizational setup and professionalism from the one introduced by the British forces. I hope our national pride, the defense forces, would rise to the occasion and they would modernize their laws, change the training philosophy, and would give priority to professionalism other than giving its attention to issues that hamper institutionalizing it so that it commands respect from the citizens and, most of all, the hierarchy must ensure that no deserving officer is deprived of his promotion and status.

Israel is a tiny State surrounded by big countries and its location is hardly visible in the world's map. Even then, its most technologically advanced military strength is commendable by the superpowers as well. Today it boasts one of the most technologically advanced military stockpiles in the world, and one of the most effective workforces. Five most deadly systems that it acquired are: Merkaba tank: F-15s I version, Thunder the most versatile and effective user of Eagle by air force: Jericho 111, most advanced ballistic missiles capable of striking the entire Middle-East, Europe, Asia and North America: Dolphin submarine. It's hard to imagine that it owns hi-tech powers and is one of the world's top weapons exporters worth approximately 6.5 billion dollars annually. A big country like India is purchasing modern hardware from it. It is the largest exporter of drones. NATO countries used Israeli drones in Afghanistan. It has developed robotic weapons like Unmanned Ground Vehicles (UGVs) for border patrols. It also installed first operational Arrow missile battery, making it the first country in the world with an operational system that can shoot down incoming enemy missiles. Now it has grown into a satellite superpower. Its newest model of top secret tank is the "Merkava MK-4". It is difficult to mention all modern weaponry it has developed.2,3,4 I mentioned this only to show that if we have the willpower we can achieve highly technological weapons and can earn foreign currency by exporting them to foreign countries instead of importing from China and other countries in exchange of hard-earned foreign currency. If such be the case it will command respect both from home and abroad.

Reference:

1. We the People, Juan Williams
2. ibid
3. ibid
4. ibid.

Abandoned Property (X)

I would be remiss in my duty if I did not give some opinions regarding abandoned properties. It is a historical fact known to all that the Biharis and other Pakistanis mainly those who were in Mohammadpur, Mirpur, Syedpur, Pahartali and scattered in other districts of then East Pakistan. They not only grabbed all businesses but also occupied properties in Dhaka, Chittagong and other big cities. The Occupation Army could not continue in power for more than six months in East Pakistan and they could not also extend their administration to the remote areas of the country without the full support, cooperation and help of these Biharis and some Bengali Razakars. These Biharis and Razakars were mainly responsible for the killing of intellectuals, professors, doctors, engineers and molestation of women. Their activities are comparable with the atrocities of the Nazis. Naturally our government promulgated a law to take control, management and disposal of property abandoned by certain persons who were not present in Bangladesh or whose whereabouts were not known, or who had ceased to supervise or manage in person their property or who were enemy alliance.1

Most of the abandoned properties were occupied by some miscreants and land grabbers and they subsequently created forged documents after collecting information regarding the owners. Some of them even went to Pakistan and created some antedated documents of agreement for sale, hiba, etc. Some of them claimed to be heirs of the owners. Some of the owners after the change of government in 1975 came to Bangladesh and obtained citizenship with the help of the Ministry of Home Affairs, sold their properties and left for Pakistan. In the case of most of the properties, I noticed that different persons claimed as the heirs of the owners by creating forged documents. During my tenure in the highest court I was able to recover about 70/80 houses in Dhanmondi, Banani and Gulshan areas after setting aside the judgments obtained from the High Court Division. Since litigations over the claim of those properties cropped up, the government with a view to resolve the disputes over ownerships promulgated a law in 19852 by creating a Court of Settlement as a forum for adjudicating the properties.

One valuable piece of property, situated in the Bara Maghbazar area, was owned by one Zafar Tehrani and the owner left the country keeping the property in an abandoned condition. Thereafter the property was claimed by two sets of claimants. One group was led by one Abdus Subhan and another by a woman, Hosne Ara Begum, who was also claiming the ownership as wife of Rafi Tehrani, son of Zafar Tehrani. Both the groups instituted different litigations both in the civil court and Court of Settlement with a view to determining their right or interest in the property. The Court of Settlement is empowered to dispose of such claims is in summary manner. They lost in the Court of Settlement and in the High Court Division and, thereafter, they obtained leave from the apex court.3

On the question of release of the property, the point of law is clear and the apex court had settled the law points. It has been held that once a property is listed either in 'Ka' or 'Kha' lists, the natural presumption is that it has been duly enlisted as abandoned property. The property may be taken to have been vested in the government and the government has no obligation either to deny the facts alleged by the claimant or to disclose the basis of treating the property as abandoned property merely because the same is disputed by a claimant.4 the onus is entirely upon the claimant. It was also decided that if a building was included in the list, it was proof of its being an abandoned property.

Since two sets of claimants were claiming the ownership of the property it apparently showed that either one party is correct, or both are fake claimants. There cannot be any claim of a property by two groups as owners thereof and this counter claim itself was enough to lead to a presumption that the government legally declared the property as abandoned. A Court of Settlement has no power to decide on the title of the parties. On the question of onus, it is the claimant who is required to prove that the property has been wrongly included in the abandoned property list.5 After a Court of Settlement decides a matter there is no remedy for appeal. The litigant may challenge the judgment in the High Court Division by a Writ of Certiorari, but the scope is very limited. If it can be shown that the tribunal erroneously maintained the declaration of the abandoned property without admitting legal evidence or rejected legal evidence or it has misconstrued the law, a Writ of Certiorari is maintainable only on an erroneous decision in respect of a matter which is within the jurisdiction of an inferior tribunal, unless such erroneous decision relates to anything collateral.

In a Writ of Certiorari if there is mere error of law, it will not confer any power on the High Court Division because it is not sitting as a court of appeal. The error must be something more than an error. It can also entertain a petition if can be shown that a judgment has been obtained by fraud or collusion or corruption or where there is an error apparent on the face of the record or where the tribunal's conclusion was based on no evidence whatsoever or the decision was vitiated by malafide. It has no power to assess the evidence as a court of appeal.

In another case6 the apex court constituted with me, Md Abdul Wahhab Miah and Syed Mahmud Hossain held that if a property was published in the list, all permissions given by the Ministry of Works allowing mutation and transfer are declared void and be treated as obtained by collusion or fraud unless the property is released from the abandoned list because if the property is not released no one can sell, exchange or mutate his name in respect of the said property. In that case, the claimant claimed the property based on oral gift followed by an affidavit acknowledging the gift and the Ministry accepted the transfer and mutation. The department can mutate the name and acknowledge the gift after the property is released from the list and not otherwise.

The first above case, Hosne Ara claimed that she was in possession of the property being the wife of Rafi Tehrani. The tribunal on assessment of the affidavit found that she created the forged document for grabbing the property. She did not make any statement that her husband subsequently gifted the property by a deed. Hosne Ara never lived with Rafi Tehrani which is evident from deed dated October 18, 1972, wherein she showed her address at Azimpur, Lalbagh. Her kabinnama is also a forged one, inasmuch as, the signature of Rafi Tehrani does not tally with the admitted signature. The tribunal held that Rafi Tehrani never gifted the property in favor of Hosne Ara. Abdus Subhan did not admit that Rafi Tehrani possessed or owned the property or that he gifted the property in favor of Hosne Ara. Rafi Tehrani in his deposition in another suit mentioned his address at Gulshan, but in the kabinnama he gave his address at Isphahani Colony. Abdus Subhan also admitted that Rafi Tehrani lived at Isphahani Colony. Hosne Ara claimed that Rafi Tehrani left for London in 1975. But Hasina Tehrani, daughter of the owner stated that he was in Bara Magh Bazar till 1975.

As Hosne Ara could not produce any paper or document of payment of tax to the City Corporation relating to the property, there was no document showing that she ever possessed the property? The alleged gift was not acted upon even if her claim of being Rafi Tehrani's wife was genuine. She admitted that she was residing at her father's house at Azimpur during the liberation war period. As she was not in possession as admitted, the oral gift was not acted upon even if it was taken that Rafi Tehrani gifted to her. She also admitted that she made various documents of sale and she had no transferable right in the property and that she had no right to claim before the Court of Settlement. None of these transfers was legal because before release of the property, she could not transfer the property. And other such transfers, she cannot claim for release of the property. So, she had no right to file a petition of claim; rather that she was set up by interested persons was clear.

On the other hand, Abdus Subhan admitted that Advocate Abdur Rashid was in possession of the property immediately after the war of liberation. From this admitted position, he was not in possession of the property on the day of promulgation of PO 16 of 1972. From his admission, it is proved that the property was rightly declared as abandoned property. Advocate Abdur Rashid was not claiming ownership of the said property. All these findings were findings of facts arrived at by the tribunal on sifting evidence. So, the High Court Division had no right to interfere with the judgment in the absence of misreading or non-consideration of the evidence. Therefore, the High Court Division rightly did not interfere with the judgment.

The appeals were heard once before, and as the court was equally divided into 3:3, with me, Syed Mahmud Hossain and Hasan Foez Siddique being in favor of dismissal of the appeals, and Abdul Wahhab Miah, Nazmun Ara Sultana, and another judge (whose name I cannot recollect now) were in favor of allowing the appeal, I constituted a larger Bench including Mohammad Iman Ali and AHM Shamsuddin Chowdhury. Before hearing of the appeals, an influential member of a powerful family of the ruling party Sheikh Kabir made a courtesy call on me. In course of the conversation he made a request about the case. I clearly told him that the principle

345

of law regarding abandoned property had already been settled by the highest court of the country and as per overwhelming decisions, there was little scope to decide any case ignoring them. Secondly, if I were to decide in favor of one of Hosne Ara, there would arise chaos and confusion and all previous decisions would need to be reviewed and, in that case, no property could be retained as abandoned property. Before the hearing was taken up, Syed Mahmud Hossain told me that this time he would be in favor of allowing the appeal. I did not make any comment but was indeed surprised on hearing his comment. Nevertheless I understood the message.

In the second hearing, the majority opinion was expressed by me and Mohammad Iman Ali, Hasan Foez Siddique and AHM Shamsuddin Chowdhury concurred with me. Even from the claim of Hosne Ara, I noticed that Zafar Tehrani had no exclusive ownership on the property. So, her claim that Zafar Tehrani gifted in favor of his son Rafi Tehrani from whom she is claiming title, but Rafi Tehrani's title was not perfect as his father had no exclusive title and, therefore, in no case she could claim the release of the property on the basis of oral gift. What is more, she admitted that she was not in exclusive possession of the entire property and therefore her claim of oral gift was not acted upon. Hence, she did not acquire any title on the basis of oral gift and, therefore, the subsequent transfer in favor of Md. Shahidul Bhuiyan and others did not confer the title on the strength of the deeds executed by her apart from the fact that she had no subsisting interest in the property.

At one stage, she also admitted that Atiqur Rahman and others took possession from her. If the statement is taken to be true, how did Shahidul Haque Bhuiyan and others get possession from her after purchase is also not clear to me? Therefore, the third-party purchasers have had no semblance of title and possession. She also claims title based on decrees passed in two suits. But the Court of Settlements on perusal of claims and other documents held that the decrees were obtained by fraud upon the court. Those were exparte decrees. A judgment obtained by fraud or collusion may be treated as nullity and the court may ignore them even without challenging the said judgment.7 A judgment obtained by forgery cannot attain finality and it can be challenged any time by any party interested by way of defense on the ground that the decree was by fraud.8

A plea of non-service of notice was taken by Hosne Ara and Abdus Subhan. If Hosne Ara or Subhan was not in possession, how could the abandoned property authority serve notices on them? The question of serving of notice arises only if someone is in illegal possession for vacating possession in favor of the government. Therefore, the tribunal was justified in not finding any fault for non-service of notice. Rafi Tehrani had other properties in Purana Paltan and those properties were released in his favor. Therefore, a plea was taken that in view of the release of those properties Rafi Tehrani was in "East Pakistan" in 1972. The order was made by the Sub-Divisional officer. It never came before any court. The apex court is not bound by any decision of any administrative officer. Moreover, if any property is scrumptiously released that would not change the abandoned character of the other property. The Purana Paltan property was not enlisted in any list, but the Magh Bazar property was enlisted.

And therefore, this enlistment of the property had presumptive value that it was abandoned property. In the minority opinion since the author realized that there is claim and counter-claim over title and possession of the property, he concluded his opinion by holding that the Court of Settlement wrongly disbelieved the possession by Hosne Ara, inasmuch as, if her whole statement is considered it would appear that Atiqur Rahaman and others did not enter in possession of the entire property in question. He failed to notice that we were not sitting as an appellate court on the judgment of the Court of Settlement. We were deciding a matter from a judgment of the High Court Division passed on a Writ of Certiorari, and he had ignored the scope of the Writ of Certiorari.

Another suicidal finding is that merely two rival parties' claim for title of the same property would not oust the jurisdiction of the Court of Settlement. The very inconsistent claim itself is a ground for dismissing the claim, because the Court of Settlement has no jurisdiction to decide title of the parties in the disputed property. Its power is summary in nature. Another serious mistake committed was that having noticed that the parties were litigating over the same property, he afforded the parties to establish their right in the civil court in suits before it. If the title is not perfect, how the learned judge can direct to exclude the property from the list of abandoned property was also not clear to me. This judgment is apparently motivated and against his own judgment because two of them (Abdul Wahhab Miah and Syed Mahmud Hossain) decided on a matter mentioned above that unless the property is released from the list, there could not be any legal transfer of the said property. He totally ignored the transfers made by Hosne Ara.

References:

1. *Bangladesh Abandoned Property (Control, Management and Disposal) Order 1972 (PO 16 of 1972)*
2. *Ordinance of 1985*
3. *Md. Shahidul Haque Bhuiyan v. The Chairman, First Court of Settlement, Civil Appeal Nos. 10 & 77 of 2003*
4. *Bangladesh v. Jalil 48 DLR (AD) 10; Bangladesh v. Ashraf Ali, 49 DLR (AD) 161; Bangladesh v. KM Zaker 88 BLC (AD) 27 and Hazerullah v. Chairman, First Court of Settlement, 3 DLC (AD) 42*
5. *Ministry of Works v. Abdul Jalil 48 DLR(AD) 10; Bangladesh v. Md. Jalil 49 DLR(AD) 26; KM Zaker Hossain v. Ministry of Works, 8 BLC(AD) 27; and Hazeullah v. Chairman, 3 BLC(AD) 42*
6. *Government v. Orex Network Ltd. 10 ADC 1*
7. *Section 44 of the Evidence Act*
8. *Gram Panchayet v. Ujagar Singh AIR (2000) SC 327*

Contempt of Court (Y)

On at least two occasions I was put in embarrassing positions after assuming the office of the Chief Justice. One incident was over the publication of some stories scandalizing the Chief Justice in person and his office in an issue of Daily Janakantha under the heading "Activities of Salahuddin Quader Chowdhury's family. The ways to escape shortened." AHM Shamsuddin Chowdhury was the junior most member of the court and during my predecessors' time, the court was to put in embarrassing situations on many occasions due the remarks and squabble with the senior lawyers over which the Chief Justice had little control. He did not maintain the decorum, norms and conduct of a judge of the highest court, especially in the presence of the Chief Justice and other senior members. If a junior member of the Bench wants to put any query to the counsel arguing the matter, it is to be with the leave of the Chief Justice, not to speak of attacking the senior lawyers in their presence. The senior counsel was in a helpless condition and looked toward the Chief Justice, but the Chief Justice had little control over the court management. It is known by all and the less I speak the better. On one occasion Dr. Kamal Hossain shouted at him and made adverse remarks saying that he was addressing the court, not to him.

I was seriously thinking over the issue of controlling him and decided that if he was kept in my court, the administration of justice will be hampered, because in this court all important cases are normally placed in the list for hearing, and, secondly, he was very slow in writing any judgment or order, if any case was assigned to him for writing the opinion of the court. He always remains busy with extraneous business which is not congenial for a judge to deal with. Sometimes he took three to four years in finalizing a two or three-page leave granting order. Md. Abdul Wahhab Miah, the senior most judge, realized that I would constitute two simultaneous Benches for disposal of matters. This was not in vogue during my predecessors' tenure, and Wahab Miah requested me not to keep AHM Shamsuddin Chowdhury in his Bench if I really constituted two Benches. Despite his request, I kept him with Abdul Wahhab Miah in his Bench for peaceful administration of judicial work.

In course of hearing the appeal of Salahuddin Quader Chowdhury against his conviction by the International Crimes Tribunal, AHM Shamsuddin Chowdhury came to see me and requested me to keep him on the Bench. I did not keep him. After the matter was taken up for hearing he again came to meet me. Normally a judge can sit in the chair kept in front of the Chief Justice's table. This time I noticed that Shamsuddin Chowdhury was standing towards the south-western corner of my desk. Despite asking him to sit, he refused to sit saying that he would leave after talking about an urgent matter. It is a prevalent practice that whenever a judge seeks permission of the Chief Justice's time for to talk, the latter does not permit anyone else to remain there. Again, he requested me to keep him in Salahuddin Quader Chowdhury's appeal hearing. My answer was an emphatic "no." Then he asked me the reason for not keeping him on that Bench. I was not supposed to give an explanation to him, but he was insisting again and again. I told him that I do not want to keep him because the matter had already been taken up for hearing, and that I had some problems with keeping him on the Bench. He again queried as to why and what type of problems I had been facing with him. Ethically no judge can show any interest to hear a case and it is the duty of the Chief Justice not to keep him in a matter if he found that the judge was interested in a particular matter, and I reminded him of this. He was greatly eager to get some clarifications from me and repeatedly kept on asking the questions.

Then I realized that he was deliberately putting those questions and met me earlier with a view to maligning me. I said, 'Yes.' He then asked me who had met and talked with me. The mode and manner of questions and his demeanor made me suspicious that he had been harboring some ill motive and that's why he was asking me the questions again and again over the same issue. I was a bit suspicious about him. The questions he put me were quoted in verbatim in the judgment. But I could not remember those at that stage. However, I understood that he was an unpredictable person and I decided not to prolong the discussion, saying that I would not discuss this issue any further, but I told him that I would not keep him on the Bench and that there was also objection for his inclusion.

It would have been better if I could reproduce the conversations between him and me, which the contemnor Swadesh Roy disclosed in his affidavit. Thereafter, hearing of Salahuddin Quader Chowdhury's appeal was over on July 16, 2015 and the matter was kept for delivery of judgment. I recollect here that Khandker Mahbub Hossain was the President of the Bar and he was the senior counsel engaged in Salahuddin Quader Chowdhury's appeal. He met me on one occasion and requested me not to keep Shamsuddin Chowdhury on the Bench. I told him that I was embarrassed by his (Chowdhury's) conduct, but I kept him on the second Bench.

The conversation between me and Shamsuddin Chowdhury was in the early stage of the hearing. But the news item was published immediately before the delivery of judgment of Salahuddin Quader Chowdhury's appeal. If the writer and publisher of the newspaper had good motive that if Salahuddin Quader Chowdhury's appeal was heard by me there was chance of influence, they ought to have published the report as soon as they got information from Shamsuddin Chowdhury that I was influenced by Salahuddin Quader Chowdhury's family. But instead they kept silent and only two or three days before the delivery of judgment they published the report. The writer forgot all norms and decorum in choosing his language against a sitting Chief Justice.

The timing of the publication of story raised the suspicion that they wanted to frustrate the delivery of the judgment. The offending portion of the report was that the writer questioned how members of Salahuddin Quader Chowdhury's family could meet one of the judges, who was in session of the matter. He then said, the Prime Minister had postponed the tour program of one judge abroad pointing fingers at me. He added that my tour to London was sponsored by BNP-Jamaat organizations. He then posed a question: "Why a disputed businessman went ahead of the tour? What had been happening there?" Then again, he said, the judge who had acquitted Tareque Rahman could not become Benazir Ahmad (DG of RAB). He could not avoid the temptation of money like Benazir Ahmad and that is why the judge--again pointing fingers at me--could not avoid Salahuddin Quader's money. He continued, ISIS has large amounts of money, which is also known to everybody, and it is because of such money, members of

351

Salahuddin Quader's family could dare to ask not to include a certain judge on the Bench.

The writer wanted to say that I had received vast amounts of money from Salahuddin Quader's family and, accordingly, I did not keep Shamsuddin Chowdhury on the Bench meaning thereby that Shamsuddin Chowdhury is the only judge who could administer proper justice in the appeal. Some portion of the remark was so offensive that the lawyer appearing for the contemnors skipped that portion of the news when he was asked to place the report. When the court asked why he was not placing the first portion of the offending report, he appeared to be embarrassed and submitted that he would make submission on this matter later. That statement was so motivated and scandalous that the writer should have been directly sent to Dhaka Central Jail.

The court issued a Suo moto notice upon the writer and publisher of the newspaper asking them why they should not be proceeded against for contempt of court.1 when the matter came up before the full Bench, excluding AHM Shamsuddin Chowdhury, the contemnors wanted him to be included on the Bench at the hearing. All the judges were satisfied on reading the recorded version between me and AHM Shamsuddin Chowdhury that the latter had surreptitiously recorded the conversation and sent the recorded portion to the contemnor. Because he was a party in the offending article the court desisted from issuing any proceeding against AHM Shamsuddin Chowdhury for the interest of justice.

The contemnors appeared and wanted long adjournments for two months. The court rejected the prayer, because contempt matters should not be dragged on for indefinite periods. Since they touch the integrity, dignity and impartiality of the court, they should be heard expeditiously with a view to restoring the confidence of the public's perception of the judiciary. The contemnors filed a petition on August 6, 2015 stating that they collected information against "Mr. Justice Surendra Kumar Sinha" and in another petition it stated that if the Chief Justice constitutes a Bench as per the will of a party of a pending appeal, judicial conscience demanded that "Mr. Justice Surendra Kumar Sinha cannot sit in a

Bench to adjudicate a matter in which directly he is a party to that subject: a party must get a fair trial and a trial cannot be said to be fair in face of apparent bias because from the audio record it appears that the honorable Chief Justice Mr. Surendra Kumar Sinha said that Swadesh Roy shall be dealt with."

In another petition it was claimed that they wanted to "cross examine Justice Surendra Kumar Sinha, the honorable Chief Justice of Bangladesh, to unearth the whole truth because as per the Constitution of Bangladesh no one is above the Constitution and "whoever you so high the law is above you." The lawyer Salahuddin Dolan by filing another application prayed on behalf of the contemnors to issue summons upon Shamsuddin Chowdhury to examine as defense witness stating that Shamsuddin Chowdhury had consented to depose in the matter. From this prayer it may be imagined as to how a dangerous person Shamsuddin Chowdhury is! All the judges of the Bench were surprised to know the intention of Shamsuddin Chowdhury.

The contemnors not only made indecent and derogatory remarks in the news item, they also continued in their attempts to scandalize the office of the Chief Justice in course of the hearing of the matter. Even they exceeded norms by expressing that the Chief Justice should not be on the Bench as they would not get fair justice ignoring that contempt matters are heard by the same Bench with which the contempt was perpetrated--but on the other hand they had no objection if Shamsuddin Chowdhury was included on the Bench. They even wanted to cross examine me saying that I was not above the law. Not only had the contemnors, their lawyer also committed contempt by making wild allegation against me. Due to his arrogant behavior and purposively malicious remarks, which had not even the remotest relevance to the merit of the case, all the judges of the Bench and lawyers present in the court room were surprised. Such mischievousness had never occurred in the history of our judicial culture. Before the court made any observation, the lawyers present in the courtroom became very annoyed at the awfully pathetic behavior shown by the contemnor's lawyer and they demanded to forcibly discontinue his submission any further. I requested the lawyers in the courtroom to calm down so that the proceedings of the court were not interrupted.

When the court wanted the contemnor's lawyer to make his submission, he said that he was feeling insecure and asked for the proceedings to be adjournment. The court having guessed his motive, namely, that he was trying to frustrate the hearing of the matter, I directed the Attorney General to provide Dolon with police protection till the matter was disposed of and, also, he should be given such protection on his way back to his residence. In the face of the level of disparagement and despicable behavior the lawyer (Dolon) portrayed standing against the highest court of the land the court showed its befitting patience that only matches the power and glory of the greatest temple of justice of the nation. The contemnors again filed another application that if AHM Shamsuddin Chowdhury were included on the Bench, they would have no objection to my inclusion on the Bench. This last application nakedly exposed their intention and motive behind seeking to cross examine the Chief Justice; secondly, to examine AHM Shamsuddin Chowdhury as witness on their behalf; and thirdly, to include Shamsuddin Chowdhury on the Bench.

The matter was initially heard before a four-member Bench, but when the contemnors filed subsequent application, I included other judges excluding Shamsuddin Chowdhury. One day Nazmun Ara Sultana along with Syed Mahmud Hossain and Hasan Foez Siddique wanted to say something to me about this contempt matter. Nazmun Ara wanted an assurance from me that if I pardoned the contemnors, they would seek unconditional apology. From her body language I came to understand that she came after discussions with the other two judges, but she was hesitating to approach the matter. I told her that before any matter was heard, I could not give any final word and that whether the contemnors would seek unconditional apology was their personal matter. If they submit such an application the court would consider it later. I had been informed by some of the judges residing in the Judges Complex that the Law Minister had visited Nazmun Ara's residence during that period at night. Therefore, my suspicion was proved correct as the Law Minister was trying to get the contemnors relieved of the charge and he wanted to demean the office of the Chief Justice because I stood in his way in interfering in the administration of justice.

In the judgment it was held that under our constitutional scheme there was no escape from the acceptance or disobedience of compliance of a direction given by a highest court in a judicial review, because it being the final court such direction is binding upon whom it is given. Non-compliance with the highest court's order not only dislodges the cornerstone of maintaining the equilibrium and equanimity of the State's governance, there would also be a breakdown of constitutional functioning of the State. It would be mayhem in all respect and the substratum of the Constitution would be broken. For achieving the establishment of rule of law the Constitution has assigned the special task to the judiciary of the country. It is only through the court that the rule of law unfolds its contents and establishes its concepts. For the judiciary to perform its duties and functions effectively and be true to the spirit with which it is sacredly entrusted the dignity and authority of the court had to be respected and protected at all cost. The only weapon of protecting itself from onslaughts to the institution was the long hand of contempt of court left in the armory of judicial repository which, when needed, can reach any neck howsoever high or far away it may be. The right to freedom of speech and expression can go far as they did not contravene the statutory limits that must prevail without any hindrance. The maintenance of the dignity of the court is one of the pertinent principles of rule of law in a democratic set up and any criticism of the judicial institution couched in the language that apparently appears to be mere criticism but ultimately results in undermining the dignity of the court cannot be permitted when found having crossed such limit.

The judiciary is the last and final path and hope of the citizens for protecting their lives, liberty, property and establishing their rights and liabilities. If any calculated scandalizing of judges is made, the hopes and aspiration of the people will be eroded. Any individual or institution which is conscious of the power of the court and adheres to it would necessarily feel that to offend a court at all in a

355

manner such that it feels it has been lowered in the eyes of the people is a matter of regret and no person or institution in a State should feel itself so great as to regard offering an apology as being beneath his or its dignity.

Scandalizing the court is to be taken to mean any act done or writing published calculated to bring a court or a judge of the court into contempt. Scandalizing the court by means of publication may be taken to mean bringing the authority of the court into disrepute. A tendency to scandalize the court or tendency to lower the authority of the court or tendency to interfere with or obstruct the administration of justice in any manner or tendency to challenge the authority of the majesty of justice is criminal contempt. Any act done, or writing published calculated to obstruct or interfere with the due course of justice or the lawful process of the court is contempt of the court. It includes scurrilous attack on the judiciary, which is taken to undermine the authority of the court and public confidence in the administration of justice. In such case no leniency can be shown to the contemnors.

Interference with the administration of justice may have the tendency to pervert the course of justice. The stream of justice should be unsullied. If an impression is created in the minds of the public that the judges of the highest court act on extraneous considerations the confidence of the whole community in the administration of justice is bound to be undermined and no greater mischief than that can be imagined. Any publication which is or is likely to have the tendency to pervert the course of justice by attempting to excite through the media prejudices, the party or their litigation while they are pending constitutes a serious type of contempt of court. When a proceeding is awaiting verdict in a court if the media publishes stories revealing the conduct of the offender or the evidence adduced against him and thereby holding him guilty, the same amounts to contempt.

The contemnors not only scandalized the office of the Chief Justice but also undermined the authority of the entire court because even if I am influenced there are other judges. I cannot deliver a judgment without their concurrence. Contempt proceedings are drawn and disposed of by the judge or the Bench against whom the contemnors make statements undermining the authority, prestige and dignity of the concerned judge. If the judge against whom aspersions are brought is a party to the proceedings no court would be able to administer justice. In that case, whenever a litigant find that a judge has taken a view which will go against him, the litigant will make wild allegations against the judge with a view to get rid of him.

The court also made adverse comments against Salahuddin Dolon due to his arrogant behavior and purposive malicious remarks toward the Chief Justice and cautioned him that he also showed contemptuous behavior. The court suspected that he had minimum knowledge as to what the Chief Justice had admitted. He was totally involved with his clients without caring as to whether the Chief Justice is maligned with derogatory words or remarks. The court found the contemnors guilty.

All the judges though were convinced that not only the contemnors, but AHM Shamsuddin Chowdhury and Dolon also committed the same contempt. About the writer, Swadesh Roy who committed a serious type of contempt, he deserved to be sent to jail. Before rising in court all the judges sat for discussion and agreed that the contemnors should be convicted. However, Md. Abdul Wahhab Miah pleaded that the delivery of the judgment should be postponed for two months claiming contemnor Atiqullah Khan Masud is a very powerful man, who has close connections with the Prime Minister and if we convict him, there would be repercussions on the part of the government. I was extremely irritated on hearing Wahab Miah's view but managed to control my exasperation and said that if we were convinced that the contemnors had committed contempt, the judgment should be delivered at once without delaying the matter. Any delay would raise various questions about the authority of the court.

All of them agreed that they should be sent to jail; and according to Abdul Wahhab Miah, we should send them to jail after some time. I told them that if we can award sentence after two months, why not on the same day fixed for judgment. After hearing Abdul

Wahhab Miah's view, some of the judges were confused. Realizing the situation, I told them that either we would acquit them of the charge of contempt or punish them. If they are apprehensive of the power of Atiqullah, a lenient view may be taken about their sentences. Accordingly, instead of sending the contemnors to jail, we took a lenient view. We sentenced them to confinement till the rising of the court with a fine of ten thousand taka each to be paid to a charitable organization. It is disgraceful for a nation that even after such conviction the Prime Minister awarded Swadesh Roy with the Ekushey Padak a few months after the conviction. She very intentionally awarded him because this writer was in the habit of writing scandalous remarks against me and, as such, he was rewarded.

After the judgment was prepared, when Abdul Wahhab Miah noticed that there were adverse remarks against Salahuddin Dolon, he requested me to exonerate him and/or to drop the adverse findings. I told him that he displayed such discourteous behavior and uttered such disparaging remarks against the Chief Justice that he should not be pardoned. In this regard, I pointed out to him an incident of Rafiqul Huq, who was the senior counsel appearing in a matter. The litigant had prepared an application expressing no confidence against then Chief Justice Khairul Haque. Rafiqul Huq in open court said that he would not file such an application in court rather he would withdraw his name from the case if he felt pressured in that regard. Wahhab Miah then requested me to show leniency in using the language. I told him that since he was requesting for the lawyer, I will not make strong remarks against him, but from his conduct, the lawyer deserved to have his license withdrawn.

Abdul Wahhab Miah agreed with my view. It appeared to me that Salahuddin Dolon had a close relationship with Abdul Wahhab Miah. This I came to know subsequently from his own version. Abdul Wahhab Miah came to me to discuss a matter and during our discussion, he volunteered that he had called Salahuddin Dolon for ascertaining as to why he had made such disparaging and wild remarks against the Chief Justice. Salahuddin Dolon told him that as the contemnors did not find any reputed lawyer to appear and contest on their behalf, ABM Khairul Haque called and pressurized him to accept the brief on behalf of the contemnors and that he did not make those remarks voluntarily, but because of the request and pressure from Justice ABM Khairul Haque he was compelled to make those remarks. Dolon added that he repented his actions.

The second contempt matter was against two cabinet ministers: Advocate Md. Quamrul Islam, MP, Minister, Ministry of Food, and Mozammel Haque, MP, Minister, Ministry of Liberation War Affairs, for their derogatory and highly contemptuous remarks made on March 5, 2016 at a roundtable discussion held at BILIA auditorium against the Chief Justice and the Supreme Court in respect to a pending appeal for judgment on March 8, 2016.

Mir Kashem Ali was sentenced to death by the International Crimes Tribunal. He preferred an appeal and the appeal was heard in my court. In course of the hearing, I noticed that the case was badly conducted by the prosecutors which enraged me. I drew the attention of the Attorney General that this type of incompetent prosecutors should be removed from the list of prosecutors and that competent lawyers should be appointed otherwise the purpose and object of setting up the tribunal would become a forum for political vendetta and corruption would be rampant. There were whispers regarding such corruption against some investigation officers and prosecutors. It was known to all that Mir Kashem Ali was a very rich man. He owned a big business house in Bangladesh. In course of hearing of the appeal, the Attorney General produced document showing that Mir Kashem Ali engaged a lobbyist in the US on payment of 25 million US dollar for frustrating the war crimes trials by creating pressure on the government through the US government. He also produced the acknowledgement receipt of payment of money. From this it could be imagined how large a fortune he had amassed.

The defects we noticed were that two prosecutors conducted the trial, and the order sheet revealed that one prosecutor examined one witness and another prosecutor examined another in the absence of the other and in this manner the entire trial was concluded. I remarked that their conduct reminds me that I have been watching a sequence less drama. If a stage drama is directed by two directors, and each directors directs one scene leaving the other scene to the other director, there would be no consistency in the sequences and the audience would not get interested in enjoying it due to lack of consistency in the sequences.

The hearing of the appeal was concluded about 15 days previously and just three days before the delivery of the judgment, I heard from some lawyers who had attended a seminar along with me in Nepal that two ministers on March 5 made contemptuous remarks against me at a roundtable touching on my remarks against the prosecutors. It was told that Advocate Quamrul Islam said that since the Chief Justice had said that the International Crimes Tribunal was being used politically, then the appeal of Mir Kashem Ali should be heard by a new Bench leaving out the Chief Justice. Since the Chief Justice had made comments about the case in open court, Islam had said, the appeal should be heard again without the Chief Justice, because whatever decision he would give would be questionable. He also said that the Chief Justice wanted to put the prosecution and investigation teams in the dock along with the accused saying that the prosecution was playing politics with this case. Such statements in open court led him (Islam) to believe that the decision would go against the Muktijoddhas. Since the Chief Justice had made such statements, there is no way that the accused could be sentenced to death and that he will either acquit the accused or reduce the sentence. In the same meeting, the other contemnor said that if the death sentence is upheld, then it will be said that the government had created pressure and if, on the other hand, the decision is otherwise, it would not be acceptable, and this dilemma had been created by the Chief Justice. He also demanded my withdrawal from the Bench, if I did not resign.

On reading the news item, I was so shocked that I did not attend the afternoon session of the seminar because no one can make any comment over a pending matter publicly. What's more, if the cabinet ministers make such remarks it would be taken as the opinion of the government. They intentionally made those remarks just immediately before the delivery of the judgment though I had made those remarks at the initial stage of hearing at which time they kept silent. On March 7 at noon, I rang the law minister. He received my call but told me that he was in a cabinet meeting. Then I told him that if he was in the cabinet meeting, it was so urgent that he should draw the attention of the Prime Minister to what I wanted to say to him. I drew his attention to the remarks of the ministers and told him that unless the two cabinet ministers seek unconditional apology and withdraw their remarks before my return, they would face severe consequences. After the cabinet meeting was over, again I contacted the Law Minister and wanted to know about the reaction of the Prime Minister. The law minister told me that the Prime Minister reprimanded them in the cabinet meeting and the matter should be dropped there and I should not commit any excess in this connection. I told the minister straightaway that I was not at all satisfied with the explanation and requested him to remain in the court at 7:00PM, at which time, I would be expecting to reach court directly from the airport.

I directed my Registry to inform all the judges to remain in my chamber at 7:00 PM. I rushed to the court directly from the airport and I was told that the Law Minister and the judges were all waiting for me. Before I discussed with the judges, I went to the waiting room where the law minister was sitting. The law minister explained to me again that the Prime Minister had rebuked the ministers openly and directed them not to make any such derogatory remarks against the Chief Justice. I told the law minister that I was not at all satisfied with this explanation and reminded him that I stood by my opinion. The law minister then suddenly made a remark which I could not even imagine. He said that if I proceeded further, the Supreme Court would have to pay the price for it. I was astounded on hearing the remarks of the law minister, but I controlled my temptation to retort and calmly said that whatever he had to say he should say in the presence of all the judges.

Accordingly, I brought him to my chamber and narrated to the judges in the presence of the law minister the discussions I had with him but refrained from pointing out the threat given by the law minister. All the judges then told the law minister that they would not say anything and that whatever decision the Chief Justice would take, he is being the guardian of the judiciary, and they would accept his (the CJ's) opinion. Then I again told the Law Minister that time was passing and unless the ministers had a press conference and expressed their apology to me by 11:00 PM, the delivery of the judgment of Mir Kashem Ali would be hampered and other consequences might also follow. I wanted to make it clear that the remarks of the two cabinet ministers against the Chief Justice would be taken as the opinion of the government and, in that case, the relationship between the judiciary and the government would be impacted. And therefore, I wanted a peaceful solution of the matter within that night.

The law minister did not make any commitment, but from his body language it seemed to us that he was not happy with my remarks and with a furious attitude he left my chamber telling me that he would inform me. After the departure of the law minister, we discussed the matter meticulously and all the judges were convinced that unless the ministers tendered an unconditional apology openly, we would take legal action against them the following day. It took us till about 11:00 PM in finalizing our decision when we departed for our homes. Before our departure, I requested the members of my Bench Syed Mahmud Hossain, Hasan Foez Siddique and Mirza Hossain Haider to come to court at 8:00 the next morning for our own discussion and asked other judges to come to my chamber at 8:30AM. It may be pointed out here that we did not discuss the result of the appeal because normally we express our opinion before the delivery of the judgment as a measure to check leakage. At 8:00 in the morning, I intimated my brother judges that the law minister did not inform me of anything. Under the circumstance, if the ministers did not withdraw their remarks, it would not be possible on my part to remain a party in the matter and deliver the judgment. I requested them to deliver the judgment without me, because it would not be proper on my part to be a party to the judgment due to those remarks of the ministers. I also told them that all the judges heard the matter at length and it would not be difficult for them to take a decision in the appeal.

At that moment all three judges in unison told me that if I withdrew my name, they would be left with no option other than to withdraw their names too from the appeal. On hearing their opinion, I was frightened and apprehended that after so much labor, all endeavors would be wasted. Then I wanted to know from them the next course of action. All of them said that they would agree with me on whatever decision I would take. I then told them that let the other judges come and we would take a decision unanimously. After the arrival of the remaining judges, I explained to them that the law minister did not contact me. I also intimated to them that I wanted to withdraw my name form the delivery of the judgment, but my brothers were not agreeable. All the judges agreed that we were left with no option other than to issue contempt proceedings against the two cabinet ministers. Accordingly, all the judges sat in court at 10:00 AM by constituting a special Bench and drew up contempt proceedings against the ministers.2

The matter appeared in the list on March 14, 2016, on which day contemnor Mozammel Haque appeared in person with his lawyer, but Advocate Quamrul Islam prayed for adjournment. The prayer was allowed, and the matter was adjourned to March 20 with direction upon the contemnors to appear in person before the court. The matter was heard for some time on that day and then it was adjourned to March 27, on which day both the contemnors appeared in the court with their counsel and expressed their unconditional apology. The court rejected their unconditional apology and decided to hear the matter on merit. In course of hearing, I queried Rafiqul Huq, senior counsel appearing for Mozammel Haque, as to whether the remarks of the ministers which were published in the issue of the Jugantar on March 6, 2016 violated their oath and directed him to place the statements of the ministers. After reading of the newspaper reports, Rafiqul Huq frankly conceded that they had violated their oath as per the Constitution. The court unanimously passed a short order on March 27 finding the contemnors guilty of gross contempt of court and sentenced them to pay fine of Tk.50,000 each to be donated to two charitable organizations. After the verdict the law minister held a press conference stating the ministers did not violate their oath and the Constitution and, therefore, they could continue as ministers.

Though all the judges unanimously found the ministers guilty of contempt of court, and their senior counsel admitted in open court that they had violated their oath, two judges, Syed Mahmud Hossain and Hasan Foez Siddique, observed that the ministers did not violate their oath. The majority opinion was delivered by Justice Muhammad Iman Ali, and the minority opinion was expressed by Justice Hasan Foez Siddique. In the majority opinion it was observed that contempt of court may be classified into three categories, namely (i) disobedience of court orders and breach of undertakings given to the court, (ii) scandalizing of the court, and (iii) interference with the administration of justice. The first category is termed as civil contempt, whereas the other two categories are contempt of a criminal nature. In the facts and circumstances of the case, since there is no allegation of any breach or non-compliance of any order of the court, the contemnors had made comments/remarks scandalizing the court or interfered with the administration of justice. Such utterances in public, by persons holding high constitutional posts, had demonstrated their utter disregard for the rule of law and decisions of the Supreme Court and hence violation of the provisions of the Constitution contrary to the oaths of their office to preserve, protect and defend the Constitution.

The judiciary is the guardian of the rule of law. The Supreme Court has been entrusted with the solemn duty of declaring the law if the same is ultra vires the Constitution. In Idrisur Rahman, 3 it was observed that "the expression of rule of law has a number of different meanings and corollaries. Its primary meaning is that everything must be done in accordance with law, in other words, it speaks of rule of law and not of men and everybody is under the law and nobody is above the law. The other meaning of rule of law is that government should be conducted within a framework of recognized rules and principles which restrict discretionary power and our Constitution is the embodiment of the supreme will of the people setting forth the rules and principles". But the most important meaning of rule of law is that the disputes as to the legality of the acts of the government are to be decided by Judges who are independent of the Executive. Everyone, however high she or he may be, must abide by the law of the land. The law of the land includes all that is law as defined and accepted as law by the Constitution. Every citizen has surrendered to the provisions of the Constitution which is the manifestation of the will of the people. There are multitudes of rights given by the Constitution to the citizens, but those are subject to restrictions imposed by law. However, the Constitution has provided for the citizen an independent judiciary which will establish the rule of law.

The Supreme Court, which has been given the power of judicial review, is the guardian of the Constitution. "In order to be effective in its capacity as guardian and for the establishment of rule of law, independence of the judiciary is imperative. The independence of the judiciary as affirmed and declared by Articles 94(4) and 116A, is one of the basic pillars of the Constitution and cannot be demolished, whittled down, curtailed or diminished in any manner whatsoever, except under the existing provision of the Constitution."4

Judges must act true to their oath of office, which they swear or affirm on taking office. It is a solemn oath and an arduous burden, which has to be borne in spite of the various vulnerabilities of the judges. Judges do not have a voice to air their grievances or to protest any vengeful attacks, verbal or otherwise. They do express their views in their judgements; they are mandated by the Constitution to say what is or is not the law. Consequently, what the Supreme Court declares in its judgement is law, until a judgement is reversed or altered by it.

The Constitution also gives the Supreme Court the power to declare what are laws within the territory of Bangladesh. Article 111 provides that the "law" declared by the Appellate Division shall be binding on the High Court Division and the law declared by either Division of the Supreme Court shall be binding on all courts subordinate to it. However, personal attacks on individual judges or imputation of improper motives to judges acting during their duty are not tolerated anywhere in the world. Scurrilous remarks about judges and scandalizing of the court are everywhere dealt with under the law of contempt of court. Fair criticism of judgments and decisions based upon objective critical analyses of the law and other decisions from home and abroad cannot be subject of contempt of court proceedings. However, criticism of the integrity of individual judges' cuts at the root of the justice delivery system, especially if the allegations are unfounded.

Insinuations and comments derogatory to the dignity of the court which are calculated to undermine the confidence of the people in the integrity of the judges constitute contempt. For the protection of organized society and maintenance of the rule of law, there is necessity of an independent and fearless judiciary in which the public will have full confidence as the dispenser of justice. Making objectionable remarks against judges may constitute contempt of court but criticism of a judgment, that is, the decision itself, cannot constitute contempt of court. Criticism of a judge in his individual capacity, per se, does not constitute contempt of court, unless such criticism goes to the root of the judiciary as an institution. It would certainly be contempt of court if the language used brings the court into disrespect or impinges upon its dignity and majesty and challenges the efficiency or competence of the judge to dispense justice. It would be contempt of court if the comments published tend to interfere with the administration of justice, especially if the comments relate to a matter which is sub-judice. About the power of the court to punish for contempt of court, Mahmudul Islam suggests that, this power has been granted not for the protection of the individual judges from imputations, but for the protection of the public themselves from the mischief they will incur if the authority of the Supreme Court is impaired.5 Scandalizing the court is not necessarily intended to attack any particular judge, but it entails publication which, although it does not relate to any specific judge, is a scurrilous attack on the judiciary as a whole, which is calculated to undermine the authority of the courts and public confidence in the administration of justice.

The Supreme Court is one of the pillars of the State machinery and is afforded dignity and respect by everyone, even the high and mighty; and rightly so. Daily thousands of litigants throng the courts in search of justice. They believe in and respect the justice delivery system. Without such reverence the judgments delivered would be ineffective and the rule of law would be rendered nugatory. Citizens of the country look to the judiciary for adjudication of their legal disputes with their neighbors as well as for enforcement of their rights enshrined in the Constitution and other laws of the land. However, if the judiciary is to perform its duties and functions effectively, to live up to the expectations of the citizens of the country and remain true to the spirit with which they are sacredly entrusted, the dignity and authority of the courts must be respected and protected by all and at all costs. The judges are the final arbiter between litigants and the public, and powerful authorities and organizations. The public always has and always will repose their faith in the justice delivery system so long as the independence and integrity of the judges is seen to be intact. For the judiciary to command the respect of the people, it is necessary that it is not undermined in any way.

Criticisms of conducts of judges, which cannot possibly have the tendency to obstruct or interfere with the administration of justice, are not contempt of courts, even though they may be libelous attacks on judges. Thus, an attack on a judge for conduct not connected with his judicial functions will not come within the mischief of contempt of court. Such an attack would inevitably also be calculated to lower the authority of the courts over which the judges so maligned happen to be presiding and thus tend to interfere with the due course of justice and the proper administration thereof.

Whether or not apology of contemnors is accepted, and if so, what sanction if any is to be imposed depends on the facts and circumstances of each case. Apologies are mere empty words if the contemnors in fact justify their action in some way. During deliberations on March 20 the court observed that usually if an apology is offered then it is normally in one or two sentences. When the contemnors say sorry and then proceed to justify why they said what they had said, then the apology is a mere device to get a lesser punishment or no punishment at all. This court has a duty to protect itself and the judicial institution from any person who will utter damaging remarks and then proffer empty apologies when taken to task for their admitted acts of destruction and desecration of the sanctity of the judiciary, which is otherwise held in high esteem by the public.

Scandalizing includes an attack upon any judge in his public capacity for such attack would be calculated to malign the judge and to lower the authority of the court over which the judge performs his judicial function. At the same time, it also amounts to interference with course of justice and the proper administration thereof. Criticism of judges of the highest court in respect of acts done in their administrative capacity, which contain improper imputation, amounts to contempt. If the Chief Justice is criticized for acts done in his administrative capacity this also amounts to contempt. The criticism should be fair and not made with oblique motives or with the object of maligning the justice delivery system and lowering the majesty of the law and dignity of the court in the estimation of the public.

In view of our constitutional scheme, non-compliance with the Supreme Court's order would not only dislodge the cornerstone maintaining the equilibrium and equanimity in the State's governance, there would be a breakdown of constitutional functioning of the State. For the judiciary to perform its duties, to function effectively and be true to the spirit with which it is sacredly entrusted, the dignity and authority of the courts must be respected and protected at all costs. The only weapon of protecting itself from an onslaught on the institution is the long hand of contempt of court left in the armory of judicial repository which, when needed, can reach any neck howsoever high or far away it may be. The maintenance of the dignity of courts is one of the pertinent principles of rules of law in a democratic set-up and any criticism of the judicial institution couched in the language that apparently appears to be mere criticism but ultimately results in undermining the dignity of the court cannot be permitted when found to have crossed the limit. The contempt jurisdiction is not exercised to protect the dignity of an individual judge but to protect the administration of justice from being maligned. Interference with the administration of justice, which may have the tendency to pervert the course of justice, has been termed as a serious type of contempt.6 Ibid

The contemnors on March 15, 2016 filed an affidavit seeking an adjournment due to Advocate Quamrul Islam's previously fixed official duties abroad to attend the FAO Regional Conference. In the same affidavit he expressed his unconditional apology and deep regret and remorse for the statements and comments made by him. In respect of the other two affidavits filed, each of them contained the contents of his affidavit in Bangla sworn before a Notary Public. In both the affidavits placed before the court the contemnors tendered unconditional apology in acknowledgement of their inadvertent failure to remain vigilant against making any statement regarding a matter pending for judgement before the court. In one affidavit one prayed for exoneration from the proceedings and, in the other, he prayed for dispensing with his personal appearance. While hearing on March 20, 2016, the contemnors each placed before the court their affidavits admitting their guilt and praying for acceptance of their unconditional apology. During deliberations, Rafiq-ul-Huq, appearing for one contemnor, was asked to place the oath of allegiance which was sworn by the ministers when taking oath of office. The Chief Justice posed the question as to what the outcome should be if the ministers breach their oath of office to protect the Constitution. He also pointed out that the admission of guilt by any member of the public is not the same as that of the contemnors who had taken oath under the Constitution.

While the hearing on March 27, 2016, two further affidavits were placed on behalf of the contemnors before the court. One contemnor expressed regret and remorse for his utterances and placed himself at the mercy of the court and prayed for acceptance of his apology and for exoneration from civil and criminal liability. The other in his affidavit also begged unconditional and unequivocal apology for his utterances and prayed to exempt him from the contempt proceeding. The Attorney General placed the statements of the two contemnors as published in the Daily Janakantha on March 7, 2016. Janakantha reported, in the meeting held on March 5, one contemnor also demanded that the Chief

Justice should step aside from the appeal hearing. The contemnors neither denied having made the statements as reported in the newspaper, which were placed before the court, nor clarified the contents of the reports which were read out in court.

During hearing any matter the judges often pose questions and ask questions in open court in order that the parties get an opportunity to clarify any fact or issue or to elucidate their contentions and submissions. These comments/queries from the Bench do not usually form part of the judgment. Keeping in mind that the matter is sub-judice before pronouncement of the judgment, it is not proper that anyone should comment on or criticize such verbal exchanges inside the courtroom. There is no wrong in critiquing a judgement once it is finally published. However, it must be borne in mind that deliberations during any hearing may not be subjected to analysis or criticism since such comments in a sub-judice matter might be prejudicial and taint the mind of the public before the judgment is pronounced. An analysis of the statements made by the contemnors showed that they did not wish the Chief Justice to continue the Bench hearing the criminal appeal of Mir Kashem Ali.

This clearly shows the intention of the contemnors to bully the Supreme Court into delivering the judgement according to their demand upholding the death penalty of Mir Kashem Ali. Their justification for the utterances was that they were Muktijoddas (freedom fighters) and were swayed by their emotions and sentiments. However, sitting Cabinet ministers should stop to think and realize the consequences of their utterances. Their justifications have watered down the quality of their apologies, which cannot be anything other than a perfunctory, face-saving exercise motivated to get a lesser punishment.

The contemnors had clearly shown their wish to remove the Chief Justice from the Bench hearing the appeal in question. Their further utterance that they must have their expected judgment shows their sheer indifference to the authority of the Supreme Court to act independently. It also shows their total disregard for the rule of law. The Constitution gives the Supreme Court authority to deliver judgments in accordance with the law, but they wished to dictate what decision should be announced by the Supreme Court for it to be acceptable to them. The said utterances show an intention to divert the course of justice in a way, come what may, which is contrary to the mandate of the Constitution which requires that every citizen should enjoy the protection of the law and be treated in accordance with law. The comments demand that the Supreme Court should decide the appeal other than in accordance with the law, and this is violative of the Constitution. They neglected their sworn duty to protect the rule of law enshrined in the Constitution. They have intentionally made the utterances and have indeed expressly admitted their guilt. They have acted in violation of the law and are in breach of their oath of office to preserve, protect and defend the Constitution. In their exuberance, they have undermined the sanctity of the institution of the judiciary by questioning the justice delivery system. The Constitution enjoins all citizens to abide by the law and makes the decisions of the Supreme Court law to be given effect to by all. They have scandalized the Supreme Court in a highly motivated manner to influence the judgment of the Court. This is gross criminal contempt and a violation of the provisions of the Constitution. The contemnors deserved no sympathy other than the lenient view taken in awarding sentence which has already been expressed. It is a criminal contempt and the ministers were convicted for criminal offence, but the Prime Minister kept them in the Cabinet. That is totally unethical.

References:

1. The State v. Swadesh Roy, 12 ADC 932
2. The State v. Advocate Quamrul Islam, MP, Minister, (Ministry of Food), and another contempt petition No. 09 of 2016
3. Bangladesh v. Idrisur Rahman, 15 BLC (AD) 49
4. Secretary, Ministry of Finance v. Md. Masder Hossain, 52 DLR (AD) 82
5. Constitutional Law of Bangladesh. Third Edition
6. Ibid

Miscellaneous Matters (Z)

I have referred to only a few decisions and left other important decisions on acquisition of property overruling the previous decisions, both in criminal and civil matters, and I cannot say anything due to lack of reference materials available to me, despite my efforts to procure the other judgments from abroad. The website of the Supreme Court is the source of collecting materials and, but suddenly it has been kept beyond the reach of the people. I really fear that if the Supreme Court is squeezed daily in this manner one day we will find it a gorgeous building minus its glory and historical pronouncements. However, from memory I could recollect some cases.

1. A matter which is very important is the construction of the Bangladesh Garments Exporters and Manufacturers Association (BGMEA) office. This building was constructed without any documentary title and without any plan being approved from the RAJUK on a portion of Begunbari Khal and Hatirjheel Lake, two natural waterbodies situated in their present location since time immemorial. These two waterbodies are connected with the Buriganga River through a canal, which plays a pivotal role in keeping the capital safe from water-logging and flood during the rainy season. The government took up a massive project in order to save, restore and preserve the remnants of those two khals, known as the "Hatirjheel-Begunbari-Project" with the sole object of beautification of the same, providing water-based amusement facilities and the construction of circular roads all around the said lakes, so that the city dwellers get a breathing space and it can be saved from the encroachers. The BGMEA constructed a 15-sorey building defying all laws of the land and thereby eclipsing the waterbody. Under such circumstances, the High Court Division issued a suo moto rule and ultimately the rule was made absolute.

2. The BGMEA then came before the apex court.1 we held that the nature of the land is a natural waterbody and, therefore, the BGMEA constructed a building which has been classified as waterbody and hence the construction was contrary to "Joladhar Ain 2000" (The Waterbody Act 2000). The object of the Ain was the proper drainage of flood and rain water in Dhaka City and therefore a conversion of the said land is prohibited by law. The said construction is also in violation of the Environment Conservation Act, 1995. The BGMEA obtained a document, but the transferor had no right, title or interest, since, the land was recorded in the name of the government. The transferor, Export Promotion Bureau, has no saleable interest in that property. Moreover, the construction was made before the deed was executed in favor of the BGMEA. Since the Export Promotion Bureau did not acquire title before December 2006, the correspondences made with the Export Promotion Bureau and the unregistered agreement executed with it did not confer any right title upon the BGMEA. Therefore, the BGMEA constructed the building illegally, by using its power of money, in violation of the law and accordingly we directed RAJUK to demolish the building within 90 days from the delivery of the judgment.

3. Hazaribagh within Dhaka City is the home of tannery factories of Bangladesh. Almost 95 percent of tanneries are located there. The factories used to tan hides and skins of animals, but none of those had any water treatment plants. So, the polluted wastage of the tanneries was released directly to the adjacent Buriganga River. Decades ago the government had allocated a separate industrial area for the relocation of the tannery industry. But the trade body of the tanneries, the Tannery Association, was delaying their move to the newly earmarked area on various pleas. Considering the devastating and suicidal impact of tannery waste on the environment, the apex court issued direction to shift those tanneries, 154 in number, with a further direction that if they are not shifted they would have to pay

pecuniary compensation to the government exchequer. That also yielded no result and accordingly we directed the authorities to disconnect the electricity and gas lines that compelled them to shift the tanneries in mid-June 2017.

4. Cabinet Minister for Public Works Engineer Mosharraf Hossain was involved in a criminal case filed by the Durinity Daman Commission (Anti-Corruption Commission). When the case was under investigation at the initial stage, he moved the High Court Division with a quashing petition. Ultimately, he got a favorable judgment from the High Court Division. The matter came up before the apex Court at the instance of Durniti Daman Commission. My primary duty was to settle the law points so that multiplication of cases can be avoided. There is another difficulty: If we maintained the judgment of the High Court Division, all offenders of criminal cases would rush for protection claiming quashing proceedings referring to our court and, in that case, it would be difficult for the investigating agency to collect evidence after a lapse of time. Though the Indian jurisdiction interferes with cases at the initial stage, we are strict in this respect. We do not want to hamper the course of justice at the initial stage on consideration of the social conditions and the appointment of judges being made in the higher judiciary without looking into the quality but of on political consideration.

5. We held that when a case is under investigation, the court has no power to take cognizance of the offence and therefore no legal case is pending in the eyes of the law. If in the investigation process by the law enforcement agencies the court interfered with the matter, there would be adverse impacts, firstly, all the accused after committing crimes would rush to the High Court Division and the net result would be after taking the stay order, they would be emboldened to commit similar crimes. The law enforcement agencies would remain a silent spectator in those cases. Secondly, if this process is allowed the number of cases would pile up in the court and, in such an event,

374

the ends of justice would be defeated. Considering the above adverse impacts, we held that High Court Division has no power to exercise jurisdiction in a pending investigation matter. Therefore, the High Court Division's power to exercise jurisdiction is ousted. We set aside the judgment of the High Court Division and directed the Durniniti Daman Commission to continue with the investigation. Naturally the minister was not happy with me.

6. Another important case which I can recollect is that of a student of Mymensingh Girls Cadet College, whose name was Sharmila Shaharin Pollen. She was 18 years old, and in the twelfth grade of the college. She was found dead in the bathroom of her dormitory on February 11, 2005. Records revealed that she was a very beautiful and attractive girl and one of the teachers of the college, who was an army officer, was trying to develop an affair with her. Pollen's father had two daughters and both the daughters were very intelligent. Pollen did achieve excellent results in the Secondary School Certificate Examination. Pollen's father was contemplating to send his younger daughter to the same cadet college. Pollen prevented her parents from sending her younger sister to the college and indirectly indicated the problems she was facing with the army officer lest her younger sister also faced the same fate. On the day of occurrence, Pollen was said to have been with her classmates, but suddenly at around 10:00 AM she disappeared. Her dead body was recovered from the toilet. The dead body was immediately sent to the Mymensingh Medical College Hospital. But when it was found that she was already dead, the authority arranged the autopsy of the victim hurriedly without informing her parents about her death. Somehow her parents on getting the news rushed to the Mymensingh Medical College Hospital when they noticed that the dead body was already kept in an ambulance for sending to her parents' home for burial. Her father was compelled to receive the dead body. The father noticed some marks of violence on the body of the victim

375

and he suspected that the death was not suicidal but homicidal, although the autopsy report procured was one of suicide. The victim's father Abul Bashar Patwary, a retired Air Force Officer from Chandpur, after procuring all information's and the letters written by the victim to her mother made a complaint alleging that her daughter was tortured and strangled to death and then her body was hanged inside the bathroom to pass it off as a suicide. In the complaint he implicated then Adjutant Major Nazmul Haque, then also an Associate Professor of Mymensingh Medical College, who conducted the autopsy, then Sergeant Nowsher-Uz-Zaman, then security guard, and then Deputy Adjutant General Major Munir Ahmed Chowdhury. There was a judicial inquiry. The proceeding was interrupted from time to time and took three to four years to conclude the inquiry. The inquiry officer recommended taking cognizance of the offence against the accused and the magistrate took cognizance of the offence against those accused. They then moved the High Court Division with a quashing petition. The High Court Division discharged the rule on April 06. The army officers filed a leave petition against the judgment of the High Court Division.

7. Just a few days before the hearing of the matter, Major General Shafiul Abedin, the DGFI chief, sought a courtesy visit to me. I allowed him, and we had discussions on informal issues but at one point of time he requested me for a favor in respect of the accused in the Pollen murder case saying that the officer had been promoted to the rank possibly of a Colonel. But as a case is pending against him, his promotion to the next higher post could not be considered. He told me that the officer is a brilliant one and he was falsely implicated in the case for which he has been facing with lot of complications in his career. Normally this type of requests comes to the Chief Justice all the time. I did not pay any heed to them. I only told him that I would investigate the matter as normally I did in such issues. When the matter was taken up for hearing, I noticed that

the victim's father had been moving heaven and earth for the past seven years to get justice from the court of law. But justice was a far cry for him. He could not put the accused in the dock. As a consolation ultimately, the offenders were brought to justice. I also noticed that he had spent a lot of money to gather reports to prove the allegations against the accused and never lost hope of getting justice. After the hearing was over, I wanted opinion of my brother judges. They unanimously told me that the petition should be dismissed, and the accused be put on trial. With a view to test the mindset of my brothers, I told them that there was a request from the hierarchy of the DGFI to do a favor for the accused. Their reply was that the officer seemed so powerful that he could reach the Chief Justice, so naturally he must have reached the magistrate and the High Court Division. But they ignored his requests. I was very happy on hearing their views and without any hesitation, I dismissed the petition. I heard later that the court indicted five accused in March last year 2016. Major Munir was said to have absconded. I hoped that my judicial officers who would hold the trial of the case shall maintain the dignity, impartiality and the glory of justice and would do the right thing in the case even if there was pressure from the hierarchy of the army keeping in mind that their predecessors were also asked for a favor, but they never bowed to the requests. There lies the beauty of the judiciary.

8. Major General Shafiul Abedin again came to meet me for some other purpose, which I will discuss later on. When I drew his attention to the Pollen murder case saying that I could not do anything in favor of the accused officer despite knowing that he was a high-ranking officer in the DGFI, but the law points were against him. I was unprepared to hear the reply from Major General Shafiul Abedin. Firstly, he lied saying that "Oh Sir! I am not interested about that case, only because of the request the Army Chief, since he had requested me, and he was interested about the case." In the other breath he told me,

"Sir, it would be easier for them to get the officer acquitted from the trial court." I was stunned on hearing him declare that when he was talking to the Chief Justice about a murder case. How this officer undermined the judiciary astounded me very much. These officers feel that they are the most powerful department of the State and their wishes will be reflected in every officer of the state. Dr. Mohiuddin Khan Alamgir and his two sons were convicted and sentenced by the Special Judge in absentia for possession of wealth beyond their known sources of income. They did not appear before the court at any point of time, but Dr. Alamgir somehow was acquitted of the charge on technical ground. One of his sons drowned to death and the other is a resident in the US. He did not challenge his conviction. On his behalf, Dr. Mohiuddin Khan Alamgir moved a writ petition in the High Court Division where the Bench was presided over by AHM Shamsuddin Chowdhury. The High Court Division quashed the conviction without following the minimum norms. Under the Durniti Daman Ain, there is provision of appeal against a conviction made by a Special Judge and in presence of alternative remedy, a judicial review is not maintainable. Secondly, if the convict does not surrender to the jurisdiction of the court of law, he cannot seek redress for his grievance in a court of law. Thirdly, a judicial review is not available at the instance of a third party against a conviction, because if such petitions are entertained, all convicts after leaving the court will resort to avoid the conviction by filing a writ petitions through their near ones. In that case the administration of justice will be denied.

9. The matter was taken before the apex court at the instance of the Durniti Daman Commission. A group of senior counsel appeared to oppose the leave petition. The council did not take the trouble of convincing the court; instead just after pointing out the facts he sat down. When a senior counsel appeared, I wanted to know from him under which principle or jurisprudential view, we would not interfere

with the judgment. If he could show anything from any jurisdiction, I would certainly give a verdict which would be historical one, but he must help us to write a judgment in favor of the accused. The counsel got the message and left the matter at the mercy of the humanitarian aspect that Dr. Mohiuddin Khan Alamgir had lost a son and the other is a citizen of the US. I told him that the law is so harsh that it does not look at the face of anyone, it looks straight, and speaks in the same language. He got the opinion of the court and resumed his seat.

10. In 2016 the administration arranged a program at the Osmani Auditorium for awarding certificates to the officers at the field level who had performed extraordinarily with a view to encouraging them. The Prime Minister was the chief guest and I was invited by the Janaproshashon Secretary. Accordingly, I attended the program. After the ceremony was over, the Prime Minister was approaching the refreshment room and I was in front of the room. She told me with a tinge of disappointment that Dr. Mohiuddin Khan Alamgir had made a lot of contribution toward the Awami League and had suffered a lot for his support. I understood why she was making such a comment. I told her that the law does not allow entertaining such manner of petition. If I allowed such petitions, all convicts including Begum Khaleda Zia would want to avail that opportunity on behalf of her son Tareque Rahman and, in that case, the ends of justice would be defeated. In this connection I cited her some examples. She understood the issues and agreed with my views.

11. Basundhara Group of Companies is one of the biggest business conglomerates in Bangladesh and, hence, one of the most powerful business houses. It has influence on the government, bureaucracy, police administration and the military. I did not hesitate to set aside the judgment of acquittal passed by the High Court Division of its Chairman Ahmed Akbar Sobhan alias Shah Alam and five

other family members and directed them to surrender to the lower court in connection with a tax evasion case.2 I also set aside the judgment of acquittal of Mofazzal Hossain Chowdhury Maya, Relief and Disaster Management Minister, who has been convicted and sentenced to 13 years with a fine of five crore taka on June 14, 2015.3 I also set aside the order of acquittal passed in favor of ex-lawmaker of the Awami League, Joynal Hazari, who has been sentenced to 10 years imprisonment by order dated August 31, 2015.4 I stayed the judgment of the High Court Division of Ashian City's Housing Project on August 22, 2016.5 I intervened in the judgments of all sensational cases of powerful persons whenever I found illegalities and, even then, a section of government sponsored media and activists started castigating me as corrupt after the verdict of the Sixteenth Amendment.

Reference:

1. BGMEA v. Government, Civil Appeal No. 1162 of 2013
2. Daily Star, March 08, 2015
3. Daily Star, June 15, 2015
4. Daily Star, September I, 2015
5. Daily Star, www.dailystar.net

Chapter 16

Legal Profession

Lawyers are valued as conscience keepers of the society. Lawyers hold a position of privilege within the society. They are expected to have knowledge about law, etiquette, norms, etc. and therefore they have power and respect from all sections of society. Their status is comparable with no other profession or service. The most significant thing is they are professionals, but their professionalism is different from other professions, like doctors, professors, teachers, dentists, architects, engineers, accountants, senior army officers, senior police officers though they are also typically included in the list of professionals. The notion of a profession involves a complex social, political and economic process.1 Professionals work for the benefit of the public, rather than for themselves.2 a common mark of true professionals is that they will work longer than their fixed hours and go to great lengths to perform their duties for their clients and to the public. If a client needs a professional's help outside the standard work hours, that professional will be obliged to help in a way that others would not. Normally lawyers do regularly work long hours to ensure that the needs of clients are met. I can remember one instance when I studied the whole night to prepare a brief of a murder case and argued the case the entire court hours the following day in the Sylhet High Court Bench in a murder case. Some police personnel were involved in it and got an order of acquittal on the question of misjoinder of charges. It is a reported case (Constable Lal Mia V. state).However the Appellate Division reversed the judgment. I did not feel any weakness or drowsiness because I concentrated my mind only on one point and, that is, I would devote Ali my endeavors to convince the court the principle of law I wanted to establish. It is devotion of a lawyer to achieve the science of law with a view to convince the court; money is sometimes immaterial to such lawyers. It is somewhat ironic that lawyers, who are often portrayed as working to enrich themselves, rely on their dedication to the public good as the ground of being a professional.3 Professionalism, critics say, is a mystique used to justify a privileged position and monopoly on a market. There are three models of professionalism, such as4:

I. Professionalism as helping the market. Professionalism enables clients to be informed about the services on offer and ensures that there is a reasonable quality of service that is reasonably paid.

II. Professionalism as promoting a public utility. This model sees professional services as being a matter of public good and argues that we need professional regulation to ensure the efficiency and quality of these services.

III. Professionalism as protection. This model recognizes the dangers that exist in a relationship between a lawyer and a client. Professionalism provides a means of ensuring that there is intervention to protect clients.

People go to lawyers for various reasons, i.e. someone who will stand up for them and argue their case and make sure that they protect the clients' rights; clients seek someone who will make sure that he is not being taken advantage of and will fight in the clients' corner. Whether the client wants the services of the lawyer to draft a plaint, complaint or a deed for ensuring someone is focused on his interests and who will have his back. A lawyer is not meant to be neutral, ensuring there is a fair outcome; rather, he is meant to represent the client's case and ensure that the client gets the best outcome possible. A lawyer is not meant to use cases to pursue his own agenda, but to enable the client to do what he wants. A client always wants a lawyer who must keep his information confidential. A client seeks legal advice about intimate issues or issues of great financial interests. The client has a right of privacy and this right is a fundamental human right. The information given to a lawyer is property or any critical matter, received by a lawyer as a fiduciary, and the fiduciary must account for gains made using the information.5

Nowadays these ethical values are declining. Some lawyers are more interested in their personal financial interest than those of their clients'. They often fail to give priority to client's interest, with exceptions. Money counts as the paramount consideration. I rarely found lawyers who had come to argue cases after proper preparation. I hardly found a leave petition which did not require filing of additional grounds, if the court wanted to grant leave. Some senior lawyers after accepting senior briefs realized that none of the grounds taken was relevant for disposal of the matter and filed additional grounds before taking up the matter. I found very intelligent junior lawyers who were called to the Bar, but they have little patience to learn from their seniors. After 6/7 months they opened independent law firms and began soliciting consultancy from different companies. Normally, it is perceived by many business houses that a law firm run by barristers would serve their purpose and engaged them as consultants. I found many good cases which the litigants lost due to ill advice, lack of proper pleadings or drafting. Pleadings are the foundation of litigation and many bad cases are won by good drafting. Young lawyers have no alternative but to learn the art of drafting. They must have sufficient knowledge on fact, law, evidence and the application of law. They have to bear in mind to be able to tackle the mass of irrelevant or false or baseless averments, and other legal contentions. They must be equipped with the understanding of some fundamentals---the distinction between: fact; law; and application of law.

"Fact" has a variety of meanings. It may signify a state of things, i.e. an existence or a motion; an event or incident or occurrence; an act, action or deed; thing or deed; an effect produced or achieved; a reality as distinguished from supposition or opinion; a truth as distinguished from fiction. Facts can be both physical and psychological. All rights and liabilities are dependent upon and arise out of facts. If pleadings do not give enough details, they will not raise an issue, and the court may reject the claims or pass a decree on admission. Lawyers should give enough effort required in relation to the application of law to the facts as admitted by the parties or, if there is dispute, to the facts as found by the court upon evidence as part of its process of fact finding.

It is said in the US that the legal profession's aristocratic character began to fade after state lawmakers started relaxing the requirements necessary to be admitted to the Bar during the early 1800s. By the second half of the nineteenth century, however, these relaxed requirements led to a kind of class struggle between the old-time aristocratic lawyers and the less refined corps of men, many of them immigrants, who began earning a living as attorneys. Justice Brewer complained in 1895 that a growing multitude is crowding in who are not fit to be lawyers, who disgrace the profession after they are in it, and who in a scramble after livelihood are debasing the noblest of professions into the meanest of avocations. The American Bar Association was founded in 1878 largely as an effort by the "best men" of the Bar to restart control over their profession, in part by raising the standards of legal education and other requirements necessary to become an attorney.6

To legal elites who believed that the proper development of the law takes centuries, legislatures--with their power to cast aside longstanding principles of common law and replace them with an entirely novel legal regime--were downright terrifying. One early president of the American Bar proclaimed that the United States could endure all its other dangers with less apprehension than the action of its federal and state legislation inspires. American Bar speakers labeled elected lawmakers as "reckless politicians" "who truckled for the unthinking vote"; "social agitators" who sought office for "self-advantage, not for the public weal"; and "professional demagogues" "who filled the land with ill-considered and impractical theories" and engaged in "gross, persistent, flagrant and sometimes corrupt dereliction."7

We saw from the above how the founding fathers of America built the nation giving top priority to the maintenance of rule of law and respect for the law; gave the citizens full power to select legislatures. But we as a nation want to stifle the judiciary all the time, instead of improving the process of legislating law neglect it by selecting legislatures the impact of which affect lawyers' standard. In this regard I would reproduce an admission of a world-famous leader who after being called to the Bar and starting to practice as a lawyer said, "It was easy to be called but it was difficult to practice at the bar. I had read the laws, but not learnt how to practice law...Besides, I had learnt nothing at all Indian law. I had not the slightest idea of Hindu and Mahommedan Law. I had not even learnt how to draft a plaint and felt completely at sea."8 Finding no alternative, Gandhi met Frederic Pincutt as per recommendation of one of his friends. Gandhi said, "I can never forget that interview. He greeted me as a friend. He laughed away my pessimism. 'Do you think, he said, 'that everyone must be a Pherozeshah Mehta? 9 Pherozeshahs and Badruddins are rare. Rest assured it takes no unusual skill to be an ordinary lawyer. Common honesty and industry are enough to enable him to make a living. All cases are not complicated. Well, let me know the extent of your general reading.' When 'I (Gandhi) acquainted him with my little stock of reading, he was, as I could see, rather disappointed. But it was only for a moment. Soon his face beamed with a pleasing smile' and he said, 'I understand your trouble. Your general reading is meagre. You have no knowledge of the world, a sine qua non for a vakil. You have not even read the history of India. A vakil should know human nature. He could be able to read a man's character from his face and every Indian ought to know Indian history. This has no connection with the practice of law, but you ought to have that knowledge.'" (Ibid)

The commercialization of the legal profession is the main root for the dearth of good professional lawyers. It was ever so commercialized as it is today. One former US Deputy Attorney General as back as about eighty years ago warned that in the US the "legal process, because of unbridled growth, has become a cancer which threatens the vitality of our forms of capitalism and democracy." He added, "In the USA 30 billion dollar is spent annually on lawyers which comes to 1.5 percent of its gross national products." In India, because of a complicated system, so also in Bangladesh, the percentage spent on lawyers may also be about 1.5 percent of our gross national product. There are three grave shortcomings of the present system in administering justice. Firstly, the commercialization of the legal process. Nani A. Palkiwala, one of the prominent lawyers and authors said, "I do not think the legal profession was ever so commercialized. When I

385

started my practice in 1946 in the original site of the Bombay High Court, if a counsel made a factual statement to the judge, it was implicitly believed to be true. You seldom heard of an affidavit filed on behalf of the government or any public authority, which did not contain the whole truth, but now all that had totally changed. Counsel often makes statements at the Bar which are factually incorrect, and affidavits are often filed, even on behalf of public authorities, which do not state the truth. Look at what was going on before the Lentin Commission, how witness after witness perjured himself. Yet there was no sign of public disgust and outrage. Unfortunately, we accept perjury as a fact of Indian life. The worst danger is not that even persons in high public office perjured themselves. The worst danger lies in public acceptance of national character. As a man who loves India not wisely but too well I asked the question – why can we not have standards as high as those of the mature democracies in the world? After all, our ancient culture is the noblest ever known."

He emphasized the shortcomings of the Indian system was that all the time the citizenry, 'their rights, they do not lay a corresponding stress on their responsibilities toward their fundamental duties which has become a dead letter. The greatest drawback of our administration of justice is delay in disposal of cases. We, as a nation, have some fine qualities, but the value of time is not one of them. There are historical reasons for our relaxed attitude to time. Ancient India had evolved the concepts of eternity and infinity. So, what do thirty years wasted in litigation matter against the backdrop of eternity! During my judgeship in the High Court Division I found litigation which had originated before my birth in 1940. I (Palkiwala) do not know what the fate of that case after my judgment was. Lawyers are entitled to earn their living, but not at such an unbearable cost to society. We must educate our lawyers better. We produce "ethical illiterates" in our law colleges and universities, who have no notion of what the public good is. The number of lawyers today in our country is about fifty thousand. By contrast, the number of practicing lawyers in Japan is about fifteen thousand. About forty thousand students appear in law examinations in Japan and only about six hundred succeed; less than two percent. So difficult is the examination they must go through. No wonder then that in Japan very few cases are filed, and disputes are mostly settled out of court. In the United States also most litigation is settled out of court and if any party refuses to settle the case and ultimately loses he is burdened with the heavy cost of the expenses of the lawyers and court time. We must therefore improve the quality of public administration which is at all time low today.

Judge Learned Hand, a renowned American judge said, "As a litigant, I should address a law suit beyond almost anything else, sort of sickness and death." Justice Douglas, another renowned judge, said that forty percent of American lawyers were incompetent. Justice Earl Warren, the former Chief Justice of the US said that fifty percent of American lawyers were incompetent disagreeing with Justice Douglas's estimate of forty percent. He believed that America was approaching a disaster area, not just a problem, he stressed that the American judicial system "May literally breakdown before end of this century." He told the American Bar Association, "The harsh truth is that we may be on our way to a society overrun by hordes of lawyers, hungry as locusts, and brigades of judges in numbers never before contemplated. The notion that ordinary people want black-robe judges, well dressed lawyers and fine paneled courtrooms as the setting to resolve their disputes, is not correct. People with legal problems, like people with pain, want relief and they want it as quickly and inexpensively as possible."

Compared to those three countries---India, Japan and USA---our condition is the less to speak, the better. When I entered the Bar there was a tradition of keeping 4 or 5 juniors by the senior advocates, sometimes more in their chambers. Seniors used to give dictation on pleadings, petitions, taught those ethics, professional conduct, etc. The juniors respected them like parents. This tradition has since been abolished. Now if a new law graduate wants to enter a senior's chamber, he will keep him provided he can bring briefs for the senior. The tradition of learning and teaching is foreign these days. The drafting of pleadings is easy now due to computers. Lawyers hardly give attention to drafting pleadings. Even lawyers couldn't draw up a bail petition properly. The responsibility is entrusted either to a junior or to a clerk who preserve proformas of some plaints, writ petitions, written statements and so on.

In our country there was a complex tussle between barrister lawyer judges and advocate lawyer judges. It continued from the Calcutta High Court, the original High Court. In the Calcutta High Court there were two Bars, one meant for the barristers and the other meant for locally educated lawyers. In Bangladesh, the tradition was maintained in a separate way. The barrister lawyers and judges used to arrange a dinner every year at the then Sheraton Hotel later renamed Hotel Ruposhi Bangla. Even the Chief Justice if he was a non-barrister was not invited to that dinner. Possibly this traditional dinner is not followed now on a regular basis. But I noticed that even though barrister advocates were affiliated with differing political ideologies, they used to maintain close contacts with each other and this was reflected even in the Bar elections. Normally, the barristers cast their votes in favor of another barrister if contest from other panel of different political ideology. This is known to all, but none discloses this difference openly. I used to enjoy the movement of the barristers and the lawyers in court even in contested matters. I also noticed that barristers appeared in court in favor of another barrister of a different political ideology if he faced litigation in court.

My senior S.R Pal told me that among the barristers practicing during the relevant time only Ashrarul Hossain and Rafiqul Haque were appearing in typical civil matters and had good conception in civil laws because during the British period the lawyers maintained the tradition of the Bar and were trained under renowned civil practitioners. The best civil lawyers I have seen were S.R Pal, Hamidul Haque Chowdhury, T.H. Khan, and M.H. Khandaker. Khandkar Mahbubuddin Ahmed, B.N. Chowdhury, M. Nurullah, Moinul Haque, Mahmudul Islam, Ahmad Sobhan and they appeared mostly in first appeals, which were treated as very complicated matters. Sirajul Haque, Zulmat Ali Khan, Aminul Haque, Abdul Malek were the best criminal lawyers. Barrister Rafiqul Huq worked with Barrister Ashrarul Hossain while Barrister Ishtiaque Ahmed and Barrister Rokonuddin Mahmud were very intelligent, had good command in language and conception in law which made them good lawyers. After Mahdudul Islam joined their chamber, they became good civil lawyers as well. But except for Barrister Ashrarul Hossain, others usually appeared in writ and company matters and conducted efficiently. Barrister Ashrarul Hossain, according to S.R Pal, grapsed civil law meticulously because he attended his articleship in a chamber of a civil lawyer in Calcutta and was trained in civil law in Calcutta High Court. Barrister Rokonuddin Mahmud was basically using one chamber with Barrister Syed Ishtiaque and Mahmudul Islam. He is basically a gifted lawyer and grasped civil law due to his knowledge and having constant touch with Syed Ishtiaque Ahmed and Mahmudul Islam. He is very sharp in his conception and has good command in English. But as a matter of fact, he appeared in very few pure civil cases. His plus point is that he is very meticulous on facts and law. Whenever he appeared in civil matters he had thoroughly prepared the brief. Similar is the case of Barrister Rafiqul Huq and Azmalur Hossain.Ther are hardworking lawyers and thorough in facts and law. They worked with Barrister Ashrarul Hossain and therefore they have deep conception in civil laws.

Even I have seen in S.R Pal that he was not in favor of filing leave petitions if he did not find merit in the case. But if due to the persistent pressure of the clients he accepts a brief, he frankly conceded that the case was covered by earlier views taken by the court and he had no case. Justice Kamaluddin Hossain while tossing the petition to the bench readers uttered, "Thank you Mr. Pal."

References:

1. *D. Nicolson and J Webb, Public Rules and Private Value: Fractured Professionalism and Institutional Ethics (2005) 12 International Journal of the Legal Profession*
2. *T. Persons, the Problems Matter: Structure in T. Persons Essays in Sociological Theory.*
3. *Legal Ethics, Jonathan Herring*
4. *John Leubsdrof, Three Models of Professional Reform (1981), 67 Cornell law Review 1021*

5. *Boardman v. Phipps (1967) 2 AC 46*
6. *Injustices, Ian Millhiser at p. 100*
7. *Matzko, Early Years, 193-194*
8. *The Law and the Lawyers, M.K Gandhi*
9. *Pherozeshah Mehta, the Best Lawyer of the Day in Bombay High Court*

Chapter 17

Interference in the Administration of Justice

I pointed out earlier that due to the interference by the Ministry of Law the administration of justice is being hampered for a long time. Even in the process of appointment of 3rd and 4th class employees in the lower judiciary, a show committee is constituted, and an examination is also conducted. This will be evident from the following case: 1 Mohammad Abul Kalam along with few others were appointed after following all procedures. They joined their respective posts and they were deputed as process servers at Kuliarchar, Bajitpur and Kishoreganj. After seven months of joining, the District Judge directed them to refund the salaries by referring to a letter of the Ministry of Law on the plea that they were appointed beyond the date fixed by the ministry. The Ministry of Law referred to a circular of the then Ministry of Establishment dated January 22, 1998, wherein it was pointed out that there was strict direction to obtain prior approval of the Ministry of Public Administration for filling up vacant posts by the Ministries/Divisions and their subordinate departments, and that the District Judge did not follow the said direction.

This circular has no manner of application to the employees of the lower judiciary. The lower judiciary is neither a subordinate department of the Ministry of Law and Justice nor the Ministry of Public Administration. It is under the Supreme Court of Bangladesh. Article 109 of the Constitution clearly provides that "the High Court Division shall have superintendence and control over all courts and tribunals subordinate to it." In the Masder Hossain case, the question was set at rest. Besides, Article 111 provides that "The law declared by the Appellate Division shall be binding on the High Court Division and the law declared by the High Court Division of the Supreme Court shall be binding on all courts subordinate to it." Here also in clear terms the question of subordination of the District Courts has been mentioned. These two provisions are clear and there is no gainsaying that all District Courts are subordinate to the High Court Division. It is not a subordinate department of the Ministry of Law and Justice.

Functionally and structurally judicial service stands on a different footing from the civil administrative services of the Republic. While the function of the civil administrative services is to assist the political Executive in the formulation of policy and in execution of the policy decisions of the government of the day, the function of the judicial service is neither of them. It is an independent arm of the Republic which sits on judgment over parliamentary, Executive and quasi – judicial actions, decisions and orders. To make them equal and to put the judicial service and civil administrative service on the same plane is to treat two unequals as equals, the court observed. The independence of the judiciary, as affirmed and declared by Articles 94(4) and 116A, is one of the basic pillars of the Constitution and cannot be demolished, whittled down or curtailed or demolished in any manner whatsoever, except under the existing provisions of the Constitution. It is to be borne in mind that the subordinate staff of the lower judiciary cannot be dissected from the judicial service because the judicial officers cannot administer justice without the supporting staff.2

The functions of the lower judiciary are altogether different from civil administrative service. The Ministry of Public Administration's circulars under memos dated March 15, 1992, May 11, 1991, and January 17, 2000, are not applicable to the District Courts and I declared that accordingly. Thereafter I issued a circular directing all courts and tribunals to fill up all vacant revenue posts without taking any permission from the Ministry of Law. Henceforth, the District Courts will be at liberty to take immediate steps to fill vacant sanctioned posts for the smooth functioning of the courts without taking prior approval or clearance from the Ministry of Law and Justice as well as the Ministry of Public Administration. The said circulars are not applicable to the lower judiciary. The Ministry of Public Administration was directed to withdraw the aforesaid circulars immediately, but it did not withdraw those.

References:

1. *Civil Petition No. 2532 of 2014, Bangladesh v. Md. Abul Kalam Azad*
2. *Secretary v. Md. Masder Hossain, 52 DLR (AD) 82*

Chapter 18

Depletion of Values

During my office I had the privilege of hearing a huge number of criminal cases. I felt more comfortable in disposing of criminal matters than civil matters. When I was in the High Court Division, being the junior most judge, I was given the task of presiding over a Division Bench with powers of criminal motions and it is taken as a challenge for a judge to tackle. A lot of controversial cases and diehard offenders come for anticipatory bail, politicians too come for anticipatory bail and the lawyers also flock to the criminal motion Benches as they get hard cash if they appear in any criminal motion matter. Initially when I joined the Bar, it was a condition precedent that the senior most judge was entrusted with second appeals because the disposal of second appeal required complicated questions of law and second appeals are normally heard by a single Bench. The senior most judge never felt insulted by exercising single Bench matters although his junior brothers were presiding over Division Benches and taking up motions. There was another precedent that the senior most judge was given the task of hearing contempt matters and contempt matters were heard by a Division Bench. Not many contempt petitions are being filed in present days. If the senior most judge is busy with single matters, the Chief Justice gave the jurisdiction to the second senior most Bench for hearing contempt matters. In those days, I noticed the judge hearing second appeal used to dispose of 10 to 12 appeals in a day and judgments were delivered in open court. Now if a senior judge is given a single Bench matter he feels undermined by the Chief Justice. Sometimes they approach the Chief Justice to give them Division Bench power on the plea that some of his junior brothers are exercising jurisdiction of powerful Benches.

Thereafter, I was given the power of hearing death references. It was the only Bench in the High Court Division. Within less than six months, I concluded hearing of all death references and the relevant section could not supply me ready death references. In death reference matters, the entire order-sheet of the trial court, the FIR, charge-sheets, "almost", seizure list, sketch map with index, confessional statements, if any, are to be printed by the BG Press. The working of the Supreme Court requires printing of daily cause list for the High Court, all forms of both civil and criminal matters are required to be printed. But the Supreme Court does not own any press. The court is totally handicapped being in the hands of the BG Press. BG Press could not prepare paper books and print forms for the lower courts in time and the court had nothing to do in this regard. When I visited the district courts there were complaints that because of shortage of forms, cases could not be made ready and the administration of justice is hampered. I also noticed that for the last 6 to 7 years no printed forms were supplied to the lower courts. I told the Ministry of Law to do the needful; but my requests were fell on deaf ears.

I wanted to set up a security press and deputed an officer to do a survey of the matter. He visited some departments of the government which own printing presses. I noticed that some departments which do not have enough work for a press but still own presses. Bangladesh Iman also has a press though it is a losing concern. At the final stage due to bureaucratic barriers and apathy of the government, I could not implement the project. A security press is necessary for many reasons and one of those is that every year the Supreme Court must pay about Tk 20 crore to print only the daily cause lists. This is total wastage of a massive amount of money. Secondly, evidence is recorded by the trial courts manually. Sometimes, corrupt BG Press officials do not properly print the paper book and omit incriminating portion in the evidence. That requires lot of painstaking work to compare the record of the court for ascertaining the correctness of the evidence printed by BG Press. As the BG Press could not supply the paper books I directed the concerned section to type the paper books to get the death references ready for hearing.

Suddenly I was given the task of hearing the Jail Appeals in open court. The practice that was being followed was that the Chief

Justice used to constitute some separate Benches for hearing jail appeals and the judges readily and happily accepted the task and disposed of jail appeals at home, mainly on weekly and long holidays. Jail appeals were never assigned to any Bench to be heard in open court. I exercised the jurisdiction for more than two years hearing jail appeals only. At one stage it so happened that I concluded hearing of all jail appeals and took up the current year's jail appeals. The relevant section could not supply me with jail appeals claiming it did not receive the lower court records. I accordingly directed the section and the concerned court to transmit the records through special messengers. I was not given the jurisdiction of writ matters at any time during my long tenure of about 11 years in the High Court Division. Only in two special matters I was made a member of the Special Bench and on those two matters I delivered judgments. I was apprehending at that time that because of lack of practical experience in original side matters, I would face difficulty if I was elevated to the Appellate Division. But my fears were erased when I heard leave petitions and appeals from the judgments of the High Court Division in writ matters particularly because I had very good concept in civil law. Moreover, when I worked as a junior of S.R.Pal's I appeared in many different matters with him and took dictation of many writ petitions. So, I had the basic foundation in original side matters also which helped me a lot in adjudicating petitions and appeals arising out of writ jurisdiction.

Since I had a knack in criminal jurisprudence, I noticed that in most of the cases though I was convinced that the accused was involved, but due to faulty investigation and prosecution, most of the accused were getting the benefit of doubt. It gave me lot of pains that because of prosecution's improper handling of the cases, sometimes due to corrupt practices of the investigation agency and public prosecution, the real offenders including accused in offences like murder, dacoity with murder, rape with murder, were benefiting getting from doubt. As a judge I cannot award a moral conviction and in dispensing criminal justice the court cannot concerned about who really is involved in the crime, but he can be given benefit of the doubt due to faulty conduct of the cases. The court cannot maintain a sentence unless it concludes on an elaborate evaluation of the materials on record that the prosecution has been able to prove the charge beyond a shadow of doubt. The defense is put to an advantageous position under the adversarial system of criminal justice. The court has no role in his regard and administers justice only based on legal evidence. Some of the judges' award conviction morally on being convinced that the accused was really an offender and that he should not be given the benefit of doubt. This is altogether wrong. Even I have noticed that in some cases in the apex court, the judges maintained the conviction on moral grounds ignoring the fundamental principles of law.

I have given conscious thoughts to the issue and noticed that the investigation agency is in the habit of diverting the real incident in some other direction keeping loopholes and sometimes due to lack of knowledge or due to corruption the prosecution ignores those defects and conducts the case as routine work. When I joined the Bar in Sylhet, I noticed that the most veteran criminal lawyers were appointed as public prosecutors and government pleaders. The District and Sessions Judge normally recommended the names of two lawyers, one for the appointment of a public prosecutor and other for government pleader, with their consent to the District Magistrate for appointment by the authority. This recommendation was the basis for the appointment. There was no interference by the political leaders in the selection process. But today's scenario is totally different. The District Judge has no role at all and the politicians make the selection. Sometimes, very efficient criminal lawyers refused the offer on the plea that he had accepted a lot of serious cases and had already taken money and at such it was not possible to accept the offer. Even then the most veteran criminal lawyers who did not to become Assistant Public Prosecutors remained on the panel and conducted the sensational cases at the request of the District Magistrate, provided they had not been appointed by the defense.

The senior lawyers at the cost of their own practice conducted such sensational cases without any remuneration because the remuneration which was provided to an Assistant Public Prosecutor was so nominal that they preferred not to submit bills after the conclusion of trials. I also noticed that Suleman Raza Chowdhury and Abdul Ahad Chowdhury, the most veteran criminal lawyers, appeared in many cases for the prosecution. The litigants sometimes brought some homegrown vegetables or a big fish or sticky rice as honorarium to the lawyers, but the lawyers refused to accept those gifts. They maintained their professional ethics that they were conducting the case on behalf of the State and ethically they could not receive any extra fees or other gifts from the clients. Still, I can recollect that the faces of the poor village litigants, particularly informants scolded by the State counsel for bringing home grown stuffs for them, their faces appeared gloomy. In fact, they did not bring those not as remuneration but as a gesture that their cases were conducted freely by the State prosecutors. They felt that they were not able to give honorarium to the lawyers of their status.

After Dhaka and Chittagong, Sylhet was a very rich Bar because a lot of people from Sylhet are residing in the United Kingdom. They are used to sending massive amounts of Pound Sterling to their kith and kin. So, Sylhet was economically rich in comparison with other districts and litigants have the capacity to pay large fees to the lawyers. During the war of liberation there were many local people who supported the Pakistani regime and they became Peace Committee members and their poor dependents were engaged as Razakars. Immediately after the independence, the government appointed Munir Uddin Ahmed as prosecutor for conducting collaborator cases. He did not receive even a single farthing and used to come to court on a manually-pulled rickshaw. He never used any motorized vehicle, although all his colleagues were maintaining automotive vehicles. If he wished to earn money he could have earned crores of taka because all the accused were moneyed persons. I knew him closely. I noticed that any offender was dared to visit his residence or wanted to influence him through someone close to him. I also noticed that my senior, Aftab Uddin Ahmed, and some other veteran criminal lawyers who exchanged lot of hot words in course of those trials with Munir Uddin, departed the court with smiling faces and exchanged views in friendship. The lawyers were so close to each other, but they could not even imagine any favor from Munir Uddin.

Abdus Subhan Chowdhury was the government pleader and vice principal of Sylhet Law College. On one occasion the Deputy Commissioner sent his judicial "peshkar" to him with a request to meet the Deputy Commissioner for an urgent discussion of a legal matter. Right at that moment Subhan Chowdhury sent his resignation letter to the Deputy Commissioner and verbally told the judicial "peshkar" that if the Deputy Commissioner had anything to discuss with him, he is being the client, must attend the lawyer's chamber. Mobarak Hossain was the Public Prosecutor for a considerable time in Sylhet. He was so honest that nobody could even imagine that he had accepted any money from the prosecution side not to speak of taking any money from the offenders for favor. This was the tradition in those days. The lawyers always maintained ethical standards. Now the Public Prosecutors and Government Pleaders are appointed mainly on political consideration and there is strong lobbying for the jobs because many party followers are interested to become Public Prosecutors and Government Pleaders. It is rumored that the Public Prosecutors and Government Pleaders are appointed in exchange of large kickbacks without caring whether the candidates can hold such offices. The State does not seem to be bothered about whether the lawyers who were going to be appointed as Public Prosecutors and Government Pleaders had the minimum knowledge in criminal or civil law. The main consideration apparently is party affiliation and money. I had rarely seen that a Public Prosecutor or Government Pleader maintaining a car, but these days it is reported that they are maintaining most expensive cars. The remuneration given to a Public Prosecutor or Government Pleader is very negligible because they are being paid at the old rate and, in the present market, it is difficult for them to maintain their livelihood with the low amount of honorarium. So, we have opened their path to openly indulge in corruption with the net result that the people are deprived of justice, while our government persists with a blind eye.

A country cannot claim to be civilized unless there is democracy, the government is formed with the mandate of the people, there is rule of law, and law is applicable to all from the president to the general public. It is not meant only for a segment of people. There cannot be a system of pick-and-chose in the administration of justice. If it is not for all, it is not justice. But if the instruments of justice are used by the government in power for ulterior motives, that country cannot be taken as a civilized one. In order to achieve this goal, all citizens have a role and they cannot avoid their responsibility. Everyone is bound to follow the rule of law--the executive, the judiciary, the bureaucracy, the police, the military— and has a role in civil administration because the politicians in power have, perhaps, unconsciously given such powers to them though it is suicidal for a nation as well as for the lawyers, the businessmen and non-governmental agencies. But the vital tasks remain the responsibility of the executive, the judiciary, the lawyers and the law enforcing agencies.

If one commits an offence, the primary role is for the police to bring him to justice, the role of the executive is not to interfere in the matter allowing the police to detect the offenders, and then there is the role of the judiciary and the lawyers. Under the prevailing system if the lawyers cannot perform their responsibilities, it is difficult for the court to administer proper justice. If the law enforcing agencies take the law in their own hands, then who will protect the citizens? The rule in such a country will be considered tyrannical and the country cannot be recognized as a civilized nation. For the last few years a new culture has been developed in our country which is unprecedented and unthinkable for a civilized world. It is called "cross firing" in the name of "encounter". Law-enforcing agencies take the law in their own hands and kill innocent persons on concocted stories of recovery of arms or alleged incriminating materials used in the commission of the alleged crimes. If this type of State sponsored crimes is allowed, no citizen is secure in the hands of the law-enforcement agencies, especially since after the incidents the Home Ministry arranges press conferences in support of such lynching. After criticism by human rights activists, social media and international organizations, it temporarily subsided but nowadays law enforcing entities again started killing of alleged drug predators.

The question is who will decide someone is a drug smuggler or dealing in drugs. If the law enforcing agencies have the final say regarding commission of an offence, then there is no need for courts. How could they know that the persons who were killed were drug smugglers and, even if it is so, who gave them the power to kill them? Under what law do they perpetrate such offences? If one is really an offender he has a right to protection and if he is found guilty he will be convicted by a court of law. His sentence will depend upon the gravity of the offence. Even in Jammu and Kashmir it is most difficult to get away by killing a terrorist by showing false encounter. It is known by all that there are ongoing terrorist activities there and the terrorists driven out the Kashmiri Pundits from Jammu, and they cannot return to their homeland. Some army officers were put to justice after judicial probes found they had killed people in fake encounters. Some even lost their jobs. There is respect for human rights, rule of law and it is possible only because there is democracy in the country, and hence the people are conscious of their rights. If there is use of excess power by the armed forces, the people raise their voice. Even then India is being criticized by international organizations for such killings of terrorists in purported encounters. We have not learned anything from our neighboring country as to what is meant by human rights, what is meant by rule of law and that a citizen cannot be killed by law enforcing agencies in any manner other than in accordance with the law.

The degree of civilization in a society can be judged by entering its prisons.1 A nation should not be judged by how it treats its highest citizens, but its lowest ones.2 "… even the vilest criminal remains a human being possessed of common human dignity".3 In order to live as human beings we have to be able to act on our judgment; wild animals aside, the only thing that can stop us from doing so is other people; and the only way they can stop us is by using physical force.4 A civilized society or country has a well-developed system of government, culture, and way of life and that treats the people who live there fairly: a fair justice system is a fundamental part of a civilized society.5 Civilizations are intimately associated with and often further defined by other socio-politico-economic characteristics, including centralization, the domestication of both humans and other organisms, specialization of labor, culturally ingrained ideologies of progress, monumental architecture, taxation, societal dependence upon farming, etc.6 Historically, civilization has often been understood as a larger and more advanced culture, in contrast to smaller, supposedly primitive cultures. Civilization concentrates power, extending human control over the rest of nature, including over other human beings. Albert Schweitzer outlines two opinions: one purely material and the other material and ethical.

Civilization has a more complex political structure, namely the State. State societies are more stratified than other societies; there is a greater difference among the social classes. The ruling class normally has control over much of the surplus and exercises its will through the actions of a government or bureaucracy. Effective government is a cornerstone of civilized societies. Whether the government is a democracy or dictatorship, a strong government is needed to enforce laws and keep people safe from foreign or domestic threats. Due to the geographical location, our main concern is not foreign threat, ours is domestic threat. A welfare state is a concept of government in which the state plays a key role in the protection and promotion of the social and economic well-being of its citizens. It is based on the principles of equality of opportunity, equitable distribution of wealth, and public responsibility for those unable to avail themselves of the minimal provisions for a good life. Emperor Ashoka of India put forward his idea of a welfare state in the 3rd Century BCE. He consciously tried to adopt it as a matter of state policy; he declared that "all men are my children" and "whatever extension I make, I strive only to discharge debt that I owe to all living centuries." Today we have forgotten all those traditions of the dawn of our civilization and the concept of running a welfare state.7

Reference;

1. *Fyodor Dostoevsky*
2. *Nelson Mandela*
3. *Justice William J. Brennan*
4. *A Civilized Society: The Necessary Conditions: Craig Biddle*
5. *Cambridge Academic Content Dictionary*

6. *Haviland, William et al. (2013). Cultural Anthropology: The Human Challenge: Solms-Laubach, Franz (2007) Nietzsche and Early German and Austrian Sociology, Walter de Gruyter.: Adams, Robert McCormick (1996) The Evolution of Urban Society: Michael Mann, The Sources of Social Power, Cambridge University Press, 1986, vol.1: Grinin, Leonid E (Ed) et al. (2004), "The Early State and its Alternatives and Analogues"*

7. *Romila Thaper (2003). The Penguin History of Early India: From the origins to AD 1300. Penguin UK. P592.*

Chapter 19

Jail Visits

I realized that if I want to make any revolutionary change in the administration of justice, I should have practical knowledge regarding conditions of the prisons and the number of prisoners, both under trial and convicts, kept in each central jail of the country, the condition of female offenders, the life term offenders, the death sentence offenders, the undefended offenders, and so on. Some of the prisoners though they preferred jail appeals, they were not be heard because of technicalities. I had come across some of those, while I was on the criminal Bench. Some of the innocent persons were also suffering life sentences, and even some of the innocent persons were serving as proxies in exchange of money on behalf of the convicts. The first visit I made was to the Sylhet Central Jail. The high officials apprised me of the conditions of the jail, from the records I came to know that more than double the number of prisoners was kept in the jail. I went through different wards of the jail. I visited the female section of the prison and noticed that some of the illiterate innocent women were suffering jail sentences for indefinite periods of time. On query to a young woman who initially expressed her indolence as if her body language was saying that the prevailing system was meaningless to her since any innocent person may be put in jail by powerful persons in exchange of money.

After much effort she opened her mouth and the story revealed by her was appalling. I cannot recollect her name. My officers noted down her name, but since I left Dhaka without bringing those notes, I have either lost them or misplaced them. Her only son was drowned by her co-wife with the help of her relations but instead she was involved in the killing of her son. She could not understand why she was languishing in jail. Another woman was put in jail in a false case by the brothers of her husband for grabbing her husband's property. There were hundreds of incidents like these. I found similar incidents in the male wards also. The jail authority thereupon arranged a "Majlish" of the prisoners both under trial and undergoing sentences, with their records. It is a practice being followed in jails that whenever a high-ranking dignitary visited a jail, those who have unblemished records and who appear to have been languishing in jail on false grounds for indefinite periods, and since the jail officials could not do justice to them because of their limitations, they drew the attention to these cases of the visiting dignitaries. I have noticed more than hundred cases which were false, and the persons were suffering in "hajat" for indefinite periods. Some of the prisoners though preferred jail appeals but they did not know the fate of their appeals. Some of the appeals which were required to be filed within 30 days under the special laws were not filed and the appeals were dismissed. On queries I came to know that as soon as a convict desired to file a jail appeal, some prisoners are deputed for filing the appeals. But the filing of appeals was delayed due to time consumed in obtaining copies of the judgments. As they could not pay extra money to get copies of the judgment they could not file jail the appeals and jail authorities could not help them. Sometimes the jail authorities obtained copies of the judgment, but by that time the time limit for an appeal had expired.

I directed the jail authorities to communicate to my Registry to supply the papers of the prisoners who intended to file appeals and about appeals filed out of time or non-availability of copies of judgment. I advised the officers that as soon as a prisoner intimated that he desired to file an appeal, though they are under obligation to file the petition along with the copy of judgment, the limitation shall run for filing appeal from the date of intimation to the jail authority and not from the date of communicating to the Supreme Court. Because those prisoners had none to look after their cases and the jail being an organ of the State, filing of the petitions by the convicts shall be deemed to have filed appeals to the proper court. As per my direction, the jail authority transmitted all the papers and I directed all the cases be heard by some Benches on Thursdays and in respect of those cases the copies of which could not be filed, I directed the Registry to direct the concerned court to immediately send for the records of those cases. Most of the cases were ultimately heard by some Benches and some of the convicts were released from custody. I have also given some guidelines to the judges while dealing with jail appeals.

I noticed many prisoners on trial who are not produced in court in petty cases for years together. They were involved in cases in Comilla and Chittagong and also implicated them in Sylhet, but these prisoners could not be produced in court outside Sylhet. This has resulted due to lack of monitoring of the cases. I directed the authority to send the prisoners to their respective districts where they were wanted for trial. I noticed that some prisoners were kept in condemned cells and on inquiry I came to learn that they are dreaded criminals. But later on, I learnt that some offenders intentionally attacked the inmates of the general ward and they were termed as dreaded prisoners and then are sent to the condemned cells where they get sufficient space for movement and sleeping.

I visited the library and noticed that the jail authority could not collect books which would be beneficial to the prisoners. Instead, some cheap religious books have been kept. I advised the jail authorities to collect books which would be useful for them to change the mindset of the offenders. A person after committing an offence is sent to jail for three purposes; deterrence, retribution, incapacitation and rehabilitation. Penology is concerned with the effectiveness of those social processes devised and adopted for the prevention of crime is the first object, via the repression or inhibition of criminal intent via the fear of punishment. Penologists have consequently evolved occupational and psychological education programs for offenders detained in prisons, and a range of community service and probation orders which entail guidance and aftercare of the offenders within the community. The importance of some measure of punishment on those persons who break the law is however maintained to maintain social order and to moderate public outrage which might produce appeals for cruel vengeance.1

The prison population has increased dramatically over the last twenty-five years. This rapid increase has created the need for development of the prisons. It is now said by some social workers that rehabilitation was the dominant model for the criminal justice system for several decades prior to the mid-1970s. However, some notable research in the field of criminal justice concluded that rehabilitation had been insufficient.2 the criminals, while doing their time, should realize the moral error of their ways and refrain from such activities in the future, once released. Essentially, a prison should be a "moral hospital."

We have not seen any change in our prison system and the authorities are treating the offenders in the similar fashion as they were treated during the British rule. The developed and the developing countries have made fundamental changes in penology. Originally this term—penology--was coined by Francis Lieber, as a section of criminology that dealt with the philosophy and practice of various societies in their attempts to repress criminal activities and satisfy public opinion via an appropriate treatment regime for persons convicted of criminal offences. Now in England it is treated as the study of the punishment of crime and prison management and in this sense, it is equivalent to correction. Penology is concerned with the effectiveness of those social processes devised and adopted for the prevention of crime by repression or inhibition of criminal intent via the fear of punishment. The study of penology, therefore, deals with the treatment of prisoners and the subsequent rehabilitation of convicted criminals. It also encompasses aspects of probation as well as penitentiary science relating to the secure detention of offenders committed to secure institutions. So, penology concerns many topics and theories including those concerning prisons, i.e. prison reform, prisoner abuse, prisoner's rights, recidivism, as well as theories of the purposes of punishment. Rehabilitation is the reintegration in the society of a convicted person and the main objective of modern penal policy is to counter habitual offending also known as criminal recidivism. Alternatives to imprisonment also exists such as community service, probation offenders, and others entailing guidance and after-care for the offenders.3

The second phase of my prison visit was to the Central Jail, Kashimpur in Gazipur, on June 29, 2017. This prison is overpopulated; three to four times more prisoners are kept therein.

In this prison, some facilities for reformation of the prisoners under the present Inspector General of Prisons Brigadier General Syed Iftekhar Uddin have been undertaken. In the jail, a modern bakery, a printing press where all the jail forms and other necessary papers are printed, a weaving section, an embroidery section, a furniture making section with canes have been set up and some other handicrafts are being made by the prisoners. I was told that the prisoners are so trained in these sections that after their release they could rehabilitate themselves without the help of outsiders.

Except overpopulation, the environment of the prison is very good. The women prisoners are privileged with learning to play musical instruments. I noticed the paucity of books in the library and found that ten to twelve young boys in similar dresses were reading religious books in a group. On enquiry I came to know that those boys were arrested on alleged incidents of terrorism and most of them were under trial prisoners. The religious books they were reading were very cheap pieces of hadiths edited by some unknown writers. I told the jail authority that these boys are misguided and if they can read this type of cheap books with misinterpretation of religion they will not be able to correct them for life after their release from custody. I hardly found any books on history, philosophy, autobiographies of great personalities, sociology and on other social topics which might give them notions of the modern world and society, so that they can get out of their conservative mindset. Accordingly, I donated one lakh taka from my budget to buy books and directed the officers to select books which would be useful for the reformation of the prisoners.

In the jail "Majlish" (a gathering with inmates) I noticed a centenarian woman was leaning on an old woman. I wanted to know about the centenarian prisoner. The IG Prisons told me that he was very concerned about the woman named Ohidunnesa. I directed to produce the woman in front of me. The woman could not sit alone not to speak of standing. She was brought to me with the help of two other women prisoners and the old woman who was also an octogenarian started crying and said that she had no grievance at all if she could have managed to release her mother-in-law. I was surprised to know that an octogenarian woman was concerned about her mother-in-law although she was not concerned about her own fate. She said that she was all along guarding her mother-in-law, sometimes her condition deteriorated due to problems with breathing. She used to urinate and defecate in her bed and the daughter-in-law would clean all those happily as if she was looking after her own ailing mother.

The jail authority also reported to me that sometimes they get calls at midnight about her breathing and other complications and doctors had to take special care of her. The octogenarian woman told me that eleven members of her family were sentenced to life imprisonment in a false case on May 14, 2000 in Chandpur. Ohidunnesa lost her husband and a son while they were undergoing the sentence. Then and there I asked the IG Prisons to produce her papers and noticed that her leave petition was also rejected by the apex court. I noted down the case and noticed that the jail leave petition was filed long after the delay and it was dismissed on the ground of time-bar. Then on my direction the jail officials preferred a review petition and the matter was heard on merit. We were surprised to notice that she was convicted on hearsay evidence and she passed orders based upon which other accused persons of her family succumbed to injuries to the victim. She was around the age of 80 years during the time of occurrence. I have seen several cases, that when there were long-standing family feuds, the older persons are also implicated on the allegation of passing orders to pounce upon the victims. It is one of those cases which had been detected on perusal of the entire record. Accordingly, we acquitted her of the charge and she was released from the jail.4 I was so satisfied when I saw her picture both in print and electronic media. A centurion innocent woman past 19 years of her life in jail without committing any crime. She ultimately came out as a free person.

As part of my jail visits I went to the Central Jail at Keraniganj. It is one of the most modern jails in Bangladesh. The construction work of the main building with other facilities was yet to be completed, but the prisoners had already been shifted there. The condemned cells were also with modern facilities and the divisional prisoners' cells were also most modern providing adequate space. But the most horrible thing was the library. I carried with me books worth one lakh taka and handed those over to the IG Prisons. Both the central jails of Dhaka are over populated. One of the most disturbing complaints I heard in Kashimpur Jail was that most of the under-trial prisoners told me about the inadequacy of prison vans. In a prison van there is accommodation for about 30 to 40 prisoners, but the jail authority carries 70 to 80 prisoners in a van. The prisoners reported to me that about three to four hours' time is taken to make a one-way trip due to traffic congestion and in the summer heat most of the prisoners fainted on their way to courts. Because the vans are not only overcrowded, they are completely closed from all sides except some holes in the upper portion of the vans. So, there was no scope for passing fresh air into the van. The movement of prisoners was in an inhuman condition and they wanted to get rid of this treatment. I reported the incident to the Home Minister and he assured me that he had already ordered for importing some prison vans and the situation would improve after arrival of those vans.

I also noticed that some under trial prisoners were not being produced in court for 5 or 6 years and they did not know the fate of their cases. Some of the suspected persons were arrested under section 54 and they remained in jail for months together for absence of police reports. I directed my officers to note those cases without waiting for the reports and directed the CMM to dispose of those cases. Later I came to know that most of the cases were filed by interested persons either to avenge a grudge or grab property. Most of those cases were disposed of within three to four months. I also noted down some old appeals which were pending due to various reasons --in some cases the relations lost interest to contact the lawyers; in some cases, the lawyers died in the meantime and nobody from the prisoners' side took interest about the cases; and in some other cases, the prisoners could not satisfy the demands of the lawyers. I noted down all the appeals and directed some Benches to dispose of them on a priority basis. All the appeals were disposed of within a very short time.

References:

1. *Rajendra Kumar Sharma, Criminology and Penology, Atlantic Publishers and Distribution.*
2. *Bertall, 2006; Martinson, 1975*
3. *Clare Obuy, Ensuring Respect of the Rights of the prisoners under the European Conventions of Human Rights, a part of their Reintegration Process.*
4. *The New Nation, Issue 20th July 2016*

Chapter 20

Inspection of Juvenile Correction Center

One day Law Minister Anisul Haque requested me to do something for the protection of juvenile offenders, particularly in respect of one Al-Amin, who hails from a very respectable family but got involved in a murder case owing to his complicity with some friends who were beyond the control of their parents. This boy had been subjected to inhuman treatment in the Juvenile Development Center, Gazipur, at the hands of inmates. Previously also I got some complaints regarding irregularities in the center by the Chairman of the Human Rights Commission. Accordingly, I decided to inspect both male and female centers secretly. In the morning of January 26, 2017, I went to the Female Juvenile Center at Konabari, Gazipur, without prior intimation, where 122 juvenile girl offenders are kept.

I spoke with the inmates in the dormitories keeping my female officers with me and recorded complaints made by the juveniles. I wanted to know from them about the reasons of their coming to the center and most of them replied that they were detained in criminal cases in compelling circumstances. I found many female juveniles, with high social status, who were detained because of marrying against their parents' will. Missing and physically challenged juveniles and floating female juveniles were also found at the center. I directed my officials to submit a report after scrutinizing the cases of the juveniles detailing the nature of offence, if any, and period of detention. Embroidery and sewing machines were there for the training of the female juveniles. Officials said that the center had also set up a library with some books. The condition of the center appeared to me congenial.

I then went to the Juvenile Development Center, Gazipur. On getting information of my inspection high officials attended the center and many media people as assembled at the gate of the center claiming there was restriction on entry of media. The media people sought my interference for allowing them to accompany me. On my direction some of them could enter subject to the condition that they would not broadcast anything in the electronic media. I found 411 male juveniles staying there. I asked the officials to ensure the release of Al-Amin Khan for appearing at the secondary school certificate examination beginning from February 2. Some male juveniles alleged that they were subjected to torture and sexual harassments by seniors who were known as "big brothers". The law minister had also made similar allegations. They said that many of them have crossed the age of 18 years, but they have not been released from the center. I found that the center has no arrangement for education above class five. There was no mechanism for consultation for the development of the juveniles detained in connection with criminal cases.

I found a playground for male juveniles, but none was seen to play there. The juveniles had complained about the standard of food. Some juveniles requested me to arrange for sending them to their families. A probe conducted by the authority found that 20 juveniles cut their hands, forehead and legs with broken glasses in September 2014 as they were subjected to torture and the superintendent detected carrying of drugs in the center. Following a High Court order, the authorities conducted a probe and it was found that some juveniles had brought drugs to the center on their way back from court. The probe also found that the juveniles were suffering from malnutrition as they were served with low quality food. Most of the juveniles complained that they were not produced before the court regularly. On inquiry I found that there were no proper transportation facilities and there was negligence of the authority in taking proper steps.

I further noticed that 6 or 7 offenders were suffering from frustration, because they could not appear in the SSC examination which was scheduled to be held in seven days. I directed my officials to note down the number of cases pending against those offenders. Except one, most of the offenders were arrested in respect of petty cases. So, I directed the Registry to arrange their bail from the Magistrate's court within one or two days so that they could sit for the examination. Later, I was reported that all the juveniles appeared in the examination. I directed the superintendent to arrange for the safety and security of the juveniles so that they are not subjected to torture at the hands of "big brothers". On hearing this from me, it appeared to me that the super had no knowledge regarding such incidents.

I talked to some victims separately, who did not want to disclose the maltreatment meted out by their "big brothers" for fear of reprisal. I assured them that they would not be ill-treated henceforth. On being satisfied with my assurance they told me that on the day of meeting their near ones or on court day, if their parents supply food and money, the "big brothers" snatched away everything. It is apt to clarify at this juncture, who these "big brothers" are. In every room 10-15 boys are kept and the boys who were in the center from before the arrival of newcomers, irrespective of age and body structure, tried to assert control over the newcomers. The authority also gave them some internal disciplinary work. I saw even a very thin and young boy had become a "big brother" in a role. The newcomers were bound to follow the direction of the big brothers. The big brothers in the center have also made an alliance among themselves and totally controlled the newcomers. They sometimes sexually molested them too. This fact was known to the administration, but they always ignored these and because of the existing circumstances the newcomers did not make any complaint. I supplied the names of the so-called big brothers to the superintendent, who was bewildered when I disclosed those incidents to him. The incidents were happening so secretly that none dared to disclose anything to the officials. Later, I came to know that some of the big brothers had been shifted to the Jessore Juvenile Center.

I found some marks of violence on some of the juveniles on their legs. On query they reported that the police tortured them and sent them to the center without cause. I was very shocked, naturally, on seeing a boy who could not walk due to severe injuries on his leg. I obliged the authority to decide for his treatment immediately. On thorough interrogation, one by one secretly and by cross checking of the authority, I came to know that most of the juvenile offenders were being utilized by the professional offenders for carrying drugs and committing robberies and banditry. The professional offenders trained these juveniles in such a way that they could enter a house in broad daylight if there was no inmate in the house through the ventilator and then they opened the door so that the professional offenders could enter. At dead of night also they broke the ventilator of the toilets by using some instruments and pushed the juveniles inside the house. After opening the door, the professional offenders sometimes used force on the inmates of the house and compelled them to assemble in the toilets and then they easily continued their acts of robbery. These juvenile offenders were getting training from the professional offenders and after becoming "big brothers" in the center subsequently they ultimately would become professional offenders. So, it was essential for the authorities to change their motivation and give proper education so that after their release they could lead an honest life.

These centers are earmarked as restricted centers. Normally media people are not allowed inside these centers. The authorities who are at the helm of affairs took the advantage of the restriction on the entry of the media to manage the centers at their whims. Sometimes social workers and NGO workers and the Human Rights Commission members visited the centers with prior permission of the authority. As they do not have any executive power or command over them, therefore, their visits yielded no fruitful result. Accordingly, I directed my officials for giving direction to the District and Sessions judges to monitor the centers by visiting at least once a month and to take necessary steps for releasing those who were kept in the centers only based on suspicion or who were detained on petty allegations. The Chief Justice may also arrange the inspection of the centers by deputing a judge of the High Court Division at least once a year. In such event, the irregularities would be addressed, and the authorities would be worried if any adverse situation developed or if steps were taken by the judges. I directed the officials to decide for the release of those offenders against whom there are minor allegations and if the parents were willing to take them back into their custody. I received replies from both the centers within a week that all my directions and suggestions had been implemented.

Chapter 21
Terrorism

Terrorism is, in the broadest sense, the use of intentionally indiscrete means to create terror among the masses of people; or fear to achieve a financial, political, religious or ideological aim. It is a term used to describe violence or other harmful acts against civilians by groups or persons for political or other ideological goals. Many people find "terrorism" is perpetrated for a political goal and deliberately target "non-combatants". Responses to the violence for any goal, worthy or not, have often involved additional violence, and ignored the reasons that led to the perpetration of those acts. Terrorism ultimately involves the use or threat of violence with the aim of creating fear not only to the victims but among the citizens in general. The attacks are carried out in such a way as to maximize the severity and length of the psychological impact. Each act of terrorism is a performance, a product of internal logic, devised to have an impact on many large audiences. Terrorists also attack national symbols to show their power and to shake the foundation of the country or society they are opposed to. This may negatively affect a government's legitimacy, while increasing the legitimacy of the terrorist organization and/or ideology behind a terrorist act.1

I came across a few cases on terrorism and diehard criminals who had faced trial of offence of murder. Some of the cases were: Ershad Sikder of Khulna, a diehard criminal; Mufti Abdul Hannan, a gang leader of terrorist activities in Bangladesh; and another case of Lakhsmipur. In the last one the terrorists charged grenade aiming a judge while he was performing judicial work in court, but luckily for the judge the grenade hit the paper weight on the table of the judge and instead of hitting the judge, turned back toward an old man in the witness box and unfortunately the witness was killed while the judge along with some officials were injured.

Now I will turn to a horrific incident organized by Mufti Abdul Hannan, in which three police personnel were killed on May 21,

2004 in a bomb blast at the gate of the shrine of Hazrat Shah Jalal, Sylhet, while Anwar Chowdhury, then British High Commissioner in Dhaka, was returning after offering his Juma prayers at the shrine. The police personnel were on duty for the High Commissioner. He was also seriously injured in the grenade attack. In this case, some crucial law points were involved. Mufti Hannan was not present at the crime scene, but he was the mastermind who had organized the killing and was the leader of the terrorist outfit Harkatul Jihad. Evidence and record revealed that Mufti Hannan supplied the grenades to the principal offender who participated in the grenade detonation. Three terrorists, Md. Sharif, Md. Shadul Alam alias Bipul and Md. Delwar Hossain Ripon gave confessional statements and Mufti Abdul Hannan made a confession in another sensational case, commonly known as the "Ramna Batomul bomb explosion case" in which many persons succumbed to injuries due to bomb blasts at dawn while the victims were attending celebrations welcoming the first day of the Bengali New Year, the Pohela Boishakh.

The question arose whether the confession of Mufti Hannan made in another case could be used in this case, and if it was admissible, what could be the procedure of admissibility of the evidence of one case to another case. As terrorist activities are hatched in secrecy, it is difficult on the part of the investigating agency to detect all the terrorists in the case. Secondly, when a person joins terrorist outfits, he changes his name and normally one terrorist does not know the actual name of another terrorist because the names remain hidden as per the direction of their leader. Mufti Hannan was a dreaded criminal, who had originally joined the Afghan war against the Soviet Union, passed many years in Pakistan and then returned to Bangladesh and organized the terrorist group Harkatul Jihad. He was involved in the killings at Ramna Batomul (Ramna Park Banyan tree); attempting to blow up Sheikh Hasina, the Prime Minister of Bangladesh at Kotali Para, while she was scheduled to deliver a speech. He had planted a powerful bomb beneath the stage for that purpose. In his confession he admitted his involvement in some other sensational cases in connection with Dhaka Ramna Police Station Case No. 46 (4)/2001.

Under the scheme of the Evidence Act, a confession is included in the category of "admission" in sections 17 to 31. A confession is admissible in evidence because the maker acknowledges a fact in issue to his detriment. The maker acknowledges his/her culpability provided it is true and voluntary. Section 24 is a rule of exclusion if the confession is not voluntary it is not admissible. It must be free from inducement, threat or promise. It must also be free from police influence. Its wording shows that prima facie a confession is to be deemed relevant without formal proof of voluntariness. The ground of reception is the same as that of "admission". The language used in this section shows prima facie that a confession duly recorded as required by law is deemed to be relevant. The expression "confession" has been defined as an admission made at any time by a person charged with a crime, stating or suggesting the inference that he committed the crime.2

Section 80 of the Evidence Act3 states about "Presumption as to documents produced as record of evidence." It states any document if produced before any court, purporting to be a record or memorandum of the evidence, or of any part of the evidence, given by a witness in a judicial proceeding or before any officer authorized by law to take such evidence or to be a statement or confession by any prisoner or accused person, taken in accordance with law, and purporting to be signed by any judge or magistrate, or by any such officer as aforesaid, the court shall presume that the document is genuine; that any statements as to the circumstances under which it was taken purporting to be made by the person signing it are true; and that such evidence, statement or confession was duly taken." Section 80 gives legal sanction to the maxim Omnia Praesumuntur rite et solemniter esse acta donee probetur in contrarium, which means, all things are presumed to have been done regularly and with due formality until contrary is proved.3(a)

When a deposition or confession is taken by a public servant, there is a degree of sanctity and solemnity which affords enough guarantee for the presumption that everything was formally, correctly and duly done. The presumption to be raised under Section 80 which deals with depositions or confessions of offenders is considerably wider than those under section 79, which provides presumptions as to the genuineness of certificates, certified copies and certified by other documents, that is to say, where a person acts in an official capacity, it shall be presumed that he was duly appointed, and it has been applied to a great variety of officers. The presumption embraced not only the genuineness of the confession but also that it was duly taken and given under the circumstances recorded therein. It deals not only with relevancy but also with proof, if it was recorded in accordance with the law. On the strength of these presumptions, it dispenses with the necessity of formal proof by direct evidence what it would otherwise be necessary to prove.

A confession by an accused in accordance with law is admissible without examining the Magistrate who recorded it since the Magistrate was a public servant who recorded the statement in discharge of his official duty if it was recorded in accordance with the law. The usual presumption arises under this section that the confession is voluntarily made. The burden is on the accused of showing that his confession is not voluntarily made. The Magistrate's mere admission in the cross-examination that he filled up the form in question-and-answer as required by Section 164 of the Code of Criminal Procedure in recording the confession, is enough that he has recorded it properly. This section dispenses with the necessity of formal proof of a confession recorded in accordance with the law. Genuineness under the section can be presumed only when the confession has been recorded substantially in the form and in the manner provided by law.

The High Court Division wrongly applied the confession of an accused in convicting the offender of a charge of criminal conspiracy ignoring the dictums of the Indian, Pakistani, Bangladeshi courts and the Privy Council. Statements made after the conspiracy had been terminated either on achieving its object or it is abandoned, or it is frustrated, or the conspirator leaves the conspiracy in between, are not admissible against the co-conspirator. Fixing the period of conspiracy is important as the provisions of section 10 of the Evidence Act would apply only during the existence of the conspiracy.4 A statement made by one conspirator in the absence of the other with reference to the past acts done in the actual carrying out of the conspiracy after it had been completed, is not admissible under Section 10. The words "common intention" signify a common intention existing at the time when the thing was said, done or written by any one of them. In Bazlul Huda, the court discarded the confessions of Farooque Rahaman, Sultan Shahriar and Mohiuddin (Artillery) observing that those confessions were not relevant facts to prove the charge of conspiracy and then on assessment of the oral evidence found that the prosecution had been able to prove the charge of conspiracy against the accused. The High Court Division wrongly applied the ratio of those cases. In view of the above consistent views expressed by the Privy Council and the Supreme Courts of India, Pakistan and Bangladesh, there is hardly any scope to consider the confessions of three accused to prove the charge under section 120B of the Penal Code. Even if the charge under sections 320/120B failed, there will be no difficulty in maintaining the sentences of the co-accused on alteration of the charge.5

As to the application of confession in one case to another case the High Court Division relied upon some cases in which it was stated that in the absence of any inhibition for such use of confession there is no reason for the court to introduce a further fetter against the admissibility of confession. The court without giving a proper explanation concluded its opinion with above few words because it did not explore the law covering the field. Accordingly, I gave a detailed guidance. "Evidence may be given in any suit or proceeding of the existence or nonexistence of every fact in issue and of such other facts as are declared to be relevant, and of no others."6 Section 5 of the Evidence Act deals with facts in issue and relevant facts. Evidence may be given in a judicial proceeding to prove the existence or non-existence of every fact in issue or of such other facts which are declared to be relevant by some other provisions of Chapter II, and of no other collateral facts. The facts necessarily involved in the determination of the issue are sometimes called res gestae. So, relevancy is the test of admissibility. Facts in issue are necessary ingredients of the litigated right or liability and they may be given in evidence as a matter of course. Whenever there is absence of direct evidence concerning facts in issue, their existence may be established as satisfactorily by circumstantial evidence as by direct evidence. The existence or non-existence of a fact may be inferred from the existence or non-existence of certain other facts.7 Admissibility of evidence is the rule and the exclusion are the exception. Evidence may be given in a case in respect of any fact which is relevant for the determination of an issue involved in it.

The object of a trial of a person in a case is to ascertain the truth in respect of the charge made against him. The court is to estimate at its true worth. In deciding the question whether certain evidence may be admissible or not, it is necessary to look at the object for which it is produced, and the point it is intended to establish; for it may be admissible for one purpose and not another.8 The object of tendering evidence is to ascertain whether the evidence is relevant for the purpose of determining the "facts in issue" or "relevant facts" in a particular case. If the real object of a judicial proceeding is to ascertain the existence of facts on which the existence of a right or liability is made, this fact may be given in evidence as a matter of course. Therefore, Section 5 should be read subject to the specific provisions governing admissibility enacted in other parts of the Evidence Act the facts connected in any of the ways mentioned in sections 6 to 25. Where a document consists of two separate parts, one of which is admissible and the other is inadmissible, the document cannot be rejected. The principle underlying in this case is that the recitals in the document which is admissible may be taken in evidence if the said recital is relevant for ascertaining the facts in issue.

The principle of law embodied in section 6 is usually known as the rule of res gestae recognized in English law. The essence of the doctrine is that a fact which, though not in issue, is so connected with the fact in issue "as to form part of the same transaction." If facts form part of the transaction which is the subject of inquiry, manifestly evidence of them should not be excluded. Such fact forming part of the res gestae should not be excluded without rendering the evidence unintelligible. Sections 6, 7, 8, 9 and 14 of the Evidence Act are treated under the heading res -gestae. It is, therefore, evident that it is an exception to the general rule that hearsay evidence is not admissible. Generally, if the fact is so connected to form part of the same transaction, the statement must have been made contemporaneously with the acts which constitute the offence or at least immediately thereafter. If there is an interval, it is enough for fabrication and then the statement is not part of the res gestae.

Stephen defines this term "as a group of facts so connected together as to be referred to by a single name, as a crime, a contract, a wrong or any other subject of inquiry which may be in issue. When facts though not strictly forming part of the same transaction may be so closely connected with it that they tend to prove or disprove or explain the transaction under inquiry. So, this provision embraces a large area of facts. A motive, preparation, the existence of a design or plan, the conduct of a party is continuance of a criminal action, but it is very difficult to prove them in precision. Section 8 states that the conduct whether previous or subsequent of any person of an offence who is the subject of an inquiry, if it is relevant and if the conduct influences or is influenced by any fact in issue or relevant fact. Normally, there is a motive behind every criminal act that is why the court while examining the complicity of an accused tries to ascertain as to what was the motive on the part of the accused to commit the crime in question.9

If a certain fact cannot co-exist with the performance of the act in question, and therefore if that fact is true of a person of whom the act is alleged, it is impossible that he should have done the act. The form sometimes varies from this statement; but its nature is the same in all forms. The consistency, to be conclusive in proof, must be essential, i.e. absolute and universal; but since in offering evidence, we are not required to furnish demonstration, only fair ground for inference, the fact offered need not have this essential or absolute inconsistency, but merely a probable or presumable inconsistency; and its evidentiary strength will increase with its approach to absolute or essential inconsistency. Section 8 declares admissible facts which are logically relevant to prove or disprove the main fact or fact in issue. The above ex-position clearly indicates the admissibility of collateral facts prove inconsistency, probability or improbability. There may be collateral facts which have no connection with the main fact except by way of disproving any material fact proved or ascertained by the other side, i.e. when they are such as make the existence of the fact so highly improbable as to justify the inference that it never existed. The language used in Section 11 of the Evidence Act appears to be a general rule. This provision should not be construed in its widest significance and as a rule. This section is controlled by section 32 of the Act where the evidence consists of statements of persons who are dead or cannot be found; but this rule is subject to certain exceptions. There is a difference between the existence of a fact and a statement as to its existence. This section makes admissible the existence of facts and not statements as to such existence, unless the fact of making that statement is a matter in issue.10

The consideration of a case upon evidence can seldom be satisfactory unless all the presumptions for and against a claim arising on all evidence offered or on proof withheld, in course of pleading and tardy production of important portions of claim, or defense, be viewed in connection with the oral or documentary proof which per se might suffice to establish it.11 Copies made from the original by mechanical processes which in themselves ensure the accuracy of the copy and copies compared with such copies refer to all copies made from the original by some mechanical process which ensures their accuracy. These are admissible in evidence.12 where a party can show that non-production was not due to his own default or neglect, secondary evidence would be admissible under this clause to adduce secondary evidence. It is not enough to show that the party who wants to use it cannot produce it because it was not registered.

The facts which are relevant to the fact in issue and describe the various ways in which facts though not in issue are so related to each other as to form components of the principal fact, i.e. as to form part of the same transaction. In determining the proximity of time; proximity or unity of place; continuity of action and community purpose or design may be taken in a wider prospective. The phrase "same transaction" occurs also in sections 235 and 239 of the Code of Criminal Procedure. Whether a series of acts are so connected as to form the part of the same transaction is purely a question of fact depending on proximity of time and place, continuity of action and unity of purpose and design. A comprehensive formula of universal application cannot be framed regarding the question whether two or more acts constitute the same transaction. The circumstances which must bear on its determination in each individual case are proximity of time, unity or proximity of place, continuity of action and community of purpose or design. A transaction may be a continuous one extending over a long period and two places. Therefore, the expression "part of the same transaction" must be understood as including both immediate cause and effect of an act or even also its co-location or relevant circumstances. I concluded my opinion that the confession of Mufti Hannan was admissible in evidence for ascertaining his complicity in the incident of killing.

References:

1. Mark Juergensmeyer, Terror in the mind of God: The Global Rise of Religious Violence (University of California Press 2003
2. Stephen in his Digest of the Law of Evidence
3. Section 80 of the Evidence Act

3(a). Proved (Ballentine's Law Dictionary).

4. Mirza Akbar v. King Emperor, AIR 1940 PC 176; Bhagwan S. Swarup v. State of Maharashtra, AIR 1965 SC 682; Zulfiqar Ali Bhutto v. State, PLD 1979 SC 53; State v. Nalini (1999) 5 SCC 283; and Bazlul Huda v. State 62 DLR(AD) 1
5. Civil Appeal Nos. 22-24 of 2010, Mobile Quader v. State
6. State of Maharashtra v. Kamal Ahmed Mohammad vakil Ansary, (2013) 12 SCC 17 and Gujrat v. Md Atique AIR 1998 SC 1686
7. Section 5 of the Evidence Act
8. Taylor v. Williams (1830) 2B & AD
9. Section 8 of the Evidence Act
10. Section 11 of the Evidence Act and Law of Evidence, Wigmore
11. Rajendra v. Sheopersun, 10M 1A (PC)
12. Section 63 of the Evidence Act

Chapter 22

Religion and Fundamentalism

People in Christian nations all over the world read not only the New Testament but also the Old Testament. The Old Testament contains the history of Israel and the teachings of numerous messiahs and prophets of that region. People in Christian nations study these so they strongly feel that they must preserve the nation of Israel and protect the teachings of God in the Old Testament. On the other hand, how do they regard Islam, which was propagated after Christianity? It is not that they do not recognize Islamic countries as valid societies and States. However, deep in their hearts, they strongly retain a belief that, from the perspective of their religious principles, Islam is a collection of teachings that are outdated.1

They do not say it outright. If they were to say that Islam represents the teachings of devils, Muslims would get furious. That would lead to more threats of multiple terrorist incidents. It is something people cannot say openly not only in Japan but in Christian nations too. There has been no decisive winner in the conflict, because the Christian civilization and the Islamic civilization, and despite three large wars during the Crusades, hostility continues to these days. From the viewpoint of Christian civilization, the Islamic world seems like a place where terrorism is rampant. Therefore, to suppress the roots of the terrorism, they believe they must not allow Islamic nations to obtain immense power. They think, "If we let Islamic countries to have nuclear weapons" what would we do when they commit terrorism with those nuclear weapons? That is why the US and UK are pushing the idea that it is acceptable for Israel to have nuclear weapons, but not the Islamic nations. However, this idea obviously comes from a sort of value judgment; a cultural value judgment influences it. Of course, it is debatable whether such a judgment is right or wrong. Israel is in a position where it could easily annihilate several hundred million Muslims surrounding it, but if these Muslims were to attack Israel they would immediately suffer a nuclear attack.2

The religions ideals of the future must embrace all that exists in the world and is good and great, and at the same time, have infinite scope for future development. All that was good in the past must be preserved; and doors must be kept open for future additions to the existing store. Religious ideals must become universal, vast and infinite. The power of religion, broadened and purified, is going to penetrate every part of human life. Through such a religion, humanity will worship at the altar of one universal divinity, at once transcendent and eminent, showering peace and blessedness on all.3

Early Buddhism reflected to some extent this philosophic and rational spirit of the Buddha, and its inquiries were based on experience. In the world of experience, the concept of a pure being could not be grasped and was therefore put aside; so also, the idea of a creator God, which was a presumption not capable of logical proof. Nevertheless, the experience remained and was real enough in a sense; what could this be except a mere flux of becoming, ever changing into something else? Hence these intermediate degrees of reality were recognized, and further inquiry proceeded on these lines on a psychological basis. Buddha, rebel as he was, hardly cut himself off from the ancient faith of the land. The difference between him and the other teachers lay chiefly in his deep earnestness and in his broad public spirit of philanthropy.

Yet Buddha had sown the seeds of revolt against the conventional practice of the religion of his day. It was not his theory or philosophy that was objected to---for every conceivable philosophy could be advocated within the fold of orthodox belief so long as it remained a theory---but the interference with the social life and organization of the people. So, inevitably, Buddhism tended to break away from the old faith, and, after Buddha's death, the breach widened.

With the decline of early Buddhism, the "Mahayana" form developed, the older form being known as the "Hinayana". It was in this Mahayana that Buddha was made into a god and devotion to him as a personal god developed. The Buddha image also appeared from the Grecian northwest. About the same time there was a revival of Brahmanism in India and of Sanskrit scholarship.

Between the Hinayana and the Mahayana there was bitter controversy and debate, and opposition to each other has continued throughout subsequent history. The Hinayana countries (Sri Lanka/Ceylon, Myanmar/Burma, and Thailand/Siam) even now rather look down upon the Buddhism that prevails in China and Japan, and I suppose this feeling is reciprocated.

Four definite schools of philosophy developed in Buddhism, two of these belonged to the Hinayana branch and two to the Mahayana. All these Buddhist systems of philosophy have their origin in the Upanishads, but they do not accept the authority of the Vedas. It is this denial of the Vedas that distinguishes them from the Hindu systems of philosophy which developed about the same time. These latter, while accepting the Vedas generally and, in a sense, paying formal obeisance to them, do not consider them as infallible, and indeed go their own way without much regard for them. As the Vedas and the Upanishads spoke with many voices, it was always possible for subsequent thinkers to emphasize one aspect rather than another, and to build their system on this foundation.

Professor Radhakrishnan3 (a) describes the logical movement of Buddhist thought as it found expression in the four schools thus. It begins with dualistic metaphysics looking upon knowledge as a direct awareness of objects. In the next stage ideas are made the media through which reality is apprehended, thus raising a screen between mind and things. These two states represent the Hinayana schools. The Mahayana school went further and abolished the things behind the images and reduced all experience to a series of ideas in their mind. The ideas of relativity and the sub-conscious self-come in. In the last stage--this was Nagarjuna's Madhyamika philosophy or the middle way--mind itself is dissolved into mere ideas, leaving us with loose units of ideas and perceptions about which we can say nothing definite.

In this way we arrive finally at airy nothing, or something that is so difficult to grasp for our finite minds that it cannot be described or defined. The most we can say is that it is some kind of consciousness--Vijayan as it is called. What was the effect of Buddha's teachings on the old Aryan religion and the popular beliefs that prevailed in India? There can be no doubt that they produced powerful and permanent effects on many aspects of religious and national life. Buddha may not have thought of himself as the founder of a new religion; probably he looked upon himself as a reformer only. But his dynamic personality and his forceful messages attacking many social and religious practices inevitably led to conflict with the entrenched priesthood. He did not claim to have been uprooted from the existing social order or economic system; he accepted their basic premises and only attacked the evils that had grown under them. Nevertheless, he functioned, to some extent, as a social revolutionary and it was because of this that he angered the Brahmin class who were interested in the continuance of the existing social practices. There is nothing in Buddha's teachings that cannot be reconciled with the wide range of Hindu thought. But when Brahmin supremacy was attacked it was a different matter. It is interesting to note that Buddhism first took root in Magadha, that part of northern India where Brahmanism was weak. It spread gradually west and north and many Brahmins also joined it. To begin with, it was essentially a Kshatriya movement but with a popular appeal. Probably it was due to the Brahmins, who later joined it, that it developed more, along chiefly to the Brahmin Buddhists that the Mahayana form developed; for, in some ways, and notably in its catholic variety, this was more akin to the varied form of the existing Aryan faith.

Buddhism influenced Indian life in a hundred ways, as it was bound to, for it must be remembered that it was a living, dynamic and widespread religion in India for over a thousand years. Even in the long years of its decline in India, and when it later practically ceased to count as a separate religion in South Asia, much of it remained as part of the Hindu faith and in the national ways of life and thought. Even though the religion as such was ultimately rejected by the people, the ineffaceable imprint of it remained and powerfully influenced the development of the race. This permanent

428

impact had little to do with dogma or philosophic theory or religious belief. It was the ethical and social and practical idealism of Buddha and his religion that influenced our people and left their imperishable marks upon them, as the ethical ideals of Christianity affected Europe though it may not pay much attention to its dogmas, and as Islam's human, social, and practical approach influenced many people who were not attracted by its religious forms and beliefs.

Much of the ritualism and ceremonials associated with the Vedic as well as more popular forms of religion, disappeared, particularly animal sacrifices. The idea of non-violence, already present in the Vedas and Upanishads, were emphasized by Buddhism and even more so by Jainism. There was a new respect for life and a kindness to animals. And always behind all this was the endeavor to lead the good life, the higher life.

Buddha had denied the moral value of austere asceticism. But the whole effect of his teaching was one of pessimism towards life. This was especially the Hinayana view and even more so that of Jainism. There was an emphasis on other-worldliness, a desire for liberation, of freedom from the burdens of the world. Sexual continence was encouraged, and vegetarianism increased. All these ideas were present in India before Buddha, but the emphasis was different. The emphasis of the old Aryan ideal was on a full and all-rounded life. The student stage was one of continence and discipline; the householder participated fully in life's activities and took sex as part of them. Then came a gradual withdrawal and a greater concentration on public service and individual improvement. Only the last stage of life, when old age had arrived, was that of sanyasi or full withdrawal from life's normal work and attachments.

Not only India but the whole of Central Asia had large numbers of huge Buddhist monasteries. There was a famous one in Balkh, accommodating 1,000 monks, of which we have many records. This was called Nava-vihara, the new monastery, which was Persianized into Nambiar. Probably at the time of the Buddha the Brahmins were the only more or less rigid caste. The Kshatriyas or the ruling class was proud of their group and family traditions but, as a class, their doors were open for the incorporation of individuals or families who became rulers. Of the remainder most were Vaishyas, agriculturists, an honored calling. There were other occupational castes also. The so-called caste-less people, the untouchables, appear to have been very few, probably some forest folk and some whose occupation was the disposal of dead bodies, etc.

The emphasis of Jainism and Buddhism on non-violence led to the tilling of the soil being considered a lowly occupation, for it often resulted in the destruction of animal life. This occupation, which had been the pride of the Indo-Aryans, went down in the scale of values in some parts of the subcontinent, despite its fundamental importance, and those who tilled the land descended in the social scale. Thus Buddhism, as a revolt against priest raft and ritualism and against the degradation of any human being and his deprivation of the opportunities of growth leading to a higher life, unconsciously led to the degradation of vast numbers of tillers of the soil. It would be wrong to make Buddhism responsible for this, for it had no such effect elsewhere. There was something inherent in the caste system which took it in this direction. Jainism pushed it along that way because of its passionate attachment to non-violence, and Buddhism also inadvertently helped in the process.

There was no side spread or violent extermination of Buddhism in India. Occasionally there were local troubles or conflicts between a Hindu ruler and the Buddhist Sangha or organization of monks, which had grown powerful. These usually had political origins and they did not make any essential difference. Hinduism was at no time wholly displaced by Buddhism. Even when Buddhism was at its height in India, Hinduism was widely prevalent. Buddhism died a natural death in India, i.e. the South Asian subcontinent; or rather it was a fading out and transforming into something else. India, says Keith, 3b has a strange genius of converting what it borrows and assimilating it. If that is true of borrowings from abroad or from allied sources, still more is this applicable to something that came out of its own mind and thought. Buddhism was not only entirely a product of India; its philosophy was in line with previous

Indian thought and the philosophy of the Vedanta (the Upanishads).

Brahmanism and Buddhism acted and reacted on each other and despite their dialectical conflicts, or because of them, approached nearer to each other, both in the realm of philosophy and popular belief. The Mahayana especially approached the Brahmanical system and forms. It was prepared to compromise with almost anything so long as its ethical background remained intact. Brahmanism made of Buddha an avatar, a God. So, did Buddhism itself. The Mahayana doctrine spread rapidly but it lost in quality and distinctiveness what it gained in extent. The monasteries became rich, centers of vested interests, and their discipline became lax. Magic and superstition crept into the popular forms of worship. Ibid

In India, says Havell, 3(C) religion is hardly a dogma, but a working hypothesis of human conduct, adapted to different stages of spiritual development and different conditions of life. A dogma might continue to be believed in, isolated from life, but a working hypothesis of human conduct must work and conform to life or it obstructs life. The very raisin d'ê·tre of such a hypothesis is its workableness, its conformity to life, and its capacity to adapt itself to changing conditions. So long as it can do so it serves its purpose and performs its allotted function. When it goes off at a tangent from the curve of life, it loses contact with social needs, and the distance between it and life grows--it loses all its vitality and significance.

Metaphysical theories and speculations deal not with the ever-changing stuff of life but with the permanent reality behind it, if such exists. Hence, they have a certain permanence which is not affected by external changes. But, inevitably, they are the products of the environment in which they grow and of the state of development of the human minds that conceived them. If their influence spreads they affect the general philosophy of life of a people. In India, philosophy, though in its higher reaches was confined to the elect, has been more pervasive than elsewhere and has had a strong influence in molding the national outlook and in developing a certain distinctive attitude of mind. Ibid

There is a common presumption in all of them: that the universe is orderly and functions according to law, that there is a mighty rhythm in it. Some such presumption becomes necessary, for otherwise there could hardly be any system to explain it. Though the law of causality, of cause and effect, functions, yet there is a measure of freedom to the individual to shape his own destiny. There is belief in rebirth and an emphasis on unselfish love and disinterested activity. Logic and reason are relied upon and used effectively for argument, but it is recognized that often intuition is greater than either. The general argument proceeds on a rational basis, in so far as reason can be applied to matters often outside its scope. Professor Keith has pointed out that the systems are indeed orthodox and admit the authority of the sacred scriptures, but they attack the problems of existence with human means, and scripture serves for all practical purposes but to lend sanctity to results which are achieved not only without its aid, but often in very dubious harmony with its tenets.

In his quotation Vincent Smith has used the words Hinduism and Hinduised. It is correct to use them in this way unless they are used in the widest sense of Indian culture. They are apt to mislead today when they are associated with a much narrower, and specifically religious, concept. The word Hindu does not occur at all in ancient literature. The first reference to it is in an Indian book, in a Tantric work of the eighth century AC, where Hindu means a people and not the followers of a religion. But the word is a very old one, as it occurs in the Avesta and in Old Persian. It was used then and for a thousand years or more by the peoples of western and central Asia for India, or rather for the people living on the other side of the Indus River. The word is clearly derived from Sindhu, the old, as well as the present, Indian name for the Indus. From this Sindhu came the words Hindu and Hindustan, as well as Indus and India.

The famous Chinese pilgrim I-tsing, who came to India in the seventh century A.C., writes in his record of travels that the northern tribes, that is the people of Central Asia, called India

Hindu (Hsin-tu) but, he adds, this is not at all a common name...and the most suitable name for India is the Noble Land (Aryadesha). The use of the word Hindu in connection with a religion is of very late occurrence. The old inclusive term for religion in India was Arya dharma. Dharma really means something more than religion. It is from the root word which means to hold together; it is the inmost constitution of a thing, the law of its inner being. It is an ethical concept which includes the moral code, righteousness, and the whole range of man's duties and responsibilities. Arya dharma would include all the faiths (Vedic and non-Vedic) that originated in India; it was used by Buddhists and Jains as well as by those who accepted the Vedas. Buddha always called his way to salvation the Aryan Path.

The expression Vedic dharma was also used in ancient times to signify more particularly and exclusively all those philosophies, moral teachings, ritual and practices, which were supposed to derive from the Vedas. Thus, all those who acknowledged the general authority of the Vedas could be said to belong to the Vedic dharma. Sanatana dharma, meaning the ancient religion, could be applied to any of the ancient Indian faiths (including Buddhism and Jainism), but the expression has been monopolized now by some orthodox sections among the Hindus who claim to follow the ancient faith.

Buddhism and Jainism were certainly not Hinduism or even the Vedic dharma. Yet they arose in India and were integral parts of Indian life, culture and philosophy. A Buddhist or Jain in India is a hundred percent product of Indian thought and culture. In later ages this culture was greatly influenced by the impact of Islam, and yet it remained basically and distinctively Indian. Today it is experiencing in a hundred ways the powerful effect of the industrial civilization, which rose in the west and it is difficult to say with any precision what the outcome will be.

Many Hindus look upon the Vedas as revealed scripture. This seems to me to be peculiarly unfortunate for thus we miss their real significance--the unfolding of the human mind in the earliest stages of thought. And what a wonderful mind it was! The Vedas (from the root vid, to know) were simply meant to be a collection of the existing knowledge of the day; they are a jumble of many things: hymns, prayers, ritual for sacrifice, magic, magnificent nature poetry. There is no idolatry in them; no temples for the gods. The vitality and affirmation of life pervading them are extraordinary. The early Vedic Aryans were so full of the zest for life that they paid little attention to the soul. In a vague way they believed in some kind of existence after death.

Gradually the conception of God grows: there are the Olympian type of gods, and then monotheism, and later, rather mixed with it, the conception of monism. Thought carries them to strange realms, brooding on nature's mystery, and the spirit of inquiry. These developments take place during hundreds of years, and by the time we reach the end of the Veda, the Vedanta (anta, meaning end), we have the philosophy of the Upanishads. The Rig Veda, the first of the Vedas, is probably the earliest book that humanity possesses. In it we can find the first outpourings of the human mind, the glow of poetry. Yet behind the Rig Veda itself lay ages of civilized existence and thought, during which the Indus Valley and the Mesopotamian and other civilizations had grown. It is appropriate, therefore, that there should be this dedication in the Rig Veda: To the Seers, our ancestors, the first path-finders!

These Vedic hymns have been described by Rabindranath Tagore as a poetic testament of a people's collective reaction to the wonder and awe of existence. A people of vigorous and unsophisticated imagination awakened at the very dawn of civilization to a sense of the inexhaustible mystery that is implicit in life. It was a simple faith of theirs that attributed divinity to every element and force of nature, but it was a brave and joyous one, in which the sense of mystery only gave enchantment to life, without weighing it down with bafflement--the faith of a race unburdened with intellectual brooding on the conflicting diversity of the objective universe, though now and again illumined by intuitive experience as: Truth is one; (though) the wise call it by various names.

During the first week of May 2013, a fanatic outfit Hefazate Islam gathered at the Shapla Chattar of Motijheel Commercial Area, Dhaka, with prior permission of the authorities for holding a religious meeting. But sometime thereafter their object and purpose found focus. The supporters of the outfit demonstrated violently encompassing the entire Motijheel area to Baitul Mokarram area, burnt valuable properties including those of floating street vendors selling religious books and burnt thousands of Qurans. None raised any objection about burning of the holy Quran. Although they claim that they are not a political organization, they organized themselves to protect "Islamic ideology". Prime Minister Sheikh Hasina commented on Saturday July 13, 2013 that Hefazate Islam Chief Allama Shafi's "comments on women" were disgusting and filthy. "I have been watching a statement of Shafi on TV for the last few days. I think his comments are extremely disgusting and dirty. Women have been given the maximum freedom and rights in Islam," she said.6 The Prime Minister made this remark while inaugurating 88 air-conditioned BRTC (Bangladesh Road Transport Corporation) buses at Ganabhaban in the morning. During the previous few days, suddenly a video clip where Allama Shah Ahmad Shafi appeared to deliver a sermon on women spread over the Internet and fueled censure by his critics. Hasina said, women's dress would depend on place, time and situation and none had the right to dictate that. "Does not he have sick a mother, sister and wife? We had to defend other mothers, sisters and wives." She added, "Islam is the religion of peace. Bibi Khadija was the first person to accept Islam, because no one was brave enough to do so. Shafi should have kept that in mind." Hasina further said, "Even Islam's first martyr was a woman--Bibi Sumaia." Hasina also criticized the BNP for patronizing the Hefazate Islam.7

State Minister for Women and Children Affairs Meher Afroz Chumki on Sunday described Hefazate Islam Ameer Allama Ahmed Shafi as a man of distorted mentality for his "derogatory and indecent remarks" about women. She saw while addressing a press conference at her office. Recently in the social media, a speech of Allama Shafi had been widely circulated, wherein he made some indecent remarks regarding women and likened them to mouth-watering tamarind (tetul). Voicing concern over Shafi's remarks the junior minister said, "By comparing women with tamarind he has humiliated not only the womenfolk but also his mother, wife, sister and daughter as well as menfolk." She said the anti-women remarks of the Hefazate have also defamed Islam as the religion has given all the rights to women to work and learn along with their male counterparts. "What Allama Shafi teaches the madrassa students is very clear from his remarks." Revealing that some two crore women are working in various sectors across the country and that they are successful in their respective fields, Chumki alleged that Hefazate Islam was trying to confine the women within the four walls as they want to turn the country into an Afghanistan or Pakistan. She also urged the people to protest the contemptuous remarks of the Hefazate chief. Replying to a query whether any legal action would be taken against Allama Shafi for his contemptible remarks, the state minister said, those who make remarks against the Constitution should be brought to justice. "I hope the government will look into the matter. As I'm also part of the government, action will be taken against him after discussion."8

The Prime Minister came down heavily on the Hefazate Islam leader Allama Shafi for his "derogatory and indecent remarks," saying, "One religious leader recently made some indecent remarks about women. I'm totally confused how a religious leader could utter such indecent remarks when Islam showed highest respect for women." Regarding remarks of Allama Shafi about women leadership, the Prime Minister said, women's dress would depend on place, time and situation and none has the right to dictate that. "We have to defend the honor of our mothers-sisters-wives. Islam is the religion of peace. Bibi Khadiza is the first person to accept Islam, because no one else was brave enough to do so. Shafi should have kept it in mind." Hasina said, "Even Islam's first martyr was a woman- Bibi Sumaiya," added.10 She also said that it was the people who will decide their leadership. But, she said, her party always believes in decency of dressing. Meanwhile, irked by "unnecessary, criticism, Prime Minister Sheikh Hasina said on Saturday that she will go for a tit-for-tat policy against those criticizing the government relentlessly over the quick rental power issue." The PM said, "She and her party always believe in decency of clothes. Let the holy Ramadan be over, let the holy Eid pass be, I'll do that I'll do that after open declaration." Describing what will be the tit-for-tat policy, Hasina said the government will stop the production of power after the generation of 3200 MW of power. "The present government has inherited this level of power generation from the BNP-jamaat alliance whine it came to power in 2009. She went on; "I think, we will go for that decision, it'll help people to realize what the present government does for power generation."

Earlier a YouTube video clip of Hefazate Islam Chief Shah Shafi created much outrage on social network sites. In the video, Shafi told his followers not to educate girls after primary level, to keep them at home and not to let women become financially independent. Shafi justified the rampant incidents of sexual harassment and violence against women, saying such things would keep happening as long as they go outside of their homes, either for studies, work or shopping. When contacted for comments the secretary general of the groups, Junayed Babunagori said the video was "fabricated." He claimed that the video was a plot to disgrace Shafi. "He never preached any such sermon," Babunagori added. However, in the video Shafi's lips are in sync with the audio. It has not been identified when, where the Hefazate leader delivered the sermon. One Akash Malik uploaded the video on July 6. According to the scroll information, it was distributed by Al-Arab Enterprise, 46 Madrassa Market, and Hathazari in Chittagong. Shafi in the lecture said his statements were quoted from the Quran and that he was following the directives of Almighty Allah. He Quoted Surah Ahazab. "The Quran says: you (women) should stay at your home --- your duty is to stay at the husband's house and safeguard property. Your primary duty is to stay and look after your family and children only, do no go out even for shopping." Shafi asked the men to educate girls only up to Class four or five. He said the girls need only that much education just to be able to handle the accounts of their husbands' earnings. Quoting the same verse from the Quran, a legal expert of the Islamic foundation, Mufti Abdullah said; "The Quran does not prohibit women from going outside. It just tells women to be decent."

Shafi is the principal of Hathazari Al Jamayetul Ahlya Harul Ulum Moynul Islam, the madrassa that provides Qawmi certificates. Formed in 2010, Hefazat's development at education policies terming them "Anti-Islamic." Hefazat resurfaced in February this year "to protect Islam from the hands of atheists" particularly those who were leading a mass movement against the war criminals at Shah Bagh in Dhaka and elsewhere. Hefazate Islam placed a 13-point list of demands that included the formulation of a blasphemy law to execute those who demean Islam, and imposing restrictions on the mingling of men and women in public. When the demands spurred public rage, Hefazate revised its demand centering women. They said they were not against women leaving their homes or working. But wanted them to wear veils and walk decently. Bangla blogs on social media were very critical and vocal on the issue. Several women's rights group and activists protested the Hefazat's remarks. In most Islamic "waaz" (religious lectures), clerics explain the Quran and Hadiths to the audience, most of whom are illiterate Muslims. In some cases, they also speak against women's current lifestyle seen mainly in the urban areas. Many people who spoke against Shafi's remarks demanded that he be punished for presenting a "wrong expiations of the Quran" and demeaning women. Some asked the government and Islamic scholars to clarify Shafi's comments. "Irrespective of one's sexual identity, education or profession, being knowledgeable is a priority in the Quran and these so-called Islamic preachers are portraying Islam in a wrong way." said the Facebook status. An organizer of "Bangladesh for One Billion Rising," a worldwide campaign against violence against women, Trimita, pointed out that the speech was nothing but "a mockery to Islam." In the clip, Shafi also raised the issue of working women's character, saying families where both the husband and wife earn an income could not be united because of those women who "earn money through adultery."11 The way Ahmad Shafi misquoted the Quran to abuse and denigrate women is repulsive. The Quran does not exhort women to stay at home and "not even to go for shopping." Contrary to Shafi's fabrication, the Quran nowhere urges men to take four wives or even justifies--let alone encourage--polygamy. Shafi's promotion of patriarchy particularly in the name of religion is as old as civilization. Pre-modern societies in history---Pagan,

438

Jewish, Christian, Hindu, Muslim and others---almost invariably promoted patriarchy by demonizing women. As Aristotle did not believe women had souls, so did many medieval Christian priests. Biblical texts, Jewish and Christian clerics, Hindu sages and monks, Muslim priests and philosophers also portrayed women as sub-human. While Saint Clement of Alexandria (150-215 AD) thought "every woman should be felt with shame by the thought that she is a woman" we find women being denigrated as "the devil's gateway" and "the root of all evil" in Christian texts; and as an object of sex or Raman "hence the pejorative "Ramani" in Sanskrit and Sanskrit based languages. Writings by some Muslim scholars are full of misogynic prescription. However, unlike the post- Renaissance and post-enlighten societies in the west, many Muslim societies are not enlightened enough to accept women as human beings deserving equal rights or opportunities. Extra- and un-Islamic practices and beliefs have crept into some Muslim societies. Although Bangladeshi women have better rights and opportunities than what their counterparts enjoy in Afghanistan and Pakistan, some clerics are against raising their voice against women's liberation and equal rights and opportunities guaranteed by the constitution. Sheikh Hasina abruptly made a U turn and when handing over of "Agartala Conspiracy case Record" in Ganabhaban stated to me that how much money she spent towards calming and bringing the followers of Hafazate in her lines of thinking? I was not prepared to hear such remarks from her lips. The issue was discussed between us was about combating terrorism in the country. She made the above comment in reply to my apprehension. I realized that all politicians of underdeveloped countries goal are almost same: though they speak about welfare of the people, their main motto are how to come to power and then to consolidate it by any means at the cost of public exchequer.

The prevalent chaos, corruption and political uncertainty in the fractured and over-polarized country have facilitated the rise of Islamist forces not long after the government's "decisive victory" against the anarchist JMB and HUJI (B) in 2006. In some leaders and their followers are collectively responsible for the disorder at the macro and micro levels. Firstly, the government and people promote three types of education--English, Bengali and Islamic--

and produce unemployable and under-employable graduates out of reach, not-so-rich and poor families. This discriminatory education has also polarized Bangladesh society between the disempowered masses and the dominant elites. The system has created social envy "vernacular elites" towards the western elites (as Oliver Roy has coined the expression), precipitating the clash of cultures and interests between people having different world visions, philosophies and interests. It is time that Bangladesh addressed its lopsided education policy for the sake of equal opportunity for all citizens. Most importantly, only modern, secular and job-oriented education can contain Islamic obscurantism and tyranny. Secondly, along with bad governance and unaccountability, both the military and the "democratic" governments since the 1970s had tolerated and even promoted political Islam.

As General Ziaur Rahman legitimized Islamic parties, so did military dictator H.M. Ershad, to legalize their rule by exploiting the religious sentiments of most of the population. The BNP under Khaleda Zia and AL under Sheikh Hasina have not lagged far behind in this regard. The successive AL and BNP governments not only failed to remove the unconstitutional amendment to the Constitution that had declared Islam as the "State Religion", but also nurtured political Islam and forged politically expedient electoral alliances with reactionary Khelafat Majlish, Jamaat-i-Islami and other Islamist groups. Surprisingly, some former "secular' and "socialist" politicians have also been serving political Islam since August 1975. Liberal democratic politicians in Bangladesh should have learned from the bad example of Pakistan, where another General Ziaul Haq started Islamizing the polity.

Finally, it is time to call a spade a spade. Political Islam in Bangladesh is not dead; it is only dormant. It must be addressed, not exploited politically. Bangladeshi leaders and people must realize that the Hefazate and Jamaat are the two sides of the same coin. Despite their mutual differences these undemocratic, fascistic, pre-modern forces can unite to the detriment of freedom, democracy, rights of women, minorities and liberal Muslims. It is distressing that so far only a handful of human rights and women's rights groups, along with the Awami League, have condemned the

"Allama" for his misogynist expositions. The BNP and all democratic forces should come forward to contain political Islam, so that Bangladesh does not experience a clash of democratic and obscurantist forces in the long run.12

In most developed countries the ideal of life is to receive education, acquire skills, take up a profession and be successful in society. The Almighty has been eliminated from State activities. And religion has been thrown out of education, under the pretext of making education academic. But in most underdeveloped countries, a totally reverse philosophy has been chosen by the authorities in power. Taking advantage of faulty laws, absence of rule of law and inadequacy in administration of justice people extract opportunities of making their fortunes by smuggling or by evasion of tax or by any other means, fair or foul. Politicians are power mongers and they want to achieve power by hook or crook. As a result, their main object is to continue in power ignoring the country's development and the welfare of the people. They utter good words for the people which they themselves do not believe. They travel abroad on the excuse of official programs at the expense of the public exchequer, often in the name of education, training and so on. But instead they buy expensive things they see in those countries thus wasting the entire public fund.

In Japan, the Ministry of Education, Culture, Sports, Science and Technology does not approve the establishment of a science university saying, "A university will be approved only if it teaches a curriculum that fits within the current academic standard." I cannot approve a curriculum "That is based on spiritual messages." Spiritual messages that are received by those from heaven or high spirits, but it is not academic study. Our case is totally different. For example our education curriculum and the universities are based in the name of religion. I believe total human destruction would be because of religion. That is why Dawkins12 (a) wrote: "What a relief it would really be if religion vanished from this world." He is skeptical that religion has any survival value, contending that its cost in blood and guilt outweighs any conceivable benefits. Russel thought "the universe is just there, and that's all."

How civilization is threatened by religion or is likely to be devastated by religion will be evident from some examples. Sri Lanka and Thailand are still adhering to Theravada Buddhism which has existed for 2000-2500 years now. On the other hand, Mahayana Buddhism is practiced in Japan, Myanmar and some other small countries. The difference is on the issue of "reincarnation" of Buddha. More specifically, whether Buddha would enter Nirvana or not. One group of followers say there is misinterpretation in the teachings of Buddhism. Now the question is who will awaken them to the truth? If you come to rectify one school of thought, there would be tussle from the other group. There is conflict between Christianity and Islam. Even in Islam there about 68 sects. Of them, the major fight is among Sunni, Shia, Qadiani, Bahai, Kurds, etc. There is also stark difference between Islam and Judaism. They were founded a long time ago in different places and their ideas and beliefs differ. One group does not believe in the existence of the other group. There is also conflict between Hinduism and Islam. One wants to dominate the other depending upon the locality and population. There are also differences among the schools of thought in Christianity. I believe--and millions of people like me believe-the preachers of these religions arrived from time to time for the welfare of the people. They propagated human values, civilization, peace, prosperity, control, cruelty and hatred in them. They spoke about values of humanity, but we misinterpreted their sermons for our self-interest.

In monotheistic religions such as Islam, Christianity and Judaism do not always play top priority in human life. In these religions, people believe that the Almighty comes before humans and thus God has the right to punish or reward human beings. So, they believe that God rewards people when they act correctly but punishes them when they do wrong deeds. There was mass killing of millions of people in Europe over religion in medieval period and thereafter they separated religion from politics. Now there is no conflict between different sects of Christianity. In England there is a blasphemy law, but we do not find any victimization of minorities at the hands of the majority. It is only because the State does not tolerate religious excesses or religious domination by the majority and instead gives priority to democracy and rule of law over religion. Similar is the case in respect of Europe except Turkey.

The US was founded on religious values. Significantly the Declaration of Independence states: "We hold these truths to be self-evident, that all men are created equal, that they are endowed by their Creator with certain unalienable rights that among these are life, liberty and the pursuit of Happiness." It is now a great democracy: after India there is rule of law, human rights and values are safeguarded. Even then President Barrack Obama had to declare in his inaugural address, "We are a nation of Christians, and Muslims, Jews and Hindus and non-believers." He stressed human values, equality, and equal treatment of all citizens and true prosperity of democracy from the religious rights. In recent days fewer people in the US are following the Christian religion and instead they give precedence to human rights, human values, maintenance of rule of law. It is evident on Sundays that mostly elderly people attend churches while few members of the younger generation go to church. As a result, many churches are being closed. In recent times in Paterson, New Jersey, three churches were sold to an organization named Muslim Ummah of North America and those were converted to mosques. Besides, a convent located at Woodland Park, New Jersey, on 60 acres of land has been sold as the nuns were not able to maintain it and now the place is being used by Berkeley College. Tolerance is the virtue of a human being and minus toleration a human is inhumane.

Now there is unprecedented terrorism over religious supremacy. ISIS, an offshoot of Al-Qaeda, invaded Iraq, Syria and Libya and took possession of huge chunks of land, declaring a Caliphate and Shariah law. This led to tragic refugee crises across the Middle East spreading all the way to Europe. Most people in underdeveloped and developed countries in general believe in spiritual Devine, the leaders of these countries do not express their opinion clearly and instead keep silent. People in developed countries with a scientific background deal with things of the world, like material and physical substances. They spend years together investigating things that can be seen with the naked eyes, they sometimes forget about invisible. Science has rapidly developed in the past two centuries.

Many citizens in modern developed countries consider religion and science antagonistic. A good number of people who abhor religion believe that religions are the cause of many wars. Actually, war occurs due to the rigid and intolerant thinking of some religious zealots. This way of thinking that human beings are built up over time and each religion is unable to revise its original teachings. Hence religions should be isolated from State activities and politics. It should be kept personal and individual. In this context I may mention the issue of installation of symbol of Justice in front of the Supreme Court building which attracted much criticism from a fanatic section of people. Justice is the legal or philosophical theory by which fairness is administered. An early theory of justice was set out by the ancient Greek philosopher Plato in his work The Republic. About ninety percent of judges was in favor of it being there. As Chief Justice I talked to each judge when I raised this point in the Full Court when only a few—maybe 5 or 6 senior judges--started murmuring about the issue and I stopped the discussion realizing their attitude.

Thereafter, considering the religious sentiment, I directed the sculpture be made in such a manner that the dignity of our culture is maintained. The Prime Minister's Office issued a letter regarding the sculpture. I was so surprised on receipt of the letter. The Judiciary is an organ of the State, not a department of the government. The letter indicated that the law and order might deteriorate because of the sculpture. Before writing the letter, the Prime Minister should have at least talked with the Chief Justice or her Principal Secretary should have talked with the Registrar General. Instead the Prime Minister's Office treated the Supreme Court as a department of the government. It was both a shameful and very much disgraceful action. I did not even feel it proper to reply. However, some senior judges pointed out that religious people may take exception when they will gather at the national Eidgah for saying prayers during Eid-ul Fitr and Eid-ul-Azha.

With a view to avoid such controversy, with an aching heart, I decided to shift Justitia and place it in front of the annexed court building. It was most surprising that the Prime Minister made comments remarking the Greek sculpture was an idol and she did not find any reason for having it. If a Prime Minister of a secular State treats a sculpture as an idol I have nothing to say in this regard; but the fact was, it was a symbol of justice in the form of a woman. It occurred to me, how being a woman herself, the Prime Minister could make such absurd comments about the likeness of another woman. There are so many sculptures in and around the University of Dhaka and lately the Election Commission planted a sculpture in front of its new building. No religious people seem to have objected to it.

Hefazate Islam chief along with some of his leaders met the Prime Minister on April 12, 2017. From the newspaper reports I came to know that the government had decided to give recognition to the certificate of Dawrae Hadith under Qaumi Madrassa Education Board as equivalent to master's degree in Islamic Studies and Arabic. If we continue to compromise with education for political reasons, it will cause disastrous consequences to the nation. There is no doubt that education is a fundamental human right, but the question is what type of education we should give to our next generation. It is also correct that across the world some children are more likely to miss on education than others. That deprivation has lifelong consequences that often mean that the next generation, too, will start out at a disadvantage. The resulting cycles of inequality and deprivation thwart the potential of both individuals and societies.

It is not enough to get children to schools; we also need to ensure that they learn to read, count and acquire the necessary life skills. Good teachers are essential to solving the crisis of inadequate learning and closing the gap between the poor and good quality education. It is therefore vital that all children have teachers who are well-trained, motivated and able to identify weak learners and are supported by well-managed education systems. Poor quality of education has serious negative impacts on children's learning. Leadership, vision and professional learning and development that contribute to high quality in some services are lacking or ineffective in poor quality services. Poorly resourced or unsafe learning environments and inappropriate teaching practices are factors in poor quality education and care.

How quality education given to a child in a developed country makes a difference is evident from my own experience. I took Tuni, aged 8, my beloved grand-daughter, for an evening walk near her house in Brisbane. Suddenly I had to cough, and some phlegm got to my throat. I spat the mucus beside the sidewalk on the grass. She was greatly surprised at my conduct and advised me not to repeat it on the road anywhere else. She emphasized that it is unhygienic and illegal and that I should keep a napkin in my pocket in case of such a necessity. It made me feel ashamed, but I also realized simultaneously the quality of education imparted to children there.

A few weeks ago, I saw the photo of the newly sculpted representation of Justitia in Dhaka University. There is something different about the depiction of Lady Justitia that stands in front of the Supreme Court. The universal picture of Lady Justitia is embedded in our minds. Her gown clad blindfolded statue holds a sword and scales in her hands. The description is quintessentially Greek for it stands as the Greek Goddess Themis, an allegorical embodiment of the moral force in judicial system. However, the sculpture on our court premises is covered in a sari, transforming her into a Bangladeshi prototype of Themis. There is a bold message resonating within it and hopefully I am not reading too much into it. I would like to comment everyone involved in it letting this sculpture go up in the same time when our education Board was busy to taking us backgrounds by responding to the demands from few religious groups.

They are now protesting to get Lady Justitia removed from the court premises. Some are questioning the rationality of a female representation of justice. Adding an ingenious point of need for gender equality in the justice system, they are asking why there would only be the sculpture of a female and not of a male too. It is well settled that the universal exemplification of morality in the judicial system is done through a woman named Justitia and we simply have abided by that. It may be pointed out that the front of Iran's top Shariah Court has a sculpture of Justitia. The Indian Supreme Court has also installed Lady Justitia in Indian attire. When we have dressed Lady Justitia in our own cultural tradition it looked ugly to someone. How funny!

There are currently less than seven percent female judges in the Supreme Court. The legal profession is highly arduous; the formative years require putting in long hours and doing the best for the seniors. It was quite logically perceived that female newcomers would be unable to put in the same number of hours as her male counterpart due to familial and societal constraints. Therefore, given the choice between a qualified female newcomer and a less qualified male one, most chambers would probably opt for the latter. The number of female law students who graduate never materialize in the same percentage in the profession. But female representation is of extraordinary significance especially when viewed against the backdrop of Santa Clara Superior Court Judge Aaron Persky's too lenient a sentence for rape accused Brock Turner13 which created a public uproar. Moreover, the US President had signed an executive order relating to women's reproductive health without any female representation. The defense to rape even in the UK, i.e. "belief in consent" is a carefully nurtured loophole in a system run by men. And finally, the infamous "Two-Finger Test" for rape identification in Bangladesh (lately declared illegal by the Supreme Court) used to put the victims under unnecessary physical violation after she had allegedly already gone through the ordeal of rape.

This brings me back to our representation of Themis. She is the epitome of our own homegrown feminism which has never bothered about any waves; it has simply been based on pulling women up in the socio-economic and political hierarchy. So, while we see a flicker of hope in the masterwork of sculptor Mrinal Haque, it shakes the interests of a few religious groups. They have had their way in injecting patriarchal norms in children's minds, now they are demanding to get the sculpture removed. To that I would like to say in the same manner as my favorite pop culture icon, the Notorious Ruth Bader Ginsberg, Associate Justice of the Supreme Court of the United States, I dissent.14 Toleration emerges because of ideas central to dominant philosophical and religious doctrines and practices; not as an antidote to them.15

We do not take lessons from Europe and America even after nearly fifty years of independence. We should not give importance to religion in the affairs of State. Not one single religion should be accorded special privileges in national life or international relation because that would be violation of the principles of democracy and the spirit of our Constitution. "No group of citizens shall arrogate to itself right and privileges which it denies to others. No person should suffer from any form of disability or discrimination because of his religion. But all alike should be free to share the fullest degree in the common life. This is the basic principle involved in the separation of church and state. The religious impartiality of the Indian State is not to be confused with secularism or atheism. Secularism as here defined is in accordance with the ancient religious traditions of India. It tries to build up a fellowship of believers, not by surrounding individual qualities to the group mind but by bringing them into harmony with each other. The dynamic fellowship is based on the principle of diversity in unity which alone has the quality of creativeness".16

The basis for human rights stands in a variety of relationships to national security and human security. If security itself is conceived as a universal individual right, the foundation of counter-terror would be the protection of the individual from both external fears and State violence. A broader notion of national security that includes the State's responsibility to ensure and provide security to its citizens implies more rights. Since terrorism is represented as a total fact to the existence of democratic societies, unilateral and preemptive actions are justified as a defense both against the hegemon and for the stability of the world order. Such perspectives are usually coupled with a reading with terrorism as war, an assertion that the threat is unprecedented and a description of strategic scenarios in which intelligence is paramount to the survival of the political order. Now it is believed by the general citizenry that acts of terrorism should be considered acts of war at the international level, and terrorists forfeit both national and humanitarian protection as enemies of mankind meriting universal prosecution by any means necessary. The ever-increasing global danger of terrorism needs stringent laws which give extraordinary powers to the law enforcement agencies. In the US President Clinton enacted the "Anti-Terror and Effective Death Penalty Act". In Bangladesh the "Santras Birodhi Ain, 2009" (Anti-Terrorism Act 2009) and "Aparadh Samporkito Bishoye Parosporik Sohayata Ain" 2012" (Criminal Related Mutual Cooperation Act, 2012) were enacted. In India there are laws like TADA and POTA. Many stringent laws to combat terrorism have been enacted conferring wide powers to the law enforcement agencies in many countries of the globe.

The most extensive domestic impact on human rights arising from the counter- terror priority after 9/11 in the US took the form of a very comprehensive legislation, namely the Patriot Act. The Patriot Act gives the government wide powers with serious potential of abuse alarming civil libertarians especially as the authority has applied it to immigrant suspects to detain them secretly without charges for a long period of time. Canada adopted its first "National Security Policy" in 2004 crafted to reflect the balance between the need for national security and the protection of old Canadian values of openness, diversity and respect for civil liberties. The alternative of combating terrorism under existing laws followed by Germany has caused debate among liberal democracies.

When the French revolutionaries stormed the Bastille, overthrew the monarchy and church, remade the calendar and executed royal and elite descendants by the thousands for the sake of a new, blank slate for humanity, Anglo-American conservative Edmund Burke felt-first of all-grief. His primary impulse was to mourn what was lost. He mourned it even though it was not his. This was not the same as defending the old order, which was, in many ways, indefensible as Burke conceded. It was simply to remind his fellow humans that society is complicated, that its structure developed not by accident but by evolution that even the most flawed bonds that tie countless individuals are not to be casually severed for the sake of inchoate ideas. Even people and societies with deeply wounded past with histories that cry out for renewal and reform, are nonetheless the products of exactly that past. They can never be wiped clean, born again, remade overnight. Even radical change requires a reckoning with the past if it is to graft successfully onto a human endeavor on life. Living in the present cannot mean being oblivious to one's own history. It means living through and beyond that history.17

If that is a conservative insight, it presses more powerfully than ever today. If the essence of conservatism is conserving, then our current moment is an extremely unnerving one. In the 21st Century, the pace of change can at times seem overwhelming. Quantum Leaps in technology have transformed how we communicate with one another and expanded everyone's access to an endless array of life possibilities. Fundamentalism means adherence to the external thought and fate. You could call secular fundamentalism ideologies. You could call religious fundamentalism the moment a living fate becomes an ideology, a doctrine; but the pattern of thought is the same. The truth embraced by fundamentalists encompasses everything. It is a total truth. It informs us not merely about the origin of the universe or what happens to us when we die, but if we follow its inexorable logic, what we are supposed to do today, in the next half hour, and tomorrow, and the next day and the next are all predetermined. In its more neurotic forms it encompasses not merely basic virtues, but even the minutiae of personal hygiene, diet, clothing, facial hair, etc. As Pascal put it: when one must have abandoned human reason to seek the deeper reason accessible only by fate. Or as the current Pope has said: "Without the light of Christ, the light of reason is not sufficient to enlighten humanity and the world."18 Ibid

For many, this kind of religious fate seems to be a form of suffocation. They observe the adherence of fundamentalist fate and they are baffled by the way in which a text or a Pope or a Mullah can determine how a person acts, thinks or even feels. Or it seems as if this State of religion been requiring some sudden 'leap' i.e. inaccessible to non-believers of beyond their understanding. God made man? An individual who lived to millennia ago being vivid in a modern person's existence, these are more engaged questions. How could a fundamentalist Jew really believe that eating an oyster will render him moral outcast? How can a Muslim blame and punish the victims of rape rather than the perpetrators? How can an Orthodox Catholic believe as a matter of infallible doctrine that the woman who conceived Jesus did not die but was physically lifted of the ground and whisked vertically above the clouds? These practices and beliefs seem odd, even unhinged to many non-believers. At the very least, they seem to imply a life half-lived, or vicariously lived, a form of oppression from without or within, an extreme difference to something inherently unknowable as if it were fully known.19 Ibid

Fundamentalism, by contrast, purposefully and relentlessly forces an unalterable, precise, external truth into the center of a person's life and demands complete obedience to it. Its core is not the individual conscience, but God himself, and the decision of the individual to surrender himself to God entirely as the premise of every action he commits and every decision he makes. When you read the text of Islamic or Christian or Jewish fundamentalists, you see references to God in almost every sentence, every thought, every argument.20 Ibid

Total purity for the world to exist in fact exactly as it exists in a book often requires mass murder and when asked to defend the worst excesses the fundamentalists can always cite the Danger of the Devil. That Devil is international Jewry, Christian infidels, Papist heresy, secular humanism, bourgeois contortions, Zionism, homosexual lifestyle, interracial marriage and so on. Take any kind of fundamentalism and you will find a Satan somewhere. The living rebukes to Holy Truth lay behind the massacre of September 11, 2001. The theology of Al-Qaeda-and it is unmistakably a theology-regards the mere existence of non-Muslims as an affront to eternal truth. This affront is made doubly offensive by the fact that the infidels so clearly prospered, while the faithful have languished. The free and vibrant societies of the West, with their market capitalism and religious pluralism appear to the latest adherence of Muslim fundamentalist paranoia as symbols of Satan.

These Satanic forces have so much power that they contaminate Muslim regimes in the Middle East and, worst of all, they help protect the Jewish people on land claimed by Islam.

Think of how the strictest of Wahhabis must see New York City: full of Jews living peacefully with Muslims, of gays with protected freedom, women able to pursue their dreams of happiness independent of male permission. It is a veritable Sodom. And the more beleaguered the Islamic fundamentalist feels the more violent he gets.21 Ibid Fundamentalists view religious idealism as the basis of personal and communal identity. They understand truth to be revealed and unified. That revealed and unified truth is internationally shocking-the more outlandish it may appear, the central to the truth it probably is. They see themselves as part of a cosmic struggle; view their political and cultural opponents as agents of evil; and envy the success of modern materialism.

Gorenberg notices Bin Laden's confidence in his 1998 statement: "We are sure of Allah's victory and our victory against the American and the Jews as promised by the Prophet (peace be upon Him); 'Judgment Day' shall not come until the Muslims fight the Jews, where the Jews hide behind trees and stone, and the tree and the stone will speak and say, Muslim, behind me is a Jew. Come and kill him."22 When asked to sum up his message Osama Bin Laden could not have been clearer: "Our call is the call of Islam that was revealed by Muhammad," he said. "It is a call to all mankind. We have been entrusted with good cause to follow in the footsteps of the Messenger and to communicate His Message to all nations," he said, it is a religious war against "unbelieve and unbelievers."23

The use of religion for extreme repression or even terror is not restricted to Islam. For most of its history, Christianity has had a worse record. From the Crusades to the Inquisition to the bloody religious wars of the 16th and 17th centuries, Europe saw far more blood spilled for religion's sake than the Muslim world's deeds and given how expressly non-violent the teachings of the Gospel are, the extremism of Christian fundamentalism in this respect was arguably more striking than Bin Laden's fundamentalist version of

Islam. Ibid Recently, American Evangelism tended to keep some distance from governmental power. The Christian separation between what is God's and what is Caesar's--drawn from the Gospels – helped restrain the inexorable theological logic of fundamentalism in America for a long time. The last few decades have proved the exception. As modernity advanced and the certitudes of fundamentalist fate seemed mocked by an increasingly liberal society, Evangelicals mobilized and entered politics. Their fate and zeal sharpened the temptation to fuse political and religious authority beckoned more insistently. The result is today's Republican Party, perhaps the first religious political party in American history.

A conservative, by contrast, will be skeptical of believers of fundamentalist and socialist ideology arguments. He will want to know from the fundamentalist who exactly came up with this "good." He will ask why he should adhere to a view of virtue which is deduced from a religion he does not share or from a "nature" he does not recognize as his own. He will ask the socialist why he is being forced to give up his own money and property for the sake of an idea of substantive equality that sounds like a surreal fantasy to him. Who guarantees either versions--that of the virtuous or that of the substantively equal? And who says what virtue is? And by whose standard do we judge substantive equality? If inequality remains after redistribution, what then? And, moreover, how do we control a State that has the power to divest me of my income and wealth and property? The conservative will just be asking the question; and will refuse to give up his freedom until he gets an answer that satisfies his skeptical soul. This is to say, he will never stop asking. And so, a political project based on virtue or substantive equality can never get started. Ibid

For conservatism's deepest roots lie in doubt; without doubt, conservatism would have little to offer the modern world. If it were just another ideology, another system of thought vying for public attention and support, it would have simply joined the queue. You want politics that will end all existential alienation? Become a communist. You want politics that will redistribute and promise social justice and inclusion? Become a socialist. You want politics that rests its defense of inalienable human rights on God-given liberty? Become a liberal. You want politics that affirms divine truth in its governance of human affairs? Visit Iran. The radical alternative to all these options is conservatism. As politics, its essence is an acceptance of the unknowability of the ultimate truth, an acknowledgement of the distinction between truth forever and what is truth for here and now, and an embrace of the discrepancy between theoretical and practical knowledge. Ibid

Robert George23 (a) argues that "there can be no legitimate claim for secularism to be a 'neutral' doctrine that deserves a privileged status in the national public philosophy." The words insisting here the proper meaning of secularism. It is not anti-religious, as is now often claimed. Definitional secularism merely argues that public institutions and public law be separated from religious dogma or dictates. A secular society can be one in which large minorities of people have deep religious faith, but in which politics deals with laws that are, as far as possible, indifferent to the convictions of citizens, and clearly separated from them. Some evangelical Christians have thrived under secularism. Think of the astonishing career of someone like Billy Graham, a man who sought to bring millions to a fundamentalist faith but who did not construct a political movement as such. Or think of the work of a group like the Salvation Army that, in a secular society, channels fundamentalist faith into social action and helps so many people in real need. In fact, the premise of secular neutrality is precisely what the christianistic right now disagrees with. Senator Rick Santorum affirms, "I don't want a government that is neutral between virtues and vice." Elsewhere Santorum writes that the defenders of secularism "are trying to instill a different moral vision--one that elevates the self, the arbitrary the individual good, above all else. And frankly, this moral vision amounts to nothing less than a new religion. A polytheistic one in which each individual is to be his own God to be worshiped." For Santorum, the alternative to politics responsive to one God is politics responsive to many, with no mechanism to distinguish between them.24

Left fundamentalists also discount the whole idea of government neutrality and want to use government power and the law to insist on their own values; racial justice, enforced tolerance, direct public funding of deeply controversial areas like abortion and the use of public schools to inculcate the dogmas of multi-culturist in children. For the fundamentalist left it is a masked design to observe obscure systematic oppression of various kinds; for the fundamentalist right, it is a shame created to obscure a secular `humanist' agenda.

The presumption that law and religion are, in many ways, motivated by the same values is an understandable one. After all there is widespread belief that the law is primarily in the business of seeking out truths and revealing the just path. Its task is to do what's fair and what's right. Judges hand down judgment and make hard decisions. These decisions make sense, but they should feel right emotionally and morally to those not only at the receiving end of the judgment, but to the rest of the citizenry, the outside witnesses of these private proceedings. This expectation of fairness, wisdom and justice is precisely what draws people to the laws in the first place--the desire for a just resolution to a conflict that simply can't be mediated elsewhere.

In religion on the other hand, most people attend churches, mosques, synagogues and temples in search of moral and spiritual guidance, among other things. They want to expand their moral vision and consciousness, wishing to anchor themselves temporarily to this world while at the same time aspiring to a moral transcendent existence. We all want to know the recipe for virtue, the secret formula for becoming a better person. Is there a way to live righteously when our daily endeavors are marked by so much personal failures?

Unfortunately, the law is not the place to find those answers. Justice may be about many things, but moral complexity of distinguishing between right and wrong, or arriving at the truth of a given situation, is neither its strength nor its ostensible mission. Courts of law are there to administer justice to efficiently streamline cases, to ensure the availability of forum that offers the chance of some relief. It's the possibility of justice that it guarantees, not the quality of that justice, not the certainty that, in the end, justice will make sense, feel right and resolve matters in a way that leaves the parties better off and reconcile to move on with their lives. The institution of law defines itself as an arbiter of legal dispute, and not as a dispenser of moral lessons or seeker of truths. It thrives on an adversarial process that only take prisoners and leaves little room for peace.25

There is a belief, for most people that the values and teachings that are embodied in both law and religion--the consciousness and ideals that are invoked in places of worships and court houses--are basically the same that they go hand in hand. In practice and in fact, however, law and religion are largely, and unfortunately, not inspired by the same values, although most of us wish to believe it.26 Ibid

In developed countries the ideal of life is, receive education, acquire skills, take up a profession and be successful in society. Almighty has eliminated from State activities. And religion thrown out of education, under the pretext of making education academic. But in under developed countries, a total reverse philosophy is chosen by the authorities in power. Taking advantage of faulty law, absence of rule of law, inadequacy of administration of justice people get the opportunity of making their fortune by smuggling or by evasion of tax or by any other means. Politicians are power monger and they want to achieve it by hook or by crook. As a result, their main object is to continue in power ignoring the country's development and welfare of the people. They utter good words to the people which they themselves do not believe. They travel abroad in group showing unnecessary programs with exchequer in the name of education, training and so on. But they give up good things in those countries in the airport and follow the old path. So, the entire moneys are wasted.

If we really want to develop our country as a welfare State we must change our attitude of self-interest, self-enjoyment, self-centeredness, self-absorbed, self-obsessed, selfishness and give importance to the State adroit to the patriotism.

References:

1. *The Laws of Justice, Ryuho Okawa, p. 100-101*
2. *Ibid p. 101*
3. *Swami Vivekananda, While Uniting peoples of Different Faiths and Religions of all over the World.*

3(a). Sarvepalle Radhakrishnan – Essays in the History of Religions by Joachim Wach.

3(b). Keith Wandell -History of Modern Philosophy, Metaphysics, Philosophy of Religion, Ethics,   Indian Philosophy

3(c). Dr. Harvell Bowman – Journal of Communication and Religion

3(d). The Early History of India by Vincent A. Smith (Third Edition)

4. *Rock Edict XII; Nikam and McKeon, 1959; 51-2*
5. *Asoka 269-32 BC*
6. *http://www.bdchronicle.com/detail/news/32/654*
7. *http://www.bdchronicle.com/detail/news/32/654#/KGYdHdf .dpuf*
8. *http://www.bangladeshchronicle.net/2013/07/chumki/calls/ allamashafi-a-man-of-distorted-mentality*
9. *http://www.bdchronicle.com/detail/news/32/654#stash.KG YdHdDfdpuf*
10. *http://archive.dhakatribune.politics/2013/jul/09/comments-women-shafi#E2%80%99s-video-creating-storm-social-media#stash-ePhLRiEd.pduf*
11. *Austin Peay, State University, Tennessee. USA*
12. *www.latimes.com/local/abcarian/la-me-abcarian-persky-stanford-20180126-story.html*

12(a). Richard Dawkins-The God Delusion, 2006

13. *Anupama Joyee, Student of Law, University of London, International Program*

14. *Human Rights India and West, Ashwini Peetush and Joy Drydyk*

15. *Sharvalli Radhakrishnan (President of India) 1955, p. 202*

16. *The Conservative Soul (Fundamentalism, Freedom and the Future of the Life, Andrew Sullivan)*

13. *Ibid*

14. *Ibid*

15. *Ibid*

16. *Ibid*

17. *The End of Days, Gerson Goteborg*

18. *The Conservative Soul, p. 59*

19. *Ibid*

23(a). Robert P. George is the McCormick Professor of Jurisprudence at Princeton and is evidently regarded as a leading Christian conservative.

20. *The Myth of Moral Justice, Thane Rosenbaum*

21. *Ibid*

22. *Ibid*

Chapter 23
Supremacy of Law

The supremacy of law was the chief characteristic citing A.V. Dicey's analysis: "La ley est La plus haute inheritance, que le roi had; car par la ley il meme et toutes ses sujets sont rules, et si la ley me fuit, nul roi et nul inheritance sera" i.e. the law is the highest estate to which the king succeeds, both he and all his subjects are ruled by it, and without it there would be neither king nor realm.1 According to Dicey, the supremacy of law was, in its term, a principle that corresponded to three other concepts and therefore implied three different and concomitant meanings of the phrase "the rule of law": (a) the absence of arbitrary power on the part of the government to punish citizens or to commit acts against life and property; (b) the subjection of every man, whatever his rank and condition, to the ordinary law of the realm and to the jurisdiction of the ordinary tribunals; and (c) a predominance of the legal spirit in English institutions, because of which Dicey explains, "the general principles of English constitution are the result of judicial decisions----; whereas under many foreign constitutions the security given to the rights of individuals results or appears to result from the general (abstract) principles of the constitution".2 Ibid

According to Dicey's idea that the absence of arbitrary power on the part of the government. Equality is an idea embodied in the Dicean description of the second characteristic of rule of law, that is, every man, whatever his rank or condition, is subject to the ordinary law of the realm. According to Dicey, only ordinary courts, in England as well as in France, could really protect citizens by applying the ordinary law of the land. Professor Hayek2(a) charges Dicey with having contributed a great deal to preventing or delaying the growth of institutions capable of controlling, through independent courts, the new bureaucratic machinery in England because of a false idea that separate administrative tribunals would always constitute a denial of ordinary law and, therefore, a denial of the rule of law.

Dicey and Hayek apparently differ only slightly in their respective interpretations of equality as the characteristic of rule of law. Both maintained that independent courts are essential to grant to the citizens equality before law. Hayek thinks that the existence of two different judiciary orders is not objectionable by itself, provided that both orders are independent of the executive. Hayek analyzed how the rule of law might be beneficial to the free market. While Dicey does not admit the existence of two different judiciary orders, one to settle disputes between ordinary citizens only and one to settle disputes between ordinary citizens and state officials on the other.

Dicey's conclusion may or may not be applicable to present circumstances, but it is a consequence of the people of equality before the law, that is, one of the principles applied by both Dicey and Hayek's interpretation of the meaning of the rule of law. Dicey wrote "the idea of legal equality or of the universal subjection of all classes to one law administered by ordinary courts has been pushed to its utmost limit." With us every official, from the Prime Minister down to a constable or a collector of taxes, is under the same responsibility for every act done without legal jurisdiction as any other citizen. The news abounds with cases in which officials have been brought before the courts and made in their personal capacity liable to punishment or the payment of damages for the acts done in their official character but more than their lawful authority. A colonial Governor, a Secretary of State, a military officer, and all subordinates, though carrying out commands of their official superiors, are as responsible for any act which the law does not authorize as in the case of any private and unofficial person.3 Ibid

All European countries, except England, adopted written Codes and written constitutions accepting the idea that precisely worded formulae could protect people from encroachments of all possible kinds of tyrants. Governments as well as courts accepted this interpretation of the idea of the certainty of the law as the precision of written formula laid down by legislatures. The Greek and the Continental notion of the certainty of the law correspond to the ideal of individual liberty formulated by the Greek authors who speak of government by laws. According to the Italian system, nobody can tell whether a rule may be only one year or one month or one day old when it will be abrogated by a new rule. All these rules are precisely worded in written formulae that readers or interpreters cannot change at their will. Nevertheless, all of them go as soon and as abruptly as they came. The result is that if we leave out of the picture the ambiguities of the text are always "certain" as far as the literal content of each rule is concerned at any given moment, but people are never certain that tomorrow they shall still have the rules they have today. This is "the certainty of law" in the Greek or Continental sense. It is a certainty in the sense that one requires to foresee that the result of a legal action taken will be free from legal interference tomorrow.4

Liberty and democracy came first in the scale of values; prosperity comes later. There is little doubt that this was also the scale of values of the Athenians. The Romans accepted and applied a concept of certainty of law. That could be described as meaning that the law was never to be subjected to sudden and unpredictable changes. Moreover, the law was never to be submitted, as a rule, to the arbitrary will or to the arbitrary power of the legislative assembly or of any one person including senators or other prominent magistrates of the state. This is the long run concept or if you prefer, the Roman concept, of the certainty of law.5

According to the English principle of the rule of law, which is closely connected with the whole history of the common law, rules were not the result of the exercise of the arbitrary will of a man. They are the object of a dispassionate investigation on the part of courts of judicature just as the Roman rules were the object of a dispassionate investigation on the part of the Roman jurists to whom litigants submitted their cases. It is now considered old fashioned to maintain that courts of justice describe or discover the correct solution of a case in the way that Sir Carleton Kemp Allen pointed out.6

Law is the enterprise of subjecting human conduct to the governance of rules. Unlike most modern theories of law, this view treats law as an activity and regards a legal system as the product of a sustained purposive effort. If we are to understand that effort, we must understand that many of its characteristic problems are moral in nature. Thus, we need to put ourselves in the place of judge faced with a statute extremely vague in its operative terms yet disclosing clearly enough in its preamble an objective the judge considered plainly unwise. Even in an attempt to offer a neutral concept of law that will not import into notion of law itself any particular ideal of substantive justice, proposes the following definition:

"The rule of law simply means the 'existence of public order.' It means organized government, operating through the various instruments and channels of legal command. In this sense, all modern societies live under the rule of law, fascist as well as socialist and liberal states."7

It is perfectly obvious that a system of legal rules may lose its efficacy if it permits itself to be challenged by lawless violence. Sometimes violence can only be restrained by violence. Hence it is quite predictable that there must normally be in a society some mechanism ready to apply force in support of the law in case it is needed. But this innocence justifies the use or potential use of force as the identifying characteristic of law. Modern science depends heavily on the use of measuring and testing apparatus; without such apparatus it could not have achieved what it has. But no one would conclude on this account that science should be defined as the use of apparatus for measuring and testing. So, it is with law. What law must foreseeably do to achieve its aims is something quite different from the law itself.8

It is precisely when the legal system itself takes up weapons of violence that it imposes on it the most significant requirements of the rule of law. In more developed nations it is in criminal cases that people are most exigent in the demand for guarantees that law must remain faithful to itself. Thus, that branch of law most closely identified with force is also that which the people associate most closely with formality, ritual, and solemn due process. This consideration explains, but does not justify, the modern tendency to see physical force as the identifying mark of law. The body of law is administering with integrity and, in case of dispute, is interpreted and applied by special courts. If an infraction is established the State pursuant to a court order levies a fine in the form of a deduction from the trader's deposit.9 Ibid

In most theories of law, the element of force is closely associated with the notion of a formal hierarchy of command or authority. Since the emergence of nation-states, however, a long line of legal philosophers, right from Hobbes through Austin to Kelsen and Somlo, have seen the essence of law in a pyramidal structure of state power. This view abstracts from the purposive activity necessary to create and maintain a system of legal rules, contending itself with a description of the institutional framework within which the activity is assumed to take place.

If we ask what purpose is served by the conception of law and a hierarchy of command, the answer may be that this conception represents the legal expression of the political nation-state. It may be answered that common sense and a concern to make the measures effective will ordinarily lead the legislature to make the laws reasonably clear, whereas the contradictions among the rules applied by the various agencies of government constitute a perennial problem.10 Ibid

If we confine ourselves to the Europe of the Twentieth Century, we might well say that in most European countries the rule of law is now nearly as well established as in England and that private individuals, at any rate who do not meddle in politics, have little to fear as long as they keep to the law, either from government or from anyone else.11

The idea of the certainty of law cannot depend on the idea of legislation if "the certainty of law" is understood as one of the essential characteristics of rule of law in the classical sense of the expression. I agree with Dicey's view of the rule of law implying the fact that judicial decisions are at the very foundation of the English constitution and in contrast to this fact is the opposite process on the Continent where legal and judicial activities appeared to be based on the abstract principle of a legislative constitution. Many western countries, in ancient as well as in modern times, have considered the ideal of individual freedom essential to their political and legal systems. A conspicuous characteristic of this ideal has always been the certainty of the law. The certainty of law is conceived in two different ways: first as the precision of a written text emanating from legislatures, and second, as the possibility open to individuals of making long-term plans based on a series of rules spontaneously adopted by people in common to be eventually ascertained by judges through centuries and generations. In the present age confusion of the meaning of "certainty and rule of law" has particularly increased because of the emerging tendency in the English-speaking countries to emphasize law making by way of legislation instead of by courts of adjudicature.12

Bureaucrats enter the scene as soon as civil servants seem to be above the law of the land regardless of the nature of that law. There are cases in which officials deliberately substitute their own will for the provisions of the law in the belief that they are improving on the law and achieving, in some way not stated in the law, the very ends they think the law was intended to achieve.13

Lord Acton viewed that "by liberty I mean assurance that every man shall be protected in doing what he believes to be his duty against the influence of authority and majority, custom and opinion."14 According to Watts, "No one should interfere with the legitimate activities of anyone else if to interfere means the use of coercion, fraud, intimidation, restraint or verbal abuse."15

References:

1. *Dicey, Supremacy of the Law*
2. *Ibid*

2(a). *Friedrich August Von Hayek, economist and philosopher, shared the 1974 Nobel Prize in Economic Science*

3. *Ibid p. 189*

4. *Freedom and the Law, Bruno Leoni*
5. *Ibid p. 84-85*
6. *Law in the Meaning, Sir Carleton Kemp Allen*
7. *Professor Friedmann, 'Law and Social Change,' (1951) p. 281*
8. *The Morality of Law, Lon L. Fuller, p. 108*
9. *Ibid*
10. *Ibid*
11. *Albert Venn Dicey, Introduction to the Law of the Constitution (8th Edition) p. 185*
12. *Law in the Meaning, Sir Carleton Kemp Allen*
13. *Bureaucracy and Civil Service Gladden*
14. *History of Freedom, Lord Acton*
15. *Union of Monopoly, V. Orval Watts*

Chapter 24

Secularism

One of the earliest articulations of political tolerance emerges from the principle of 'Ahimsha' or non-violence interpreted as a political principle, in contrast to merely an individual's ethical virtue. This is first developed by Buddhist Emperor Ahsoka.A As early as the 3rd century BC Ashoka's edicts declare respect for all perspectives, philosophers and religions as an implication and requirement of the principle of Ahimsha. Political toleration, recognition and respect for various philosophical and religious doctrines and practices arise from principles internal to these Buddhist traditions. This is radically different both conceptually and historically, from how political toleration and the related notion of secularism emerged in Europe. As the quintessential political ideal, toleration grew out of the bloodshed of the Reformation and the 30 years' war (1618-1648). It emerges from religious factions within Christianity and its inability to cope with internal differences as a result, import, of claims to absolute truth. The birth of political neutrality and the separation of church and State, secularism, and indeed liberalism itself, have roots in this bloody conflict. But this is not the case here. Ashoka realizes the importance of tolerance as it is intrinsic to Buddhist practice. Indeed, it is after his conquest of Kalinga and the horrors of war, for which he himself was responsible, that Ashoka constructs a political interpretation of 'Ahimsha'; he expands the principle from a personal virtue to a political virtue.

King Priyadarshi honors men of all faiths, members of religious orders and lay men alike with gifts and various marks of esteem. Yet he does not value either gifts or honors as much as growth in the qualities essential to religions of all faiths. This growth may take many forms, but its root is guarding one's speech to avoid extolling one's own faith and disparaging faiths of others improperly or, when the occasion is appropriate, immoderately. The faiths of all others deserve to be honored for different reasons. By honoring them, one exalts one's own faith and at the same time performs a service to the beliefs of others. By acting otherwise, one injures his own faith and thus the faith of others. But if a man extolls his own faith and disparages another because of devotion to his own and because he wants to glorify it, he seriously injures his own faith. Therefore, concord alone is commendable, for through concord men may learn and respect the conception of Dharma accepted by others. The King desires men of all faiths to know each other's doctrines and to acquire sound doctrines. Those who are attached to their faiths should be told that Priyadarshi does not value gifts of honors as much as growth in the qualities essential to religion in men of all faiths. Many officials were assigned to tasks for this purpose – the officers in charge of spreading the Dharma; superintendent of women in the royal household; the inspectors of cattle and pasture lands; and other officials. The objective of these measures is the promotion of each man's faith and glorification of Dharma

Secularism is the principle of the separation of government institutions and persons mandated to represent the state from religious institutions and religious dignitaries. One manifestation of secularism is asserting the right to be free from religious rules and teachings or, in a State declared to be neutral on matters of belief, from the imposition by government of religion or religious practices upon its people.1 Another manifestation of secularism is the view that public activities and decisions, especially political ones, should be uninfluenced by religious beliefs or practices.

Secularism draws its intellectual roots from Greek and Roman philosophers such as Epicurus and Marcus Aurelius; from Enlightenment thinkers such as John Locke, Denis Diderot, Voltaire, Baruch Spinoza, James Madison, Thomas Jefferson, and Thomas Paine; and from more recent freethinkers and atheists such as Robert Ingersoll, Bertrand Russell, and Christopher Hitchens. It shifts the focus from religion to other "temporal" and "this-worldly" things with emphasis on nature, reason, science, and development. The purposes and arguments in support of secularism vary widely.2 In European laicism it has been argued that secularism is a movement toward modernization, and away from traditional religious values (also known as secularization).

This type of secularism, on a social or philosophical level, has often occurred while maintaining an official State Church or other State support of religion. In the United States, some argue that State Secularism has served to a great extent to protect religion and the religious from governmental interference, while secularism on a social level is less prevalent.3

The Italian law professor Alberico Gentile (1552–1608) has been the first to divide secularism from canon law and Roman Catholic theology. The term "secularism" was first used by the British writer George Jacob Holyoake in 1851.4 although the term was new, the general notions of freethought on which it was based had existed throughout history.

Holyoake invented the term secularism to describe his views of promoting a social order separate from religion, without actively dismissing or criticizing religious belief. An agnostic himself, Holyoake argued that "Secularism is not an argument against Christianity; it is one independent of it. It does not question the pretensions of Christianity; it advances others. Secularism does not say there is no light or guidance elsewhere but maintains that there is light and guidance in secular truth, whose conditions and sanctions exist independently, and act forever. Secular knowledge is manifestly that kind of knowledge which is founded in this life, which relates to the conduct of this life, conduces to the welfare of this life, and is capable of being tested by the experience of this life.5

Barry Kosmin of the Institute for the Study of Secularism in Society and Culture breaks modern secularism into two types: hard and soft secularism. According to Kosmin, "The hard secularist considers religious propositions to be epistemologically illegitimate, warranted by neither reason nor experience." However, in his view of soft secularism, "The attainment of absolute truth was impossible and therefore skepticism and tolerance should be the principle and overriding values in the discussion of science and religion."6

The departure from reliance on religious faith to reason and science marks the beginning of the secularization of education and society in history. According to Domenic Marbaniang, secularism emerged in the west with the establishment of reason over religious faith as human reason was gradually liberated from unquestioned subjection to the dominion of religion and superstition.7 Secularism first appeared in the west in the classical philosophy and politics of ancient Greece, disappeared for a time after the fall of Greece, but resurfaced after a millennium and half in the Renaissance and the Reformation. He writes:

"An increasing confidence in human capabilities, reason, and progress, that emerged during the Italian Renaissance, together with an increasing distrust in organized and state supported religion during the Reformation, was responsible for the ushering of modernity during the Enlightenment, which brought all facets of human life including religion under the purview of reason and thus became responsible for the freeing of education, society, and state from the domination of religion; in other words, the development of modern secularism."8

Harvey Cox explains that the Enlightenment hailed nature as the "deep reality" that transcended the corrupted manmade institutions. Consequently, the rights of man were not considered as God-given but as the de facto benefits of Nature as revealed by Reason.9

Secularism and secularization are positive goods which must be defended as foundations of liberal democracy because they enhance the broad distribution of power and oppose the concentration of power in the hands of a few. Therefore, they are opposed by authoritarian religious institutions and authoritarian religious leaders.10

One manifestation of secularism is asserting the right to be free from religious rule and teachings or, in a State declared to be neutral in matters of belief, from the imposition by the government of religious practices upon the people.11 in political terms, secularism is a movement towards the separation of religion and government. This can refer to reducing ties between a government and a State religion replacing laws based on scriptures with civil laws, and elimination of discrimination based on religion. The positive ideal behind the state is equality of all people--each person should be free to realize their excellence and breaking down the barriers of class and caste. A secular state is generally considered out-of-place in mainstream politics (Weasel). In a secular state religion has no place in the affairs of the state. Maharaja Ranjeet Singh of the Sikh Empire in the first half of the 19th century successfully established secular rule in the Punjab and in his Durbar, he had Sikhs, Muslims and Hindus representatives heading the Durbar.12

References:

A. *Asoka 269-32 BC*

B. *Rock Edict XII; Nikam and McKeon, 1959; 51-2*

1. *Secularism and Secularity: Contemporary International Perspective, Edited by Barry A. Cosmin and Ariela Keyson, Institute of Secularism in Society and Culture, 2001*

2. *Yaniv Rozani Citing Domenic Marbani in Regulating the Eternal: The Paradox of Entrenching Secularism in Constituting, Michigan Law Review 253. 2017 p. 324*

3. *Feldman, Noah (2005), Divided by God, New York City*

4. *Yavuz, Hakan M and John L Esposio (2003) Turkish Islam and the Secular State. ISBN 0-8156-3040-9*

5. *Holuaoke G.J (1986) English Secularism: A confession of Belief, Library of Alexandria, p. 48*

6. *Kosmin Barry, Hard and Self Secularist and Hard and Soft Secularism*

7. *Ervin Budiselie, Christian Wilness for the 21st Century: Contemporary, yet Orthodox and Radical, p. 404*

8. *Demenic Marbeniang, Secularism in India, A Historical Analysis*

9. *Harvey Cox, the Secular City: Secularization and Urbanization, 2013*

10. *Secularism 101--History, Nature, Importance of Secularism by Austine Cline*

11. *Secularism and Secularity; Contemporary International Perspectives by Barry A. Kosmin and Ariela Keysar, Hartford, T*

12. *K.S Duggal, Ranjjeet Singh: A Secular Sikh Sovereign.*

Chapter 25

Democracy

Normally people's comprehension of democracy is that it is "majority rule." If you ask to them what political equality means, they will reply "one person, one vote." But neither majority rule nor one person one vote has the kind of historical or constitutional pedigree that most people assume. Most states until the 1960s flouted the principle of one person, one vote either by design or through inaction. Many states retained legislative district boundaries first drawn at the turn of 20th century long after their population had shifted dramatically. The idea behind "one person, one vote" was not merely to ensure abstract equality among individual voters. Whereas male apportionment often gave numerical minorities a stronghold of government decision making "one person, one vote" was intended to assure that "in a society ostensibly grounded on representative government, --- a majority of the people of a State could elect a majority of that State's legislature.1 Moreover Chief Justice Warren thought that one person, one vote would help ensure that henceforth elections would reflect the collective public interest ---- rather than the machinations of special interests."2

Anthropologists have identified forms of proto-democracy that date back to small bands of hunter gatherers that predate the establishment of agrarian, settled societies and still exist virtually unchanged in isolated indigenous groups today. In these groups of generally 50-100 individuals, often tied closely by familial bonds, decisions are reached by consensus or majority and many times without the designation of any specific chief.2 (a) Given that these dynamics are still alive and well today, it is plausible to assume that democracy in one form or another arises naturally in any well-bonded group or tribe.

These types of democracy are commonly identified as tribalism, or primitive democracy. In this sense, a primitive democracy usually takes shape in small communities or villages when there are face-to-face discussions in a village council or with a leader who has the backing of village elders or other cooperative forms of government.2 (b) This becomes more complex on a larger scale, such as when the village and city are examined more broadly as political communities. All other forms of rule – including monarchy, tyranny, aristocracy, and oligarchy – have flourished in more urban centers, often where there were concentrated populations.2(c)

Another claim for early democratic institutions comes from the independent "republics" of India, sangha's and ganas, which existed as early as the 6th century B.C. and persisted in some areas until the 4th century. The evidence for this is scattered, however, and no pure historical source exists for that period. In addition, Diodorus—a Greek historian who wrote two centuries after the time of Alexander the Great's invasion of India—mentions, without offering any detail, that independent and democratic states existed in India. Modern scholars note the word democracy at the time of the 3rd century B.C. and later suffered from degradation and could mean any autonomous state, no matter how oligarchic in nature.2(d)

Key characteristics of the gana seem to include a monarch, usually known as the Raja, and a deliberative assembly. The assembly met regularly. It discussed all major state decisions. At least in some states, attendance was open to all free men. This body also had full financial, administrative, and judicial authority. Other officers, who rarely received any mention, obeyed the decisions of the assembly. Elected by the gana, the monarch apparently always belonged to a family of the noble class of K'satriya Varna. The monarch coordinated his activities with the assembly; in some states he did so with a council of other nobles.2 (e) The Licchavis had a primary governing body of 7,077 rajas, the heads of the most important families. On the other hand, the Shakyas, Koliyas, Mallas, and Licchavis, during the period around Gautama Buddha, had the assembly open to all men, rich and poor.2 (f) Ibid

Scholars differ over how best to describe these governments, and the vague, sporadic quality of evidence allows for wide disagreements. Some emphasize the central role of the assemblies and thus tout them as democracies; other scholars focus on the upper-class domination of the leadership and possible control of the assembly and see an oligarchy or an aristocracy.2 (g) despite the assembly's obvious power, it has not yet been established whether the composition and participation was truly popular. The first main obstacle is the lack of evidence describing the popular power of the assembly. This is reflected in the Artha' Shastra, an ancient handbook for monarchs on how to rule efficiently. It contains a chapter on how to deal with the sangas, which includes injunctions on manipulating the noble leaders, yet it does not mention how to influence the mass of the citizens—a surprising omission if democratic bodies, not aristocratic families, actively controlled the republican governments.2(h)

Another issue is the persistence of the four-tiered Varna class system. The duties and privileges on the members of each caste—rigid enough to prohibit someone sharing a meal with those of another order—might have affected the roles members were expected to play in the state, regardless of the formality of the institutions. A central tenet of democracy is the notion of shared decision-making power. The absence of any concrete notion of citizen equality across these caste system boundaries leads many scholars to claim that the true nature of ganas and sanghas is not comparable to truly democratic institutions.

Indian media had a historic advantage in comparison to its counterparts elsewhere. Having been in the vanguard of the struggle against British colonial rule it can claim to be one of the principal stakeholders in India, the democratic republic. Testifying to the deep sense of engagement that the Indian press had with its lively reporting and perspectives that journalists, columnists and editors brought to India's freedom struggle and the intense public debate in editorial columns over the shape and direction of the future independent state. It is a matter of public recognition and axiomatic that India's parliamentary democracy would necessarily have to be anchored to the postulates of secularism, pluralism, and democracy if India's diverse cultural, religious, ethnic and linguistic strands were to cohere together as a single national unit.

Indian democracy has been fundamentally enriched by the historical presence of a lively argumentative tradition. Philosopher and economist Amartya Sen has observed that "India has been especially fortunate in having a long tradition of public arguments, with toleration of intellectual heterodoxy," thereby enabling it to make particularly effective connections with democracy and choose a resolutely democratic constitution.2(i) Democracy, notes Sen, is "intimately connected with public discussion and interactive reasoning: And to the extent such a tradition can be drawn on, democracy becomes easier to institute and also to preserve." He argues, the tradition of India "applies not merely to the public expression of values, but also to the interactive formation of values, illustrated for example by the emergence of Indian form of secularism."2(j) Ibid

An important body of literature suggests that stable democracies are apt to check the spread of violence by their strong civil societies.2 (k) civil society fosters democratic values and identities by challenging the centralization and abuse of power within the political society. Cohen and Arato, for instance, conceive of civil society as a "self-limiting, democratizing, movement seeking to expand and protect spaces for both negative liberty and positive freedom".2(l) India was among the first major country in the world to recognize and provide for the right of cultural collectivities – with diverse religious, linguistic communities, casts and tribes living in the country. This represents a significant and creditable initiative on the part of democratic India's early political leaderships, because at the time the Indian State framed these policies, most of the western and third world states had not consciously acknowledged in their policy framework the internal diversities in their societies. The democratic framework of the Indian Constitution gave recognition to diversity and accepted that the political community consisted of several different communities.

Watergate Hotel, one of Washington DC's plushest hotels, has entered the political lexicon as a term synonymous with corruption and scandal because of the events of 1972 presidential election in the United States. So-called burglars broke into the Democratic

Party National Committee offices at the Watergate Complex and it was believed that President Richard Milhous Nixon was deeply involved in the incident as well as in the subsequent cover up. He is one of the most fascinating political figures of the 20th century, and he was also a known figure to the people of Bangladesh because he directly supported the Pakistani regime during the liberation war of Bangladesh in 1971. Actions following the break-in at the Watergate were heavily influenced by the media, particularly because of the work of two reporters from the Washington Post, Bob Woodward and Carl Bernstein. The scandalous activities included "dirty tricks" such as bugging the offices of political opponents and people of whom Nixon or his officials were suspicious including extensive illegal activities against the Democratic Party.

The FBI reported the Watergate break-in was part of a massive campaign of political spying and sabotage by the Nixon reelection committee. Nixon created a new conspiracy for the cover-up which began in March 1973 and fully formed in May and June 1973 operating until his presidency ended on August 9, 1974. On March 1, 1974 a grand jury in Washington indicted several former Nixon aides who became known as the Watergate Seven. The issue of access to the tapes, which Nixon kept when discussing anything in the Oval Office, went to the United States Supreme Court. The court unanimously ruled on July 24, 1974 that claims of executive privilege over the tapes were void and ordered the President to release the tapes to the special prosecutors. The tapes revealed several crucial conversations that took place between the President and his counsel John Dean. In this conversation Dean summarized many aspects of the so-called Watergate case describing it as a "cancer on the Presidency."

On February 6, 1974 the House of Representatives approved giving the Judiciary Committee authority to investigate to impeach the President. The House Judiciary Committee by a majority recommended the 1st article of impeachment against the President: obstruction of justice. Ultimately, President Nixon had to resign with the following words: "I have never been a quitter. To leave office before my term is completed abhorrent to every instinct in my body. But as president, I must put the interest of America first. America needs a fulltime President and a fulltime Congress, particularly currently of problem we face at home and abroad. To continue to fight through the months ahead for my personal vindication would almost totally absolved the time and attention of both the President and the Congress in a period when our entire focus should be on the great issues of peace abroad and prosperity without inflation at home. Therefore, I shall resign the Presidency at noon tomorrow. Vice President Ford will be sworn in President at that hour in this office."3

This speech speaks volume about American value, patriotism, democracy, nationalism and the reasons of influence of America over the world. It also exhibits that internal economic development took precedence over the personal interest of the President. It may be taken a simple thing for people like ours and in our country that if one candidate secretly records the political opponent's strategies is a fraud as "White House had prior knowledge of the burglary."

How do the American citizens value democratic institutions? The Washington Post ran a story around from a Justice Department source saying that the new Attorney General Jeff Sessions had on two occasions met the Russian Ambassador, Sergey Kislyak. It relates to the last presidential election that installed Donald Trump in the White House. The documents allegedly say, "There was continuing exchange of information during the campaign between Trump surrogates and intermediaries of the Russian government." It was treated obviously extremely serious and if there is any evidence that anyone affiliated with the Trump campaign, communicated with Russian government during this campaign, what will you do? "We will of course investigate and pursue any and all illegal actions," a confuse Sessions answered a question he was not asked. It was revealed that a well-connected lawyer from Moscow, who was likely a Russian agent, an associate of Azerbaijani Russian oligarch Aras Agalarov; a US music promoter who manages Agalarov's son, a Russian pop-star; and a Russian government lobbyist in Washington walked into Trump Tower. Their purpose in visiting the campaign headquarters of a presumptive major party nominee for the president was to meet with three highly placed people in the campaign. The Russians were offering a dump of negative or even incriminating information about their Donald Trump's opponent. "The meeting included campaign Chairman Paul Manafort, and the campaign's most influential voice, Jared Kushner, because: (a) a high level conspiracy was being coordinated; (b) Manafort and Kushner, not taking the campaign very seriously, and without a thought of any consequence her, were merely entertained by the possibility of dirty tricks; (c) the three men were united in their plan to get rid of Lewandowski-with Don Jr. as the hatched man-and, as part of this unity, Manafort and Kushner need to show up at Don Jr's silly meeting.4

A democracy is a political system or a system of decision or a system of decision-making within an institution or organization or a country, in which all members have an equal share of power.5 Modern democracies are characterized by two capabilities that differentiate them fundamentally from earlier forms of government: the capacity to intervene in their own societies and the recognition of their sovereignty by an international legalistic framework of similarly sovereign states. Democratic government is commonly juxtaposed with oligarchic and monarchic systems, which are controlled by a minority and a sole monarch respectively.

Democracy in its earliest forms is generally associated with the efforts of the ancient Greeks and Romans who were themselves considered the founders of Western civilization by the 18th century intellectuals who attempted to leverage these early democratic experiments into a new template for a post-monarchical political organization.6 The extent to which these 18th century democratic revivalists succeeded in turning the democratic ideals of the ancient Greeks and Romans into the dominant political institution of the next 300 years is hardly debatable, even if the moral justifications they often employed might be. Nevertheless, the critical historical juncture catalyzed by the resurrection of democratic ideals and institutions fundamentally transformed the ensuing centuries and has dominated the international landscape since the dismantling of the final vestige of empire following the end of the Second World War.

Modern representative democracies attempt to bridge the gulf between the Hobbesian "State of nature" and the grip of authoritarianism through "social contracts" that enshrine the rights of the citizens, curtail the power of the state, and grant agency through the right to vote.7 Ibid While they engage populations with some level of decision-making , they are defined by the premise of distrust in the ability of human populations to make a direct judgement about candidates or decisions on issues.

According to the classical concept of democracy as it was formulated toward the end of 18th century in England, the democratic process was assumed to permit the people to decide issues for themselves through elected representatives in Parliament.19 Nevertheless, it is generally admitted that, according to the classical theory of democracy, Parliament was conceived of as a committee whose functions "would be to voice, reflect, or sent the will of the electorate. Ibid. Dicey recognized that the language of Austin was therefore as correct regarding "political" sovereignty as it was erroneous in regard to what he termed "legal" sovereignty and stated that "the electors are part of and the predominant part of politically sovereign power. As things now stand, the will of the electorate, and certainly of the electorate in combination with the Lords and the Crown, is sure ultimately to prevail on all subjects to be determined by the British government. The matter indeed may be carried a little further, and we may assert that the arrangements of the constitution are now such as that the electors shall by regular and constitutional means always in the end assert themselves as the predominant influence in the country.20

The principle of representation, in England as well as in other countries, was extended practically too all the individuals in a political community, at least to all the adults belonging to it. But three great problems arose which needed to be solved if the representative principle was actually to work: (1) that of making the number of citizens entitled to choose representatives correspond to the real structure of the nation; (2) that of getting candidates to stand for the office of representatives who were adequate exponents of the will of the people represented; and (3) that of adopting a system of choosing representatives that would result in their adequately reflecting the opinions of the people represented. Ibid

John Stuart Mill pointed out the fact that representation cannot work unless the people represented participate in some way in the activity of their representatives. Representative institutions are of little value, and may be mere instruments of tyranny or intrigue, when the generality of electors are not sufficiently interested in their own government to give their vote, or, if they vote at all, do not bestow their suffrages on public grounds, but sell them for money, or vote at the back of someone who has control over them or whom for private reasons they desire to propitiate. Popular election, as thus practiced, instead of a security against misgovernment, is but an additional wheel in the machinery.21

Democracy is government by consent and when laws are made to overcome an evil or provide a facility or otherwise ameliorate it is the voice of the people, and the discipline of a democratic society demands that he conform to the norms of behavior so set by law. The erosion of the sense of obedience to law will eventually undermine democratic life itself.

The superintendence, direction and control of the preparation of electoral rolls for elections to the office of president and parliament and the conduct of such elections shall vest upon the Election Commission which shall hold elections of members of Parliament. There is also provision in Article 118(4) that "The Election Commission shall be independent in the exercise of its functions and subject to this Constitution and any other law." Independence (of the Election Commission) is meant to show that our Constitution in clear terms has given power to the Election Commission to hold elections independently. That being so, why are there controversies for a long time for holding free and fair national parliamentary elections? Do we really want free and fair elections? The answer is possibly "No". And that is only because of a lack of political will of the political party in power. It always wants to continue in power by any means. When such a political party remains in the opposition for any reason, it will raise the issue of neutral elections. This proves that our politicians do not allow the Election Commission to work independently. When it comes to power they set up a commission in such a manner that it will be subservient to their will and wishes keeping an eye on the next election.

Democracy as highlighted in the Preamble of our Constitution and provisions of elections contained in Part VII of the Constitution have been de facto liquidated. Right from the Magura bi-election, almost all elections, even after amendment to the Constitution providing provision for Non-party Caretaker Government for holding free and fair elections, also did not work due to lack of foresight of our political leaders. No government in power ever tried to develop democratic institutions to work independently. Only the rich can afford to contest elections, only communal forces and corrupt methodologists can nominate candidates or save policies. A small percentage of people in the voters' list can buy and become winning candidates. Money matters in the elections, and communalism too, make the clear majority in the constituency a mockery. Money and muscle power are now regularly used in local government elections. Few countries, if any, have ever experienced the bloodshed we witnessed in the last Union Parishad election. The violence primarily was not with the opposition political activists but among the activists of some political party. The opposition cannot match them without the blessings of the administration. As a result, the genuine, neutral and honest people who have no money and muscle power cannot even dream of participating in the process of local government elections. What is the path then that we have taken?

The confidence of the people in the democratic process is almost zero. This is not a good sign for a nation. We cannot present a free, fair and peaceful election in a similar manner to what the military junta presented to the nation in 1970. Nowhere in recent days could the people cast their votes freely and impartially, and there is not a single example that can be cited anywhere in the country that officials entrusted with the task of conducting free and fair elections were not partisan.

In 2014 one of the main political parties did not participate in the national parliamentary election on the plea that the Election Commission was not impartial, and it would be a futile attempt to participate in such a mockery of an election with persons nominated by the ruling party as Election Commissioners. Their apprehension proved true. Firstly, the voter turnout in that election was so meagre that in most cases only about 5 percent of voters turned up at certain polling centers. 153 Members of Parliament were declared elected unopposed, which is unprecedented in the history of democracy in the world. Some of the candidates wanted to withdraw their nominations apprehending the outcome but they were not allowed that liberty. Hussain Muhammad Ershad withdrew his nomination but it was not accepted only to show that at least the Jatiya Party participated in the election. However, his younger brother Golam Quader's withdrawal of nomination was accepted because he was not the president of the party. Subsequent bi-elections and local elections proved that the apprehension of the opposition was true and that the political party which formed the government itself was shaky of the outcome of the election. From their conduct after the elections it appeared that within two years there would be another election. But predictably, after consolidating power it forgot the past and continued in power with the help of a superpower of the sub-continent.

Thereafter, a reign of terror was let loose by the opposition political parties: killing hundreds of people by setting fire to vehicles and other terrorist activities. The ruling party took the advantage of the mistake committed by the opposition party and managed to draw sympathy of the international community. Similar type of elections was also conducted by the said opposition political party when it was in power in 1996. But that political party could not stay in power for more than two months. During that time the present ruling party, the Bangladesh Awami League, was in the opposition, but it did not commit similar atrocities in the country. If the political parties both in power and the opposition do not take lesson from their past and use money and muscle power to win over the election officials, the entire democratic system is bound to collapse. If once the system is made unworkable, it would be difficult for the nation to restore it. The people will lose confidence in the system. The net result would be, even if we develop our economic condition, we would not command any respect in the international arena because we could not allow the people to elect their representatives. We would be treated as an uncivilized country in their estimation. It is a disgrace for our nation that even after 47 years of independence we could not hold a free and fair election till now although we fought for a democracy and sacrificed much blood under the Pakistani regime to attain our goal of democracy. The neighboring countries which were less important to us economically, socially and politically, like Nepal, Bhutan, Sri Lanka, Maldives, Pakistan and even Afghanistan can hold free and fair election.

Taylor points out, democracies, "therefore, require a relatively strong commitment on the part of their citizens. In terms of identity, being citizens must rate as an important component of who they are: in other words, the modern democratic states need a healthy degree of what used to be called patriotism, a strong sense of identification with the polity and willingness to give of oneself for its sake. That is why the states try to inculcate patriotism and to create a strong sense of common identity even where it did not previously exist. And that is why one thrust of modern democracy has been to try to shift the balance within the identity of the modern citizen, so that being a citizen will take precedence over a host of other poles of identity, such as family, class, gender, even (perhaps especially) religion."22

The Economist Intelligence Unit (EIU), of the UK, compiled an index that intends to measure the state of democracy in 167 countries, of which, 166 are sovereign states and UN members based on 60 indicators grouped in five different categories measuring pluralism, civil liberties and political culture. The index categorizes countries as one of four regime types: full democracies, flawed democracies, hybrid regimes and authoritarian regimes updated for 2010. Bangladesh was in the third category of "Hybrid regime" along with countries like Liberia, Uganda, Iraq and

Palestine. If the index of 2014 election was taken, there would have been little doubt if castigated our country as "Authoritarian" and placed in the last group.22

I conclude this chapter with the words of a jurist Jerome Frank who frankly and fort erringly explains that he had "Little patience with or respect for, the suggestion, I am unable to conceive - That in a democracy, it can ever be unwise to acquaint the public with the truth about the working of any branch of government. It is wholly undemocratic to treat the public as children who are unable to accept the inescapable shortcomings of our judicial system which are capable of being eliminated is to have all our citizens informed us to take the system now functions. It is a mistake, therefore, to try to establish and maintain through ignorance public system for our courts."

There are some great leaders around the globe who fought for the equal rights of their citizens; equal protection of law; democracy; rule of law; and independence of their respective countries. Among them George Washington, Mohan Das Karm Chand Gandhi, Bangabandhu Sheikh Mujibur Rahman and Nelson Mandela. Of them except Gandhi, other three became heads of the State of their countries. Gandhi became Brahmachari (renunciation of worldly affairs). He denounced to become the Prime Minister of India after Independence. He nominated Jawaharlal Nehru as the Prime Minister. The other three leaders became the presidents of their respective countries. George Washington was the first President of the USA for eight years (1789-1797). Under his Presidency, he shaped the country under Federal Government and the balance of power between the federal Government and the States. He also secured the freedom of thought and the conscience of the people of the USA. He also laid the foundation of democracy in the country and after completion of two tenures he stepped down although there was no constitutional mandate. Therefore, he is being revered by his citizens. Nelson Mandela became the President of South Africa for one term of six years. Before he assumed in power, the country was ruled by minority whites and eighty percent of the country's wealth belonged to those minority people. He shaped the country in such a manner that there was no communal disturbances and he brought the country under democracy, established the rule of law, freedom and liberty to people; and then he stepped down. He did not remain in power for an indefinite period. His beliefs for the causes of the people have been reflected in his presidency. Therefore, these three national leaders are respected all over the world as undisputed global leaders for humanity, rule of law, and democracy. On the contrary, Bangabandhu Sheikh Mujibur Rahman though fought for equal protection of law, rule of law, and for democracy; he opted to become the President of the war-torn country; but failed to institutionalize the democracy, rule of law and fundamental rights of the citizens. He was the undisputed leader who had fought his entire political career for the democracy and equal rights for the citizens of the country. He was the one who could lay the foundation of democracy and the rule of law, but the most tragedy part of our country is that instead of institutionalizing them he throttled democracy, rule of law and freedom of thought and conscience. He wanted to shape the country under authoritarian rule. That is why we are still fighting for the democracy and the rule of law. If he had given the substratum of democracy and the rule of law, he would have been revered as the most powerful leader like George Washington, Mahatma Gandhi, and Nelson Mandela.

References:

1. *Reynolds, 377 US @ 565*
2. *G. Edward White, Earl Warren; A Public Life, p. 337*

2(a). Fire and Fury, Michael Wolf

2(b). Democracy OED online: Oxford University Press

2(c). Morris I, the Measure of Civilization, Princeton University Press

2(d). Olson, M (1983), Dictatorship, Democracy and Development, American Political Science Review

2(e). Ibid

2(f). Political System, Encyclopedia Britannica online

2(g). Democracy, Encyclopedia Britannica online

2(h). Diodonus, Encyclopedia Britannica online

2(i). Larsen, 1973, p. 45-46

2(j). Robinson, 1997, p. 22

2(k). Ibid

2(l). Bongard-Levin 1996, p. 61-106

(m). Trautmann T.R, Koutillya and the Artha Shastra

2(n). Nobel Laureate Amartya Sen on Democracy

2(o). Robert Putnam, Bowling Alone. The Collapse and Revival of American Community

2(p). Jeal L. Kohen and Andrew Arato, Civil Society and Political Theory (Cambridge Press, 1992)

> 3. *Bruno Leon, Freedom and Law, p. 112*
> 4. *Diecy, Introduction to the Study of the Constitution*
> 5. *John Stuart Mill, Considerations on Representative Government*
> 6. *Democracy index, Wikipedia*

Chapter 26

Separation of Power and Independence of Judiciary

Before democracies developed in the Western and developed countries, the Crown exercised autocratic authorities over the colonies, but the American Founding generation was determined to prohibit the concentration of government power in the hands of one person or one body. As an essential precaution in favor of liberty, the American framers created a government that separates the power to make law from the power to execute the law and further separates those powers from the power to try individuals for violating the law. While departing from the Articles of Confederation to create the office of the president, the American Constitution conspicuously omits any analogue to the dispensing power invoked by British monarchs to disregard Acts of Parliament and instead directs the president to "Take Care that the Laws be faithfully executed."1 James Madison, one of the Founders explained that "The accumulation of all power--legislative, executive and judiciary, in the same hands, whether of one, a few, or many, and whether hereditary, self-appointed, or elective, may justly be pronounced the very definition of tyranny."2

The system disperses power among the three branches of government and it does so not by making them "wholly unconnected with each other" but by "giving to each a constitutional control over the others."3 The Founders recognized that the Executive must act with dispatch and strength in war, but they were deeply concerned about the risk of concentrating too much power in Executive hands.

The constitution of India does not, anywhere, clearly indicate that the three organs of the State--Legislature, Executive and Judiciary--have earmarked separate jurisdictions with no power to anyone of them to encroach on to the field of the other. But such separation of powers has been seen to be the "basic structure' by the Supreme Court in the Keshavananda Bharti case.4 The three organs must act within their allotted sphere which is called balancing the powers for the benefit of the people in whom in a democratic polity the constitution vests sovereignty. In our Constitution also, people's sovereignty has been recognized in the following words in the Preamble and Article 7 of the Constitution:

"To maintain its supremacy as the embodiment of the will of the people of Bangladesh" and again it is said, the Constitution is "the solemn expression of the will of the people." The separation of powers between the three organs being for balancing each other's power, each organ has right to object to alleged enforcement by the other organ onto its field.

There is no controversy on the principle that Legislature is elected, Executive is appointed, and Judiciary is selected. Law making, law enforcing, and judging are distinct permissible constitutional processes requiring three distinct expertise. Legislature sometime is too populist and theoretical. Executive is over-realistic as it has to face complicated situations in applying law; and the Judiciary is highly idealistic in its approach to the problems before it. The three organs of a state, therefore, must function from the experiences and wisdom of each other with the purpose of achieving the foremost common constitutional goal of guaranteeing fundamental human freedoms to the citizens of a democratic country. If the Legislature seeks guidance from the Executive and keeps up the ideals recognized by the Judiciary based on the interpretation of the constitution it can legislate well and perform better in its law-making exercise. If the Executive in application of laws keeps in view the spirit of the law, it can enforce it effectively and make it beneficial to the people for whom the given law is made. If the judiciary seeks guidance from the Legislature and Executive in taking decisions on controversies and social conflicts brought before it, its super-idealism will be tempered by realism.5

A debate was surfacing in the United States as to the power of the president to declare war in times of emergency he being the Commander-in-Chief ensures unified control of the Armed Forces.

While reserving to Congress the power to declare war, the Founders certainly expected the president to repel sudden attacks without prior Congressional authorization.6 In Hamdan the court rejected the notion of preclusive presidential power by saying: "Whether or not the President has independent power, absent Congressional authorization to convene military commissions, he may not disregard limitations that Congress has in proper exercise of its own war powers places on his power."7 However Justice Bleyer observed that nothing prevents the president from retuning to Congress to seek the authority he believes necessary.8 Justice Jacson's dictum was that "with all its defects, delays and inconveniences, men have discovered no technique for long preserving free government except that the executive be under the law, and that the law be made by parliamentary deliberations."9

The Romans accepted and applied a concept of the certainty of law that could be described as meaning that the law was never to be subjected to sudden and unpredictable changes. The law was never to be submitted as a rule, to the arbitrary will of the arbitrary power of any legislative assembly or of any one person, including senators or other prominent magistrates of the state. This is the long-run concept.10

Separation of powers, often imprecisely used interchangeably with the trias politica principle, is a model for the governance of a State. Under this model, a State's government is divided into branches, each with separate and independent powers and areas of responsibility; the powers of one branch are not in conflict with the powers associated with other branches. The typical division is into three branches as mentioned above, which is known as trias politica model. It can be contrasted with the fusion of power in some parliamentary systems where the Executive and Legislature are unified. Separation of powers, therefore, refers to the divisions of responsibilities in two distinct branches to limit any one branch from exercising the core functions of another. The intent is to prevent the concentration of power and provide for checks and balances. Aristotle first mentioned the idea of a "mixed government" or hybrid government in his work "Politics" where he drew upon any of the constitutional forms in the city states of ancient Greece. In the Roman Republic, the Roman Senate, Consuls and Assemblies showed an example of a mixed government according to Polybius.11

The term "tripartite" system is commonly ascribed to French Enlightenment political philosopher Baron Deed Montesquieu, though he did not use such term, in reality he referred to "distribution of power". Montesquieu described the various forms of distribution of political power among a Legislature, an Executive, and a Judiciary. Montesquieu's approach was to present and defend a form of government which was not excessively centralized in all its powers in a single monarch or a similar ruler, a form of government known then as "aristocracy". He based this model on the constitution of the Roman Republic and the British constitutional system.12 Montesquieu took the view that the Roman Republic had powers separated so that no one could usurp complete power.13 In the British constitutional system Montesquieu observed a separation of powers among the monarch, parliament and the courts of law.

In every government there are three sorts of power: The Legislative; the Executive in respect to things dependent on the law of nations; and the Executive regarding matters that depend on the civil law. By the first, the prince or magistrate enacts temporary or perpetual laws, and amends or abrogates those that have been already enacted. By the second, he makes peace or war, sends or receives embassies, establishes the public security, and provides against invasions. By the third, he punishes criminals, or determines the disputes that arise between individuals. The latter we shall call the judicial power, and the other, simply, the executive power of the state."14

He argues, quite explicitly, that each power should only exercise its own functions: "When the Legislative and Executive powers are united in the same person, or in the same body of magistracy, there can be no liberty; because apprehensions may arise, lest the same Monarch or Senate should enact tyrannical laws, to execute them in a tyrannical manner. Again, there is no liberty if the judiciary power be not separated from the Legislative and Executive. Were it joined with the Legislative, the life and liberty of the subject would be exposed to arbitrary control; for the judge would be then the legislator. Were it joined to the executive power, the Judge might behave with violence and oppression. There would be an end of everything, were the same man, or the same body, whether of the nobles or of the people, to exercise those three powers, that of enacting laws, that of executing the public resolutions, and of trying the causes of individuals."15

Separation of powers requires a different source of legitimization, or a different act of legitimization from the same source, for each of the separate powers. If the Legislative branch appoints the Executive and Judicial powers, as Montesquieu indicated, there will be no separation or division of its powers, since the power to appoint carries with it the power to revoke. The Executive power ought to be in the hands of a Monarch, because this branch of government, having need of dispatch, is better administered by one than by many: on the other hand, whatever depends on the legislative power is oftentimes better regulated by many than by a single person. But, if there were no monarch, and the executive power should be committed to a certain number of persons, selected from the Legislative body, there would be an end of liberty, by reason the two powers would be united; as the same persons would sometimes possess, and would be always able to possess, a share in both.16

Australia does not maintain a strict separation between the Legislative and Executive branches of government—indeed, government ministers are required to be members of Parliament—but the Federal Judiciary strictly guards its independence from the other two branches. However, under influence from the American constitution, the Australian constitution does define the three branches of government separately, and this has been interpreted by the judiciary to induce an implicit separation of powers.17 State governments have a similar level of separation of powers, but this is generally based on convention, rather than constitution.

India follows constitutional democracy which offers a clear separation of powers. The judiciary branch is independent of the other two branches with the power to interpret the Constitution. Parliament has the Legislative powers. Executive powers are vested with the President who is advised by the Union Council of Ministers headed by the Prime Minister. The Constitution of India vested the duty of protecting, preserving and defending the Constitution with the President as common head of the Executive, Parliament, Armed Forces, etc. not only for the union government but also the various State Governments in a federal structure. All three branches have "checks and balances" over each other to maintain the balance of power and not to exceed the constitutional limits.18

In Italy the powers are separated, even though the Council of Ministers needs a vote of confidence from both chambers of Parliament that represents a large number of members (almost 1,000)19 Like every parliamentary form of government, there is no real separation between Legislature and Executive, rather a continuum between them due to the confidence link. The balance is protected by Constitution between these two branches and, obviously, between them and the judiciary branch, which is independent.

A multiparty system of Parliament that must either form a minority Executive or a coalition Executive functions as a perfectly good system of checks and balances even if it was never a stated goal for the introduction of multiparty system in Norway. The multiparty system came about in response to a public outcry of having too few parties and a general feeling of a lack of representation. For this reason, we find very little on the topic of separation of powers or checks and balances in the works of Norwegian political scientists today.20

The development of the British constitution, which is not a codified document, is based on this fusion in the person of the Monarch, who has a formal role to play in the Legislature (Parliament), which is where legal and political sovereignty lies, is the Crown-in-Parliament, and is summoned and dissolved by the

Sovereign who must give his or her Royal Assent to all Bills so that they become Acts, the Executive (the Sovereign appoints all ministers of His/her Majesty's Government, who govern in the name of the Crown) and the Judiciary (the Sovereign, as the fount of justice, appoints all senior judges, and all public prosecutions are brought in his or her name).

Although the doctrine of separation of powers plays a role in the United Kingdom's constitutional doctrine, the UK constitution is often described as having "weak separation of powers" (A. V. Dicey), despite its constitution being the one to which Montesquieu originally referred to. For example, in the United Kingdom, the executive forms a subset of the legislature, as did— to a lesser extent—the judiciary until the establishment of the Supreme Court of the United Kingdom. The Prime Minister, the Chief Executive, sits as a member of the Parliament of the United Kingdom, either as a peer in the House of Lords or as an elected member of the House of Commons (by convention, and as a result of the supremacy of the Lower House, the Prime Minister now sits in the House of Commons) and can effectively be removed from office by a simple majority vote. Furthermore, while the courts in the United Kingdom are amongst the most independent in the world, the Law Lords, who were the final arbiters of judicial disputes in the UK sat simultaneously in the House of Lords, the upper house of the legislature, although this arrangement ceased in 2009 when the Supreme Court of the United Kingdom came into existence. Furthermore, because of the existence of parliamentary sovereignty, while the theory of separation of powers may be studied there, a system such as that of the UK is more accurately described as a "fusion of powers".

Until 2005, the Lord Chancellor fused the Legislature, Executive and Judiciary, as he was the ex-officio Speaker of the House of Lords, a government Minister who sat in Cabinet and was head of the Lord Chancellor's Department which administered the courts, the justice system and appointed judges, and was the head of the Judiciary in England and Wales and sat as a judge on the Judicial Committee of the House of Lords, the highest domestic court in the entire United Kingdom, and the Judicial Committee of the Privy

Council, the senior tribunal court for parts of the Commonwealth. The Lord Chancellor also had certain other judicial positions, including being a judge in the Court of Appeal and President of the Chancery Division. The Lord Chancellor combines other aspects of the constitution, including having certain ecclesiastical functions of the established state church, making certain church appointments, nominations and sitting as one of the thirty-three Church Commissioners.

These functions remain intact and unaffected by the Constitutional Reform Act. In 2005, the Constitutional Reform Act separated the powers with legislative functions going to an elected Lord Speaker and the Judicial functions going to the Lord Chief Justice. The Lord Chancellor's Department was replaced with a Ministry of Justice and the Lord Chancellor currently serves in the position of Secretary of State for Justice. The judiciary has no power to strike down primary legislation and can only rule on secondary legislation that it is invalid about the primary legislation if necessary.

The greatest expression of the separation of powers was incorporated in the United States Constitution. The founding fathers included features of many new concepts, including hard-learned historical lessons about the checks and balances of power and the then-new concept of separation of powers. Similar concepts were also prominent in the state governments of the United States. As colonies of Great Britain, the founding fathers considered that the American States had suffered an abuse of the broad power of parliamentarism and monarchy. As a remedy, the US constitution limits the powers of the Federal Government through various means the three branches of the Federal Government are divided by exercising different functions, and are separated in origin by separate elections, each branch controls the actions of the others and balances its powers in some way.

In the United States Constitution, Article 1 Section I gives Congress only those "legislative powers herein granted" and proceeds to list those permissible actions in Article I Section 8, while Section 9 lists actions that are prohibited for Congress. The vesting clause in Article II places no limits on the Executive branch, simply stating that "The Executive Power shall be vested in a President of the United States of America." The Supreme Court holds "the judicial power" according to Article III, and it established the implication of judicial review.22

The presidential system adopted by the Constitution of the United States obeys the balance of powers sought, and not found, by constitutional monarchy. The people appoint their representatives to meet periodically in a legislative body, and, since they do not have a king, the people themselves elect a preeminent citizen to perform, also periodically, the Executive functions of the state. The direct election of the head of state or of the executive power is an inevitable consequence of the political freedom of the people, understood as the capacity to appoint and depose their leaders. Only this separate election of the person who must fulfill the functions that the constitution attributes to the president of the government, so different by its nature, and by its function, from the election of representatives of the electors, allows the executive power to be controlled by the Legislature and submitted to the demands of political responsibility.23

Judicial independence is maintained by appointments for life that erases very soon any sense of dependence on the Executive, with voluntary retirement and a high threshold of dismissal by the Legislature, in addition to a salary that cannot be diminished during their service. The Federal Government refers to the branches as "branches of government", while some systems use "government" to describe the Executive. The Executive branch has attempted24 to claim power arguing for separation of powers to include being the Commander-in-Chief of a standing army since the American Civil War, executive orders, emergency powers and security classifications since World War II, national security, signing statements, and the scope of the Unitary Executive.

"In order to lay a due foundation for that separate and distinct exercise of the different powers of government, which to a certain extent is admitted on all hands to be essential to the preservation of liberty, it is evident that each department should have a will of its own; and consequently, should be so constituted that the members of each should have as little agency as possible in the appointment of the members of the others. Were this principle rigorously adhered to, it would require that all the appointments for the supreme Executive, Legislative, and Judiciary magistracies should be drawn from the same fountain of authority, the people, through channels having no communication whatever with one another. Perhaps such a plan of constructing the several departments would be less difficult in practice than it may in contemplation appear. Some difficulties, however, and some additional expense would attend the execution of it. Some deviations, therefore, from the principle must be admitted. In the constitution of the judiciary department in particular, it might be inexpedient to insist rigorously on the principle: first, because peculiar qualifications being essential in the members, the primary consideration ought to be to select that mode of choice which best secures these qualifications; secondly, because the permanent tenure by which the appointments are held in that department, must soon destroy all sense of dependence on the authority conferring them. It is equally evident, that the members of each department should be as little dependent as possible on those of the others, for the emoluments annexed to their offices. Were the executive magistrate, or the judges, not independent of the legislature in this particular, their independence in every other would be merely nominal."25

The three branches in the German government are further divided into six main bodies enshrined in the Basic Law for the Federal Republic of Germany:

Federal President (Bundespräsident) – formally Executive, but mainly representative in daily politics. Federal Cabinet (Bundesregierung) – executive. Federal Diet (Bundestag) & Federal Council (Bundesrat) – bicameral legislature. Federal Assembly (Bundesversammlung) – presidential electoral college (consisting of the members of the Bundestag and electors from the constituent states). Federal Constitutional Court (Bundesverfassungsgericht) – judiciary

Besides the constitutional court the judicial branch at the federal level is made up of five supreme courts—one for civil and criminal cases (Bundesgerichtshof), and one each for administrative, tax, labor, and social security issues. There are also state (Länder / Bundesländer) based courts beneath them, and a rarely used senate of the supreme courts.26

Public power is a public trust and the paramountcy of accountability to the people is democratically imperative. The judiciary is no exception to this fiduciary necessity so that the common people shall have access to justice system which must hear the grievance of any citizen and give him/her appropriate remedy as provided in the Constitution. So long unity and fraternity are basic to the rule of law, any citizen is a neighbor to his/her fellow citizen and shares his/her cause of action. The law of locus standi is therefore expansive and wherever there is an injury which affects the people at large or a member thereof it is never narrow and anyone not visibly with sincere concern is at home in court when he sues espousing a community grievance or public cause. This is the root rule of Public Interest Litigation, ideologically socialistic and paradigmatically sound. "We the people" have resolved to secure all citizens justice--social and economic--and liberty, equality and fraternity. To deny this collective fate is to defy the Republic's foundation.27 whoever be the sovereign, must be obedient to the law. Again, the content of law must be such as to reflect the current opinion of the community on what is right and good and ought to be done and, in this sense, it cannot be an arbitrary fiat of a ruler. Law must harmonize interests in such a manner that the greatest good of the greatest number is promoted and peaceful life and progress ensured. In fact, it should be in close touch with the people's lives, aims and aspirations lest it should drag the people down.28 Ibid

A lone dictator did indeed have a monopoly of power, but he maintained it with a regime of constant terror and fear. You never knew when a soldier would come knocking on your door at night; or when a son or daughter would be dragged off the street and tortured and murdered; or when a father or brother might be conscripted with a gun barrel in his back. Such a monopoly of force is almost as bad as complete anarchy. It is unpredictable, violent, terrifying, and psychologically stultifying. Enduring a dictatorship is life lived as trauma. The question then becomes: how do we sustain order by granting some entity of monopoly of force and yet remain protected against that entity as well? The answer is that the monopoly of force must somehow be constrained and restricted to ensuring the security of everyone alike. This not an easy fit and its achievement in human history has been remarkably rare and fleeting. Most human beings have never enjoyed such a stable and free. Hobbes did not. Neither did Montagu. They both lived in countries that were, at the time they wrote, torn apart by civil and religious warfare. Oakeshott, for all his bohemian tendencies, fought in uniform in a war to protect his own civilization against Nazi tyranny and lived to see the capital city of his own land bombed into rubble. Socrates was executed for the crime of free thinking while Machiavelli lived in fear of the Princes he tried to teach. The great imaginers of security and freedom knew security and terror well.29

A very important conclusion to be drawn is that the rule of law in the classical sense of the expression cannot be maintained without securing the certainty of law, conceived as the possibility of long run planning on the part of individuals regarding their behavior in private life and business. Bureaucrats enter the scene as soon as civil servants seem to be above the law of the land regardless of the nature of that law. There are cases in which officials deliberately substitute their own will for the provisions of law in the belief that they are improving on the law and achieving, in some way not stated in the law, the very ends they think the law was intended to achieve. There is often no doubt about goodwill and sincerity of the official in these cases.30

No direct democracy could solve the problem of avoiding both coercion and uncertainty since the problem is not itself related to direct or indirect participation in the law-making process through legislation resulting from group decisions. This warns me also of the comparative futility of all attempts to secure more freedom or more certainty for individuals in a country as far as the law of the land is concerned by letting them participate as frequently and as directly as possible in the law-making process through legislation by universal adult suffrage, proportional representation, referendum, initiative, recall of representative, or even by other organizations revealing purported public opinion about as many subjects as possible and making the people more efficient in influencing the political behavior of the rulers.31

Judicial independence is the concept that the judiciary needs to be kept away from the other branches of the government. That is, courts should not be subject to improper influence from the other branches of government or from private or partisan interests. Judicial independence is vital and important to the idea of separation of powers. Different countries deal with the idea of judicial independence through different means of judicial selection or choosing judges. One way to promote judicial independence is by granting life tenure or long tenure for judges, which ideally frees them to decide cases and make rulings according to the rule of law and judicial discretion, even if those decisions are politically unpopular or opposed by powerful interests. This concept can be traced back to 18th century England. In some countries, the ability of the judiciary to check the legislature is enhanced by the power of judicial review. This power can be used, for example, by mandating certain action when the judiciary perceives that a branch of government is refusing to perform a constitutional duty or by declaring laws passed by the legislature unconstitutional.32

The development of judicial independence has been argued to involve a cycle of national law having an impact on international law, and international law subsequently impacting national law. This is said to occur in three phases: the first phase is characterized by the domestic development of the concept of judicial independence; the second by the spread of these concepts internationally and their implementation in international law; and the third by the implementation in national law of these newly formulated international principles of judicial independence.33

A notable example illustrating this cycle is the United Kingdom. The first phase occurred in England with the original conception of judicial independence in the Act of Settlement 1701.34 The second phase was evident when England's concepts regarding judicial independence spread internationally, and were adopted in the domestic law of other countries; for instance, England served as the model for Montesquieu's separation of powers doctrine,35 and the Founding Fathers of the US Constitution used England as their dominant model in formulating the Constitution's Article III, which is the foundation of American judicial independence.36 Other common law countries, including Canada, Australia, and India, also adopted the British model of judicial independence37

The International Association of Judicial Independence and World Peace produced the Mt. Scopus International Standards of Judicial Independence between 2007 and 2012. These built on the same association's New Delhi Minimum Standards on Judicial independence adopted in 1982 and their Montréal Universal Declaration on the Independence of Justice in 1983. Other influences they cite for the standards include the UN Basic Principles of Judicial Independence from 1985, the Burgh House Principles of Judicial Independence in International Law (for the international judiciary), Tokyo Law Asia Principles, Council of Europe Statements on judicial independence (particularly the Recommendation of the Committee of Ministers to Member States on the independence, efficiency and role of judges), the Bangalore Principles of Judicial Conduct 2002, and the American Bar Association's revision of its ethical standards for judges.38

Independence of the judiciary is taken as an essential prerequisite for guaranteeing the basic rights and freedom acknowledged by modern society. The essence and core of judicial independence consists in creating a congenial atmosphere for impartial adjudication by the courts, free from any constraints, interference and influence direct or indirect. It is a universally accepted principle that justice should not only be done but seen to be done. It is possible only when it is realized by the people that the judiciary has the necessary freedom to act to deliver justice evenhandedly – however mighty the parties before it may be. The courts should be able to discharge their functions independently without fear or favor, implying that the judicial system should not be exposed to external influences--actual or apparent--and pressures from within the judicial hierarchy itself. It also implies functional independence from the administrative point of view.

The aim is to facilitate unbiased, fair and efficient dispensing of justice to those who come to the courts so that public confidence in the administration of justice is preserved and fostered. The guarantee of judicial independence is primarily meant to benefit the public at large. It is important to realize that the independence of the judiciary is founded on public trust and that judicial independence ought to be the culture and pervading norm of a democratic government. In the Montreal Declaration it was stated, "Judges individually shall be free, and it shall be their duty to decide matters before them impartially in accordance in their assessment of the facts and their understanding of the law without any restriction, influences, inducements, pressures, threats or interferences, direct or indirect, from any quarter or for any reason."39

Judicial independence should be viewed from the twin perspectives of individuals and institutional independence. Individual judge's independence lies in career advancement, security of tenure, salaries and other conditions of service, immunity from civil and criminal action and, above all, freedom to decide cases according to one's conscience. Institutional independence embraces administrative and financial independence, effective enforcement of judicial decisions and the protection of individual judge or institution from being scandalized. The task of judicial independence is not complete without a discourse on judicial accountability. No public institution or public functionaries is exempt from accountability, although the degree or manner of enforcing accountability may vary. Credibility and confidence in the appointment process is a key feature of confidence in the judicial system as a whole. The selection of the best among eligible persons in keeping with the needs of a pluralistic society is the desideratum. The process must be independent, transparent and fair.

The larger the power, the greater the responsibility founded on this touchstone. The independence and accountability of the judiciary obligates the judges to a high code of integrity, good behavior and scrupulosity, with no immunity of liability to public criticism and legal action in case of culpable delinquency on and off the Bench. American jurist judge Jerome Frank wrote that "in a democracy, it can never be unwise to acquaint the public with the truth about the working of any branch of government. It is wholly undemocratic to treat the public as children who are unable to accept the inescapable shortcomings of manmade institutions: the best way to bring about the elimination of these shortcomings of our judicial systems which are capable of being eliminated is to have all our citizens informed as to how the system now functions. It is a mistake, therefore, to try to establish and maintain, through ignorance, public esteem for our court."

Judicial accountability is also an idea of balancing the concepts of judicial independence. It is a debate of the day that judicial accountability must be developed consistent with the principle of judicial independence. Judicial accountability cannot be on the same level or measure as the accountability of the Executive or Legislature. This is so because of the very nature of the function and role of the judiciary. Certainly, judiciary is not an exception to the norm of accountability. Absolute judicial independence without any obligation for its conduct or performance is the antithesis of democracy. Judicial independence is a constitutional value and a norm of democratic governance cannot be dissociated for the obligation of the judiciary to account for its conduct. It has been observed by Supreme Court of Canada that "public confidence in and respect for the judiciary are essential to an effective judicial system and, ultimately, to the democracy founded on the rule of law. Many factors, including unfair and uninformed criticism, or simple misunderstanding of the judicial role, can adversely influence public confidence in and respect for the judiciary. Another factor which is capable of undermining public respect and confidence is any conduct of judges, in and out of court, demonstrating lack of integrity. Judges should, therefore, strive to conduct themselves in a way that will sustain and contribute the

501

public respect and confidence in their integrity, impartiality, and good judgement."40

There are different classifications of judicial accountability attempted in scholarly treaties and research papers. However, without getting into the nuances let us accept the principle that judicial independence and judicial accountability to the public need to be harmonized and viewed as complementary principles. When we talk of judicial accountability we have in view the inbuilt safeguard in the system; those which have developed as healthy conventions. We think of mechanisms in place to investigate the complaints or representations of the seekers of justice, to check malpractices in the judicial system and to deal with judges indulging in corruption, misuse of power and improprieties. Another set of accountabilities is the posting of judicial officers in the subordinate judiciary. In India this issue of accountability does not pose much problem. There is a well-entrenched complaint mechanism in India. The complaints against ministerial staff and subordinate judiciary are handled at various levels in the hierarchy. There is a vigilance organization in every High Court. The High Court exercises administrative control over District and Subordinate courts under Article 235 of the Constitution. Disciplinary action can be initiated, and enquiries held by the High Court against District Judges and other members of the subordinate judiciary for acts of misconduct, dereliction of duties, etc. and major as well as minor penalties can be imposed by the High Court.41

In Bangladesh, it is far different. Never and during my tenure was I not able to persuade the Executive to leave the accountability of the judges of the lower judiciary in the hands of the High Court Division. Though the language of Article 235 of Indian Constitution is Pari Materia of Article 109 of our Constitution, but all disciplinary actions are being initiated and are inquiries held by the Executive. If any proposal is sent for taking disciplinary action against a subordinate judicial officer, the Ministry of Law keeps the matter in abeyance. Even when serious allegations are brought to its notice it turns a blind eye to such matters. In such a scenario the Supreme Court is subjected to severe embarrassment all the time.

It is imperative for a country if it believes in the independence of the judiciary to give total financial independence to it. The proper distribution of national wealth including government spending on the judiciary is a prerequisite for an independent judiciary. In traditional and in some developing countries, spending on the judiciary is controlled by the Executive. Bangladesh is one such country. The entire expenditure of the lower judiciary is controlled by the Executive and the Supreme Court has no hand in it. This undermines the principle of judicial independence, because it creates a financial dependence of the judiciary on the Executive. It is important to distinguish between two methods of corruption of the judiciary; i.e. the state through budget planning, and privileges being the most dangerous and private. State corruption of the judiciary can impede the ability of businesses to optimally facilitate the growth and development of a market economy.

The apex court in this regard observed Ibid that the financial independence of the Supreme Court is inextricably connected with the functioning of the subordinate judiciary. As the High Court Division has a controlling and supervisory role it has a consultative role connected with the subordinate judiciary. Financial independence of the Supreme Court can be secured if the funds allocated to the Supreme Court in the annual budget can be disbursed within the limits of the sanctioned budget by the Chief Justice without any interference by the Executive, i.e. without seeking the approval of the Ministry of Finance or any other Ministry. The Chief Justice will be competent to make appropriations of the amounts from one head to another, create new posts, abolish old posts or change their nomenclature, to upgrade or downgrade as per requirements, provided the expenditure incurred falls within the limits of budget allocation. To ensure financial discipline an accounts officer of the Accountant General's office may be deputed in the Supreme Court for pre-audit and issue of checks. Thus, the Executive control over the financial independence of the Supreme Court will be eliminated.

The second essential condition of judicial independence is security of salary and other remuneration, and, where appropriate, security of pension. The right to salary and pension of subordinate judiciary should be established by law and there should be no way in which the Executive can interfere with that right in a manner to affect the independence of subordinate judicial officers. The third essential condition is institutional independence of the subordinate judiciary especially from Parliament and the Executive. It must be free to decide on its own matters of administration bearing directly on the exercise of its judicial functions. The judiciary must be free of actual or apparent interference of the Executive arm of the government. It must be free from powerful non-governmental interference like pressure from corporate giants, business or corporate bodies, pressure groups, media, political pressure.

On behalf of the Judicial Officers Association, a writ petition was filed challenging the action of the Executive purporting to incorporate "Judicial Service" within the Bangladesh Civil Services and two orders of the Ministry of Finance suspending and cancelling an earlier order regarding the pay and allowances of the judicial officers. The case in commonly known as Masder Hossain case.42 Till 1974 the subordinate judiciary was totally independent.43 Article 109 states: "The High Court Division shall have superintendence and control over all courts and tribunals subordinate to it." Article 116 states, "The control (including the power of posting, promotion and grant of leave and disciplines) of persons employed in the judicial service and magistrates exercising judicial functions shall vest in the Supreme Court." In 1975, the word "President" was substituted for the word "Supreme Court"44 Later on, an amendment to Article 116 was made and by this amendment, the words "And shall be exercised by him in consultation with the Supreme Court" have been added after the word "President".45 By addition of the word "President" and addition of some other words after the word President, the Executive made a hotchpotch in the administration and control, including posting and promotion, of judicial officers of the lower judiciary. Keeping Article 109 intact Article 116 carries no meaning at all. Either Article 109 be deleted, or Article 116 be restored to its original if the Executive really wants judicial officers to work independently. In the Fifteenth Amendment, Article 115 was also substituted for the old 115. Under this substituted provision, the president has been vested with the primary power, distinguished from contingent power, to frame rules about appointment of persons to the offices in the judicial service or magistrates exercising judicial functions.

The apex court held that this rule-making power of the president is constitutionally different in content and fact from "the contingent rule-making power of the president in the proviso to Article 133 of the Constitution." The apex Court termed this power as "contingent rule making power by citing example of this power which are available in Articles 62 (2), 75 (1) (a), 79 (3), 85, 127 (2), 120 (2), proviso to Article 33, Articles 138(2) and 147 (i) (b)." The president has also some other powers of approval prior or subsequent rule to be framed by the authority as per Articles 107(1) and 113(1).The primary and plenary power of framing rules of Parliament with the approval of the president and this will have immediate legislative effect, say, Article 55(6) of the Constitution. Upon a thorough exploration of almost all relevant provisions of the Constitution, the court held that the power of the president under Article 116, in effect the Prime Minister or the chief political Executive of the country in view of Articles 48(3) and 55(2), the president wields control over the presiding officers of subordinate courts in a variety of fields. The Prime Minister becomes the real wielder in this regard. The Prime Minister being a political person is vested with the Executive Power needed to check on such a sweeping and absolute power. The primacy of the views of the Supreme Court shall not be disregarded by the Executive for it is the Supreme Court, not the political Executive, which is the best judge of judicial matters and judicial officers, and under Article 116 the views and opinions of the Supreme Court on any matter shall get primacy over the views and opinions of the Executive.

The court also formulated 12 guidelines to be observed by the Executive, of them Clause 7 and 8 are very relevant. They state: (7) "It is declared that in exercising control and discipline of persons employed in judicial service and magistrates exercising judicial function under Article 116 the views and opinions of the

Supreme Court shall have primacy over those of the Executive." (8) "The essential conditions of judicial independence in Article 116A, elaborated in the judgment, namely within (1) security of tenure, (2) security of salary and other benefits and pension, (3) institutional independence from the parliament and the executive shall be secured in the law or rules made under Article 133 or in the executive orders having the force of rule."

Except for England, all countries are guided by written constitutions which are the primary law of their land. The Executive, the Legislature and the Judiciary as well as the citizens are bound to respect the mandates of the constitution. If anyone disrespects or disregards or flouts or in any way either by innuendo or otherwise neglects any of the provisions of the constitution, s/he cannot claim to be a true citizen of that country because he does not respect the supreme law of the country. In the United Kingdom the monarch heads the country, and it follows constitutional conventions which are as good as a constitution. All nations adore, respect and give allegiance to their respective constitutions. Neither a president nor a prime minister or any organ of the State can disregard the constitution and as per mandates of the constitution all persons holding constitutional posts are bound to subscribe to an oath or affirmation pledging to preserve, protect and defend the constitution. Only judges of the apex court take the oath adding "to protect the law". Under the scheme of every constitution, the three organs of the State are completely independent, and none is subservient to another. But in a country like Bangladesh the parliament is totally controlled by the Executive.

If we look at American history, we find although President Eisenhower respected the rule of law and ordered troops to Little Rock to enforce a Supreme Court order46 he was privately unamused by Chief Justice Warren's most famous opinion. "Southern whites," Eisenhower told Warren at a White House dinner, "are not bad people. All they are concerned about is to see that their sweet little girls are not required to sit in school alongside some big overgrown Negroes."47 Eisenhower later described Warren's appointment as the "biggest damn-fool mistake I ever made."48 Chief Justice Earl Warren was a Republican and he was Governor of California for three terms. So, President Eisenhower never expected that Chief Justice Earl Warren would give a verdict against the right leaning policy of the government. Though he was not happy with the judgment, President Eisenhower did not demean or show any disrespect to Chief Justice Earl Warren, rather the President invited him to a dinner. His only remark was it was his "biggest damn-fool mistake."

It is expected, as did Chief Justice Earl Warren, that every person holding the exalted office of the Chief Justice of a country should respect the constitution and his oath. If he respects the constitution and his oath, he must show allegiance to the constitution, maintain the rule of law and uphold the independence of the judiciary. Otherwise he should not assume the office because, being the head of the judiciary, if he shows partisan behavior democracy and the rule of law is bound to be buried by his hands. He will not command respect from the other judges, the subordinate judges and the people. He will bury the judiciary. Therefore, Chief Justice Earl Warren completely abandoned Lochnerism 48(a) (The Lochner era is a period in American legal history from 1897 to 1937 in which the Supreme Court of the US is said to have made it a common practice "to strike down economic regulations" and the broader idea that judges should set the nation's economic policy – as a unanimous court announced in 1955.

Those days are long past. When the US Supreme Court uses the Due Process Clause of the Fourteenth Amendment to strike down state laws, regulates business and industrial conditions, because they were unwise, improvident or out of harmony with a school of thought. For protection against abuses by the legislatures, the people must resort to the polls, not the courts."49

It is generally noticed that many in the least developed and developing countries after assuming power by hook or by crook government functionaries do not show any respect to the people or pay any attention to the problems of the people. A selfish attitude for personal advancement and personal ambition are the greatest hindrances in reaching out to the needy. During British rule the administration was mainly concerned with maintaining law and order. The constitutional government of a free nation means a joint effort of people, in and outside government, to achieve human development and for it to achieve constitutional goals of equality, justice and dignity of everyone. For constitutional governance, therefore, the mindset from "everyone unto himself" to "concern for others" must be developed. But it seems, the government departments and offices are busy dealing with files and rotating them while the problems of men behind the files are totally forgotten. One fails to understand why a retired person must approach a tribunal for getting his legitimate pension dues. There is so much talk of rampant corruption in every department of the state that the increasing work load in the Anti-Corruption Bureau is testimony to the fact that corruption is a contagious disease and eating up the very vitals of our administrative bodies. The reason seems to be individual self-aggrandizement, insensitivity and lack of human values in the administration.

Unless we develop a check-and balance-concept for the next generation, it will not be possible to achieve human development, for which the constitution requires commitment of the people in and outside the government and their joint effort. During the British Rule the concept was of foreign rule and citizens were ruled. In the constitutional governance of a free nation, both the rulers and ruled are citizens of the same country. Those in government should realize that they are not merely holders of public offices, they must enlighten citizens themselves and must show concern for others to work for human development for achieving the goal set up in the constitution. Swami Ranganathanada in his book "Democratic Administration in Light of Practical Vedant" says, "The slave element which went into the veins during the British period continues even after attaining freedom. Those in the government behave as if they are rulers and the citizens whom they are dealing with are the ruled or their subjects. The Constitution vests sovereignty in the people. It includes citizens who are in the government. They must change their mindset. They are not rulers and the people with whom they deal are not ruled through them. They exercise governmental power for the people and they in the true sense are their servants."50

The essence and core of judicial independence consists in creating a congenial atmosphere for impartial adjudication by the courts. This atmosphere should be preserved both in the higher and lower judiciary free from any constraints, interference and influence, direct or indirect. It is only possible when people will realize that the judiciary has the necessary freedom to act to deliver justice evenhandedly. It also implies functional independence from the administrative point of view. The aim is to facilitate unbiased, fair and efficient dispensation of justice to those who take shelter of the court, so that the public confidence in the administration of justice is preserved and fostered. The guarantee of judicial independence is primarily meant to benefit the public at large and not so much the individual judges. The independence of the judiciary is founded on public trust and it is important to realize that the judiciary is performing its responsibilities without any semblance of interference by the Executive. If there is influence or restriction or inducement or pressure or threat or interference either directly or indirectly from any quarter, there cannot be an independent judiciary. That is why it is recognized in the international arena that the judiciary shall be independent of the Executive and the Legislature and the judges shall enjoy immunity from any sort of harassment for acts and omissions done in their judicial capacity. If it is the basic concept of independence of judiciary, the primary duty is to set up an independent judicial system about appointment, posting, promotion, financial benefits and other perks and it is also recognized as a fundamental principle by the UN Resolution of 1985. The core and primary essence is to institutionalize the judiciary. Institutional independence embraces administrative and financial independence, effective enforcement of judicial decisions and protection to the individual judge and institution from being scandalized.

Institutionalization has many facets, but the Chief Justice must be alert to see whether any organ of the State is trying to intrude into affairs of the judiciary. I noticed at one time that the parliamentary standing committee issued a letter to the Supreme Court directing the Registrar General to attend its meeting for a discussion over the backlog of cases. When my attention was drawn to the matter I directed him not to attend the meeting because it is none of the business of the Standing Committee. It was pointed out to me that the previous Chief Justices used to send Registrar. I told him that they were wrong and advised him to write a letter pointing out that the Standing Committee would not call the Registrar General for discussions relating to internal matters of the judiciary. Then again, the committee wrote another letter which was also ignored. This way the committee continued writing such letters. The Law Minster requested me to send the Registrar General saying that since Sujanjit Sengupta, a senior parliamentarian, had written the letter, his wishes should be respected. I told him if I direct the Secretary of Parliament to attend the Supreme Court for a discussion regarding the business of the parliament, for instance, due to lack of quorum Parliament cannot properly transact business, would the Speaker of Parliament send the Secretary? The Law Minister kept silent. It was very painful when it was pointed out that ABM Khairul Haque, instead of ignoring the request of the Standing Committee, had been regularly attending its meetings. I told the minister that it was Haque's assessment if being the former Chief Justice he attended meetings of the Standing Committee, he was degrading his office and he should have kept that in mind. But I would be the last person to attend such meetings. He could not control his anger and blurted out that I have been under the "sovereign parliament." I was extremely shocked to hear his comment. He had no idea about the meaning of sovereignty.

The government increased the pay scale of civil servants by gazette notification dated December 15, 2015 with retrospective effect from July 1, 2015 but judicial officers' pay scale was published by gazette notification dated April 13, 2016 after much tussle with the government because the government always neglected the judiciary. Government officials started drawing enhanced salaries from December 2015, but judicial officers got theirs after four months and it was after I had given an ultimatum that the gazette was published. Regarding the enhancement of salaries of the President, Ministers and Judges were settled in the same cabinet meeting and before such meeting the Law Minister discussed with me regarding the judges' salary. I supplied him with the mode of increase of emolument by writing before his decision. But three separate Bills for President, Speaker and Deputy Speaker and Ministers were passed on May 5, 2016 by Act 19 of 2016, The President's (Remuneration and Privileges) (Amendment) Act 2016, Act-20 of 2016, The Prime Minister's (Remuneration and Privileges) (Amendment) Act 2016, Act 21 of 2016, Speaker and Deputy Speaker (Remuneration and Privileges) (Amendment) Act 2016, Act 22 0f 2016, The Ministers, Ministers of State and Deputy Ministers (Remuneration and Privileges) (Amendment) Act 2016, Act 23 of 2016, Members of Parliament (Remuneration and Allowances) (Amendment) Act 2016, but the Supreme Court Judges Pay Bill was stalled on the ground that unless I would agree to send the Registrar General for discussions, the Bill would not be placed in the house.

The President, the Prime Minister, the Speaker and Ministers started drawing new salaries, but the judges were deprived of the new pay scale. Finding no alternative, I wrote a demi official (DO) letter addressed to the Speaker reminding her that it is not desirable for any tussle between Parliament and the Judiciary and requested her to pass the Judges Remuneration and Privileges Amendment Bill. I also reminded her of the deadlock that had been created between the Judiciary and the Uttar Pradesh Legislature over powers, privileges and immunities of the State Legislature.50 (a) this letter also yielded no result and ultimately, I brought the matter to the Prime Minister's notice, but she gave no satisfactory reply. Then I told her that while the president, prime minister, ministers, parliament members, officers and employees of administrative services were enjoying the festivities and benefits, the judges were being deprived from those benefits. Some of the judges also expressed their frustration that they were being deprived of the benefits, but they could not raise the issue with me. On getting scent of some of their dissatisfaction in a full court meeting while discussing on miscellaneous agenda I reminded the judges that prestige and dignity cannot be assessed by money; that I am the last person who would surrender to the wishes of the Executive; and that the government would be bound to give our increased salaries one day. Possibly this remark was communicated to the ministers by some of the judges and ultimately the Bill was passed as the Supreme Court Judges (Remuneration and Privileges) (Amendment) Act, 2016 (Act No. XXXIX of 2016). The judges got their benefits more than six months after the President and the Prime Minister got their benefits!

Except Bangladesh, I cannot recollect of any country that has a constitution and democracy and yet the judiciary is under the direct control and discipline of the Executive. After the delivery of judgment in the Masder Hossain case, fourteen years had elapsed, but the Executive did not promulgate the disciplinary and conduct rules for the officers of the subordinate judiciary. Even no step was taken in this regard, although the government has been claiming that the lower judiciary is independent. After I assumed office as the Chief Justice, I directed the Ministry of Law to submit the draft disciplinary and conduct rules. After taking adjournments for about six months, the concerned Ministry submitted a draft copy of Disciplinary Rules without the Conduct Rules, which was a verbatim reproduction of the Government Servants (Appeal and Disciplinary) Rules 1985. It was in direct conflict with the Masder Hossain verdict, particularly the Directive No-7. Accordingly, the Full Court directed the Ministry to submit modified rules in conformity with the directive given in the Masder Hossain judgment.

The government submitted the new rules, but they were in fact almost like its earlier rules. So, I constituted a powerful committee headed by the senior most judge of the Appellate Division, Md. Abdul Wahhab Miah. The committee submitted a comparative chart showing the provisions which conflicted with Masder Hossain and modified the draft copy with different colors which ought to be added and/or substituted in place of the one prepared by the Ministry. The Full Court constituted with the Chief Justice, Md Abdul Wahhab Miah, Nazmun Ara Sultana, Syed Mahmud Hossain, Muhammad Iman Ali, Hasan Foez Siddique, Mirza Hossain Haider, Muhammad Nizamul Haque and Mohammad Bazlur Rahman--a nine-member Bench by order dated August 20, 2016, by quoting guidelines No. 1 and 7 in Masder Hossain observed that the government had accepted the guidelines and separated the Magistracy, but the lower judiciary could not function independently under the control and supervision of the Supreme Court in the absence of Disciplinary and Conduct Rules. Since the copy of the rules prepared by the government was not in conformity with the above guidelines, it observed that the draft copy prepared by the Ministry of Law is marked as appendix A and the modified copy in conformity with Masder Hossain case was appendix B. The office printed the same separately to identify the portion recommended by the government and the parts modified by the Committee. The words and figures printed in red color were the modifications made by the committee. To remove any doubt or confusion, the office also printed a corrected copy, which was marked as appendix C, and which should be published in the gazette.

The Court by order dated May 11, 2015 observed that in the absence of Conduct Rules, if service rules are prepared, no action could be taken against any judicial officer and, accordingly, it directed the government to supply the copy of Conduct Rules. Till date the government did not communicate the draft copy of the Conduct Rules. Accordingly, as per direction of the Chief Justice the committee prepared the Conduct Rules marking it as appendix D. Conduct Rules are indispensable for implementing the service rules and it has been prepared in conformity with the prevailing norms that are being followed by the judicial officers with certain modifications. While preparing the modified draft Rules the Committee noticed that there was inconsistency in the "Bangladesh Judicial Service (Service Formation, Appointment and Suspension, dismissal and removal) Bidhimala, 2007," and not in conformity with guideline No.7 in Masder Hossain, inasmuch as, under the prevailing rules, it is provided in rule 7 that no officer can be suspended by an officer other than one below the rank of the appointing authority. The appointing authority of judicial officers is the President. By providing this provision no action can be taken against any judicial officer even if he is found guilty of corruption or insubordination by the Supreme Court promptly. This has hampered the administration of justice. This anomaly should be removed for maintaining the rule of law. This has also caused various complications in the administration of justice.

Accordingly, the Committee prepared an amendment in the said rules, which will augment the administration of justice. The proposed amendment was communicated by marking it as appendix E.

The order was passed by the nine-member Bench and order was communicated to the government hoping that the government would publish the gazette notification by November 6, 2016. The Ministry did not publish the gazette notification and instead sat on the matter. I requested the Law Minister to have a cup of tea. The Law Minister pointed out that the court had undermined the President by making certain observations in the order. On hearing his remark, I was greatly surprised and noticed the audacity of the Law Minister in questioning the propriety of the court's order. But I did not retort to his remark and told him that we would look into the matter later on, but we must talk about the rules. If the order of the court is not correct or amounts to demeaning the President, the remedy for the government is to file a review petition. I told him that I have quoted the order of the court and there I find nothing demeaning to the President. Moreover, the President is not above the law. The Law Minister's objection was only to delay the process. I explained to him meticulously with reasons behind those modified provisions. On hearing me he did not have any answer and said that he would publish the gazette notification very soon.

When the Law Minister visits the Chief Justice, he informs the media people that he was going to meet the Chief Justice. This time also both electronic and print media reporters were waiting at the porch of the Supreme Court. On query from the media, the Law Minister told them that there were fruitful discussions with the Chief Justice and whatever differences were there between the judiciary and the executive about the rules had been settled amicably. There was no difficulty in publishing the gazette notification. The Law Minister also assured me that he would publish the gazette notification within a week. The Law Minister's remarks were widely covered by the media. At that time, I attended a program arranged by the Sylhet Bar in which I said that we are getting the Disciplinary Rules for the judicial officers within a week. However, in fact all statements of the Law Minster, that the differences between the government and the Supreme Court in finalizing the rules had been minimized, were a myth which I noticed later.

The Law Minister wasted one year by showing various pleas. He never told the media that there were differences between the Supreme Court and the Law Ministry. The Attorney General also intimated to the court that so far, the rules were concerned, they were in the hands of the Law Minister and that he had no hand in it. The court was totally helpless in the hands of the Law Minister and I was of the view that without taking any punitive action against the persons who were involved in the matter, it would be proper to somehow get the rules published in the gazette. All my endeavors failed due to the rigid attitude of the Law Minister. Whenever he met me he appeared to me very cordial and pretended that the rules were in the final stage for examination before final publication in the gazette. I had never come across any Law Minister who blatantly makes such false statements to a Chief Justice. All the time he failed to honor his words, which he gave to me not only over the publication of the gazette, but also about the appointment of judges in the High Court Division and elevation of judges to the Appellate Division. On every occasion of his visit, he used to make requests for some cases and I got information from reliable sources that he was in the habit of requesting the judges of the High Court Davison in respect of some cases. During my tenure as judge, I found three Law Ministers and I never found that Abdul Matin Khasru and Shafique Ahmed requesting on behalf of any case at any point of time. The previous two Ministers regularly attended the Ministry from morning to 5:00 PM, but Anisul Haque hardly attends his office in the Ministry every day. The net result was that all decisions on urgent matters are kept pending for months together due to his absence from the Ministry.

When I was compelled to leave the country, I learnt from the media that there was fruitful discussion between the Law Minister and judges of the Appellate Division headed by Justice Md. Abdul Wahhab Miah, then performing the functions of the Chief Justice, and resolved the differences and that the gazette notification would be published soon. I believed on hearing the news that there was no scope for discussion again after the approval of the modified copy of the rules in open court by a nine-member Bench. Such an order cannot be altered privately by five judges in the chamber. Without reviewing the order dated August 28, 2016, the judges cannot take any decision. To my utter surprise, the government published the rules in a gazette notification on December 11, 2017 and the court accepted the rules. Somehow, I collected a copy of the rules and on reading them I was totally bewildered. The rules are verbatim repetition of the rules which were initially prepared by the Ministry and those are in total conflict with Masder Hossain and the order dated August 28, 2016.

The crucial point in a dispute over the rules between the Supreme Court and the Ministry is over the question of primacy on all matters of judicial officers performing judicial functions in courts and tribunals and judicial magistrates. A look into the rules clearly shows that the Executive has primacy over the Supreme Court despite clear directives in Masder Hossain, which separated the Judiciary form the Executive. The government has kept the lower courts under its control. To make the point clearer, in the process of taking disciplinary action against a judicial officer, who would be the "appropriate authority' in deciding it? In the definition column, the term "Superior Authority" means in proper cases the "Appropriate Authority", the Supreme Court, and in case of officials on deputation the authority that controls them. So, the officers on deputation are kept totally outside the control of the Supreme Court although they are put on deputation with the Supreme Court for a limited period. "Appropriate Authority" means, it was stated, the President or the Ministry or Division entrusted within the scope of the rules of business formulated under Article 55(6) of the Constitution. All other provisions relating to enquiry and departmental proceedings; filing of departmental case; issuance of first and second show cause notices; imposition of minor or major penalties; attachment of an officer during the period of suspension; the appointment of enquiry officer or committee; the objection against the enquiry officer; consideration of enquiry report; second show cause notice and final decision; enquiry and other steps regarding physical or mental incapacity of an officer; the procedure for enquiry and issuance of notice in case of desertion of service; procedure for filing criminal case; and the chapter regarding appeal and review are kept with the Executive. The Executive has primacy while the Supreme Court's role is advisory.

Masder Hossain's case was decided as back as on December 2, 1999, and since then almost two decades have elapsed. The government filed review against the judgment which was also dismissed. The law does not permit a second review. The judgment has attained finality, and the government accepted the judgment and implemented about eighty percent of the directives. The government has estopped from deviating from the guidelines given in Masder Hossain. The prime and principal point decided in the case was the complete separation of the Judiciary from the Executive; and in respect of disciplinary actions the primacy should be with the Supreme Court over the Executive. The above opinion was expressed keeping mind the substituted provisions of Article 116 after rejecting the submission made at the Bar. The court observed that under the scheme of the Constitution, the President has only two powers contained in Clause (3) of Article 48 of the Constitution. Though in Article 116 the control (including the power of posting, promotion and grant of leave) and discipline of persons employed in the judicial service shall vest in the President, in effect this power remains with "the Prime Minister or the chief political executive of the country, in view of Articles 48 (3) and 55 (2). The President wields control over the presiding officers of subordinate courts in a wide variety of fields. The Prime Minister has therefore become the real wielder of power in this regard. The Prime Minister being a political person in whom is vested the Executive Power of the Republic needed a check on such sweeping and absolute power," the court observed. "Article 116 and 116A will be only making binds. What is that teeth? Are mere meaningful and substantive consultations and full disclosure of all connected facts during consultations enough? These are no doubt essential and necessary requirements in the process of consultation, but the end-result shall be the primacy of the views and opinion of the Supreme Court, which the Executive shall not disregard, for it is the Supreme Court, not the political executive, which is the best judge of judicial matters and judicial officers.

Under Article 116 the views and opinions of the Supreme Court on any matter covered by that Article shall get primacy over the views and the opinions of the Executive."

Though in Masder Hossain the court in clear terms observed that Parliament had blundered in forgetting that neither it in exercise of its power under Article 136 nor the President in exercise of his power under the proviso to Article 133 of the Constitution can usurp the primary rulemaking of the President in respect of appointment of persons in the judicial service and that when laws are made by Parliament, either the Presidential Rules go out of existence or they exist to the extent not in conflict with the laws made by the parliament. The contingent rule-making power of the President are contained in Articles 62(2), 75(1) (a), 79(3), 85, 127(2), 128(3), 138(2), 147(1) (b) and proviso to Article 133 of the Constitution. The President is also designated as a rule approving authority, such as Articles 107(1) and 113(1) of the Constitution.

Article 115 provides another example of such a direct, primary and plenary power of the President to make rules about appointments of persons to offices in the judicial service or magistrates exercising judicial functions. Parliament has no authority to make laws or the government has no authority to pass orders or frame rules under our Constitution on this subject. The rule-making power of the President in relation to appointments include the rule-making power to create a judicial service in the first place, to prescribe qualifications for appointment, the manner or method of recruitment, and all pre-appointment matters to be covered by Rules. If the executive power to appoint includes the power to suspend or dismiss, and if 1Article 115 gives the President rule-making power in respect of appointment, then why the word 'appointments' in Article 115 should not be given its full meaning, both in the Executive and rule-making spheres and why the rule-making power of appointment should not extend to rule-making power to suspend or dismiss. Reading Articles 115 and 116 together it is clear that the President will make rules regarding suspension and dismissal under Article 115 and frame rules in such manner that he will leave the control to himself to be exercised in the manner contained in Article 116. If Articles 109 and 116 are read together, they mean that the real control over the courts and tribunals and their presiding officers will be exercised by the High Court Division. A rule-making power cannot be so easily implied when the makers of the Constitution did not lack in expression while bestowing an authority with rule-making power in Articles 62(2), 79(2)(3), 113(2), 115 and proviso to Article 133. Therefore, Article 116 contains only executive power and the manner of its exercise. The President can exercise nothing more than that.

In arriving at such a conclusion, the court held that "conferment of legislation or rule-making power has to be specific and definite" as per the Constitution. A rule-making power cannot be so easily implied when the makers of the Constitution did not lack in expression while bestowing an authority with rule-making power as in Articles 62(2), 79(2)(3), 113(2), 115 and 116. Article 115 contains both Executive and legislative powers to the extent described by the court earlier, but Article 116 contains only an Executive Power and the manner to exercise it. The Constitution, therefore, clearly intended that the rules of recruitment and appointments of persons to such offices and the control and discipline of them shall be regulated in a manner different from their services to government by Part IX of the Constitution. Over and above, Article 116A confers on such person's independence in exercise of their judicial functions that was not there in the earlier provisions governing the field. The provisions show the judicial service as a class apart from the executive and administrative civil services of the Republic. Articles 133 and 136 are applicable to them, but they are to be treated as a class apart from the other services of the Republic as a distinct entity, never to be treated alike or merged or amalgamated with any other service, except with a service of allied nature. The apex court left no stone unturned while expressing its opinion. Those findings are past and closed and cannot be realized from them. Any deviation from them is tantamount to violation of the Constitution. If the judges cannot comprehend the tenor and meaning of the opinions, they cannot hold the office of the highest court.

Therefore, the Ministry, particularly the Law Minister, Law Secretary and the judges of the court flouted the findings, directions and guidelines in Masder Hossain and/or failed to comprehend the ratio in Madsder Hossain and thereby their acts are violation of the Constitution. The five-member Bench which approved the rules have not only betrayed the judiciary for fear of reprisal by the Executive but also trampled upon the judiciary. The Bidhimala of 2007 is also not in conformity with the guidelines in Masder Hossain. The five-member Bench cannot ignore, nullify and/or review any order or judgment passed by a nine-member Bench. Therefore, the order accepting the Disciplinary Rules by the Bench is per-in curium and has no force of law. It is a misfortune that these judges compromised with their conscience which is disgraceful, shameful and violated the judicial norms.

References:

1. *US Constitution, Article II Section 3*
2. *The Federalist No. 47 (James Madison)*
3. *The Federalist No. 48*
4. *Keshwananda Bharati v. State of Kerala, AIR 1973 Sc 146*
5. *The Principle of Constitutional Interpretation by Justice D.M Dharmadhikari (2004) 4 SCC Journal 3, Working a Democratic Constitution-The Indian Express, by Granbelly, Austin*
6. *The Records of the Federal Convention of 1887 @ 318*
7. *Hamdan v. Ramsfield, 548 US 557 (2006)*
8. *343 US @637 (Jackson J concurring)*
9. *Youngstoyn, 343 US 655*
10. *Freedom and the Law, p. 83-84*
11. *Histories, Book 6, 11-13*
12. *The Spirit of the Laws, 1748*
13. *The Roman Republic in Monlesquiew and Rousseau, Schiendler, Ronald, Monlesquieu's political writings (2012) and Loyd, Marshal Davies (1998), Polybus and Founding Fathers, The Separation of Powers.*
14. *The Spirit of the Laws, 1748*
15. *Australian Communist Party v. Commonwealth (1951) HCA 5 Aust LII*
16. *Indian Constitutional Law, LexisNexis Butterworths Wadhwa, Nagpur, page 912*

17. D. Argondizzo-G. Buonomo, Spiglature intorno allattuale bicameralisomo e proposte per quello future, in Monodoperaio.net.aprile 2014, p. 9
18. Wikipedia
19. Wikipedia
20. Constitution of the United States and Marbury v. Madison, 5 US (1 Cranch) 137 (1803)
21. Garcia-Trevijano, Anlanio, A Pure Theory of Democracy, Translated by University of America
22. Bruce P. Frohnen, George W. Carey, Constitutional Morality and the Rise of Quasi-Law, Harvard University Press 2016
23. James Madison, The Federalist Paper 51
24. Wikipedia
25. Justice B.R Krishna Iyer, Law and Life, page-90
26. Ibid
27. The Conservative Soul, p. 235
28. Freedom and the Law, p. 95-96
29. Ibid
30. Wikipedia
31. The normative cycle of shaping judicial independence in domestic and international; The mutual impact of National and International Jurisprudence and Contemporary Practical and Conceptual Challenges (2009), 10 Chicago Journal of International Law
32. Wikipedia
33. Ibid
34. Ibid
35. Ibid
36. International Association of Judicial Independence and World Peace-International Project of Judicial Independence Retrieved 11 October 2014
37. Montreal Declaration, 10 June 1983
38. Moreau-Berube v. New Brunswick, Judicial Council (2002) 209 DLR (Fourth Series)
39. Human Values and Human Rights, Justice D.M Dharmadhikari, p. 304
40. Secretary, Ministry of Finance v. Md. Masder Hossain, 52 DLR (AD) 482
41. Articles 109 and 116 of the Constitution
42. The Constitution (Fourth Amendment) Act, 1975
43. The Constitution (Fifth Amendment) Act, 2011
44. Brown v. Board of Education, 347 US 483 (1954)

45. Charles J. Ogletree, *All Deliberate Speed, Reflections on the First half Century of Brown v. Board of Education*

46. Alden Whiteman, *Earl Warren, 83, Who led High Court in Time of vast Social Change, Is Dead*, NY Times, July 10, 1974

47. *Williamson v. Lee Optical of Oklahoma, Inc* 348 US 483, 488 (1955)

48. Extracts *Human Values and Human Rights*

48(a). Lochner era is a period in American legal history from 1897 to 1937 in which the Supreme Court strikes down economic regulations

49. Ibid

50(a) AIR 1965 SC 745

Chapter 27

Constitution: Sixteenth Amendment Case and its Aftermath

After the introduction the parliamentary form of government by the Constitution (Thirteenth Amendment) Act, 1991, the Westminster form of government was established in Bangladesh. But the government then in power could not conduct a free and fair election. All bi-elections were contravened. There was agitation by the Bangladesh Awami League for introducing a system for holding the national elections under a Non-party Neutral Caretaker Government. The then Prime Minister told the media that "there was no impartial person other than a child or a lunatic." In one sense, she was correct. But, no credible elections under a government could be organized and they had become farcical. All elections are turned 'antonyms'. They were merely eyewash. The Constitution has a chapter on the Election Commission and, in black and white, the Election Commission is independent and impartial. But the question is why there cannot be a free and fair election under any political party in power? This must be clarified first.

Keeping a provision in the Constitution and giving power to an agency conducting its business independently and impartially is one thing, but unless the institution is manned by persons who are not impartial, no credible and impartial election under him can be held impartially. It is a practice prevalent in our country that the Election Commissioners are appointed from amongst retired persons. So, they feel that their selection is a bonus after retirement and thus they must perform their responsibilities as per the desire of the government in power. If such a process can continue, there cannot be any credible and fair election with Election Commissioners because they are chosen on consideration of their line of thinking, political ideology and connections with that political party. No government ever tried to institutionalize the

Election Commission. All political parties when they come to power want to fill the Election Commission with their own men without caring for democracy or the organization.

That is why it has been said, the government in power did not allow any department or organs under the Constitution to work independently and to institutionalize them. If the selection process is flouted one cannot expect impartial treatment from the department even if the Constitution provides otherwise. So, it is to be understood in that sense. The Bangladesh Awami League committed a blunder in demanding introduction of a system of Non-party Caretaker Government after the expiry of the tenure of the government for a period of three months for holding national election. There was provision of composition of a Non-party Caretaker Government2 with a Chief Adviser at its ahead and not more than 10 other advisers, all of whom shall be appointed by the President. The Chief Adviser and the other Advisers shall be appointed within fifteen days after Parliament is dissolved or stands dissolved and the date on which the Chief Adviser is appointed. The Prime Minister and his/her cabinet who were in office immediately before Parliament was dissolved or stood dissolved, shall continue to hold office as such. The President shall appoint a person who among the retired last Chief Justices and who are qualified to be appointed as an Adviser, provided that if such retired Chief Justice is not available or is not willing to hold the office of Chief Adviser, the President shall appoint as Chief Adviser the person who among the retired Chief Justices of Bangladesh retired next before the last retired Chief Justice. If no retired Chief Justice is available or willing to hold office as Chief Adviser, the President shall appoint who a Chief Adviser from among the retired Judges of the Appellate Division who retired last provided that if such retired judge is not available or willing to hold office as Chief Adviser the President shall appoint a Chief Adviser from among the citizens of Bangladesh who are qualified to be appointed as Advisers.

However, if the above provisions cannot be given effect to, the President shall assume the functions of Chief Adviser. The Non-party Caretaker Government shall discharge its functions as an interim government and shall carry on routine work and routine functions of the government with the aid and assistance of persons in the services of the Republic; and, except in the case of necessity for the discharge of such functions, it shall not make any policy decisions.3

These provisions are so vague, indefinite and lacking in of precision in the process of selection of Chief Adviser and Advisers that the President exercised his function as in a presidential form of government without checks and balances in a system run by a Westminster type of government. Firstly, the President was elected by a political party. The political parties had no confidence even in his members of Parliament. So instead of holding election of the President by secret ballot, the voting of President was to be done by raising hands on the open floor of Parliament by an amendment to the Constitution only to deter party members from voting for the opposition candidate, even if the opposition candidate is more capable, impartial and popular. The members were compelled to vote for the one who is selected by the party hierarchy. The natural consequence is that no person of moral integrity and dignity, even he believes in political philosophy of a political party, can be selected as its candidate. Only a diehard partisan politician would be selected as the party candidate.

This was proved when Prof. Badrudduzza Chowdhury, a veteran physician and a progressive-minded cultural personality, could not continue in the office of President only because from his conduct and deeds he showed some impartiality. Under the prevailing system, the President is a titular head of the State having no executive power other than the appointment of the Prime Minister and the Chief Justice only. But these two functions are also taken as per advice of the chief of the party which commands the highest number of votes in Parliament and nominates him as the Prime Minister. Therefore, he cannot move beyond the party decisions. In the absence of the Prime Minister, he practically represents the interim government and conducts business for the interest of the political party to which he belongs. Therefore, he cannot choose an impartial Chief Adviser and other Advisers.

Moreover, the political party in power would look for the judge to be elevated to the Appellate Division keeping in mind his date of retirement so that he could be appointed as Chief Justice who retired last before the expiration of the tenure of the government. Naturally, the political parties try to bring politics in the process of elevation of judges to the Appellate Division with a view to serve their purpose. Judges who are not involved in politics but are suddenly compelled to get involved in political activities for running a government even for a limited period of three months would perform political activities within and outside the country. There were bad provisions for the selection of Advisers in the Non-party Caretaker Government and, most of all, the difficult task for the President was the selection of a Chief Adviser from the citizens of Bangladesh, if he (the President) could not select one from amongst the Chief Justices or judges of the Appellate Division who had retired last. Though the functions of the Caretaker Government were to carry out only routine work of the government without entering policy decisions, it is seen in each period of selecting the Chief Adviser and Advisers, there was chaos and confusion. During one of such government, the Chief of Army was about to take over power and the country was put in serious lawless situation but somehow or other the situation was tackled.

One Chief Adviser made dramatic changes in the administration immediately after taking oath in Bang Bhaban even before formation of his Cabinet. Questions were raised from different quarters as to how he could take such decisions before assuming his office and after taking advice from his advisers. He gave an explanation that as he was about to be appointed as Chief Adviser, he had done some "field work" of his own. A retired Chief Justice is not supposed to know which officers are neutral and which are not unless and until he takes advice from his advisers or other sources. If he had decided something before taking oath of office, it was certainly from a section of officers who were not on good terms with the immediate past government. So, from that moment he became not an impartial head of a Caretaker Government. He must have served the purpose of some interested quarter. Even if it is assumed that he was not partisan, his conduct raised suspicions among a section of the people that he was partisan. That proved that the interim government was not a neutral government, but a partisan one. Soon thereafter, the caretaker Chief formed a commission to recommend cases which were filed on alleged political considerations. This power does not come within the scheme of a Caretaker Government because it is a political decision. It is reported that as per recommendations of the commission he had formed, about three thousand diehard criminals were released from custody. There was strong resentment from one political party against the actions of the Caretaker Government, but little attention was given to the objections. There was allegation also in the selection of some of the Advisers.

In the selection of the next Caretaker Government the President, without following Clauses (3) (4) and (5) of Article 58C, assumed the office Chief Adviser of the Caretaker Government. It was now when one political party, the Bangladesh Awami League, protested the appointment of Justice K.M Hasan, the retired Chief Justice. According to that party, he was a politically partisan person. If the Chief Justice is politically motivated and partisan, what would be the consequences of the judgments delivered by him? So, politics was brought into the appointment process of judges. There was much agitation against his appointment leading to loss of lives. After assumption of office by the President, the situation turned more complex. One political party raised serious objections against the appointment of the Chief Adviser and his Advisers, it continued for months together and ultimately the Army had to intervene in the matter and the President was compelled to declare Emergency in the country, but such a declaration of Emergency by the President was unconstitutional.4

A proclamation of Emergency can only be declared by the President if he is satisfied that a grave emergency exists in which the security or economic life of Bangladesh, or any part thereof, is threatened by war or external aggression or internal disturbance, for a period of 120 days provided such proclamation is countersigned by the Prime Minister prior to its proclamation for its validity. There was no Prime Minister working at that time. Though there was internal disturbance in the country, it was due to the partisan role of the President for which the country should not be burdened with an Emergency. Because of the imposition of Emergency, all fundamental rights were suspended. One may pose a question that if during the subsistence of a Caretaker Government, there was threat of aggression externally or serious internal disturbance, what would the President do since there was no Prime Minister during that time? These are very intricate constitutional points and before the constitutional amendment there should have been detailed discussion among the political parties and with the constitutional experts. Parliament ought to have debated the matter and made corresponding amendment to Article 141A.

There was no scope for such discussion as one of the biggest political parties was not represented in Parliament and the constitutional amendment was brought in haste and was passed within a very short time. The country was brought under some sort of mini-martial law and during the long tenure of the Caretaker Government of about two years, the interim government made many policy decisions and promulgated laws which were not within the ambit of the Caretaker Government. The military was at the helm of affairs and the Caretaker Government was used as a rubber stamp. Almost all leading political leaders including heads of the two biggest political parties were arrested and a huge number of cases were filed against them. Kangaroo courts were set up in the Jatiya Sangsad Bhaban to hold trials of offences of corruption against them.

A writ petition was filed challenging the vires of the Constitution Thirteenth Amendment5 as public interest litigation. The High Court Division discharged the rule holding that the amendment was intra vires of the Constitution. However, one member of the Bench suspected as to whether under the new system there was possibility of holding an impartial election even if the prime minister was not in office since the government's men and machinery would be used by such government to influence the election result in favor of the political party to which the prime minister belonged. This was the major factor necessitating the passing of the government. I held that the constitutional law or the constitutional convention and rules did not develop in Pakistan. Our founding fathers committed to the people to present a modern democracy, a constitution where the fundamental rights of the citizens will be enshrined, democracy will flourish and be practiced, and the rule of law will prevail. But within a short time, the people found the leaders were concentrating power and acted against the spirit of democracy. The rulers whittled down conventions and morality. No constitutional set up, either the Executive or Parliament or Election Commission or the Judiciary, could function. It is wrong to say that to achieve democracy Parliament may bring amendments to the constitution.

Can Parliament amend the Constitution by changing the basic structure of the Constitution? Can it bring a system by which the parliamentary form of government is converted to the presidential form of government for consolidating and institutionalizing democracy? The system introduced by the amendment was so vague that the question of choosing a Chief Justice who had retired last under Clause (3) of Article 58C had been raised by one of the main political parties. If there is objection against the selection of another Chief Justice, who retired last before the last Chief Justice, by another political party the President had no option other than to appoint the Chief Adviser from among the judges of the Appellate Division. If there are similar objections against such judges of the Appellate Division who retired last, clearly then there would be a deadlock, chaos and confusion in the process of selection of the Chief Adviser. If no consensus is reached among the major political parties to select a citizen, the President would assume the office who is none but elected by the members of a political party who had a majority in Parliament.

A written constitution is the source from which all governmental power emanates, and it defines its scope and ambit, so that each functionary would act within their respective fields. No power can be claimed by any functionary which is not to be found within the constitution nor can anyone transgress the limits thereof. We had followed the path of Pakistan. Instead of flourishing democracy, the rulers in Pakistan tried to concentrate their powers instead by presenting a constitution after partition and acted against the spirit of democracy. The rulers whittled down the conventional morality. No constitutional set up either the Executive or Parliament or Judiciary or Election Commission could function. This is reflected in the historical background of Pakistan.6 I found no difference between the Pakistan's political episode after partition and ours after independence. Though we got a good constitution immediately after independence, the persons who fought for democracy, rule of law and the constitution whittled down the Constitution itself. From that point, we started heading in a similar manner and it continues even today.

Previous Caretaker Governments had changed almost the entire administration which raised the question as to the modality of their actions, as if they transacted business of the government like elected governments. This violation of the Constitution would continue so long the system would exist. There are inconsistencies between Article 56(4) and 58A which tend to cloud the order, length and the manner of governance by a Caretaker Government. In a democratic polity after the dissolution of Parliament, the existing government is entrusted with the role of interim government. The Prime Minister does not lose the representative character even after dissolution of Parliament, as is evident from Articles 56C (4), 57 (3), 73 (3), (4) & (5). The President is entrusted with power of defense portfolio. Therefore, in the parliamentary form of government, the President shall exercise the Executive power of the government, which is contrary to Article 55(2). Also, Article 58B (3) is not in pari-materia with Article 55(2) in view of Clause 58B (2) which provides that "The Caretaker Government shall be collectively responsible to the President." Though the President is not in the true sense the representative of the people in the sense the Presidents of the United States and the France are as they are elected by the people. In our case the President is not answerable to the people but answerable to Parliament. Therefore, he cannot wield the power that is being used by the Prime Minister under Article 55(2). The system reverted to a system which functioned prior to the Constitution (Twelfth Amendment) Act, 1991.

Democracy being a vague term, its connotation varies from country to country, though the Thirteenth Amendment suspends the representative government for a short interregnum period. Due to the lack of transparency in the selection process of the Election Commissioners, the Commission could not function independently and if the independence of the Election Commission is ensured in ultimately then attention should be given to the quality of persons manning the Election Commission. If the selection process is not transparent, there cannot be any free and fair election in the country. It is a shame for a nation that a political party which can run the country for five years cannot present a parliamentary election impartially and fairly. It is also disgraceful for such a political party which stands in the way of holding free and fair elections. No self-respecting nation can even imagine that such political parties will run the country for five years, if it cannot conduct a free and fair election. The character and content of parliamentary democracy in the ultimate analysis depend upon the quality of persons who function in the legislature as representatives of the people. Elections are a barometer of democracy and the contestants are the lifeline of the parliamentary system and its set up.

If we want to achieve free and fair elections, the institutionalization of al democratic institutions is a pre-condition. Without improving democratic institutions no election can be conducted freely and fairly. The Election Commission has been given the responsibility of superintendence, direction and control of the conduct of elections. So, if the Executive really wants to hold a free and fair election, Part VII of the Constitution under the heading "Elections" should be amended empowering the Election Commission with such powers as are necessary for holding a free and fair election. The Election Commission should be equipped with all facilities and allowed to function independently with a view to restoring the people's confidence. Right persons should be appointed to the office of the Election Commission after consultation with all political parties. The Election Commission should be preserved and protected from political interference.

I failed to understand that the Thirteenth Amendment to the Constitution was made to restore the people's confidence in a democratic process which is devoid of substance on the constitutional and jurisprudential point of view. If an executive government can ensure free and fair election, there is no need for providing any independent Election Commission in the Constitution. The founders entrusted the task upon the Election Commission and not upon the executive government. For achieving the constitutional mandate for holding free and fair election, Article 126 says that "the Executive authority shall assist the Election Commission in the discharge of its function." But no corresponding power has been given to the Election Commission like Article 112 of the Constitution, which contains in Part VI under the heading "Judiciary". The Executive authority acts in aid of the Supreme Court whenever a direction or order or a declaration is made by it since the Supreme Court has been given the arms to investigate and punish for any contempt for violation of such order or direction, a power that is lacking in the Election Commission. The Election Commission has not been given any magistracy power for an offence punishable under Sections 175, 175, 180 and 228 of the Penal Code. It should be allowed to take penal action against government servants entrusted with election responsibilities if they violate any order or direction. If any officer is deputed to the Election Commission, the EC then should have power to take disciplinary action against him and the Commission should also be giving the full power to transfer any public servant during the interregnum period. It should also be afforded with staff and employees according to its requirement.

If any public servant is given on deputation to the Election Commission, such officer must be guided by the disciplinary rules of the Commission. It is difficult to conceive that the Executive Government will not follow the direction of the Election Commission in the interest of holding a free and fair election which is a basic feature of the Constitution. If the Executive really wants to hold a free and fair election, Parliament should make corresponding amendments in Part VII of the Constitution. Parliament instead of making necessary amendments in the Election Commission Chapter introduced a hotchpotch system dismantling the parliamentary form of government. A constitution should not be allowed to remain in a hotchpotch condition. A provision in the constitution which creates chaos, confusion and anarchy should be removed. I concluded my opinion with the observation that the holding a free and fair parliamentary election is the main issue of the day. So the next two parliamentary elections may be held under the existing system in light of the observations made subject to the condition that the selection of the Chief Adviser should be made not from the Chief Justices retired last or from the retired last judges of the Appellate Division in according to Clauses (3) & (4) of Article 58C with the hope that Parliament shall enact laws during this period by amending the Constitution for institutionalizing and equipping the Election Commission for conducting free and fair national parliamentary elections.

The day I took oath as an additional judge in the High Court Division, I kept in my mind that I would have to face many challenges every day and I would give priority to my office other than anything else---even at the cost of my family life, mainly because I had sacrificed much in my long-cherished profession which I developed day-by-day with much hard work and devotion. This profession gave me everything--my status, recognition as a reputed lawyer among my contemporaries, financial stability from zero to the owner of a four-storey house in the capital's Dhanmondi area and maintaining a vehicle with a chauffeur which was rare in those days. It all was a dream for most lawyers in those days, but somehow, I attained them. I was the fortunate one because of my association with the best lawyers, both in the district court and the highest court, and my sacrifices in family life. So, I had kept in mind that there was no scope to retreat from my beliefs. I knew that every judge took oath to preserve, protect and defend the Constitution and the law. There always has been controversy surrounding that office and it is bestowed by the Constitution to take every challenge whatever might be the consequence. I kept in mind that when a serious question of the correctness of any constitutional point arose it was emphatically the province and duty of the judiciary to say what the law is. My firm principle for which I assumed the new office was to uphold the Constitution. One of such challenge involves measuring executive and legislative actions against the Constitution whenever such actions were first brought within the sphere of controversy, and then properly brought within the judicial review jurisdiction of the court. I was conscious that a person who sat in court must have known that there always has been and, probably, always will be controversy surrounding that office. It is inherent in the office of a judge of the highest court. Accordingly, I must have been prepared for the attacks upon me. I ventured to express the hope that my decisions always will be controversial, because it is the nature of the human dominant group in a country like ours to keep pressing for further domination. And unless I had the fiber to do justice to the weakest, vulnerable, women and children of the country, regardless of the pressure brought upon me, we can never achieve our goal of life, liberty, freedom and well-being for everyone. I was prepared to express my opinion that the court's process is more available to the public than those of the other branches of the government, i.e. the Executive and Parliament.

In the original Constitution of 1972, the procedure for removal of judges of the Supreme Court was kept with Parliament since December 16, 1972, but despite such provisions, no separate law was promulgated by Parliament providing the procedures for such removal and a dead provision continued till January 25, 1975. On that date the Constitution was drastically amended.7 Clause (2), new Clause (2) to Article 96 were included providing that a judge may be removed from his office by the President on the ground of misbehavior or incapacity after giving him an opportunity of being heard. So, before the amendment there was no law regulating the removal of a judge and after the amendment, a judge was equated with a private servant making a provision that he may be removed by the President directly by giving him a show cause notice. The entire mechanism for removal of a judge was with the Chief Executive of the State. There were no checks and balances. The then government hurriedly implemented the amendment because the government was toppled by a military regime after brutally killing Bangabandhu Sheikh Mujibur Rahman and other members of his family on August 15, 1975. So, we did not get any outcome of those two systems.

534

The military regime amended this provision for removal of judges by adding Clauses (3), (4), (5), (6), (7) to Article 96. Under the amended provision, in place of removal of a judge by the President, a new system was introduced providing for a Supreme Judicial Council consisting of the Chief Justice and two next senior judges who shall inquire into the incapacity or conduct of a judge and shall prescribe the Code of Conduct to be observed by them. If the Council reported to the President that in its opinion a judge had ceased to be capable of properly performing the functions of his office or has been guilty of gross misconduct, the President shall pass the order of removal. Under this provision, in place of the President who was the appointing authority, the full power was given to the Supreme Judicial Council. In the selection of the Supreme Judicial Council, a proviso was also added to the effect that if a member of the Council is absent or is unable to act due to his illness or against whom the proceeding was initiated, the judge who is next in seniority to those who are members of the Council shall act as such a member. The Chief Justice shall be the Chairman of the Council by dint of his office. But the powers have been given equally to the Commission in deciding. In the earlier provision, the removal was only on the ground of proved misbehavior or incapacity, but in the next amended provision the horizon was further expanded to the effect that if any judge is found guilty of gross misconduct, he would be subjected to inquiry by the Council. The President shall direct the Council to enquire against a judge either from any information received from the Council or from any other source. This is very significant, inasmuch as, the Supreme Judicial Council shall function every day regarding the capacity of a judge to function properly or his guilt of misconduct. They may also suo moto hold an inquiry and may report to the President. If the President is satisfied that the information given by the Council is enough, he may proceed according to the Constitution. Since the Council retains the power all along, it may supervise the conduct of judges which was totally absent earlier.

Three vital questions arise from the above discussion: that there was a removal mechanism of judges by Parliament in the 1972 Constitution; it was not acted upon in the absence of any law. The

Judges have not tested the merit or demerit of this system. The second provision was most dictatorial and undignified for a judge it cannot be acceptable in a civilized world. Nowhere in the world there was such a system in practice. This was totally under the control of the Executive. The next one was though promulgated by a Martial Law regime, the system was more transparent, inasmuch as, the senior most judges of the Supreme Court who are at the helm of affairs of the administration of justice would oversee the conduct or misconduct or behavior of judges. Under this system two judges were compelled to resign when they came to know that the Supreme Judicial Council was acting against them and one judge was removed on the recommendation of the Supreme Judicial Council. So, the system was implemented, and it yielded good result. It would had been better if any impartial body was created as the one in England, but when the Executive all the time wanted to appoint more judges of its liking irrespective of their credibility, capability, capacity and acceptability, it is difficult to implement in our country. The Executive never wanted any independent and impartial judge in the higher echelon. It wanted to serve their purposes by appointing judges leaning toward them. They are not at all concerned about the independence of the judiciary; rather they are interested in how to use the judiciary against the opposition political parties. If a selection process is fair, all wrongdoings will be eliminated from the administration and the people will be benefitted thereby.

This martial law promulgated system could work even after declaring the Constitution Fifth Amendment void.8 Parliament after a thorough examination by its Standing Committee on the Ministry of Law, Justice and Parliamentary Affairs for scrutiny and taking opinion from the experts passed the amendment to the Constitution. The bill was placed in Parliament on June 30, 2011.9 in this amendment the Preamble, Articles 19, 47, 65, and 66. 72, 80, 82, 93, 117, 118, 122, 123, 125, 129, 139, 141A, 147, 152, First Schedule, Third Schedule, Fourth Schedule of the Constitution were amended; Articles 2A, 4A, 6, 8, 9, 10, 12, 38, 42, 44, 61, 70, 94, 95, 96, 97, 98, 99, 100, 101, 102, 103, 104, 105, 106, 107, 108, 109, 110, 111, 112, 113, 116, 142, 145A, 150 were substituted; Articles 7A, 7B, 18A, 23A and the Fifth Schedule were added; and Article 58A and Part XIA were omitted. From the above, it is apparent that the Constitution was drastically changed by the Tenth Parliament. It was not merely a technical or clerical amendment made in haste as claimed by the Attorney General; rather it was passed after meticulous examination by the experts.

In this amendment Article 96 has been retained in a similar language as the martial law regime had promulgated it. It is not only this provision which Parliament has retained, it also retained the expression "Bismillahir Rahmanir Rahim" at the prefix of the Preamble, the citizenship in Article 6, some laws, particularly the Acquisition and Requisition of Immovable Property Ordinance, 1982 which involves the right to property has also been retained. Some other provisions were also kept in the Fifteenth Amendment. The Supreme Judicial Council mechanism introduced by the Constitution Fifth Amendment was retained despite declaration by the highest court that all actions taken, and laws promulgated from August 15, 1975 to April 9, 1979 were void.

Thereafter, by the Constitution Fifteenth Amendment Article 96 was redrafted verbatim. But all on a sudden this provision has been substituted10 again by the Sixteenth Amendment. By this amendment, a judge may be removed by the President pursuant to a resolution of Parliament supported by a majority of not less than two-thirds of the total number of members of Parliament on the ground of proved misbehavior or incapacity. About misbehavior or incapacity, it is provided that the parliament by law will regulate the procedure of relating to the misbehavior or incapacity of the judge. No law has been prepared by Parliament nor has any opinion of the stakeholders been taken by Parliament before such amendment. ABM Khairul Haque and Suranjit Sengupta are the main architects in reintroducing the provisions contained in the 1972 Constitution and convinced the Prime Minister, who was totally against such change. When I came to know about the move I cautioned ABM Khairul Haque in a seminar at the Judicial Training Institute not to give ill advice to the government pointing out that certainly he did not want to cripple the judiciary because he was also the Chief Justice. He introduced a doctrine in similar fashion as Dr Muhammad Munir had paved the way in legitimatizing martial law in Pakistan by taking an opinion of Hans Kelsen "nor and grund norm" in the name of "pure theory of law". According to ABM Khairul Haque, there cannot be any change in the basic structure of the Constitution in restoring a provision contained in the original Constitution. He also paved the way of a dictatorial regime to rein in the higher judiciary at a time when the Supreme Court is continuously pressurizing the Executive to give full independence to the lower judiciary by amending Article 116 with a view to allowing the judges to administer justice independently.

This amendment has been challenged in the High Court Division by Advocate Asaduzzaman. A Special Bench with Moyeenul Islam Chowdhury, Quazi Reza-ul Hoque and Md. Ashraful Kamal heard the matter for over six months because of repeated time taken by the government for filing affidavit. The judges of the Supreme Court were kept without any disciplinary rules since September 22, 2014. There were also no disciplinary rules for the lower judiciary after the separation of judiciary in 2007, and a deadlock was created in the judiciary. During the hearing, the Law Minister came to meet me with a draft copy of the law for my opinion. I told the Law Minister that it was not proper for the government to promulgate the law during the hearing of the constitutional amendment and that I would not give any opinion until the matter was finally disposed of on merit. Ultimately, the hearing of the matter was concluded on May 5, 2016, they fixed for CAV (Court Awaiting Verdict). After conclusion of the hearing, the judges met for discussions and unanimously decided that the rule would be made absolute declaring the amendment to the Constitution void. The judges also unanimously assigned the task of writing the opinion of the court to Moyeenul Islam Chowdhury. As various constitutional law points arose, and arguments continued for months together and as the final judgment could not be prepared by Moyeenul Islam Chowdhury, the judges decided to pass a short order on May 5, 2016, and all the three judges prepared a short order on May 4, 2016.

Suddenly, Justice Quazi Reza-ul Hoque came to meet me on emergency basis in the late afternoon of May 4, 2016 with a broken heart and a pale-looking face. I wanted to know the reason for his coming. Quazi Reza-ul Hoque simply handed over to me a visiting card of an army officer, whose name I cannot recollect, who was a DGFI officer and deputed to the Supreme Court. He told me that the said officer met him in his chamber and pressured him to deliver the judgment in favor of the government. Quazi Reza-ul Hoque was so annoyed with conduct of the officer that he directed him to leave the room at once. Reza-ul Hoque simply said to me that as I am the guardian of the judiciary, he brought the incident to my knowledge for doing the needful. I was so shocked after hearing him that I called the Attorney General and the Law Minister. I requested the Attorney General to intimate the incident to the Prime Minister and that I want to see that in my administration of justice no such incident recurs in future. He assured me that he would inform the matter to the Prime Minister. Later, the Law Minister came, and I handed over the officer's visiting card and told him that it is a deplorable incident that the DGFI is exerting pressure on the judges for delivery of a judgment in favor of the government and narrated to him the incident with Reza-ul Hoque. When the Law Minister saw the visiting card, it appeared to me that he knew the officer. He took the card and assured me that no such incident would happen in future. One day I had the occasion to meet the Prime Minister at a function and I requested her to direct the DGFI officers not to interfere in the administration of justice. The Prime Minister remained silent.

After the pronouncement of the judgment on May 5, 2016, Moyeenul Islam Chowdhury and Quazi Reza-ul Hoque came to meet me. Both their faces were pale and they expressed their helplessness in the administration of justice. Then they narrated a pathetic story they had experienced prior to the rising to the court. When the judges were just about to rise in the court for pronouncement of the judgment, Md. Ashraful Kamal told Moyeenul Islam Chowdhury that the short order should be modified and that he would give a dissenting opinion. Both Moyeenul Islam Chowdhury and Quazi Reza-ul Hoque expressed their dissatisfaction and said to him that they would declare judgment only by substituting the word "majority" for the word "unanimous". They told me that till late evening, Md. Ashraful

Kamal was with them and it was beyond their imagination that he would change his mind in such a manner at night. Everything then became clear to me: the DGFI officials had changed the mind of Md. Ashraful Kamal.

Quazi Reza-ul Hoque maintained his integrity and did not succumb to the pressure whereas Md. Ashraful Kamal possibly could not overcome the pressure.   In this connection, I remember a very amusing incident I had enjoyed in the judges' lounge on one occasion when the judges were assembled there. Abdul Wahhab Miah was all the time talkative and could exchange views with all the judges irrespective of their position, which was of course admirable. He was able to gossip with lawyers and judges for hours together. I am just quite the opposite and sometimes I had to face criticism of my conduct that due to my reservations, none of the judges could talk with me freely. They felt comfortable talking with Abdul Wahhab Miah. He congratulated Moyeenul Islam Chowdhury and Quazi Reza-ul Hoque for their contribution to the Sixteenth Amendment judgment openly, but he could not notice that Md Ashraful Kamal was standing just behind them. Abdul Wahhab Miah's voice was always high and all of us noticed that Md. Ashraful Kamal's face became a bit ashen at that moment. Adbul Wahhab Miah then realized that Md Ashraful Kamal was also standing there and then he hugged him saying, "Oh! You were also a member of the Bench. No matter you gave a dissenting opinion." We all found the incident enjoyable.

We, the senior judges, were concerned about the attitude of the government and had to talk occasionally that if judiciary is to survive, the appeal against the Sixteenth Amendment should be heard and disposed of in presence of the present strength of the Appellate Division because within a short period Nazmun Ara Sultana, Abdul Wahhab Miah and I would retire serially. There would be a vacuum in the Appellate Division for the time being because of lack of experienced judges. So, we decided to dispose of the appeal expeditiously. Most of the judges in the meantime read the judgment of the High Court Division and understood the points argued at the Bar and opinions expressed by the judges. Some of the Judges started studying laws by themselves unofficially; I came to know this from a statement of a brother judge. For obvious reasons, I am not inclined to disclose his name, lest his future career be put in jeopardy. He told me, "Sir, I studied a lot of decisions regarding the independence of the judiciary of different jurisdictions of the world and wanted to write something of my own so that it would be easier for me to write my opinion promptly after the hearing of the appeal." I dissuaded him from indulging such a practice for two reasons. Firstly, we have not heard the matter yet, and before hearing of the matter it was unethical for a judge to form any opinion; and secondly, if for any reason, his opinion is leaked, it would put him in an embarrassing position, which might be suicidal for him.

I advised him that whatever might be the result of the appeal, I am of the view that he should not write anything because he has a bright future which should not be ruined. The matter, however, accordingly appeared on the list in the full court. I kept in mind that a very crucial constitutional point was involved in the matter; it ought to be heard by all the judges. I was convinced that the Attorney General would try to delay the disposal of the matter because the government from its highest level wanted my opinion earlier regarding the matter, but I declined to express it. Hence the Attorney General wanted to delay the disposal in the High Court Division. One day he hinted to me that I should not become late Tajuddin Ahmed, the main architect of our out-liberation struggle. If a leader like Tajuddin Ahmed did not lead the provisional Mujibnagar government, our history could have been otherwise. I realized the message of the Attorney General. The government was bent upon retaining its power of the removal mechanism of the judges of the Supreme Court with it and that, if it was not possible, the responsible judge or judges would be dealt with severely. He told me that I had a lot of achievements in the judiciary since all sensitive decisions were given by me including decisions on abandoned properties, revenue matters, Bangabandhu murder case, jail killing case, all appeals against offences of crimes against humanity were also given by me. I had also brought discipline to the judiciary and that after such achievement I should not take any risk to become a villain in the estimation of the government. I heard his opinions but did not give much importance to his them

541

because I gave priority to the independence of the judiciary and I did not compromise with my conscience and was ready to face any eventuality if its independence was secured.

At a State banquet arranged at Hotel Sonargaon in honor of a head of State, as usual, I reached the venue fifteen minutes before the arrival of the Prime Minister. There the Prime Minister came in front of me and reminded me about the Sixteenth Amendment case which had then been taken up for hearing in the High Court Division. This was the first occasion the Prime Minister approached me about a case. I told her that normally I did not interfere in any matter pending before the High Court Division or lower courts, which she knew. I reminded her that being the guardian of the judiciary, it is expected by all the judges that the Chief Justice should maintain his decorum, dignity and independence. Furthermore, as a person, I did not like to interfere in the administration of justice. Only in one or two cases which came to my knowledge from other sources that those cases were delayed due to the interference of the opposite parties who were very powerful persons, I talked with the judges concerned for expeditious hearing without allowing adjournments. So, I told the Prime Minister that after the judgment, the matter would come before us when I would investigate the matter.

Before hearing of the appeal, I knew the Attorney General's attitude when he wanted to avoid the hearing of the appeal expeditiously. Accordingly, I thought over the matter once again, although I did not fix my mind about the merit of the matter. It was my contemplation that I would conclude the hearing within two to three months after allowing two adjournments. One of the most significant parts for a presiding judge of a court is the art of controlling court management and case management. If the presiding judge does not have enough experience in court management, it is difficult for him to dispose of any complicated matter particularly in cases where the lawyers would show temper or adopt devices to somehow make me angry so that the matter is not heard by me. By this time, I had developed the art of managing them without using any harsh language. It is necessary for every judge to keep control the court's proceedings. I thought about the matter and chalked out a plan on how to expedite the hearing. I decided that on the first day I would engage some senior lawyers as amicus curie taking it for granted that the Attorney General would seek adjournment. This would speed up hearing because normally in constitutional matters it was advisable to hear senior advocates.

The Attorney General prayed for eight weeks adjournment for his preparation. I did not give any reply but from my right-side Abdul Wahhab Miah was whispering to me to give him a short adjournment since it was the first occasion. I told him to keep quiet and then started giving dictation to the Bench readers observing that since the Attorney General had prayed for adjournment for his preparation, let Mr. T.H Khan, Dr. Kamal Hossain, Mr. M. Amirul Islam, Mr. Abdul Wadud Bhuiyan, Barrister Rokan Uddin Mahmud, Barrister Azmalul Hossain, Mr. A.J Mohammad Ali, Mr. A.F. Hassan Ariff, Mr. M.I Faruqui and Barrister Fida M. Kamal be requested to appear in the matter as amici curie with direction to submit written arguments one week before the next date fixed for hearing and that they would be allowed to argue only for five minutes each. I directed the office to serve paper books to the amici within 24 hours and adjourned the matter for two weeks. Thereafter, on two occasions, the Attorney General took adjournments, and then I told him that if he goes on taking adjournments I would have no option other than to hear the amici curie, who had in the meantime submitted their written arguments and attended court for arguments on each date.

The Attorney General got the message and assured me that he would argue the case on the next date. On the first day of hearing, the Attorney General raised the objection that the court had selected amici curie in an unbalanced manner, inasmuch as, most of the lawyers were against the government's line of thinking. I cautioned the Attorney General not to bring politics into the court and told him that all counsel appointed were most competent lawyers as the court thought fit. They were not engaged in arguing on any political issue rather to help the court and if he had any suggestion to add more lawyers, I would not have any objection. The Attorney General could not supply any name. Later, Abdul

Matin Khasru prayed for inclusion of his name as intervenor. I allowed him to appear and place his argument. The hearing was concluded in 11 working days. The last day of hearing was June 1, 2017. I adjourned the matter for delivery of the judgment on July 3, 2017.

After rising from the court, I requested the judges to come to my chamber for a discussion with them about the matter pointing out that after a lengthy hearing our memory is fresh and that if they express their opinions we could deliver the final judgment on July 3, 2017. I reminded them that Nazmun Ara would retire within a few days and we could take her signature before her retirement. I had the firm belief that the government would create pressure upon the judges but if we give our final verdict before such maneuvering it would be easier on my part to deliver a unanimous opinion. Abdul Wahhab Miah protested my view saying that we would not express anything prior to July 3, on which date we would express our opinions. I tried to persuade the judges to take into consideration that apart from the facts and law points there would was nothing left to express opinions on. I also pointed out that it is a practice being followed by every superior court on the globe that whenever a complicated case is heard and kept for delivery of judgment after a long time or in cases where the court keeps the matter as CAV (court awaits verdict), the court normally delivers the signed judgment on that day. The judges could not agree, and it was a big blunder committed by them.

On July 1, 2017, in the morning I got a call on my private mobile phone and the caller identified himself as the military secretary to the President and requested me to come to Bang Bhaban for a talk with the President at 7:30 PM as desired. I was a bit surprised that the military secretary or any other high-level official had never contacted me directly earlier. Previously on all occasions, the military secretary contacted the Registrar General and then the Registrar General brought the matter to my knowledge and subsequently conveyed my opinion to the government. Even when I was in the High Court Division, the military secretary had contacted the Registrar General requesting him to ask me for a cup of tea with the President. This time I noticed an exception. I had very cordial relationship with the President. I along with my wife was invited to the Bang Bhaban privately for dinner previously. We enjoyed the company of the President, who appeared to me to be a very simple and open-minded gentleman par excellence. He does not hold back and starts talking many internal family matters and about the corruption of government's ministers, MPs and some judges. He had mentioned about some files which were sent for his approval, but he refused to approve them when he found that the proposals were unethical, immoral or illegal. He even told me that he had advised the Prime Minister that such files should not be sent to him for approval. He spoke about the corruption in the judiciary and encouraged me to rein in the corruption. He gave me some examples of some high-level personnel known to him from boyhood who had become billionaires and some of them had also declared having "black money" by taking advantage of government schemes. Whenever we met the first charge against me used to be why I had not visited him for a long time! Why did I not I send "boudi" (my wife) to Bang Bhaban for spending time with his wife. He is so simple a person that all the time he addressed my wife as "boudi" although by age and position he did not have to address my wife in that manner. To speak the truth, I would have hesitated to address in such manner. However, he is a spineless power monger politician. He does not believe in ethics and morality. He has a quality which is lacking in many politicians and it is his royalty to his master.

Normally, I did not address any of my junior friends' wives in that manner. There lies the simplicity of President Abdul Hamid. He was possibly the junior most MNA elected in the 1970 election, and since then he was never defeated in any election in his constituency. When we talk, sometimes I forget that I am gossiping with a President. On one occasion, I learnt from the media that he had said he got "referred mark" in one subject in his graduation for which he could not get admitted to Dhaka University. These displays his simplicity---someone who does not suppress anything and suggests to the students that to become a great man only higher division and higher qualification would not make a person to occupy a higher position in the country. One requires devotion, honesty, sincerity and ambition to become a great man. The first quality of a person is to be honest and sincere in his responsibility. I salute him for these qualities. Socrates did not have any institutional education, but till now he is regarded as the greatest philosopher ever born. Rabindranath Tagore never crossed the matriculation level, but he is regarded one of the best litterateurs. Mrs. Indira Gandhi never had an academic degree, but she became a great leader of India. Poet Quazi Nazrul Islam had no academic background, but he is regarded as the greatest Rebel Poet in Bengali. Obviously academic qualification was never a criterion to become a great personality.

Going back to the Military Secretary's call, subsequently I got a text message from him from phone number: 01730090095. The text message read:

"Assalamu Alaikum, Sir, with reference to our mobile conversation yesterday, I am reminding you once again about your call on with Honorable President today at Bangabhaban at 1930 hours. With profound regards. Major General Md Sarwar Hossain, Military Secretary to President"

I was very much anxious on receiving the above text message. Never had I received any direct invitation from someone of such a high level. After I became the Chief Justice, all communications were made through my Registry. Either it was through the Registrar General or my private secretary. I checked my office whether there was any invitation from the Bang Bhaban for the evening. I was told that the office had not received any such invitation. I could not understand why the invitation was made so secretly. One of my closest aides told me that it might be that the program was arranged secretly. Whatever explanation offered to me, I could not be satisfied. At any event, I reached Bang Bhaban five minutes ahead of the scheduled time. The Military Secretary received me at the porch and took me to his room. It confused me further. I had visited Bang Bhaban alone many times earlier. While in the High Court Division once and after becoming the Chairman of the Judicial Service Commission on many occasions, and from the date of my appointment as the Chief Justice I was there numerous times. Every time I was taken to a special room reserved for the purpose. I visited many rooms of the Bang Bhaban, even the inner residential section as a private guest. There are some waiting rooms in Bang Bhaban. Besides the President's Office on the ground floor, there are rooms for officers. I was hesitating whether I should sit in the room of the President's Military Secretary or not. I felt insulted and was also thinking of turning back instead of waiting there.

The Military Secretary was requesting me to have a seat. The room was so poorly arranged that if I sat in the sofa, then just in front of me the MS would be sitting in his chair separated from me only by his desk. It was not at all appropriate for a Chief Justice to sit there. The Military Secretary appeared to me very anxious and sometimes he went out and came back and requested me to sit. He wanted to serve tea or coffee. I said, "No, thanks." Sometimes he wanted to talk with me. I sat for a moment and then stood up and started reading the names of former military secretaries displayed on the wall. I wanted to know the name of one who was posted there during the emergency period. I got the name and noted it down. This way I passed about 45 minutes. My mental condition at that time was very anxious. Then I was taken to the President's room. I was stunned on seeing the persons present there. Besides the President, Prime Minister Sheikh Hasina, Law Minister Anisul Haque and Attorney General Mahbubey Alam were present.

After exchanging wishes, we took our seats. The Prime Minister raised the point regarding the Sixteenth Amendment judgment. What I had suspected proved true. I told the Prime Minster in a very polite manner that on a previous occasion also all of us sat together in that particular room when a deadlock was created due to non-cooperation of the Ministry. I could not transfer any honest officer to Dhaka and Chittagong and District Judges to the district courts. I also could not execute any modernization project of the judiciary, and I had to face embarrassing position in public meetings due to the telephonic pressures created by the ministers on the courts for making favorable orders. The meeting yielded no result. I pointed out to her that a deadlock condition persisted regarding the postings of District Judges, Chief Judicial Magistrates and other responsible posts in different districts. The ministry recommends corrupt and disputed officers for those posts. Many of the responsible posts are lying vacant for more than six months.

The Law Minister started making up totally false stories even ignoring his commitments made to me earlier. Then I drew the attention of the Prime Minister that people like Dr. Mizanur Rahman, Chairman of the Human Rights Commission, and Prof. Dr. Abul Barakat spoke against the Law Ministry's telephonic direction in such a manner that finding no other alternative I assured them that there was no such incident since my assumption of the office of the Chief Justice. Now the lower judiciary was totally under the Ministry's control and if the superior judiciary is also surrendered to the government there would be anarchy in the country. The Law Ministry says that they did not interfere, not to speak of directing any officer for granting bail. I had made some enquiries on getting complaints and produced the papers for the Prime Minister.

I stated that if this process is allowed it would be very difficult on my part to manage the judiciary with dignity. I even told her that I had asked the Minister that if he had any personal interest in a case in respect of any accused, he should not allow the officers of the Ministry to give direction over telephone. I also pointed out that whenever a proposal for transfer of an officer to Dhaka comes to me, I made enquiries about the officer and when I ascertained that the officer did not possess a good reputation, I suggested that he be accommodated in the Ministry. The Prime Minister simply said, making requests over the phone is not proper and the proposal of the Chief Justice was good. I told the Prime Minister that all the time the officers of the Law Ministry were directing the Magistrates and Sessions Judges for granting bails even to veteran criminals.

I candidly told the Prime Minister that I had hinted to the Law Minister that if Article 116 is restored to its original position there would be no difficulty in resolving the disciplinary and removal mechanism of the judges in the higher judiciary, because eighty percent of the people have to go to the lower judiciary and it is our

548

highest responsibility to bring some discipline to our lower judiciary. In the lower judiciary a dual administration is operating creating a total deadlock and if the higher judiciary is left with the Executive, public perception of the judiciary would suffer profoundly.

The Prime Minister told me that Article 116 cannot be restored because Bangabandhu himself changed it with the Fourth Amendment. When I got this firm view from the Prime Minister regarding Article 116, I wanted to know from her how the judiciary could be handled and controlled. She advised me that the situation should be resolved through mutual discussions. I knew that the Prime Minister has a soft corner for the Law Secretary without knowing his real character, because he has acquired the quality of convincing one within a short period of time, but I refrained from disclosing this and told her that under the present set up it was not at all possible for resolving any difference mutually, because all the time the Law Ministry wanted to push corrupt officers into responsible posts with a view to serving their purpose.

The Prime Minister requested me to somehow give the verdict in favor of the government. I told her that even if I express opinion in favor of the government, there would not be any certainty that the High Court's judgment would be set aside, because we had not discussed the matter. Our opinions would be disclosed just before the pronouncement of the judgment. So, aside from myself, there were six other judges. I don't know about their opinions. The Prime Minister, the Law Minister and the Attorney General were repeatedly pressing me to give my opinion alone in favor of the government, even if the other judges gave their opinions against the government. When I was unmoved, the Prime Minster lost her temper. Then abruptly she expressed her dissatisfaction towards me stating that she had all information's regarding me. The first point she raised was that why I declined to furnish information to the Durniti Daman Commission in reply to its letter regarding Justice Md.Jaynul Abedin.She stated that this judge submitted report in his judicial probe in favor of the then government regarding the 21st August incident post judicial inquiry. He was a diehard pro- BNP judge and that due to Supreme Court's report he could not be prosecuted regarding corruption. Her second charge was that why I delivered judgment in respect of Muslim Cotton Mills of Gazipur in favor of A.K. Azad. He is a corrupt businessman. I was bewildered on hearing such charges as if she was harboring the view that the Appellate Division is an organ of her government. The Prime Minister appeared to me blind for retaining power and her only object was how to control the Supreme Court for coming to power in the next election. Her approach was unethical and unconstitutional, but I guessed, she kept her blind eyes towards what is right or wrong.

The Attorney General was not only pressurizing me but was also making entreaties to change my mind. He reminded me that I had delivered so many extraordinary judgments that the government would remember me forever. But for one judgment I should not give up all my achievements. I was very offended on hearing the entreaties of the Attorney General but controlled my annoyance. Though unethical, the Prime Minister and the Law Minister could request me for political reasons, but the position of the Attorney General was completely different. The Attorney General is the chief law officer of the State and it was always his duty to remain impartial. He is not the Attorney General of the government only, rather in the true sense he is the "Attorney-General for Bangladesh."11 He is not only for the prosecution, but he also must see the interest of the defense. Whenever he found that the government was wrong in some matter, his duty was to advice the government properly and prevent the government from doing anything wrong. He should not take merit of the appeal personally. The office of the Attorney General is very high, and he must command respect from all segments of people. I controlled my temptation to point out the dignity, integrity and impartiality showed by M.C. Setalvad, the first Attorney General of India, for which he is regarded as one of the best and respectable Attorneys General of India. However, I would point out here that on one occasion he turned down the request of Jawaharlal Nehru to appear in Nanabati's case in the Supreme Court when he found that the government gave unethical privilege to him despite his conviction for murder.

All the time I found the President was silent, making one or two comments only. The matter reached a point of heated debate. But I told the Prime Minister that she would not be able to show any example in the world, including Pakistan, India and Sri Lanka, where the Chief Justice had voluntarily offered to resign. But I was the only one who wanted to step down and had informed her when I had raised the issue that I was handicapped by the hand of the Law Ministry in all matters relating to posting of any honest officer in a responsible post. And since the President was right before us, I wanted to step down at that very moment if she insisted that I express my opinion in favor of the government. The Prime Minister then said why you would resign. Whatever might be the result of the appeal, I should continue till the date of my retirement.

That evening the meeting was so secretly done that we were served with only tea and some light refreshments and though it got to around 11:30 PM we were not served with dinner because it was such a sensitive matter that possibly with a view to maintaining the secrecy, no dinner was arranged. I was hungry and tired, and I could not even keep my balance. The Prime Minister then stood up and said, the Chief Justice had not eaten anything, and he had his court in the morning. We then departed after the Prime Minister's departure. On my way home I felt like my vehicle was on my head and I was sitting upside down. My head was spinning, and I was feeling faint. I could not realize when I reached my residence. After my vehicle stopped at the porch, Salem, my long-time driver called out, "Sir, get out of the car." Then I realized that I had reached home. Somehow, I strolled upstairs and retired to my bed taking a glass of water. Reading my body language and seeing my face, my wife helped me change my clothes and did not request that I eat my dinner.

As usual I got up at 5:00 AM and though I was too weak because of mental pressure and also because I had not eaten the previous night, I went for a walk keeping in mind that I had been entrusted with an onerous responsibility for the judiciary and unless I perform my responsibilities correctly, the judiciary will be ruined and, in that case, I would be held responsible. In the battlefield if the commander retreats, his force is bound to perish. I figured if I took a walk to forget the previous night's episode and fatigue I would be able to generate enough energy. I thought throughout my walk for an hour that it was not the time to break down and that I should rise to the occasion. Otherwise, I would put the judiciary in a shameful condition which would jeopardize my entire career's achievement and the belief that I had been preserving throughout my life. After a shower, prayers and having breakfast as usual, I reached court at 7:45 AM and waited for the arrival of my brother judges, who were supposed to come by 8:00 AM as directed earlier. I realized that I had fifteen minutes time to think over the matter.

It was my normal practice that when I reached the court a full jug of green tea used to be served by my personal assistant. While sipping the tea, I wanted to evaluate the situation and decided that I would not show any sign of mental agony or pressure to them and I firmly believed that at the Bang Bhaban there was at least one discussion with some judges prior to my discussion and that was the reason I was kept in the office of the Military Secretary. The other room located in the northern block was used as the venue for the discussion. Accordingly, I was taken to the southern block to the Military Secretary's office which was toward the western side opposite to the President's outer office. I felt confirmed that the restless movement of the Military Secretary was due to such a meeting. One crucial matter surfaced in my mind that at least two of the judges would dissent in the matter and if that would happen what would be my next course for meeting the eventuality. Because I had read the mindset of all the judges earlier, I believed that all, but one was in favor of dismissing the appeal. But previous evening's incident led me to believe that there were maneuvers on the part of the government and what I apprehended was going to be true. I wanted the opinion of the judges on the last day of the hearing only keeping in mind that before any maneuvering from the government, I should secure their opinions. I did not want to waste any moment because the time passing fast. I decided that unless we reached a unanimous opinion, I would defer the delivery of the judgment. I have that capacity and control over the judges and if I decide to defer the judgment, nobody would raise any question.

Within a few minutes all the judges took their seats. I pretended as if nothing had happened to me over the judgment and I behaved with them in my usual fashion. I directed that coffee be served to all the judges and directed my staff not to allow anyone inside my chamber without my prior permission over the phone. I made a very short revelation of facts and the manner of how the Sixteenth Amendment appeal reached the highest court for hearing. I also apprised the judges of the overall problems I have been facing in administering justice. Then I wanted the opinion of the judges. The usual practice is to take the opinion first from the junior most judge, but this time I broke the tradition and told the judges that I would start taking opinion from the senior most judge. Then I looked toward the senior most judge sitting on the left, i.e. Md. Abdul Wahhab Miah. He made a very short opinion in favor of dismissing the appeal. Then I looked to Nazmun Ara Sultana and she supported Md. Abdul Wahhab Miah. Then I turned my face toward Syed Mahmud Hossain on my left who, keeping his head low, said that he would allow the appeal. Then I turned my head toward Mohammad Iman Ali. His opinion was not in either direction but toward a middle path for disposal of the appeal with observations. When I looked at Hasan Foez Siddique he expressed his opinion for allowing the appeal. Then I wanted to know the opinion of Mirza Hossain Haider. He concurred with the senior most judge. So, the picture became clear to me. What I had guessed the day earlier and even on the last day of hearing proved true. I recollected why I had pressurized them to express their opinions. If I had decided to allow the appeal by a majority decision it would have been suicidal because Mohammad Iman Ali was leaned toward the middle path. The government under such circumstances could avoid the majority opinion of the High Court Division.

In the meantime, Md. Abdul Wahhab Miah started pleading with Syed Mahmud Hossain and Hasan Foez Siddique. Nazmun Ara Sultana joined him. I realized that the more they would try to convince them, the more those judges would remain firm in their opinions because I realized what had happened the previous evening. They could not ignore the Prime Minister's request because the carrot was dangling near their mouth. Unless they were motivated afresh, it would be difficult to change their opinions. In that case, all my efforts would be frustrated. I knew the mindset, the integrity and dignity of all the judges. I directed Abdul Wahhab Miah and Nazmun Ara Sultana not to make any comment. I started talking with Justice Hasan Foez Siddique because he would be my first target. I knew him very well and I realized that he would be a soft target for me. If I can change his mind, it would be easier for me to convince Syed Mahmud Hossain. If I could obtain their opinions, the other one would be much easier for me.

I said to Justice Hasan Foez Siddique, "Look at me. I have nothing to gain or nothing to lose if the judges' removal mechanism is left with the Executive, because I was leaving the judiciary very soon." I reminded him how I mentored him, trained him, and kept my trust in him with the expectation that one day he would lead the judiciary. In the present muddled conditions of the lower judiciary, and the conduct of Parliament members that we had been facing every day, was it possible for them to administer justice with whatever dignity of the higher judiciary would be left with them? Did he want to bury the judiciary? They (the political authorities) are so greedy they want to control everything from madrassas to schools to colleges to Union Parishads and Upazila Parishads instead of giving their attention to the law-making process for which they were elected. We had also rejected bail for some of the lawmakers. The democratic institutions are in total shambles. In addition, because of the degradation of morality of some judges of the High Court Division we hardly find any standard judgments from the High Court Division. I drew his attention to the conduct of some of the judges and, over those matters, we had already expressed our helplessness in open court among ourselves. Now the judges are directly under our control and even at this stage we are unable to rein them, and if they could remain under the present members of parliament what consequences would they face?

It appeared to me there was a bit of change in his body language. Then I took up the issue with him again and started reminding him of the glory, prestige and integrity he has been harboring in him. His elder brother is a judge in the High Court Division and he has nothing to lose. After talking on some other issues, which I refrain from disclosing, he told me that if we formulate the Code of Conduct of the Judges, he would agree with the majority. I told him that was exactly the right matter he had raised, and I was also thinking of promulgating the Code of Conduct in the judgment so that it could not be changed easily, and all the judges would be bound to follow the Code of Conduct because of the Constitution.12 Hasan Foez Siddique agreed with me.

Then I turned to Syed Mahmud Hossain. I knew that he would be a very soft target if I could change the mind of Hasan Foez Siddique. I reminded him of one fact which I used to tell him regularly when I found him alone. I also pointed out to him how I nurtured him from the stage he was a practicing lawyer, how I treated him all the time and used to advise him on many matters, but without disclosing elaborately in the presence of all. I had the firm conviction that he could not disown my contribution in him reaching his present position. In the true sense I used to give guidance to both Syed Mahmud Hossain and Hasan Foez Siddiqui. One was weak in criminal matters and another in civil matters. I encouraged them to write judgments on subjects they were weak in and explained to them the law points involved in those matters. Their only grievance against me is that I was so prompt in arriving at conclusions that they could not follow me. I used to explain to them the points in question and then told them to read minutely the decision on the point which I had mentioned to them on the spot.

He kept his head down and after 8 to 10 minutes of my conversation with him, Mahmud Hossain simply moved his head expressing "yes". Then and there I stood up and hugged him and said softly, keeping my mouth close to his ear, that he would be succeeding me. Finally, my efforts worked. Then I took on Mohammad Iman Ali and it took me 2 or 3 minutes and while I reminded him that all of us were deciding something for the cause of the judiciary keeping in mind the poor litigants. He was an activist for women and children related issues. What purpose would it serve if he proceeded toward a neutral path? Would this government constitute a neutral body as in the UK? It would be a far cry. Md. Abdul Wahab Miah and Nazmun Ara Sultana joined me and within three minutes we were able to change his opinion. By this time, it was around 10:30 AM.

I noticed the sounds of murmuring of the lawyers from which I understood that the court was full of lawyers and media people were also waiting for our opinion. I rushed to my chair and noted down the order of the court. Abdul Wahhab Miah was asking me what I had been writing. I told him that I was writing the short order. He then said, since we are unanimous, we need not pass any short order. I told him that "you would not understand for what reason I am writing the short order." After writing the short order, I called for our jamadars. After taking putting on our gowns we sat in court. There was pin-drop silence in the room though it was packed. I directed the Bench reader to take down the order of the court. I switched on the microphone and declared, "The appeal is dismissed unanimously."

Normally we did not use the word "unanimous" when we allowed or dismissed any matter, but this time, I used this word intentionally. It was a Monday and when we delivered our opinion the Cabinet meeting was ongoing. Later, I learned from a Minister who was very close to me that immediately after pronouncement of the order, the Law Minister communicated the message into the Prime Minister's ear that the appeal was dismissed unanimously. The Prime Minister only remarked, "Unanimous!" After rising from the court, we again sat for discussion. I took the opinion of the judges whether anyone was interested to add any opinion to the judgment, meaning thereby that as a precedent, the Chief Justice always delivers this type of constitutionally important judgments. All the judges unanimously expressed their opinion that there would be one judgment to be written by me. I congratulated all the judges and directed them to sit in their respective courts. Nazmun Ara Sultana was supposed to retire on July 7, 2017. So, I decided to prepare and finalize the judgment by July 6, 2017.

I started my dictation the same day and told the judges that I would not sit in court for preparing my opinion. On July 5, 2017 I gave copies of my opinion to all the judges saying that they should read the judgment properly and if they found any mistake in the language, tense or spelling, they were at liberty to correct them and we would sign the judgment either on July 6 or July 7, before Nazmun Ara Sultana took off her robe for the last time. On Thursday July 6, 2017, I requested the judges for a cup of tea during recess hour and wanted to know how far they had perused my judgment, because it had to be signed at midnight if possible. I wanted Nazmun Ara Sultana to sign before she took leave at which Mohammad Iman Ali requested me to add a few words of his own and the other judges said that it was such a long judgment that they could not read the entire judgement thoroughly. So, it was not possible on their part to finalize the judgement in course of the day. I then told them that I dictated the judgment sparing court's afternoon session and even then, they expressed their inability. Nazmun Ara Sultana appeared a bit embarrassed and said that she would not put her signature on the judgment; instead her opinion would be "I agree". After two or three days, Hasan Foez Siddique requested me to add something of his own. I asked him not to do so particularly in this case on consideration of his future. Even then he expressed his eagerness to add something saying that it was a historical judgment and he wanted to participate in it. So, I agreed. Then Syed Mahmud Hossain requested me that he too wanted to add something, at which I was a bit surprised.

All the time, but especially in sensational cases, he wanted to avoid writing judgments particularly in appeals against the judgments of the International Crimes Tribunal. I persuaded him to deliver at least one judgment on many occasions. But he would express his inability to endorse any judgment stating he would write judgements other than in those cases.

Anyhow, then Abdul Wahhab Miah also wanted to add his own opinion and then Mirza Hossain Haider said that if everyone expressed their opinions, he would also do so. The moment Abdul Wahhab Miah wanted to add something, I had reasons to believe that some maneuvering was going on in the matter and my draft

557

copy of the judgment had been communicated to the government by any one of them and, I firmly believed I knew who had supplied the draft copy to the government. All the time I was requesting my brother judges to maintain utmost secrecy about our talks and opinions on legal matters, but it did not yield any result. Because all my discussions regarding improvement of the judiciary or transfer or posting of any officer to a responsible station were leaked to the Law Ministry before we actually took any steps. On one occasion, I requested the judges by holding my palms together, "Please, don't disclose anything about whatever we have discussed." I reminded them that we were judges of the highest court and the Almighty has given us enough power, but if we are unable to maintain secrecy it will be suicidal for the judiciary. After occupying such exalted office, we should maintain secrecy, integrity and dignity for the sake of the judiciary and the institution. I also reminded them that in India, the UK and the US, Supreme Court judges maintain total secrecy. This I knew personally during my visits and there are also books on the subject. But unfortunately, we could not maintain the standard. I told them that by doing such things we were demeaning ourselves in the estimation of those to whom we leak our secret talks. All my entreaties obviously fell on deaf ear.

On the question of secrecy Justice Earl Warren wrote many court decisions have a strong impact on the economy of the nation, or at least some part of it. Because, as a rule, the court deals only with the facts of a given case, such reverberations might not even be known to the court. If words were to escape prematurely from the conference room as to the outcome of a case, dire results might follow. Those with unauthorized information might prosper greatly while the uninformed might be bankrupted. Some of the cases radically affect the stock market. Then he concluded, "I can say with great relief that there never was a leak during my sixteen years on the court."12(a)

He established new jurisprudence on constitutional law and the meaning of a constitution of a great nation. The phraseology of the Constitution of US confirms and strengthens the principle, supposed to be essential to all written constitutions that a law repugnant to the constitution is void; and that courts, as well as other departments, are bound by that instrument. He proceeded, that for any wrong the law would afford a remedy. This truism had to be qualified by recognition of the direction of the Executive to act without hindrance in the discharge of his duties. If a law would be in opposition to the constitution; if both the law and the constitution apply to a case so that the court must either decide to that case conforming to the law, disregarding the constitution; or conforming to the constitution, disregarding the law; the court must determine which of these conflicting rules govern the case. This is of the very essence of judicial duty. He explained that the province of the judicial departments to say what law is. And answered that those who apply the rule to a case must of necessity expound and interpret that rule. If the two conflict with each other, the courts must decide on the operation of each. 12(b)

When Earl Warren delivered the historic Brown decision regarding the practice of segregating children in public schools, he was influenced by John Marshall in Marbury and Oliver Wendell Homes who had disappointed Franklin D. Roosevelt who castigated the court publicly for not following his policies and advocated the recall of controversial decisions of the Supreme Court by popular vote. FDR was disappointed because Justice Oliver Wendell Homes, his first appointee and one of the giants of court history, failed to support his position in an important anti-trust case .12(c) To speak the truth, I too was influenced by John Marshall, Oliver Wendell Homes and Earl Warren, the great jurists and towering figures in American judicial history, who shaped the nation into a habitable one preserving and protecting human rights and values by their strong pronouncements ignoring the threats of three powerful US Presidents.

Going back to our own issues, after reading the judges' separate pronouncements, I had no doubt that the Law Minister and ABM Khairul Haque had again appeared on the scene for maneuvering my opinion because mine was a philosophical opinion and I had travelled to the root of the matter without caring about the manners which were being followed. I reminded of Chief Justice Marshall when he was fighting with the powerful Executive in 1803. Except

Mirza Hossain Haider, all other judges fell in the trap of the government. Even after Syed Mahmud Hossain and Hasan Foez Siddique's opinions, I did not rectify my opinion to meet those points, which I will discuss later. Abdul Wahhab Miah traveled in a middle-way without touching any point expressed by me. When five separate judgments appeared before me, the question arose as to the endorsement of Nazmun Ara Sultana on the philosophy of law as set down by me. No judge is permitted, after retirement, to sit with the sitting judges for discussion even if he or she was a party to the judgment. So, naturally, except my draft copy, no copy of the other opinions was given to her and she was not invited to any of the sessions of discussion on the judgment. I did not add anything despite reading the dissenting statements on the assumption that mine was the longest judgment and if I made any attempt to add something, the judgment would require to be rewritten in majority portions. So, I opted not to express any opinion on those points.

As per tradition, Nazmun Ara's endorsement would be placed after the opinion of Abdul Wahhab Miah, because of seniority. She had no opportunity to read the opinion of Md. Abdul Wahhab Miah; she had read my opinion only. So, naturally, I told my officers to make the endorsement of Nazmun Ara Sultana to the effect that "I agree with the judgment prepared by the learned Chief Justice in place of the expression 'I agree'." I added those lines on the assumption that if her endorsement "I agree" is added it would be presumed that she was agreeing with the views of Abdul Wahhab Miah. But she did not read his opinion. Even after delivery of my opinion, when we met on July 6, 2017, she did not say anything that she was not agreeing with any part of my judgment. After the signing of the judgment, when it was published on the website, she expressed her anger to Mirza Hossain Haider as to why he had put his signature in her endorsement without her consent. Mirza Hossain Haider disclosed to me later about the comment of Nazmun Ara. I made no comment to him. It is the practice that only the Chief Justice has the power to assign any judge to sign on behalf of any judge after retirement or death. The Chief Justice is entrusted with this power by the Constitution and the Rules and by convention. This practice is being followed since 1861. Most of the judges retired before signing the decree. If any decree is required to be drawn up pursuant to the judgement of the High Court Division, the Chief Justice assigns some of the judges to sign on behalf of the retired judge or a judge who is not alive. After resignation of Latifur Rahman and Foyze and some other judges, the Chief Justice allocated their judgments for rewriting and signatures. Even in the Appellate Division, after the retirement of AHM Shamsuddin Chowdhury and Mohammad Mozammel Hossain, the former chief justice, they could not finalize and sign a huge number of judgments. Their judgments were rewritten and signed by judges assigned by me.

In my opinion I expressed that the moot question that was raised in the appeal and which requires a clear answer is whether the Constitution (Sixteenth Amendment) Act, 2014 has violated the basic structure of the Constitution. It is indeed the crux of this appeal. Apparently, this question may look very harmless and straightforward, but in fact it is not that simple an issue to answer. Rather the answer to this question involves some immensely complex and unfathomably deep issues and events which have taken place in our political history during the last seven decades (1947-2016) in general and during the last four and half decades (1971–2016). If it had been a simple challenge of a constitutional amendment it would have been much easier to answer and give a verdict; but since this question has a long and checkered history, the answer should not be a short verdict containing only the core opinion of the court.

It involves one of the fundamental debates common to any democratic polity: if the removal mechanism of the judges of the Supreme Court is given to Parliament, whether the independence of the Judiciary will be affected and/or hampered. The independence of the judiciary is intertwined with democracy and the Rule of Law, the Political Culture and the Economic Development of the country. The first-ever modern democracy in history, the U.S., also went through this similar debate and it took couple of hundred years to refine a sound politico-judicial culture which gives stability in exercise of State power. Even after 220 years of the foundation of their Republic, the debate is not over yet. But for the U.S., this unfinished debate does not mean incompleteness or chaos; rather every time they are creatively exploring different options for more coherent, sound and harmonious ways to devise, define and redefine their democratic institutions so that their society becomes more stable and capable of delivering the pledges inscribed in their Constitution. This is a creative evolution of a political community which goes ahead with the life of that community with a healthy check and balance mechanism intertwined with trial and error.

But history also has some paradoxes. Not all political communities can withstand the unpredictable waves of this creative trial and error process in their political life. All cannot withstand this test of time because it is not only a strong economy, not only skyscrapers, not only large and long bridges that guarantee a country's stability and augmentation, rather most importantly it requires "collective political wisdom". A most unfortunate country in this world is that which possesses all that have been mentioned earlier but does not possess "collective political wisdom". What is meant by "economic prosperity" for a nation is a relative notion which changes from century to century, but what does not ever change is the notion of wisdom on which the invisible structure of the nation is built. I will come to this point of "collective political wisdom" in a later part.

Exercising power under a written constitution is as if working with a jigsaw puzzle. This is a tiling puzzle that requires the assembly often of oddly shaped interlocking and tessellated pieces. Each piece usually has a small part of a picture on it; when complete, the jigsaw puzzle produces a complete picture. The modern State machinery is undoubtedly complex, the separation of powers is not absolute. Therefore, it often overlaps creating a puzzling situation but through the design of the constitution, it puts things in an orderly manner so that nothing remains separated or disintegrated forever. All judicial review— all manner of adjudication by courts— is itself an exercise in judicial accountability; accountability to the people who are affected by a judge's rulings. This accountability is evidenced in critical comments on judicial decisions when a judge behaves, as he should, as a moral custodian of the constitution. Judges perform their functions and enhance the spirit of constitutionalism. They should realize the solemnity and importance of the functions reposed on them by the constitution. "The ideal judge of today, if he is to be a constitutional mentor, must move around, in and outside court, with the constitution in his pocket, like the priest who is never without the Bible (or the Bhagavad Gita). Because, the more you read the provisions of our constitution, the more you get to know of how to apply its provisions to present-day problems."13

Two weeks after hearing William Marbury's Commission as a justice of the peace, John Marshall pronounced the most important decision in the US Supreme Court's history. Marshall effectively amended the constitution by assuming the power of judicial review for the Supreme Court allowing it to void an Act of Congress it deemed unconstitutional. Nowhere in the American Constitution had the framers written "that a law repugnant to the Constitution is void" or given the Supreme Court the power to void a law. In Marbury, the Supreme Court declared both the President and Secretary of State guilty of violating the Constitution, and for the first time, it voided part of an Act of Congress.13(a) President Jefferson claimed in Marbury, "Nothing in the Constitution has given them the right...to decide what laws are constitutional and what not." Such powers "would make judiciary a despotic branch."14 After Marbury, the Supreme Court established itself as the supreme arbiter of the Constitution and American laws and the Federal judiciary as the third co-equal branch of the Federal Government alongside the Executive and Legislative branches.

On October 16, 1951 Liaquat Ali Khan, the first Prime Minister of Pakistan, was assassinated. "A tussle for grabbing power among persons who held positions of advantage in the Government thereupon ensued and under its weight the foundation of the State started quivering." On October 24, 1954, Ghulam Muhammad, the handpicked Governor General, by a proclamation dissolved the Constituent Assembly and placed armed guards outside the Assembly Hall. In accordance with the opinion given by the Federal Court a new Constituent Assembly was elected, and a Constitution ultimately came into force on March 23, 1956.15

Henceforth the edifice of democratic institutions was whittled down and never restored. An absence of democratic institutions leaves its impact on the rule of law and thereby affects the institutionalization of the judiciary. A new theory of "basic democracy" was introduced subsequently. The country gradually but surely slid toward autocracy. The people's basic human rights were ignored. The bureaucracy was at the helm of affairs in place of the people's power. Ultimately the edifice of an independent country became non-existent within a few years. It was an eminent lesson because a country must be run on the wishes of the people, not on the wishes of a bureaucracy.

Our Constitution is intimately linked in a symbolic way with our liberation struggle and it is most significantly not a document but a stream of history with its meaning coming from the silt deposited by historical experience over the years. While drafting our Constitution, our Founding Fathers' most forceful and explicit commitments to human freedom, dignity and equality emerged from the liberation struggle. Thus, democratic self-determination is the source of power. They kept in mind that every Bangladeshi, every lover of liberty and independence swears by the blood of the liberation struggle, never to ignore the sacrifices. Therefore, the meaning of "we the people" mentioned in the beginning of the Preamble of the Constitution of Bangladesh has a different meaning than of the same phrase that has been used in the Preamble of the Indian Constitutions and our Constitution must be interpreted in that context. One may pose a question as to the meaning of the term "constitution."

Constitution may be defined as to body of rules and maxims in accordance with which the power of sovereignty is habitually exercised. A constitution is valuable in proportion to its suitability to the circumstances, desires, and aspirations of the people, and as far as it contains within it the elements of stability, permanence and security against disorder and revolution. Ultimately it is valuable only to the extent that it is recognized and can be enforced. Although every State may be said in some sense to have a constitution, the term constitutional government is only applied to those whose fundamental rules or maxims not only applied to those shall be chosen or designated to whom the exercise of sovereign powers shall be confined, but also impose efficient restraints on the exercise for the purpose of protecting individual rights and privileges, and shielding them against any assumption of arbitrary power.16

Nothing in the original constitution of the United States aimed to eliminate slavery, even in the long run. No clause in the constitution declared that "slavery shall cease to exist by July 4, 1876, and Congress shall have power to legislate toward this end." However, the preamble to our Constitution indicated the future principles of the State that "through a democratic process a socialist society, free from exploitation --a society in which the rule of law, fundamental human rights and freedom, equality and justice, political, economic and social dignity, will be secured for all citizens." It was also declared to safeguard, protect and defend the Constitution and maintain the supremacy of the will of the people of Bangladesh so that we may prosper in freedom.

The first word of the first sentence of the Preamble to our Constitution of the People's Republic of Bangladesh is "We". The strength of a nation lies in this word and in the spirit of "WE". This "we ness" is the key to nation building. A community remains a community so long all those who belong to the community can assimilate themselves in this mysterious chemistry of "we ness"- the moment they are elevated to this stage they become a "nation". And our Founding Fathers very rightly understood, realized and recognized this quintessential element of nation building, and therefore the first sentence they in the Constitution is: "We, the people of Bangladesh, having proclaimed our independence on the 26th day of March 1971 and, through a historic struggle for national liberation, established the independent, sovereign People's Republic of Bangladesh."

Thus, if we carefully investigate the philosophy of our political existence we unfailingly see that the citizens of our country are woven by a common thread referred to as "We the people". And the solemn expression of the will of the people is the supreme law of the Republic, i.e. the Constitution. The triumph in 1971 was obvious because the feeling of "we ness" was unbreakable. There were numerous conspiracies to break this unity, but the enemy utterly failed to inject even the slightest shred of doubt among us. Now that we are living in a free, independent and sovereign country, however, we are indulging in arrogance and ignorance which threaten the very precious tie and thread of "We". We must get rid of this obnoxious "our men" doctrine and the suicidal "I alone" attitude. Not party allegiance or money but merit alone should be given the highest priority at all levels of national life and in institution building. Any person who is making tremendous sacrifice and humongous contribution for development and social progress must be recognized. And in doing so we must only see his or her contribution to this society, not to his/her political color or inclination. If we cannot get ourselves out of this narrow parochialism and cannot overcome the temptation of party nepotism, then this will be the biggest assault on the very foundation of our liberation war--and the rock-solid idea of "We" which brought us our long-cherished independence. To immortalize this momentum, the word "we" have been put in the very first sentence of our Constitution as the very first word of this sagacious document.

Antonio Lamer, the 16th Chief Justice of Canada, once described the preamble, while interpreting judicial independence, as "the Grand Indents Hall to the Castle of the Constitution".17 The framers of their Constitution clearly stated this philosophy, aims and objectives of the constitution and to describe the qualitative aspect of the polity the Constitution is designed to achieve.18

The words "historic struggle for national liberation" mentioned in the Preamble of our Constitution clearly indicated that our Parliament would not do anything by way of amendment to the Constitution ignoring the spirit of the sacrifice of millions of people. By the same token, we should not make any change in our historic document about the democratic process, fundamental rights, equality and justice, and rule of law, which should predominate in the administration of the country. These basic principles should be institutionalized -- not curtailed lest the sacrifice of the martyrs is nullified. This Preamble was changed by the military rulers and by the Constitution Fifth Amendment case the court restored it to its original position. Though the qualifying words "for national liberation" ended with "national independence" it should not be comprehended that our national liberation or independence is over; rather quite the opposite -- it is a continuing process to achieve the august goals for which our martyrs sacrificed their lives. "Liberty and Justice for all" stated that two centuries later Eleonore Roosevelt opened a new chapter in US history by expanding the way of American's think about who qualifies for the protection under the Founding Father's idea of natural rights. As First Lady, from 1933-1945, she used the White House bully pulpit "to make the case that all human beings– both men and women, Jews as well as Christians, West Virginia coal miners and Japanese Internees during World War II, blacks as well as whites, refugees' asylum and provides immigrants--are born with God given, natural right to personal liberty.19

This is what I believe is expressed by "We the People" mentioned in our Preamble. There is no doubt that the elected representatives of the Bangladesh Awami League led the liberation struggle, but people from all walks of life, like laborers, workers, fishermen, housewives, prisoners, educationalists, students, industrialists, intellectuals, Police, Army, Ansars, EPRs and supporters of other political parties participated, except a few religiously fanatic ideologues and their evil companions. Our liberation war was not an isolated event rather it was an all-engaging phenomenon, turning every one essentially into a freedom fighter. Some of them directly fought face to face in the battlefield - some of them supported with logistics - some of them encouraged them to achieve their goal - some of them travelled across the world to let people know of the horrific atrocities perpetrated by the military junta and their cohorts—some of them made the international community aware of the real picture so that they could support our cause— some of them collected money by different means to support the freedom fighters—some of them who could not cross the border gave shelter to the freedom fighters—some of them played a dual role and secretly sent messages and information to the freedom fighters.

The Constitution is, as the solemn expression of the "will of the people, the supreme law of the Republic, and if any other law is inconsistent with this Constitution that other law shall, to the extent of the inconsistency, be void." (Article 7) Now a very natural question may arise: in the Constitution who has been given the responsibility to declare a law void in case it conflicts or is "inconsistent" with Article 7 of the Constitution? Has this power been given to the Executive? The answer is an emphatic "no". Has this power been given to Parliament? The answer again is an emphatically "no". This heavy burden of scrutinizing the constitutionality of any law made by Parliament or the administrative body of the State has been rested upon the shoulder of the Supreme Court. For that matter the Supreme Court has been assigned with the power of "judicial review" by the Constitution itself.

The Supreme Court will stand firm and aloof from party politics and political theories. It is unconcerned with the changes in government. The court stands to administer the law for the time being in force, has goodwill and sympathy for all, but is allied to none. Occupying that position, we hope and trust it will play a great part in the building up of the nation, and in stabilizing the roots of civilization which have twice been threatened and shaken by two World Wars and maintain the fundamental principles of justice which are the emblem of God. The journey of judicial review on constitutional amendments in India started from the First Amendment Act, 1951, which had inserted Article 31B.20 Six years later in 1973, a larger Bench of thirteen judges considered the validity of some of the later amendments, the Twenty-Fourth, Twenty-Fifth and Twenty-Ninth Amendments to the Constitution. The case was practically based on considering the correctness of the decision of Golaknath.21

Since there was division by six into six, Khanna agreed with none of the 12 judges and decided the case midway between the two conflicting views holding that (a) the power of amendment is limited; it does not enable Parliament to alter the basic structure or framework of the Constitution; and (b) the substantive provision of Article 31C, which abrogates the fundamental rights, is valid on the ground that it does not alter the basic structure or framework of the Constitution. In interpreting a constitutional document the meaning and intention of the framers of the constitution must be ascertained from the language of that constitution itself; with the motives of those who framed it, the court has no concern.22 A constitution must not be construed in a narrow or pedantic manner, rather that construction which is most beneficial to the widest possible amplitude.23 Constitutional expert Dr. Wines wrote24 generic interpretation "… asserts no more than that new developments of the same subject and new means of executing an unchanging power do arise from time to time and are capable of control and exercise by the appropriate organ to which the power has been committed … while the power remains the same, its extent and ambit may grow with the progress of history." Hence it will be seen that suppositions as to what the framers might have done if their minds had been directed to future developments are irrelevant and that the question whether a novel development is or is not included in the terms of the constitution finds its solution in the application of the ordinary principles of interpretation, namely, what is the meaning of the terms in which their intention has been expressed.25

The court kept in mind the doctrine of severability to limit the application of judicial verdict and observed that in doing so the court can modify or even dismantle a legislation in the interest of justice. The court in such circumstances did not subscribe to the notions that all acts of the usurpers are illegal and illegitimate. The court took into consideration the acts, relevant things and legislative actions which are useful or which acts, things, deeds tend to advance or promote the need of the people or all acts, things and deeds which are required to be done for the ordinary functioning of the State or the acts, things, deeds and legislative matters which would augment the independence of the judiciary and welfare of the people, etc. This had been done in Pakistan as well as in Bangladesh. The independence of the judiciary is one of the basic features of the Constitution and the basic features of the Constitution cannot be changed, altered or amended.

Marshall had similar problems during Presidents Jefferson and Andrew Jackson's administrations. During Jefferson's administration by his historical pronouncement in Marbury and during Andrew Jackson's administration because of the great "Cherokee Nation" who fought Andrew Jackson in 1788. In the suit John Marshall, on March 18, 1831, in another historic judgment pronounced that the Cherokees were a sovereign nation and rejected Jackson's claim that they were subject to State law. The Indians were "domestic dependent nations" he ruled, subject to the United States as a ward to a generation.25(a) In spite of these, today he is regarded as the most towering figure in US judicial history. Chief Justice Taney, following Marshall from 1833 to the Civil War, had severe difficulties due to the outgrowth of the troublesome slavery question. And even in this century the two Roosevelts brought the force of their administrations to bear upon the court. Theodore Roosevelt castigated the court publicly for not following his policies. Franklin D. Roosevelt, angered by decisions of the court during his administration, sought Congress increase the number of justices by adding one for each justice over the age of seventy, of whom there were then six, thus enabling him to bring the number to the maximum of fifteen as fixed by the Bill. Called by its proponents as the Court Reorganization Bill and by its opponents as the Court Packing Bill, it was killed in committee and did not reach the floor in either house. Every man who has sat on the court must have known at the time he took office that there always has been and, in all probability, always will be controversy surrounding that body. It is inherent in the court's work.

If we look at the foundations of the English legal system, we find that the Judiciary as an independent third branch of the State still survives as an ideal, though not as part of the British Constitution. Whatever critics of Dicey's theory of the "Rule of Law" may say of our time and generation, it cannot be doubted that common law played a tremendous part in the events which led up to the establishment of the modern British constitution and with it the English way of life and thought.27 When Parliament was showing an arbitrary temper comparable with that of the Stuart Monarchy in the Seventeenth Century, Wilkes appealed, not in vain, to the common law. At the same time, when the English government was refusing to grant to their American colonies the rights for which Parliament had fought nearly a hundred years before, the framers of the United States Constitution saw so clearly the true place of law in the government of the people that they conferred upon the Supreme Court the power to declare invalid the acts of the President or of Congress. This is the lesson for the present age. If people are to live in peace and enjoy their liberties and, because this is a corollary to all liberties, observe their obligations, there must be law, and to declare it, law courts presided over by independent judges who will administer justice indifferently to all men.

With the passage of time, the judicial accountability system has been dramatically changed in respect of the United Kingdom. The procedure to be adopted is in the following manner: In terms of regulating misconduct in the judiciary, the Executive still plays a central role, sharing the responsibility for judicial complaints and discipline jointly with the Lord Chief Justice (LCJ) under detailed procedures set out in the Concordat and implemented in the Judicial Discipline (Prescribed Procedure) Regulations 2006. The old Lord Chancellors enjoyed considerable discretion over judicial discipline, though the department was generally thought to handle dismissals and discipline "with considerable natural justice" with a "quiet word" often used to encourage judges to step aside. Today, the responsibility for complaints is shared between the LCJ and the Lord Chancellor, supported by a Judicial Conduct Investigations Office (JCIO) staffed by civil servants.

The Lord Chancellor is accountable to Parliament for the operation of the discipline system. The JCIO filters out unfounded or trivial complaints, referring serious ones to a nominated judge who acts as a further filter and then to an investigating judge. This triage system ensures that non-trivial complaints receive proper consideration and that judges are investigated by their peers. If at the end of the process the LCJ and Lord Chancellor wish to take disciplinary action, they must refer the case to a review body composed of two judges and two lay members. The LCJ and Lord Chancellor must decide jointly on disciplinary sanctions but cannot take any action more severe than that recommended by the review panel. At the end of the process only the Lord Chancellor can formally remove a judge from office, and only at Circuit Judge Level and below. For Judges of the High Court level or above, the decision to dismiss must be approved by both Houses of Parliament (this has not occurred since 1830). There is also a process for reviewing the JCIO process itself. Complaints of judges can raise concerns about the handling of a complaint (but not the merits of the decision made) with the Judicial Appointments and Conduct Ombudsman (JACO). Allegations of serious misconduct remain very rare amongst the senior judiciary. That said the JCIO and the JACO receive significant numbers of complaints--an average of around 1,700 per year. This, in turn, requires significant resources: the JCIO has fifteen staff and the JACO ten. A significant proportion of complaints received (normally 50 per cent or more) relate to judicial decisions rather than alleged misconduct and are dismissed for this reason. Between 2008 and 2013 and average of fifteen court judges were disciplined each year for misconduct. A similar number (eighteen) resigned. The average figure for judges removed from office is very low-- less than two per year.28

Though the United Kingdom is the only country which functions under an unwritten constitution, the Executive, the Monarch, the Parliament and the Judiciary are working side by side without intrusion of powers by one organ on the other. It is found that even in the absence of any constitution and disciplinary mechanism a judge of the High Court was removed about 187 years ago. After the passing of the Constitution Reform Act, 2005, the relationship between Parliament and the Judiciary has undergone a structural change. The removal of the UK's highest court of appeal from the House of Lords formally separated the judges from the legislature and this has inevitably changed the institutional architecture within which judges and parliamentarians interact. But the provisions of the Act do not tell the whole story of those changes which did not begin and end in 2005. The removal of the Law Lords was a critical moment, but practices shaping relations between Parliament and judges were changing even before then and have evolved since. There will always be tensions between Parliament and the Courts. Recent years have provided several high-profile examples: sustained wrangling over the proper scope of judicial review in human rights and national security cases; the role of the European Court of Human Rights; and the boundaries of parliamentary privilege. Decisions by courts in relation to human rights and judicial review are often points of friction between judges and politicians. After the creation of the UK Supreme Court, the roles of President and Deputy have been clearly defined.29 Ibid

On the question of judicial accountability and judicial discipline it is said that "the court is largely self-regulating." The Constitutional Reform Act in UK provides that the justices hold office during good behavior but may be removed on the address of both Houses of Parliament. Given that no judge has been removed by Parliament since 1830, this is a measure of last resort that is unlikely to be used. Although not required by statute to do so, the court's first leadership team introduced a complaint procedure. Complaints relating to the effects of the court's judicial decisions are inadmissible, but anything disclosing grounds for further consideration are referred to the President, who can decide to take no action or to resolve the complaint informally.

If formal disciplinary action is considered, the President must consult with the Lord Chancellor. Formal action involves a tribunal consisting of the Lord Chief Justice, the Lord Chief Justice of Northern Ireland and the Lord President (head of the Scottish judiciary), plus two independent members nominated by the Lord Chancellor. After the tribunal delivers its report, the Lord Chancellor must decide whether to remove the justice by laying the necessary resolution before both Houses of Parliament. This change has been made to announce the judges' independence. In respect of Scotland and Northern Ireland, the judges enjoy much greater autonomy over judicial complaints and discipline than do their counterparts in England and Wales. In each jurisdiction, the investigation of complaints against judges is done for the most part by the judiciary. However, a key difference is that in England and Wales the Lord Chancellor still plays a central role: The Lord Chief Justice and the Lord Chancellor must cooperate both in the making of rules and in reaching disciplinary decisions.

The very first and the only case in India that involved the impeachment motion and the Inquiry Committee formed against V. Ramaswami of the Supreme Court found him guilty because of gross abuse of his financial and administrative powers as the Chief Justice of the Punjab and Haryana High Court and criminal misappropriation of property. The impeachment motion was however vanquished, as it did not attain a special majority Lok Sabha as required. Another such motion was initiated against Chief Justice Dina Karan of Sikkim High Court who then resigned his post. Parliamentary Standing Committee reports on the Judicial Standards and Accountability Bill, 2010 (JSAB) during impeachment motions against Justices Sen and Dina Karan in India came in for severe criticism from the Campaign for Judicial Accountability and Reforms (CJAR). The resignations of Justices Sen and Dina Karan have exposed the inadequacies of the prevailing system to make judges answerable for their omissions and commissions because of the inherent politicization of the parliamentary mechanism. The fact that tainted judges can simply evade parliamentary scrutiny and censure by resigning is a telling commentary on the lacunae in the legal and constitutional provisions in regard to impeachment.

In respect of a judge of the High Court in Sri Lanka, Section 111 provides that "the Judge of the High court shall- 2(b) be removed and be subject to the disciplinary control of the President on the recommendation of the Judicial Service Commission." So, in respect of removal of High Court Judges the President shall exercise the power on the recommendation of the Judicial Service Commission, an independent body. Chief Justice Shirani Bandaranayke was impeached by Parliament in January 2013 by President Mahinda Rajapaksa only because she gave a ruling against the government in reprisal for inconveniently declaring unconstitutional part of its legislative agenda including one against a Bill proposed by Basil Rajapaksa, then Minister for Economic Development and brother of President Mahinda Rajapaksa. On November 6, 2012, 14 charges were made against Bandaranayke including professional and financial misconduct and abuse of power. Even though the Speaker revealed these charges which Chief Justice Bandaranayke had denied and refused to resign from her office, a Parliamentary Select Committee (PSC) was formed with seven ruling party MPs along with 4 opposition MPs to conduct an inquiry and the PSC found Bandaranayke guilty on account of a few charges which was enough to remove her from office. All the four opposition MPs withdrew from the Committee rejecting the reports saying, "This was not an inquiry--it was an inquisition." The report was first sent to the President and later to the Parliament for vote on the impeachment motion. Meanwhile, people opposed the removal of the Chief Justice. On January 1, 2013, the Supreme Court ruled that the PSC had no power to investigate the allegations against the Chief Justice and the impeachment was therefore unconstitutional. Chief Justice Bandaranayke appealed against the PSC and on January 11, 2013, the Court of Appeal quashed the PSC's findings declaring the impeachment unconstitutional. Chief Justice Bandaranayke continually refused to recognize the impeachment and lawyer groups refused to work with the new Chief Justice. Chief Justice Bandaranayke's controversial impeachment drew much criticism and concern from within and outside Sri Lanka. After the change of the government on January 28, 2015, she was reinstated and she herself resigned on the following day.

In respect of Malaysia, during Mahathir Mohamad's tenure as Prime Minister in 1982, several constitutional amendments were made to severely weaken the institutional strength of Malaysia's judiciary. Mahathir was a dominant political figure, winning five consecutive general elections and fending off a series of rivals for the leadership of United Malays National Organization (UMNO) party elections in 1987 and matters then came to a head when Mahathir Mohamad, who believed in the supremacy of the Executive and Legislative branches, became Prime Minister. This crisis was very well known as a judicial or constitutional crisis. The history of parliamentary impeachment in the Asian region does not create any favorable impression until it can bring political intervention in the judiciary to an end, as further enunciated in a report of the International Bar Association's Human Rights Institute (IBAHRI).

Devi prasad Singh depicted the real picture of India regarding the criminal background of parliamentarians stating that the trend of nomination of candidates with criminal records is on the rise. He said the 1996 Legislative Assembly in Uttar Pradesh did not reverse but may have increased the 1993 trend. Not only did the BJP, the BSP and the SP gave tickets to dozens of candidates against whom legal proceedings had been instituted (33, 18, and 22 respectively), but a certain number of BJP, BSP and Congress MLAs amongst them became ministers when the BJP formed the government, first jointly with the BSP, then alone, from October 1997. This was achieved by recruiting dozens of MLAs from the BSP and the Congress (and offering up to a few hundred thousand rupees per MLA), with a ministerial post for each. Thus, the Uttar Pradesh cabinet finally comprised 92 members. The BJP Chief Minister, Kalyan Singh, tried to project himself as clean and set up a Special Task Force (STF) in 1998 to capture or liquidate criminals. However, public enemy number one then was Sri Prakash Shukla who appeared to have colluded with at least eight ministers of Kalyan Singh's government; they protected him, making the task of the STF more complicated30 Uttar Pradesh is not the only state where the entry of the criminals into politics has accelerated in the last few years. Bihar is certainly as seriously affected as Uttar Pradesh. In 2000, 31 Legislative Assembly Members had criminal records ranging from murder to dacoity. Most of them contested as Independents, but there were BJP, Congress, and RJD and Samata candidates as well. Maharashtra is also suffering from the same disease. During the municipal elections in 1997, 150, 72 and 50 candidates with past or present difficulties with the law (Godbole 1997) were fielded from Mumbai, Nagpur and Pune respectively. Andhra Pradesh is not lagging either. In 1999 an NGO called Lok Satta Election Watch released a list of 46 candidates contesting elections to the Lok Sabha or the Legislative Assembly with, allegedly, some criminal background. Delhi is also new in this circle of most criminalized states. In fact, Delhi is gradually taking over from Mumbai as the crime capital of India. This city-state tops the list of number of crimes per head, with 527 in 1996 (against 121 in Bihar) and in terms of percentage change, with a plus 55 per cent change in 1996 over the quinquennial average of 1991:5 out of 81 Legislative

Assembly candidates in 1998, 120 had more than two criminal cases registered against them, and out of 69 MLAs 33 had criminal cases against them.31

Those countries' experiences with parliament–led mechanisms for removal of judges of the higher judiciary are pathetic, politicized and unworkable. The systems being followed are not working and all these countries are facing a lot of criticisms from home and abroad even though the social and economic conditions of those countries are much better and their experience in democracy is more mature than ours. We did not have any democracy from 1947 till 1971. We had only three and half years' democratic government after independence in 1971. Then the country experienced the worst nightmare in history— not only the Father of the Nation but also his entire family (except two daughters) including a minor boy of four years, were brutally killed. The country again fell in the hands of the guns and generals who established a reign of terror through martial law, and it continued till 1990. After much sacrifice and through a tremendous mass uprising the military demagogue was ousted from power and the country again returned to its usual course of parliamentary democracy. But the system could not work properly due to the apathy of the government then in power to hold free and fair elections. In the Sixth Parliamentary election, the biggest political party which led the liberation struggle did not participate and Parliament could not survive for more than two months. After a huge agitation, the government was compelled to amend the Constitution.

The Constitution (Thirteenth Amendment) Act, 1996 incorporating a system of Non-Party Caretaker Government for holding free and fair election was passed, but it did not take long time to discover that this system had some incurable inherent weaknesses. Again, the country went through another saga of military backed caretaker government in the garb of Emergency for two years. It was also due to the lack of foresight of the politicians in power and their apathy to institutionalizing democracy. By the Thirteenth Amendment, Articles 58B, 58C, 58D, 58E were inserted and Articles 61, 99, 123, 147, 152 were amended. Form 1A was also inserted in the Third Schedule of the Constitution. Under the amended provision, a Non-party Caretaker Government shall wield the Executive power of the Republic, but it shall discharge its functions as an interim government and shall carry on the routine functions of the government without any power of making any policy decision during the period from the date on which the Chief Adviser of such government entered upon office after Parliament was dissolved or stands dissolved by reason of expiration of its term till the date on which a new Prime Minister entered upon his/her office after the constitution of the parliament. The mechanism for choosing the Caretaker Government had been provided in Article 58C. There was controversy over choosing of the Chief Adviser of the government. The country had to experience an attempted coup d'état by the Chief of Army Staff which had resulted in his removal during one interim government period. Ultimately this constitutional amendment was challenged in the High Court Division. The matter came before the court and by a majority the court was of the view that the amendment ultra vires the Constitution. In the majority opinion, the court was of the view that two parliamentary elections may be held under the Caretaker system subject to the condition that the selection of the Chief Adviser should not be made from amongst the last retired Chief Justices or retired judges of the Appellate Division, in accordance with Clauses (3) and (4) of Article 58C. The court gave the above direction keeping in mind that by keeping this system there was politicization in the selection of the Chief Justice and, alternatively, the Election Commission should be empowered and institutionalized so that the parliamentary elections can be held fairly. The court noticed that in every national election, the political party which lost the election questioned the impartiality of the election and the biggest opposition party did not cooperate in the 10th parliamentary election.

The court was of the view that the government should strengthen the Election Commission with all powers for holding free and fair parliamentary elections and that there should be automatic filling up of the vacancies in the Election Commission without the intervention of the government. None of the succeeding governments took any step in this regard. Even the opposition political party has not also raised this point either in Parliament or in any forum with the net result that the Election Commission has not been institutionalized yet.32 unless the national parliamentary election is held impartially and independently, free from any interference, democracy cannot flourish in the country. In the absence of credible elections, a credible parliament cannot be established.

As a result, our election process and the parliament remain in infancy. The people cannot repose trust upon these two institutions and if these institutions are not institutionalized to gain public confidence and respect, no credible election can be held. In the absence of a free and fair election, the parliament cannot be constituted with wise politicians and this may impede institutionalization of the parliament itself. If the parliament does not mature enough, it would be a suicidal attempt to give it the power to remove judges of the higher judiciary. The Judiciary should not be made answerable to Parliament. Even after having two chambers, India cannot properly transact the business of a parliamentary removal mechanism while ours is totally different – there is one parliament and the parliamentarians are under the obligation to vote as per direction of its hierarchy even if there is free and fair election.

In addition, the political parties should be cautious in selecting their candidates for the national elections. As noticed above, even in a mature democracy, where an election mechanism has been institutionalized and the parliamentarians are elected in free and fair voting, they could not yet properly transact the business of removal of judges of the highest court impartially. It is expected in a country operating as a constitutional democracy the following indispensable constituents would exist: (a) purity of election, (b) probity in governance, (c) sanctity of individual dignity, (d) sacrosanctity of rule of law, (e) independence of judiciary, (f) efficiency and acceptability of bureaucracy, (g) credibility of institutions like the judiciary, bureaucracy, Election Commission, Parliament, (h) integrity and respectability of those who run those institutions. After the delivery of the judgment by the High Court Division, the Supreme Court noticed from both print and electronic media reports that Members of Parliament while discussing on the floor of the house criticized the judgment and the judges questioning their propriety in declaring the amendment ultra vires the Constitution by using unparliamentarily language.

This proved again that our parliamentary democracy is immature and to attain maturity there is necessity of practicing parliamentary democracy continuously for at least 4 or 5 terms with the participation of all major political parties. The Members of Parliament in India and Pakistan did not react against any verdict given by their highest court and accepted the verdicts of the Supreme Courts even though some decisions were sensational. Clause (3) of Article 65 of our Constitution made provisions for fifty reserved seats for women in Parliament, who are not directly elected by the people. The Constitution (Fifteenth Amendment) Act, 2011 inserted a new provision as Clause (3A) to Article 65 which provided the following for the remaining period of the parliament in existence at the time of the commencement of the Fifteenth Amendment: "Parliament shall consist of three hundred members elected by direct election provided for in Clause (2) and fifty women members provided for in Clause (3)."

In a democracy, based on the rule of law, it is now the expectation of every citizen that all aspects of the government ought to be highly accountable. As a matter of fact, it should be remembered that the judiciary has historically been one of the most accountable organs of the State. The concept of judicial accountability can broadly be said to refer to the notion that judges or those who sit in judgment over others need to account for their judicious and injudicious conduct. The emerging right to democratic governance has come with a call for accountability of all public institutions. The legislature is composed of members who represent an electorate. They are accountable to this electorate. The Executive branch also has, at the end of the day, to account to those who put them in office. In their day to day functions, judges experience tremendous pressure. They are to review the decisions of both the Legislature and the Executive branch of the government. It is again, a concept of democratic governance to guarantee judicial independence, which requires that the judiciary must, in the performance of its function, be free from any interference, be it political, parliamentary, administrative, executive or otherwise. This principle of non-interference permeates all who sit on the Bench.

The present Article 70 has been substituted by the Constitution Fifteenth Amendment. The majority of the Members of Parliament come from political parties. The political party which gains a majority in Parliament forms the Cabinet headed by the Prime Minister. Article 55(2) gives the executive power of the Republic to the Prime Minister in accordance with the Constitution. Article 55(4) says that all executive actions of the government shall be expressed to be taken in the name of the President and clause (6) of Article 55 provides that the President shall make rules for the allocation and transaction of the business of the government. Under Article 48, clause (3), the President in the performance of all his functions, save only that of appointing the Prime Minister and Chief Justice, shall act in accordance with the advice of the Prime Minister. From the above, this provision boils down to: a political party through the process of election secures most of the seats in the parliament under the banner of a political party becomes majority members. The leader of said political party who commands the support of the majority of the Members of Parliament forms the Cabinet which runs the government. The theoretical separation of power is completely diluted here because the members who are in the majority in the parliament legislate and the Cabinet which is formed from among them discharge the function of the Executive part of the government. Therefore, legislation and administration fall in the hands of the same group of Members of Parliament. In that view of the matter, Article 70 in any format ensures adherence of Members of Parliament belonging to a party to abide by the party's instructions.

If Articles 7, 22, 94(4), 102 and 112 are read together, it becomes clear that the Supreme Court is independent, separate and is the guardian of the Constitution and it is an organ of the State. It is not merely a court. If this position is taken to be true, the parliamentary removal mechanism introduced by the Sixteenth Amendment would be an embargo upon the judges to uphold the supremacy of the Constitution as well as it will create imbalance between the organs of the State and thereby jeopardize the independence of the Judiciary. The Constitution itself delineates and demarcates the difference and contains in separate compartments different provisions, some of which relating to the judges of the Superior Judiciary as constitutional functionaries holding an office and the other to the various services holding posts based on cadres governed by separate rules. There are various provisions in the Constitution which establish and protect the independence of the Judiciary as a basic feature in its sweep and as an inherent element of the rule of law. With all that, I think, the bedrock of independence lies in the personalities who handle the inter-relation with the changing concepts of rights and liberties, and in a sense, the continuing life itself for the time being.

Removal of judges from office should be an event rarely to take place if their entry in the judiciary is properly made after detailed scrutiny as required for getting the selection done with best quality of head, heart and courage with judicial discipline and conviction for rule of law and equal justice with the backbone that never to yield to any power or favor, however tempting or convenient it may seem and in strict adherence to the rule of law, being an integral part of the independence of judiciary. For ensuring rule of law through a rigorous judicial selection process and high standards of ethical conduct can help avoid the need for the use of a removal mechanism. These are basics to be borne in mind, but the Executive ignores the criteria in the selection process as is seen all the time. Besides the risk that a judge may become mentally or physically incapacitated while in office, there is always the danger of the rare judge who engages in serious misconduct and refuses to resign when it becomes clear that his or her position is untenable. On the other hand, there is the threat to judicial independence when the removal process is used to penalize or intimidate judges. The challenge is to strike the correct balance between these concerns. It is to be ensured that the removal process cannot be used to penalize or intimidate judges. Removal from office is a very serious form of judicial accountability. The Judiciary must be seen to be independent. Public confidence hinges upon both these requirements being met. Judicial independence serves not as an end, but to safeguard our constitutional order and to maintain public confidence in the administration of justice. The three core characteristics of judicial independence are: security of tenure, financial security, and administrative independence which have emerged from the various decisions as considered by it. But in fact, the Sixteenth Amendment has affected the security of tenure of the judges of the Supreme Court, a core characteristic of judicial independence.33

The Judiciary being a sagacious organ of the State must apply laws, interpret them and the Constitution, and decide disputes between individuals, and between individuals and the State, and finally deliver justice. The State is being run by its Executive branch and the Executive acts in its own sphere of activity. But it is one of the biggest litigants. Making policies and executing them come within the sphere of the Executive. But in executing the policies, there are situations where the court is required to interfere in exceptional cases, like the present one. If the policy decision is one of violation of fundamental rights or interference with the independence of the Judiciary or in violation of any provisions of the Constitution, the courts will not hesitate to interfere and intervene in the matter. Similarly, if the policy decision violates an Act of Parliament or the rules made thereunder, the courts will not remain as silent spectators – they will certainly intervene in such acts. Whenever a constitutional matter comes before this court, the meaning of the provisions of the Constitution comes for interpretation. Though there is no implied limitation on the power of Parliament to amend the Constitution but by insertion of Article 7B, the power is circumscribed. An amendment will be invalid if it interferes with or undermines the basic structure. Therefore, the validity of an amendment to a constitution is not to be decided by the touchstone of Article 26, but only based on violation of the basic features of the Constitution.34

According to the Constitution Fourth Amendment the control, including posting, promotion, leave and discipline of persons employed in the judicial service are to be exercised by the President. Though there was a provision for consultation in exercising this power, but practically this consultation is meaningless if the Executive does not cooperate with the Supreme Court. Moreover, this amendment is in direct conflict with Article 109, which provides that the High Court Division shall have superintendence and control over all courts and tribunals subordinate to it. If the High Court Division has superintendence and control over the lower judiciary, how can it control the officers performing judicial work if the Executive controls the posting, promotion and discipline and takes disciplinary action, is not clear to me. Thus, the Sixteenth Amendment is a colorable legislation. Where the power of Parliament is limited by the Constitution or Parliament is prohibited from passing certain laws. But Parliament sometimes makes a law which in form appears to be within the limits prescribed by the Constitution but which in substance transgresses the constitutional limitation and achieves an object which is prohibited by the Constitution. It is then called a colorable legislation and is void on the principle that what cannot be done directly cannot also be done indirectly.

The underlying idea is that although a legislature in making a law purports to act within the limits of its powers, the law is void if in substance it has transgressed the limits resorting to pretense and disguise. The essence of the matter is that legislature cannot overstep the field of its competence by adopting an indirect means. Adoption of such an indirect means to overcome the constitutional limitation is often characterized as a fraud on the constitution. The entire question is one of competence of the legislature to enact a law. A law will be colorable legislation if it is one which in substance is beyond the competence of the legislature. A mala fide exercise of discretionary power is bad as it amounts to abuse of discretion.35 With a view to avoiding any misgiving and confusion I formulated the Code of Conduct in exercise of power under Article 96 of the Constitution.36

Though the higher judiciary is totally independent, the process of selection of judges is not impartial. So even if the institution is independent, the persons manning the institution are not impartial. Even then some of them rise to the occasion and express opinions on the question of independence of the Judiciary. Justice Krishna Iyer in his "Law & Life" pointed out that appointment of judges should not be disappointments of the robbed brethren. There must be specific criteria consistent with the socialistic, secular and democratic values as set out in the preamble. In the process of scanning candidates their character, class and commitments and versatility should be investigated after due publicity and never as a secret deal. Every qualified member of the Bar in the country should be considered for selection and this opportunity will be real only if the public is made aware of prospective vacancies and conditions of selection. Dialectical materialism saturated with moral content must be the guiding principle of the appointing committee. Along with them I add that only being a qualified member of the Bar should not be the criterion for the selection. The candidate's family background too must be taken into consideration, particularly the educational background. There cannot be any selection unless at least two generations, if not three, must be educated, and this is fundamental for consideration. This is my assessment on a thorough assessment of the past and present judges.

Some of the judges feel they are not independent because of their political beliefs. It will be a bit blot on the independence of judiciary. In developed countries, 80 to 90 percent lawmakers have law backgrounds. Even in India 30 to 40 percent lawmakers have law background. In our country less than 10 percent of the lawmakers have background in law. Most lawmakers have business or are attached to business houses. About 30 to 40 percent have criminal records and naturally they have litigation pending in the courts. Article 70 of the Constitution says, no Member of Parliament who was nominated as a candidate of a political party shall vote against that party. If he votes against any bill placed by the political party in power or votes against on any issue he will be disqualified to be a member of that political party. So, it cannot be said that the Members of Parliament are independent at present either. There are provisions of impeachment of judges in different countries, but the constitutions of those countries are totally different. For example, in the US any member can vote against his party on any issue. Almost in all European countries the same principle is applicable.

In India a provision like Article 70 of our Constitution exists, but no comparison can be made with them because India has a tested democracy since 1937. Bangladesh has been ruled by dictators and martial law administrators as well. In 1970 there was a peaceful election, but the people could not enjoy the fruit of democracy because a dictator did not want to hand over power to the political party that was victorious. This led the people to take arms in their hands and ultimately the country was liberated. After the independence the country could not be run democratically for more than two and a half years. The elected government pushed the country toward an undemocratic system. So, we did not taste democracy even after a peaceful election. Just immediately after the liberation of the country, the question of removal of judges did not arise at all mainly because the entire country was in a devastated condition. The government in power was busy in rebuilding the country. Citing a provision contained in the 1972 Constitution the government wanted to travel back to 1972 provision. The condition of 1972 does not exist now, and the higher judiciary cannot be placed in the hands of Parliament because our constitution was achieved with the sacrifice of millions of martyrs. There is a difference in the meaning of the expression "We the People" used in the Preamble to our Constitution with the expression "We the People" contained in the Indian Constitution because India achieved independence through negotiations. The expression "We the People" used in US Constitution may be comparable to ours because the US also achieved independence after sacrificing many lives. In the US the people's representatives, either in the lower house or in the upper house, are elected by the people. Even a party's candidates are selected by the people. No member of the two main political parties can contest any election directly unless s/he is selected by delegates or constituents of that locality. In our country, a candidate of a political party is not selected by the people or councilors of that political party. They are selected by the leaders of that political party. So, a candidate for a parliamentary seat can directly participate in the election without being nominated by the councilors of that political party.

The ultimate result is that if for any reason a political party can raise a wave of popularity, a candidate even having a bad reputation with a criminal background can be elected on such a wave. Under such circumstances if a Member of Parliament is not selected by its councilors and ultimately not elected by the electorate by testing his popularity, he cannot claim to be a representative of the people. Our Constitution says, the country will be run by the people's representatives, but this representation is totally absent. We never try to choose our Members of Parliament as per the mandate of the Constitution based on "We the People". If any deviation is made from the mandate of the Constitution it will be contrary to the Constitution. Based on consideration of a deep reverence of our judicature some pathological facets of public concern designed to transform of the great constitutional instrumentality. Justice Holmes said: "Law is the business to which my life is devoted, and I should show less than devotion if I did not do what in me lies to improve it, and, when I perceive what seems to me the ideal of its future, if I hesitated to point it out and to press toward it with all my heart."37

We amended the Constitution changing its basic character, infringing on the fundamental rights, suppressing the rule of law and interfered with the independence of the Judiciary. This process started with the Fourth Amendment. Instead of expanding the horizon in the augmentation of decentralization of power and safeguarding the rule of law, independence of the Judiciary, fundamental rights and democracy we curtailed basic human rights, rule of law, independence of the Judiciary and democracy. On the other hand, American amendments were made for the betterment of the people and democratic rights, equal opportunity for education and for other benefits. The American Constitution had survived a civil war, presidential assassinations and economic crises. The framers wanted the amendment process to be difficult: there have been 10,000 attempts, 33 have passed Congress, and only 27 have passed both in Congress and the States. Amendments may be proposed in two ways; first by Congress with two-thirds of each house supporting; and second by delegates at a national convention that is called by Congress at the request of two-thirds of State Legislatures. Till this day only the first method has been used. For ratification of amendments there are two methods: firstly, three-fourths of State Legislatures must approve; secondly, citizens elect delegates to the convention where three-fourths must approve. The second approach was only used with the Twenty-First Amendment.

From the date of ratification of the Constitution we have made 16 amendments to it till 2014. The world's oldest constitution is the American Constitution and till date they have made only 27 amendments and the amendments were made for enhancing the rights of the citizens. The 12 amendments are the early adjustments to the constitution. Amendments 1-10, passed in 1792, have protected some rights from government infringement and they are called Bill of Rights. The Eleventh protects certain law suits. The Twelfth fixed the presidential election process. The Thirteenth Amendment ended slavery (1865). The Fourteenth Amendment defined citizenship, expanded due process and established equal protection (1868). The Fifteenth Amendment prohibited denying the right to vote because of race, color and previous servitude (1870). The American Sixteenth Amendment permitted passage of income tax (1913). The Seventeenth Amendment provided for direct election of US Senators (1913). The Eighteenth Amendment prohibited production, transportation, and sale of alcohol (1919) (in 1933 the 21st Amendment repealed the prohibition.) The Nineteenth Amendment gave women to the right to vote (1920). The Twentieth Amendment changed the dates of the presidential and congressional terms (1933). The Twenty-Second Amendment created the presidential term limit (1951). With the Twenty-Third Amendment Washington DC got to vote in presidential elections (1961). The Twenty-Fourth Amendment banned poll tax (1964). The Twenty-Fifth Amendment established rules for presidential succession (1967). The Twenty-Sixth Amendment lowered the voting age to 18 years (1971). The Twenty-Seventh Amendment set the rules for Congressional pay.

So, all the amendments to the US Constitution were made keeping in mind the protection of citizens' rights, not reducing their rights or taking away their rights. On the other hand, we approached toward the back instead of going forward. Chief Justice Warren while giving his ruling in Brown on May 17, 1954, stated in his autobiography that Marshal arrived at the Supreme Court to hear the Brown ruling. He, seated with associate justices of the court, read the decision out loud. "In approaching this problem, we cannot turn the clock back to 1868 when the (Fourteenth) Amendment was adopted, or even to 1896, when Plessey vs Ferguson was written. We must consider public education considering each: present place in American life: we conclude that, in the field of public education, the doctrine of 'separate but equal' has no place. Separate educational facilities are inherently unequal."38 On the other hand, we turned back to 1972 overlooking the fundamental change that had taken place in the preceding forty years in the country. Every country is looking forward, not backward, and wants to institutionalize its state organs phase by phase so that the people can enjoy the fruits of independence and safeguard their inherent rights; but ours is totally opposite. We are attempting to go toward the medieval age.

In constitutional matters, particularly in case of a matter challenging the constitutionality of an amendment to the constitution, the court is not concerned with any particular issue, because for giving interpretation of the constitutionality of an amendment, the court is bound to explore different provisions of the constitution and give its opinion. This is an established practice being followed since 1803 in Marbury. The court is required to see a more perfect independence, establish justice, ensure democratic tranquility, promote the general welfare and, most of all, and protect the constitutional safeguards. Whenever a question arises concerning the constitutionality of a power, the first question the court is required to see is whether the power is expressed in the constitution. If it is, the question is decided. If it is not expressed, the next inquiry must be whether it is properly an ancient to an express power and necessary to its execution. If not, Parliament cannot exercise it. Law cannot remain static. The court must evolve new principles and lay down new norms which would adequately deal with new problems which arise for protecting the citizens against abuse.

References:

1. *Bangladesh v. Advocate Asaduzzaman Siddique CLR, Special Issue-2017*
2. *Article 58C of the Constitution*
3. *Articles 58C, 58D of the Constitution*
4. *Part IXA, article 141A of the Constitution*
5. *Civil Appeal No. 139 of 2005 (Thirteenth Amendment case)*
6. *Yusuf Patel v. Crown, PLD 1955 FC 387; State v. DOSSO, PLD 1958 SC 533 and Asma Jilani v. Government of Punjab, PLD 1972 SC 139*
7. *The Constitution (Fourth Amendment) Act, 1975*
8. *Khandker Delwar Hossain v. Bangladesh Italian Marble, Civil Petition No. 1944 of 2009*
9. *The Constitution (Fifteenth Amendment) Act, 2011*
10. *Gazette Notification, September 22, 2014*
11. *Article 64(1) of the Constitution*
12. *Article 111 of the Constitution*

12(a). *The memories of Chief Justice Earl Warren, P.284*

12(b). *The Constitution and Chief Justice Marshall by William F. Swindler, P. 31-32*

12(c). *Earl Warren (Ibid) P. 334*

13. *Before Memory Fades, Fali S. Nariman*

13(a). *John Marshall – P-210*

14. *Annals of Congress, II; 434-436; Thomas Jefferson to Abigail Adams, September 11, 1804; 12:162*
15. *Asma Jilani v. Government of Punjab; PLD 1972 SC 139*
16. *Calhoun, Disquisition on Government Works, i, 11 Cooly, Constitutional Limitation, 8th Edition 4*
17. *Provincial Court Judges (1997) 3 SCR 3*
18. *Anwar Hossain Chowdhury v. Bangladesh, 34 DLR (AD) 1*
19. *Juan Williams in the book "We the People", Chapter 7*
20. *A.K Kaul v. Union of India, (1995) 4 SCC 73*
21. *Keshwananda Bharati v. State of Kerala, AIR 1973 SC 1461*
22. *In re 1938 (1939) FCR 18, 36, (39)*
23. *James v. Commonwealth, (1936) AC 578*

24. Dr. Wines

25. R.V Brislan; P (1935) 54 CLR 262

25(a). Cherokee Nation v. Georgia, excerpted from Andrew Jackson and his Indian Wars by Robert V. Remini, reprinted by Viking Penguin and Joseph C Barke, "The Cherokee Cases: A Study in Law, Politics and Morality" 21 Stanford L. Rev 500

26. Memories of Chief Justice

27. Historical Introduction to English Law, Co. Litt of 183b.

28. The Politics of Judicial Independence in the UK's Changing Constitution, p. 58-59

29. Ibid

30. Law and Reality, Devi Prasad Singh

31. The Hindustan Times, 26 October 1998; The Hindu, 3 September 1999, 23 November 1998

32. Abdul Mannan Khan v. Bangladesh, 64 DLR (AD) 169

33. Latimar House Guidelines

34. M. Nagraj v. Union of India, (2006), 8 SCC 212; Keshwananda (Supra); Bangladesh v. Idrisur Rahman, 15 BLC(AD) 49; Anwar Hossain Chowdhury (Supra), Indira Nehru Gandhi v. Raj Narayan, AIR 1975 SC 2299

35. Punjab v. Gurdial Singh, AIR 1980 SC 319

Chapter 28

Ethical Values of Judges of the Highest Court and the politicians

I used to discuss the problems being faced by me with the judges regularly and took their opinions. It happened earlier during my long tenure in the Appellate Division. I had worked with five Chief Justices and none of them discussed with fellow brother judges regarding matters related to the administration of justice. I kept in mind the advice given by the ATM Afzal, the former Chief Justice, that Kamal Uddin Hossain, also a former Chief Justice, used to invite him when he was in the High Court saying that whenever he had time after court hours to sit beside him for observing the administrative work because he would be the Chief Justice one day and that the judges had no experience in administrative work. Whenever any problem had arose in any district court, I called them during recess time and took their advice. I noticed that all our discussions became known to the ministry. I could not rectify the problem. I requested the judges not to disclose anything to others, but my request did not yield any result. When I could not keep anything secret, I reminded the judges that they are judges of the highest court and the honor bestowed on them is comparable with none in the country, but all my requests went unheeded. There were a lot of important matters in which the government or a minister is interested, and we had to discuss them but all our discussions were leaked.

In the Sixteenth Amendment matter all the judges expressed opinions that the Chief Justice would speak for the court as a convention and this fact is admitted by Md. Abdul Wahhab Miah in his opinion observing, "My Lord, the learned Chief Justice, was supposed to speak for the court." But the judges made a U-turn after circulation of my opinion. Immediately after the pronouncement of the judgment, ABM Khairul Haque called an unprecedented press conference on August 5, 2017 attacking the judgment and me personally. He said, whatever the Chief Justice said is as a headmaster and other judges have accepted those as his views. It is shocking to see how a former Chief Justice is not only demeaning but also undermining the other judges of the highest court. He might have a personal dislike for me, because I rescued him many times, but what about the other judges? I find no proper language to make any comment on his uncourteous remarks. When reporters queried Khairul Haque regarding the irrelevant remarks he had made about the Fifth Amendment case, he avoided the question saying that he had called the press conference over the judgment of the Sixteenth Amendment.

ABM Khairul Haque and Anisul Haque, the Law Minister, used similar languages in their press conferences. It would have been fair to criticize my opinions by writing articles if they had the courage to do so. But why indulge in character assassination of the sitting Chief Justice? They exceeded all norms even though they are members of the same family. They caused much loss to the judiciary. Thereafter, the judges one by one, except two, started expressing opinions of their own. It was clear to me that there was a lot of string pulling going on. Someone was pulling strings from behind the screen and the puppets were performing giving lot of joy to the audience. I was asking myself which path we had chosen: to go forward or backward. Second question surfaced in my mind was that there must be an end of every act, thing or deed. Should we stop at certain stage or we would travel endless future? If it being so, I don't believe so, what would be the fate of our next generation? History nurtures personal and collective identity in a device of world. People discover their place in time through stories of their families, communities and nation. These stories of freedom and equality, injustice and struggle, loss and achievement, courage and triumph shape people's personal values that guide them through life. History is the foundation for strong, vibrant communities. A place becomes a community when wrapped in human memory as told through family stories, tribal traditions, and civic commendations as well as discussions about our roles and responsibilities to each other and the place we call home.

History helps people envision a better future. Democracy thrives when individuals convene to express opinions, listen to others and take actions. Weaving history into discussions about contemporary issues clarifies differing perspectives and misperceptions, reveals complexities, grounds competing views in evidence and introduces new ideas; all can lead to greater understanding and viable community solutions. History, saved and preserved, is the foundation for future generations. Historical knowledge is crucial to protecting democracy, rule of law, human rights and human values. By preserving authentic and meaningful documents, artifacts, images, stories and places, future generations have a foundation on which to build and know what it means to be a member of the civic community. (https://www.historyrelevance.com/value-history-statement/)

Values are beliefs shared by individuals or a community about what is important or valuable. Ethics are the action and manifestation of values. I have no regret about our politicians who have been ruling our country since 1972; they intentionally may ignore or forget or pretend to forget the past because power makes them blind. But what about our judges? Did they forget Dr. Muhammad Munir or Dr. FKM Munim, former two Chief Justices of Pakistan and Bangladesh? General people may not remember them or even if they remember, they may not know their past stories but, I believe, our judges of the highest court know them. Did they not consider Badruddin Ahmed Siddiky, former Chief Justice of East Pakistan who had refused to administer the oath of Governor General to Tikka Khan during the martial law period in 1971? If the two former Chief Justices of the highest courts are compared with the latter, who was not as highly qualified as they were, yet his weight and integrity is far more than of the two combined. If they have intentionally forgotten the sagacity and lessons of our history, it is a suicidal act for the Judiciary.

Syed Mahmud Hossain and Hasan Foez Siddiqui observed that I made observations regarding Article 116 of the Constitution which was not an issue at all in the appeal. Both said, I travelled beyond the issues involved in the matter. I am sorry to say, they have little conception of judicial review on constitutional issues. Possibly they could not comprehend the Fifth Amendment, Eighth Amendment and Masder Hossain, not to speak of Kesavanada and

Marbury. I strongly believe and still hold the view that their opinions were made to be given from a certain corner in the same manner as they did in the case of two Ministers in a contempt proceeding. I would be happy if they had read the opinions of the above five historic cases. They would get their reply. All those judgments have been accepted by all and no question arose about reviewing them. Arbitrary or biased decisions or other terrible blunders and grave misjudgments by judges, unless there are correcting agencies, may result in crimes without punishment. When it comes to expounding on constitutions, an old document of continuing vitality, judges are supposed to use traditional tools of judicial analysis--text, meaning, original understanding and decided precedent. In John Marshall's words, "To say what the law is "but how you apply an Eighteenth century document to the Internet, DNA testing, electronic surveillance, smart phones, video games, social media, gay marriage, affirmative action, whether capital punishment with lethal injection with or without an effective anesthetic is cruel and unusual" and other societal and technical phenomena, dreamed at the time of the Constitution, without some over-reaching philosophy as to where you are headed?

"Politics plays a really significant role in shaping our judicial system," writes Maya Sen, a political scientist at Harvard's Kennedy School of Government. She argues that this is because the appointing authority takes account of ideology in the judicial selection process. Sen concludes that the bottom line is the recent conservatism favoring the politicization of the courts. She notes that conservatives have worked hard to develop qualified judicial candidates with a rightist point of view, principally through the federalist society, a conservative organization active on law school campuses, before which Alito, Thomas, and Scalia have spoken.1 I need not make any further comment about them.

It is a certainty that the US Supreme Court justices, even those of the highest intellectual quality, such as the nine on the present Court, tend to make political decisions. As Scalia observed: "Judges have been known to be politically partisan."2 Their religion, their professional training, their personal life experience informs their political leanings like everyone else's.3 Justice Brandies saw law not as a system of artificial reason but as a logical extension of ethical ideals with freedom at its core. He bristled at the willingness of his colleagues to endorse the government's use of wiretap technology to gather evidence and argued passionately for an individual's "right to be let alone". His ringing dissent is still one of the most quoted opinions in court history. "Men born to freedom are naturally alert to repel invasion of their liberty by evil minded rulers," he wrote, and added, "the greatest danger to liberty lurk insidious encroachment by men of zeal well-meaning but without understanding." He might have been writing about the democratic surveillance activities of NSA today.4 Was Brandies a legalistic jurist who woodenly applied the text of the Constitution to the case before him or was he the judge Bishop Canon predicted who would find it "difficult" when it was a conflict between the law and a "sound public policy and for the moral and material welfare of the State, to be entirely unbiased when it comes to a decision"? 5

Antonin Scalia believes that the Constitution is "enduring", if not dead. This means it looked at the text and the original understanding, not some liberal notion of an evolving "living" constitution that means whatever the justice would like it to mean. A professor of Near Eastern Studies at Princeton remarked, "Scalia interprets the constitution the same way that ISIS interprets Shariah."6

Scalia believes that the text of the Constitution, and the original understanding of its meaning at the time of ratification, and how courts have interpreted it, ought to be the decisive factors in interpretation, not the personal view of an individual justice, who wants the Constitution to mean what he or she would like it to mean.7 The Judiciary in the US, after a long debate in Marbury, is now established as a coequal branch of government, serving as a "check and balance" mechanism on the Executive and the Legislative branches of the government. The Constitution was to become a living document with the court, the guardian of the Constitution. As Marshall observed in 1918, "We must not forget, it is a Constitution we are expounding.8 The Court would use this newly acquired power sparingly. Still, the camel's nose was in the tent. Marshall kicked partisan Supreme Court all in the early days of America with the sine qua non for establishing judicial power for centuries to come and the Court was presently exercising this power by making policy choices are more politically than legally informed. Their Court asserted its jurisdiction to curtail the excesses of other branches of government and to order compliance with its mandates. If the Court was ever to protect and define the basic constitutional rights of unpopular minorities, it required this appropriation of awesome judicial power to interpret and define the law. And the indispensable feature was the power to make all the people, including the Executive branch of the government to submit to its mandate. Thus, began the rule of law in the United States of America.9

It is the essence of judicial duty that the court must determine which of the provisions is inconsistent with law or another provision of the Constitution, and the court must decide that case in conformity with the law and must expound and interpret the Constitution. The concept of judicial review is pronounced as an inherent or necessary and proper power of the court, ordinary judicial review of unconstitutional matters is the very essence of the court's jurisdiction. After the Marbury decision the principal criticism of the government was that it was itself a dictum masquerading as a rule of decision – that the doctrine was not essential to the disposition of the case.

A constitution is understood to grow and evolve over the time as the conditions, needs and values of society change. Such evolution is inherent to the constitutional design because the framers intend the document to serve as a general charter for a growing the nation and a changing world. Hence constitutional interpretations must also be informed by contemporary norms and circumstances, not simply by its original meaning. The text of the constitution must be construed to have the capacity to adapt to a changing world, otherwise the rights declared in words may be lost.10 The constitutional governance of a free nation means the joint effort of the people, in and outside the government, to achieve human development and to attain the constitutional goals of equality, justice and dignity of everyone. For constitutional governance the mindset from "everyone unto himself" to "concerned for others" must develop. In the constitutional governance of a free nation both the rulers and the ruled are citizens. Those in government should realize that they are not merely holders of public offices. They must be enlightened citizens themselves and must show concerns for others to work for human development for achieving the goals set out in the constitution. An elected government, therefore, must be made accountable and answerable to an unelected body of legal experts comprising the Judiciary so that merely on the strength of votes, minority rights and rights of individuals are not snatched away or interfered with. This is one very important role expected of the judges of constitutional courts, who must act as watchdogs for the protection of fundamental human rights of citizens.11

Justices are not elected, and their mandate flows from the constitution's texts and their duty is to interpret it in good faith. Holmes's philosophy was that the personal element in a great judge really matters; that law is more like a skyscraper under construction with judges in their own way and legislatures in their own way gradually building new beams, making new laws to meet the need of an evolving society.12 Human beings, Oliver Wendell Holmes Jr. thought, build the law. He said, "The life of the law" has not been logic; it has been experience: the felt necessities of the time, the prevalent moral and political theories, institutions of public policy, avowed or even unconscious, and even the prejudices which the judges share with their fellow men, have had a good deal more to do with them than syllogisms in determining the rule by which men should be governed.13 The judges make the law out of what they discover, and that law is the will of the justices trying to do that which is right.14

While drafting the Constitution of India the members of the Constituent Assembly were enthusiastic supporter of a powerful Judiciary. They had established an excellent reputation during the long period of British rule. Indeed, a strong case can be made from the statement that the greatest legacies of the British Raj were an impartial and independent judiciary and a widespread belief in the rule of law. Many regarded the Supreme Court of the United States as the model to emulate in India. The US Supreme Court under the leadership of Chief Justice Marshall assumed the power declaring a law unconstitutional and it is thus the Supreme Court established its own supremacy over the Executive and Congress. The Indian Constitution, unlike the English constitution, recognizes the court's supremacy over the legislative authority, but that supremacy is a very limited one, for it is confined to the field where the legislative power is circumscribed by legislation put upon it by the constitution itself. Within this restricted field, on a scrutiny of the law made by the Legislature, it can declare it void if it is found to have transgressed the constitutional limitations.15 This was the first case in which the Supreme Court was called upon to interpret the new constitution, the first to involve the fundamental rights, the first to involve the controversial Preventive Detention Act, the first in which an individual bypassed all lower courts and took his grievance directly to the Supreme Court, and the first in which the Supreme Court, in the exercise of its new powers, declared unconstitutional a portion of a parliamentary enactment.

The Supreme Court words are final, not because it is infallible; it is infallible because it is final. The Constitution vests vast power to the apex court to enforce fundamental rights, to do complete justice in any cause or matter pending before it and to punish any contempt itself. Civil and judicial authorities are obligated to act in aid of the Supreme Court. And the law declared by it is constitutionally conclusive save on review or reversal by a larger Bench or by a valid constitutional amendment. So, it can cause and review executive actions if they are contrary to constitutional law, declare ultra vires legislation or other violation by Parliament beyond constitutional jurisdiction and jurisprudence. Such being the impregnable immensity of the highest tribunal's authority, this plenary, paramount power process is a public trust. Naturally in a democracy power and accountability are blended integrally. The independence of the Judiciary does not exalt it into an imperium in imperia since supremacy belongs to the highest judiciary which is a sublime sentinel on the quivered, a few pregnant posers arise which demand sensitive and sensible answers turned to the values of the socialist, secular, democratic Republic.16

References:

1. *"Why Judges Tilt to the Right" by Adam Liptak, New York Times, February 1, 2015*
2. *Morison v. Olson, 487 US 654, 730 (1988)*
3. *Supremely Partisan, page 29*
4. *277 US 438 Act 471 (1928)*
5. *Supremely Partisan, page 125*
6. *Supremely Partisan, page 193*
7. *Ibid, page 195*
8. *Mcculloch v. Maryland 17 US 316, 407(1819)*
9. *Supremely Partisan, page 82*
10. *Olmstead, 277 US @ 472-473*
11. *Human Values, page 345*
12. *Proceedings of American Philosophical Society, Vol 91 No. 5, pages 405-420*
13. *Oliver Wendell Holmes, Jr, The Common Law*
14. *Chaffe, "Do Judges Make or Discover Law?" page 420*
15. *A.K Gopalan v. State of madras (1950) SCR 88,*
16. *Justice V.R Krishna Iyer, Law and Life, pages 286-287*

Chapter 29
Character Assassination

Character assassination is a deliberate process that destroys the credibility and reputation of a person, institution or nation. Agents of character assassinations employ a mix of open and covert methods to achieve their goals, such as raising false accusations, planting and fostering rumors and manipulating information. It may involve exaggeration, misleading half-truth or manipulation of facts to present an untrue picture of the targeted person. It is a form of defamation and can be a form of ad hominem argument. It is the deliberate destruction of an individual's reputation. The effect of character assassination driven by an individual is not equal to that of a state-driven campaign. The state-sponsored destruction of reputation, fostered by political propaganda and cultural mechanisms, can have more far-reaching consequences. One of the earliest signs of a society's compliance to loosening the reins on the perpetration of crimes with total impunity is when a government favors or directly encourages a campaign aimed at destroying the dignity and reputation of its adversaries, and the public accept its allegations without question. Generally, official dehumanization has preceded the physical assault on the victims.1

In his press conference in the first week of July 2017 the Law Minister attacked me in filthy language. He said, the Chief Justice delivered the judgment with an ulterior motive. He used smutty words while criticizing the Chief Justice of Bangladesh. For observance of 15th August, a public meeting was called in Dhaka at Suhrawardy Uddyan in which the Ministers including the Prime Minister made unprecedented remarks against me. On August 22, 2017, the Prime Minister talked to the victims and survivors of August 21st grenade attack following a program marking the day at Krishibid Institute, Dhaka. She slammed me for comparing Bangladesh with Pakistan. She said that Justice Sinha should have quit before making such a comparison and defaming Parliament. "I will say this: everything can be tolerated, but comparing Bangladesh with Pakistan cannot be acceptable," she said. Hasina asked the people to judge the comparison with Pakistan posing a question why, "Bangladesh would be compared with Pakistan and Pakistani prime minister." She said, "There would be no benefit in giving me such a threat."

According to the parliamentary system, the President is elected by Members of Parliament including women lawmakers while the President appoints the Chief Justice, she said. She added that if the lawmakers were not elected, how the President would be elected. "When you (Chief Justice) make criticism in this regard you will have to accept the others. So, you should have stepped down before making such comments." Hasina said, there were many contradictions in the verdict. "I am going through the verdict and taking notes. By the grace of the Almighty, she remarked in the Jatiya Sangsad comparing Bangladesh with Pakistan was very insulting. "So, I seek justice from the people, as their court is the biggest one and none can ignore it," she said.2

These statements proved beyond doubt that she was making statements as per advice of the sycophants because she is totally detached from the public and the law. The sycophants misquoted my remark in court on a day which was fixed for supplying the gazette notification relating to the Disciplinary Rules for the judicial officers. As the Attorney General was taking repeated adjournments, I reminded him saying "look at Pakistan, not to speak of other countries, which had no rule of law at all, they too had separated the lower judiciary in 1973." Some lawyers of Awami League family misquoted my statement to the reporters at the Bar and the reporters confronted the Attorney General asking whether I had made such a statement. The Attorney General told the reporters that I did make such a statement. Even then the Prime Minister accepted the sycophant's statement. The Prime Minister was fearing that I would take legal actions against the persons whose names were published in the Panama Papers in the same manner as the Supreme Court of Pakistan took cognizance against the Pakistani Prime Minister Nawaz Sharif and debarred him from continuing as the Prime Minister of Pakistan.

It is a fact that we defeated Pakistan and that Pakistan had no democracy and is run by autocrats, even then the government made the lower judiciary completely independent in 1973, and its higher judiciary has been exercising its power independently since the time of Chief Justice Iftekhar Chowdhury. There was some rumor about political interference, but he fact remains that the Supreme Court declared a powerful sitting Prime Minister (Nawaz Sharif) corrupt and unfit to continue in the office of Prime Minister. We did not find any uproar on the floor of Parliament after such a judgment and still Nawaz Sharif's party continued to run the government. Did we in Bangladesh make any effort to hold an enquiry about the Panama Papers? Why was the Prime Minister so apprehensive on hearing the remarks on the Pakistan episode? The Prime Minister was not properly advised which is evident from her remarks about the appointment of Chief Justice by the President. She failed to comprehend a Westminster type of parliamentary government. There is no scope under this system for election of women members by Members of Parliament because under the parliamentary system all members are required to be elected by the people. This reservation of 50 parliament seats for women and their election by an indirect method is not recognized in the Westminster system. This is in fact not election but selection. Moreover, the appointment of Chief Justice by the President is not a favor, rather it is the constitutional obligation of the President. She failed to distinguish between the constitutional obligation of the President and election of the President.

On September 14, 2017, there was a discussion for about five and half hours in Parliament in which some lawmakers and Ministers not only attacked me but also mounted coordinated assaults on my character which was not only unconstitutional but also contrary to the Rules of Procedure, which they totally ignored. The Prime Minister again echoed the statements of ABM Khairul Haque and stated that other judges put their signatures on what I had written, but they did not do it from their heart. It is an unfortunate remark coming from the lips of the Chief Executive of the country. The Prime Minister failed to comprehend the consequences of her remarks about the judges of the highest court. If the Chief Executive of the country demeans the judges of the highest court, the public perception about them would be affected adversely and, in that case, the people would lose faith in the institution of the judges of the apex court of the country. Secondly, the Constitution has given her the executive power of the State and she took oath under that Constitution. Yet at the same time she ignored the Constitution by demeaning the judges of the highest court, who also took oath under the Constitution.

The Prime Minister was also ill-advised regarding the President's power under the Constitution. Her remark that the Chief Justice was trying to take the power of the President was completely incorrect and gravely misleading. The issue was resolved as far back as on December 2, 1999, about 19 years back, and the government had acquiesced to it. As per the Constitution, besides the two specific powers of the President his other powers have been precisely dealt with in Masder Hossain. About the President's power of control, including some enumerated subjects and discipline of persons employed in the judicial service and magistrates exercising judicial functions, are neither Executive power nor Legislative powers. A rule-making power cannot be so easily implied when the makers of the Constitution did not lack in expression while bestowing an authority with rule-making power. So, the question of taking the power of the President or usurpation power of the President does not arise at all.

I did not make any comment regarding the unconstitutional and uncourteous remarks made by the Prime Minister, Ministers and Members of Parliament and instead remained silent in the interest of the Judiciary lest the judiciary and administration of justice are affected. In this connection I feel tempted to quote some valuable words of a renowned judge of the US, Justice Stone, who had observed: "...While unconstitutional exercise of power by the executive and legislative branches of the Government is subject to judicial restraint, the only check upon our own exercise of power is our own sense of self-restraint."4

In such circumstances, I was shocked and deeply perturbed and, with a view to regain mental strength, I wanted to join the Asia Pacific Region Chief Justices conference in Japan and to pass 5 or

6 days with my younger daughter in Canada before joining the conference. Though my decision to join the conference was taken about six months ago, I decided not to join the program under the changed circumstances. After one day of arriving in Canada, the Indian dailies, the Hindu and the Indian Express, in their issues dated October 14, 2017 published reports criticizing the government's role over the verdict of the Sixteenth Amendment. The newspapers focused on the criticism made by the ruling party. I had given a second thought over the matter and realized that if the publication of news by international media continues over the verdict and me personally, the image, dignity and prestige of the office of the Chief Justice would be destroyed. So long I would continue in the office the criticism will continue and, in that case, no Chief Justice will be able to perform his responsibilities independently. In that case the Judiciary will be seriously affected. It is one of the main objects of the Executive to somehow dominate the judiciary. Accordingly, I decided to step down mainly claiming though seven judges constituting the Bench unanimously pronounced the verdict maintaining the High Court Division's judgment, the Prime Minister criticized me alone in unsophisticated language which also too strong, misquoting my remarks made in the course of hearing a matter and also without comprehending my opinion about the Sixteenth Amendment. Not only the Prime Minister, Ministers and her party men were making comments attacking me personally. It was only because there was none in the country to challenge her authority and she does not tolerate anyone who has any courage to speak against her desire and certainly never in front of her. Another aspect she could not forget was that I had managed to change the opinion of two judges after they were convinced by her. It amounted to interference in the administration of justice by the Chief Executive.

Accordingly, I communicated with the Attorney General over phone expressing my intention that I had decided to step down and to intimate my decision to the Prime Minister. About 4 or 5 hours thereafter, Dr. Gowhar Rizvi, adviser to the Prime Minister on International Affairs, rang me and said that the Prime Minister told him that I should not to resign and that I must continue in my office till retirement. Not being satisfied with his version I again contacted the Attorney General over phone when the latter wanted to know from me whether Dr. Gowhar Rizvi talked with me. When I responded in the affirmative, he told me that whatever Dr. Gowhar Rivi said was the correct message from the Prime Minister. I was therefore confirmed that as soon as I communicated my decision to the Attorney General, he met the Prime Minister without delay and in the discussion Dr. Gowhar Rizvi was also present to whom the Prime Minister had assigned the task of communicating her views to me. This also convinced me that the Prime Minister had given serious thought the issue. Accordingly, she possibly she engaged Gowhar Rizvi with a view to ascertaining the news items published in the two prominent Indian newspapers and thought that such criticism might be suicidal to her government's image. Accordingly, the government's view was communicated through an adviser of the rank of a Cabinet Minister. Then I left for Japan. The valedictory session of the conference was held on September 20 or 21 2017. I was given a hearty ovation after my speech at the conference and my mental condition improved slightly. Accordingly, I decided to visit Hiroshima on September 22, 2017 and expressed my desire to our Ambassador for making necessary arrangements for the visit. The Ambassador told me that an officer would accompany us in the short tour.

Immediately after the conference in the late afternoon a representative of the DGFI intimated to me that I should not return to the country and I must go to Australia or Canada for the time being until they decided about my next course of action. I wanted to know from him how he got my contact number and how could I be assured of the truth of his information. In reply he told me that the DGFI was monitoring my programs and that the chief of the department directed him to communicate their decision. I told him that I had no ticket and enough money for such a visit and I could not go legally. Then he replied that the ticket and money would be arranged by the DGFI. I was both surprised and shocked at such news and told him that I would return to the country at any cost. After some time, the officer told me that in that case I should return after seven days. I was surprised to note that the DGFI had the final say over the Prime Minister. Secondly, an elite intelligence agency of the country exceeded its norms by regulating the affairs of the Chief Justice of a country. Even they did not follow any ethics, decorum or even the law. A Chief Justice leaves the country with the prior permission of the President, because in the absence of the Chief Justice, the President is required to assign the functions of the Chief Justice to the next senior most judge of the Appellate Division. If I had to leave for another country for seven days without the permission of the President, I would violate the law. Lastly, I understood the object of the last direction for overstaying for seven more days only; it was to suit the purpose of the Law Secretary. After the superannuation of Law Secretary Abu Saleh Skeikh Mohammad Johirul Haque, the government extended his tenure for two more years without consultation with the Chief Justice, even without any intimation to the Supreme Court and his order of extension was stayed by the High Court Division. The judgment obtained a stay order from the judge-in-chamber, and the matter would appear in the court on the reopening day for hearing.

There was a proposal for the extension of the retirement age of the District Judges for two years due to shortage of Senior District Judges. The proposal was made from the highest level of the judiciary and the government initially accepted the proposal. But due to the pressure of the secretaries, the Prime Minister ultimately retracted from her earlier decision. Now after retirement any officer in the administration can have his/her tenure extended by the government for two years. But a District Judge is not an officer in the civil administration service and the rules of extension are not applicable to a judicial officer and it had been settled in the Masder Hossain case. The Law Secretary's tenure was extended treating him as an officer in the civil administration service. The law does not permit to extend the tenure of a judicial officer because it is different from administrative service and the decision is contrary to the case of Kazi Habibul Awal, because the law Secretary was deputed in the Ministry as District Judge.5

The members of the judicial service are a class apart from the executive and administrative civil services of the State. Though Articles 133 and 136 of the Constitution are applicable to them, they are to be treated as a class apart from the other services of the State as a distinct entity, never to be treated alike or merged or amalgamated with other services. I told Syed Mahmud Hossain, who was assigned by me to perform as Judge in Chamber, to refer the Law Secretary's matter in the court so that it could be heard by the full court in view of the decision in Habibul Awal. Normally in constitutional and some complicated matters, like this one, it is a condition precedent that the Judge in Chamber would not make any interim order regarding the matter that is to be heard in open court. Whenever the Chief Justice directs a Judge in Chamber, he cannot disobey the direction because he has been given power by the Chief Justice. This time Syed Mahmud Hossain, disobeying and violating decorum and precedents, made an interim order of stay and fixed the matter for hearing after reopening in October 2017. I guessed that with a view to avoid me in the hearing of the matter, the DGFI wanted me to overstay for seven days abroad.

When I finally disobeyed the direction given by the DGFI, I was directed to cooperate with an army officer at Singapore Airport because I was returning to Bangladesh via Singapore and there was about five hours' transit time in Singapore. I wholly refused that proposal also. On September 23, 2017 at noon I landed at Changi Airport and was received by our High Commissioner. In the VIP lounge a tall young person with short cropped hair came with the High Commissioner to the lounge. Immediately thereafter the High Commissioner left the VIP room I wanted to know the identity of the person. But without disclosing his identity, he told me that he wanted the welfare of the country and wanted to say me a few words for the betterment of the country. On sensing his audacity, I rebuked him. Then he said that he was a government employee and was bound to obey the direction of his superior officer and I should not take any exception to him. Then he disclosed his name and rank as Lt. Colonel Md. Nazimuddoulah. I was then convinced that he was a DGFI officer with whom I was directed to talk in Tokyo. Since he apologized, I behaved properly with him and wanted to know about other matters. He did not dare to discuss any other issue and again expressed his apology for his conduct saying that he was a very junior officer in comparison to the position of a Chief Justice. I was feeling so uncomfortable by this incident at

Singapore Airport that after boarding the aircraft I was totally unmindful and could not realize when I landed at Dhaka Airport around 11:00 PM.

At the boarding bridge I noticed that 4 or 5 persons in civil dress escorted me and followed me on my way and one of them told me that they wanted to talk with me in the VIP lounge over a cup of tea. I was very much saddened from the incident in Singapore and as soon as I saw those persons, I was convinced that they were officers of the DGFI. I was fatigued due to my long journey coupled with the incidents happening one after another and practically I could not eat anything on the plane. So naturally I was very enraged by their behavior. I flatly refused their request and got into my car. When I was about to enter my car, the officer told me that they would follow me as a precaution for my security. I told them that whatever they wish they could do, it did not matter to me.

The entire way home I did not talk to my wife despite her query about the identity of those persons and, realizing my mental condition, she did not disturb me. Reaching home, I changed my clothes hurriedly, took two sleeping pills, drank a glass of water and went to bed. The whole night I could not sleep. As the situation evidently was turning more unpleasant I was convinced that a serious conspiracy had been hatched during my stay in Tokyo. I was thinking how I ought to face the upcoming situation. I was also convinced that even the Prime Minister's opinion had been negated by the DGFI. Either that or the Prime Minister had indicated to them to humiliate me because otherwise they could not have gone to this extent. This was possible as it was directly handled by the Prime Minister. In this connection, I remembered another incident during the Emergency period. But there was a difference between the two. In 2008 there was Emergency in the country and the Army was at the helm of affairs. I was a judge in the High Court Division. Even then when I took a strict decision not to obey the DGFI's direction they retreated. This time no Emergency had been declared and though I am the Chief Justice and despite the Prime Minister's decision that I should continue in office till retirement, the DGFI was determined to challenge my

609

status and position. I was also wondering who had control of state power: The Prime Minister or the DGFI. I thought that it must be with the latter otherwise they could not have taken such audacious steps. Keeping these things in mind I had decided that I would not show any weakness outwardly.

During the Durga Puja I used to enjoy all the five days in my village home. This time I decided to pass two days in my village and another two days in Dhaka because it would be the last Durga Puja during my entire tenure of judgeship. As per previous decision, I returned to Dhaka on the day of "nabami puja" and visited Dhakeswari Temple for offering my prayers to the Deity. The media on knowing my program assembled in the Dhakeswari complex and on the following day the news was carried, both in electronic and print media, giving importance to my visit to the temple. The following day I went to Bang Bhaban at noon to participate in the reception arranged by the President on Bijoya Dashami on September 30, 2017. We exchanged greetings as usual and the President told me that I should not leave without taking sweets arranged in the Darbar Hall. I went to the Darbar Hall and found the Indian High Commissioner. We were talking in the middle of the hall when two officers, presumably from the army, interrupted us and requested me to take some sweet. As I was again and again disturbed, I realized that the army personnel did not want me to talk to the Indian High Commissioner. Hence then I left Bang Bhaban without eating anything.

On the following morning, I decided to complete my pending judgments and orders and from the early morning I began working in my ground floor office. At around 11:00 AM the Registrar General informed me that all the judges of the Appellate Division headed by Md. Abdul Wahhab Miah wanted to meet with me. I told him to ask them to come at 5:00 PM. After some time, the query arose in me why all the judges wanted to meet me. With a view to remove suspicions, I directed my personal assistant to connect with Mirza Hossain Haider. I told him to meet me, but the latter told me that he was in a meeting with Md. Abdul Wahhab Miah along with the other Judges at his residence. On hearing this from him, I was confirmed that an organized conspiracy was being hatched. Then I told him to hand over the phone to Md. Abdul Wahhab Miah and I told him that since all the judges were with him I told him to come at once with them to my residence instead of coming at 5:00 PM. Abdul Wahhab Miah then told me that they were in a meeting and required half an hour more to finish the meeting and they would come then.

At 12:00 noon when they came Md. Abdul Wahhab Miah told me in a faltering voice that on the previous night the President had called them for dinner and except Mohammad Iman Ali all the judges of the Appellate Division and the Law Minister went. The President disclosed to them some allegations against me, which were serious, and the President directed them not to sit with me in court. He further told me that he (Wahab Miah) read the allegations till 2:00 AM and thought over the matter seriously. They advised me that I should not come to court reminding me that if I go to the court, they along with all the judges of the High Court Division would not attend the conventional ceremony of meeting the lawyers at the Supreme Court lawn on the reopening day on October 3. From the last sentence I had no doubt in my mind that in the meantime they had somehow contacted with some judges of the High Court Division of their line of thinking and told them not to cooperate with me. On hearing his voice, I felt sick, but I did not show any reaction and behaved normally. I could not even imagine hearing such words from none other than all the judges of the highest court with whom I had delivered judgments unanimously, but in my absence, they were all influenced by the government and fell in its trap. It was beyond my comprehension that these judges would betray me. They failed to understand that they have betrayed with their own conscience and thereby destroyed the image of the Supreme Court. My strength came from my puisne brothers. We all stood for the independence of the Judiciary and delivered the judgment on the Sixteenth Amendment unanimously. But they had taken a U-turn.

Despite my availability in Dhaka, they attended the dinner with the President without me and without giving any intimation to me. The President also knew that I was in Dhaka and I had met him in the afternoon. Even then he did not invite me to the dinner. So, it was clear to me that all the judges, except one from the Appellate Division, hatched a conspiracy with the President and the Law Minister. Or in the alternative, the Law Minister hatched the conspiracy with the help of the DGFI and convinced the President to arrange a dinner for the judges and before that he took the judges into confidence as part of the conspiracy behind my back. I realized that when the senior most judges in the country decided something, it would be simply a futile attempt to change their attitude.

If they had no ill motive, instead of discussing among themselves in the morning at Md. Abdul Wahab Miah's residence, they would have discussed with me to face the situation. They have already made up their minds. If they were clear in their conscience they would not have fallen into the trap of the government and attended the dinner without me. The judges did not disclose anything about what type of serious complaints were against me. After hearing Md. Abdul Wahhab Miah, I developed a sense of hatred to speak with them and told them to leave me alone. After their departure, I was thinking of strategies to overcome the situation, but I had none to consult with after the new developments. I did not exactly know what the allegations were against me. For ascertaining the allegation, I called Mirza Hossain Haider to meet me again. When he came I asked him whether he knew what allegations were leveled against me. He said, he had no direct idea about them, but the President had handed over some papers to Md. Abdul Wahhab Miah. I requested him to inform me about those after perusal of the same if possible. He again went to Md. Abdul Wahab Miah's residence and tried to find out the allegations. After a few hours, he returned and reported that I had sent four crore taka to my younger daughter equivalent to 30,000 Canadian dollars. I asked him whether he believed the allegations that I siphoned crores of taka to Canada pointing out that even if the allegations were taken as true, 30,000 Canadian dollars comes to eighteen lakh taka in Bangladesh currency, then where from they believed that I siphoned off crores of taka. He then said he did not think over the matter, now I realized that the allegations were false.

Some crucial questions arise from the above decision of the judges of the highest court. They had totally ignored their own opinions in the Sixteenth Amendment verdict. They had unanimously formulated the Code of Conduct of the Judges to the effect, amongst others, that "justice must not only be done but it must also been seen to be done; that the behavior and conduct of a higher member of the judiciary must reaffirm the people's faith in the impartiality of the judiciary and that any act of a judge, whether in official or in personal capacity, which erodes the credibility of his perception has to be avoided."6 Did they not then violate their own code of conduct? Again they said (a) "If a complaint is received by the Chief Justice from anybody or any other sources that the conduct of a Judge is unbecoming of a judge, that is to say, the judge is unable to perform his/her judicial work due to incapacity or misbehavior, the Chief Justice shall hold an enquiry into such activities with other next senior most judges of the Appellate Division and if the Chief Justice or anyone of the other judges declines to hold preliminary enquiry or if the allegations are against anyone of them, the judge who is next in seniority to them shall act as such member and if such enquiry found that there is prima facie substance in the allegation the Chief Justice shall recommend to the President what to the president (b) A complaint against a judge shall be processed expeditiously and fairly and the judge shall have the opportunity to comment on the complaint by writing at the initial stage. The examination of the complaint at its initial stage shall be kept confidential, unless otherwise requested by the judge. (c) All disciplinary action shall be based on standards of judicial conduct."7

The Judges totally ignored the Code of Conduct which they formulated only three months ago. If the judges of the highest court of the country are purchased or influenced by a government so cheaply, what would be the fate of the general litigants? What they said was that they were called for a dinner by the President at night and the latter had handed over some allegations against me saying that the allegations were serious and that they should not sit with me in court. So, they either acted as per order of the President or they believed that the allegations were serious enough in nature and that there was no need for any inquiry since the President had told them so. Did they not violate their oath and the Constitution by adhering to the request of the President? They themselves overruled the Sixteenth Amendment judgment without affording the Chief Justice to know the allegations, not to speak of affording me any opportunity to comment on the allegations. If the process is so simple, why should there be hearing of any constitutional matter in open court consuming valuable time of the court at the cost of public exchequer and taxpayers? They left nothing more for the Court to consider in any matter, because they can decide the fate of the Chief Justice of the country as per advice of the President. If the judges are satisfied with a lavish dinner that the Chief Justice is corrupt, they can do so against any other judge. Even their own fate or anyone of them may face such eventuality if the government decides to do so by compelling the other judges. Also, such questions arise: Whether any judge is safe in their hands? Whether any individual is safe in their hands to get justice? If the Chief Justice does not get justice, who else would get justice under the present set up?

They established a new convention which is unheard of in the judicial arena anywhere in the world that if the Executive does not want any judge or Chief Justice on any ground, there is no need to hold any enquiry by an impartial body as per the Constitution. Why did we fight for the independence of the lower judiciary right from 1999? Why then are the conduct and disciplinary rules necessary for the judges of the lower judiciary? If the Chief Justice is helpless, how the judges of the lower judiciary will get justice? Even the judges treated the Chief Justice as less than a private servant who can be compelled to resign at their whim, caprice and wishes. An employee in the administration is entitled to protection under the Rules of 1985 but a Chief Justice is not entitled to any such protection! Under these circumstances whether any judge of the Supreme Court can act or administer justice impartially? Any judge may be removed at the wish of the government by adopting the same policy. Then what is the Constitution for? They trampled on the Constitution which was written with the blood of martyrs. I feel ashamed to speak about them. They acted as stooges in the hands of the Executive. They also crushed the independence of the Judiciary. The hopes and faith of the citizens in the Supreme

Court, which is known as temple of justice, had totally been demolished and shattered by these Judges.

The President toward whom I had personal respect and whom I adored as a gentleman par excellence, who had dedicated his entire life to the cause of the people and achieved many things in his life, including glorifying the offices of the Speaker and the President, proved himself as a stooge in the hands of the Prime Minister or DGFI. He has no capacity to stand for his conviction and performed as a handpicked pliable person. He did not show any respect to his oath to faithfully discharge the duties of the office of President of Bangladesh. According to the Constitution, he subscribed to an oath to preserve, protect and defend the Constitution, and that he will do right to all manner of people according to law. Whether he faithfully discharged the office of President? Or whether he preserved, protected and defended the constitution? I had believed that he was a gentleman par excellence, but it was artificial. How could he dictate the judges of the highest court not to sit with the Chief Justice, meaning thereby, he wanted to create a deadlock in the highest court of the country? His conduct was unethical and unconstitutional. Apparently, he did not even think of the consequences that would follow if I did not follow the judges' opinion and go to court. I gave the priority of the Judiciary and instead of creating a chaotic situation in the highest judiciary remained silent.

The Prime Minister was away from the country on that day. I thought by this time the President had acquired vast knowledge on the Constitution because he was a lawyer and held constitutional posts for a long time. I had mentioned the command in constitutional law of the Indian President, but now I firmly believed whatever our President had done or achieved, the highest office of the country was not his achievement, but it is because he had reposed trust upon the Prime Minister or the Prime Minister found in him faithful. He also did not care and recognize constitutional value at all. He violated his oath and the Constitution by directing the judges of the highest Court not to sit with the Chief Justice even after knowing that the Chief Justice has done nothing other than disregarding an unethical request. Instead of inviting the judges, if he had any respect in his office, he could have told me about what was happening in the afternoon when I met him for exchanging greetings on Bijoya Dashami. If he had no time at that moment, he could have told me to wait for some time for a short discussion. Or he might have hinted to me to meet him at his convenient time on the same day. Since he arranged a dinner for the judges the same evening, he certainly had information from someone, but he concealed it from me. His silence proved that he was occupying the office of the President just ornamentally. If he could behave with the Chief Justice in such an unethical, unconstitutional and rude manner, a person with whom he had exchanged views many times, then how will an ordinary citizen get good treatment from him?

It is very difficult for me to believe that the President had invited the judges of the Appellate Division secretly for compelling them not to sit with me. If the Chief Justice is faced with such an unethical conduct from the President, who had dealt with the Chief Justice, where will the people go and get justice is not known to me. He was worse than Professor Lajuddin Ahmed as he did not behave with me in this manner.

A president of a country is not an ornament, but he is the Head of State and the Supreme Commander of the defense forces of Bangladesh. By dint of such office, during a crisis period, he would lead the country. It is expected from a President of a country to follow the Constitution and not behave like an ordinary worker of a political party. If I had committed a serious offence of misconduct or an unethical act, the Constitution has provided the procedure for taking legal action. If I had corrupted and misused my office why did the DGFI try to prevent me to return to Bangladesh? If the DGFI is used against the Chief Justice and all affairs of the State are resolved through this force, why have we kept a Constitution? If the DGFI is above the law, then who will enquire against them if they commit any offence? If a Chief Justice can be kept in solitary confinement by this force, it may be taken that they are above all. If I have committed a serious offence why was I allowed to leave the country instead of proceeding against me in accordance with law, is not clear to me. It is also not clear to me why I was compelled to file my resignation at Singapore Airport? Why was not my resignation accepted earlier? These are required to be disclosed to the public otherwise this type of incidents will continue, and such incidents are suicidal for a nation.

The Judiciary is very delicate and sensitive organ of the State. The President appoints the Chief Justice of Bangladesh, but it is not a grace or reward given to the appointee. It is the constitutional obligation of the President or the Chief Executive of the government and he cannot expect any undue advantage or privilege from the Chief Justice due to such appointment. He becomes the Chief Justice of Bangladesh after taking oath and the Chief Justice cannot be a Chief Justice of the court if he shows any favor to the political party which appoints him. The office of the Chief Justice is an institution and he is the guardian of the Judiciary, a vital organ of the State. Under the constitutional framework, the Supreme Court works as a watchdog for the constitution and the government. This court has constantly tried to respond to the problems and tribulations of the people of Bangladesh from whom the constitutionalism is derived and whose aspirations it seeks to serve without escaping criticism. All the time the court attempts to establish itself in the consciousness of the people of Bangladesh.

The Supreme Court is created by the Constitution and it is the only organ of the State on whom the hopes of each citizen of the country depend. That cannot be destroyed; otherwise the substratum of the country will be destroyed.

The Supreme Court has been created for the governance of the Judiciary at its helm by the Constitution to realize the expectations on an enduring basis for all times to come. It is one of the organs which safeguards the ultimate hopes and aspirations of the citizens of the country and the Constitution has been drawn up keeping the above objectives in mind. After the abolition of the Privy Council in 1949, the Supreme Court of Pakistan was created. It was as inevitable as it was historically compelling that the Supreme Court had to be a new nation's court established by the people of the country to participate in the future life and fortunes of nations. But from the very inception of the court it could not fulfill the hopes of the citizens. After Bangladesh's independence in 1971, the new Constitution came into being in 1972. So, it was historically imperative that the Supreme Court of Bangladesh must be a Bangladesh Court established at the high cost of the sacrifices of the martyrs which will preserve and protect the future life and fortunes of the Bangladeshi nation.

After the independence numerous measures taken by the governments of different political parties did not find favor with the Supreme Court. The legislation of the Indemnity Ordinance, the declaration of martial law twice, the setting up of six permanent High Court Divisions in different districts, the Bangladesh Civil Service (1-Organization) Order, 1980 purporting to incorporate the Judicial Service within the Bangladesh Civil Service as one of the cadre services; the Constitution Fifth, Eighth, Thirteenth and Sixteenth Amendments, all of them were struck down by this court whenever it found that those were ultra vires the Constitution on different issues. None of the governments was happy with the Supreme Court's decisions, but the court did not hesitate to give those decisions ignoring the government's angry eyes. No government, alien or indigenous, relishes frequent court rulings when they state that its measures are unconstitutional.

The framers of our Constitution were insistent not only that the judiciary be independent of the Executive and Legislative, but also that it be composed of the most competent people available. Hence, the minimum qualification for appointment to the Supreme Court is set forth in the Constitution. In addition to being immune from personal attacks by Parliament or anybody, the Supreme Court in order to maintain the dignity of the court and protect it from malicious and tendentious criticism, it was empowered to punish for contempt itself. On several occasions, the Supreme Court has invoked this power, the most notable case being that of Mahmudur Rahman, the publisher and editor of the daily Amar Desh, and Atiqullah Khan, publisher, and Swadesh Roy, assistant editor of the daily Jana kantha, and two Cabinet Ministers Advocate Quamrul Islam and Md. Mozammel Haque. During the martial law and Emergency, the Supreme Court was bitterly criticized for not defending the civil liberties of the citizens when it was called upon to do so. The court overcame those criticisms later by declaring all black laws unconstitutional and legislations void and rose to the occasion.

On October 2, 2017, I came to court in the morning for finishing my unfinished work. At 11:30 AM my private secretary Anisur Rahman informed me that the Director General of DGFI Major General Md. Saiful Abedin wanted to meet me at 12:00 noon. I permitted him to come. The officer came in time and wanted to know why I misbehaved with his officer at Singapore Airport. I was stunned looking at his body language and the way he charged me directly as if I am a subordinate officer. I was thinking how the officer could get such audacity to charge the Chief Justice. He told me that should I know after my Sixteenth Amendment judgment, the BNP was so happy that they distributed sweets among themselves. They exchanged text messages that they were coming to power soon. He could show me video which he recorded. I told him that it is none of my concern who comes to power. If anyone panicked with their conduct that reflected his weakness and it is the weakness of the government. He further told me that there is none between him and the Prime Minister, and what he said can be taken as the version of the Prime Minister and he followed her direction. He then said, "Sir, take four months holiday till January 31, 2018." I declined and asked him in what capacity he was directing me. I then said I had talk with Dr. Gowhar Rizvi and I will not do anything without talking with the Prime Minister. He said the Prime Minister would not talk with me. I told him that on the day of Eid-ul-Azha the Prime Minister had told me that she would discuss with me what had happened. On hearing this, the DGFI chief appeared shaky. Then he told me that there were allegations against me. On hearing this, I shouted, "What! You're exceeding your limits. Who gave you the power to talk like this?" He said that without proof he had not said anything. I said that I was surprised at his audacity. Thereafter he left my office.

Though I showed my temper and courage to the DGFI chief, at the same time I realized that I could not fight with this "mighty person" who had a gun and purse, but I have none of those. My strength depended on my brother judges, but they had gone against me. I was informed that the entire Supreme Court building was occupied by DGFI officials in plainclothes. My officers were trembling in fear. On the following day, I came to know that the DGFI personnel entered the IT section of the court and removed the video of the DGFI chief from the CCTV. My secretary Anis requested me that I should not take any decision which would deteriorate the situation.

I realized from his body language that they were facing with a lot of problems, but they were not disclosing all to me. I realized that all the judges were against me and if the administration was totally hostile to me, how could I survive? Finding no other alternative, I decided to go on leave for one month only instead of three months for the interest of the judiciary. I decided to talk with the Prime Minister in this regard. My leave petition was prepared by the DGFI officials as I came know. Because normally my secretary prepares my applications but this time he was under constant guard by them. After signing the application, I left for my residence at noon. After returning home I noticed that my security was tightened. I was completely kept in a condition of house arrest. No outsider could enter my house. The Supreme Court Bar members wanted to meet me on the following day, but they were not allowed. My relatives who came to meet me were detained at the gate, they were interrogated, their photos were taken and then some of them could enter. One day, a helper of my house was physically assaulted when he could not promptly answer their queries. On October 3, 2017, the DGFI chief wanted to know from me over phone if I wanted to be admitted to a hospital. But I did not want to go to any hospital. I told him that I would not go to the hospital because I was not sick – I could not pretend to be a sick person. He then said that it would have been better if I went to the hospital. From that moment, a doctor from the BSMMU, an orthopedic and a cardiologist used to visit my residence as per direction from the DGFI. Of them, I could remember the name of Prof. Sajal Banarjee of the Cardiology Department. I noticed, they came empty handed without even bringing their stethoscope. I joked with them why they had come to see a patient without bringing their basic instruments. They looked toward me helplessly and pretended to smile.

I had no work at home, so I had to talk with them for hours together over tea and coffee. They expressed their helplessness. I told them that why they were so unsteady when the Chief Justice was not. The problem lay with the Chief Justice, not with them. On hearing this, they lowered their heads and made no comment. In fact, I felt pity for them because they were compelled to visit my residence without any just cause compromising with their valuable time. One day Anisul Haque, the Law Minister, came to visit me. I wanted to know the purpose of his visit. He said that he had come to see me. I was enraged and told him, "Don't be a hypocrite. Whatever you want to say, say specifically. The Judiciary cannot run in this way and convey this message to the Prime Minister." The Law Minister responded by saying he would convey my message to the Prime Minister. When my nephew came to meet me from Uttara he was detained for three hours at the gate and was not allowed to enter the house. One of my staff was physically assaulted when he refused to give them his cell phone number. I told the Law Minister, what sort of nonsense his people were doing, pointing out those incidents.

On October 5, 2017, at around 10:00 PM, my secretary Anis intimated me that the DGFI chief wanted to meet me at my residence. As I was going to bed at that time, I prevented him from visiting at an odd hour. The officer requested my secretary that he would come only for a few minutes and I finally allowed him to come. At 10:30 PM the officer came and wanted to know that since I was supposed to go abroad, why had I not gone? I reminded him that without meeting with the Prime Minister, I would not go anywhere. I knew that the Prime Minister would return on October 7. He told me that I must leave the country by October 6, 2017. He would arrange my ticket. I declined his proposal. Then he left my residence saying that I must leave the country either on October 7 or 8. After this unpleasant discussion Dr. Gowhar Rizvi rang me. My wife told him about the arrival of the DGFI Chief. I called Gowhar Rizvi and wanted to know why these sorts of unwanted incidents were happening. On hearing all that had occurred, he was stunned and told me that he would meet me on October 6. He came accordingly, and I reminded him that he had prevented me from stepping down; but the DGFI chief was saying otherwise. He told me that he had communicated what the Prime Minister told him to convey to me. On hearing the pressure created by the DGFI to leave the country, he told me that what this officer was telling me was false. I told him that the Judiciary cannot run in such a manner. I requested him to arrange a meeting with the Prime Minister. He assured me that after the return of the Prime Minister, he would arrange a meeting on priority basis. Dr. Gowhar Rizvi thereafter did not inform me anything. Obaidul Kader also assured me about a meeting but later both remained silent. I understood their helplessness and therefore opted not to contact them and sparing them all embarrassment.

Then I realized that whatever the DGFI chief was saying was correct and he was working as per the direction of the Prime Minister. I was convinced that the Prime Minister did not allow me to resign while I was in Canada with a view to humiliate at the hands of military officials. Either that or she was also helpless in their hands. She was also victimized by them during the Emergency period, but she had forgotten her past. The Law Minister did not intimate anything to me either. At one stage I noticed that no one was receiving my telephone calls. I was totally confined without any connection with anybody. Even if I send for someone for a discussion, they did not show any courage to meet me and expressed their helplessness. If someone came to meet me they were interrogated in such a manner at the gate that they were compelled to go back. Under such circumstances I decided to leave the country to get some relief from the suffocating condition. Initially I decided to go to Australia. On October 5, 2017, a reporter of Zee News from Singapore contacted me over phone and wanted to know my condition. I did not make any adverse remark about Bangladesh but told her that our judiciary is totally independent. All the time, even in such a critical period, I tried to uphold the image of the Judiciary.

After taking the President's permission to leave for Australia I decided to leave the country on October 13, 2017. But before my departure I wanted to have dinner with my friend Abdur Rashid and called him. He replied that he had come to know that a lot of ordeal had to be faced at the gate of my residence, so I should inform the gate about his arrival at 7:00 PM. accordingly, through my personal assistant, I conveyed the message to the security officials at the gates. Despite such intimation, the security personnel stopped his vehicle in front the gate and even after knowing his identity, he was compelled to come out of the vehicle, his cell phone number was noted down and he was asked the reason for his visit. After they took his photograph he could enter my house. He expressed his displeasure to me and charged me that despite intimation he was subjected to face much humiliation. I expressed my apology and said that it was beyond my control and assured him that I had indeed informed the security officials about his arrival for dinner. I was informed that from the evening a huge number of media people had assembled outside the gates of my residence. I was expected to travel on a Singapore Airlines flight at 11:00 PM. I was told that the situation was deteriorating, and it would be difficult on my part to leave the house without speaking with them. So, I decided to speak with the media at the time of my departure from home. I had previous bitter experience that my statements were misquoted by the media. So, in the late afternoon I directed my secretary Anisur Rahman to meet I and I printed a statement in which I mentioned two things: my health condition was good. And as the Law Minister had hinted on the previous day, which I came to know from the media, that he wanted to change the Supreme Court administration as well, my second point in the statement was that I was apprehensive about the independence of the Judiciary. Before making this statement when I wanted to come out of my vehicle at the gate, due to the pressure of the media people my vehicle's flag stand and side mirrors were broken. After handing over my written statement to the reporters I headed for the airport.

All this time I was pressurized from the very beginning by the DGFI to say that I was sick. When they failed to get me admitted to a hospital, they tried to send me abroad for treatment. Their intention became clear to me later. It was a device of the Law Minister, who had never dealt with the Constitution, and had only dealt with some criminal matters previously. So, in his estimation, on a bare of reading Article 97 of the Constitution, he realized that if I took leave on the ground of some ailment or got admitted to a hospital it would be easier for the government to assign Justice Md. Abdul Wahab Miah to perform the functions of the Chief Justice. Otherwise, it would be difficult to digest the criticism from the Bar and the intelligentsia. I had performed the duties of the Chief Justice many times when my predecessor was out of the country on several occasions. Normally I performed routine work only and did nothing related to the administration of the Judiciary. Official records also show that no judge performing the office of the Chief Justice interfered with any policy matters in the administration of the Judiciary mainly because in the absence of the Chief Justice the senior most judge performed his responsibility, but he had not taken the oath as Chief Justice. The Chief Justice takes an oath separately administered by the President and his functions are clearly mentioned in the Constitution and in the Rules.

This was the practice being followed over a long period of time. But this time, everything was different. From the day I was confined to my official residence, Justice Md. Abdul Wahab Miah wanted to behave as if he was the Chief Justice. He started to issue threats to all officers calling them one by one and telling them that there were allegations about them and that the government was not happy with their conduct. He became the mouthpiece of the government and wanted to satisfy the government particularly the Ministry of Law. He traveled to the extent that on two occasions Justice Bhabani Prasad Singha and Justice Md. Ruhul Quddus came to meet me in the evening. On getting this information, Justice Md. Abdul Wahab Miah displayed his displeasure to Justice Ruhul Quddus and said that Justice Bhabani Prasad Singha was related to me, but why would he, Ruhul Quddus, visit me.

After my arrival in Singapore, I came to know from the media that on the following day the Supreme Court website had published news stating that there were serious allegations of corruption against me. I came to understand that because I told the media that I was not sick, the Law Minister was angered and got the news published on the website of the Supreme Court. After opening the mouth of the Prime Minister, Ekattur TV, a loyalist of the political party in power, organized talk shows with political puppets of the government and started propaganda of alleged corruption against me. It also took similar actions when the contempt matter against daily Jana kantha and its reporter was initiated. The court called for the CD of the talk show then, but at the request of the Law Minister I did not take any step. The President also told the judges by inviting them to a dinner that there were serious allegations against me. During my tenure I had delivered judgments against many powerful and rich persons of the country, like the chairman of Bashundhara Group, chairman of Jamuna Group, Asian City, Fantasy Kingdom , owners of the Chittagong ship breaking companies, Ragib Ali of Sylhet and also had nullified the judgments of the High Court Division regarding valuable properties situated in Gulshan, Banani, Motijheel, Dhanmondi and Maghbazar areas and yet now the President, the government not and its sponsored media were trying to malign me as corrupt. If their claim is true, then from whom had I taken illegal advantage? And these allegations came only after the pronouncement of the Sixteenth Amendment judgment. Following that verdict, the government desperately tried to assassinate my character only to justify their unjustified and unusual actions against me.

I had a plot of land allotted by RAJUK at Sector-10 in Uttara, just contiguous to Ashulia road. I constructed a six-storey building with loan taken from the Bangladesh House Building Corporation. When the loan plus my cash in hand did not meet the construction cost, I took one and half crore taka from two of my close friends and relatives on condition of giving two apartments to them. During the construction, both my wife's and my life were targeted four times. I luckily survived at Sylhet Circuit House and my wife survived in my village home. Thereafter, my security was tightened. My village home was brought under CCTV coverage and a strong police force was permanently deployed at my home for guarding even during our absence. Though there were two incidents of attacks on my house the government had withdrawn the entire security force. I would have to engage a private security firm to protect the house because it is located toward the southeast border of our village and there was no residence toward south. At any time, the house could also be destroyed by the miscreants, but it was not possible to deploy private security on my part. So, I felt insecure to stay at the newly constructed building because armed robberies are being committed there during day time as well although it was constructed with a boundary wall hoping that after retirement I would stay in that village home. Now it is not secured. If I stay at my village home who will give my security? Why my and my wife's life are threatened again and again. Why I was targeted again and again. No minister is so targeted although he is in the government. No one has any contribution in the affairs of the country other than to satisfy his "Apa". Why the State shall bear so much expenses against his security, and other benefits if he has no contribution in the welfare of the country. If someone risking his life works for the country and ultimately his acts are not recognized none would work for the interest of the country. It is not a matter of political will of a party but for the interest of the country. It is the responsibility of the State to give protection to citizens who have dedicated their life to the interest, cause and security of the country. Someone who performs such work it is not for the interest of the political party in power, rather it is in the interest of the State.

If a country wants to command respect in the international arena it should recognize those who worked for the country. The political party in power should work beyond its parochial mindset if it really loves the country and wants to build the country as a civilized and welfare country. All great nations recognized those who dedicated their lives to the cause of the people and the country. But Bangladesh seems to be an exception. The government took advantage of my services and after their purpose was served they just tossed me away. The young Robert Moses wanted to reform the city and state government to improve living conditions in New York in the mid-nineteenth century. Along with him William Levitt contributed to the development of the city. The Power Broker author Robert Caro cast Moses as a bullying maniac and one of the American history's greatest villains for destroying New York City's neighborhoods. Villain or hero, it was Moses who paved the way for the major civic centers, parks, beaches, bridges, tunnels and parkways of today – creations that are the basis of modern suburban life. The iconic skyscrapers and super-highways that define American cities today are the product of his mind. He transformed a Queen's ash dump into a beautiful park ground for the 1964 World's Fair and cleared the lane for Manhattan's Lincoln Center for the Performing Arts, home of the New York Philharmonic, the New York City ballet and the Metropolitan Opera. It was Moses who gained control of the land and attracted private funding necessary to bring the United Nations Headquarters to New York City. 7(a) Today not only the people of America recognize him as the architect of America's development but others too because all world leaders attend the United Nations Headquarters every year and most crucial international issues are decided there by world leaders.

I approached the near ones from whom I had taken money to build the house saying that they had purchased the apartments in the hope that they would live with me jointly. So, with prior approval of sale for six crore taka, I entered into an agreement for sale and wanted to execute the sale deed. But the purchaser wanted a registered agreement and an irrevocable power of attorney to sell the house. She and her husband represented that they purchased it for profit but if the deed is registered, they would have to pay a large amount toward RAJUK's transfer fee and registration costs. The purchaser repaid the House Building Finance Corp. outstanding loan, obtained non-encumbrance certificate, paid the money taken from the two persons against two apartments, and the balance amount of four crore taka was given by pay orders. I deposited the pay orders in my account, and purchased a duplex apartment for me, another for my elder daughter and paid money by checks from my account and the balance amount has been kept in fixed accounts in the Sonali Bank, Supreme Court branch, in my name and my younger daughter's name as she was not willing to purchase apartment in Dhaka.

I and my wife have been submitting returns to the Income Tax Department regularly. The amount of receipt and payment including fixed deposits has been shown in our income tax return. Am I a fool who will receive four crore taka in pay orders in my official account which I have been maintaining for about thirty-nine years? Am I not entitled to sell property in case of need because I was the Chief Justice? Did I suppress anything in my tax return? Why not those propagandists mention about my tax returns and claim there are inconsistencies in my returns and statement of accounts? Against that backdrop is it ethical to generate rumors and propaganda against a Chief Justice? It appears it is possible only for those who want to usurp power and continue to remain in power without the people's mandate to use state machinery against a Chief Justice because he spoke out about rule of law and democracy. So long I delivered judgments which went in their favor I was a good person, but the moment I spoke for the common people I became corrupt. Did they initiate any inquiry based on the Panama Papers? Less than forty-eight hours after the first story was published, Iceland's Prime Minister resigned, a Ukrainian politician had called for the impeachment of its President, Pakistan's Prime Minister Nawaz Sharif was compelled by its apex court to step down, Austrian and Australian governments started investigations against its nationals. But significantly we kept quiet. We also did not make any inquiry against the Food Minister who bought rotten wheat from Brazil without letting know our Embassy officials about the purchase although it was mandatory. When the news was published, the Food Minister wanted to involve the Embassy, but the Embassy refused his overtures. I do not want to disclose many things about corruption because I had maintained a complaint box and I did indeed receive many documents.

I could not believe how a judge like Md. Abdul Wahab Miah, whom I trusted and gave an independent Bench and also made him chairman of all committees constituted by me in all judicial programs, which my predecessor did not give to me during his tenure, could publish on the Supreme Court Website about my alleged corruption without disclosing to me following the advice of his two junior judges and Anisul Haque. Justice Abdul Wahab Miah turned into an obliging puppet in the hands of the Law Minister who had those preposterous allegations put on the website---but no directive or any circular or any news regarding the judiciary is circulated on the website without the direction of the Chief Justice. I was the sitting Chief Justice on that day also.

But Justice Abdul Wahab Miah bypassing the Chief Justice directed the allegations to be published as per the wish of the Law Minister. I was reminded of the picture of Khandker Mushtaque Ahmed at that time. Justice Md. Abdul Wahab Miah was a carbon copy of Khandker Mushtaque Ahmed. Bangabandhu had to give his life believing Khandker Mushtaque Ahmed and disbelieving the most articulate architect of our independence Tajuddin Ahmed. On the following day, I heard that Justice Abdul Wahab Miah had not only withdrawn almost all judicial officers from the Supreme Court Registry, they were in fact sent to the remotest corners of Bangladesh, which he could not do so. If this process is allowed, then any judge while performing the functions of the Chief Justice can change the entire administration of the Supreme Court at the direction of the Law Ministry when the Chief Justice goes abroad to attend a seminar. The same principle could be applicable to the President, the Prime Minister and the Speaker.

If anyone of them leaves the country, they must hand over charge to the next senior person as per the Constitution. Suppose if the President leaves the country for seven days, the Speaker is supposed to perform in the office of the President. If the Prime Minister left the country and if Parliament is in session the Deputy Leader of the House will take over for the period of the Prime Minister's absence. Similarly, if the Speaker leaves the country, the Deputy Speaker performs the responsibilities of the Speaker. Given this fact, would they want changes in the administration during such interregnum periods? These issues possibly raised queries from different corners and the Law Minister held a press conference placing Article 97 of the Constitution and said that the person in charge had the power to make such changes. Thereafter I came to know that Abdul Wahab Miah started transferring many judicial officers ignoring the established precedence I had developed: no officers should be transferred from a station if his spouse is working in the same station. Even those transfer orders were not taken with the approval of the GA Committee, which is the only authority to transfer judicial officers from one station to another. He had assented to the list sent by the Law Ministry and thereby not only violated the Constitution, but also violated the law and convention. I posted and deepened on those officers after taking proper information taken from different corners against the Ministry's opposition and one das changed everything by a signature.

He fell in love with the power of the office of Chief Justice to such an extent that he was desperately implementing all wishes of the Ministry of Law ignoring that he could not cross the barrier of elevating in the Appellate Division for a long time. Anisul Haque had faced a lot of criticism for recommending his name for the Appellate Division. During his tenure in the Appellate Division, Abdul Wahab Miah proved that he was a fanatical person and therefore, in no case would the Awami League make him the Chief Justice of Bangladesh. This was known to us for a long time. The government used him to reach their goals by dangling the prospect of the office of Chief Justice in front of him.

His most shocking act during this time related to my wife's travel from Dhaka to Australia by Singapore Airlines flight on October 17, 2017. Despite intimation the Supreme Court did not send any message to the relevant government offices regarding her travel itinerary. Rather my secretary Anis had to send a message from his private mail. Naturally the Bangladesh High Commission in Singapore did not provide her protocol any service. She was travelling as the wife of the Chief Justice. She noticed an officer of the High Commission in the airport, but he did not come forward to receive her. She traveled from one terminal to another at dawn as an ordinary passenger by traveling on two commuter trains. Since previously she had always traveled with official protocol she faced great consternation as a transit passenger from Singapore airport to Australia. She overcame the problems by asking unknown persons to show her the right direction at the airport.

On her arrival at Brisbane Airport, she shed tears on seeing me. I realized that she had been made to suffer. I was much angered and prayed to the Almighty that no spouse of any Chief Justice or holder of a constitutional post should ever be made to undergo such types of humiliation in future. If the judges of the highest court act as agents of the government, how can officers of the lower judiciary perform their judicial work independently? They demolished the substratum of the judiciary which had been built by eminent judges and Chief Justices by sweat and hard work while the existing higher officials destroyed all that had been attained in a day for their personal gain. I wanted to resign on repeated occasions. When I realized that I could not perform my responsibility independently, I wanted to be allowed to resign by the President and Prime Minister in the presence of the Law Minister and Attorney General at Bang Bhaban on two occasions, and lastly from Canada but this time too I was not allowed, I now realized, with a view to humiliate me as a measure of taking revenge for the Sixteenth Amendment judgment. The Prime Minister had committed a blunder: she did not humiliate Chief Justice Surendra Kumar Sinha, she has intentionally scandalized the office of the Chief Justice, an organ of the State, and tarnished the image of the Judiciary as a whole. She debased a Chief Justice who is the guardian of the Judiciary, as per advice of the Law Minister, Law Secretary and DGFI. This became clear to me on a bare reading of her mindset. I analyzed her mind on different occasions as I had the privilege of exchanging views with her exclusively twice, on each occasion for more than three hours, and I understood her frame of mind.

Some columnists expressed their apprehensions over the ongoing ordeal I had been facing with. Shahdeen Malik in his commentary under the heading "Tenuous: Task of Tallying Law with Even" on October 18, 2017 wrote: "The Sixteenth Amendment has replaced Article 96 with a new Article 96. The original Article had a provision for a Supreme Judicial system --- by scraping the Sixteenth Amendment, the Supreme Court revived the Supreme Judicial Council – it has been reported that the honorable President summoned four judges of the Appellate Division to Bang Bhaban and apprised them of 11 allegations against Chief Justice SK Sinha. Further reports have it that five judges later called on Chief Justice SK Sinha in this connection – yet we note that several judicial officials in the Supreme Court administration have been sent en masse to Panchgarh, Thakugaon, Lalmonirhat, Saatkhira, Barguna and other remote districts. So long we had known that when government changes certain government officials are frowned upon by the new political government. Loyalists of the old government are sidelined. It is quite exciting to see that these great ideals of political governments are now being applied to the judicial administration too.

Ali Reaz[8] wrote commented under heading "Sinha Saga: More Questions than Answers": "The statement by the Supreme Court issued a day after the Chief Justice left Dhaka for Australia 'on Leave', raises questions one can hardly avoid. The statement alleges that the Chief Justice faces '11 charges'… we are aware of the background of the tension between the Chief Justice and the government since the release of the full copy of the Sixteenth Amendment annulment appeal verdict on August 1; they require no repeating. However, we shouldn't forget the unkind reactions of the ruling party leaders inside and outside the parliament. The visits of Awami League leaders to the Chief Justice's official residence immediately after the verdict were reported in the press. The vitriol against the incumbent Chief Justice was unprecedented in the history of the country. Those who followed the event closely before the episode began to unfold would be remiss if they didn't recall the statement of a disgruntled retired Supreme Court justice who prophesied that Sinha not only will 'have to resign but also leave' the country. The conspiracies between the government's statements, communicated by the Law Minister and the Attorney General and repeated ad nauseum for at least a week by ruling party supporters, that Chief Justice Sinha was sick and that he sought leave for said reason were debunked by the Chief Justice's statement on his way to the airport for his flight to Australia. 'I am well,' he said in a written statement; he didn't contest the news that he sought the leave. But he said he would return to the court. The opposition political parties and others said that 'he was forced to seek a leave.' … the timeline suggests a leak if not a construction. The 'allegations' of his misdeeds never featured in public conversations or in the official narrative until August 1, 2017, the day the full Supreme Court verdict with observations about the state of governance was released. Instead, previously Sinha was praised, among other things, for being the first non-Muslim Chief Justice in Bangladesh, a Muslim majority country."

He also wrote: "The statement claims that the CJ was confronted by his peers and failed to provide 'satisfactory' answers. If one was unaware of the impeachment procedure of judges, s/he would get the impression that there is an informal process of disciplining justices. The irony that lies here is that it was the justices who unanimously agreed, not too long ago, that the disciplinary procedure should be in their hands instead of in the hands of Parliament members that it should be a formal process and it should be through the Supreme Judicial Council. Why was such a process not contemplated? To whom was the decision communicated? Was such intimation necessary? Should the justices have waited and simply not sit? We won't know the answers to these questions. The anxiety of the Executive branch of being restrained which led to the 16th Amendment prompted the situation, and the judiciary's last-ditch effort to save it from encroachment was the essence of the verdict."

Syed Badrul Ahsan wrote an article on October 18, 2017 under the heading "Commentary: The Unedifying Debate around Justice Sinha", 88c said, "The demarcation of territory between the Judiciary and the Executive in Bangladesh is getting blurred of late. One does not require much wisdom to comprehend the inglorious way in which the ruling political class had effectively created a crisis over the role, or non-role as the case might be, played by the Chief Justice in an interpretation of the law and the Constitution. Justice Surendra Kumar Sinha, having been pushed into hot water over the judiciary's decision to scrap the Sixteenth Amendment to the Constitution has now gone, or been made to go abroad. ...that begs the question: who drafted the letter which the Law Minister flaunted only weeks ago before the media about the head of the judiciary asking for leave? If we are to take the Minister's word for it – that Justice Sinha did indeed write and sign that letter – how does the government explain this new narrative of the Chief Justice's not being physically unwell at all? Unfortunately, in the aftermath of Justice Sinha's departure for Australia we remain in the dark about the nature of the crisis, about the probable fallout from it on national politics. No one is arguing that the Chief Justice is innocent or that he is guilty of everything he is being accused of. What exercises the public mind though is the nature of the fury which the ruling dispensation has been directing at Justice Sinha since the judgment over the Sixteenth Amendment came to pass. And then remember, if you will, the gamut of condemnation, and vilification the Chief Justice has been compelled to go through considering the judgment. All of that has been ugly. The beauty which characterizes the relationship of the Legislative, Executive and Judicial branches of the State, one to the other, has gone missing. Here is how it all happened: A retired Judge of the Appellate Division in unprecedented fashion, went public with his opinion that the Chief Justice would be compelled to leave the country; a former Chief Justice, at present presiding over the Law Commission, publicly criticizes the Chief Justice over the judgment in the Sixteenth Amendment case; the country's Agriculture Minister, not willing to be left behind, held out the threat that Justice Sinha would either have to leave the country or undergo psychological treatment at the mental hospital in Pabna; in the Jatiya Sangsad, the Chief Justice was subjected to some of the worst abuse and vilification a public figure has suffered through in this country. It was unfair, for here were our lawmakers running down the head of the judicial branch, knowing full well that the latter had little opportunity, given the nature of his office, of defending himself or responding to their questions about his performance or character or both."

Dr. S Chandrasekharan in an article 88d uploaded on https://www.eurasiareview.com under the heading "Bangladesh: A Judgment Gone Awry" wrote: "It was surprising that the whole establishment of Sheikh Hasina went against a judgment of the Chief Justice of the Supreme Court on the annulment of 16th Amendment of the Constitution. The Chief Justice was literally hounded out. He has gone on a month's medical leave, though it is very unlikely he would return after leave. He was due to retire on February 1 next year. By making personal attacks on the Chief Justice, the Bangladesh government has not brought itself any glory as these amounted to an attack on the judiciary itself! They have left a bad taste avoidable and certainly the Bangladesh judiciary is as independent as any other similar organization elsewhere. The judgment was unanimous and all, but one wrote an individual judgment, and the verdict was that the 16th Amendment was violative of the basic structure of the Constitution. The judgment of the Chief Justice was the longest with over 400 typed pages and one could see the erudition and the sincere efforts made by the judge in concluding that the parliamentary members are not yet fit to take on the power of removing the judges. While the conclusions may be right, the words chosen by him were rather strong. He said, 'Parliamentary democracy is immature and to attain its maturity, there is a necessity of practicing parliamentary democracy continuing for 4 or 5 terms!'

At another point the Chief Justice opined that 'No nation is made of or by one person'--a statement misconstrued by the critics as a direct assault on the Father of the Nation Bangabandhu. But the Chief Justice had followed this sentence with a reference to the 'Sonar Bangla' by the Father of the Nation—Bangabandhu Sheikh Mujibur Rahman. This was conveniently left out by the critics.

"On the issue of elections of fifty women members to Parliament, the Chief Justice went out of the way to suggest direct election and not through Parliament and this was criticized by the Prime Minister herself. In all, the judgment made good reading with historic references from all over the world and a study is a must to all those aspiring students doing constitutional law. The Chief Justice admits that Judges being humans do (make) mistakes some of which could be unintentional-- and his case was one such. There was no doubt that the judgment angered many individuals including the present Finance Minister Abdul Muhith. Initially word was sent round in ruling party circles not to comment on the judgment. The correct response was that of the Law Minister who said, "We do not agree but we respect the verdict." But the whole scenario changed when the Prime Minster herself criticized the judgment in very strong terms and said that the Chief Justice should have resigned! This opened the floodgates. One senior Minister said that the sitting judges are "immature." Another said that the Chief Justice should be sent to a lunatic asylum. A third one said that the judgment was perhaps written by another English knowing editor or by the ISI of Pakistan. Yet another called the Chief Justice a Razakar who helped the then government in the liberation struggle. This perhaps was the unkindest cut of all.

"The spirit of moderation and tolerance for fellow individuals appear to have vanished. There is no doubt that the Chief Justice in his enthusiasm has failed to understand the creed or the DNA of the people around him. Yet no one can deny that the role of the Judiciary in Bangladesh has been glorious, professional with integrity. The right thing to do would be to get the Chief Justice back to his work after the leave. In the past he has delivered many profound judgments and he should be respected for his honesty, diligence and integrity."

The Country Reports on Human Rights Practices for 2017, of the United States Department of State, Bureau of Democracy, Human Rights and Labor, published a forty-one-page report 88c on Bangladesh. In the summary report some of the critical points raised are very crucial for Bangladesh. I quote some of those: "The most significant human rights issues included: extrajudicial killings, torture, arbitrary or unlawful detentions, and forced disappearances by government security forces; restrictions on civil liberties, including freedom of speech, press, and the activities of nongovernmental organizations (NGOs); a lack of freedom to participate in the political process; corruption; violence and discrimination based on gender, religious affiliation, caste, tribe, including indigenous persons, and sexual orientation and gender identity also persisted and, in part, due to a lack of accountability. There were reports of widespread impunity for security force abuses. The government took limited measures to investigate and prosecute cases of abuse and killing by security forces. Public distrust of police and security services deterred many from approaching government forces for assistance or to report criminal incidents. Suspicious deaths occurred during raids, arrests, and other law enforcement operations. Security forces frequently claimed they took a suspect in custody to a crime scene or hideout late at night to recover weapons or identify conspirators and that the suspect was killed when his conspirators shot at police. The government usually described these deaths as "crossfire killings," "gunfights" or "encounter killings," terms used to characterize exchanges of gunfire between the Rapid Action Battalion (RAB) or other police units and criminal gangs. A domestic human rights organization, Ain-O-Salish Kendra (ASK), reported that security forces killed 162 individuals in "crossfire". Another domestic human rights organization, Odhikar, reported that security forces killed 118 individuals extra judicially in the first 10 months of the year [2017]. On May 12, 2017, RAB forces allegedly shot and killed Rakibul Hasan Bappi and Lalon Molla in Goalanda Upazila, Rajbari District. According to RAB, the men died during a gunfight that occurred during a RAB raid of a meeting of the Purba Banglar Communist Party, a banned organization. On September 8, Islam's family said that RAB arrested Islam at a tea stall at Singarhat Bazar and later detained him in his home, where RAB members allegedly tortured him. RAB members then took him to Rajshahi Medical College Hospital, where he died on September 9 [2017]. The hospital reported injuries to multiple areas of Islam's body, according to press reports.

"Terrorists committed killings in three separate terror incidents in March, all of which were claimed by ISIS. On March 17, a suspected suicide bomber infiltrated a RAB barracks and killed one person. On March 24, a suicide bomber killed two individuals at a police checkpoint near Dhaka's Hazrat Shahjalal International Airport. On March 25, eight individuals were killed and more than 40 injured in two blasts during a raid on a suspected ISIS safe house in Sylhet. ASK stated there were 60 enforced disappearances during the year. Authorities took into custody in August 2016 the sons of three former opposition politicians convicted by Bangladesh's International Criminal Tribunal. Authorities alleged they were conspiring to prevent the execution of one of their fathers, but they were never charged with a crime. Authorities released Humam Quader Chowdhury seven months later, but Mir Ahmed Bin Quasem and Amaan Azmi remained missing at year's end. During the year Odhikar reported security forces tortured approximately 12 persons to death.

"Authorities sometimes held detainees without divulging their whereabouts or circumstances to family or legal counsel, or without acknowledging having arrested them in the first place. The most significant among such units are the Counter Terrorism and Transnational Crime Unit (CTTCU), the Rapid Action Battalion (RAB)--a mostly counter-terrorism focused Special Mission Unit--

and the Detective Branch. The military, which reports directly to the prime minister (who also holds the title of minister of defense), is responsible for external security. The military may also be "activated" as a backup force with a variety of domestic security responsibilities when required to aid civilian authorities. The Directorate General of Forces Intelligence (DGFI) and National Security Intelligence (NSI) are the two primary intelligence agencies with overlapping responsibilities and capabilities. Media reports asserted that the DGFI and, to a lesser degree, the NSI engaged in politically motivated violations of human rights.

"There is a functioning bail system, but police routinely did so with impunity, despite a May 2016 directive from the Supreme Court's Appellate Division prohibiting rearrests of persons when they are released on bail in new cases without producing them in court. Unlike in the past year, when police engaged in a mass arrest campaign, reportedly arresting 14,000 individuals including a purported 2,000 opposition-party activists, during the year police made periodic arrests of opposition activists on various charges. On September 23, the Daily Star newspaper reported delays in recruitment of judges, which were hampering judicial proceedings and leading to a substantial case backlog, rendered 397 positions of lower court judges, including 51 district judges, vacant. More than 2.7 million cases were pending with the lower courts and 400,000 cases were pending with the High Court Division of the Supreme Court. The law provides for an independent judiciary, but corruption and political interference compromised its independence. In 2014 Parliament passed the 16th Amendment, affording it the right to remove judges. During the year the Supreme Court ruled the amendment unconstitutional, and the chief justice's resulting public dispute with parliament and the prime minister resulted in the chief justice's resignation and departure from the country. The chief justice claimed the government forced him to resign, while the government denied the charge. The government continued to pursue corruption charges against the chief justice at year's end, which human rights observers alleged were politically motivated. Human rights observers maintained that magistrates, attorneys, and court officials demanded bribes from defendants in many cases, or they ruled based on influence by or loyalty to political patronage networks. Corruption and a substantial backlog of cases hindered the court system, and the granting of extended continuances effectively prevented many defendants from obtaining fair trials.

"Intelligence and law enforcement agencies may monitor private communications with the permission of the Ministry of Home Affairs, but police rarely obtained such permission from the courts to monitor private correspondence. Human rights organizations alleged the Special Branch of police, the National Security Intelligence, and the Directorate General of Forces Intelligence employed informers to conduct surveillance and report on citizens perceived to be critical of the government," the US State Department Country report stated.

Law Minister Anisul Haque hinted to me on many occasions about my selection process reminding me that he along with the Prime Minister and the President were present at Bang Bhaban while taking decision as the only minority Chief Justice of Bangladesh. He wanted to say, as I was given such an opportunity to occupy the most prestigious office, I should not do anything which may put the government in embarrassment. On hearing those remarks on repeated occasions, I asked him why he was making such comments. I asked him if I ever approached anybody to appoint me as the Chief Justice. He admitted that I did not approach anybody else for my appointment. But the government had no alternative at that time. It was under compulsion that the government appointed me. The government also got the fruits of my appointment. Citizens of the country realized within six months of my appointment that I was the correct and proper selection. I can claim without hesitation that my selection was a right decision for the Bangladesh Awami League. During my tenure, I delivered judgments on most of the sensational cases risking my life and I can claim without any hesitation that no chief justice ever delivered so many judgments on critical law points as I delivered alone. I had reconsidered almost all inconsistent judgments by constituting larger Benches so that the litigants, the lawyers and the courts are not confused over our verdicts. I brought discipline to the lower judiciary, as also to the then Supreme Court. The highest number of cases, both in the lower and higher courts, was decided during my tenure. I compelled all the judges to sit and rise from the courts in time. The present government is the biggest beneficiary of my impartial pronouncements in respect of revenue matters, abandoned properties, settling and giving guidelines regarding the employees of development projects, Bangabandhu killing and Jail killing cases and, most of all, almost all appeals of offenders of crimes against humanity were decided by me and I also settled the law points. On the contrary, I was rewarded by being called a corrupt Chief Justice when I did not succumb to the government's pressure on the Sixteenth Amendment case and then they used the media to assassinate my character and that too toward the end of my tenure. I was not allowed to retire in the usual course; I have been humiliated at the hands of DGFI who treated me as less than an ordinary citizen only because I did not allow the Supreme Court to become subservient to the government.

I was compelled to leave the country with a suitcase without taking any money. I invested the entire money which I got by selling the house for purchasing apartments. I could not imagine that I would be forced to leave the country and remain as a stateless citizen abroad. If I had any ill motive I could have sent the money abroad earlier. My income tax returns will prove my claim. Initially I stayed one month with my elder daughter in Brisbane, Australia. I led a comfortable life there because I had the company of my grandchildren, but even such a happy life did not permit me to continue there because of my conscience. No dignified parent wants to live with their daughters' family for an indefinite period. So, I went to Canada but on reaching there I realized that it was also a wrong decision. I stayed in a small studio with a kitchen, bathroom, bedroom and living room all accommodated in one room. Such a place is enough for a single person. Moreover, it was costly and beyond my capacity; instead I was putting a heavy financial burden on my daughters. In Toronto, Canada, I could not move about freely because I ran into many Bangladeshis who wanted to talk with me whenever they saw me. In fact, I was genuinely surprised to experience that every Bangladeshi citizen knew me and wished to take a photograph. They offered me anything when they saw me at a supermarket. It was an embarrassing situation I faced there. I was cautioned by some of my well-wishers that it would be better for me not to stay in Toronto. My younger daughter is living in Manitoba in Canada, but she is also staying in a one-room apartment with her husband. It is also not suitable for me. Under these circumstances I thought it proper to stay with my younger brother Dr. Ananta Kumar Sinha. But he was staying in Boston, Massachusetts. However, I compelled him to shift to Paterson, New Jersey, a largely undeveloped old city where most of the Bangladeshi citizens who are living there are doing so because of the cheaper cost of living. The water is polluted because of industrial wastes and drinking water has to be bought from the market. I stayed two months in a basement, thanks to the generous gesture of Md. Afzal Miah, a resident of my locality in Bangladesh, who volunteered and requested me to stay in his basement. Many Bangladeshis living in Paterson know where I am staying and most of them are hailing from Sylhet. It was a humiliating situation for a Chief Justice of a country to be living as a floating stateless person. I can barely come out on the street for a walk because whenever a Bangladeshi sees me, out of their intrinsic generosity, he expresses his sympathy and wants to help me. Everyone wants to meet me and wanted to know the "real story." I felt embarrassed to disclose anything to anyone. Simultaneously I felt helpless and consequently a feeling of humiliation also swept over me.

After all a Chief Justice, whether in office or retired, carries with him the integrity, dignity, personality and nationalism of the country. Otherwise there would arise adverse repercussions in the minds of the citizens of the country to which he belongs. I do not like to stay as a stateless person but then the million-dollar question is whether my life is safe and secure in Bangladesh if I do return to my country? From the conduct of the government none of my well-wishers are encouraging me to return to the country fearing for my safety. I have given much thought to the situation and realized that while in office as the head of an organ of the State, I did not get my due status, independence, office and instead was confined to my residence by the security forces. After resignation, what would be my fate if I return? If I am kept on house arrest, it would be a suicidal one. I was not allowed to talk with anybody while in office and now after coming out of the country I cannot talk with anybody else except my wife because none of my officers and well-wishers is receiving my phone calls fearing reprisal. I heard that DGFI officials are constantly threatening them. All my telephones are monitored by them. Even my close relations are now avoiding me, as they are constantly threatened by the DGFI officials.

I absolutely understand the manner of pressure being brought to bear on the officers who had worked with me by the intelligence department. Many of them have been sent to the remotest corners of the country. It is learnt that false departmental proceedings are being initiated against some of them. What offence have they committed? There was no blemish in their career earlier. If there was nothing against them then, why they are subjected to inhuman mental pressure only because they worked in my administration and they followed my directions. Can that be an offence? In the government's estimation I might have committed "wrong" because I did not compromise with the independence of the Judiciary. They did not want the Judiciary to work independently--they wanted it to be subordinate the government; they wanted it under the control of the Executive.

Syed Aminul Islam is one of the most efficient senior officers who had rendered valuable services to the government for about four years as Joint Secretary under a Secretary although he was senior to the Secretary. He accepted it and he was humiliated to the extreme, but he did not protest. I rescued him, appointed him as the Registrar and then made him the first Registrar General because of his performance. The Law Minister wanted to elevate him to the Bench in the first batch of appointments in place of Farid Ahmed Sibli, because he was not liked by the Secretary. Though I appointed Sibli as additional judge, he was not confirmed. He was the most competent judge in the batch. His fault was he was not liked by the law secretary. On query the law minister told me that while he worked as Additional Registrar, he helped the then government in filing criminal case against Sheikh Hasina as reported by law secretary. Syed Aminul Islam has been posted to a most undignified post which is not befitting for a Registrar General instead of elevating him to the Bench. They rewarded Zakir Hossain as Registrar General who had worked as Registrar under me because he acted as agent of the government by leaking secret documents to the ministry. My secretary Anisur Rahman is one of the most brilliant officers in the Judiciary. Not only he has been transferred to a remotest district, he is subjected to humiliation, a report from a reliable source said, only because he worked with me. Was working for a Chief Justice his fault? He had to totally cut off all contacts with me due to pressure.

All my family members including my wife were kept far from my administration as a measure to avoid controversy. My wife is now totally isolated. She stayed one month in Australia, but she also felt uncomfortable to stay in our elder daughter's home. These are the values of my wife too. She received no assistance from the Supreme Court administration. If the former acting Chief Justice or the present Chief Justice do not protect the judicial officers and if the CJ performs as per dictates of the Law Ministry, they may be benefitted personally for the time being, but they must realize that power does not remain permanently, but their performance will remain in the history of the Judiciary. I made it clear to the media at the time of my departure that I would return to the country very soon and my heart and mind are yearning for my return for continuing with my charity work. But who will give me security? One day the government wanted my services and strengthened my security. Today I am its most hated person. It is only because I spoke about the independence of lower judiciary and wanted the Supreme Court to keep out of its control. The Prime Minister could not forget the pangs of the proceeding initiated against her by the apex court for derogatory remarks when she was the Prime Minister for the first time. But the reality is: Does my absence outside the country enhance the image of the country or diminish it?

Why is the government worried about my presence in the country? If I get this type of conduct from the government, how innocent will people get proper treatment from the government? The Chief Justice himself did not get justice while in office, would he then get justice when out of office? Will he get security from the government? Would the intelligence agency which stood in my way in completing my tenure allow him to live in peace? The Prime Minister announced in a public meeting that the people will judge my act in future? What for? Is it only because the Sixteenth Amendment judgment? Or for remarks made during hearing regarding the independence of the judiciary? If the Prime Minister could not tolerate a remark made by me against the government in a court case, can any opposition politician be secure after criticizing her? If the Chief Justice could not speak for the Judiciary, who will speak on its behalf? Given the evolving backdrop will any other Chief Justice dare to speak for the independence of the Judiciary in future? If he cannot, the next question then is, what type of judiciary does the government want? I leave these crucial questions for the people to answer and give a solution for the survival of our next generation with dignity.

Aniruddha Roy, the honorary Consul General of Belarus, a reputed businessman was picked-up from Dhaka's Gulshan at 4:30 PM after holding a meeting with his bank officials. He has been a CIP for the last six successive years; he has higher degree in leather technology. I had no acquaintance with him previously. He introduced himself to me in the Officers' Club two years back when I visited the place to attend Saraswathi Puja. I had opened a complaint box after my assumption in the office of Chief Justice. In the complaint box many complaints were submitted regarding a variety of issues. My Registry scrutinized the complaints, and those which they thought worth considering they drew my attention to them. Aniruddha Roy sent a complaint alleging that Rahmatullah, a Member of Parliament from Dhaka and President of Awami League Dhaka north chapter forcibly took his signature on share transfer form and letter of resignation from the office of Managing Director of a leather factory FB Footwear and garments factory Foot Bed Footwear in Gazipur. Rahmatullah was a shareholder of the leader factory, but Roy set up it and he managed it. I told the incident to Barrister Fazle Nur Taposh, MP, to amicably settle the dispute. But he failed to resolve the problem. Aniruddha Roy did not receive a single farthing. He has only one son who is autistic. His wife tried her best to improve their son's condition but with no result. Accordingly, she was very upset and

Aniruddha Roy could not give time to the family because of his business. Roy had close relationship with some Cabinet Ministers and Secretaries and he was known to be a perfect gentleman.

Aniruddha's wife rushed to my residence after two days when she failed to trace her husband. She appeared to me in an abnormal state and could barely speak and was wailing for an hour. She narrated the incident and told me that she spoke to Minister Tofail Ahmed and some other Ministers. Tofail Ahmed assured her that Aniruddha Roy was alive and in safe custody. Therefore, it was known that he was in the custody of the DGFI. Aniruddha's wife was pointing her finger at Rahamatullah and two other gentlemen, one possible Mahin who had a joint leather and knit business in Narayanganj, Hazaribagh and Savar areas. They are RMM Knit Clothing, RMM Sweater factory and RMM Leather Industries in Bangladesh. She said that she would give up all the properties if needed. Though Rahmatullah had taken Roy's signature on the share transfer form it was not transferred by the Registrar of Joint Stock Companies. Her version was that I would be able to get Roy released him. She added that if Aniruddha Roy did not survive, her future with an autistic son would be doomed. On hearing everything I was awfully shocked, and I told her that I would make my best efforts to get her husband released. I contacted different authorities but did not get proper response. I had also been facing problems, so I could not help her anymore.

After staying one month in Brisbane, I decided to stay in Canada. By this time, I was informed that if I returned to Bangladesh my life would be in danger. So on November 5, 2017, I left Brisbane via Singapore hoping to have my medical checkup there because, there would be no certainty when I would be able to consult my doctors in Singapore. My departure from Singapore was for the morning of November 8, 2017. In the meantime, Lt. Colonel Md. Nazimuddoula contacted me at my hotel and told me that he was directed by senior officers to resolve our problem respectably. I talked with Awami League leader and Minister Obaidul Kader, whom I had known from earlier days, over phone. He also assured me to solve the problem after discussions with the Prime Minister. But ultimately, he did not give any feedback.

After two days Obaidul Kader sent information with Prof. Rafiqur Rahman, a central committee member of the Awami League, that I should take long leave till my superannuation on January 31, 2018. I realized that Obaidul Kader failed to persuade the Prime Minister and felt embarrassed to speak with me and conveyed the message through Prof. Rahman. I did not give any reply to him and stuck with my decision. In such a situation, Lt. Colonel Nazimuddoula requested me to extend my date of departure to November 7, 2017. Due to his persistent entreaties, I changed my ticket to November 10 subject to the condition that the government would give an official announcement that the allegation of corruption brought against me was based on misinformation and that Aniruddha Roy be released. I told him in clear terms that I do not want to resign or retire keeping the wild allegations over my head. I had the impression that Aniruddha Roy was abducted by his partners, but later I got confirmation from Lt. Col Nazimuddoula that he was in their custody. Police also intimated to the wife of Aniruddha by tracking his phone that he was kept somewhere in Kachukhet in Dhaka Cantonment area. All negotiations with the officers failed due to the attitude shown by the DGFI that it would not publicly declare that allegations brought against me were untrue. He made repeated entreaties till the evening of November 10. I told him in clear terms that the question of persuasion does not arise at all because I did not commit any wrong and did not want to step down keeping the allegations over my head.

These facts clearly proved that for reasons not known to me the Prime Minister was convinced that my presence in Bangladesh would be suicidal for her. Right from Tokyo the DGFI hierarchy wanted to keep me away from the country despite the direction of the Prime Minister in Canada only a few days ago. No allegation was brought against me other than those disclosed by Abdul Wahhab Miah orally on October 1, 2017, that there were serious allegations against me till the day after I left for Australia. Whenever I disclosed that I was not sick, Md. Abdul Wahhab Miah published on the official website of the Supreme Court that there were serious allegations against me. If I had committed any sort of misconduct, why was the government eager to send me abroad? It was its prime responsibility to proceed according to the

Constitution against me and to prevent me from leaving the country to face prosecution. This proved that an ill motive propelled the policy makers of the government. At 10:00 PM on November 9, 2017 when all our discussions had failed, the officer frankly told me, "Sir, you know, and I also know that the allegations are false. The authority did not get any wrongdoing against you after a thorough investigation." He also expressed one sentence which, I believe, was from heart, saying, "Sir, people like you are suffering, but the corrupt people are always winning." I had no doubt about what he wanted to say and by pointing fingers at whom. He left at 10:00 PM after taking dinner with me seeking unconditional apology that he could not help resolving my problems although he tried his best honestly and sincerely. From his body language this officer appeared to me to be a sincere one.

Around 2:30 AM of November 10, 2017, I heard the doorbell. I had not slept all night. So I got up and fount Lt. Colonel Md. Nazimuddoulah and he sought my permission to enter my room. He said, "Sir, the DGFI has released Aniruddha Roy and if you wish you can talk with him over phone." He then told me that he was kept at an undisclosed location and if I resigned it could lead to Aniruddha's release. I refused the proposal saying that unless the government announced the allegations against me were false, I would not resign. Again, he requested me with clasped palms that he knew I was an honest and efficient Chief Justice of Bangladesh and he treated me like his father. Hence, he wanted to resolve the problem honorably and that he was making the request at his own risk. He said, he was convinced after talking with me that I was an extraordinary gentleman that he had ever seen. He also told me that unless I resigned Aniruddha Roy would again be taken by the DGFI and dishonest persons, who are at the helm of affairs in the government, would again prevail upon the Prime Minister and in that case all efforts would be frustrated. From the conduct and conversation with this officer, I had developed a soft corner for him and felt that this officer was different from the others of the department.

I told him that I could not make any decision without discussing with my wife and daughters. He told me that in Bangladesh many things can be done which are not possible in any other country and the best example was what the government had done with me. I told him that I would make my decision in Canada. He then expressed his apprehension that those Ministers would frustrate the efforts if more time passed. I noticed that I had consumed a lot of time in the conversation and my departure for the airport was almost near. It was around 5:00 AM and my flight would depart at 8:00 AM. He assured me that the High Commissioner had already reached the airport with other officers and he would take all necessary measures for my boarding and candidly requested me to give a dictation at the hotel prior to my departure so that he could type it at the hotel and take my signature at the airport. I handed him the resignation letter which I had prepared in Australia, which reads as under:

Toronto, November 8, 2017

The Honorable President

People's Republic of Bangladesh

Sir,

After the pronouncement of the verdict annulling the Sixteenth Amendment to the Constitution, there has been a series of unprecedented scathing speeches and remarks made by some members of the Cabinet and political leaders in power against the Chief Justice. These scornful, indecent and disrespectful remarks had clearly undermined the authority of the office of the Chief Justice and the Judiciary and are a deliberate and vicious attempt at scandalizing the position of the Chief Justice. This disparaging and vengeful reaction against the judgment had embarrassed me to an extent where it has made it impossible for me to continue in the office of the Chief Justice. Furthermore, the forces in power intentionally created an unspeakable situation compelling me to leave the country against my wishes.

Therefore, to ensure and uphold the exalted office of the Chief Justice and the image of the Judiciary, I hereby resign from the office of the Chief Justice.

The officer read the letter into his cell phone to his higher authority. The higher officer requested him to replace some words with softer language so that they could be spared any unnecessary stigma. I refused to change the language. In the meantime, the officer handed over the phone to me to speak with Aniruddha Roy. I heard Roy's voice telling me, "Sir, looking at the face of my autistic son please sign the letter in the language of the officer." And he started wailing. On hearing his voice I felt helpless as if I had lost my sense of thinking. Then I handed over a copy of the resignation letter with some modified language and told the officer that if he could print it after making the corrections, I would put my signature at the airport. I reached the airport VIP lounge around 6:45 AM. I was received by the High Commissioner at the airport and he told me that he had already intimated the authority that just before the take off the plane, the Chief Justice would aboard, because he is in an emergency work at the airport. In the meantime, the officer returned with my resignation letter. I told him that before signing it I would like to speak to Aniruddha about his release. I wanted to know from where he was talking. He said that he was talking from Dhanmondi playground. I told the officer that I would not give my resignation in this manner till I was convinced that Aniruddha Roy was taken to his residence and I wanted to talk with his wife. After a few minutes they gave the phone to his wife. She was also wailing and making entreaties to me to tender my resignation in exchange for the life of her husband. The DGFI chief told me that unless I followed their instructions Aniruddha Roy would have to face some serious consequences. I realized that it was nothing, but systematic and organized state terrorism perpetrated by an elite force keeping hostage a perfect gentleman and their treatment was so cruel that it could be compared with none other than the Gestapo Force of Hitler. They may even kill Aniruddha Roy and members of my family. Aniruddha and his wife's wailing touched my heart, but I told them that unless he was taken inside the house and saw his son, I would not put my signature on the letter. Meanwhile my departure hour was nearing fast. Aniruddha Roy then told me, "Sir, I am on the stairs of my house." On being satisfied that he was released, I signed my resignation letter after making some corrections in it. I did not minutely read the resignation letter but handed it over to the High Commissioner with a request to communicate with the President.

These incidents were not only startling but beyond comprehension. This traumatic night would remain memorable throughout my life. I could not imagine a government of a civilized country would behave with a sitting Chief Justice in such manner by using its elite force to remain in power, particularly a leader like Sheikh Hasina, the daughter of Bangabandhu Sheikh Mujibur Rahman. I could not imagine or even believe my eyes that the leader I had seen very closely with much cordiality could be so cruel toward me. I thought over the matter again and again and concluded that she was an educated and mature politician and possessed many good qualities; she had committed no wrong. But the power in her hands made her rude and cruel; she was hungering for power and wanted to remain in power by any means. She forgot her past when she returned to Bangladesh in 1981 after the assassination of her father. Being the eldest daughter, she could not see her parents' and siblings' bodies including that of Russel, a mere child.

Surely, she fought for democracy, rule of law and independence of the judiciary for her survival and reorganized the Bangladesh Awami League from shambles to one of the biggest and organized political party of the country. She alone could not remain in power for such a long period of time without the assistance of many of us, but the moment she consolidated her power without taking a mandate of the people, she became rude. She herself did not believe in 2014 that she would remain in power till 2018 and, that is why, by breaking all norms she hurriedly took oath before expiry of the previous term and even before dissolving the Ninth Parliament. All that was possible only due to the weakness of the opposition political party, the support of a neighboring regional superpower and the judiciary's role. Everybody assumed that there would be fresh elections within two years. But all assessments proved false due to the unconditional support of the neighboring powerful country, India.

India should realize that it has made many positive contributions to Bangladesh but at the same time there is dark side also. During the crisis period in 1971, India not only gave shelter of ten million refugees, it had also shed the blood of its soldiers in the liberation struggle and withdrew its soldiers as soon as Bangabandhu requested them to withdraw their troops. The black chapter is that it is behaving as "big brother" with us instead of being an "elder brother." It has diverted waters from all rivers flowing into Bangladesh causing serious environmental and ecological imbalance in our country particularly in Northern Bangladesh. The balance of trade and commerce is also lopsidedly in favor of India and these have caused much anxiety among most of the people. It has been purposely and intentionally supporting a government which has no respect for democracy, rule of law and human rights. Corruption is rampant, forced disappearances of citizens by security forces are a regular feature, and violation and discrimination based on gender, religion, affiliations are persistent. The government is run largely with the support of the security services. Terrorism is increasing daily and the more the government will depend on the security forces as a tool to remain in power, the more terrorism and fanaticism will rise.

People cannot be ruled with the help of security forces consistently violating the civil rights of the citizens. No autocratic government can rule the country for an indefinite period. Unless democracy and the rule of law are established, the sentiments of the people will keep rising against the tyrannical government and it will go against India as well, because India is seen to be propping up an autocratic government for its own interests. If India does not draw lessons events in Nepal and Sri Lanka, one day it will face two Pakistan's, and in that case, its sovereignty could come under threat.

I am surprised to notice how selfish and self-absorbed people can be and how hungry for power some can be. A few days ago, I was respected, loved and adored by many except 2 or 3 Ministers and some powerful business houses against whom I had taken legal actions. The scenario changed overnight on July 3, 2017 as soon as I expressed my opinion for the independence of the Judiciary. Moreover, I have my constitutional right to express my opinion without fear and favor. My opinion may not be liked by the ruling party, but the way the politicians expressed their anger just cannot be accepted in the 21st Century. Stuff like this was common in the medieval period when a judge had to give his life for his impartiality. Even in 1803, the US President did not treat Justice John Marshall in the manner our Prime Minister behaved with me in 2017. According to these critics, I expressed my opinion with the ill motive of toppling the government by hatching a conspiracy. What conspiracy do they want to mean: a secret plan by a group to do something unlawful or harmful or a plot, scheme, plan, mechanism, ploy, trick, ruse, subterfuge, collusion, and intrigue in connivance? Is anyone of these applicable to me? If I managed to convert the opinions of two judges upon whom the government had reposed its trust that cannot be taken as unethical. This is part of our practice. I convinced those enumerating reasons, with personal command of law and with superiority in knowledge. This under no circumstances can be treated as an offence. Both judges possess higher degrees than what I possess, and they have also acquired a lot of experience in judgeship. In fact, at one point I taught them as I would students with a view to making them mature in the administration of justice so that they could lead the Judiciary in my absence.

If I had committed any wrong, my opinion may be reviewable. But how does any question of conspiracy come up? The authority in power went to such extent that it directed all the state entities to abandon me. As a result, I had to cancel a program in New York when one of the organizers told me frankly that it was an embarrassing position for them to keep me as the chief guest on the occasion. Even if they officially did not declare anything, in the world of technology nothing can be kept secret. They could not cause any harm to me. But the government's meanness focused to them. Is it a believable story that an army officer directly threatens the Chief Justice of a country? And it did not stop there. They were continuously issuing threats to the members of my family. Today they successfully managed to topple me but morally they could not belittle me. They set a very bad precedent which would have far-reaching consequences in future. So long I was in office, the Supreme Court was totally independent, and the lower judiciary was also getting a modicum of independence, but the moment I was compelled to leave the country, the entire scenario changed. The Supreme Court is like a department under the Ministry of Law. It is truly suicidal for the nation. We did get the original Supreme Court which existed before 1982. Once an institution is broken, it is very difficult to bring it back to its original position. It is normally said, it is easy to break a building but difficult to return its original shape by repairing it.

If democracy matures and is institutionalized, the people will be conscious of their rights. The United States was successful in spreading the ideologies of democracy, liberation, fundamental human rights, and market economies, and the people are enjoying the results. They achieved these goals not in a day. They practiced and believed them for the wellbeing of its citizenry. A country like ours also speaks about these ideologies but does not follow them because the persons in power want to remain in power by any means. Their line of thinking and methods differ. We claim that we have a democracy and we describe our county as a "People's Republic" but these words are not reflected.

So, the words "People's Republic" in the country's name are incongruous and have no connection with democracy. "Justice" in the strict sense is generally determined by rule of law. But if the persons in power do not adhere to rule of law or rule of law is not used in the real sense in all spheres of the nation, the government is bound to be transformed into an autocracy. It uses the machinery of the law as an instrument for remaining in power, to consolidate its power, to suppress the wrongdoings by its followers, and to suppress those who oppose its wrongdoings. The expression "People's Republic" has become meaningless. The government passes new laws with a view to suppress the opposition parties and those laws no longer reflect the will of the society.

A crime does not always and everywhere mean something definite. There are differences between nations; an act may be considered a crime in one country, but not in another. While we do let the law decide what is wrong, it varies from country to country. Generally, we say justice is determined by law; but it is not applicable to some countries and Bangladesh is not an exception. Constitutionalism essentially means creating a constitution and the laws under it and carrying out the politics of a nation based on them. In a constitutional democracy, the constitution cannot restrict democracy. The people of our country are sovereign and as an expression of their sovereignty they have created a Constitution which contains democracy, rule of law, equality, secularism and socialism. A constitution has a section that protects fundamental human rights, and a section that defines the framework of the nation. Most nations also set the principle of separation of powers among three branches of the State. So, a constitution protects the right of the people and outlines the principles of the government. There are aberrations in most third world countries and Bangladesh is one of them. Gandhi in his "The Story of My Experiments with Truth"9 said, "Men cannot for a moment without consciously or unconsciously committing outward 'himsha' the very fact of his living, eating, drinking and moving about-necessarily involve some 'himsha', destruction of life, be it ever so misrule. A votary of 'ahimsha' therefore remains true to his faith. If the spring of all his actions is compassion, if he shuns to the best of his ability the destruction of the tiniest creature, tries to save it, and thus incessantly strives to be free from the deadly will 'himsha'. He will be constantly growing self-resistant and compassion, but he can never become entire free from outward 'himsha'."

When an autocrat rules a country, he perceives himself as the all-powerful master. He is the one who can save the nation, build the nation, build the infrastructure of the country, he is the architect of the development of the country and under him the country is developed so promptly that people are happy with him. He will talk of rule of law to be maintained by all. But he sees himself above the law. In South Africa, when a minority group ruled the country, the original Africans and Indians were divided into different groups. One segment was grouped as "Musalman

654

merchants", who would call themselves "Arabs". Another was that of Hindus, and yet another of Parsi clerks. The white men called the largest community that composed of Tamil, Telegu and North Indians indentured and freed labourers "coolies" or 'Samis". Sami is a Tamil suffix occurring after many Tamil names meaning a master. Whenever an Indian resented being addressed as Sami and had enough wit in him, he would try to return the compliment: "You may call me Sami, but you forget that Sami means a master. I am not a master!" Some white men used to get angry, swear at the Indian and, would even belabor him; for Sami to him was nothing better than a term of contempt.

Gandhi stated that he was known as the "Coolie Barrister". The merchants were known as "coolie merchants". This attitude even persisted in the West Pakistani mind and they treated East Pakistanis as such. The rulers and their cohorts behaved with the Bengalees as if they were inferior citizens. That's why Sheikh Mujibur Rahman agitated on the six-point program. Sheikh Mujibur Rahman dreamt of a country free from exploitation – "a society in which the rule of law, fundamental human rights, and freedom, equality and justice, political, economic and social order will be secured for all citizens." Did we attain those even after 47 years of independence? There is existence of one political party in Parliament. There is no semblance of democratic practice in the country. In the last local government election about 122 persons were killed. Free and fair national election is a far cry. Innocent people are being killed every day by miscreants, on one side, and in the hands of law enforcement agencies under the rubric encounters. Terrorism is rising day-by-day, but the government is reluctant to admit the links of those terrorists with ISIS or Al-Qaeda outfits although they commit crimes in similar patterns by using the same technology. I fail to understand why we feel shy to admit this. By not making these connections public we embolden them to recruit, implement and commit terrorist activities. This terrorism can be curbed immensely if we give proper education to our new generation, practice democracy in the country and maintain rule of law in all aspects.

Rule of law is not a fundamental principle our rulers are concerned about. They trampled the Constitution and have no respect for it. Even if the apex court gives an interpretation or direction upon the Executive relying upon a provision of the Constitution, they ignore it as if it is subservient to the government. Ministers usually give interpretations and the meanings of the Constitution according to their sweet will ignoring the court. Truly speaking there is a vacuum of a constitutional government and a constitutional organ of the State is absent or not working according to the Constitution.

After my resignation at Changi Airport in Singapore under compulsion, I came to learn from the print media that my resignation was accepted on November 10, 2017. Part IV of the Constitution under the heading "The Executive" contains Chapter 1-The President who is practically a titular head of the State and the executive power of the Republic shall be exercised by or on the authority of the Prime Minister [Article 55 (2)]. The Executive chapter includes the Prime Minister and the Cabinet; local government; the defense services; the Attorney General. The Legislature chapter contains Parliament, Legislative and financial procedures and ordinance making powers. The Judiciary contains the Supreme Court; the subordinate courts; administrative tribunals. Article 94 explains details about the establishment of the Supreme Court. Clause (2) says: "The Supreme Court shall consist of the Chief Justice, to be known as the Chief Justice of Bangladesh, and such number of other judges as the President may deem it necessary to appoint to each division." So, the composition of the Supreme Court must be with the Chief Justice and other judges. In the absence of the Chief Justice, the composition of the Supreme Court cannot be complete. In the absence of the complete composition of the Supreme Court--an organ of the State--the country cannot legally function and there was vacuum in the administration of justice by "The Judiciary" under Part VI of the Constitution after November 10, 2017, if my resignation was really accepted on that day.

A similar point arose about the composition of the Durniti Daman Commission Ain, 2004. During the last caretaker government (2007-2008) there was no Anti-Corruption Commission in accordance with Section 5 for a considerable period. In the absence of the Commission, its secretary issued notice upon some offenders under Section 26 (1) of the Ain to submit wealth statements. If no of a wealth statement is submitted by the notice receiver, the failing party will be guilty of offence under sub-section 2 (s) of Section 26.10 The apex court held that the notice was void and that the conviction of an offender for non-submission of wealth statement was also void for non-composition of the Commission as per law.

This provision of law is a subordinate legislation. Even then in the absence of the constitution of the full Commission, there would not be any difficulty in transacting the business of the State causing serious vacuum in the administration of justice because there is no limitation for filing a criminal case against an offender. However, if an Organ of the State remained incomplete, even for a day, the acts, things, deeds done during this interregnum period by that Organ of the State would be void. There would be a constitutional vacuum of the State. The composition of the Supreme Court in the absence of the Chief Justice is incomplete till the period a new Chief Justice enters his office. Therefore, it is a constitutional obligation of the government to appoint a Chief Justice whenever the office of the Chief Justice falls vacant. This practice is being followed since 1935.

After the appointment of the Chief Justice, he subscribes to an oath under Article 148 of the Constitution and the appointment of the new Chief Justice is effective on the day following the retirement, resignation or removal of the sitting Chief Justice. The Law Minister said that until a new Chief Justice was appointed, the President has the power to appoint a temporary Chief Justice under Article 97 and that the President had legally appointed Md. Abdul Wahab Miah to perform the functions of the Chief Justice. He also stated that all functions of the Chief Justice can be performed by the temporary Chief Justice in view of the words "those functions" used in Article 97. If the Chief Justice is absent, because of illness, or any other cause, is unable to perform the functions of his office, then the question of performing "his Office" comes up until some other person enters upon that office, or until the Chief Justice resumes his office. But in the absence of the Chief Justice, how "his" functions can be performed or "his" office can be performed by the next senior most judge? This Article 97 must be read along with Article 94 of the Constitution then a clear meaning can be inferred. Article 97 without Article 94 cannot carry the correct meaning of the composition of the Supreme Court.

The Attorney General in this connection said that the appointment of the Chief Justice is the prerogative power of the President and this power can be exercised by him at any time he deems fit. The President is not above the Constitution and he must perform his constitutional obligation in accordance with the Constitution. These opinions are contrary to the Constitution and devoid of substance. The Law Minister and the Attorney General had created a deadlock by giving ill-advice out of ignorance to the government. A country cannot be run in such a manner with persons having stunning dearth of knowledge on constitutional matters and laws of the country.

In bidding farewell to the readers some words of V.R Krishna Iyer regarding Jerome Frank (of the US) who has expressed the idea in classic diction: 11

"Some politicians, and a few jurists, urge that it is unwise or even dangerous to tell the truth about the judiciary, Judge Jerome Frank of the US Court of Appeals sensibly explained that he had little patience with, or respect for, that suggestion. I am unable to conceive that, in a democracy, it can ever be unwise to acquaint the public with the truth about the workings of any branch of the government. It is wholly undemocratic to treat the public as children who are unable to accept the inescapable shortcoming of manmade institutions the best way to bring about the elimination of those shortcomings of our judicial system which are capable of being eliminated is to have all our citizens in front as to how that system now functions. It is a mistake, therefore, to try to establish and maintain, through ignorance, public esteems for our courts."

When I was driven out of the country, I had decided to write my memoirs disclosing the facts that compelled me to leave the country. Whenever I met people close to me I was confronted with a question about the facts leading to my unfortunate ordeal. But then there was Allama Iqbal's lines to inspire me:

"Jahan mein ehle-e-imaan soorat-e-khursheed jeetay hain,

Idhar doobey, udhar nikley; udhar doobey,idhar niklay"

"In this world, men of faith and self-confidence are like the sun,

They go down on one side to come up on the other."

References:

1. *Character Assassination I Cuba. Miami: Original Books p.12.ISBN 978-1-6137-974-0*
2. *Bangladesh Sangbad Sangha, August 22, 2017*
3. *Article 48(3) of the Constitution*
4. *United States v. Butter 297 US 1*
5. *Bangladesh v. Kazi Habibul Awal 13 BLD (AD) 1, Civil Appeal No. 111 of 2008*
6. *Conduct No. 17, Code of Conduct*
7. *Conduct No. 38, Code of Conduct*

7(a). *We the People, Juan Williams, P-130-133*

8. *Professor Ali Riaz, Politics and Government, Illinois University*
9. *The Story of My Experiment with Truth.*
10. *Durnity Daman Commission v. Dr. Mohiuddin Khan Alamgir, 62 DLR (AD) 290*
11. *Justice Krishna Iyer, "Law and Life" P 34*

Printed in Great Britain
by Amazon